Reading Archaeology

Reading Archaeology
An Introduction

edited by

ROBERT J. MUCKLE

 UNIVERSITY OF TORONTO PRESS

Previously published by Broadview Press 2008 © Robert J. Muckle

Library and Archives Canada Cataloguing in Publication

Reading archaeology : an introduction / [edited by] Robert J. Muckle.

Includes bibliographic references.

ISBN 978-1-55111-876-5

1. Archaeology—Textbooks I. Muckle, Robert James

CC165.R42 2007   930.1   C2007-903914-6

We welcome comments and suggestions regarding any aspect of our publications—please feel free to contact us at news@utphighereducation.com or visit our Internet site at www.utppublishing.com.

North America
5201 Dufferin Street
North York, Ontario, Canada, M3H 5T8

2250 Military Road
Tonawanda, New York, USA, 14150

ORDERS PHONE: 1-800-565-9523
ORDERS FAX: 1-800-221-9985
ORDERS E-MAIL: utpbooks@utpress.utoronto.ca

UK, Ireland, and continental Europe
NBN International
Estover Road, Plymouth, PL6 7PY, UK
ORDERS PHONE: 44 (0) 1752 202301
ORDERS FAX: 44 (0) 1752 202333
ORDERS E-MAIL: enquiries@nbninternational.com

The University of Toronto Press acknowledges the financial support for its publishing activities of the Government of Canada through the Canada Book Fund.

This book is printed on paper containing 100% post-consumer fibre.

Printed in Canada

Contents

Preface

There are several ways to learn about archaeology. Listening to lectures, participating in discussions, watching films, visiting websites and blogs, lurking on listserves, and participating in fieldwork, for example, are all good. Reading, however, remains essential.

Reading Archaeology: An Introduction has multiple purposes and is eclectic by design. The previously published articles and chapters in this collection were chosen to ensure a good sampling of readings that would correspond to topics commonly covered in archaeology courses, stimulate interest, and introduce readers to the nature of scholarly, semi-scholarly, and popular literature in archaeology.

For those looking to pair this volume with a standard introductory textbook, *Introducing Archaeology* (Robert Muckle, 2006), also published by Broadview Press, is a good fit as it follows a similar thematic organization.

Acknowledgements

M any people deserve recognition for the production of this volume: the authors of all the selections for making archaeology so interesting, accessible, and thought provoking; the copyright holders for allowing them to be reproduced in this volume; and the people in editorial and production at Broadview Press who have in somewhat of a magical fashion taken my wishes and turned them into reality. I am especially grateful for the guidance of anthropology editor Anne Brackenbury and for the copy editing of Catherine Dorton, who makes me look like a better writer than I really am.

Recognizing and Reading Archaeological Literature

Virtually all college and university students are aware that reading is important. Many, however, are unfamiliar with the various kinds of writing that make up the literature in academic disciplines, including archaeology. This Introduction explores the major kinds of archaeological literature and provides some tips on how to recognize and read them most efficiently.

Students need to understand the nature and diversity of archaeological literature for a few practical reasons. Throughout their college or university studies, they will be required to write research papers with the provision that scholarly sources be used. So learning how to differentiate between scholarly literature and popular or semi-scholarly sources is essential. Also, to effectively read archaeological literature, students will need to use various reading strategies, which are outlined here. Choosing a reading strategy based on recognizing the kind of literature can save students many hours of time spent in frustration when preparing for class or doing research papers.

Although the focus here is recognizing and reading archaeological literature, the information is transferable to other academic disciplines as well.

What Is Archaeological Literature?

The phrase "archaeological literature" means different things to different people. For some, archaeological literature refers to only that which is considered scholarly, such as articles in academic journals, usually written by university professors. Others take a broader view of what constitutes archaeological literature and include a wider range of sources, such as printed works on topics of archaeological interest in semi-scholarly and popular publications. It is this broader view that is represented in this reader.

Only rarely are works written by people not trained in archaeology considered part of archaeological literature. Exceptions have included the writing of some journalists, science writers, amateurs, and those trained in other disciplines, especially if they are reporting on original research and adhering to the principles of good scholarship.

Periodicals and books are the two primary avenues for archaeological literature. The term *periodical* is used in library and information science to denote a publication that is published on a regular basis, such as daily, weekly, monthly, quarterly, three times a year, twice a year, or annually. Major kinds of periodicals include journals, magazines, newsletters or bulletins of associations, and newspapers. In academia, designating a periodical as a journal indicates an academic or scholarly content. Indeed, many scholarly periodicals include the word *journal* in the title of the periodical.

Periodicals that focus on archaeology number in the thousands. After consolidating their resources, a group of libraries in Great Britain now lists more than 2,000 periodicals of interest to archaeologists. This list excludes many periodicals that focus on areas outside of Europe, so it is reasonable to think that the number is significantly higher, especially when smaller, regional publications are factored in. A list of major periodicals of interest to archaeologists is included as an appendix to this reader.

As with periodicals, thousands of books focus on archaeology. Most non-scholarly or popular books about archaeology are published by commercial publishers, large and small. Scholarly and semi-scholarly books are published by university presses, associations of professional archaeologists (e.g., the Society for American Archaeology), or commercial publishers.

Many resources are available to students to help them distinguish between scholarly and popular sources. College and university libraries, for example, often have print or online guides, usually focusing on periodicals. However, for archaeology students, the guides usually oversimplify the diversity of places where archaeological writing can be found. Many kinds of writing fall somewhere in between scholarly and popular, and are called semi-scholarly. Each of these three major kinds of archaeological literature is described in the following section.

Three Kinds of Archaeological Literature

The boundaries between the three categories of archaeological literature—scholarly, semi-scholarly, and popular—are often blurred. What some classify as semi-scholarly, for example, will be considered popular by others. There is no consensus or standard, absolute factor that can be used to classify a piece of writing. While peer review is a constant in scholarly literature, it may also be found in semi-scholarly or popular literature. What follows should be considered the general characteristics or trends of each of the three major kinds of archaeological literature.

SCHOLARLY ARCHAEOLOGICAL LITERATURE

Scholarly archaeological literature, also known as academic literature, is published in two primary forms: journal articles and books. It is the major way of communicating scholarly research. So, most scholarly writing is undertaken by university professors and graduate students working on their master's degree or Ph.D. quite simply because it is they who are conducting the research.

This type of writing is expected, and in some cases it is demanded, in order to obtain tenure at a university. Writing a scholarly article or book is often the last major stage of an archaeological research project, and writing about one's project for the larger community of archaeologists is considered to be an archaeological ethic.

Good scholarly writing usually takes considerable time. It is not unusual for an archaeologist to spend weeks or months crafting an article and a year or more on a book. It is standard practice that scholarly journals do not pay authors for their contributions. Authors may receive royalties on scholarly books, but considering that most are destined for research libraries rather than bookstores and personal sales, the amount of money earned tends to be negligible. The real reward for scholarly writing is in knowing that your work contributes to the advancement of the discipline and enhances your recognition as an archaeologist and scholar. More practically, for those beginning their professional careers, scholarly writing helps one find and maintain employment as an academic.

Scholarly writing in archaeology generally follows the format of most scientific writing. This includes an introduction that outlines why the research project was important, a review of other published literature on the same topic, a description of the methods of research, the results of the research, and a discussion of the results. Scholarly articles typically refer to several dozen or more other published works on the topic (cited within the article and listed at the end).

Archaeological scholarly writing in articles and books usually

- provides reporting of primary (original) research,
- uses specialized language (i.e., jargon), specific to archaeology,
- is written with an expectation that the reader has at least a broad familiarity with the topic,
- cites many sources within the article and includes extensive, up-to-date bibliographies or references,
- is evaluated by peer review by other archaeologists prior to publication to ensure the work meets high standards of scholarship,
- identifies the author as well as their academic affiliation,
- contains many references to other publications on the topic, some of which may be in foreign languages and the gray literature,
- is often indexed in academic library databases,
- usually has major headings throughout an article or chapter,
- refers to all figures and tables in the main part of the article,
- makes the goals, methods, results, and conclusions of research explicit, and
- includes an abstract: a brief summary of the article usually between the title and introduction to the article.

Of course, if an article is published in a scholarly journal, that is a good indication that it is scholarly. However, for those near the beginning of their studies in archaeology, it is not always self-evident whether a journal qualifies as scholarly or not. Some common characteristics of scholarly journals include

- authors that vary from issue to issue,
- editorial boards that include professors from universities, often identified in the beginning pages of an issue or on the journal web page,
- publication by a professional association of archaeologists or a scholarly publisher, often identified in the beginning pages of an issue or on the journal web page,
- continuous pagination throughout an entire volume, rather than within each issue (e.g., only the first issue of the volume or year begins with page 1),
- electronic archiving,
- availability through electronic search engines focusing on scholarly works, such as scholar.google.com.,
- absent or minimal advertising,
- images in black and white rather than color,
- availability by subscription only, appearing only rarely on newsstands.

Each scholarly journal tends to focus on a particular area within archaeology, such as a place, time period, or method, which can usually be ascertained by the journal title. Journals are also associated with different levels of prestige. For example, for archaeologists working in North America and focusing on method, theory, and prehistory, the premier journal is considered to be *American Antiquity*. For those working in the field of historic archaeology in North America, *Historical Archaeology* is considered the premier journal. Examples of other journals with relatively high prestige include *Antiquity*, *Archaeometry*, *Asian Perspectives*, *Geoarchaeology*, *Journal of Anthropological Archaeology*, *Journal of Archaeological Method and Theory*, *Journal of Archaeological Research*, *Journal of Archaeological Science*, *Latin American Antiquity*, and *World Archaeology*.

Scholarly articles also appear in journals that focus on the broader discipline of anthropology, which in North America is often considered to encompass archaeology as a subfield. The most prestigious of these include *American Anthropologist* and *Current Anthropology*. Prestigious interdisciplinary journals such as *Nature* and *Science* also publish articles on archaeology.

Scholarly books come in a variety of forms,

including theses, dissertations (book-length treatments of a student research), monographs, and edited volumes. As part of the process of obtaining a master's degree or Ph.D. in archaeology, students are generally required to undertake primary research, usually including field and laboratory work, and describe it in a thesis or dissertation. Scholarly books on a narrow topic by a single author are often referred to as research monographs, or simply monographs. An edited volume consists of a series of individual chapters, each written by a different author or group of authors. Such books sometimes consist primarily of works originally published elsewhere. Edited volumes are compiled by the editor, who invites a variety of authors to contribute a single chapter on a topic. The topic may be quite narrow, and the book may be a compilation of papers presented at a single session at an academic conference. The topic may also be broad, such as the archaeology of religion or gender.

If in doubt, the name of the publisher may be a clue as to whether a book should be considered scholarly or not. Most university presses focus their publication program on scholarly works, although it would be a mistake to assume that the work is necessarily scholarly because it was published by a university press. Many commercial companies, such as Blackwell and Routledge, also focus on publishing scholarly archaeology books.

SEMI-SCHOLARLY ARCHAEOLOGICAL LITERATURE

Semi-scholarly literature falls between the rigors of truly scholarly writing, which is primarily for those familiar with the topic and academic in style, and popular writing, which is mainly for the general public and usually in a mass media format, such as newspapers or widely circulated magazines. Semi-scholarly writing typically focuses on simply sharing results of research rather than explaining a phenomenon or making significant contributions to archaeological method and theory.

The amount of time to undertake scholarly writing is usually measured in weeks, months, and years, but the amount of time required for semi-scholarly writing can often be hours or days (unless it is a book). This is one of the primary reasons why a considerable amount of semi-scholarly literature is written by non-university based archaeologists, who, unlike university archaeologists, rarely have the time or resources to produce true scholarly literature.

The four major forms of semi-scholarly archaeological literature are (i) works produced by archaeologists primarily for other archaeologists and those in related fields, and appearing in trade or professional publications, (ii) project, field, and laboratory reports, (iii) works produced by archaeologists for other archaeologists, students, and the lay public in books and popular magazines, and (iv) text and reference books in archaeology, produced for students and professionals.

Works written by archaeologists primarily for other archaeologists and those in related fields are often in the form of brief reports, comments, forums, essays, opinions, and reviews. This sort of archaeological literature is likely to occur in publications such as *The SAA Archaeological Record*, targeted at professional archaeologists and presented as a benefit of membership in the Society for American Archaeology.

Semi-scholarly writing by archaeologists for archaeologists or those in related fields shares these characteristics:

- it often appears in a periodical explicitly described as a newsletter, magazine, or bulletin of an association of professional archaeologists, anthropologists, or those in heritage-related fields;
- it usually lacks the rigor of true scholarly writing (i.e., lacks abstract, has little or no context, lacks formality of academic writing);
- it may contain advertisements and color illustrations;

- the articles are usually much briefer than scholarly writing;
- it may not include in-text citations and bibliographies;
- it may not include the dissemination of primary research; and
- it cites relatively few or no sources.

Project, field, and laboratory reports are perhaps the most common type of writing by archaeologists, but these reports usually remain unknown to most researchers, and even when they do know about them, they are often difficult to find. With rare exception, every archaeological project requires a written report, and the time and other costs for writing are usually built into the project budget. Reports are usually required of funding. It is also a long-standing ethic that archaeologists write reports of their work and make them available. Such works, whether on the overall project or a particular aspects of field and laboratory research, are often prepared for clients, governments, and aboriginal groups. These reports typically are written in the same style as scholarly work, but lack the extensive citations and discussions found in such works.

Works produced by archaeologists for a wide audience consisting of other archaeologists, students, and the educated lay public is the form in which the distinction between scholarly, semi-scholarly, and popular writing is most blurred. Many books, for example, are targeted at both those in or studying the profession of archaeology and the lay public, and this is often reflected in the writing. While maintaining some aspects of academic writing, these kinds of books tend to use less specialized terminology, provide fewer or no references, and are written in a more informal style than purely academic publications. Some contributions in such periodicals as *Archaeology, Expedition, National Geographic*, and *Scientific American* may also be considered semi-scholarly, especially if the article is written by an archaeologist, reports on original research, is peer reviewed, or provides references.

Textbooks, reference books, manuals, and case studies are usually considered semi-scholarly. Authors are usually paid a royalty on sales, but as with most other kinds of writing in archaeology, the real reward is in sharing and contributing to the discipline, especially considering the relatively small market. Major publishers of these kinds of books include both university and commercial presses.

POPULAR ARCHAEOLOGICAL LITERATURE

Archaeological writings targeted at the general public are often termed *popular* and are found in both periodicals and books. One form includes articles written for newspapers and popular magazines such as *Time, Discover*, and *The Economist*. Some may consider periodicals such as *Archaeology, Expedition, National Geographic*, and *Scientific American* to be popular, while to others they are semi-scholarly. Generally, if a reporter, journalist, or anyone not trained in archaeology writes the article and if it is appearing in a periodical not clearly scholarly, the article will be considered popular. Articles by journalists are often based on presentations at conferences that they attend, press releases, or recently published reports.

Archaeological writings in the popular press (e.g., magazines and newspapers) are often characterized by

- authors who are not identified,
- authors who are not trained in archaeology,
- secondary reporting, such as articles based on a press release or presentation at a conference,
- little if any specialized language or assumption of basic knowledge of the topic,
- few if any citations of sources or no bibliography,
- a writing style that often uses quotes extensively,
- little or no attention paid to the goals or methods of research, or other relevant background information, and

- boxed-text features, side bars, and illustrations that do not directly correlate to the article (i.e., no reference is made to them in the main article).

Often, popular journals that include articles on archaeology
- are available at retail locations as well as by subscription,
- are produced by a commercial publisher,
- are printed on glossy paper,
- begin new pagination for each issue (i.e., each issue of the same volume or year begins with page 1),
- contain extensive advertising, and
- feature color photos on the cover and in the interior.

A WORD ABOUT GRAY LITERATURE AND ARCHAEOLOGY LITERATURE ON THE WEB

Archaeologists frequently refer to "the gray literature," which is a body of archaeological writing that remains largely unknown beyond a small group and is generally difficult to access. This includes unpublished reports on archaeological investigations to governments and clients, master's theses, Ph.D. dissertations, bulletins and newsletters of various professional and public groups, and local popular publications including newspapers. Sometimes gray literature is referred to as "non-conventional literature." Gray literature is rarely indexed in libraries and thus usually remains unknown, despite that it often contains significant information.

Over the past few decades, the amount of archaeological research done outside of academia, such as in cultural resource management or CRM (which involves investigating an area before it will be disturbed by construction), has burgeoned. So too has the amount of gray literature, especially the production of field and laboratory reports. It is the rare archaeological project that concludes without a written report. Most academic archaeologists working in universities are expected to produce scholarly literature, and they are often given time to do so. However, no such expectation falls upon those working in the CRM industry. Indeed, due to the significant amount of time it takes to produce truly scholarly works, it is not a reasonable expectation for those working outside of academia. Thus, while archaeological gray literature continues to increase, the wider community's lack of access to it often remains a problem. Some agencies have begun cataloging and archiving the gray literature in their offices and repositories with the goal of making it available on the Web, but this is likely to represent less than 1 per cent of the many thousands of reports considered part of the gray literature. Perhaps one of the most useful ways archaeologists have found to access the gray literature is to make enquiries about potential gray literature for their topic of interest on Internet listserves, such as HISTARCH.

Many kinds of archaeological works appear on the Web, and much of it does qualify as scholarly. Purely Web-based scholarly journals, such as *Internet Archaeology*, do exist and many scholarly journals publish both in print and online. Some journals provide immediate access to the issue online, while others require a waiting period of one or more years after print publication before they allow their issues to be viewed online.

Many websites focus on archaeology, but it would be dangerous to assume that they all contain archaeological literature without some kind of critical evaluation. Similarly, some very lengthy and insightful comments often appear on listserves and blogs, but without taking a critical look at them, it is inappropriate to consider them archaeological literature. Some of the things to consider when evaluating writing on the web are the credentials of the author (e.g., Is he or she an archaeologist who is considered expert in the particular topic?) and the website host (e.g., Is the site hosted by an academic institution or association of professional archaeologists?). One should remember that unless the writing is associated with an academic journal, contributions on the Web are unlikely to have gone through a proper, scientifically sound, peer-review process and are thus unlikely to qualify as "scholarly."

Reading Archaeological Literature

A successful college or university student should be familiar with various kinds of reading. These include skim reading, narrative reading, reading for content, and critical reading, also known as deep reading or reading for meaning.

SKIM READING

Skim reading can be a very important tool for archaeological literature of all kinds. If the work has been written well, then focusing on the title, the abstract (if there is one), the major section headings, the first paragraph of each major section, and the captions to figures and tables can be an efficient way to begin reading a selection. For example, if the selection is being read to find appropriate sources for a research paper, then skim reading is a very efficient method. Skim reading should enable a reader to have a general idea of an article or book chapter within a few minutes, and it is probably the most common way of reading for both students and professionals in archaeology. The sheer number of articles and books on most topics of archaeological interest is so vast that it just isn't reasonable to expect a thorough reading of each. After skim reading, most archaeologists will then make a decision whether to proceed to one or more of the following stages of reading: narrative, reading for content, or critical reading.

Another advantage of skim reading is that even if you know you should be reading to extract content or reading critically, it provides a mental preparation for what's ahead.

NARRATIVE READING

As with skim reading, narrative reading can be a useful tool to quickly determine the value of the writing and prepare for what lies ahead. Narrative reading is probably closest to what most would regard as reading for pleasure. It requires little forethought; the reader simply follows along and attempts to grasp the big picture without getting lost in the details (as one typically does when reading a novel or article from a popular magazine for pleasure). Sources written in anticipation of being read in a narrative style generally fall into the categories of popular and semi-scholarly literature. Often, professors who ask students to read a textbook chapter before coming to a lecture are anticipating the student will do a narrative reading so they have a broad familiarity with the topic.

READING FOR CONTENT

Reading for content requires care and time. Much of the semi-scholarly and all of the scholarly literature is written with the expectation that readers will be extracting information useful for their own studies. Most textbooks, for example, are written to provide information, not pleasure, although I suppose it is possible to have both. Practical tips for reading for content include the following:

- Allow plenty of time for reading.
- Skim read or do a narrative read first to prepare mentally for what is ahead.
- Know the kinds of information you are seeking so you don't get bogged down with irrelevant information.
- Be prepared to mark the paper (unless it is a borrowed copy, of course) either with your own system or some standard symbols, highlighting such things as the thesis, important results, conclusion, and key points.

CRITICAL READING

Reading critically, also known as "reading for meaning" and "deep reading," is the highest level of reading a college or university student will encounter. Critical reading does not necessarily mean that one must find fault with the writing. Mostly, critical reading involves evaluating how well an author presents the information and attempting to identify the unstated biases of the author (i.e., reading between lines). Critical reading often requires making inferences on the reader's part.

Practical tips for critical reading include the following:

• Allow plenty of time.
• Read for content first to become familiar with the material.
• Determine the explicit purpose of the writing (i.e., goals, objective, thesis).
• Carefully pick out the evidence used to support the thesis or argument.
• Distinguish the kinds of evidence used for support (e.g., scholarly versus non-scholarly).
• Determine if the article flows logically.
• Identify the assumptions of the author (both the stated and unstated ones).
• Identify any bias of the author (e.g., methodological, theoretical, geographical, temporal, or political).

Of course, the more one knows about archaeology, the easier it should be to do a critical reading, especially when it comes to evaluating whether the author did an adequate job of presenting the background and identifying theoretical and methodological bias.

However, novices to scholarly archaeological literature should still be able to critically evaluate the literature by examining how a selection follows the standard model of scientific writing. Ask the following questions:

• How well has the Introduction been written? For example, does it introduce the topic, background, and thesis? Does it include the nature of the problem being investigated and the rationale for the study?
• How well has the background information been presented? Are there references to other works on the same general topic? Is there enough information to provide a reasonable context for the research being reported? (The background should provide enough information that the general problem being studied and the rationale for the study are understood.)
• How well are the methods of research detailed?
• How well are the results presented? Are the results clear?
• How well are the results discussed? Are the implications of the results, such as supporting an hypothesis, clear?

Concluding Comments

This volume contains 29 selections from published scholarly, semi-scholarly, and popular literature. The selections were chosen to enhance the reader's appreciation of both the discipline of archaeology and the nature and diversity of archaeological literature. Each selection has a brief introduction that includes some questions to guide reading and usually a bit of context, such as information on the general topic, the author(s), and the publication in which the selection originally appeared. The questions have been included with the expectation that readers will primarily be reading for content. Of course, it would also be a good exercise to use the criteria in this Introduction to categorize each selection as scholarly, semi-scholarly, or popular, and to attempt a critical reading.

Situating Archaeology: Past and Present

Introduction

The selections in Part 1 were chosen to provide insight into the diverse nature of archaeological thought, practice, and writing, past and present. The first two pieces offer some historical context for archaeology: "Ethnical Periods" by Lewis Henry Morgan exemplifies the intellectual climate of the late 1800s, a time when archaeology was emerging as a scholarly discipline, and David Silverman's "The Curse of the Curse of the Pharaohs" provides a view of the non-scholarly aspects of early archaeology. The remaining selections represent an overview of the diversity of archaeological thought and practice in recent times.

"Ethnical Periods"

LEWIS HENRY MORGAN

T his selection is the first chapter in *Ancient Society or Researches in the Lines of Human Progress from Savagery through Barbarism to Civilization* by Lewis Henry Morgan, originally published in 1877. Morgan trained and practiced as a lawyer in the United States but spent much of his time studying and writing about Native Americans. In this chapter, Morgan outlines what he sees as the seven basic stages of human development, beginning with the lowest stage of savagery and culminating with civilization. This proposed sequence of progression came to be known as the unilinear or unilineal theory of cultural evolution. Morgan's theory became widely but not universally accepted by academics and the non-aboriginal populations of North America and Europe. It arose at a time when many people were questioning what we now recognize as prehistoric cultural artifacts and sites from Europe and elsewhere and the extreme cultural diversity of living groups of people being "discovered" by Europeans. Morgan's theory hypothesized that the prehistoric remains were remnants of societies who subsequently progressed through some

or all of the stages, and the cultural diversity of living people was evidence that some aboriginal groups were slower to progress and thus were examples of the various stages of savagery and barbarism in modern times.

From an archaeological perspective, Morgan's theory was pivotal. Some consider it to be the second major archaeological theory, the first being the development of the three-age system (the Stone, Bronze, and Iron ages). Since the theory was based on material evidence of technology and subsistence, which archaeologists tend to focus on, it became attractive to many.

Morgan's theory was not without criticism however, and the work of archaeologists and anthropologists in the late nineteenth and early twentieth centuries totally discredited the theory. It is now commonly accepted that societies may efficiently adapt and evolve in many different ways and that adopting a new kind of technology or subsistence strategy is not always a benefit. Readers are cautioned that while Morgan's theory is of historical interest, it is no longer considered valid.

Questions to Guide Reading

What are the seven statuses identified by Morgan? What are the technological and dietary characteristics of each?

The latest investigations respecting the early condition of the human race are tending to the conclusion that mankind commenced their career at the bottom of the scale and worked their way up from savagery to civilization through the slow accumulations of experimental knowledge.

As it is undeniable that portions of the human family have existed in a state of savagery, other portions in a state of barbarism, and still other portions in a state of civilization, it seems equally so that these three distinct conditions are connected with each other in a natural as well as necessary sequence of progress. Moreover, that this sequence has been historically true of the entire human family, up to the status attained by each branch respectively, is rendered probable by the conditions under which all progress occurs, and by the known advancement of several branches of the family through two or more of these conditions.

An attempt will be made in the following pages to bring forward additional evidence of the rudeness of the early condition of mankind, of the gradual evolution of their mental and moral powers through experience, and of their protracted struggle with opposing obstacles while winning their way to civilization. It will be drawn, in part, from the great sequence of inventions and discoveries which stretches along the entire pathway of human progress; but chiefly from domestic institutions, which express the growth of certain ideas and passions.

As we re-ascend along the several lines of progress toward the primitive ages of mankind, and eliminate one after the other, in the order in which they appeared, inventions and discoveries on the one hand, and institutions on the other, we are enabled to perceive that the former stand to each other in progressive, and the latter in unfolding relations. While the former class have had a connection, more or less direct, the latter have been developed from a few primary germs of thought. Modern institutions plant their roots in the period of barbarism, into which their germs were transmitted from the previous period of savagery. They have had a lineal descent through the ages, with the streams of the blood, as well as a logical development.

Two independent lines of investigation thus invite our attention. The one leads through inventions and discoveries, and the other through primary institutions. With the knowledge gained therefrom, we may hope to indicate the principal stages of human development. The proofs to be adduced will be drawn chiefly from domestic institutions; the references to achievements more strictly intellectual being general as well as subordinate.

The facts indicate the gradual formation and subsequent development of certain ideas, passions, and aspirations. Those which hold the most prominent positions may be generalized as growths of the particular ideas with which they severally stand connected. Apart from inventions and discoveries they are the following:

I. Subsistence,
II. Government,
III. Language,
IV. The Family,
V. Religion,
VI. House Life and Architecture,
VII. Property.

First. Subsistence has been increased and perfected by a series of successive arts, introduced at long intervals of time, and connected more or less directly with inventions and discoveries.

Second. The germ of government must be sought in the organization into gentes in the Status of savagery; and followed down, through the advancing forms of this institution, to the establishment of political society.

Third. Human speech seems to have been developed from the rudest and simplest forms of expression. Gesture or sign language, as intimated by Lucretius, must have preceded articulate language, as thought preceded speech. The monosyllabical preceded the syllabical, as the latter did that of concrete words. Human intelligence, unconscious of design, evolved articulate language by utilizing the vocal sounds. This great subject, a department of knowledge by itself, does not fall within the scope of the present investigation.

Fourth. With respect to the family, the stages of its growth are embodied in systems of consanguinity and affinity, and in usages relating to marriage, by means of which, collectively, the family can be definitely traced through several successive forms.

Fifth. The growth of religious ideas is environed with such intrinsic difficulties that it may never receive a perfectly satisfactory exposition. Religion deals so largely with the imaginative and emotional nature, and consequently with such uncertain elements of knowledge, that all primitive religions are grotesque and to some extent unintelligible. This subject also falls without the plan of this work excepting as it may prompt incidental suggestions.

Sixth. House architecture, which connects itself with the form of the family and the plan of domestic life, affords a tolerably complete illustration of progress from savagery to civilization. Its growth can be traced from the hut of the savage, through the communal houses of the barbarians, to the house of the single family of civilized nations, with all the successive links by which one extreme is connected with the other. This subject will be noticed incidentally.

Lastly. The idea of property was slowly formed in the human mind, remaining nascent and feeble through immense periods of time. Springing into life in savagery, it required all the experience of this period and of the subsequent period of barbarism to develop the germ, and to prepare the human brain for the acceptance of its controlling influence. Its dominance as a passion over all other passions marks the commencement of civilization. It not only led mankind to overcome the obstacles which delayed civilization, but to establish political society on the basis of territory and of property. A critical knowledge of the evolution of the idea of property would embody, in some respects, the most remarkable portion of the mental history of mankind.

It will be my object to present some evidence of human progress along these several lines, and through successive ethnical periods, as it is revealed by inventions and discoveries, and by the growth of the ideas of government, of the family, and of property.

It may be here premised that all forms of government are reducible to two general plans, using the word plan in its scientific sense. In their bases the two are fundamentally distinct. The first, in the order of time, is founded upon persons, and upon relations purely personal, and may be distinguished as a society (*societas*). The gens is the unit of this organization; giving as the successive stages of integration, in the archaic period, the gens, the phratry, the tribe, and the confederacy of tribes, which constituted a people or nation (*populus*). At a later period a coalescence of tribes in the same area into a nation took the place of a confederacy of tribes occupying independent areas. Such, through prolonged ages, after the gens appeared, was the substantially universal organization of ancient society; and it remained among the Greeks and Romans after civilization supervened. The second is founded upon territory and upon property, and may be distinguished by a state (*civitas*). The township or ward, circumscribed by metes and bounds, with the property it contains, is the basis or unit of the latter, and political society is the result. Political society is organized upon territorial areas, and deals with property as well as with persons through territorial relations. The successive stages of integration are the township or ward, which is the unit of organization; the county or province, which is an aggregation of townships or wards; and the national domain or territory, which is an aggregation of counties or provinces; the people of each of which are organized into a body politic. It taxed the Greeks and Romans to the extent of their capacities, after they had gained civilization, to invent the deme or township and the city ward; and thus inaugurate the second great plan of government, which remains among civilized nations to the present hour. In ancient society this territorial plan was unknown. When it came in it fixed the boundary line between ancient and modern society, as the distinction will be recognized in these pages.

It may be further observed that the domestic institutions of the barbarous, and even of the savage ancestors of mankind, are still exemplified in portions of the human family with such completeness that, with the exception of the strictly primitive period, the several stages of this progress are tolerably well preserved. They are seen in the organization of society upon the basis of sex, then upon the basis of kin, and finally upon the basis of territory; through the successive forms of marriage and of the family, with the systems of consanguinity thereby created; through house life and architecture; and through progress in usages with respect to the ownership and inheritance of property.

The theory of human degradation to explain the existence of savages and of barbarians is no longer tenable. It came in as a corollary from the Mosaic cosmogony, and was acquiesced in from a supposed necessity which no longer exists. As a theory, it is not only incapable of explaining the existence of savages, but it is without support in the facts of human existence.

The remote ancestors of the Aryan nations presumptively passed through an experience similar to that of existing barbarous and savage tribes. Though the experience of these nations embodies all the information necessary to illustrate the periods of civilization, both ancient and modern, together with a part of that in the Later period of barbarism, their anterior experience must be deduced, in the main, from the traceable connection between the elements of their existing institutions and inventions, and similar elements still preserved in those of savage and barbarous tribes.

It may be remarked finally that the experience of mankind has run in nearly uniform channels; that human necessities in similar conditions have been substantially the same; and that the operations of the mental principle have been uniform in virtue of the specific identity of the brain of all the races of mankind. This, however, is but a part of the explanation of uniformity in results. The germs of the principal institutions and arts of life were developed while man was still a savage. To a very great extent the experience of the subsequent periods of barbarism and of civilization have been expended in the further development of these original conceptions. Wherever a connection can be traced on different continents between a present institution and a common germ, the derivation of the people themselves from a common original stock is implied.

The discussion of these several classes of facts will be facilitated by the establishment of a certain number of Ethnical Periods; each representing a distinct condition of society, and distinguishable by a mode of life peculiar to itself. The terms *"Age of Stone," "of Bronze,"* and *"of Iron,"* introduced by Danish archaeologists, have been extremely useful for certain purposes, and will remain so for the classification of objects of ancient art; but the progress of knowledge has rendered other and different subdivisions necessary. Stone implements were not entirely laid aside with the introduction of tools of iron, nor of those of bronze. The invention of the process of smelting iron ore created an ethnical epoch, yet we could scarcely date another from the production of bronze. Moreover, since the period of stone implements overlaps those of bronze and of iron, and since that of bronze also overlaps that of iron, they are not capable of a circumscription that would leave each independent and distinct.

It is probable that the successive arts of subsistence which arose at long intervals will ultimately, from the great influence they must have exercised upon the condition of mankind, afford the most satisfactory bases for these divisions. But investigation has not been carried far enough in this directly to yield the necessary information. With our present knowledge the main result can be attained by selecting such other inventions or discoveries as will afford sufficient tests of progress to characterize the commencement of successive ethnical periods. Even though accepted as provisional, these periods will be found convenient and useful. Each of those about to be proposed will be found to cover a distinct culture, and to represent a particular mode of life.

The period of savagery, of the early part of which very little is known, may be divided, provisionally, into three subperiods. These may be named respectively the *Older*, the *Middle*, and the *Later* period of savagery; and the condition of society in each, respectively, may be distinguished as the *Lower*, the *Middle*, and the *Upper Status* of savagery.

In like manner, the period of barbarism divides naturally into three sub-periods, which will be called, respectively, the *Older*, the *Middle*, and the *Later* period of barbarism; and the condition of society in each, respectively, will be distinguished as the *Lower*, the *Middle*, and the *Upper Status* of barbarism.

It is difficult, if not impossible, to find such tests of progress to mark the commencement of these several periods as will be found absolute in their application, and without exceptions upon all the continents. Neither is it necessary, for the purpose in hand, that exceptions should not exist. It will be sufficient if the principal tribes of mankind can be classified, according to the degree of their relative progress, into conditions which can be recognized as distinct.

I. Lower Status of Savagery

This period commenced with the infancy of the human race, and may be said to have ended with the acquisition of a fish subsistence and of a knowledge of the use of fire. Mankind were then living in their original restricted habitat, and subsisting upon fruits and nuts. The commencement of articulate speech belongs to this period. No exemplification of tribes of mankind in this condition remained to the historical period.

II. Middle Status of Savagery

It commenced with the acquisition of a fish subsistence and a knowledge of the use of fire, and ended with the invention of the bow and arrow. Mankind, while in this condition, spread from their original habitat over the greater portion of the earth's surface. Among tribes still existing it will leave in the Middle Status of savagery, for example, the Australians and the greater part of the Polynesians when discovered. It will be sufficient to give one or more exemplifications of each status.

III. Upper Status of Savagery

It commenced with the invention of the bow and arrow, and ended with the invention of the art of pottery. It leaves in the Upper Status of Savagery the Athapascan tribes of the Hudson's Bay Territory, the tribes of the valley of the Columbia, and certain coast tribes of North and South America; but with relation to the time of their discovery. This closes the period of Savagery.

IV. Lower Status of Barbarism

The invention or practice of the art of pottery, all things considered, is probably the most effective and conclusive test that can be selected to fix a boundary line, necessarily arbitrary, between savagery and barbarism. The distinctness of the two conditions has long been recognized, but no criterion of progress out of the former into the latter has hitherto been brought forward. All such tribes, then, as never attained to the art of pottery will be classed as savages, and those possessing this art but who never attained a phonetic alphabet and the use of writing will be classed as barbarians.

The first sub-period of barbarism commenced with the manufacture of pottery, whether by original invention or adoption. In finding its termination, and the commencement of the Middle Status, a difficulty is encountered in the unequal endowments of the two hemispheres, which began to be influential upon human affairs after the period of savagery had passed. It may be met, however, by the adoption of equivalents. In the Eastern hemisphere, the domestication of animals, and the Western, the cultivation of maize and plants by irrigation, together with the use of adobe-brick and stone in house building have been selected as sufficient evidence of progress to work a transition out of the Lower and into the Middle Status of barbarism. It leaves, for example, in the Lower Status, the Indian tribes of the United States east of the Missouri River, and such tribes of Europe and Asia as practiced the art of pottery, but were without domestic animals.

V. The Middle Status of Barbarism
It commenced with the domestication of animals in the Eastern hemisphere, and in the Western with cultivation by irrigation and with the use of adobe-brick and stone in architecture, as shown. Its termination may be fixed with the invention of the process of smelting iron ore. This places in the Middle Status, for example, the Village Indians of New Mexico, Mexico, Central America and Peru, and such tribes in the Eastern hemisphere as possessed domestic animals, but were without a knowledge of iron. The ancient Britons, although familiar with the use of iron, fairly belong in this connection. The vicinity of more advanced continental tribes had advanced the arts of life among them far beyond the state of development of their domestic institutions.

VI. Upper Status of Barbarism
It commenced with the manufacture of iron, and ended with the invention of a phonetic alphabet, and the use of writing in literary composition. Here civilization begins. This leaves in the Upper Status, for example, the Grecian tribes of the Homeric age, the Italian tribes shortly before the founding of Rome, and the Germanic tribes of the time of Caesar.

VII. Status of Civilization
It commenced, as stated, with the use of a phonetic alphabet and the production of literary records, and divides into *Ancient* and *Modern*. As an equivalent, hieroglyphical writing upon stone may be admitted.

RECAPITULATION

Periods	Conditions
I. Older Period of Savagery,	I. Lower Status of Savagery,
II. Middle Period of Savagery,	II. Middle Status of Savagery,
III. Later Period of Savagery,	III. Upper Status of Savagery,
IV. Older Period of Barbarism,	IV. Lower Status of Barbarism,
V. Middle Period of Barbarism,	V. Middle Status of Barbarism,
VI. Later Period of Barbarism,	VI. Upper Status of Barbarism,
	VII. Status of Civilization,

I.	Lower Status of Savagery,	From the Infancy of the Human Race to the commencement of the next Period.
II.	Middle Status of Savagery,	From the acquisition of a fish subsistence and a knowledge of the use of fire, to etc.
III.	Upper Status of Savagery,	From the Invention of the Bow and Arrow, to etc.
IV.	Lower Status of Barbarism,	From the Invention of the Art of Pottery, to etc.
V.	Middle Status of Barbarism,	From the Domestication of animals on the Eastern hemisphere, and in the Western from the cultivation of maize and plants by Irrigation, with the use of adobe-brick and stone, to etc.
VI.	Upper Status of Barbarism,	From the Invention of the process of Smelting Iron Ore, with the use of iron tools, to etc.
VII.	Status of Civilization,	From the Invention of a Phonetic Alphabet, with the use of writing, to the present time.

Each of these periods has a distinct culture and exhibits a mode of life more or less special and peculiar to itself. This specialization of ethnical periods renders it possible to treat a particular society according to its condition of relative advancement, and to make it a subject of independent study and discussion. It does not affect the main result that different tribes and nations on the same continent, and even of the same linguistic family, are in different conditions at the same time, since for our purpose the *condition* of each is the material fact, the *time* being immaterial.

Since the use of pottery is less significant than that of domestic animals, of iron, or of a phonetic alphabet, employed to mark the commencement of subsequent ethnical periods, the reasons for its adoption should be stated. The manufacture of pottery presupposes village life, and considerable progress in the simple arts.[1] Flint and stone implements are older than pottery, remains of the former having been found in ancient repositories in numerous instances unaccompanied by the latter. A succession of inventions of greater need and adapted to a lower condition must have occurred before the want of pottery would be felt. The commencement of village life, with some degree of control over subsistence, wooden vessels and utensils, finger weaving with filaments of bark, basket making, and the bow and arrow make their appearance before the art of pottery. The Village Indians who were in the Middle Status of barbarism, such as the Zuñians the Aztecs and the Cholulans, manufactured pottery in large quantities and in many forms of considerable excellence; the partially Village Indians of the United States, who were in the Lower Status of barbarism, such as the Iroquois, the Choctas, and the Cherokees, made it in smaller quantities and in a limited number of forms; but the Non-horticultural Indians, who were in the Status of savagery, such as the Athapascans, the tribes of California and of the valley of the Columbia, were ignorant of its use.[2] In Lubbock's *Pre-Historic Times*, in Tylor's *Early History of Mankind*, and in Peschel's *Races of Man*, the particulars respecting this art, and the extent of its distribution, have been collected with remarkable breadth of research. It was unknown in Polynesia (with the exception of the Islands of the Tongans and Fijians), in Australia, in California, and in the Hudson's Bay Territory. Mr. Tylor remarks that "the art of weaving was unknown in most of the Islands away from Asia," and that "in most of the South Sea Islands there was no knowledge of pottery."[3] The Rev. Lorimer Fison, an English missionary residing in Australia, informed the author in answer to inquiries, that "the Australians had no woven fabrics, no pottery, and were ignorant of the bow and arrow." This last fact was also true in general of the Polynesians. The introduction of the ceramic art produced a new epoch in human progress in the direction of an improved living and increased domestic conveniences. While flint and stone implements—which came in earlier and required long periods of time to develop all their uses—gave the canoe, wooden vessels and utensils, and ultimately timber and plank in house architecture,[4] pottery gave a durable vessel for boiling food, which before that had been rudely accomplished in baskets coated with clay, and in ground cavities lined with skin, the boiling being effected with heated stones.[5]

Whether the pottery of the aborigines was hardened by fire or cured by the simple process of drying, has been made a question. Prof E.T. Cox, of Indianapolis, has shown by comparing the analyses of ancient pottery and hydraulic cements, "that so far as chemical constituents are concerned it (the pottery) agrees very well with the composition of hydraulic stones." He remarks further, that "all the pottery belonging to the mound-builders' age, which I have seen, is composed of alluvial clay and sand, or a mixture of the former with pulverized fresh-water shells. A paste made of such a mixture possesses in a high degree the properties of hydraulic Puzzuolani and Portland cement, so that vessels formed of it hardened without being burned, as is customary with modern pottery. The fragments of shells served the purpose of gravel or fragments of stone as at present used in connection with hydraulic lime for the manufacture of artificial stone."[6] The composition of Indian pottery in analogy with that of hydraulic cement suggests the difficulties in the way of inventing the art, and tends also to explain the lateness of its introduction in the course of human experience. Notwithstanding the ingenious suggestion of Prof. Cox, it is probable that pottery was hardened by artificial heat. In some cases the fact is directly attested. Thus Adair, speaking of the Gulf Tribes, remarks that "they make earthen pots of very different sizes, so as to contain from two to ten gallons, large pitchers to carry water, bowls, dishes, platters, basins, and a prodigious number of other vessels of such antiquated forms as would be tedious to describe, and impossible to name. Their method of glazing them is, they place them over a large fire of smoky pitch-pine, which makes them smooth, black and firm."[7]

Another advantage of fixing definite ethnical periods is the direction of special investigation to those tribes and nations which afford the best exemplification of each status, with the view of making each both standard and illustrative. Some tribes and families have been left in geographical isolation to work out the problems of progress by original mental effort; and have, consequently, retained their arts and institutions pure and homogeneous; while those of other tribes and nations have been adulterated through external influence. Thus, while Africa was and is an ethnical chaos of savagery and barbarism, Australia and Polynesia were in savagery, pure and simple, with the arts and institutions belonging to that condition. In like manner, the Indian family of America, unlike any other existing family, exemplified the condition of mankind in three successive ethnical periods. In the undisturbed possession of a great continent, of common descent, and with homogeneous institutions, they illustrated, when discovered, each of these conditions, and especially those of the Lower and of the Middle Status of barbarism, more elaborately and

completely than any other portion of mankind. The far northern Indians and some of the coast tribes of North and South America were in the Upper Status of savagery; the partially Village Indians east of the Mississippi were in the Lower Status of barbarism, and the Village Indians of North and South America were in the Middle Status. Such an opportunity to recover full and minute information of the course of human experience and progress in developing their arts and institutions through these successive conditions has not been offered within the historical period. It must be added that it has been indifferently improved. Our greatest deficiencies relate to the last period named.

Differences in the culture of the same period in the Eastern and Western hemispheres undoubtedly existed in consequence of the unequal endowments of the continents; but the condition of society in the corresponding status must have been, in the main, substantially similar.

The ancestors of the Grecian, Roman, and German tribes passed through the stages we have indicated, in the midst of the last of which the light of history fell upon them. Their differentiation from the undistinguishable mass of barbarians did not occur, probably, earlier than the commencement of the Middle Period of barbarism. The experience of these tribes has been lost, with the exception of so much as is represented by the institutions, inventions and discoveries which they had brought with them, and possessed when they first came under historical observation. The Grecian and Latin tribes of the Homeric and Romulian periods afford the highest exemplification of the Upper Status of barbarism. Their institutions were likewise pure and homogeneous, and their experience stands directly connected with the final achievement of civilization.

Commencing, then, with the Australians and Polynesians, following with the American Indian tribes, and concluding with the Roman and Grecian, who afford the highest exemplifications respectively of the six great stages of human progress, the sum of their united experiences may be supposed fairly to represent that of the human family from the Middle Status of savagery to the end of ancient civilization. Consequently, the Aryan nations will find the type of the condition of their remote ancestors, when in savagery, in that of the Australians and Polynesians; when in the Lower Status of barbarism in that of the partially Village Indians of America; and when in the Middle Status in that of the Village Indians, with which their own experience in the Upper Status directly connects. So essentially identical are the arts, institutions and mode of life in the same status upon all the continents, that the archaic form of the principal domestic institutions of the Greeks and Romans must even now be sought in the corresponding institutions of the American aborigines, as will be shown in the course of this volume. This fact forms a part of the accumulating evidence tending to show that the principal institutions of mankind have been developed from a few primary germs of thought; and that the course and manner of their development was predetermined, as well as restricted within narrow limits of divergence, by the natural logic of the human mind and the necessary limitations of its powers. Progress has been found to be substantially the same in kind in tribes and nations inhabiting different and even disconnected continents, while in the same status, with deviations from uniformity in particular instances produced by special causes. The argument when extended tends to establish the unity of origin of mankind.

In studying the condition of tribes and nations in these several ethnical periods we are dealing, substantially, with the ancient history and condition of our own remote ancestors.

Notes

[1] Mr. Edwin [sic] B. Tylor observes that Goquet "first propounded, in the last century, the notion that the way in which pottery came to be made, was that people daubed such combustible vessels as these with clay to protect them from fire, till they found that clay alone would answer the purpose, and thus the art of pottery came into the world."—"Early History of Minkind [sic]," p. 273. Goquet relates of Capt. Gonneville who visited the southeast coast of South America in 1503, that he found "their household utensils of wood, even their boiling pots, but plastered with a kind of clay, a good finger thick, which prevented the fire from burning them."—Ib. 273.

[2] Pottery has been found in aboriginal mounds in Oregon within a few years past.—Foster's "Pre-Historic Races of the United States," I, 152. The first vessels of pottery among the Aborigines of the United States seem to have been made in baskets of rushes or willows used as moulds which were burned off after the vessel hardened.—Jones's "Antiquities of the Southern Indians," p. 461. Prof. Rau's article on "Pottery," "Smithsonian Report," 1866, p. 352.

[3] "Early History of Mankind," p. 181; "Pre-Historic Times," pp. 437, 441, 462, 477, 533, 542.

[4] Lewis and Clarke (1805) found plank in use in houses among the tribes of the Columbia River.—"Travels," Longman's Ed., 1814, p. 503. Mr. John Keast Lord found "cedar plank chipped from the solid tree with chisels and hatchets made of stone," in Indian houses on Vancouver's Island.—"Naturalist in British Columbia," I, 169.

[5] Tylor's "Early History of Mankind," p. 265, "et. seq."

[6] "Geological Survey of Indians," 1873, p. 119. He gives the following analysis: Ancient Pottery, "Bone Bank," Posey Co., Indiana.

Moisture at 212° F.,	1.00
Silica,	36.00
Carbonate of Lime,	25.50
Carbonate of Magnesia,	3.02
Alumina,	5.00
Peroxide of Iron,	5.50
Sulfuric Acid,	.20
Organic Matter (alkalies and loss),	23.60
	100.00

[7] "History of the American Indians," Lond. Ed., 1775, p. 424. The Iroquois affirm that in ancient times their forefathers cured their pottery before a fire.

"The Curse of the Curse of the Pharaohs"

David Silverman

One of the most significant discoveries in the history of archaeology was that of the tomb of Tutankhamun, popularly known as King Tut, found in Egypt's Valley of the Kings by Howard Carter in the early twentieth century. Not only did this discovery lead to a more complete understanding of ancient Egypt, it also catapulted archaeology into the realm of popular culture, including the notion of curses associated with mummies.

In this selection, David Silverman tackles the notion of the curse of Tutankhamun. Silverman is a professor and museum curator at the University of Pennsylvania. The article originally appeared in a 1987 issue of *Expedition*, which is published by the University of Pennsylvania Museum of Archaeology and Anthropology. Although many articles on the subject have been published in more recent years, they lack the archaeological background and the details of media involvement that this one has and add little to the conclusions it reached.

Questions to Guide Reading

Who were King Tut, Howard Carter, and Lord Carnarvon?
In what year was the tomb of King Tut discovered and excavated?
What were the implications of selling the exclusive rights to publication about the discovery?

"Cursed be those that disturb the rest of Pharaoh. They that shall break the seal of this tomb shall meet death by a disease which no doctor can diagnose." (Inscription reported to have been carved on an Egyptian royal tomb)

Throughout the centuries, ancient Egypt and its civilization have often been referred to in terms of the dark and mysterious. Encounters with its strange customs have frequently led people, both ancient and modern, to have misconceptions about this land. The Greeks acknowledged that much ancient wisdom, such as the basics of mathematics, architecture, art, science, medicine, and even philosophy, ultimately derived from the Egyptians; but they still had some difficulty in understanding, accepting, or even dealing with the alien and unfamiliar aspects of the religion. Greek historians often wrote about the mysterious ways in which the Egyptians worshipped their deities, such as this note by Herodotus: "There are not a great many wild animals in Egypt ... Such as there are—both wild and tame—are without exception held to be sacred" (II, 65). He also wrote a disclaimer: "I am not anxious to repeat what I was told about the Egyptian religion ... for I do not think that any one nation knows much more about such things than any other" (II, 4). Of course he then goes on to state: "[The Egyptians] are religious to excess" (II, 35-39).

Egypt *was* different from much of the rest of the ancient world, with its pantheon of fantastic deities, part animal, part human; its rulers who were understood to be gods on earth; its bizarre funerary practices that paid unheard of attention to the preparations for an afterlife; and its enigmatic script that was written with recognizable pictures, but remained unreadable and therefore mysterious to the uninitiated. As a result, Egypt managed to inspire both awe and fear in the foreigner who came into contact with its culture.

Today, the products of Egyptian civilization that have survived the passage of more than 3000 years provide a visible monument to its advanced state. Such accomplishments, however, often evoke suspicion rather than respect. Thus there are people who prefer to believe that Egyptian building techniques, literature, art, and mathematics derived from an alien culture from outer space, rather than to accept the documented evidence of their earthly origin. This and other equally inaccurate theories are espoused by people fondly referred to by Egyptologists as "pyramidiots." But while some modern ideas about ancient Egypt are based on a mixture of misguided awe and respect, others appear to have originated under less innocent circumstances. One of the most persistent examples of the latter type is the so-called curse of the pharaohs.

An Egyptologist Cursed

During the last hundred years or so, the phrase "curse of the pharaohs" has been used to describe the cause of a large assortment of ills. These range from natural disasters to a mild stomach disorder that often plagues tourists to Egypt (also known as "pharaoh's revenge," or "gippy tummy"—derived from "Egyptian tummy"). I became personally involved with this curse (I mean that supposedly written by or for the pharaohs), when I became Project Egyptologist for the Treasures of Tutankhamun Exhibit that traveled across the United States from 1976 to 1979.

Charged with writing the text that appeared in the exhibit, I conducted research on all aspects of the discovery, excavation, and recording of Tutankhamun's tomb and its contents. Naturally, I came across several references to the famous "curse of King Tut." But before I had begun to deal with that matter on more than a superficial level, I came into contact with the "curse of the curse of King Tut." My first published newspaper interview consisted of a few descriptive paragraphs about the exhibition that carried this headline: "Beware the beat of the bandaged feet, as the ancient Egyptian saying goes." Of course there was no such saying in ancient Egypt. I vowed that the next time that I met with a reporter I would be more careful: I had to be assured that the tone of the column would be as professional as possible and the content totally accurate.

Within a matter of weeks I was interviewed again, when the crate containing Tutankhamun's funerary mask was opened. I was circumspect, cautious, and at my scholarly best. Moreover, the entire discussion was taped; this way, I thought, I would be sure that the real facts behind the curse of King Tut were included, and any misunderstandings avoided. Afterward I waited expectantly for the newspaper to appear. The front page was as accurate as I could have hoped, but on the follow-up, the headline read: "Egyptologist admits there was a curse." In fact, this line did bear some relationship to what I had said. In discussing the deaths of those associated with the tomb of King Tut I had remarked: "It is true that everyone who enters the tomb will die, just as it is true that everyone who crosses Woodlawn Avenue (a main thoroughfare on the University of Chicago campus) will eventually die." I never expected to have my remark edited in such a creative way and taken out of context.

While this kind of misinformation may seem innocuous enough, there were several other articles that gratuitously included unsubstantiated "facts", such as that which appeared in the *Washington Post* (March 16, 1977): "'Cursed be those that disturb the rest of the pharaoh' read an inscription on his tomb." There was in fact no curse on either the walls of the tomb or on any object found inside it. So, you may well ask, if there was no curse, how is it that there are so many of them attributed to the tomb and its owner? In the case of the articles written during the latest King Tut exhibit, I venture to say that most if not all references to the curse derived from ignorance and a desire for a catchy headline—not necessarily in that order.

The Troubles of Carter and Carnarvon

From the time of the discovery of the young pharaoh's tomb in 1922 it was surrounded by controversy. The original concession granted to the excavators by the Egyptian government called for some division of the finds between the host country and the excavator, as had been the custom in the past. In the end, such a division was precluded, primarily because of the desirability of keeping together the contents of a nearly intact tomb that was such an important part of the heritage of the country, not to mention the magnitude of the discovery, its impact on the world, and its effect on our knowledge of the past. While Lord Carnarvon, the sponsor of the expedition, hardly needed nor indeed expected vast remuneration for his archaeological efforts, there was the question of the cost of six years of field work conducted for Carnarvon by Howard Carter before the tomb was discovered. Moreover, there were six and one-half more years of work ahead in order to clear the tomb, and then four years of work to be completed in the laboratory before the last of the artifacts would leave the Valley of the Kings for the Cairo Museum.

In a stunning move that was calculated to deal with all of his problems (not the least of which was the overwhelming demand for information from the press), Lord Carnarvon sold the exclusive rights to publish anything about the tomb to the *Times* of London. By this action, Carnarvon was able not only to offset the costs of previous and future work at the site, but also to avoid constant interruptions by the press. In the past, members of the expedition had been badgered to utter distraction by reporters hungry for stories about an event that had aroused the interest of the public; now, reporters no longer had direct access to such sources. This is not to say that the *Times* withheld all information: it did give out stories—but only *after* they appeared in the *Times*, with the result that all other newspapers were always at least a day behind the *Times* with any news about the boy king.

This situation angered the press, but they were not the only ones who were disgruntled. In an effort to keep tourists from interrupting those who were trying to record and clear the tomb, Carter and Carnarvon had barred virtually all but a select few from the excavation. Some officials of the Antiquities Service, other Egyptologists, and political figures from Egypt and around the world could not gain access to the tomb easily. Such secrecy caused rumors to flourish, the most malicious of which referred to the planned theft of some objects. Unfortunately, there may well have been a bit of truth to these stories, and some authors claim that a few artifacts now in the collections of museums outside Egypt may have originated in Tut's tomb!

Conversely, one of the objects that remained in the collection and is now on exhibit in the Cairo Museum may not have come from its designated find spot. A head of Tutankhamun portrayed as the god Nefertem emerging from a lotus depicts one of the ancient creation myths. According to Carter's later published reports, it was found in the corridor to Tut's tomb; this location, however, really did not make much sense, since all similar objects were found in the Treasury. Carter did not include any real information about the head in his original field reports, nor did he note it in the first volumes of his book. In fact, the figure was "discovered" in a neighboring tomb (used for storage) when a committee of officials visited the site during Carter's absence. It was carefully wrapped, and stored in a crate with labels from a European provision shop. Despite these irregularities, no scandal emerged, and the apparently hastily devised version of its origin has become the official story: it was found in debris in the corridor, where it had been left by (ancient) thieves.

While the media missed out on this particular episode, they did have a field day when Lord Carnarvon died on May 6, 1923—less than a year after the discovery of the tomb. There were all sorts of versions of the specific "curse" to which Carnarvon's death could be attributed, but most tried to relate it to an inscription of warning in the tomb. Some of the reporters had the aid of disgruntled Egyptologists, who had not only been denied access to the tomb, but also any information about it. Since there was no love lost between Carter and Carnarvon and some of their scholarly colleagues, there was always someone who was willing to provide information about certain objects or inscriptions in the tomb, based solely on published photographs. In this manner, many inscriptions could be construed as curses by the public, especially after a "re-translation" by the press. For example, an innocuous text inscribed on mud plaster before the Anubis shrine in the Treasury stated: "I am the one who prevents the sand from blocking the secret chamber." In the newspaper, it metamorphosed into: "... I will kill all of those who cross this threshold into the sacred precincts of the royal king who lives forever."

Such misrepresentation proliferated, and soon curses were being found in all of the inscriptions. Since few people could read the texts and thereby check the original, the reporters were safe. They could (and did) publish a photograph of the large golden shrine in the Burial Chamber, together with a "translation" of the accompanying inscription: "They who enter this sacred tomb shall swift be visited by wings of death." The carved figure of a winged goddess that accompanied the shrine would no doubt reinforce the "translated" threat. In reality, the texts on this shrine come from The Book of the Dead—a collection of spells intended to ensure eternal life, not to shorten it!

Poor Lord Carnarvon. His death, rather than promoting the peace and quiet that he wished for himself and his colleague Howard Carter, resulted in more interest in, and scandal and intrigue about, the discoverers of King Tut. Every newspaper around the world carried a story about Lord Carnarvon's death from the mysterious and ominous forces unleashed from the tomb that he was responsible for opening. All sorts of related phenomena were also attributed to the action of the curse upon the defiler of the tomb. For example, all the lights in Cairo were reported to have gone out at the precise moment of Lord Carnarvon's death. The loss of electricity in Cairo, however, was not an uncommon occurrence, and is an experience that most tourists to Egypt have encountered several times.

Carnarvon's son, Lord Porchester, added to the mystery by recounting that his father's dog, at home at the family castle Highclere, let out a pitiful cry at the moment of its master's death, and then it too died. It appears, however, that Lord Porchester was in India at the time of his father's death, so the story of the dog's demise must have been related to him, not actually seen by him. It is pertinent to note that the estate of the deceased Lord Carnarvon continued to reap the benefits of the arrangement made with the *Times* of London, receiving a percentage of the profits realized from the sale of stories. Keeping the interest of the public at fever pitch was a lucrative business for both the *Times* and Carnarvon's estate. During the Chicago portion of the recent exhibition (April 15-August 15, 1977), Lord Carnarvon's heir stated that although he did not know if there was a curse, he wouldn't take one million pounds to enter the tomb. The real story behind the death of Carnarvon is not quite so dramatic, if no less tragic. It appears that he died of an infection that caused blood poisoning, and that the origin of this infection was a mosquito bite on the cheek, cut open by a razor during shaving.

Corroboration for Tutankhamun's curse mounted as people died who could be associated in some way with Carnarvon or with the tomb. More rational explanations of these deaths were overlooked by the reporters, who could finally get a scoop and not have to wait for the *Times* to present their facts. Throughout the world, the story of the death of Carnarvon was recounted in detail, though not necessarily with accuracy. The press began to have a field day after the death of Carter's conservator (A.C. Mace of the Metropolitan Museum of Art); the fact that Mace had had pleurisy for a long time did not appear to affect the storytellers. So another man fell to the curse. A friend of Carnarvon's who was infirm and elderly was the next to succumb. Then the Egyptologist, archaeologist, and writer Weigall (whom Carter and Carnarvon had attempted to keep out of the tomb under any circumstances) died too, supposedly from the curse. An Egyptian prince was murdered in London by his jealous French wife—another victim! Soon the papers carried stories of curators and workmen from museums all over the world, who had neither visited the tomb nor come into close contact with any of its contents, but had nevertheless been struck down. Nervous people began cleaning out their basements and attics and sending their Egyptian relics to museums in order to avoid being the next victim.

Times have not changed. About 15 years ago, the Director General of the Egyptian Antiquities Department (Dr. Gamal Mehrez) died; he had been chronically ill, but his death was attributed to the movement of King Tut's treasures for an exhibition in England. Even more recently, I had to testify for the prosecution at the trial of a man who had murdered his wife because (the defense claimed) he had been cursed by an Egyptian object that had come into the couple's possession.

Carter, it should be noted, died in bed of natural causes at the age of 67 (March 2, 1939), more than 17 years after he discovered the tomb of Tutankhamun.

Some Real Egyptian Curses

All of the fabrications and exaggerations described above neglect two points. The first is that there may well have been some natural phenomena in Tut's tomb (or any tomb, for that matter) that could cause disease, for example, molds or spores. It is a fact that paleopathologists and microbiologists now suggest that mummies be examined by people wearing gloves and masks to prevent the spread of any infection. Indeed, the Philadelphia *Inquirer* recently ran an article on this topic, entitled "Thesis: Fungi, not a curse, killed the finders of King Tut's Tomb" (July 30, 1985). Of course, this theory does not account for Carter's remarkable resistance to the micro-organisms, not to mention the workers and scientists attached to the project, officials, and tourists who also survived.

The second point is that the ancient Egyptians did in fact use curses. Most of them are couched in the form of threats, and they occur mainly on the monuments of private citizens rather than on those of royalty. This interesting observation may indicate that royalty had protection against its enemies through other sources. In fact, most of the curses come from inscriptions on the walls of private tombs of the Old Kingdom, during a time when the royal tombs (pyramids) were decorated with a set of spells called Pyramid Texts that were meant as aids, advice, and directions for the king. Because of their size, prominence, and the existence of a large group of priests attached to the funerary complex, the royal funerary monuments obviously had the protection they needed.

Royal curses, when they do occur, are directed more toward this life than the next. There is an address at Deir el Bahri by Thutmose I to the court of his daughter, the reigning pharaoh Hatshepsut: "He who will adore her, he will live; he who will speak evil in a curse against her majesty, he will die" (Sethe 1906:15 ff). Somewhat distinct are the "execration texts" that occur on pottery bowls and figurines from the end of the 12th-13th Dynasty. These are curses against foreign states or peoples that might act or had already acted against Egypt. At appropriate times, the objects with their curses were ritually smashed.

Amenhotep, son of Hapu, was a remarkable figure from the 18th Dynasty, who was later deified (in the 21st Dynasty). A mortuary temple which was built in his honor was protected by a rather lengthy and detailed curse:

> As for [anyone] who will come after me and who
> will find the foundation of the funerary tomb
> in destruction ...
> as for anyone who will take the personnel from
> among my people ...
> as for all others who will turn them astray ...
> I will not allow them to perform their scribal
> function ...
> I will put them in the furnace of the king ...
> His uraeus will vomit flame upon the top of their
> heads, demolishing their flesh and devouring
> their bones.
> They will become Apophis [a divine serpent who is
> vanquished] on the morning of the day of the year.
> They will capsize in the sea which will devour
> their bodies.
> They will not receive honors received by virtuous
> people.
> They will not be able to swallow offerings of the
> dead.
> One will not pour for them water in libation ...
> Their sons will not occupy their places, their
> women will be violated before their eyes.

> Their great ones will be so lost in their houses that
> they will be upon the floor ...
> They will not understand the words of the king at
> the time when he is in joy.
> They will be doomed to the knife on the day of
> massacre ...
> Their bodies will decay because they will starve and
> will not have sustenance and their bones will
> perish. (British Museum Stele 138; Varille 1968)

Important decrees could also be protected by threats, especially in regard to specific individuals already proclaimed guilty, as this indictment shows:

> As to any king and powerful person who will forgive
> him, he will not receive the white crown, he will not
> raise up the red crown, he will not dwell upon the
> throne of Horus of the living. As for any commander
> or mayor who will petition my lord to pardon him,
> his property and his fields will be put as offerings for
> my father Min of Coptos. (Sethe 1959:98, 16ff)

It is clear that while the Egyptians rarely made the kind of curses that you find in the headlines, they did understand the power of negative thinking and saying. Their curses are hardly a mystery, hardly an enigma. Their suggestive remarks and threats were meant to dissuade those who might act against them. The means by which this was accomplished was the written word, so important in all aspects of Egyptian culture. The curse would survive as long as the monument on which it was written.

Some Non-Royal Curses

Most genuine Egyptian curses take a particular form, and, once established, the pattern remains intact. Those placed on private tombs during the Old Kingdom are usually preceded by a statement such as: "As for any [here is put the title of any one of several professions] who will pass by this monument, may he say a 1000 of ... [a variety of provisions]; He will receive ... [one of several benefactions]." Then follows the threat:

As for anyone who will:

do something evil against this my grave

seize a stone from this my tomb

remove any stone or any brick from this my tomb

enter this tomb in impurity

enter upon these my images in impurity

(the last two can be embellished with: "after he has eaten the abomination which the beneficient ones detest")

which is then followed by the punishment:

he will be judged regarding it by the great god.

I will wring his neck like a goose [or like a bird] and cause those who live upon earth to fear the spirits who are in the West.

I will exterminate his survivors.

I will not allow their farms to be occupied.

Other forms of threat do occur: "As for anything which you shall do against this my grave, the like shall be done against yours."

Examples of curses from the Middle Kingdom are rarer, perhaps in part because of the use of protective spells that occur in the Coffin Texts.

Every man who will interfere with this my stela, I will be judged with him in the place where judgement is made. (Sethe 1959:87, 17-18).

As for any people [a variety of professions] who will make a disturbance in this tomb or who will destroy its writings or who will do damage to its images, they will fall to the wrath of Thoth. (Sethe 1959:88, 1-3)

Less formulaic are the warnings that occur in the Letters to the Dead, in which those on earth ask the spirits of the dead for aid and advice. Sometimes the living press the issue with a threat: "Am I being injured in your presence? ... who then will pour out water for you?" (Gardiner and Sethe 1929:4).

Even private letters can contain expressions of ill will such as that written by one Middle Kingdom woman from el Lahun to another, with the closing expression: "May you be [sick] when you read this." One of the most touching examples of this type of inscription is the threat written by a mother during the Ramesside Period, who had adopted servants as her children and wanted to assure their position:

She said: "As Amon endures and as the Ruler endures, I make the people whom I have recorded freemen of the land of Pharaoh. Should a son of a daughter or a brother or a sister of their mother or their father contest with them—except for this son of mine, Pendiu—for they are no longer slaves to him, but are brothers and sisters to him, being freemen of the land—may a donkey copulate with him and a female donkey copulate with his wife, if anyone shall call one of them a slave ..."—in the presence of very numerous witnesses. (Translation based on Gardiner 1940:23ff)

Such sentiments are paralleled in a later curse, from the Ethiopian period:

As for the one who will cause this [document?] to remain, his son will remain on his place—one after another. Neither his images nor his name shall be obliterated forever and ever. As for the one who will obliterate [this decree] the power of the goddess Neit will come into being against him forever and ever. His son shall not be caused to remain on his place and a donkey will copulate with him, a female donkey with his wife and his children, and he will fall to the flame from the mouth of Sekhmet. (Translation based on transcription of the stela in Spiegelberg 1903:191-92)

References

Edel, Elmar
1944
"Untersuchungen zur Phraseologie der ägyptischen Inschriften." *Mitteilungen des Deutschen Archäologischen Instituts, Abteilung (Kairo)* 13:1-90.

Gardiner, Alan
1940
"Adoption Extraordinary." *Journal of Egyptian Archaeology* 26:23.

Gardiner, Alan H., and Kurt Sethe
1928
Egyptian Letters to the Dead. London: Egypt Exploration Society.

Griffith, F.L.
1898
Hieratic Papyri from Kahun and Gurob. London: Bernard Quaritch.

Helck, Wolfgang
1975
"Fluch." *Lexikon der Ägyptologie* 2, Lieferung 2. Wiesbaden: Otto Harrassowitz.

Herodotus
1954
The Histories. Tr. Aubrey de Sélincourt. Reprint. Baltimore: Penguin Books, 1965.

Hoving, Thomas
1979
Tutankhamun, the Untold Story. New York: Simon and Schuster.

Sethe, Kurt
1906
Urkunden der 18. Dynastie. Urkunden des ägyptischen Altertums IV. Leipzig: J. Hinrichs.
1959
Ägyptische Lesestücke. Hildesheim: Georg Olms.

Spiegelberg, W.
1903
"Die Tefnachthosstele des Museums von Athen." *Recueil des Travaux* 25:191-192.

Vandenberg, Phillipp
1975
The Curse of the Pharaohs. Tr. Thomas Weyr. Philadelphia: J. Lippincott.

Varille, Alexandre
1968
Inscriptions concernant l'architecte Amenhotep fils de Hapu. Bibliothèque d'Études 44. Cairo: Institut Français d'Archéologie Orientale.

"From Theory to Theme Parks and the Man on the Moon: Archaeology in Contemporary Academia, Industry, and Popular Culture"

Robert J. Muckle

This article is based on a presentation given at the annual meeting of the American Anthropology Association in 2004. The presentation highlighted recent trends and items of interest in archaeology to an audience composed primarily of anthropologists and anthropology students broadly familiar with archaeology but who don't necessarily specialize in it.

Robert Muckle, who is also the editor of this volume, is a professor of archaeology at Capilano College in Canada. This selection was originally published in a 2005 issue of *Teaching Anthropology/ SACC Notes*, a periodical published by the American Anthropological Association and the Society for Anthropology in Community Colleges.

Questions to Guide Reading

What is the nature of the debate about the place of archaeology within academia?
What topics of academic research interest are covered in the article?
What is the nature of archaeological work and interest within the heritage industry?
What concerns archaeologists about the way archaeology is portrayed in popular culture?
What are the traditional and contemporary rationalizations for archaeology?

Introduction

Archaeology in the early 21st century is considered, discussed, rationalized, theorized and practiced in many contexts. Recent developments in three of these contexts—academia, industry and popular culture—are the focus of this paper.

It is an interesting time in archaeology. A cursory examination of mainstream archaeological literature could easily lead someone to think that archaeology just continues to plod along with the same old debates and research interests. Delving deeper into the published literature, purveying the titles of books in press and perusing conference programs, discussions on listserves and the on-line and printed information from organizations of professional archaeologists, however, may lead to a contrary view.

To be sure, many of the age-old debates and research interests in archaeology continue, but there are emergent subfields and many new areas in which archaeologists have been giving voice. These include such matters as intellectual property rights, theme parks, television programs and the archaeology of outer space. When some of these areas have been covered in years past, they were often discussed in a whimsical manner and could legitimately be relegated to the 'fringe.' Now, it just isn't so.

The first section of this paper—Archaeology in Academia—covers the debate about the proper place of archaeology in academia and the inroads the post-processualist school has made in mainstream archaeology. It includes emergent subfields, a few areas of long-standing archaeological interest such as the peopling of the Americas and the origins of agriculture, and a new focus on space heritage. The second section—Archaeology in Industry—includes the various terms used for archaeologists working outside of academic settings. It also covers how archaeologists are going beyond their traditional role in the industry of finding, documenting and assessing the significance of archaeological sites to becoming much more involved with the marketing of heritage.

The third section—Archaeology in Popular Culture—briefly covers the concern archaeologists have about the portrayal of archaeology as it affects student pre-conceptions and the direction of research. The fourth section—Other Contexts and New Rationalizations—provides a brief overview of archaeology in the contexts of politics and global social movements; it also provides some contemporary rationalizations for archaeology.

ARCHAEOLOGY IN ACADEMIA

For those who may not be aware, considering archaeology as one of the fields of anthropology is pretty much an American phenomenon. The debate about whether American archaeology should stand alone or continue to be considered as one of the fields of anthropology has a long and continuing history.

Just because the American Anthropological Association recently published a volume of papers called *Archeology is Anthropology* doesn't mean there is a consensus of opinion among archaeologists. A look at other organizations may provide other conclusions. In March 2004, the periodical *The Archaeological Record*, published by the Society for American Archaeology, produced a special issue on the status of American archaeology. One of the papers is from a one-time professor of archaeology and now a university president, who essentially argues that within universities, anthropology as a whole is in a period of descending status. Archaeology, it is argued, would thus be well served by breaking from anthropology and tying itself to the 'harder' sciences, where institutional investment is growing. Others have made similar arguments, suggesting that association with the social sciences and humanities carries with it a '*malignancy of post-modernism*' that doesn't serve archaeology very well.

Other recent and interesting contributions on the relationship between archaeology and anthropology include those by Liz Brumfiel (2003), Ian Hodder (2003), and Michael Rowlands (2004). I think these are particularly interesting for the different perspective each provides. Brumfiel, an archaeologist and current president of the American Anthropological Association, not surprisingly outlines the benefits of collaboration between archaeologists and cultural anthropologists. Hodder, probably the most influential archaeologist of the last two decades, writes from his history of training and building his career in Britain and Europe and only recently taking up a position in the Department of Cultural and Social Anthropology at Stanford. Those who follow developments in archaeology are undoubtedly aware that Hodder is generally credited with leading the post-processual movement, which at one extreme is anti-scientific. Interestingly, Hodder recognizes that one of the disadvantages of archaeology being considered a subfield of anthropology in North America is that it likely impedes developments in archaeological science. Rowlands, an anthropologist, writes from Britain, where anthropology and archaeology are generally distinct. He suggests that a convergence is occurring there as social and cultural anthropologists appear to be rediscovering material culture.

In regard to theory, there is a good overview article on issues and theory in North American archaeology by Michelle Hegmon (2003) in a recent issue of *American Antiquity*. She states that there is little explicit discussion of theory in North American archaeology. However, it is clear that the post-processualists or the 'processual-plus' school, as some are now calling it, have been making significant inroads in archaeological research being conducted by those based in American universities. Archaeological research now often focuses on such things as gender, ethnicity, agency and symbols. There has also been a trend towards replacing such phrases as '*cultural evolution*' with '*pathways to complexity*' or '*pathways to power*.' In a similar vein, instead of writing about social or political organization, archaeologists are now writing increasingly about '*organizational strategies*.'

Two recently emergent subfields of archaeology that are receiving considerable attention are community archaeology and indigenous archaeology. Although once community archaeology was considered to include work with descendant communities, it is now largely considered to be archaeology focussed on local, often non-indigenous communities, usually with the interests of the community front and center. The Society for Anthropology in Community Colleges (SACC) sponsored a session on community archaeology at a recent AAA meeting, and the papers were published in this periodical (9:1, 2002). This type of community archaeology was also the focus of a recent theme issue in the journal *World Archaeology*; and a couple of books have just come out on this sort of community archaeology (Derry and Malloy 2003, Shackel and Chambers 2004).

The field of indigenous archaeology is receiving much attention, both in North America and throughout the world. What will likely become a standard in the field is a book called *Indigenous Archaeologies*, set to be published in 2005 and based on a series of papers presented at the 2003 World Archaeology Congress. One of the themes

of indigenous archaeology has to do with intellectual property rights. There is an excellent article on this in a recent issue of *Current Anthropology* (Nicholas and Bannister 2004).

In terms of academic research interests, considerable attention in recent months has been focussed on the possibility of pre-Clovis peoples in the Americas. Much on this topic has recently appeared in the popular press, and a November 2004 *Nova* program detailed the possible connections between the Solutrean of Upper Palaeolithic Europe and the Clovis peoples of the Americas via an Atlantic Ocean crossing. Bruce Bradley and Dennis Stanford, the leading proponents of the Solutrean-Clovis connection, have outlined their views in a recent issue of *World Archaeology* (Bradley and Stanford 2004). Things may change, but it would be an overstatement to say that the archaeological community in general accepts a Solutrean-Clovis connection.

Another find related to possible pre-Clovis peoples in the Americas that has received considerable attention in the popular press relates to the Topper Site in South Carolina. Since 1998, archaeologist Al Goodyear has been excavating allegedly pre-Clovis deposits there. The results of some radiocarbon dates came back in mid-November 2004, suggesting an antiquity of about 50,000 years. The archaeological community is awaiting some scholarly publication, and until then the jury is still out. Certainly, at this point, not all are convinced. Some are claiming the so-called 'artifacts' are not artifacts at all; and some have expressed doubt that the material used for dating was cultural.

With the possibility of pre-Clovis and despite the claims of trans-Atlantic crossings or entries via the south Pacific, the majority opinion still holds that the first people in the Americas came from Asia via the area around the Bering Strait. Research over the past few years has increased doubt about an ice-free corridor passage and increased the likelihood of a migration down the west coast of Alaska and Canada. Research is showing that even during the glacial maximums, some areas could have supported human populations prior to 12,000 years ago. One site that has received considerable attention is Port Eliza on the west coast of Canada. Here it has become evident that the between 16,000 and 14,000 years ago, the environment supported a variety of birds, fish and mammals.

On a global scale, the emergence of domestic foods continues to be an area of much interest in archaeology. Archaeologists are increasingly considering that domestication may have occurred for reasons other than population pressure. Some archaeologists have been making the case that the first domestic foods were forms of wealth that were used exclusively or at least primarily in feasting contexts. Brian Hayden (2003) provides a good overview of this in a recent issue of *World Archaeology*. *Current Anthropology* has released a supplement to its November 2004 issue focussing specifically on agricultural origins and dispersals into Europe.

A relatively new area of archaeological interest is outer space, or 'space heritage.' This emerging interest is sometimes known as exo-archaeology, and includes everything from the documentation of the material remains of space exploration, to space junk and the search for extraterrestrial landings on earth. I don't know of any books devoted exclusively to exo-archaeology, but I suspect they will inevitably come along. The last introductory level textbook I used had a box feature on it. There are chapters in recently published books about it, sessions on it were held at both the 2003 World Archaeology Congress and the 2004 meetings of the Society for American Archaeology, and the program for the 2004 AAA meetings shows some planned paper presentations on it.

The part about the 'man on the moon' in this paper's title comes from an interesting project by archaeologists seeking to document and protect some of the artifacts and features such as footprints on the moon, particularly at Tranquility Base. Apparently, UNESCO does not wish to include it on their list of World Heritage sites, and the United States does not wish to declare it a National Historic site.

In regard to space junk, Bill Rathje, who forged his career in archaeology by studying contemporary American refuse, has been one of the leading archaeologists to write on space junk, focussing on the nature and danger of it (e.g. Rathje 2001).

I feel compelled to comment on some recent archaeological research done at the alleged alien spacecraft landing site in Roswell, New Mexico. In 2002, a professional archaeologist participated in a project involved with the search for evidence. Apparently, the project was funded and broadcast by the Sci Fi television channel. Not surprisingly, there was no convincing evidence of an alien spacecraft landing, at least by archaeological standards.

ARCHAEOLOGY IN INDUSTRY

The vast majority of professional archaeologists now make their careers in the heritage industry, which is sort of an umbrella phrase for all the work archaeologists do outside of college, university or museum settings. It is otherwise commonly known as *cultural resource management* or *C.R.M.* in North America; *archaeological resource management* in the United Kingdom; *archaeological heritage management* in the rest of Europe; and *cultural heritage management* in Australia. Other phrases it is currently known by include *client-based archaeology* and *compliance archaeology*. It also includes components of *public archaeology* and what used to be known as *conservation archaeology*, *rescue archaeology* and *salvage archaeology*.

One way of viewing the heritage industry is that it has three primary components. One component focuses on convincing the public of the value of heritage and the legislation to protect it. Archaeologists have traditionally not been very active or influential in this regard, although this is beginning to change. Most of the major associations, for example, have been prominent in their concern for the heritage of Afghanistan and Iraq. The World Archaeology Congress is positioned as a dominant player in this component of the heritage industry and has recently been weighing in on some proposed heritage legislation in the United States, much to the chagrin of some American archaeologists.

Another component of the heritage industry focuses on the investigation and assessment of heritage. This is where almost all of the work for archaeologists is: finding the sites, documenting them and assessing their significance. A recent estimate puts the number of people in this field at about 10,000 for the United States alone.

The one other component of the heritage industry focuses on the representation of heritage for the public. Traditionally, this has been left to those working in public education, tourism, other commercial enterprises or government. Recently, however, archaeologists have started to become much more involved with this component of the industry, particularly in regard to critiquing the marketing of heritage. Several examples of this can be found in the book *Marketing Heritage: Archaeology and the Consumption of the Past* (Rowan and Baram 2004). Particular criticisms found in this book as well as other sources include such things as the appropriation of culture, the trafficking of artifacts and the representation of the past through 'living museums' and archaeology theme parks.

There are some living museums and archaeology theme parks that are generally considered to be fairly good. Most of these are in Europe. The Jorvik Viking Centre in England, where even the smells are recreated, usually gets good reviews from archaeologists, as does ARCHEON in the Netherlands, where people journey through prehistoric, Roman and Medieval periods.

One of the common criticisms that archaeologists level is that living museums and theme parks usually provide a much too sanitized version of the past. Even Colonial Williamsburg, which works very closely with the archaeological community, is not free from this criticism. The problem, as some critics note, is that people often think they are really learning by going to the parks and museums—at least this is what they claim on surveys. It is sort of like going to the movie rather than reading the book.

A couple of theme parks seem rather out of the ordinary. One is the recently opened Holy Land Experience in Florida, which was apparently designed to give all those who want to visit the Holy Land the chance without the danger. I haven't been there myself, but it is apparently more than a bit slanted to the Christian view.

Another new theme park, recently opened in Switzerland, is called Mystery Park. It is very strongly associated with Erich von Daniken, who has now allegedly sold more than 60 million books documenting the notion that the Egyptian pyramids, Mayan art, Nazca lines, the statues of Easter Island and other things are the result of visits to Earth by extraterrestrials. I haven't been there yet myself, but an editor of the journal *Archaeology*, who did get the opportunity to visit earlier this year, wrote that it has to be "the most bizarre archaeological experience on the planet" (Powell 2004).

ARCHAEOLOGY IN POPULAR CULTURE

Archaeology has been firmly embedded in popular culture for quite a long time. Archaeologists have frequently made comment on it, but until recently there really hasn't been any kind of scholarly interest in it. This is now beginning to change. There is a smattering of recent short articles, often whimsical, but some expressing real concern, about archaeology in popular culture, two books that I know of (Russell 2002, Holtorf 2005) and an academic session on it planned for the 2005 meetings of the Society for Historical Archaeology.

The general sense I get is that archaeologists are becoming increasingly concerned about the way that archaeology is portrayed in popular culture. The principal concerns are that (i) since the portrayal of archaeology is usually very biased, we have to deprogram the students coming into our classes, and (ii) the popular perceptions of archaeology may increasingly determine the direction of archaeological research.

I think most of us who have been teaching for a while can appreciate how popular culture influences student preconceptions. Several years ago it wasn't uncommon for at least a few students entering an archaeology course for the first time to be thinking they would be learning about dinosaurs; that happens much more rarely now. Asking students to name an archaeologist, real or fictional several years ago would rarely progress beyond "Indiana Jones." Now, in addition to Lara Croft, I hear a plethora of names associated with television programs, ranging from *Star Trek: The Next Generation*, to *Relic Hunter*, *Babylon 5* and *Dr. Who*. A short time ago during a class discussion on Mesoamerican civilizations, I learned that one student who had been making what he thought were useful contributions learned everything he knew about the Olmec from an episode of *The Simpsons*.

I think most archaeologists recognize that popular culture has been affecting research for a very long time. We recognize, for example, that much of the research documented in media through television documentaries and print articles are funded by that media, with the knowledge that it will be good entertainment. I have to remind my own students on occasion that *National Geographic* usually funds the research described in their programs and the magazine.

A principal concern is that the proportion of research directed by media involved in popular culture may increase significantly, with research ultimately being led by what makes good television rather than what makes good archaeology. Some would say that it has already happened. It is becoming increasingly the case that television is determining the kind of research that is being done. For example, the Discovery Channel funded the recent research determining that the Ice Man, who died in the Italian Alps 5,000 years ago, was murdered (Fagan and Rose 2003).

There is also a concern that as media may direct the types of research archaeologists do, funding for archaeology from traditional sources may decrease.

This is based on the knowledge that popular culture usually portrays archaeological research as interesting but largely irrelevant to the contemporary world. Thus, politicians and others ultimately in charge of dispersing funds for pure research may find it easier to cut back on archaeology. The reasoning is that if the public generally sees archaeology as dispensable, so too will the funding agencies.

OTHER CONTEXTS AND NEW RATIONALIZATIONS

Although beyond the intended scope of this paper, I want to point out that there are other ways to contextualize archaeology and new ways to rationalize archaeology that rarely appear in textbooks and other media.

In addition to academia, industry and popular culture, I often contextualize archaeology in the frameworks of politics. Much has been written on how archaeology has been used to create a sense of cultural superiority and/or national identity in some not-so-subtle ways (e.g., Nazi Germany). New avenues of interest include examinations of how mainstream media dealing with archaeology tends to promote European and American values. They also reveal the damaging impact of political regimes and conflicts, past and present.

Archaeologists have become firmly associated with a few global social movements, including feminism, indigenous empowerment and environmentalism. The relationships appear to be mutually beneficial.

Traditional rationalizations for archaeology, such as "it is intrinsically interesting, all knowledge is good, and so that we can learn from the past," often just don't cut it anymore. One can imagine students in a classroom, saying something along the lines of "Oh, come on. Not even historians use that 'so we can learn from the past' bit anymore."

There are several rationalizations that seem to be accepted more readily. These include (i) providing a context for current events, such as explaining the conditions under which warfare appears to occur; (ii) providing a framework for investigation, including documenting heritage and forensic applications; (iii) assessing claims, including those of prehistoric use and information coming from those with real or perceived economic, social, and ideological agendas; (iv) the economic value, especially in regions where governments, corporations, and individuals are economically dependent on the heritage industry; and (v) on a very practical level, bringing an awareness of and offering solutions to some important problems of living in the early 21st century, such as marking nuclear waste sites.

References

Bradley, Bruce and Dennis Stanford.
2004. The North Atlantic Ice-Edge Corridor: A Possible Palaeolithic Route to the New World. *World Archaeology* 36 (4).

Brumfiel, Elizabeth.
2003. It's a Material World: History, Artifacts, and Anthropology. *Annual Reviews Anthropology* 32: 205-223.

Derry, Linda and Maureen Malloy (ed).
2003. *Archaeologists and Local Communities: Partners in Exploring the Past*. Washington, DC: Society for American Archaeology.

Fagan, Brian and Mark Rose.
2003. Ethics and the Media. In *Ethical Issues in Archaeology*, edited by Larry Zimmerman, Karen Vitelli, and Julie Hollowell-Zimmer, pp 163-176. Walnut Creek, CA: Altamira.

Gillespie, Susan D. and Deborah L. Nichols (ed).
2003. *Archeology Is Anthropology*. Archeological Papers of the American Anthropological Association, Number 13.

Hayden, Brian.
2003. Were Luxury Foods the First Domesticates? Ethnoarchaeological Perspectives from Southeast Asia. *World Archaeology* 34: 458-469.

Hegmon, Michelle.
2003. Setting Theoretical Egos Aside: Issues and Theory in North American Archaeology. *American Antiquity* 68: 213-243.

Hodder, Ian.
2003. *Archaeology Beyond Dialogue*. Salt Lake City: University of Utah Press.

Holtorf, Cornelius.
2005. *From Stonehenge to Las Vegas: Archaeology in Popular Culture*. Walnut Creek, CA: Altamira.

Nicholas, George and Kelly P. Bannister.
2004. Copyrighting the Past? Emerging Intellectual Property Rights Issues in Archaeology. *Current Anthropology* 45 (3): 327-350.

Powell, Eric.
2004. Letter From Switzerland: Theme Park of the Gods? *Archaeology* 57.

Rathje, W.L.
2001. Archaeology of Space Garbage. *Scientific American* February, 2001.

Rowlands, Michael.
2004. Relating Anthropology and Archaeology. In *A Companion to Archaeology*, edited by John Bintliff, pp 473-489. Oxford, UK: Blackwell.

Rowan, Yorke and Uzi Baram (ed).

2004. *Marketing Heritage: Archaeology and the Consumption of the Past*. Walnut Creek, CA: Altamira.

Russell, Miles (ed).

2002. *Digging Holes in Popular Culture: Archaeology in Science Fiction*. Oxford, UK: Oxbow.

Shackel, Paul and Erve Chambers (ed).

2004. *Places in Mind: Public Archaeology as Applied Anthropology*. New York: Routledge.

"Garbology: The Archaeology of Fresh Garbage"

W.L. RATHJE

One of the most interesting developments in archaeology over the past few decades has been the increasing attention given to the material remains of recent times, including investigations of refuse from households and landfills.

This selection was written by W.L. Rathje, the foremost expert in the archaeological study of contemporary refuse, and it originally appeared in the edited volume *Public Benefits of Archaeology*, published in 2002. Rathje is a professor emeritus at the University of Arizona and a consulting professor at Stanford.

••

Questions to Guide Reading

What has the archaeology of contemporary garbage revealed about the contents of landfills?
What principal conclusions have been reached from analyzing contemporary refuse?
What is meant by "Parkinson's Law of Garbage"?

••

Gold cups, jade beads, mummies, temples lost in rainforests. To me, these were the essence of archaeology. How I longed to become an archaeologist and to journey back to the days of our ancient ancestors by following breadcrumb trails of artifacts they had left behind. When I was nine, that was the archaeology I dreamed about as I drifted to sleep beside my dog-eared copy of *The Wonderful World of Archaeology* (Jessup 1956).

Fourteen years later I found myself in graduate school and immersed in the stifling smell of dusty potsherds, the quiet punctuated every so often by the thunderous explosions of 200 or 300 broken pieces of pottery being poured out of linen bags onto masonite laboratory tables. These potsherds had become my path to ancient lives. By this time

I had learned enough of archaeology's arcane secrets to appreciate fully the stories that could be told by potsherds and other commonplace discards about a society's rise and fall and its day-to-day existence. I was, in fact, excited to be systematically and scientifically analyzing the vast expanse of discards to discover replicated patterns of human behavior that we can still recognize today. At the time, I believed I was about to add my own small piece to understanding the puzzle of the Classic Maya collapse (see Rathje 1971, 1973). By 1968 that was the archaeology I dreamed about when I dozed off late at night on top of my well-worn copy of *Uaxactun, Guatemala: Excavations of 1931–1937* (Smith 1950).

Today, twenty-seven years later still, I look back on my past dreams of archaeology with a bemused smile, my hands full of fresh garbage and my mind dancing with thoughts of the calories from fat in our diet or of the recyclables mixed into garbage instead of separated for curbside collection. As for today's dreams—who could fall asleep while perusing the Environmental Protection Agency's Report 530–R-96–001, *Characterization of Municipal Solid Waste in the United States: 1995 Update* (Franklin Associates 1996)?

What happened to my visions of archaeology? Nothing, really. Diverse as they appear, the three perspectives pivot upon the same point: coming to understand some basic threads in the fabric of humanity—which our ancestors wove into us and which we are likewise weaving into our descendants—by touching as a person and by measuring as a scientist the artifacts people make and leave behind. With this personal preamble as background, I will now describe the history, nature, and public benefits of a type of archaeology called garbology, which I believe is currently adding one small piece of understanding to help solve the puzzle of the human enigma.

"Buried Alive: The Garbage Glut" was the cover headline of *Newsweek*, November 27, 1989. "Are We Throwing Away Our Future with Our Trash?" had been the title of the "American Agenda" segment of *ABC Evening News with Peter Jennings* on December 2, 1988. In the late 1980s, the amount of garbage America generated had reached crisis proportions for the media and its public. The vast majority of refuse was sent to landfills, and those landfills were filling up and closing down. Where was the garbage to go?

Concerned citizens, convinced that action had to be taken without delay, quickly identified garbage culprits among the discards that visibly shocked them everyday—litter. Editorials in prestigious newspapers, such as the *New York Times*, echoed popular perceptions that fast food packaging, disposable diapers, and plastic grocery bags were singularly responsible for "straining" our landfills. Public officials in communities nationwide proposed banning the

accused perpetrators. In the meantime, into what kinds of holders were responsible folks to put their burgers, hot coffee, groceries, and infants? Oddly enough, the answer was not clear, because in all the commotion there had been few facts presented about what actually was in garbage and landfills. It was at this point that a new kind of archaeologist, the garbologist studying fresh garbage, was able to unearth a few relevant facts that began to fill the information vacuum surrounding our discards.

At the time, workers around the country were regularly digging into landfills to install methane vents, but no one paid much attention to the refuse that was exhumed in the process. After all, it was just smelly, disgusting garbage. The smell and look of discards were not deterrents to archaeologists, who always expect to get their hands dirty. To archaeologists, in fact, contemporary garbage is a gold mine of information. No society on earth has ever discarded such rich refuse—much of it packaging, which identifies its former contents by brand, type, cost, quantity, ingredients, nutrient content, and more. Yielding to this temptation, between 1987 and 1995 archaeologists from the Garbage Project at the University of Arizona systematically excavated, hand-sorted, weighed, measured for volume, and recorded thirty tons of contents from fifteen landfills around North America—located from California to Toronto and from the deserts of Arizona to the Everglades of Florida. The information that emerged from these "digs" was unexpected (see Rathje 1989, 1991; Rathje and Murphy 1992a).

In contrast to all of the concern directed at fast food packaging and disposable diapers, the archaeological data demonstrated that both items *together* accounted for less than 2 percent of landfill volume within refuse deposited over the last ten years. Even more surprising, because of industry-wide "light-weighting"—that is, making the same form of item but with less resin—plastic grocery bags had become thinner and more crushable, to the point that a hundred plastic bags consumed less space inside a landfill than did twenty paper bags. If all three items of central public concern had been banned and had not been replaced by anything, the garbage archaeologists were certain that landfill managers would not have noticed the difference.

At the opposite end of the spectrum of contents were materials that occupied large portions of landfill space but received little public attention. Construction/demolition debris (C/D) was one. Because of definitional issues, C/D was not even included in the EPA's national estimates of the refuse going to municipal solid waste (MSW) or standard community refuse landfills. Nevertheless, C/D accounted for 20 percent or more of excavated refuse by volume in Garbage Project digs and was the second largest category of discarded materials recovered from MSW landfills.

The largest category occupying MSW landfill space was paper. This was true for refuse buried in the 1980s as well as for refuse dating as far back as the 1950s, because in most landfills, paper seemed to biodegrade very slowly. As a result, by volume nearly half of all of the refuse excavated by the Garbage Project has been newspapers, magazines, packaging paper, and nonpackaging paper, such as computer printouts and phonebooks.

Not long after the Garbage Project's first reports of its landfill digs, the energy directed at passing bans was largely redirected toward curbside recycling. A number of communities began placing emphasis on reuse and recycling programs for C/D. Paper recycling promotions started stressing the need to keep paper out of landfills because it did not biodegrade as quickly as most of us had once hoped. An association of state attorneys general determined from dig data that several products claiming to be biodegradable, including some brands of disposable diapers and plastic garbage bags, did not biodegrade in landfills, and the false advertising of these products was eradicated. All of this was evidence that some crucial views about garbage on the part of policy planners, the media, and the public had changed—and that garbology had been validated as a new kind of archaeology, one that could make an immediate public contribution.

The Rationale for Garbage Archaeology

For as long as there have been archaeologists, there have been jokes, cartoons, and stories guessing at what it would be like for an archaeologist to dig through our own refuse (see Macaulay 1979). While often humorous, such speculations are based on a serious rationale: if archaeologists can learn important information about extinct societies from patterns in ancient garbage, then archaeologists should also be able to learn important information about contemporary societies from patterns in fresh garbage. The pieces of pottery, broken stone tools, and cut animal bones that traditional archaeologists dig out of old refuse middens provide a surprisingly detailed view of past lifeways, just as all the precisely labeled packages and the food debris and the discarded clothing and batteries in modern middens reveal intimate details of our lives today.

During the summer of 1921, A.V. Kidder seemed to understand this when he took the trouble to observe the artifacts that were coming out of a trench being cut for a sewer line through a "fresh" garbage dump in Andover, Massachusetts. From at least this point onward, archaeologists have studied contemporary urban refuse informally and sporadically in class exercises and methodological experiments. A variety of subspecialties—ethnoarchaeology, historic sites archaeology, industrial archaeology, and experimental archaeology—have been edging ever closer to analyzing what citizens of the industrialized world discarded last year, last month, and even yesterday. All archaeologists are aware that contemporary rubbish will inevitably be studied in due course by traditional archaeologists in the same manner we now study the middens of Troy and Tikal, perhaps in a hundred or so years from now.

If indeed there are useful things to learn from an archaeological study of *our* garbage—things that can enrich human lives and minimize the undesirable environmental consequences of the industrialized world—why wait until we (and I literally mean you and I) are all dead and buried to find out? This was what a group of students and I thought when we founded the Garbage Project at the University of Arizona in the spring of 1973. Today all of us who are a part of the project, including codirector Wilson Hughes, who was one of the founding students, are still thinking along these same lines. Garbology now!

After nearly three decades of sorting, recording, and interpreting MSW, garbology, or the archaeological study of contemporary urban refuse, has become a recognizable subspecialty within archaeology and other behavioral sciences (Thomas 1979; Fagan 1985, 1991a, 1991b; Podolefsky and Brown 1993; *American Heritage Dictionary* 1992; *Oxford Dictionary* 1995; Encyclopaedia Britannica 1996; Turnbaugh et al. 1996; Rathje in press). Perhaps the defining characteristic of all garbology digs is that they combine traditional concerns of archaeological method and theory to produce results that are immediately relevant to understanding and mitigating current social dilemmas (see Rathje 1996). The highly publicized "garbage crisis" more or less had the Garbage Project's name on it and made it relatively easy to convince the public at large that the study of contemporary refuse provided a significant contribution to society. The crisis did not erupt in the media, however, until the *Mobro* garbage barge sailed in 1987 and gained an enduring place in the nation's environmental consciousness when it wandered for weeks looking for a place to dump its cargo.

Fresh Sort Rationale and Results

The Garbage Project's first data collection format, called the Regular Sort, was designed to sample and record household pickups of fresh refuse (a *pickup* is all of the materials placed out by a single household on one regular refuse collection day). From the beginning, project procedures have rigorously protected the anonymity of the households discarding the refuse sampled.

Solid waste managers have been characterizing wastes by material composition (paper, plastic, glass, etc.) and weight since the 1880s. To these traditional measures, the Garbage Project added a series of innovations, including records from package labels (brand, cost, solid weight or fluid volume of original contents, specific type of contents, packaging materials) and more detailed breakdowns of broad refuse categories, such as "food waste" (which was separated into "once-edible food" versus "food preparation debris," both being identified by specific food item; see Hughes 1984). Because of their exacting level of detail, the Regular Sort data files documenting residential refuse are ideal for analyzing the role of specific household behaviors in generating wastes. Today the Garbage Project's fresh refuse records, compiled from a long-term ongoing study in Tucson, Arizona, and short-term studies in five other cities, form a one-of-a-kind database now spanning close to thirty years.

Garbage Project studies of fresh refuse have consistently documented a few basic patterns in the way we interact with the material world around us. First, *what people say they do and what they actually do are often different.* For example, while respondents rarely report to interviewers that they waste any food at home, nearly three decades of Garbage Project studies have documented that households generally waste about 15 percent of the solid food they buy (Rathje 1976, 1986; Fung and Rathje 1982). Such misreports characterize a broad range of household behaviors. In other words, people who are interviewed or fill out surveys do not accurately report how much food they waste, what they eat and drink, what they recycle, or the household hazardous wastes they throw away (see Rathje and Murphy 1992a, 1992b).

This discovery, of course, is not a great surprise. It is common knowledge among behavioral scientists that any methodology depending upon the accuracy of answers people give to interviewers or on surveys suffers from problems of informant bias (Webb et al. 1966). Respondents may not be able to recall specific behaviors accurately and quantitatively, such as how many ounces of green beans they ate the day before or how often they discard a half-full container of pesticide; and even if respondents can recall behaviors accurately, such as beer drinking or changing the oil in their cars, they may not want to admit to the specifics.

At this point it should be noted that systematic garbage sorts avoid informant biases. Refuse data, like virtually all archaeological data, are quantitative: packaging and commodity wastes can be weighed, measured for volume, and chemically analyzed, and their labels can be read for further information, all without relying upon the memory or honesty of respondents. When refuse is identified by specific household (as opposed to recording only the generating household's census tract), the Garbage Project obtains permission for its sorts from the discarders. Even under these conditions of self-awareness, project analyses show that, except for fewer alcohol containers, discards adhere to the same patterns found in garbage collected anonymously at the census tract level (Ritenbaugh and Harrison 1984).

Although independent of informant-based distortions, refuse analysis is susceptible to other forms of bias. The most obvious one is garbage disposals, and the Garbage Project has included studies not unlike those of ethnoarchaeology, to develop correction factors for ground-up food (Rathje and McCarthy 1977). Other biases include people who drop off recyclables at buy-back centers and the fact that behavior can only be characterized at the household level and not for individuals.

Overall, the advantages of garbage sorting as an alternative to self-reporting and as a quantitative measure of behavior outweigh its limitations, and the first pattern identified—that self-reports differ from refuse records—has opened up a broad new research arena.

The second conclusion drawn from refuse analysis is that *there is clear patterning in the differences between what people report they do and what they actually do*. This conclusion was drawn from a number of Garbage Project studies designed to verify consumer responses to various kinds of diet questionnaires by comparing self-reports about food use against packaging and food debris in fresh refuse. One specific self-report/refuse pattern the Garbage Project has documented is the "good provider syndrome": a female adult reporting for a household as a whole has a tendency to overreport everything the household uses by 10 to 30 percent or more. Another pattern is the "surrogate syndrome": to find out how much alcohol is consumed by household members, do not ask a drinker; drinkers consistently underreport their alcohol consumption by from 40 to 60 percent. Instead, ask a nondrinker; nondrinkers report accurately what drinkers drink (Johnstone and Rathje 1986; Dobyns and Rathje 1987). The second conclusion is again no real surprise.

Unlike the first two, the third conclusion was full of surprises: the differences between respondent reports and the material remains in refuse frequently indicate directly opposed behaviors. To be more specific, *respondents normally report rational behaviors, while their actual behaviors often appear irrational*. One of the best examples of this kind of counterintuitive relationship between self-reports and refuse occurred during the highly publicized "beef shortage" in the spring of 1973. At this time, when consumers were complaining bitterly about high prices and erratic availability, the Garbage Project was recording the highest rate of edible beef waste it has ever documented (Rathje and McCarthy 1977).

Several other instances of this kind of counterintuitive report/refuse pattern have been documented. In 1977, the Garbage Project gave meat fat its own separate category. Using the long-term Tucson database, the Garbage Project determined that in 1983 people began cutting off and discarding much larger than normal quantities of the separable fat on fresh cuts of red meat; at the same time they also bought less fresh red meat. Both actions seemed to be responses to a National Academy of Sciences study which was widely reported in the media and which identified fat from red meat as a cancer risk factor (Committee on Diet, Nutrition, and Cancer 1983). There was just one problem. The consumers under study replaced the fresh red meat in their diet with processed red meat—salami, bologna, sausage, hot dogs, etc.—which contained large quantities of hidden fat, so that the level of fat intake in the diet did not fall; instead, it stayed the same or rose (Rathje and Ho 1987).

A third case involved household hazardous wastes (Rathje et al. 1987). In 1986 Mann County sponsored a "Toxics Away! Day" to collect household hazardous wastes, such as used motor oil and unused pesticides. The Garbage Project recorded residential refuse two months after the collection day and compared it to household discards sorted before the collection day. The results were completely unexpected: there were nearly twice as many potentially hazardous wastes recorded in the refuse *after* the collection day than there had been beforehand. The data clearly demonstrated that all of the increase in hazardous wastes was due to the discarding of large quantities of items from only a few households (such as three or four half-full cans of paint or several full containers of pesticide in just one pickup). The Garbage Project's interpretation was that the media activity surrounding the collection day had made people aware of potentially hazardous commodities in their homes. For those who missed the collection day, however, no other appropriate avenue of discard had been identified. As a result, some residents disposed of their hazardous wastes via the only avenue available to them—their normal refuse pickup. The same pattern was verified in subsequent studies in Phoenix and Tucson (Rathje and Wilson 1987). The lesson learned: communities that initiate hazardous waste collection days should inform residents of future collection times or of other avenues for appropriate discard.

Counterintuitive interview/refuse patterns of this kind indicate that consumers may not be aware of how much their reported behaviors differ from their actual behaviors and that the Garbage Project is beginning to document a previously unmeasurable phenomenon in the gap between what people think is happening and what is really going on. Such studies have already led to some general principles of the differences between people's awareness of their behavior and their actual behavior (see Rathje 1996).

The Garbage Project's contribution to understanding more clearly the relationship between what people report and what they do (Rathje and Murphy 1992a; Rathje 1996) is based entirely on the use of archaeological methods and theory to document actual behaviors quantitatively from refuse. This is the grist of any archaeologist's mill, and the validity of the Garbage Project's data records and interpretations is based upon a hundred years of previous archaeological studies analyzing refuse to reconstruct behavior.

For a hundred years, archaeologists have also been studying refuse in attempts to count the number of people who lived within particular sites or regions at particular times. The Garbage Project has now done the same thing at the request of the federal government. The U.S. Census Bureau has long been aware of the criticism that its interview-survey methods lead to significant undercounts of ethnic minorities, especially young adult males, who may be undercounted by 40 percent or more. In 1986 the Quality Assurance Branch of the Census Bureau funded a study to answer the question: Could the Garbage Project count people based on the types and quantities of residential refuse they generate? The answer was yes (Rathje and Tani 1987). For any unit of time, the overall weight of total refuse discarded (minus yard wastes, which change markedly between suburbs and inner cities) varies directly with the number of resident discarders. The Garbage Project converted quantities of refuse thrown out per week to numbers of people by using per-person generation rates documented in test areas. Overall, a series of garbage-based estimates of population came within 5 percent of the actual number of residents. The Garbage Project now stands ready to verify census counts with a method that does not violate subjects' anonymity.

Ongoing Research

During the last two decades, researchers in the Garbage Project have worked on a large number of specialized topics similar to the census study, all of which are the focus of continuing inquiry. Landfill excavations, for example, are gauging the impact of recycling programs on the volume of wastes that reach landfills. The first reported results indicated that Toronto's "blue box" curbside recycling program has conserved some 20 percent of landfill space in the metropolitan area since 1982 (Tani et al. 1992).

Recovery of 2,425 datable, readable newspapers from Garbage Project excavations dramatically changed the view that biodegradation is commonplace in landfills. To understand better why biodegradation does and does not occur in landfill environments, the Garbage Project has so far conducted four cooperative digs involving microbiologists and environmental engineers from the University of Arizona, University of Oklahoma, University of Wisconsin–Madison, Argonne National Laboratories, and Procter and Gamble's Environmental Laboratory (Suflita et al. 1993).

Recently, the Garbage Project has initiated several studies integrating fresh and landfill data on hazardous wastes in MSW. The heavy metal assays of fines (that is, finely crushed samples) are being compared with detailed item-by-item lists (such as 2 light bulbs, 1 drain opener can, two newspapers, etc.) of the refuse identified within each 150-pound landfill sample. The goal is to determine the rate of movement of heavy metals in commodities and inks and other hazardous wastes from refuse into the landfill matrix (Rathje et al. 1992).

Garbage Project Students and Staff

The Garbage Project does not consist merely of systematic records compiled by hands-on sorting of household garbage; it is also made up of the sorters and project staff attached to the hands. While many people find the results of our studies interesting, most of them also find the sorting process itself revolting. A few market researchers realized in the 1950s that household refuse contained useful information, but after repeated experiments they found that they could not pay people to sort refuse. Those hired either quit quickly or kept sloppy records. Who would possibly be willing to rummage through someone else's smelly trash and keep accurate records of its contents? That is a good question.

The answer is a matter of public record. *Rubbish!* (Rathje and Murphy 1993—the paperback edition of Rathje and Murphy 1992a) contains a list of more than 900 university students and others who sorted refuse with the Garbage Project between 1973 and 1991. The intimate archaeological view these and subsequent sorters have had of the materials discarded from households much like their own has provided them with a unique perspective; and while they do not preach to others, they are enthusiastically dedicated to providing everyone possible with the same insights they have drawn from their own hands-on sorting of residential refuse.

In attempting to share results, we at the Garbage Project have focused most directly on schools, museums, and other avenues of access to students. The rationale is that the archaeology of our own society will mean the most to the young people who can do the most with archaeological insights. Currently, project members are especially proud of two endeavors. The first is the compilation of *The WRAP (Waste Reduction Alternatives Program) Resource Manual* (Dobyns and Hughes 1994), which has been distributed to schools throughout Arizona and the United States. The manual is designed to help students and teachers learn how their individual behaviors produce significant quantities of garbage and how they can make changes that will greatly decrease that garbage. The second endeavor resulted in "The Garbage Dilemma," an interactive video on permanent display in the Hall of Science in American Life at the Smithsonian's National Museum of American History. The video was the product of cooperation among Garbage Project staff, the Smithsonian's design staff, and the Chedd-Angier Production Company. Schools and museums—not landfills—are the kinds of environments where we hope Garbage Project results will eventually come to reside.

Garbology in the Twenty-First Century

What has set the archaeologists of the Garbage Project apart from other behavioral science researchers is that all of our studies have been grounded in the hands-on sorting of quantifiable bits and pieces of garbage, in place of collecting data through interview-surveys, government documents, or industry records. In other words, the Garbage Project is studying consumer behaviors directly from the material realities they leave behind rather than from self-conscious self-reports. The exhaustive level of detail Garbage Project student sorters use to record data has also set the studies apart from other data sources. Many local plans by engineering consultant firms and even by solid waste managers are based on national characterizations of solid waste generation, which involve estimating residential and other discards by using government and industry records of solid waste production—items of questionable validity—together with an untold number of untested assumptions. Even if national estimates are accurate, they are available only at the level of categories of material composition—so much plastic, glass, aluminum, paper, steel, and so on. But how can anyone plan with these data? Most of these materials come from the packaging with which people emerge from stores; but no one goes shopping for five ounces of glass, three ounces of cardboard boxes, or eight ounces of aluminum cans. Instead, they shop for a jar of Best Foods mayonnaise, a box of Cap'n Crunch cereal, and a twelve-pack of Bud Light beer. This brings us back full circle to our item-by-item Regular Sorts of fresh refuse. In other words, in contrast to virtually all other sources of information, the Garbage Project looks at refuse the way all archaeologists do—as the material result of human behavior.

Ultimately, the contribution of the Garbage Project comes down to one simple component: in order to understand and mitigate important problems, we must first become aware of the problems and measure their material impact. Measuring material impacts can lead to some surprising results. Consider the greatest irony of the so-called garbage crisis.

Since 1987 communities everywhere have been promoting recycling, reuse, source reduction, and everything else they can to decrease the amount of refuse being discarded. At the same time, to cut collection costs and reduce worker injuries, many communities have converted to automated systems that depend on standard-sized garbage containers. The containers that most families used to buy for themselves were usually sixty gallons in size, about what one person could carry a short distance. The new standardized containers have wheels and are one-third bigger, ninety gallons, to accommodate the needs of the largest families. By all accounts, the result of these changes has been that recycling is increasing and on-the-job injuries are down. So far, so good.

The Garbage Project hands-on sorts, however, add another dimension—a darker side that no other source has mentioned (Rathje 1993). When the Garbage Project first studied Phoenix residential refuse, the city of Phoenix, unlike Tucson, already had an automated system. Garbage Project personnel were surprised to discover that Phoenix households discarded nearly double the refuse thrown out by households a hundred miles away in Tucson. The mystery was greatly clarified when the city of Tucson switched to the automated system and its household refuse generation rate increased by more than one-third. At this point, the Garbage Project identified a "Parkinson's Law of Garbage" with implications for every city's solid waste management strategy (Rathje 1993).

The original Parkinson's Law was formulated in 1957 by C. Northcote Parkinson, a British bureaucrat, who concluded, "Work expands so as to fill the time available for its completion." Parkinson's Law of Garbage similarly states, "Garbage expands so as to fill the receptacles available for its containment."

Parkinson's Law of Garbage is really quite simple. When people have small garbage cans, larger items—old cans of paint, broken furniture perpetually awaiting repair, bags of old clothing—are not typically thrown away. Rather, these materials sit in basements and garages, often until a residence changes hands. But when homeowners are provided with plastic mini-Dumpsters, they are presented with a new option. Before long, what was once an instinctive "I'll shove this in the cellar" becomes an equally instinctive "I'll bet this will fit in the dumper."

The Garbage Project has compared the components of Tucson residential refuse collected before and after mechanization. Solid waste discards went from an average of less than fourteen pounds per biweekly pickup to an average of more than twenty-three pounds. The largest increase was in the yard waste category, followed by "other" (broken odds and ends), food waste, newspapers, and textiles. The first pickup of the week was substantially heavier than the second, reflecting the accomplishment of weekend chores, and the discards in that pickup were loaded with consistently larger quantities of hazardous waste than the Garbage Project has come to expect in a typical load. These findings suggest that the introduction of 90-gallon containers should be of concern for three reasons.

First, the increase in discarded newspaper suggests that one counterproductive result of larger containers may be a lower participation rate in any form of recycling. For those who find separating out recyclables a bother, the 90-gallon bin is a no-penalty means to circumvent the issue. Likewise, the increase in "other" and textiles could mean that people are using the bin as an alternative to the donation avenue, whereby unwanted resources wind up with the Salvation Army and other charities, or even as an alternative to yard sales.

Second, the substantial increase of hazardous waste indicates that the large bins are a convenient alternative to storing toxic items at home until they are used up or until the next household hazardous waste collection day.

Third, at the same time as all-out recycling programs are being implemented to try to decrease the flow of garbage, collection techniques are being installed that may unwittingly be *increasing* the overall flow of garbage to an even higher rate.

The evidence for Parkinson's Law of Garbage is not yet conclusive. The only way to know whether it is a behavioral pattern is through hands-on garbology. This archaeological research question is important to answer for the method and theory of archaeology, for culture history, and for our cities' immediate economic and environmental future. Garbologists, grab your gloves and face masks! One day the results of your efforts may be enough to convince Indiana Jones to turn his trowel on his own discards—and then recycle them.

References

The American Heritage Dictionary of the English Language. 1992. 3rd ed. Boston: Houghton Mifflin.

Committee on Diet, Nutrition, and Cancer, Assembly of Life Sciences, National Research Council. 1983. *Diet, Nutrition, and Cancer.* Washington, DC: National Academy Press.

Dobyns, S., and W.W. Hughes. 1994. *The WRAP (Waste Reduction Alternatives Program) Resource Manual.* Phoenix: Final Report to the Reduce, Reuse, and Recycle Grant Program, Arizona Department of Environmental Quality.

Dobyns, S., and W.L. Rathje (eds.). 1987. *The NFCS Report/Refuse Study: A Handbook of Potential Distortions in Respondent Diet Reports.* 4 vols. Final Report to the Consumer Nutrition Division. Washington, DC: U.S. Department of Agriculture.

Encyclopaedia Britannica. 1996. *Yearbook of Science and the Future.* Chicago: Encyclopaedia Britannica.

Fagan, B.M. 1985. *The Adventures of Archaeology.* Washington, DC: National Geographic Society.

———. 1991a. *Archaeology: A Brief Introduction.* 4th ed. New York: Harper Collins.

———. 1991b. *In the Beginning.* 7th ed. New York: Harper Collins.

Franklin Associates. 1996. *Characterization of Municipal Solid Waste in the United States: 1995 Update.* Publication no. 530–R-96–001. Washington, DC: Environmental Protection Agency Office of Solid Waste.

Fung, E.E., and W.L. Rathje. 1982. How We Waste $31 Billion in Food a Year. In *The 1982 Yearbook of Agriculture,* ed. J. Hayes, 352–57. Washington, DC: U.S. Department of Agriculture.

Hughes, W.W. 1984. The Method to Our Madness. *American Behavioral Scientist* 28(1): 41–50.

Jessup, R. 1956. *The Wonderful World of Archaeology.* Garden City, NY: Garden City Books.

Johnstone, B.M., and W.L. Rathje. 1986. Building a Theory of the Difference between Respondent Reports and Material Realities. Symposium on "Different Approaches to Using Food Consumption Data Bases for Evaluating Dietary Intake." Institute of Food Technologists Annual Meeting, Dallas.

Macaulay, D. 1979. *Motel of the Mysteries.* Boston: Houghton Mifflin.

New York Times Editors. 1988. Serious about Plastic Pollution. In "Topics of *The Times.*" *New York Times,* January 8.

Oxford Dictionary and Usage Guide to the English Language. 1995. Oxford: Oxford University Press.

Podolefsky, A., and P.J. Brown (eds.). 1993. *Applying Anthropology: An Introductory Reader.* 3rd ed. Mountain View, Calif.: Mayfield Publishing Company.

Rathje, W.L. 1971. The Origin and Development of Lowland Classic Maya Civilization. *American Antiquity* 36(3): 275–85.

———. 1973. Classic Maya Development and Denouement. In *Classic Maya Collapse,* ed. T.P. Culbert, 405–54. Albuquerque: University of New Mexico Press.

———. 1976. *Socioeconomic Correlates of Household Residuals: Phase 1.* Final Report to the Program for Research Applied to National Needs. Washington, DC: National Science Foundation.

———. 1986. Why We Throw Food Away. *Atlantic Monthly* 257(4): 14–16.

———. 1989. Rubbish! *Atlantic Monthly* 246(6): 99–109.

———. 1991. Once and Future Landfills. *National Geographic* 179(5): 116–34.

———. 1993. A Perverse Law of Garbage. *Garbage* 4(6): 22–23.

———. 1996. The Archaeology of Us. In *Encyclopaedia Britannica's Yearbook of Science and the Future—1997,* ed. C. Ciegelski, 158–77. Chicago: Encyclopædia Britannica.

———. In press. Archaeology and Solid Waste Management. In *The Oxford Companion to Archaeology,* ed. B. Fagan. New York: Oxford University Press.

Rathje, W.L., and E.E. Ho. 1987. Meat Fat Madness: Conflicting Patterns of Meat Fat Consumption and Their Public Health Implications. *Journal of the American Dietetic Association* 87(10): 1357–62.

Rathje, W.L., W.W. Hughes, D.C. Wilson, M.K. Tank, G.H. Archer, R.G. Hunt, and T.W. Jones. 1992. The Archaeology of Contemporary Landfills. *American Antiquity* 57(3): 437–47.

Rathje, W.L., and M. McCarthy. 1977. Regularity and Variability in Contemporary Garbage. In *Research Strategies in Historical Archaeology*, ed. S. South, 261–86. New York: Academic Press.

Rathje, W.L., and C. Murphy. 1992a. *Rubbish! The Archaeology of Garbage*. New York: Harper Collins.

———. 1992b. Beyond the Pail: Why We Are What We Don't Eat. *Washington Post*, June 28.

———. 1993. *Rubbish! The Archaeology of Garbage*. New York: Harper Perennial.

Rathje, W.L., and M.K. Tani. 1987. *MNI Triangulation Final Report: Estimating Population Characteristics at the Neighborhood Level from Household Refuse*. 3 vols. Final Report to the Center for Survey Methods Research. Washington, DC: Bureau of the Census.

Rathje, W.L., and D.C. Wilson. 1987. Archaeological Techniques Applied to Characterization of Household Discards and Their Potential Contamination of Groundwater. Paper read at the Conference on Solid Waste Management and Materials Policy, New York City.

Rathje, W.L., D.C. Wilson, W.W. Hughes, and R. Herndon. 1987. *Characterization of Household Hazardous Wastes from Marin County, California and New Orleans, Louisiana*. U.S. EPA Environmental Monitoring Systems Laboratory, Report no. EPA/600/x-87/129, Las Vegas.

Ritenbaugh, C.K., and G.G. Harrison. 1984. Reactivity and Garbage Analysis. *American Behavioral Scientist* 28(1): 51–70.

Smith, A.L. 1950. *Uaxactun, Guatemala: Excavations of 1931–1937*. Publication no. 588. Washington, DC: Carnegie Institution of Washington.

Suflita, J.M., G.P. Gerba, R.K. Ham, A.C. Palmisano, W.L. Rathje, and J.A. Robinson. 1993. The World's Largest Landfill: Multidisciplinary Investigation. *Environmental Science and Technology* 26(8): 1486–94.

Tani, M.K., W.L. Rathje, W.W. Hughes, D.C. Wilson, and G. Coupland. 1992. *The Toronto Dig: Excavations at Four Municipal Solid Waste Disposal Sites in the Greater Toronto Area*. Toronto: Trash Research Corporation.

Thomas, D.H. 1979. *Archaeology*. New York: Holt, Rinehart and Winston.

Turnbaugh, W.A., R. Jurmain, H. Nelson, and L. Kilgore. 1996. *Understanding Physical Anthropology and Archeology*. 6th ed. Minneapolis/St. Paul: West Publishing Company.

Webb, E.J., D.T. Campbell, R.D. Schwarts, and L. Sechrest. 1966. *Unobtrusive Measures: Nonreactive Research in the Social Sciences*. Chicago: Rand McNally.

"Using the Past to Protect the Future: Marking Nuclear Waste Disposal Sites"

Maureen F. Kaplan and Mel Adams

Since the 1980s, the government of the United States has been consulting with scholars to determine the best way to mark nuclear waste sites so that people in the future will recognize the danger. This selection outlines how some well-known archaeological sites and monuments can help with this project and provides examples of how archaeology can be used in non-traditional ways. The article originally appeared in 1986 in the periodical *Archaeology*, a popular publication of the Archaeological Institute of America. Maureen Kaplan is an archaeologist, and Mel Adams is a scientist who has been involved in nuclear waste disposal.

Archaeologists continue to make recommendations on how to mark high- and mid-level nuclear waste at proposed repositories, and these efforts are occasionally reported in the popular press. These reports generally restate or present minor variations to recommendations described in this article, but they don't provide the archaeological context that this piece provides.

....

Questions to Guide Reading

What were the methods the researchers used? What were the three basic steps? What criteria did they use when choosing monuments?
What six archaeological sites and monuments did the researchers consider?
What lessons did the researchers learn from their investigations? How have these lessons affected the recommendations?

....

In today's nuclear age, the safe disposal of nuclear waste is naturally on the minds of both the public and the scientific community. A major concern is the possibility of human disturbance of the disposal site at some time in the future. One relatively simple approach to preventing this is *marking* the site to inform potential intruders of its contents and dangers. In designing the best possible marking system, archaeology is playing an important and revolutionary role. Because archaeology deals with man-made monuments and messages that have survived for extended periods of time, scientists are turning to the past to learn what allows information to survive and to incorporate this knowledge in the design of marking systems for nuclear waste disposal sites.

Archaeological guidelines in fact have been the focus of research performed by The Analytic Sciences

Corporation (TASC) for the US Government Office of Nuclear Waste Isolation (ONWI) in Columbus, Ohio, and with Rockwell Hanford Operations (Rockwell) in Richland, Washington. For the last five years the project for ONWI concentrated on the problem of the disposal of "high level wastes"—the spent fuel from power reactors or what remains after the reusable uranium and plutonium have been removed. No permanent site for the disposal of these wastes has yet been chosen, but for most areas under preliminary study, burial is envisioned to take place in a deep mine (450 to 550 meters). This will then be resealed, so that intrusion would require a culture with a level of technology similar to our own.

For Rockwell, work concentrated on a design for disposal sites for the radioactive wastes located at the Hanford Site, a 1500-square-kilometer area in southeastern Washington near a bend in the Columbia River. Established in 1943 as a national security area for plutonium production, it now operates under the Department of Energy. In 1968, 311 square kilometers were set aside as an Arid Lands Ecology Reserve, and during the 1970s the area north of the Columbia River was designated a wildlife refuge. As the name of the ecology reserve indicates, the Hanford Site is located in a desert-like region, a shrub-steppe grassland with an average annual rainfall of 116 millimeters that does not percolate very deeply into the soil.

Environmental conditions are important for understanding past nuclear waste management practices at Hanford, many of which were established decades ago. Only a tiny portion of the site area (less than 0.01 percent) was set aside for waste disposal. Prior to 1970, in these areas low activity liquid wastes from the reprocessing of irradiated fuel were allowed to percolate into the soil at the bottom of deep trenches or similar engineered structures. The higher activity wastes were held in single-shell concrete tanks with metal linings. (Tank wastes have recently been dried to minimize the amount of material that could leak into the soil once the tanks fail.) Solid wastes, such as contaminated trash, tools and equipment, were buried in trenches during this period. Since 1970, these early disposal practices have been improved or discontinued, but Rockwell is still wrestling with the question of disposing of the pre-1970 material. A draft environmental impact statement (EIS) has been prepared and is under public review for the final disposition of the wastes at the Hanford Site.

Over the years, safety analyses for the disposal of highly radioactive wastes have resulted in the realization that an otherwise effective disposal system can be circumvented by human interference, such as deep drilling or growing deep-rooted crops. In light of this, the draft regulations proposed in 1982 by the Environmental Protection agency (EPA) state that "the disposal system shall be identified by the most permanent markers and records practicable to indicate the dangers of the wastes and their location." The EPA regulations propose 10,000 years as the most effective time period. (Radioactive materials decay over time, unlike most chemically toxic wastes.)

In using archaeology to design the most permanent markers practicable, three steps were taken. First, we analyzed some ancient markers or monuments, and then we identified the factors in the marking system. Finally, we used archaeological data to develop accelerated testing procedures for proposed materials. The ancient monuments were chosen to represent a variety of cultures and climates, so that the monuments and their survival are not keyed to a particular culture, and to ascertain the effect of climate on survival. We also chose monuments that were at least 1,000 years old, that is, monuments that showed an ability to survive for at least one millennium.

The Fourth Dynasty pyramids at Giza, Egypt, are an obvious starting point. They have already survived nearly half the EPA's suggested 10,000-year time frame. The purpose of the pyramids, who built them, and their contemporary condition are accurately described by several later historians including Herodotus, Pliny the Elder, and the twelfth-century Arab, Abd el Latif. Even without this information, the sarcophagi within the pyramids and the texts on the walls of the later Sixth Dynasty pyramids would proclaim their funerary purpose.

Arguing against the use of a pyramid type of marker is the fact that the pyramids have survived because of their massive size, and that each pyramid marks only a single spot. We hope to delineate a whole area, and building a pyramid to cover its entire surface is impractical. If a smaller pyramid were to be built, saying "do not dig here," drilling could occur next to it without contradicting the warning.

Stonehenge in England was the second ancient marker investigated. This magnificent monument on Salisbury Plain is the culmination of nearly a millennium of use and remodeling, and is an example of a man-made marker that has lasted for nearly 5,000 years in a moist climate. Stonehenge may be very useful for a marking system because of the redundancy of its standing stones, which are much more efficient in delineating an area than the pyramids. The use of multiple components means that the plan of an area can be reconstructed even though some of the components are missing. Stonehenge has lost approximately one-third of its stones, yet there is no debate about its plan. But unlike the pyramids, there is no contemporary written information associated with Stonehenge, which has severely limited our understanding of the monument.

The situation is quite different at the Acropolis in Athens, for which we have surviving contemporary texts. We know, for example, that Pericles (died 429 BC) was the prime mover in the decision to rebuild the Acropolis on a monumental scale after peace was made with Persia. There has never been any doubt that the major buildings of the Acropolis had a religious purpose. Today, the Acropolis is an excellent example of ancient monuments that have suffered far more from the hands of man than from the ravages of nature. Acid rain is dissolving the marble sculptures and buildings. The caryatids on the Porch of the Maidens of the Erechtheion have been replaced by casts. The steel bolts and girders of the early 1900s that replaced the old iron ones

are weakening and expanding as they corrode. This extra stress has led to cracking of the marble in which the steel is embedded. In some places this has created an immediate danger of collapse—a solemn warning to those who propose technologically advanced materials that have not had the chance to undergo the test of time.

The Great Wall of China is another monument that has lasted for over 2,000 years. Built by the order of Qin Shi Huang Di, the wall was begun in 221 BC and completed in 210 BC. Construction methods differed along its 1,850-mile length, depending on the local building materials. In the east, where stone was plentiful, a foundation of rubble was laid without mortar. The wall was built of dry, tamped earth (*terre pise*) and the upper level was covered with brickwork. In the later Ming period (AD 1368–1644), granite foundation stones as large as 4.25 by 1.25 meters were used. The rubble of earthen core of the walls was faced with either brick or stone. Farther west, the wall cuts across wide expanses of loess soil, with little stone for building. The very fine loess was mixed into a slurry and poured between frames to create the wall, which was faced with stone or brick when possible. In several areas, two strips of loess were removed, leaving a rampart of earth. Stone was used again in the westernmost segment.

During its history the Great Wall has been breached and repaired but never forgotten. Its history is contained in a body of literature ranging from poems about its beauty to tales of the horrors endured by the conscripted laborers who built it. Because it was built with bricks, the Wall has needed continual maintenance over its lifetime. For the Rockwell project, it is important to note that the Wall received this care because it served a purpose for the rulers of the country. The marking system for the Hanford disposal site will also serve a public, protective function. Although it will be designed to need as little maintenance as possible, the Great Wall indicates the possibility that the marking system could be updated and repaired by future generations, should this be required.

We also turned to the Nazca lines, a collection of lines, geometric forms, and semi-naturalistic figures found on the desert floor near the town of Nazca in southern Peru (see A. Aveni article in ARCHAEOLOGY July/August 1986). The Nazca lines are drawn on an enormous scale. Single lines may run more than 10.5 kilometers, and one cleared trapezoid measures nearly 800 by 100 meters. The lines are made possible by a set of geological circumstances. Wind erosion across the desert floor carried off the dusty surface soil, leaving behind a "pavement" of pebbles and boulders. Over time these stones developed "desert varnish," a brownish-black coating of iron and manganese oxides formed by the *in situ* decomposition of the rock. Formation of this varnish is very slow, and may have begun as far back as the Pleistocene period about 10,000 to 30,000 years ago. The underlying soil, however, remained pale in color. Picking up a stone exposes the light-colored soil underneath it, and picking up a row of stones creates a light-colored line. Obviously these lines are a frail phenomenon and undergo rapid degradation when people drive or walk over them. Since many tourists now attempt to see them, they are deteriorating rapidly. Still, the Nazca lines are an example of the potential survivability of even a fragile phenomenon in a suitably remote location.

The last marker we investigated was the Serpent Mound in Ohio, an embankment of earth in the form of an uncoiling serpent. Archaeologists speculate that the Serpent Mound was built by the Adena Indians (800 BC-AD 100). In its present state of restoration, the Serpent Mound consists of two parts, the serpent and an oval shape in front of its mouth. A small mound of burned stones lies in the center of the oval. The length of the serpent is 380 meters, and its height, generally 1.25 to 1.5 meters, tapers until the tail terminates in a bank about 0.3 meters high. The core is made of stone and clay. For our purposes, the Serpent Mound is an example of what *not* to do. Obviously, the serpent form meant something to the builders, but the meaning has been lost to us. We may take this as a warning that marking a site with symbols or pictures alone may not be sufficient to convey all the information to future investigators. The Serpent Mound has no parallel in the United States. Likewise, there may be only one high-level waste repository in this country. Developing a unique symbol for a possibly unique high-level waste repository could be futile, since the symbol would have no points of reference or comparison for its future viewers.

How do we summarize the lessons learned from ancient markers? Foremost is the importance of contemporary written records to the future understanding of any of those monuments. Languages will change, and we cannot predict which of those in contemporary use will be readable or recognizable several millennia from now. Still we must include written messages to insure the possibility of reconstructing the information at some future time. It appears that only language—as opposed to pictures and symbols—may be capable of carrying higher levels of information and details. Symbols may be of use only in the relative short-term, when their cultural contexts are still understood. For example, if we see an uninscribed statue of a woman wearing a helmet and carrying a shield, we still recognize it as Athena, goddess of wisdom. But the use of symbols with associated texts will give generations in the far future the possibility of regaining the meaning of the symbol. The combined use of pictures and languages is also likely to create a symbiotic effect in recovering the intended information. In other words, the marking system should incorporate symbols, pictures and languages to convey its warning and information.

We have also learned that the materials that survive are natural ones—earthworks and stone. This is not an effect of the technological level of the cultures that built the monument; metals were in common use when most of these ancient markers were built. But there are metals which, although certainly durable, are unlikely to survive because of their intrinsic value; they show a disturbing tendency to be recycled. The Parthenon once bore a set of bronze shields erected by Alexander the Great and an inscription by Nero (AD 54–68), which we know about only from the written records and the holes left by the mounting pins. Archaeological evidence is important for indicating the difference between "survivability" and "durability" of materials.

The Nazca lines indicate that the primary emphasis of the marking system should be on detectability at eye level. There is also a subtle relationship between the size and placement of the individual components and the size of the entire monument. Stonehenge, the Acropolis, the pyramids, and the Serpent Mound can all be taken in at a single glance. The patterns and forms of the monuments are immediately perceptible. The inability to perceive a monument in its entirety may hamper the investigator's ability to understand it. This phenomenon may explain why the stone circle of Avebury, which is far larger than Stonehenge, is less widely known. The component parts of Avebury are small compared to the scale on which they are set, and it is easy to stand in one part and not realize that the remaining section of the monument exists. We can see that the components of the marking system must be scaled to a size and placed in such a manner that one person standing on the site recognizes the overall pattern.

Using the information from ancient monuments, we can draw up a preliminary marking system for a nuclear waste disposal site. Its primary feature is a series of monoliths ringing the perimeter of the disposal site. The placement of these monoliths should allow an investigator to stand at one monolith and see the next one on either side. Each monolith will be inscribed with a series of symbols, pictures, and languages to convey a warning and information about the site. A sufficient number of monoliths should be used so that the placement pattern can be identified even if some are lost. Repeating the information on every monolith provides the system with a great deal of redundancy, which allows us to be able to lose a few monoliths without jeopardizing the ability of the system to convey information.

For Rockwell, small subsurface markers are included in the design in addition to the large surface markers. The barrier designs are such that a house with a basement could be built on top of the barriers without reaching the wastes. Any construction on the site, however, is not a desirable situation, so three layers of subsurface markers are included in the proposed barrier designs. The first layer is meant to work its way to the surface by erosion, root action or animal action. These markers are meant to be found before any serious human intrusion into the barrier occurs. They are modeled in principle on the ubiquitous potsherds that allow an archaeologist to tell when a site was occupied even before excavation begins. The two lower levels of markers provide extra security should the first set be ignored or overlooked.

Archaeological information has also been used to suggest materials and sizes for the various components of the nuclear waste site. Stone is suggested for the perimeter monoliths. Since marbles, limestones and sandstones are already deteriorating in today's acid rain, they are not acceptable. The types of stone mentioned *least* in conservation literature are those which are hard, compact, non-brittle and relatively homogeneous, such as granite and basalt. While these are difficult to work, they are also more difficult to deface. The form of the monolith should be tapered to shed water and make it more difficult to reuse. Its surface should be polished so that water cannot collect in the numerous small crevices and pits of an unfinished surface. A raised band around the edge will protect the inscription from severe wind erosion. To draw on another ancient example, the façade of the Treasury at Petra in Jordan is probably in better condition than other façades at the site because it is recessed into the cliff wall.

As for size, we propose a guideline of at least twice human height; objects this size are more commonly left at the site rather than transported to a museum. For an upper threshold, the largest stones at Stonehenge are 7.6 meters and stand six meters above the level of the plain. Like the stones at Stonehenge, the surface markers should be monoliths; the one-piece construction minimizes surfaces where corrosion can begin and makes it more difficult to disassemble and reuse the marker.

For the subsurface markers, there is an additional factor to consider. They must be sufficiently distinguishable from the surrounding barrier materials to be noticed by an unobservant intruder. For these markers, stone is set aside in favor of pottery, which with its nearly 8,000-year history has withstood the test of time. Oxides can be mixed into a light-firing body to create eye-catching colors. We propose that the subsurface markers be made in yellow and magenta, the colors of the radiation warning signs currently in use world-wide. The designs are impressed so that even if the glaze fails, the information can still be obtained. A disc or lenticular shape with a 12-centimeter diameter and one centimeter at its widest point is proposed.

The messages to be placed on the markers are still in the development stage. The preliminary design has the front of the monolith bearing two symbols as well as text. One symbol is the radiation warning trefoil, which has been in international use for nearly three decades and spans several cultures. Another symbol, developed on the basis of international driving signs, shows a person digging at a barrier mound and a diagonal line across it. This is an attempt to convey the concept of "do not dig here." The front of the surface monolith would also bear the message "Danger. Radioactive Waste. Do Not Dig Here." This message is repeated in the six languages of the United Nations and the language of the Yak'ma Indians, the native inhabitants of the Hanford region. We do not know, nor can we predict, which language will be recognizable in the future. But as in the case of the Rosetta Stone, where three languages appear together, we will significantly increase the likelihood that one of seven will be recognizable. When the French engineers found the Rosetta Stone they could read the Greek immediately, and the hope is that one of our seven languages will be understood, and will help to decipher the repeated message in the other six.

One side panel of each surface marker will be devoted to a larger explanation of the site and its wastes, again repeated in seven languages. A sample text for the Hanford Site could be: "This area contains disposal sites for long-lived radioactive wastes. Each disposal site is marked by a raised mound of earth and rock. These mounds are designed to keep water, animals and humans away from the dangerous material. Do not build houses on the mounds. Do not dig for water within the area outlined by these markers. The soil below the mounds does not cause immediate sickness or death. Disturbing the mounds may cause exposure of humans to radioactivity which may result in cancer and death. Illness may not occur until several years after exposure. These disposal sites were built by the United States Government in (date)." The other side panel will be devoted to a pictorial description of the Hanford Site, a drawing showing each surface marker and barrier mound.

The subsurface markers will bear a subset of the information presented on the surface markers. Prototype markers have been tested for resistance to environmental stresses. The reverse side bears the radiation warning symbol and the message "Do Not Dig Here. Hazardous Waste Below." The obverse bears the "Do Not Dig" pictograph. Although only one language appears on each subsurface marker, the same message appears in multiple languages on the larger surface markers. In this way, we hope that each group of markers will reinforce the other.

Another part of the Rockwell project involves the use of archaeological information to identify degradation mechanisms for the marker materials. We know that the prime agent of stone decay is water, and two minor agents are wind erosion and stress relief. The criteria for the surface marker stone include hardness, which lowers susceptibility to wind erosion; to reduce the effects of windblown particles, the inscriptions on the marker will be recessed. Stress relief is due to quarrying operations that remove confining stresses on the rock and cause it to expand to its original, pre-stressed condition. This can lead to microcracking, and in extreme cases to buckling. These effects can be mitigated by storing the stone blocks for a few months before they are worked into final shape.

Water can degrade stone in several ways. As we know, acid rain is already dissolving many limestones and marbles. Freezing is detrimental when the water within the rock expands to the point of fracturing it. Salt action is extremely destructive, even to rocks resistant to other forms of decay. A testing cycle that incorporates these causes of stone decay has been developed for the surface markers. Since the efflorescence and sub-florescence of salts (the formation of crystals on or just below the surface) also cause the deterioration of pottery, the subsurface markers are likewise subjected to this testing cycle. The review of archaeological data has resulted in the design requirement of excellent drainage around each surface marker to minimize salt intake. It may also be desirable to immerse each marker in water to leach out entrapped salts before it is placed at the disposal site.

Our research has made it abundantly clear that a carefully thought-out marking system will be required for a high-level waste repository, wherever it is built. A marking system will be required at the Hanford Site if the on-site option is chosen for the final disposition of wastes. All of this research by Rockwell is being performed to assess the viability of this on-site option; it is not a decision to implement it. And archaeology continues to assist in the task of designing the most permanent markers. While none of the designs are final, archaeological data can still offer considerable information for this all-important task—nothing less than using the past to protect future generations from today's deadly wastes.

"Identifying Victims after a Disaster"

RICHARD GOULD

One of the many practical but non-traditional ways that archaeology is applied in the contemporary world is in forensic studies. In this selection, Richard Gould describes some of the recent contributions made by archaeologists working for the United Nations and at disaster locations in the United States.

Gould, an archaeologist, is a professor at Brown University, and this article was originally published in a 2005 issue of *Anthropology News*, a periodical of the American Anthropological Association.

Questions to Guide Reading

How have archaeologists been involved recently in forensics, both in the United States and around the world?

Why is archaeological method and theory valued in the context of forensics?

After Hurricane Katrina struck the Gulf coast I was deployed to the area for 17 days by the national Disaster Mortuary Operations Team (DMORT). The first week I volunteered identifying victims in Gulfport, Mississippi. The remaining time I assisted recovering human remains from hospitals, nursing homes and schools in New Orleans and St Bernard Parish. In New Orleans we recovered 48 victims at Memorial Hospital, mainly elders.

Many responders to the disaster, such as myself, are still coming up for air. At the same time, the aftermath of Katrina—both the long recovery process and our analyses of the event—has only just begun. And while it is too soon to come to any conclusions about the role of anthropology in responding to the hurri-

cane, one thing is obvious: anthropologists will continue to become an increasingly important part of major disaster recovery operations.

Disaster Anthropology

Anthropologists join funeral directors, medical examiners, coroners, pathologists, medical records technicians and transcribers, finger print specialists, forensic odontologists, dental assistants, x-ray technicians, mental health specialists, computer professionals, administrative support staff and security and investigative personnel in volunteering with DMORT. As part of its national response plan to disasters, the Federal Emergency Management

Administration calls on DMORT to identify victims and provide assistance to families. Since 1996 when Congress passed the Family Assistance Act, this humanitarian role of forensics and DMORT has continued to become central to the work of identifying victims of disasters. The Family Assistance Act was passed in response to families who had lost loved ones in airline incidents. These families testified they had received inadequate treatment, often left wondering the fate of those they lost. The act requires all public and private entities operating in the US to have a plan to assist families, in part by providing them with the information to help them grieve, in the event of a disaster.

Many DMORT volunteers have years of experience in rapidly responding to disasters. Gina Hart, a forensic anthropologist from the New Jersey State Medical Examiner's Office, was a well of expertise in Gulfport, drawing from her past work for the UN in identifying victims of ethnic violence and human rights abuses in Bosnia. Forensic work is based on a powerful method: comparing pre- and post- mortem data to identify a person. The resulting information not only assists families, but it constitutes evidence that can later be used in a court case. In Gulfport we had our challenges, largely, because like in Bosnia and other areas torn by disaster, there was little ante-mortem data available to us. Dental records were destroyed by the storm, or perhaps never even existed.

Before the processing of human remains can begin, or the forensic work, the remains must first be recovered from the field. It is in this role that the importance of archaeology is emerging. I often joke that I am an archaeologist pretending to be a forensic anthropologist. There is some truth to this. Yet, the need for archaeologists in recovering field remains and helping to carefully record the scene where remains are found cannot be ignored. An archaeologist's questions about the linking of material remains to a carefully documented field site can only strengthen the work of accurately and rapidly identifying remains. As insurance claims are processed and the question is asked—was it the storm, flood or

something else that killed this person—carefully recorded details of the scene are vital, along with the careful treatment of the recovered remains.

Standards of Evidence

All forensic investigations share similar standards of evidence. They all assume that evidence recovered at a crime or disaster scene must be documented and maintained under control from the point of collection to the courtroom or to the medical examiner's office in an unbroken evidentiary chain. This is usually referred to as the "chain of custody" (or "chain of evidence"). Evidence collected in this way for medical and legal purposes must be able to withstand challenges in the court of law, which may be very different from a scholarly context or what can be called the "court of history."

Although forensic anthropology is a profession of long-standing, the role of forensic anthropologists has been expanding dramatically since the World Trade Center disaster in 2001. Since Sept 11, not only have queries about forensics as a profession increased, but the scope of anthropological investigations and recoveries has shifted into the realm of humanitarianism—especially at mass-fatality disaster scenes. Prior to Sept 11 the focus of forensics was largely in terms of investigation, or providing evidence for courts of law, rather than its humanitarian role in assisting grieving families.

Forensic anthropology, or the "CSI model" after the popular television program, has been applied, for example, for decades to standard crime-scene investigations, often involving the FBI or Bureau of Alcohol, Tobacco, Firearms and Explosives.

Human rights archaeologists have played a major role in investigating the fate of "disappeared" individuals in places like Argentina or Guatemala or assisting the UN to identify victims of genocide in places like Rwanda or Bosnia. Primarily these efforts have aimed to provide evidence of atrocities for tribunals of leaders who ordered mass killings.

Since the mid-1980s, US-government sponsored

teams involving trained archaeologists and anthropologists have ventured into remote areas, especially in Asia and the Pacific. The teams deployed by the US Army Joint POW/MIA Accounting Command locate, document and recover the remains of US military personnel who were missing in action during past conflicts. Once identified, these remains and personal effects are repatriated to their families whenever possible.

Forensic science, of course, has proved valuable in the more traditional archaeological arena of human history and prehistory, where issues such as ancient cannibalism among Indians of the American Southwest and the events surrounding the Battle of the Little Bighorn have been studied in detail. Human osteology has always been an essential part of research and teaching in the evolution of human origins and in biocultural anthropology, and it shares many of the same principles with forensic anthropology. Indeed, focusing on empirical evidence in both the courts of history—where anthropological and archaeological theory provide frameworks for interpretation—and law—where evidence must be tightly linked to claims of guilt or innocence—can only strengthen the general standards of archaeology and anthropology in all realms.

Balancing Act

The aftermath of the World Trade Center disaster was perhaps the most painful period in the history of New York City. To say that it was a "life-changing experience" now seems trite, but it was. Forensic anthropologists volunteering with DMORT conducted round-the-clock operations near the Office of the Chief Medical Examiner (OCME) to identify victims. This was a daunting task. There were extraordinary amounts of fragmented and commingled human remains.

It was also apparent that large amounts of fragmented human remains were scattered over wide areas of lower Manhattan beyond Ground Zero, and much of this was lost during the city cleanup. There

was clearly a need for trained field teams of archaeologists to work in these areas to recover remains, personal effects, office documents, and other materials in a forensically controlled manner. This did not happen, however, until a trial recovery excavation a few months later under an invitation from the OCME demonstrated that such recoveries were possible. This volunteer team of field archaeologists, Providence Police and other members of the Rhode Island community, known as Forensic Archaeology Recovery (FAR), continues to train regularly and to deploy as needed. Arguably, so much vital evidence was lost outside Ground Zero that the number of WTC victims identified so far from human remains stands at just under 60%. For archaeologists and forensic anthropologists, the World Trade Center was one of the first "wake-up" calls that there was a need to strengthen the field recovery remains as a first step in identifying victims.

A year after this trial effort, a terrible fire destroyed "The Station" nightclub in West Warwick, Rhode Island, killing 100 people and leaving over twice as many horribly burned or injured. Although small compared with the WTC, the aftermath was similar in its effects. Rhode Island is a small community, and many people who have lived here for a while had close ties with the fire victims. Once again, DMORT assisted the local authorities—in this case the State Medical Examiner's Office—with the result that all of the fire victims were identified within three days. This was my first deployment with DMORT, and as a learning experience it was like drinking from a fire hose. Then FAR was called to "The Station" site by the Rhode Island State Fire Marshal's Office and performed forensic recoveries there for the next 11 days, finally closing the site.

In this case, FAR's primary task was to recover personal effects and enter them in custody to go to the Medical Examiner's lab for eventual repatriation to the victims' families. Another equally important task, however, was to "clean up" the site. The Fire Marshal explained that after the police lines and fences come down after a major fire, people swarm over the site collecting everything they can find—including human remains. It may be hard to imagine, but it happens. We agreed that we would not let it happen in this case, and by the end of the operation nothing of that nature was left there for people to collect. This was a service to our community that we had never envisioned beforehand, but it demonstrated the value of controlled forensic archaeology at a disaster scene in a way that had major, positive effects within our community.

The experiences of major disasters in the scope of Sept 11, "The Station" nightclub fire and Hurricane Katrina have shown us that disaster anthropology is as much a humanitarian mission as it is an exercise of anthropologists' professional and academic skills. Those of us who participate in this work train like maniacs to prepare for the very thing we dread most, but when it happens we would not want to be anywhere else.

"The Craft of Archaeology"

Michael Shanks and Randall H. McGuire

For students new to archaeology, this article may be a bit challenging, but it does provide a useful glimpse into the nature of the field. The piece originally appeared in a 1996 issue of *American Antiquity*, published by the Society for American Archaeology.

Michael Shanks is one of the most thought-provoking archaeologists of recent decades and is often identified with the post-processual archaeology that emerged out of Great Britain in the 1980s, where he spent the early years of his career before moving to the United States. Shanks is now a professor in the department of classics at Stanford. Randall McGuire is a professor in the anthropology department at the State University of New York, Binghampton.

Questions to Guide Reading

What are the perceived problems with the state of archaeology?

What do the authors mean when they imply that archaeology is a mode of production?

On what basis do the archaeologists claim that archaeology is not taken seriously?

How do the authors distinguish archaeology as it was traditionally defined from the "new archaeology" of the 1960s and modern archaeology?

What is archaeology's craft?

What are some of the ways that archaeology is divided by task and gender?

What do the authors mean when they describe the "factory model" of production in archaeology?

What are the primary advantages of considering archaeology as a craft?

The idea of archaeology as craft challenges the separation of reasoning and execution that characterizes the field today. The Arts and Crafts Movement of the late nineteenth century established craftwork as an aesthetic of opposition. We establish craft in a Marxian critique of alienated labor and we propose a unified practice of hand, heart, and mind for archaeology. The debates engendered by postprocessual archaeology have firmly situated archaeology in the present as a cultural and political practice. Many, however, still do not know how to work with these ideas. We argue that a resolution to this dilemma lies in thinking of archaeology as a craft. This resolution does not provide a method, or a cookbook, for the practice of archaeology, as indeed the core of our argument is that attempts at such standardization lie at the heart of the alienation of archaeology. Rather, we wish to consider archaeology as a mode of cultural production, a unified method practiced by archaeologist, "client" public, and contemporary society.

Anglo-American archaeology today appears to be in a state of disarray, rent by a host of splits and divisions and troubled by doubts and uncertainties (Bintliff 1993; Flannery 1982). In the theoretical arena ongoing debates pit processualists against postprocessualists, scientists against humanists, evolutionary theory against history, and an interest in generalizing against an interest in the particular (Preucel 1991; Yoffee and Sherratt 1993). Many scholars have difficulty moving from these polemical controversies to the doing of archaeology; they are plagued by doubt as to the relationship between theory and practice. There is uncertainty about how to connect academic archaeology, rescue archaeology, and cultural resource management, or how archaeology should relate to the public interpretations and uses of the past (Barker and Hill 1988; Chippindale 1986; Chippindale et al. 1990; Leone et al. 1987). Witness the lack of dialogue and lack of institutional connection between academics and field-workers (Athens 1993; Duke 1991; Hunter and Ralston 1993; Schuldenrein 1992). Archaeologists debate the nature of the relation between past and present, and these debates take on political significance in the issues of reburial and ownership (McBryde 1985; McGuire 1992). Should a universal archaeology-for-all, based on an objective knowledge of the past, be sought? Or should scholars build local archaeologies relative to the interests of different and often contentious social agendas (Gathercole and Lowenthal 1989; Layton 1989a, 1989b)? At the base of this disarray lie fundamental questions concerning the character of the discipline, questions that seem to leave us with many incommensurable archaeologies.

The aim of this paper is to offer a new point of view on these questions. We seek to rethink these polarizations in a more productive and less polemical way than we, and others, have considered before. We do not propose another new archaeology. Nor do we seek to mark yet another set of oppositions to bedevil the field. Instead we want to look at what it is that archaeologists actually do and to ask how they might make more of it.

Archaeologists take what's materially left of the past and work on it intellectually and physically to produce knowledge through reports, papers, books, museum displays, TV programs, whatever. In this archaeology is a mode of cultural production or technology with a raw material (the fragmented past, result of formation processes) and with theories and methods that allow (or indeed hinder) the production of what archaeologists desire, whether it is an answer to a research hypothesis, general knowledge of what may have happened in the past, or a tool in a political armory in the present. We will consider the character of such modes of cultural production.

We will look at archaeology as a human activity that potentially links human emotions, needs, and desires with theory and technical reasoning to form a unified practice, a "craft of archaeology." Our argument is not that archaeology should be a craft, but that good archaeology has always been a craft: a socially engaged practice which is not alienating, which edifies and provides diverse experience. Our intention is therefore not so much to draw an analogy as to outline those structures which, if given more importance, would make of archaeology a richer and more edifying practice.

Craft and Its Connotations

The term "craft" invites caricature. Comfortable middle-class people in smocks expressing themselves in activities that once were the livelihood of the working class and known as trades. Housewives sitting at the kitchen table in their Colonial Revival homes lovingly painting wooden geese, cows, or pigs in country-home correct, Sherman-Williams milk-paint colors. These crafts are arty, complacent, conservative, and safe. Craft has undertones of regressive ruralism—getting back to the securities of pre-industrial village life and community, the creation of James Deetz's (1977) communal, natural, *Small Things Forgotten* way of life in the suburbs. People surround themselves with crafts to create the illusion of a simpler traditional life. They may take up crafts as hobbies or pastimes: physical activities with clear untaxing guidelines in which they can lose themselves and escape.

It is for these reasons that craft work may not be taken seriously. Traditional and safe, homely and affirmative, craft work is not considered challenging, avant-garde, and critical, such as the work in the fine art galleries and the great art museums. In the discourse of "fine art," craft does not speak of the genius of an individual that has broken the bounds of convention and stretched the horizon of creativity. Rather, it comforts us with familiar forms executed with skill and technique to be judged by price and decorative appeal. The artist is envisioned in the studio making art in creative bouts and seemingly effortless flurries of activity. We see the craftsperson in the workshop patiently absorbed in the manufacture of objects. The identity of the artist lies in creativity, the identity of the craftsperson in labor. Art is intellectual and singular; craft is practical and everyday. Craft and art both create things of beauty, and share in the quality that we call creativity, but craft remains somehow less than art. This division of art and craft is partly institutionalized in the distinction between "fine" and "applied" arts, a decidedly western and post-Renaissance categorization (Dormer 1988, 1990, 1994; Fuller 1990).

Archaeology often is not taken seriously, both by the general public, which sees it more as recreation than work, and by colleagues in other scientific disciplines, who see it more as a technical skill than a discipline, more as craft than art. The physicist stands by the chalkboard locked in thought and then in a flurry of equations and a shower of chalk dust discovers a new principle. The archaeologist digs patiently in the dirt, absorbed in labor until slowly the discovery emerges from the earth. We associate most scholarly disciplines with a subject: biology with the study of nature, geology with the study of the earth, math with the study of numbers, and physics with the study of the laws of nature. Archaeology is most often associated in popular literatures with an activity: digging in the earth, Most of the sciences are defined in terms of an intellectual program, archaeology in terms of a type of labor. Although prehistoric archaeology in Britain has a sense of identity, at least according to its practitioners, still the usual image associated with the discipline is the excavator on site, an occasionally romantic figure, snatching pieces of the past from irrecoverable loss in a muddy ditch. In the United States archaeology is usually part of anthropology, but like craft to art, it is often thought of as the lesser part.

Archaeology was traditionally defined in terms of its practice. You were an archaeologist if you did archaeology by digging in the earth (Flannery 1982). Some scholars, such as Gordon Willey and V. Gordon Childe, wrote great summaries that synthesized what the field archaeologists had found but rarely did they do the actual digging. The New Archaeology of the 1960s challenged this equation of archaeology with technique. It sought to make archaeology more legitimate as an intellectual pursuit; a nomothetic science we could all be proud of. New Archaeologists wanted it to be more than a set of techniques, and they elevated theory to a pursuit that directed fieldwork. This desire considerably inflated one of the divisions that we live with now—particularly the separation of the theoretical from the dirt-digging archaeologist.

Consider the following set of divisions. They do not precisely coincide, but they are at the heart of an alienated division of labor that has been so important in the development of our western society. This division of labor separates thinking from doing and segregates those who think from those who do in a hierarchy of labor (Braverman 1974; Hounshell 1984; and Noble 1984 provide standard histories; Ollman 1971 is a powerful philosophical critique; Harding 1986 and Haraway 1989 contribute feminist positions on the issue).

art	craft
theory	practice
reason	execution
decision	implementation
creativity	technique
truth	beauty
cognitive	affective
intellect	emotion
knowledge-that	knowledge-how
masculine	feminine
scientific research	management

Science and fine art are here (paradoxically) united in that each claims the intellectual high ground in opposition to what is considered the more practical pole of the duality. It is in this system that the division between theoretical and rescue archaeology, for example, finds its roots in western political economy.

Humans must think to act, and action invokes thought. The alienation of art from craft, reason from action, and theory from practice breaks apart those things that are naturally joined in human action, and makes one pole of the unity less than the other. Thus this system of oppositions may be described as ideological.

The Arts and Crafts movement of the turn of the century sought to restore the unity of thinking and doing. The practitioners constructed craft as an aesthetic, a philosophy, in opposition to this alienation. A.W. Pugin and John Ruskin had established earlier in the nineteenth century a strong link between ethics and design. The movement is particularly associated in England with the work and writings of William Morris as a reaction against factory manufacture and the industrial revolution. Arts and Crafts guilds were set up by A.H. MackMurdo, C.R. Ashbee, William Lethaby, and Walter Crane. Visionaries such as Gustav Stickley and Elbert Hubbard brought the movement to the United States. In their guilds and companies they championed craft and workshop-based labor where tools served the craftsperson, as opposed to the machine-based labor of industrial capitalism where workers served machines. Arts and Crafts communities of workers such as the Roycrofters of East Aurora, New York, sought to break down the opposition of management and workers, designers and laborers. Craft was to be art in society, art not separated from life (Institute of Contemporary Arts 1984; Thompson 1977; Tillyard 1988).

We suggest that the notion of craft that developed in the Arts and Crafts movement mends those rips in modern archaeology: reason from execution, theory from practice. It focuses our attention on the labor that unifies all the different archaeologies as craft. Craft unifies theory and practice; in this unity neither pole can be the lesser. Thus craft erodes notions of hierarchy in archaeology including those that lead to inequalities based on gender. We will also show how it redefines archaeology in a way that escapes the gender-stereotyped images of the archaeologist as either a discoverer or a puzzle solver. In the discovery image the hero, usually male, risks life and limb to discover or uncover archaeological knowledge in exotic and dangerous lands (Gero 1991:2). In the puzzle-solving image the archaeologist, again usually male, takes the pieces, the facts about the past provided by secondary specialists, often female (Gero 1985), and assembles these pieces to solve the puzzle of the past.

Craft: A Sketch of Positive Cultural Production

Craft is productive work for a purpose: it is utilitarian, and avoids a separation of reasoning from the execution of a task. Craft is holistic. Craft resists this separation of work from what is produced because it is opposed to labor that separates reasoning from execution (as in management and workers) and divides activity into discrete tasks (as on an assembly line). Craft involves a rediscovery of subjugated knowledge, the recovery of practices made marginal in the rational organization of productive routines. The potter at the wheel must conceptualize the form desired even while pulling that form up from the lump of clay. The reasoning and labor of making pottery combine in the craft of throwing the pot and are embodied in the pot. The throwing of pots is at once an abstract intellectual activity and a concrete labor.

Craft is located within productive relations, both economic and cultural. It crucially involves a dialogue with its "client" or community, whose interests the craft serves. The potter serves clients who want certain items, yet shapes those wants by expanding on the needs and aesthetics found in the community. To do this the potter must be part of and participate in the life of the community to gain the knowledge, awareness, acceptance, and opportunity necessary for such a dialogue.

Craft involves an immediate and practical unity of the intellectual or cognitive and the emotive or expressive. The pot must first be created as an abstraction in the mind, but throwing the pot is a sensuous activity that is emotive and expressive. For the transformation of the pot from an abstraction to a concrete object to succeed, the craftsperson must respect and understand the properties of the craft material and incorporate an aesthetic—this is the interpretation of purpose and material within "style." The potter must understand the elasticities and limitations of the clay, master a set of techniques, and be able to use an aesthetic sense to apply these techniques to the clay and make a pot. Craft is a process of interpretation and involves taste and the judgment of quality: it is a process of design.

The judgment of craft involves criteria that are social, technical, and aesthetic. Craft items are utilitarian: they serve needs, and these are social needs. Our social position and background help determine which vessel forms we will need for our table, in what number, and for what purpose. A finished teapot can be judged on technical criteria—is it free from cracks: does the lid sit level on the teapot; and does the tea flow freely from it? But it must also meet some sense of aesthetics, be pleasing to the eye and to the hand. The complex terms imposed by interpretation and taste apply to these judgments on the labor and products of craft. To conceive archaeology as craft invokes these aspects of this sketch: a labor both cognitive and expressive, which involves reason and execution and which applies to social and practical interests, whether these are addressed or not.

Archaeology as Craft

We believe craft is latent within archaeology—a potential that is already with us and that we need to recognize.

A craft of archaeology manufactures archaeological knowledge. Archaeologists are not heroes who overcome great adversity to discover facts about the past: nor do they merely act as detectives gathering the facts of the past and assembling them like so many pieces of a puzzle. Rather archaeologists craft facts out of a chaotic welter of conflicting and confused observations: they modify them and reformulate them out of existing knowledge. Here we refer to the considerable and growing body of work in the sociology and philosophy of science, which contends that facts, objectivity, and scientific truth are social achievements and are the result of what scientists and archaeologists do. Objectivity and truth do not exist as abstract attributes of the material world, but are real, material, and located in our (scientific) relationship with the world (Gero 1991; Haraway 1989; Harding 1986; Knorr-Cetina 1981; Knorr-Cetina and Mulkay 1983; Latour 1987; Latour and Woolgar 1979; Lynch 1985; Pickering 1992; Wylie 1991). The crafting of archaeological knowledge, like any scientific enterprise, requires great skill and creativity. The discipline of archaeology—method, theory, and philosophy—cannot be reduced to a set of abstract rules or procedures that may then be applied to the "real" world of archaeological data. We do not simply "discover" the facts, a single story, or account of the past, and the pieces of the puzzle do not come in fixed shapes that only allow a single solution. The craft of archaeology involves application of discipline to particular purpose: it is a logic of particular archaeological situations. The craft of archaeology is the skill of interpreting purpose, viability, and expression.

Purpose

Purpose refers to the social and other significance of archaeological projects. Archaeological knowledge, we contend, is made rather than discovered or assembled. This making entails a relationship with a client or customer for whom the craftworker labors. It necessitates a dialogue with that community so that the work will fit the need. Archaeological knowledge, as the product of archaeological practices, is utilitarian and incorporates purposes that may be established in dialogue with others and in the interpretation of need. These purposes and needs relate to specific communities that the craft of archaeology may serve: the government, the academy, a local village community, a city council, a Native American nation. This is an application of interests, in every sense of the word. Different interests may involve different archaeological products. In most cases the archaeologist must serve more than one community, and a single project may entail or require multiple products. Such an interchange between archaeologist and client community is not one way. Archaeologists are not simply to accept the terms and interests of the client. A good work of craft enhances, alters, and creates new possibilities of experience, however modestly.

The work of the potter is a mediation or reconciliation of various spheres of interest and need. To produce work that is irrelevant to a community may be an expensive indulgence, even while perhaps adhering to a notion of avant-garde art. Yet to create something which simply panders to the supposed interests and fancies of the market can be an empty consumerism. There is also the community of fellow potters within which craftspersons ponder all aspects of the production of works in clay. Some of these musings are perhaps esoteric and of little interest to wider communities.

The most respectable and edifying work of craft, we suggest, is one produced when the potter takes the needs and interests of the "client" or customer and interprets these in a way that answers purpose while giving something more. The new teapot serves its purpose and pours tea, but the skill of the potter may succeed in providing it with a surface and form that enhance its use. It may be entertaining perhaps. It may provide satisfactions or vicarious experiences, and refer also to distinctive "styles." The potter's skill in making such an edifying teapot has many origins. One is certainly the character of the dialogue within the community of potters: the debate and polemic around styles, form, and surface, as well as more mundane information exchange.

So too with archaeology. A discipline that simply responds to its own perceived needs and interests, as in the idea of an academic archaeology existing for its own sake ("disinterested knowledge"), is a decadent indulgence. But it is important nonetheless to respect the autonomy of the discipline and the community formed by archaeologists, if only de facto. The academy may well be a valid community served by the archaeologist; or it may not be. It depends on the dialogues within, their character, range, and creativity. And, of course, it is in the interests of archaeologists to enable dialogue as a context for creative work. Such liberal and democratic values of and within an autonomous academy are worth restating, especially given the pressure to wholly accommodate archaeological practice to external interests.

So a craft of archaeology challenges a consumerist approach to archaeology. We commonly see such an approach in some cultural resource management in the United States and in the "heritage movement" more generally. Archaeologists define the consumer of archaeological knowledge either in terms of limited but powerful interests (such as companies and firms needing to comply with legislation) (Fitting 1978) or in broad sweeping generalizations (such as the general public) that obscure and deny many varied interests (DeCicco 1988; Hills 199; Knudson

1989). In the first case the archaeologist is called on to produce a very limited product to minimize the costs for the client, and in the second the archaeologist is asked to package what we have learned so that it will appeal to a mass market. Craft archaeology fosters an active dialogue between the discipline and those that it serves. A craft archaeology should find its clients among the diversity of communities and interests that it studies, works in, lives in, and draws funding from (Potter 1990).

Viability

Whatever the craftworker wishes to do, the work must be viable and practical. Craft of necessity responds to the raw material, which dictates much of what the craft product will be. The archaeologist also needs a good technical understanding of the past and a respect for material objectivity. The facts of archaeological knowledge are created from observations of a reality, and the archaeologist must recognize that reality and master the technical aids that assist or allow us to observe it. But this does not mean giving absolute primacy to the object past. In the interplay between archaeological craftworker and object, both are partners in the final product. The archaeologist gains familiarity through working with the artifacts from the past, which defy this familiarity through their resistance to classification and categorization. The archaeological record can never quite be captured or pinned down—there's always more.

Is this not also the experience of the potter? Even after a lifetime's work with clay, familiarity seems so partial and superficial. There is always so much more in the inert mineral body. Tight control of processing can achieve predictable results, as in industrial production. But this is a deadening and alienating of the craft encounter with clay. In the genuine dialogue the clay always replies somewhat unpredictably, perhaps in the response of the body to firing, spectacularly in the varied response of surface finishes and glazes. Much of the craft is in interpreting and channeling the quality of response, the resistance.

We might ask why so much of the archaeological work done under the headings of cultural/archaeological resource management or rescue archaeology seems so wooden, uninteresting, and simply boring, especially when it has not always been this way. In the early 1970s many creative individuals struggled with the new imperatives of this work to craft an archaeology that served a mix of new and old interests. Those early years witnessed many exciting successes, and an equal number of dismal failures, that led to a call for a uniformity of product (McGimsey and Davis 1977). As a result, the craft was lost in much of this work and replaced by standardized procedures, evaluative criteria, and the routinized practice of industrial production (Paynter 1983; Raab et al. 1980). The extent to which organizations such as the Institute of Field Archaeologists (IFA) in the United Kingdom (founded in the early 1980s), with its Board of Trade approval and codes of practice (IFA 1988, 1990), escapes such routinization is a debated point. Interesting, exciting, and valuable research survives only where individuals resist the alienation of industrial work and struggle to do craft.

Should the ideal of archaeological work not be a craft ideal—the notion of apprentices working with their teachers to master the doing of archaeology? The current reality of archaeology seldom fits this ideal because managers have broken apart tasks, and they expect individuals to specialize in a particular activity. The end result of this deskilling is that only those individuals managing or directing the work understand and can control the whole process (Paynter 1983). Rewards are differentiated according to imposed levels of task: interpretation over recovery, for example, with project directors reserving for themselves or controlling what is considered the more prestigious. The workers themselves are placed at the bottom of a top-down control hierarchy that seeks to maximize efficiency and profit instead of guiding apprentices to mastership. This is where the lessons of the Arts and Crafts movement are important. Unlike our analogy to the lone potter, that movement sought to integrate groups of workers and managers preforming specialized tasks in a craft production. This was accomplished by cross-training individuals in various tasks, involving all in the decision-making process, and giving each individual control of their own segment of the work process. In this craft production knowledge and skills were shared, individuals contributed to the design and decision-making process in terms of their levels of skill and involvement, and individuals managed their tasks rather than the tasks managing the individuals. We suggest this approach should be applied to archaeological practice in order to confront the reality of an industrialized archaeology.

Expression

Archaeologists have largely down-played or even denigrated the expressive, aesthetic, and emotive qualities of archaeological projects over the last three decades as they sought an objective scientific practice. Yet most of us cherish the experience of holding a just-recovered artifact, contemplating its beauty, feeling the tactile pleasure of its shape, and pondering the minor flaws and the unique peculiarities of form that reflect the person that made it. Many of us prize the solitude and oneness with nature that we experience on a survey transect through farmland or the desert, or the physical and emotional feeling of well-being, material accomplishment, and deserved rest we experience at the end of a day of excavation. In popular imagination archaeology is far more than a neutral acquisition of knowledge; the material presence of the past is an emotive field of cultural interest and political dispute. It is this that motivated most of us to be archaeologists, maintained us through the toil and struggle of becoming archaeologists, and sustains us as we do the myriad of other things we must to do to make a living as archaeologists. Archaeological labor is social as well as personal; it relates to the social experiences of archaeological practice and of

belonging to the archaeological community and a discipline or of academic discourse.

It is mainly the expressive and emotive dimension of archaeology that attracts wider communities. Expression and emotion is what makes archaeology such a (potentially) significant feature of cultural politics. We clearly see this in the experiences of the World Archaeological Congress (WAC) in Southampton, England, in 1986 and Delhi, India, in 1994. Issues of academic freedom and apartheid greatly shaped the Southampton congress (Ucko 1987), and extraordinary scenes of violence erupted, partly over religious difference, at the end of the Delhi congress.

Craft is essentially creative: taking purpose, assessing viability, working with material, and expressing interpretation to create the product that retains traces of all these stages. The creative element in craft contains an aesthetic of skill and of workmanship. Craft's expressive dimension is also about pleasure (or displeasure) and is certainly not restricted to the intellectual or the cognitive. The genuine craft artifact embodies these emotions, and the response to it is a multifaceted one. Pleasure is perhaps not a very common word in academic archaeology, but a craft archaeology must recognize its role and embody it in the product we make. This means addressing seriously and with imagination the questions of how we write about the past, how we address our activities as archaeologists, and how we communicate with others (Hills 1993; Hodder 1989; Hodder et al. 1995; Tilley 1990).

Designing Archaeologies

In the craft of archaeology the past is designed, yet it is no less real or objective. Some archaeologists fear a hyper-relativism. They think that if knowledges of the past are constructed then anything may be done with the past. They worry about how the past can be constructed when its reality happened in its own present. Recognizing that we as archaeologists craft our knowledge of the past is not, however, the same as saying we make up the past. The realities of the past constrain what we can create, just as the clay constrains the potter when she makes a teapot. We do not worry if a teapot is real or not because it was created by human hands. We are more commonly concerned with whether it is pleasing to the eye, and if it works or not.

Hence the question of archaeological design is "What kind of archaeology do we want, and will it work?" The craft object, the product, is both critique and affirmation; it embodies its creation, speaks of style, gives pleasure in its use, solves a problem perhaps, performs a function, provides an experience, signifies, and resonates. It may also be pretentious, ugly or kitsch, useless, or untrue to its materials and creation. In the same way each archaeology has a style; the set of decisions made in producing an archaeological product involves conformity with some interests, percepts, or norms. As with an artifact, the judgment of an archaeological style involves multiple considerations. We need to consider its eloquence, that is, how effective and productive it is. We should also make an ethical appraisal of its aims and purposes and possible functions. Technical matters are implicated, of course, including how true it has been to the material past, and the reality and techniques of observation that it uses to construct facts. Judgment refers to all these aspects of archaeology as craft: purpose, viability, and expression.

In the skill of archaeology, hand, heart, and mind are combined; it is an embodied experience. In such a skill know-how is as important as know-that. Archaeology as craft implies notions of apprenticeship and mastery, rather than the application of (cognitive and abstract) method. Formalized method can never substitute for skill. This is also to recognize the importance of experience (in every sense) and of subjective knowledge and familiarity with archaeological materials. Important also is the social and political character of the archaeological community, the context for mastering these skills. Craft values wisdom more than technical knowledge, more than

the right, or correct, answer. Wisdom involves knowledge, insight, judgment, and a wise course of action.

A Unified Discipline

We propose that archaeology could form a unified discipline in its craft. Archaeology's craft is to interpret the past. The archaeologist is one of contemporary society's storytellers. Archaeologists forge interpretations that provide systems of meaning between past and present in order to help orient people in their cultural experiences. This skill is the basis of the archaeologist's authority, because everyone has not mastered the craft of dealing with the past archaeologically. The craft of archaeology unifies the discipline through its practice, both in terms of uniting the activities of archaeology and in terms of divisions that appear to divide us.

We use the present tense here, but a hierarchy of archaeological practice presently exists giving the highest position to those who discover the knowledge, assemble the puzzle, or instruct us in how these things are to be done (Gero 1985)—the "archaeological theorists." Lower positions are accorded those who support the discoverer, and provide the pieces of the puzzle to be assembled. In this scientific mode of commodity production the higher levels of analysis each appropriate the products of the lower in their practice so that the theorist is accorded greater renown than the prehistorian, the field director a higher position than the laboratory assistant, and the synthesizer more attention than the faunal analyst. We divide the practice of archaeology into those of us who manage and sit on committees, synthesize, generalize, and theorize and those of us who sort, dig, and identify. As Gero (1991) points out, this hierarchy does more than just rank activities; it has a more profound social dimension.

Embedded in this hierarchy of practice is a gender division of labor that relegates women's knowledge and production or practices gendered feminine to the lower rungs of the hierarchy of practice thus depreciating them as real contributors.

There is also another mode of scientific production centered around a growing class of "archaeological engineers," scientific technicians whose standing is related to their control of scientific analysis, usually of materials. Much central and university funding has been invested in Great Britain in this form of archaeological science, and special funds exist in the U.S. National Science Foundation to equip such research. The distinction between the two forms—theorists and engineers—of archaeological science is analogous to that between physics and engineering (Latour 1987).

We would contrast the modern hierarchy of practice with a unified practice of archaeological craft where there is a range of endeavors from the interpretive to the technical, to the practical, to the creative. Each of the different activities necessary to craft archaeological knowledge embodies some mix of these endeavors, labors of the hand, heart, and mind, There is no single correct route to the final product—the archaeological work. There is no hierarchy of archaeological practices, from washing sherds to theory building; the craft involves both theory and more modest operative functions. The skill and the experience accord both significance and respectability. All archaeological activities can be reconciled in terms of their contribution to unalienated practice and their relation to the elements of archaeology's craft: purpose, viability, and expression. All archaeological activities are subject to judgment and critique on this basis.

The craft of archaeology unifies all archaeologies but does not reduce them to a single thing. Archaeology as craft must lead to multiple archaeologies and diverse archaeological products as it enters into dialogues with different interests and communities. As such, archaeology has a practice, a topic, and obligations, but no necessary methodology. The craft of archaeology has particular responsibilities to both past and present, rooted in the character of archaeological experience and not in an archaeological rule book or cookbook (Shanks 1995).

To celebrate a creative diversity of archaeological results that attend to different needs automatically opposes those impulses to get on with doing archaeology and oppose the impulse to cut out the critical reflection. By celebrating the diversity of archaeological research addressing different needs, we are resisting the impulse to simply get on with "doing archaeology" and to reflect critically about our profession. What is there to fear from an examination of our practices, the interests and desires they attend, and the emotive worlds they serve?

To the question "What is archaeology?" we would answer that it is archaeology's craft—the skill of interpreting archaeological experiences and situations—that makes us archaeologists and not sociologists or historians. It is archaeology as a craft, a mode of cultural production, that makes archaeology different from digging ditches.

The Political Economy of Archaeology

Much of what we have said in this essay concerns the political economy of archaeology, the discipline, its organizations, and its practices. We hope we have made it clear that such matters are inseparable from the structure of contemporary society. Our following remarks are brief, intending to sketch fields of debate rather than provide definitive comment.

The oppositions that bedevil archaeologists are not foibles peculiar to our discipline and practice; rather they originate in the pervasive alienation of contemporary capitalism. The separation of reason from action and theory from practice found in archaeology is at the root of modern life. The maximization of profits dictates that complex crafts be deskilled, or broken down into constituent parts, enabling minimally trained individuals to complete work rapidly. This deskilling divorces knowledge from practice: each worker comprehends one small piece of production while high-level managers oversee and understand the entire process. This factory model of production permeates most aspects of our lives and consciousness. In Christmas movies even the elves work on an assembly line with Santa Claus as the benevolent manager. The shifts in the United States and United Kingdom to a "Post-Industrial" or "Information Age" have only furthered this alienation as the training and technical know-how to control "knowledge" has increased and the need for the skilled craftsperson declined (Bell 1974; Grint 1991; Touraine 1971).

Our discussion also provokes debates on the cultural politics of higher education and its institutions. Thinking about archaeology as a technology of cultural production forces us to consider the proper role of university courses in archaeology, and of the research efforts of academics. The traditional home of archaeology has been in the academy, but today the vast majority of archaeologists do not work in the academy. Instead they are employed in some aspect of contract or rescue archaeology, or in public planning. It remains the case, however, that all archaeologists pass through the academy to receive the credentials needed to practice archaeology. The academy has always had an ambiguous position in the United States and the United Kingdom. On the one hand, it ultimately derives from an ecclesiastic model of the life of the mind aloof from the grubby realities of day-to-day life. On the other hand, public monies finance the academy, and with this funding comes the expectation that the academy will pragmatically serve society (Giamatti 1988; Kerr 1964; Rosovsky 1990). Current conservative educational policies tend to champion this expectation.

The academy has always resisted the factory model of production and sought instead a community of scholars. This community models itself on medieval guild principles of long apprenticeship (graduate school and junior faculty status) to be followed by master status (tenure). Scholars, having proven themselves through an arduous process, are granted security and freedom to pursue their intellectual interests freely. Students embrace a liberal education freeing their minds to explore, and to connect with others in a search for truth (Giamatti 1988:109). This model is, of course, the ivory tower, and it implies an academy estranged from society.

In the public universities of the United States, and in the tradition of the red-brick universities of England, the community-of-scholars model persists alongside, and often in conflict with, the principle that the university exists as a business to serve society (Kerr 1964: Giamatti 1988). National and state governments fund the academy to further economic development and address the needs of the state. Universities do this by training professionals (doctors, lawyers, teachers, engineers, military officers, and others) and by conducting research related to the technical advance of farming, manufacturing, and war. The public tends to regard the university as another level of education necessary for children to enter the middle class. Governments in Great Britain and the United States have responded to the general economic decline that began in the mid-1970s by stressing the public service obligations of the university. They have put greater emphasis on business models to structure the university. In the United States university administrations have become enamored with management models such as "Total Quality Management." These models treat the university as a business, marketing a product to consumers (the students) and demand more accountability from faculty as to their time and effort.

Neither of these models is conducive to archaeology as craft. The self-indulgence of the ivory tower leads us not to the discovery of truth, but rather to the creation of esoteric knowledge of interest to a few. In the last decade a profusion of authors have arisen to denounce the academy as wasteful, and the professorate as lazy, and to call for universities that serve the public interest (Bloom 1987; Sykes 1988). They wish to reduce the university to a factory that efficiently produces uniform, dependable, monotonous products: practical knowledge to advance industry, and uncritical, technically trained students to staff it (Lynton and Elman 1987).

The factory model has firmly taken hold in contract or rescue archaeology. Increasingly in the United

States, competing profit-taking private firms dominate this realm of archaeological practice. In the United Kingdom archaeology has been opened up to developer funding (Department of Environment 1990; Welsh Office 1991). The largest arena of archaeological practice has largely abandoned the apprentice model in favor of the factory approach.

The traditional scheme of archaeological fieldwork was an apprentice structure where students learned through participation under a master (Joukousky 1980:27). Archaeologists undertook fieldwork with two fundamental goals; to gain knowledge of the archaeological record and to train students to become masters. While contract and rescue archaeology began in this idealistic setting, it did not always serve this type of archaeology well: there were a number of spectacular failures, such as the New Melones project in California, that led to calls for a more businesslike approach (Cunningham 1979; Walka 1979). By the late 1970s apprenticeship had given way to the scientific management models of factory labor.

The scientific paradigm of the New Archaeology aided in this transformation. The New Archaeologists were (and many remain) openly contemptuous of the mastery model (Flannery 1982; Redman 1991). They advocated instead a "scientific" approach based on specialist teams. This encourages a hierarchy of both effort and reward.

Today contract and rescue archaeology exist in a highly competitive realm that exaggerates the importance of efficiency. The factory model of production maximizes efficiency by standardizing the product, and by breaking tasks down into component activities (Paynter 1983). Efficiency maximizes profit and leads to greater top-down control. Once the task of archaeology has been broken down into its components, only the managers at the top can control the whole process. In both the United States, and in the United Kingdom, national and government institutions now audit archaeological services, and dictate the form and content of reports (Cunliffe 1982, 1990; Department of Environment 1975; English Heritage 1991; Society of Antiquaries of London 1992). While there are strong arguments, of course, for quality control and standardization, the negative results have included a degenerative homogenization of the archaeological product, and in many arenas the dulling of creativity and satisfaction in the work.

Ultimately issues of the sociology and politics of education, and of the organization of archaeological practices, should be placed within the context of large-scale changes in society. These may be summarized as the shift to economic structures of flexible accumulation from managed "Fordist" economies (Harvey 1989; Rose 1991). The considerable debate over the character of postmodernity deals with the effects of these changes (Shanks 1992; Walsh 1992). Obvious features of the changes in archaeology are the rise of the heritage industry, the commercial exploitation of the material past, and the tying of academic effort to outside interest. Floating labor forces servicing contract archaeology, competitive bidding (tendering) (Swain 1991), and the rise of archaeological consultants (Collcutt 1993) are further aspects of this new political economy of archaeology.

The Politics of Craft

We cannot think a craft archaeology into existence, or create it through some act of pure will. Nor can we with a wave of our hand transform the larger political and economic structures that archaeology exists within. In this section we will gather some comments about the implications of a craft archaeology.

A first step, however, must be to critically discuss and debate what the goals of archaeology should be. Through such debate we can consider alternative practices for archaeology and learn how to "do" a craft archaeology. We face the same problems as the Arts and Crafts movement of a hundred years ago. We may do well to look at the successes, and the ultimate failure, of this movement as a place to start.

We would begin with the realization that a craft archaeology is subversive, in that it requires us to resist the dominant structures that shape contemporary archaeological work. We have commented that work done in a contract or rescue context is often dull and uninspired. Yet this is not always the case; there are many examples of exciting, interesting, and creative research done in these contexts. In all of these cases, however, the archaeologists had to resist the pressures for routinization, and work beyond the specifications of contracts and laws. They either sacrificed efficiency and profit, or put in extraordinary efforts over and above what they were paid for. Such exciting work does not result from the structure of the enterprise but rather in spite of it.

Breaking hierarchies of expertise and managerial authority may involve new management structures, and new project designs. There is a need for the "experts in the trench"—archaeologists who bring technical and scientific specialized knowledge to the point of the trowel, rather than delegating technical reporting as a post-excavation task. Computerization already allows for much of what happens in the lab or research office to occur on-site, and in the hands of those who excavate. Data collection should not be so radically separated from analysis and interpretation because we may search for methodological strategies that allow flexible renegotiation of project aims and objectives in the light of finds in the field (Shanks and Hodder 1995).

Fundamental to an archaeological craft that recognizes itself as cultural production is the relative positioning of communities of workers and their publics. It is people who practice and "consume" archaeology, and there is need to take careful, and sensitive, account of the characteristics of their communities. This brings us to a most important aspect of archaeological craft: our obligation to take responsibility for what we do and produce. A craft archaeology cannot hide its interests behind a notion of knowledge for its own sake, detached from the needs and interests of contemporary communities.

Conclusions

As craft, archaeology can be both science and humanity. The place of science is that of technical understanding of the material past and of opening archaeological awareness to the empirical richness of the things found—from the mineral inclusions and character of a clay fabric revealed in petrological examination, to the variability within a ceramic industry explored in statistical analysis.

But analogy with craft also shifts concern away from epistemology and methodology (which pose the question of how to achieve a true and objective image and explanation of the material past and have been the focus of so much attention in the last 25 years). Judgment of archaeological work need have little to do with method and adherence to a particular epistemology of how to achieve "knowledge" of the past. Judgment and assessment occur according to contribution to an archaeological practice that is not alienated.

The shifts from epistemology and method can also overcome the split between the subjective and objective elements of archaeology, the empirical and expressive, in that the labor of craft is a constant dialogue between archaeologist and material, archaeologist and community—an expressive and interpretive experience within which the past is created.

To conceive archaeology as craft is also to confirm the importance of theory, but not so much as an abstract model of procedure, belief, explanation, or description. Archaeology is now familiar with the format of many papers: they begin with a theoretical statement, premise, or argument that is then "applied" to a body of material. Being theoretically aware, however, is less about this "top-down" application. It is rarely good to make pots by beginning with an abstract aesthetic and then applying it to a piece of clay. Theoretically informed practice is simply being reflective, applying critique (aesthetic, philosophical, ethical, political, whatever) to the practice at hand. Looking at pottery decoration may also require examination of ideas such as style, ideology, indeed, art and craft, which inform an interpretive and creative understanding of material.

Finally, the analogy with craft points to the importance of recent developments in archaeological work, calling for a more humanist discipline which accepts the place of subjectivity and the affective. But rather than splitting the discipline into objectivists and relativists, scientists and historians, processualists and postprocessualists, we can effect a reconciliation and dialogue, and a unity of diversity through the concrete sensuous practice we experience as archaeology.

References

Athens, J.S.
1993 Cultural Resource Management and Academic Responsibility in Archaeology; A Further Comment. *SAA Bulletin* 11(2):6–7.

Barker, F., and J.D. Hill (editors)
1988 Archaeology and the Heritage Industry. *Archaeological Review From Cambridge* 7(2).

Bell, D.
1974 *The Coming of the Post-Industrial Society*. Heineman, London.

Bintliff, J.
1993 Why Indiana Jones Is Smarter than the Postprocessualists. *Norwegian Archaeological Review* 26:91–100.

Bloom, A.
1987 *The Closing of the American Mind*. Simon and Schuster, New York.

Braverman, H.
1974 *Labor and Monopoly Capital: the Degradation of Work in the Twentieth Century*. Monthly Review Press, London.

Chippindale, C.
1986 Stoned Henge: Events and Issues at the Summer Solstice, 1985 *World Archaeology* 18(1):38–58.

Chippindale, C., P. Devereux, P. Fowler, R. Jones, and T. Sebastian
1990 *Who Owns Stonehenge?* Batsford, London.

Collcutt, S.
1993 The Archaeologist as Consultant. In *Archaeological Resource Management in the UK: An Introduction*, edited by J. Hunter and I. Ralston, pp. 158–68. Alan Sutton, Dover, England.

Cunliffe, B.
1982 *The Report of a Joint Working Party of the Council for British Archaeology and the Department of the Environment*. Department of the Environment and Her Majesty's Stationery Office, London.

1990 Publishing in the City. *Antiquity* 64:667–71.

Cunningham, R.D.
1979 Why and How to Improve Archaeology's Business Work. *American Antiquity* 44:572–74.

DeCicco, G.
1988 A Public Relations Primer. *American Antiquity* 53:840–56.

Deetz, J.D.
1977 *In Small Things Forgotten*. Anchor Press, Garden City, New York.

Department of the Environment
1975 *Principles of Publication in Rescue Archaeology*. Report by a Working party of the Ancient Monuments Board for England. Committee for Rescue Archaeology (The Frere Report), Her Majesty's Stationery Office, London.
1990 *Planning Policy Guidance Note 16: Archaeology and Planning*. Her Majesty's Stationery Office, London.

Dormer, P.
1988 The Ideal World of Vermeer's Little Lacemaker. In *Design After Modernism*, edited by J. Thackara, pp. 135–44. Thames and Hudson, London.
1990 *The Meanings of Modern Design*. Thames and Hudson, London.
1994 *The Art of the Maker: Skill and its Meaning in Art, Craft and Design*. Thames and Hudson, London.

Duke, P.
1991 Cultural Resource Management and the Professional Archaeologist. *SAA Bulletin* 9(4):10–11.

English Heritage
1991 *The Management of Archaeological Projects*. 2nd ed. Historic Buildings and Monuments Commission and Her Majesty's Stationery Office, London.

Fitting, J.E.
1978 Client Orientated Archaeology: A Comment on Kinsey's Dilemma. *Pennsylvania Archaeologist* 48:12–25.

Flannery, K.V.
1982 The Golden Marshalltown: A Parable for the Archaeology of the 1980s. *American Anthropologist* 84:265–79.

Fuller, P.
1990 The Proper Work of the Potter. In *Images of God: Consolations of Lost Illusions*. Hogarth, London.

Gathercole, P., and D. Lowenthal (editors)
1989 *The Politics of the Past*. Unwin Hyman, London.

Gero, J.
1985 Socio-politics of Archaeology and the Women-at-Home Ideology. *American Antiquity* 50:342–50.
1991 Gender Divisions of Labor in the Construction of Archaeological Knowledge in the United States. In *Archaeology of Gender*, edited by N. Willo and D. Walde, pp. 96–102. University of Calgary, Calgary, Alberta.

Giamatti, B.
1988 *A Free and Ordered Space: The Real World of the University*. W.W. Norton, New York.

Grint, K.
1991 *The Sociology of Work: An Introduction*. Blackwell Polity, Cambridge.

Haraway, D.
1989 *Primate Visions: Gender, Race, and Nature in the World of Modern Science*. Routledge, London.

Harding, S.
1986 *The Science Question in Feminism*. Open University Press, London.

Harvey, D.
1989 *The Condition of Postmodernity*. Basil Blackwell, Oxford.

Hills, C.
1993 The Dissemination of Information. In *Archaeological Resource Management in the UK: An Introduction*, edited by J. Hunter and I. Ralston, pp. 215–24. Alan Sutton, Dover, England.

Hodder, I.
1989 Writing Archaeology: Site Reports in Context. *Antiquity* 62:268–74.

Hodder, I., M. Shanks, A. Alexandri, V. Buchli, J. Carman, J. Last, and G. Lucas
1995 *Interpreting Archaeology: Finding Meaning in the Past.* Routledge, London.

Hounshell, D.A.
1984 *From the American System to Mass Production 1800–1932: The Development of Manufacturing Technology in the United States.* Johns Hopkins University Press, Baltimore.

Hunter, J., and I. Ralston (editors)
1993 *Archaeological Resource Management in the UK: An Introduction.* Alan Sutton, Dover, England.

Institute of Contemporary Arts
1984 *William Morris Today.* Institute of Contemporary Arts, London.

Institute of Field Archaeologists
1988 *By-Laws of the Institute of Field Archaeologists: Code of Conduct.* Institute of Field Archaeologists, Birmingham, England.
1990 *By-Laws of the Institute of Field Archaeologists: Code of Approved Practice for the Regulation of Contractual Arrangements in Field Archaeology.* Institute of Field Archaeologists, Birmingham, England.

Joukousky, M.
1980 *A Complete Manual of Archaeology.* Prentice-Hall, Englewood Cliffs, New Jersey.

Kerr, C.
1964 *The Uses of the University.* Harvard University Press, Cambridge, Massachusetts.

Knorr-Cetina, K.D.
1981 *The Manufacture of Knowledge.* Pergamon Press, Oxford.

Knorr-Cetina, K.D., and M. Mulkay (editors)
1983 *Science Observed: Perspectives on the Social Study of Science.* Sage, London.

Knudson, R.A.
1989 North America's Threatened Heritage. *Archaeology* 42:71–73, 106.

Latour, B.
1987 *Science in Action: How to Follow Scientists and Engineers Through Society.* Open University Press, London.

Latour, B., and S. Woolgar
1979 *Laboratory Life.* Sage, Beverly Hills, California.

Layton, R. (editor)
1989a *Conflict in the Archaeology of Living Traditions.* Unwin Hyman, London.
1989b *Who Needs the Past? Indigenous Values in Archaeology.* Unwin Hyman, London.

Leone, M.P., P.B. Potter, Jr., and P.A. Shackel
1987 Toward a Critical Archaeology. *Current Anthropology* 28:283–302.

Lynch, M.
1985 *Art and Artifact in Laboratory Science: A Study of Shop Work and Shop Talk in a Research Laboratory.* Routledge and Kegan Paul, London.

Lynton, E.A., and S.E. Elman
1987 *New Priorities for the University.* Jossey-Bass Publishers, San Francisco.

McBryde, I. (editor)
1985 *Who Owns the Past?* Oxford University Press, Oxford.

McGimsey, C.R. III, and H.A. Davis (editors)
1977 *The Management of Archaeological Resources: The Airlie House Report.* Special Publication. Society for American Archaeology, Washington D.C.

McGuire, R.H.
1992 Archaeology and the First Americans. *American Anthropologist* 94:816–36.

Noble, D.
1984 *Forces of Production: a Social History of Industrial Automation.* Knopf, New York.

Ollman, B.
1971 *Alienation.* Cambridge University Press, Cambridge.

Paynter, R.
1983 Field or Factory? Concerning the Degradation of Archaeological Labor. In *The Socio-Politics of Archaeology,* edited by J.M. Gero, D.M. Lacy, and M.L. Blakey, pp. 17–30. Department of Anthropology. University of Massachusetts, Amherst.

Pickering, A. (editor)
1992 *Science as Practice and Culture.* University of Chicago Press, Chicago.

Potter, P.B.
1990 The "What" and "Why" of Public Relations for Archaeology: A Postscript to DeCicco's Public Relations Primer. *American Antiquity* 55:608–13.

Preucel, R. (editor)
1991 *Processual and Postprocessual Archaeologies: Multiple Ways of Knowing the Past.* Center for Archaeological Investigations. Southern Illinois University, Carbondale.

Raab, M.L., T. Klinger, M.B. Schiffer, and A. Goodyear
1980 Clients, Contracts, and Profits: Conflicts in Public Archaeology. *American Anthropologist* 82:539–51.

Redman, C.L.
1991 In Defense of the Seventies. *American Anthropologist* 93:295–307.

Rose, M.A.
1991 *The Post-Modern and Post-Industrial: A Critical Analysis.* Cambridge University Press, Cambridge.

Rosovsky, H.
1990 *The University: An Owners Manual.* W.W. Norton, New York.

Schuldenrein, J.
1992 Cultural Resource Management and Academic Responsibility in Archaeology: A Rejoinder to Duke. *SAA Bulletin* 10(5):3.

Shanks, M.
1992 *Experiencing the Past: On the Character of Archaeology.* Routledge, London.
1995 *Classical Archaeology: Experiences of the Discipline.* Routledge, London.

Shanks, M., and I. Hodder
1995 Processual, Postprocessual and Interpretive Archaeologies. In *Interpreting Archaeology: Finding Meaning in the Past,* edited by I. Hodder, M. Shanks, A. Alexandri, V. Buchli, J. Carman, J. Last, and G. Lucas, pp. 3–29. Routledge, London.

Society of Antiquaries of London
1992 *Archaeological Publication, Archives, and Collections: Towards a National Policy.* Society of Antiquaries, London.

Swain, H. (editor)

1991 *Competitive Tendering in Archaeology*. Rescue Publications/Standing Conference of Archaeological Unit Managers, Hertford.

Sykes, C.J.

1988 *ProfScam: Professors and the Demise of Higher Education*. Regnery Gateway, Washington, DC.

Thomas, J.

1995 *Time, Culture and Identity: An Interpretive Archaeology*. Routledge, London.

Thompson, E.P.

1977 *William Morris: Romantic to Revolutionary*. Merlin, London.

Tilley, C.

1990 On Modernity and Archaeological Discourse. In *Archaeology After Structuralism*, edited by I. Bapty and T. Yates, pp. 127–52. Routledge, London.

1994 *A Phenomenology of Landscape: Places, Paths and Monuments*. Berg, Oxford.

Tillyard, S.K.

1988 *The Impact of Modernism 1900–1920: Early Modernism and the Arts and Crafts Movement in Edwardian England*. Routledge, London.

Touraine, A.

1971 *The Post-Industrial Society: Tomorrow's Social History: Classes, Conflicts and Culture in the Programmed Society*. Translated by F.X. Leonard Mayhew. Random House, London.

Ucko, P.

1987 *Academic Freedom and Apartheid: The Story of the World Archaeological Congress*. Duckworth, London.

Walka, J.J.

1979 Management Methods and Opportunities in Archaeology. *American Antiquity* 44:575–82.

Walsh, K.

1992 *The Representation of the Past: Museums and Heritage in the Postmodern World*. Routledge, London.

Welsh Office

1991 *Planning Policy Guidance Note 16: Archaeology and Planning*. Welsh Office, Cardiff.

Wylie, A.

1991 Beyond Objectivism and Relativism: Feminist Critiques and Archaeological Challenges. In *Archaeology of Gender*, edited by N. Willo and D. Walde, pp. 17–23. University of Calgary, Calgary, Alberta.

Yoffee, N., and A. Sherratt (editors)

1993 *Archaeological Theory: Who Sets the Agenda?* Cambridge University Press, Cambridge.

PART 2

Ethics, Legislation, and Intellectual Property Rights

Introduction

The articles in this section explore some of the issues surrounding archaeological work and the regulations that guide it in the early twenty-first century.

Virtually every country in the world has enacted legislation to protect archaeological sites and artifacts. As a result, new career strands (i.e., cultural resource management, or CRM) and considerable opportunities have emerged for archaeologists, who are often employed to carry out the work now legislated to be done in advance of development projects.

As the quantity and kinds of archaeology have changed over the past few decades, so too have the ethical issues that archaeologists face. In order to guide them through these dilemmas, most associations of professional archaeologists have developed codes or principles of ethics. Discussions on issues such as the relationship between archaeologists and indigenous peoples are prevalent in all kinds of archaeological literature, including the popular, semi-scholarly, and scholarly.

"Private Property–National Legacy"

Mark Michel

This selection provides a brief view of some of the effects of federal laws governing archaeological resources in the United States. It was originally published in a 2003 issue of *The SAA Archaeological Record*, a periodical of the Society for American Archaeology. Mark Michel is president of the Archaeological Conservancy, a nonprofit organization dedicated to acquiring and preserving archaeological sites.

. . . .

Questions to Guide Reading

How does the United States differ from other countries in regard to the ownership of archaeological resources?

In the United States, who owns archaeological resources on federal land, on Indian reservations, and on private property?

What are the two effects of the Archaeological Resources Protection Act of 1979?

What makes archaeology perhaps unique among scientific disciplines?

What are the major concerns of the Archaeological Conservancy?

. . . .

The United States is virtually alone in the world in giving ownership of archaeological resources to the fee owner of the land. Most countries, like Mexico, Italy, and Israel, invest ownership of the national patrimony in all of the people, no matter where it is found. Other countries have less stringent laws, but carefully protect antiquities even if found on private property. But in the U.S., ownership of archaeological resources—artifacts, structures, even human remains—goes with the ownership of the land. The federal government owns the archaeological sites on its land, states and localities own the sites on their lands, Indian tribes own archaeological resources on their reservations, and private owners own whatever is on their farms, ranches, and subdivisions. The vast majority of the nation's archaeological heritage is therefore privately owned. You might ask, "What does that mean?" In most cases, it means that private owners can do whatever they like with the archaeological site. While publicly owned sites have been seriously impacted by looters, those on private land have been devastated, mainly by development, modern agriculture, and professional looters.

Identifying the Problem

No one has a good idea of how much of our archaeological heritage still exists, but the few estimates that are available are appalling. For example, in 1880 the Bureau of Ethnography estimated there were 20,000 burial mound sites in the Ohio and Mississippi River valleys. It is estimated that fewer than 200 survive today, and those on private lands are still without protection. Just within the past few years, at least four important Anasazi ruins in the Mesa Verde area have been totally destroyed by looters, and it was perfectly legal because they were located on private land.

One of the effects of the Archaeological Resources Protection Act of 1979 has been to greatly diminish illegal looting on public lands. As a result, legal looting on private lands has increased correspondingly. Professional looters buy "looting rights" or sometimes even the sites themselves. One trick used in the Southwest has been to buy a site at a high price, with little or no down payment, then loot the site and default on the mortgage. In the well-known case of Slack Farm, Kentucky, the looters reportedly paid the owner $10,000 for rights to loot a Mississippian cemetery. In New Mexico, looters recently paid landowners to use backhoes at several Zuni sites. Legal efforts to stop them failed.

Whereas other countries have taken possession or at least control of their antiquities, two factors make that unlikely in the U.S. First is the very powerful American belief in the sanctity of private land. No other nation in the world gives such unassailable protection of private property rights. Second, the dominant group in our society, people of European heritage, are unrelated either biologically or culturally to most of the nation's archaeological remains. As one state senator told me when I explained that we should protect our national heritage, "Son, it may be part of your heritage, but it ain't part of mine." Not surprisingly, the two largest archaeological organizations in the U.S. (Archaeological Institute of America and Biblical Archaeological Society) deal with European and Middle Eastern archaeology.

Yet, in recent years, progress has been made in protecting privately owned sites by legal restraints. A number of states have recently passed burial protection statutes. In 1989, for example, New Mexico passed a law that makes it a felony to disturb any burial without a permit issued by the State Historic Preservation Office. More and more large states and cities have adopted subdivision regulations that require sites to be either mitigated or preserved within new subdivisions. Tucson, Arizona has led the way by requiring that developers either scientifically excavate or preserve sites in large new developments in this archaeologically rich region. On the other hand, Pennsylvania recently repealed a law protecting unmarked graves.

The Genesis of the Archaeological Conservancy

While legislation to regulate the digging of archaeological sites may pass court review, no one that I know believes ownership of the resource rests anywhere but with the owner of the land. To do otherwise would violate the Constitutional prohibition of a taking of property without just compensation. A prohibition against digging on private land may do likewise.

It was with this in mind that the Archaeological Conservancy was founded in 1980 with the premise that the most effective way to preserve archaeological sites on privately owned land was to buy them. It is a thoroughly American idea—if you want to protect or control some land, then the most effective way to do that is to own it. If you have fee simple ownership, then you hold the cards. If a highway department wants to put a road through your site, then they have to take you to court and prove their need. If a looter trespasses on your property to steal some valuable artifacts, then he is committing a felony. It is something that everyone in America understands.

Another guiding principle of the Conservancy is the belief in "conservation archaeology." Archaeology is perhaps unique among scientific disciplines in that it destroys its own research base in the course of doing research, and yesterday's archaeologist, no matter how competent, missed many clues. It is very difficult, if not impossible, to go back and do it again once a site is dug up. Archaeological methods, however, improve every year. Because modern technology has many applications for archaeologists, it is important that information remain in situ for new techniques and new insights. The Conservancy is therefore like a museum, only instead of storing artifacts on shelves, we store them in the ground.

How the Archaeological Conservancy Works

The first step in the Archaeological Conservancy's site protection process is to evaluate and prioritize potentially endangered sites. Much of the data to accomplish this are readily available. Each state has a State Historic Preservation Officer (SHPO) established under the Historic Preservation Act of 1966. Our selection process begins by asking a SHPO to develop a list of the most important sites in their state in need of protection. Professional and amateur archaeologists are consulted as well. Once that list is complete, we field-check the sites to see what condition they are in today. Often, no one has checked on these sites for many years, and more than once we have unhappily found that an important site no longer exists.

We then apply practical tests to the resulting list of sites. How endangered is each site? How much time does it have left before it is completely destroyed? Are similar sites available? What is the attitude of the owner? How much is it going to cost? One of the first states in which we began to operate was Ohio. We received excellent support from the SHPO and archaeological community, and we wanted to build on the past accomplishments of preservation by the Ohio Historical Society. The SHPO provided us with a list of about 20 sites and we began to work. Many of the great "Moundbuilder" sites of Ohio were gone, destroyed by urban development or modern

agriculture, making the preservation of those that remained even more important. Our first target was the famous Hopewell Mounds Group, the type-site of the Hopewell culture (100 B.C. to 400 A.D.). We were able to purchase the site, and it is now part of the new Hopewell Culture National Historical Park.

The Historic Preservation Act of 1966 authorized federal matching grants to organizations like the Conservancy to acquire privately owned sites. This funding was cut off in 1981, never to reappear. The Conservancy nevertheless continues to identify, acquire, and preserve sites in an ever-expanding area of the U.S. By the end of 2002, it had completed more than 255 projects in 27 states, and book value of the property acquired reached $18 million. Field offices currently operate in Albuquerque, Sacramento, Columbus, Washington, and Atlanta.

In 2000, the Conservancy launched a $4 million fund-raising drive to buy highly endangered sites around the country. Known as the Protect Our Irreplaceable National Treasures (POINT) program, it is allowing us to buy highly threatened sites for cash. Today, the Conservancy has about 25,000 contributors from across the nation, and publishes *American Archaeology* magazine, the only popular magazine covering the archaeology of the Americas.

Once a site has been acquired, the Conservancy stabilizes the ruins to protect against erosion and other natural causes of site deterioration and prepares a 100-year management plan that sets guidelines for future research. Volunteers play a large role in both stabilization and preparation of the management plan. Preventing looting is one of our biggest concerns. We fence most of our preserves in order to visually and legally establish boundaries. No fence will keep a looter off a site, but if a looter knows that he or she will go to jail if caught inside our fence, they will think twice about it. We set up a regular patrol system, mainly using volunteers. After this point, most archaeological preserves need little care. In the eastern U.S., we like to keep preserves in grass and prevent dense brush from overrunning the site. This is usually accomplished with an agreement with a neighboring farmer to cut hay or graze cattle on the preserve. A well-trimmed preserve prevents erosion and discourages looters who are deterred by a "cared for" site with little cover for hiding their illegal activities.

The Future of Archaeological Site Preservation

The Archaeological Conservancy has proved that private acquisition works. We have demonstrated that archaeological sites on private lands can be preserved in the U.S. by using the oldest American tradition, ownership of the land. In 1980, we purchased four sites; today we protect 30 sites each year. In the next decade, we plan to expand this program even further. More encouraging is the fact that other groups are following our example. Local land trusts in New York, Louisiana, and California have moved to acquire and preserve local archaeological sites. It is also time for the federal and state governments to join in the permanent preservation of the nation's prehistoric legacy. Archaeological sites are usually small and relatively cheap. The average private site can be bought for about $40,000. At this rate, 1,000 sites—approximately 25 per state—could be purchased for only $40 million. If ten years were taken to accomplish that, the national cost would be a mere $4 million per year.

Various states have already begun to invest in their cultural heritage with innovative programs to establish archaeological preserves. Arizona makes matching grants to the Conservancy and others to acquire and preserve endangered sites, as does Colorado. South Carolina has gone even further, identifying the 100 most important archaeological sites in the state and starting to systematically acquire them. The fiscal impact of managing a national preserve system could be lessened through a partnership of private organizations, state governments, museums, and universities. Once established, preserves are relatively easy to maintain and protect. Volunteer site stewards can oversee them, as they do in Arizona and elsewhere.

Some skeptics would say that this plan protects only a fraction of archaeological resources in the U.S. However, it would be a large proportion of the sites with good integrity and ample depth for sustained research. Besides, what is the alternative? To continue to stand by and do nothing while the best of America's prehistoric patrimony is destroyed? Preserving the remains of America's archaeological legacy is a race against time. Every day, more of these sites are destroyed and along with them the information that would someday tell of the great cultures of prehistoric America. Our experience confirms that the most effective way to preserve these privately owned resources is to set them aside as permanent preserves. It is a big job, and government and the private sector must work together to get it done.

"Can You Dig It? The Growing Importance of Ethical Considerations Is Transforming Archaeology"

Anonymous

This selection introduces readers to a few of the major ethical concerns in archaeology today. The article is a good example of popular writing in archaeology. It originally appeared in a 2002 issue of the weekly magazine *The Economist* and has no identifiable author.

Questions to Guide Reading

What are the three broad ethical concerns covered in the article?
Who was Giovanni Belzoni?
What ethical and legal issues emerged from the discovery of Kennewick Man?
Why are archaeologists concerned about looting and private ownership of artifacts?
What is the basis of the claim that archaeologists are not always standing on firm ethical ground?
What is the conservation model of archaeology? Why is such a model important?

The first-world-war battlefields of Belgium and France are dangerous places where, even today, unexploded shells lurk, making excavation a potentially lethal activity. But as archaeologists pick up their trowels, they must consider more than their personal safety. For the trenches, dugouts and tunnels—many containing human remains and personal belongings—are ethical minefields too. In a paper in this month's *Antiquity*, Nicholas Saunders, an anthropologist at University College, London, says that archaeologists on these battlefields face a concentration of all the issues that have concerned archaeology in the past ten to 15 years.

These ethical concerns fall into three broad areas. First, there is the question of how to treat human remains. Over the past few years, archaeologists have often come into conflict with indigenous peoples over the custody and handling of excavated human remains. In Belgium and France the situation is particularly complex because the allied armies included soldiers from a variety of faiths and ethnicities, including Africans, Indians, Australians and Native Americans, all of whose traditions may prefer to treat remains differently.

Next is the question of ownership of artefacts. In the case of first-world-war sites, local people armed with metal detectors routinely collect medals and other memorabilia. The sale of such items, says Dr Saunders, has provided an important source of income ever since refugees first returned to the area after the conflict. Archaeologists, though, regard such activities as looting. Around the world, the general question of who has the first claim on buried items—local people, the descendants of the original owners or archaeologists—is deeply controversial.

A third ethical problem concerns the preservation of sites. Should battlefields be left alone as memorials, redeveloped for tourism, or preserved for the archaeologists of the future? Archaeologists increasingly consider the third option: in recent years, they have become more selective about what and where they dig, so that they do not preclude investigations by subsequent generations.

In short, archaeologists' investigations frequently pit their interests against those of other people, and the concerns of the present against the possible concerns of the future. As ethical considerations come to matter more, there has been a change in the way the public sees archaeologists, and the way archaeologists see themselves. "We went through a period when we thought 'Hey, we're scientists, we should be the number one priority here'," says William Lipe, an archaeologist at Washington State University in Pullman. "But most of us have now come to see it differently."

Archaeology is now changing dramatically, says Karen Vitelli, an archaeologist at Indiana University. Dr. Vitelli also chairs the ethics committee of the Society for American Archaeology (SAA) and is editor of a forthcoming book on archaeological ethics. She was one of the first archaeologists to integrate the study of ethics into archaeological training, and it has now, she says, become a standard part of many degree courses. At the same time, archaeological societies around the world (including the SAA) have adopted codes of ethics to regulate their members. What has brought about this transformation?

Skeletons in the Closet

Ethics and archaeology began to collide relatively recently. The modern discipline traces its roots back to the gentleman amateurs of the early 19th century, who brought statues, columns, mummies and trinkets back as souvenirs from their travels around the Mediterranean. Subsequent generations of archaeologists have tended to regard men such as Giovanni Belzoni—a one-time circus strong-man who shipped Egyptian antiquities back to the British Museum in London—as little better than tomb-robbers.

Belzoni was the first European to enter the temple at Abu Simbel. He rediscovered the entrance to the Great Pyramid and found five tombs in the Valley of the Kings, including that of Seti I. An excerpt from his best selling book of 1820 gives a flavour of the antiquarian practices of the time:

> Surrounded by bodies, by heaps of mummies in all directions; which previous to my being accustomed to the sight, impressed me with horror ... I was choked with mummies, and I could not pass without putting my face in contact with that of some decayed Egyptian; but as the passage inclined downwards, my own weight helped me on; however, I could not help being covered with bones, legs, arms and heads rolling from above. Thus I proceeded from one cave to another, all full of mummies piled in various ways, some standing, some lying, some piled on their heads. The purpose of my researches was to rob the Egyptians of their papyri; of which I found a few hidden in their breasts, under their arms, above their knees, or on the legs, and covered by the numerous folds of cloth that envelop the mummy.

By the early 20th century, however, archaeologists had begun to adopt the methodology of science. Increasing emphasis was placed on the accurate measurement and description of sites and publication of results in archaeological journals. Technological advances—such as the advent of radiocarbon dating—led to further refinements, and the "new archaeology" movement of the 1960s promoted quantitative methods such as statistical analysis. The transformation of archaeology, from tomb-robbing by amateurs into a coherent scientific discipline, was complete.

Paradoxically, the ethical arguments over the treatment of human remains, the ownership of artefacts and responsibility to future generations, all stem in part from archaeology's new-found scientific authority. Having eschewed their dubious forebears, archaeologists reinvented themselves as respectable scientists in search of truth. Who could argue with that?

Bones of Contention

Plenty of people, it turned out. Archaeologists' most public conflicts have been with indigenous peoples over the appropriate treatment of human remains. The most infamous example is that of Kennewick Man, a 9,300-year-old skeleton found in 1996 in a riverbank near the town of Kennewick in Washington state. Intriguingly, its skeletal characteristics are very different from those of modern Native Americans, making Kennewick Man of particular interest to archaeologists trying to understand the peopling of the Americas.

Five Native American tribes, however, claim Kennewick Man as an ancestor under the provisions of the Native American Graves Protection and Repatriation Act (NAGPRA). This law was passed in 1990 to allow Native Americans to remove ancestors' bones, and objects associated with burials and religious practice, from museum collections. A legal battle has rumbled ever since. Granting the remains of Kennewick Man to the Native Americans would deny archaeologists access to an important source of information; but granting them to the scientists would amount to a direct repudiation of the Native Americans' oral history, which is thought to go back 10,000 years.

The passing of NAGPRA demonstrated that science's authority over the dead is not absolute. However scientifically respectable their methods, archaeologists have been forced to acknowledge that they do not operate in a vacuum, and must take the values of others into account, not least because they will otherwise be denied access to important data. Attitudes are changing as a result. Dr. Vitelli says that several of her students who are

studying bioanthropology, which involves the examination of skeletal remains, are now questioning whether they want to continue in that field, for both ethical and practical reasons.

Kennewick Man, and other similar cases, are not entirely representative. In some cases, indigenous peoples and archaeologists have co-operated and reached compromises. Donald Ryan, an archaeologist at Pacific Lutheran University in Tacoma, Washington, gives one example of how things are changing. Working with Egyptian archaeologists, he excavated six tombs in the Valley of the Kings during the 1990s, including one previously explored by Belzoni. Once their work was complete, the archaeologists cleaned up the tombs, many of which had been ravaged by floods and looting. They placed the mummies in new wooden boxes and sealed the entrances. As a result, says Dr. Ryan, it was felt that a bit of order and dignity had been restored.

Before they break ground, archaeologists should talk to local people and try to identify areas where their interests coincide, suggests Dr. Vitelli. "It's very hard for many of us, since it means giving up control and authority," she says.

Artefacts on eBay

Another area where archaeologists have invoked their scientific authority is to take a firm stand against looting. Looters irretrievably destroy evidence about the context in which artefacts are found, even if the artefacts are subsequently recovered. Similarly, archaeologists have spoken out against the trade in antiquities. Ancient artefacts sold as *objets d'art* fetch high prices and thus provide an incentive for looters—who are armed and violent in some cases.

In addition to the damage and loss of context caused by looting, private ownership of artefacts can prevent archaeologists from gaining access for research purposes. It may also prevent future archaeologists from verifying previous findings. This, notes Mark Lynott, an archaeologist at the National Park

Service's Midwest Archaeological Centre in Lincoln, Nebraska, is vital if archaeology is to be truly scientific. To avoid appearing either unscientific or complicit with the activities of looters, many archaeologists choose deliberately to ignore data from objects in private collections—whatever their significance. Archaeologists remain divided over how museums should acquire and display ancient artefacts of uncertain provenance, for fear that this might encourage looters.

A recent twist to the antiquities trade has come with the advent of Internet auction houses such as eBay. A number of archaeological societies, including the SAA and the Archaeological Institute of America, have asked online auction houses to outlaw the trading of antiquities, to little effect. The problem with policing this trade is that many items have been in private hands for decades, or even centuries, and were originally acquired under very different circumstances. As it is not possible to put the objects back into the ground, says Dr. Vitelli, the trading of these items is tolerated. But this provides a loophole for unscrupulous dealers: even though many countries now strictly control the export of antiquities, dealers can simply claim that an item is from an old private collection.

In February, Frederick Schultz, an antiquities dealer, was found guilty by a New York court of conspiring to receive stolen Egyptian antiquities. Mr. Schultz claimed that the items he was offering for sale came from the 1920s collection of an Englishman called Thomas Alcock. The US Attorney's Office concluded that "the evidence at trial established that the 'Thomas Alcock Collection' was a complete fiction." Mr. Schultz has launched an appeal.

This case, though, has heartened archaeologists. The fact that a New York court was prepared to uphold an Egyptian patrimony law banning the trade in antiquities unearthed since 1983 is seen as an important victory for opponents of antiquities trading. Furthermore, says Dr. Lynott, the discussion over the ethics of trading antiquities has started to change attitudes. The debate has marginalised the people

who are willing to engage in such trade. Even so, says Dr. Vitelli, it is not clear that archaeologists' opposition to antiquities trading has helped to save sites or to diminish looting.

Moreover, when it comes to the provenance of antiquities, archaeologists themselves are not always standing on terribly firm ethical ground. Many of the items in museums today were, after all, removed by people like Belzoni. "I look at objects in the British Museum, think about how they were removed, and think that's really horrible," says Dr. Lynott. "But had they not been removed at that time, they might not be available for study today."

Belzoni was working within the laws of the period. And at the time he was plundering the Valley of the Kings, local Egyptians were merrily using mummies as firewood. The dilemma for archaeology is that carting off artefacts for display in museums on the other side of the world smacks of cultural imperialism; but so does demanding that indigenous people treat artefacts in a way that western archaeologists approve of.

Between Past and Future

Alongside the debates over the handling of human remains and artefacts, archaeologists have also been grappling with their responsibilities to future practitioners of their science. A central paradox of archaeology is that discovery involves destruction; investigation requires intrusion. Where should archaeologists draw the line when deciding how much of an important site to excavate, if they are not to hinder future investigations?

If the field is scientifically healthy, says Dr. Lipe, archaeologists will ask new questions in future and have better methods. Dr. Lipe is one of the pioneers of the "conservation model" of archaeology. This is a logical outgrowth of the new archaeology movement of the 1960s, and stresses the careful, well justified and frugal use of archaeological resources, in contrast to the exhaustive excavation of important sites.

Most archaeologists, says Dr. Lipe, have had the experience of trying to discover something new about a site that was completely excavated—only to find that the question they wanted to ask had not occurred to the original archaeologists. The intellectual health of the field, he says, depends on being able to address new questions or readdress old ones. "Archaeologists must be conservative in how they themselves use the archaeological record, as a matter of ethics."

This approach has been bolstered by the advent of non-destructive geophysical surveying techniques—such as ground-penetrating radar—that enable archaeologists to identify and target small areas of interest. Progress in analytical techniques also means that archaeologists can learn a great deal from small amounts of material, provided it is carefully chosen. The result is a move away from the complete excavation of sites towards a more selective, sampling approach.

Belzoni's Last Laugh

It is deeply ironic that it has taken so long for archaeologists, investigators of the relics of the past, to recognise that archaeological standards, too, are products of their time. Dr. Lynott says these are changing almost from year to year. Changing values mean that every generation of archaeologists inevitably regards its predecessors as crude and insensitive. "We see this looking back just a generation or two—we don't have to go back as far as Belzoni," he says.

Future archaeologists may be less critical of Belzoni. Dr. Ryan believes Belzoni has been unfairly vilified. He points out that Belzoni went to the trouble of making detailed measurements, drawings and maps of the tombs he found, which was more than most of his contemporaries did. In a period when there were no archaeological standards whatsoever, Dr. Ryan argues, Belzoni was not merely a man of his time, he was far ahead of it.

Today, archaeology is in the midst of a second metamorphosis. Having transformed itself inter-nally—into a science—it is now being reshaped by external social, cultural and political forces. But it is still a work in progress. "What we're seeing now is the emergence of additional voices that have legitimate claims on what is done to and with the archaeological record," says Dr. Lipe. Dr. Vitelli, meanwhile, insists that her students regard the current debate as a chance to reinvent archaeology. For example, the investigation of first-world-war battlefields (which have yet to receive much attention from professional archaeologists) offers a chance to develop new approaches in which the interests of all parties are taken into account. Such battlefields are unique, notes Dr. Saunders, because they provide an opportunity to perform archaeological investigations within the context of an abundance of historical documents—personal letters, diaries, maps, photographs and military records. "We have an opportunity here to create a new kind of archaeology—to make it anthropologically informed from the beginning," he says.

Double standards abound, however. Dr. Saunders' suggestion in 1999 that soldiers' remains and artefacts on first-world-war battlefields should be treated in the same way as those of Australian Aborigines or Native Americans was, he says, initially greeted with bewilderment. But things are starting to change. Already, there are signs of compromises between professional archaeologists, and amateur investigators and relic collectors.

Today, amateurs acknowledge the need to seek respectable backing. One amateur group, known as The Diggers, began investigating battlefields near Ypres in 1992. Its members do not claim to be professionals, but the group operates under a licence from Belgium's institute of national archaeology, works with a local museum, and deals with human remains in conjunction with the Commonwealth War Graves Commission.

Widespread public enthusiasm for all things archaeological—another relatively recent development—also gives archaeologists cause for optimism about the future. To illustrate how much things have changed during the course of her career, Dr. Vitelli gives the example of the Franchthi Cave in southern Greece, a site with deposits spanning the period from 30,000 BC to 3,000 BC. Dr. Vitelli worked at the site during the 1970s and, 30 years later, having become involved in archaeological ethics, she returned to the local village of Koilada and offered to give a talk about what had been found. The mayor approved and Dr. Vitelli ended up speaking to a packed house in the village school.

"It was standing room only: priests, teachers, schoolchildren. They stayed for an hour-long talk in 98-degree heat," she says. "They were interested in learning about us and why we came to their village. The mayor realised they weren't ready for it 30 years ago. And neither were we. And now we all are."

"Society for American Archaeology Principles of Archaeological Ethics"

Society for American Archaeology

Most associations of professional archaeologists have a code of ethics that stipulates how members in good standing should conduct their work. Reproduced here are the principles of ethics of the Society for American Archaeology, which is the largest association of professional archaeologists in North America. These principles were originally published in a 1996 issue of the society's scholarly journal, *American Antiquity*.

....

Questions to Guide Reading

What is meant by "stewardship"?
How can archaeologists be stewards of the past?
What do the SAA's principles say about commercialization?
What are the three ways archaeologists are encouraged to participate in public education and outreach?
What is meant by "intellectual property"? How should archaeologists deal with it?
What do the SAA's principles say about public reporting and publication?
How are archaeologists encouraged to work actively to preserve and maintain long-term access to archaeological collections, records, and reports?

....

At its April 10, 1996, meeting the Society for American Archaeology Executive Board adopted the Principles of Archaeological Ethics, reproduced below, as proposed by the SAA Ethics in Archaeology Committee. The adoption of these principles represents the culmination of an effort begun in 1991 with the formation of the ad hoc Ethics in Archaeology Committee. The committee was charged with considering the need for revising the society's existing statements on ethics. A 1993 workshop on ethics, held in Reno, resulted in draft principles that were presented at a public forum at the 1994 annual meeting in Anaheim, California. SAA published the draft principles with position papers from the forum and historical commentaries in a special report distributed to all members, *Ethics in American Archaeology; Challenges for the 1990s*, edited by Mark J. Lynott and Alison Wylie (1995). Member comments were solicited in this special report, through a notice in *SAA Bulletin,* and at two sessions held at the SAA booth during the 1995 annual meeting in Minneapolis, Minnesota. The final principles presented here are revised from the original draft based on comments from members and the Executive Board.

The Executive Board strongly endorses these principles and urges their use by all archaeologists "in negotiating the complex responsibilities they have to archaeological resources, and to all who have an interest in these resources or are otherwise affected by archaeological practice" (Lynott and Wylie 1995:8). The board is grateful to those who have contributed to the development of these principles, especially the members of the Ethics in Archaeology Committee, chaired by Lynott and Wylie, for their skillful completion of this challenging and important task. The bylaws change just voted by the members has established a standing committee, the Committee on Ethics, to carry on with these crucial efforts.

Principle No. 1: Stewardship

The archaeological record, that is, in situ archaeological material and sites, archaeological collections, records and reports, is irreplaceable. It is the responsibility of all archaeologists to work for the long-term conservation and protection of the archaeological record by practicing and promoting stewardship of the archaeological record. Stewards are both caretakers of and advocates for the archaeological record. In the interests of stewardship, archaeologists should use and advocate use of the archaeological record for the benefit of all people; as they investigate and interpret the record, they should use the specialized knowledge they gain to promote public understanding and support for its long-term preservation.

Principle No. 2: Accountability

Responsible archaeological research, including all levels of professional activity, requires an acknowledgment of public accountability and a commitment to make every reasonable effort, in good faith, to consult actively with affected group(s), with the goal of establishing a working relationship that can be beneficial to all parties involved.

Principle No. 3: Commercialization

The Society for American Archaeology has long recognized that the buying and selling of objects out of archaeological context is contributing to the destruction of the archaeological record on the American continents and around the world. The commercialization of archaeological objects — their use as commodities to be exploited for personal enjoyment or profit — results in the destruction of archaeological sites and of contextual information that is essential to understanding the archaeological record. Archaeologists should therefore carefully weigh the benefits to scholarship of a project against the costs of potentially enhancing the commercial value of archaeological objects. Wherever possible, they should discourage, and should themselves avoid, activities that enhance the commercial value of archaeological objects, especially objects that are not curated in public institutions, or readily available for scientific study, public interpretation, and display.

Principle No. 4: Public Education and Outreach

Archaeologists should reach out to, and participate in cooperative efforts with, others interested in the archaeological record with the aim of improving the preservation, protection, and interpretation of the record. In particular, archaeologists should undertake to: (1) enlist public support for the stewardship of the archaeological record; (2) explain and promote the use of archaeological methods and techniques in understanding human behavior and culture; and (3) communicate archaeological interpretations of the past. Many publics exist for archaeology including students and teachers; Native Americans and other ethnic, religious, and cultural groups who find in the archaeological record important aspects of their cultural heritage; lawmakers and government officials; reporters, journalists, and others involved in the media; and the general public. Archaeologists who are unable to undertake public education and outreach directly should encourage and support the efforts of others in these activities.

Principle No. 5: Intellectual Property

Intellectual property, as contained in the knowledge and documents created through the study of archaeological resources, is part of the archaeological record. As such it should be treated in accordance with the principles of stewardship rather than as a matter of personal possession. If there is a compelling reason, and no legal restrictions or strong countervailing interests, a researcher may have primary access to original materials and documents for a limited and reasonable time, after which these materials and documents must be made available to others.

Principle No. 6: Public Reporting and Publication

Within a reasonable time, the knowledge archaeologists gain from investigation of the archaeological record must be presented in accessible form (through publication or other means) to as wide a range of interested publics as possible. The documents and materials on which publication and other forms of public reporting are based should be deposited in a suitable place for permanent safekeeping. An interest in preserving and protecting in situ archaeological sites must be taken into account when publishing and distributing information about their nature and location.

Principle No. 7: Records and Preservation

Archaeologists should work actively for the preservation of, and long term access to, archaeological collections, records, and reports. To this end, they should encourage colleagues, students, and others to make responsible use of collections, records, and reports in their research as one means of preserving the in situ archaeological record, and of increasing the care and attention given to that portion of the archaeological record which has been removed and incorporated into archaeological collections, records, and reports.

Principle No. 8: Training and Resources

Given the destructive nature of most archaeological investigations, archaeologists must ensure that they have adequate training, experience, facilities, and other support necessary to conduct any program of research they initiate in a manner consistent with the foregoing principles and contemporary standards of professional practice.

"Copyrighting the Past? Emerging Intellectual Property Rights Issues in Archaeology"[1]

George P. Nicholas and Kelly P. Bannister

This article, outlining some of the major issues about intellectual property rights in archaeology, was originally published in a 2004 issue of the journal *Current Anthropology*. George Nicholas is a professor of archaeology at Simon Fraser University. Kelly Bannister is a professor in the school of environmental studies at the University of Victoria.

Questions to Guide Reading

What is meant by the phrase "intellectual property rights," in general and in the context of archaeology?

How do the authors define archaeology and its concerns, goals, and products?

Why do the authors describe archaeology as a contemporary sociocultural phenomena?

What are the potential points of concern about intellectual property rights in archaeology?

On what basis are archaeological sites considered to be cultural property and intellectual creations?

How have artifacts and sites been used as symbols of national identity and symbols of the identity of indigenous peoples?

What is meant by the phrase "traditional systems of knowledge"? How is it manifested in the archaeological record?

What is meant by the appropriation, commodification, and objectification of the past? What are some examples?

What is the primary advantage and primary drawback to having archaeologists control the information derived from the archaeological record?

What are some of the ways indigenous groups are seeking to control access to and use of their past through contracts and protocols?

How are indigenous groups seeking to control intellectual property through ownership mechanisms?

Rights to intellectual property have become a major issue in ethnobotany and many other realms of research involving Indigenous communities. This paper examines intellectual-property-rights-related issues in archaeology, including the relevance of such rights within the discipline, the forms these rights take, and the impacts of applying intellectual property protection in archaeology. It identifies the "products" of archaeological research and what they represent in a contemporary sociocultural context, examines ownership issues, assesses the level of protection of these products provided by existing legislation, and discusses the potential of current intellectual property protection mechanisms to augment cultural heritage protection for Indigenous communities.

"Intellectual property" is defined by Dratler (1994:1–2) as "intangible personal property in creations of the mind." Intellectual property rights are legal rights to precisely defined kinds of knowledge. In general, intellectual property laws "protect a creator's expression in artistic and literary works, the proprietary technology in inventions, the words and symbols used to identify products and services and the aesthetic aspects of product designs" (Cassidy and Langford 1999:1).

Intellectual property rights are a rapidly expanding topic of discussion in academic and other circles and a major issue in ethnobotanical and other research involving Indigenous communities.[2] Interested parties represent a convergence of natural and social scientists from government, academia, and industry, members of Indigenous communities, lawyers, corporate representatives, environmentalists, and others. Key concerns expressed by these diverse parties relate to the sociocultural, ethical, and economic aspects of current intellectual property rights legislation, among them the implications of patenting higher life forms (e.g., CBAC 2001, 2003). For the most part, archaeologists have yet to find themselves thrust into this complex milieu. We argue that archaeologists should examine whether and in what ways intellectual-property-rights-related issues are relevant to their research, particularly when claims to such rights may be made by Indigenous peoples affected by that research.

The absence of archaeologists from the intellectual property rights debate may be linked to the complexity of the issues and to the challenges of defining "intellectual property" beyond the realm of technological innovation with commercial application. Such is the case with living systems, where what qualifies as intellectual property and is protectable by law is continually being debated and tested, often in the courts.[3] Of particular relevance to archaeology is the application of the idea of intellectual property rights to the protection of the cultural knowledge and property[4] of Indigenous societies. This application is complicated by a lack of consistent terminology across interested or affected parties, Indigenous and non-Indigenous alike. For example, what is it that needs protecting and from whom? As Mann (1997:1) notes, "No one definition [of indigenous knowledge] has been universally endorsed or accepted by either Aboriginal or non-Aboriginal peoples in Canada. What is clear, however, is that indigenous knowledge as a concept concerns information, understanding, and knowledge that reflects symbiotic relationships between individuals, communities, generations, the physical environment and other living creatures, and the spiritual relationships of a people." Likewise, according to the Union of British Columbia Indian Chiefs (Hampton and Henderson 2000:ii), "There is no universally accepted definition for cultural property.... Most academic commentators assert that Indigenous knowledge issues are stretching the existing legal categories so that only a fuzzy line exists between intellectual, spiritual and culture rights." The foregoing largely concerns living people, but what of deceased societies? Archaeological research involving Indigenous societies tends to blur past and present.

National and international laws protecting cultural and intellectual property are often seen as inconsistent with emerging views on what aspects of Indigenous cultural knowledge and heritage require protection. According to Battiste and Henderson (2000:145), the problem involves "negotiating with the modern concept of property" in that Eurocentric legal approaches "treat all thought as a commodity in the artificial market" whereas Indigenous societies tend to see property as "a sacred ecological order" that should not be commodified. They suggest further (p. 250) that intellectual property laws have

> problems dealing with forms of knowledge in the area of high art or high technology (e.g., computer software and biotechnology). The major push for amendment of the law comes from the top, so that areas such as computer technology or biogenetic engineering are receiving a lot of attention, and the law is gradually being altered to accommodate these forms of knowledge. Culture and knowledge on the "bottom"—where Indigenous knowledge is so often situated—tend to be ignored.

The perceived inadequacy of applying existing laws to the protection of Indigenous cultural knowledge and heritage has led to recommendations for the expansion of legal definitions and protection mechanisms and calls for alternative and complementary nonlegal ones. For example, Janke (1998:3) proposes the term "Indigenous cultural and intellectual property rights" to refer to "Indigenous people's rights to their heritage," wherein "heritage comprises all objects, sites and knowledge, the nature or use of which has been transmitted or continues to be transmitted from generation to generation, and which is regarded as pertaining to a particular Indigenous group or its territory." Artifacts, archaeological sites, and some types of information generated by archaeological research clearly fit this definition. In fact, there is a notable similarity between a statement from Hampton and Henderson's discussion paper that "generally, cultural property is anything exhibiting physical attributes assumed to be the results of human activity" (2000:ii) and definitions of an archaeological site as "any place where objects, features, or ecofacts manufactured or modified by human beings are found" (Fagan 1997:478) and "any place where material evidence exists about the human past" (Thomas 1998:95).

In this paper we explore the concept of Indigenous cultural and intellectual property rights in an archaeological context. The central questions posed are: What relevance do intellectual property rights have to archaeology? What forms do these rights take? How might future claims to intellectual property affect archaeology? We begin by describing the "products" of archaeological research and explaining what they represent in a contemporary sociocultural context. We assess the level of protection of these products provided by existing legislation (specifically, cultural heritage acts) and the potential of current intellectual property protection mechanisms to augment that protection. Our focus is on knowledge and its physical manifestations (such as images and "art") that are derived from or otherwise pertain to the past.

We consider also whether and in what way our understanding of these emerging issues in archaeology can be informed by trends in related disciplines such as anthropology and ethnobotany. One possibility is that Indigenous peoples may seek control of the knowledge and other products of archaeological research conducted in their traditional lands—perhaps much as they have of the results of ethnobotanical research on their traditional knowledge and plant medicines (Bannister 2000, Bannister and Barrett n.d., Brush and Strabinsky 1996, Greaves 1994, Posey and Dutfield 1996). In our final section we turn to this related academic field for insights and comparative examples.

The scope of this paper ranges from local to international. Our examples are drawn from Canada (particularly British Columbia, where intellectual property rights are an important topic in current treaty negotiations), the United States, Australia, and elsewhere. The implications for archaeology are of regional significance and global interest.

Michael Brown's (1998) article "Can Culture Be Copyrighted?" provides an initial point of reference for our discussion.[5] Copyright is one of several legal instruments under statutory and common law that can be used to enforce exclusive rights in the marketplace in creations that meet certain legal criteria (i.e., novelty and material fixedness). In particular, copyright protects the physical expression of ideas but not the ideas themselves or any substantive or factual information. Ownership of copyright is established by the author's fixing the work in a material form and is used to protect rights to novel literary, artistic, dramatic, or musical works (as well as computer software). Protection is for a limited term (e.g., in Canada, the life of the author plus 50 years).[6] Rather than suggesting that copyright is the only—or the most appropriate—tool for protecting rights to intellectual property in archaeology, our title questions the common perception that this is the case. Other forms of intellectual property protection that may be relevant to archaeology include patent, trademark, industrial design, and trade secret.[7] Arguably, some of these mechanisms already have approximations in Indigenous societies—for example, family or clan ownership of songs, stories, or motifs and possession by healers of specialized medicinal knowledge that is not widely shared within the community. While ownership is not a Western[8] concept, these examples of Indigenous ownership are not given legal status in most countries. It is important to distinguish between creations that are legally protectable under current legislation and those that are not. Opportunities or pressure (internal or external) to exploit ownership rights and privileges for commercial purposes present challenges to many Indigenous communities—particularly elders, traditional healers, storytellers, and other knowledge holders, who must often reconcile their reservations about sharing cultural knowledge with the wider society (thereby contributing to recognition and potential commercial development, as well as misappropriation or misuse) with cultural beliefs and responsibilities that embody sharing. Such challenges are complicated by a widespread lack of understanding of what can and cannot be legally protected. Archaeology will not move beyond being a colonialist enterprise unless it actively seeks to understand the underlying issues of ownership and control of material and intellectual property as related to cultural knowledge and heritage.

Material property issues have certainly arisen in archaeology and will continue to frame key aspects of the discipline. Especially contentious are the repatriation of artifacts and reburial of human remains (e.g., Bray 2001, Ferguson 1996, Mihesuah 2000, Rose, Green, and Green 1996). Issues related to intellectual property have been less prominent,[9] although trends in other fields suggest that this will soon change. This is particularly true in former colonized lands such as the Americas, Africa, and Australia, where the archaeological record is mostly the product of the ancestors of the present Indigenous population(s) and not that of the dominant culture. Archaeological research in the latter context is often seen as appropriating Indigenous knowledge and rights or affecting the sanctity of Indigenous beliefs—even when the archaeologists involved believe that they are working to the benefit of Indigenous communities.

The Products of Archaeological Research and Their Protection

Archaeology is the study of human behavior and history through material culture. It is concerned with what happened in the past, when it happened, and the processes by which things changed and with the application of that knowledge in the modern world. The archaeological record is made up of both the individual and the cumulative responses of humans to a suite of social, demographic, cultural, and environmental opportunities over the course of hours, years, or millennia. Archaeologists seek to discover and explain this record and the cultural diversity it represents. The products of archaeological research thus constitute scientific knowledge in the sense of understanding the (past) world in new ways and at the same time reflect the knowledge of Indigenous cultures. Archaeology is also very much a contemporary sociocultural phenomenon that seeks to locate, create, classify, objectify, interpret, and present the past in ways that reflect the particular views of its practitioners (see Pinsky and Wylie 1995).[10] A key concern in contemporary archaeology is the degree of participation and control that Indigenous peoples have over the archaeological *process*. In Canada, for example, control issues have centered on the limitation of access to sites in traditional territories by way of a permit system (e.g., Denhez 2000). Little attention has been paid to the *products* of archaeological research.

Aside from unearthed artifacts, what is it that archaeological research produces? In its many forms, archaeology establishes chronology and precontact history (as a supplement or a corollary to oral history) and illuminates the processes by which things have changed. Specific products of archaeological research take the form of site reports, site, artifact, and feature descriptions and classifications, radiocarbon dates, and faunal remains, among other materials. These are analyzed to produce information on past technologies, dietary patterns, land-use patterns, environmental settings, demographic trends, social relationships, and other topics. Such studies may have a very short-term focus (e.g., reconstruction of life at a particular time and place) or a very long-term focus (e.g., shifts in dietary practices over millennia). A central question raised by consideration of intellectual property rights is whose property these products are and how they are protected.

The lack of explicit consideration of these issues in archaeology to date is partly the result of a societal perception that the outcomes of archaeology have limited practical application. While information of substantial public value may be produced, archaeologists often have difficulty communicating the contemporary relevance of their field.[11] Intellectual property rights issues may be especially relevant in cases where the benefits of archaeological research are based directly upon Indigenous cultural knowledge, such as the recognition and restoration of raised-field farming (Erickson 1998) and *chinampas* farming (Coe 1964) in Central and South America. In such cases, the issues faced by archaeologists may include (1) publication and ownership of copyright in books, reports, and articles, (2) access to, public disclosure of, and ownership of copyright in photographs of artifacts, (3) fiduciary duties related to the secrecy of sacred sites, which could also include copyright in maps, (4) ownership, secrecy, and publication of traditional knowledge that may result from archaeological research, and (5) ownership of, copyright in, or trademarks related to the artifacts, designs, or marks uncovered during archaeological research. Archaeological sites represent the major physical manifestation of cultural heritage for all human societies. Despite broad concerns with preserving sites, buildings, and objects of historical or cultural value, the degree of preservation and protection varies from country to country and between different states, provinces, and territories. In the United States, for example, there is extensive federal cultural heritage legislation, but archaeological sites on private property are generally not protected (Patterson 1999). The Native American Graves Protection and Repatriation Act (NAGPRA), which protects human remains and "associated funerary objects, unassociated funerary objects, sacred objects, and cultural patrimony," also excludes private property.[12] In Canada, federal legislation is very limited, with most heritage protection being conducted at the provincial level. For example, under the British Columbia Heritage Conservation Act of 1996, all archaeological sites, whether on public or private lands, are protected in principle. There is no provision for site identification surveys for all proposed developments, and therefore many sites are lost. Likewise, artifacts are not covered and are openly bought, sold, or traded at flea markets, auctions, and other venues.[13] Whatever the level of legislated heritage protection, protection of archaeological materials in the United States and Canada is based exclusively on the notion of physical property (e.g., artifacts and sites).

General legislation protecting intellectual property is, however, extensive in both countries. Thus, it is worth exploring intellectual property rights from the perspective of determining whether any aspect of them offers additional protection to archaeological resources and/or provides new avenues that Indigenous peoples can pursue to protect their cultural and intellectual property. Certain products of archaeological fieldwork and research are the result of the creative works of past Indigenous societies. Do they qualify as intellectual property in a legal sense? Should the descendants[14] of those responsible for the archaeological record have rights to that record?

To date, applications of intellectual property rights in fields closely related to archaeology such as anthropology and ethnobotany have largely been concerned with protecting traditional knowledge and the related biological resources (see Bannister 2000, Bannister and Barrett n.d., Brush and Stabinsky 1996, Greaves 1994, Posey and Dutfield 1996). Is access to a site by archaeologists any different from access to traditional knowledge and plant resources by ethnobotanists? From the point of view of archaeology, traditional knowledge can be understood as incorporating historic/modern land-use and health practices, oral and written histories, and expressions of worldview. One reason that little attention has been paid to archaeology may be that only limited material expressions of potential intellectual property are preserved in the archaeological record and even that material tends to be so old as to make issues of ownership moot from a legal perspective. For example, Brown (1998:196) notes,[15]

> The principal goal of intellectual property laws ... is to see that information enters the public domain in a timely fashion while allowing creators, be they individuals or corporate groups, to derive reasonable financial and social benefits from their work. Once a work enters the public domain, it loses most protections. I am free to publish *Uncle Tom's Cabin* or to manufacture steel paper clips without paying royalties to their creators, whose limited monopoly has expired. The same principle applies to prehistoric petroglyphs or to the "Mona Lisa," both of which have become part of our common human heritage, whatever their origins.

Brown's comments raise two important points that require further examination. First, many Indigenous groups simply do not accept that their archaeological past is first and foremost part of a shared human heritage—at least at the expense of their claims to it. Second, intellectual property protection has a limited time span after which the intellectual property becomes part of the public domain. If "time" is considered largely a Western construct (Gould 1987, Zimmerman 1987), the phenomenon it represents may be perceived differently in Indigenous cultures. In Western society time is viewed as linear and worldview is characterized by a series of clear dichotomies: past/present, real/supernatural, male/female, good/evil, and so on. In many Indigenous societies, however, not only is there greater flexibility in classifying the world but the basic conception of time may be significantly different (e.g., Williams and Mununggurr 1989).[16] Where there is no cognitive separation between past and present, ancestral spirits are part of the present. This conceptual difference requires us to avoid an exclusively Western orientation in interpreting prehistoric lifeways (as in evaluating site significance and the implications for cultural resource management practices), and this presents a major challenge to the fundamentals of intellectual property law. In other words, the petroglyphs that Brown refers to may be *timeless*. Thus, intellectual property laws that are constrained by Western conceptions of time may be severely limited in utility and appropriateness to Indigenous cultures.

Given the products of archaeological research, what are potential points of concern with regard to intellectual property rights? If other academic disciplines are any indication, the concerns of the descendants of the people responsible for the archaeological record may include appropriation, misrepresentation, or misuse of knowledge, loss of control of knowledge, and loss of access to the products of research or their benefits. Non-Indigenous researchers,[17] for their part, fear loss of control, censorship, or restrictions on use of knowledge—concerns that relate to suppression of academic freedom and restrictions on publication, which, in turn, may affect academic credentials, promotion, and continued research funding. The issues are not limited to efforts of Indigenous peoples to control their own past but also surface in religious contexts. In Israel, archaeology and related research have been severely limited by objections of ultra-Orthodox Jewish groups over the sanctity of human remains. As a result of a 1994 ruling by the Israeli Attorney General, all human remains must be "immediately handed over to the ministry of religious affairs for reburial" (Balter 2000:35). This has effectively halted most physical anthropology, and it extends to remains not affiliated with the modern Israeli population, including early human remains.

The issue of censorship will likely be raised more frequently as Indigenous peoples in many parts of the world regain greater control over their affairs. Academics are often complacent about their "freedom" until it is threatened. With freedom, however, comes responsibility. Most problems relating to publication of archaeological data can likely be avoided with some conscientious forethought and proactive effort. For example, where the potential for conflict exists, researchers will do well to work closely with community participants from the start and make clear what the project goals and products will be. Researchers should also be clear about how the products of their research may constitute intellectual property and whose property this will be.

Claire Smith (1994:96) offers the following position:

> My view is that Barunga people have the right to censor any aspect of my research that they find distressing or offensive. However, in order to avoid extensive censoring of the research I designed its parameters in consultation with them. Having done this, I do not believe that Barunga people have the right to decide whether the research as a whole should be published, unless we had negotiated this provision prior to the research being undertaken.... Nor do I agree with some Aboriginal people who maintain that results of

research should be owned by indigenous people.... In my opinion the intellectual property arising from the research belongs to the researchers involved though they have an overriding responsibility not to offend the people with whom they work.

The question raised is whether the intellectual value or creative contribution of the cultural knowledge being disclosed exceeds that of the research or transcription process. This issue is at the heart of editorial control, restrictions on publication, and claims to intellectual property. Who owns the intellectual property arising from the research is in some cases institution- or funder-specific. The policies of most academic institutions may be characterized generally as "institution as owner" or "inventor as owner," the former clearly limiting the discretionary power of an individual researcher on the matter (Bannister 2003).

The desire of many Indigenous peoples to control or censor information about their past may have two triggers. One is the largely political motivation to regain control over their own affairs; the other is a response to the unwillingness of some archaeologists to listen to and/or integrate Indigenous perspectives and interpretations into their own. As Whiteley (1997:203) notes, "Archaeologists ... have more often than not systematically excluded the knowledge and interpretations of living Pueblo descendants—as they have with non-Western indigenous peoples worldwide.... The intellectual grounds for exclusion, particularly in the now old 'new archaeology,' exalt cold 'scientific analysis' of mute material remains over indigenous oral histories: Natives need not apply." Essentially, the validity of the power inequities inherent in the conventional academic research approach (i.e., the archaeologist as expert on Indigenous culture) is in dispute. It is instructive to examine some commonalities between academic and Indigenous communities in the general concerns noted previously. The ultimate risk to both sides is *loss of control* of knowledge. An obvious tension between the different actors exists in terms of the importance, potential utility, and meaning of knowledge. In archaeology at least, this tension is better understood when knowledge is seen as both part of cultural *property* and integral to cultural *identity*. From this perspective, the appropriation and commodification of knowledge acquire added complexity, and control of knowledge becomes vital to cultural integrity.

Archaeological Research Products as Cultural and Intellectual Property

Every human society is the embodiment of a particular system of knowledge. The cultural knowledge possessed by contemporary Indigenous societies is part of a compendium of wisdom that extends back through time, a significant portion of which is represented in archaeological materials and information. This information not only reflects what happened and when it happened in the past but is symbolic of cultural identity and worldview still important to many of the descendants of the sites' creators. Archaeological sites thus constitute not only cultural property but intellectual creations, raising questions of how archaeologically derived knowledge contributes to cultural identity and what aspects of cultural identity qualify as intellectual property. Here we are referring not to archaeological approaches to cultural identity (i.e., using archaeology to define ethnicity [e.g., Shennan 1989]) but rather to the appreciation of archaeological material as a component of cultural identity (Jones 1997) that makes the products of archaeology potential forms of intellectual property. Archaeological sites and materials fit the above-mentioned definitions of Indigenous cultural and intellectual property proposed by Janke (1998) and Hampton and Henderson (2000) in their contributions to cultural identity, worldview, cultural continuity, and traditional ecological knowledge.

Cultural Identity

Archaeological artifacts and sites have long served as symbols of national identity worldwide. Stonehenge is not only one of the best-known archaeological sites in the world but also strongly associated with British identity (see Golding 1989). When Rhodesia gained independence in 1980 and became Zimbabwe, it took its new name from an archaeological site and chose as its national symbol a carved soapstone bird from that site. In many parts of the world, Aboriginal communities relocated by government mandate, epidemics, or other factors have retained a strong association with their former homes, whether through occasional visits or through oral histories (e.g., Kritsch and Andre 1997, Myers 1986). Artifacts and heirlooms also play a vital role in the identity of Indigenous peoples, serving as a link both to past generations and to the systems of knowledge that sustained them. This may help to explain the widespread use of, for example, arrowheads—objects that have likely not been in use for a century or more—in the contemporary logos of many Aboriginal groups in North America.

Aboriginal peoples may choose to represent themselves or seek confirmation of their cultural identity by continuing to use (or, in some cases, adopting) precontact objects or traditions (e.g., Merrill, Ladd, and Ferguson 1992). These may include architecture, traditional foods and cooking practices, and rock art imagery. In the Interior Plateau of British Columbia, the image of the semisubterranean pit house (fig. 1) is widely used by the Secwepemc (or Shuswap) people on letterhead, signage (fig. 2), sweatshirts, and promotional items. Fullscale reconstructions of pit houses are found in Aboriginal heritage parks and communities; some individuals have even built and seasonally use their own pit houses. Underground pit-cooking (a practice well-documented in the archaeological record) continues, although only infrequently, and pit-cooked food is prized (Peacock 1998). Pictographs are also widely viewed by Secwepemc and other Plateau peoples as an important part of

G. NICHOLAS

FIGURE 1: Reconstructed pit house, Secwepemc Museum and Heritage Park, Kamloops, B.C.

their heritage (e.g., York, Daly, and Arnett 1993), although no new ones have been painted for many generations. Among other things, pictographs provide an expression of worldview and clear indications of a distinctive Aboriginal presence in the landscape.

Worldview

Certain types of archaeological sites and artifacts, such as pictographs, petroglyphs, medicine wheels, vision quest sites, and burial sites, have long been associated with the worldviews of Indigenous peoples. While few of these are still in use today, those that are reflect continued use since precontact times; offerings are left at sacred places today much as they have been for possibly millennia (e.g., Andrews and Zoe 1997). In Australia, the National Aboriginal Sites Authorities Committee distinguishes two types of Aboriginal sites: (1) archaeological sites, whose significance is defined "on the basis of scientific enquiry and general cultural and historical values," and (2) "sites which are the tangible embodiment of the sacred and secular traditions of the Aboriginal peoples of Australia." It is noted that the latter sites may include the former and that the "relative significance of these sites may only be determined by the Aboriginal custodians" (NASAC 1991, cited in Ritchie 1994:233).

The role of these types of sites is not necessarily static but reinterpreted or even augmented to meet current needs. Dreamtime sites are places in the landscape where ancestral beings went about creating the land and all it contained, including themselves (see Stanner 1998). To Aboriginal Australians, the Dreaming is a timeless phenomenon relayed through oral traditions linked to specific places and objects. While most of these tell how things came into being, they also reflect contemporary issues. As noted by Chatwin (1987:12), almost anything "can have a Dreaming. A virus can be a Dreaming. You can have a chickenpox Dreaming, a rain Dreaming, a desert-orange Dreaming, a lice Dreaming. In the Kimberleys they've now got a money Dreaming." Contemporary influences on traditions are also found in North America. Offerings left at sacred places often include tobacco, pebbles, and food, as well as coins and other "modern" items.

Such versatility is also seen in rock art, which may include both an objective record of life in the past (e.g., animals seen) and a subjective one (e.g., personal visions, dreams, magic). These images may be interpreted differently today from when they were created.[18] In some places, the tradition continues of repainting or even painting over old images (e.g., Chaloupka 1986).

Mortuary practices and the treatment of human remains are also expressions of worldview, and the reburial issue goes to the core of worldview and cultural identity in indigenous societies everywhere (e.g., Bray 2001, Carmichael et al. 1994, Davidson, Lovell-Jones, and Bancroft 1995, Zimmerman 1997). Cemeteries have long been important places in the cultural landscape and served as territorial markers. Some cemeteries have been in use for thousands of years (O'Neill 1994). Such locations are of importance to the associated contemporary Indigenous communities and may also play a significant role in land claims and political movements.

Cultural Continuity

Cultural continuity may be reflected in the occupation of the same lands for millennia, in the retention of the technologies used in the past to produce the same household goods (e.g., ceramics in the American Southwest), and in other ways (e.g., Jones 1997). Archaeological sites serve as important personal and societal touchstones (i.e., as links between past and present) that reaffirm basic values and provide a sense of place. This is indicated by Chase's (1989:17) observations on the significance of pre-contact archaeological sites for North Queensland Aboriginal people in Australia. In cases where the colonial experience and a century or more of acculturation have dramatically changed the lives of Aboriginal peoples, there often remain core cultural values that indicate the persistence of traditional beliefs and worldview. These may take the form, for example, of a strong emphasis on family values and respect for community elders.

The strong connection between cultural continuity and Indigenous claims to land and cultural or archaeological materials has significant implications for the recognition of ownership in matters of repatriation and reburial. However, the continuity may sometimes be more apparent than real; as a result of population movements in the distant past or historic federal tribal relocation and the often capricious nature of tribal boundary recognition, one group may occupy a territory that contains the archaeological record of another. Even in central Australia, where until recently the effects of colonialism were limited, the degree of relatedness between the Aboriginal Australian groups mapped by Tindale (1974) and their late Pleistocene predecessors in the area merits examination.

Where cultural discontinuities are recognized in the archaeological record, residents of the area may deal with this information in different ways. For example, the group may lack any concrete knowledge of earlier residents and accept the entirety of the local archaeological record as its own; some Secwepemc

FIGURE 2: Example of stylized pit house used as the logo of the Secwepemc Museum, Kamloops, B.C.

people insist that their ancestors *always* lived in pit houses and harvested salmon when the archaeological record suggests that these are later Holocene developments (Nicholas 2003). Alternatively, the newcomers may recognize the legacy of an earlier occupation and integrate knowledge of ancient unrelated beings into their histories and worldviews as Hamann (2002) has documented for Meso-america. Finally, the group may consciously co-opt the archaeological record for cultural or political reasons, as is the case with current Navajo claims to Anasazi archaeological sites.

Traditional Ecological Knowledge

"Traditional ecological knowledge" has been described as an Indigenous system of knowledge that is based on observation, testing, and replicated results and therefore directly comparable with "science." Berkes (1993:3) defines the term as "a cumulative body of knowledge and beliefs, handed down through generations by cultural transmission, about the relationship of living beings (including humans) with one another and with their environment. [It] is an attribute of societies with historical continuity in resource use practices; by and large, these are non-industrial or less technologically advanced societies, many of them Indigenous or tribal." Traditional systems of knowledge have become an important subject of intellectual property rights (e.g., Simpson 1999) and are increasingly recognized by both Indigenous and non-Indigenous people as a manifestation of the acquired knowledge of particular Indigenous societies. This body of knowledge includes not only the intellectual tradition itself (i.e., the information preserved and transmitted) but also the traditional use sites that are the geographic expression of that knowledge.

Archaeological sites by any definition are traditional use sites, and therefore the knowledge represented at these sites is worth considering in the context of cultural and intellectual property. Various types of sites (e.g., fish weirs) represent the operation or practice of past land-use and resource-harvesting practices that, in turn, are the embodiment of traditional ecological knowledge, while those of a particular region collectively reflect compositional and distributional changes that occurred over millennia as past occupants responded to shifts in the natural and social environment. Traditional ecological knowledge is also frequently used by archaeologists to locate archaeological sites (e.g., Greer 1997). Site information is typically obtained through interviews with elders and community members or from published ethnographies.

Should intellectual components of the archaeological record such as these be protected as proprietary? If so, by whom? No explicit protection exists under any provincial or state heritage protection mechanisms in Canada or the United States. Most archaeologists, in fact, may not recognize an intellectual component at all. However, the situation is likely very different for those with a vested interest in their own heritage sites. In Australia, for example, Aboriginal peoples have expressed concern that "the focus of cultural heritage laws is on tangible cultural heritage, such as specific areas, objects, and sites. The intangible aspects of a significant site, such as its associated stories, songs, and dreaming tracks,

are not protected" (Janke 1998:xxiv; also Roberts 2003). Even if an intellectual component is recognized, an argument may be made that the great age of most archaeological sites puts this information in the realm of shared heritage, thus making its exploitation legally acceptable. In the following section we return to the two-sided issue of control of knowledge in archaeology and evaluate threats to Indigenous cultural and intellectual property rights through appropriation and commodification—taking and affixing a price to what many would consider inalienable and priceless.

Appropriation and Commodification of the Past

Appropriation and commodification of cultural knowledge and property affect the cultural identity and integrity of contemporary Indigenous societies. Should cultural knowledge and property be protected from such exploitation? If so, should protection be from outside interests only or from all users, including Indigenous peoples themselves? Mutability (distortions) and transferability (easy dissemination) may be reasons to explore the usefulness of intellectual property mechanisms for protecting some aspects of cultural knowledge and property from exploitation. But what if Indigenous groups want to exploit their own past for commercial gain?[19] Should intellectual property laws be used discriminately to protect the past—to support Indigenous rights? We do not address these important and complicated questions here. Rather, our aim is to raise issues and outline potential consequences of appropriation and commodification of artifacts and information with the intention of informing and stimulating discussion in this growing area of concern.

Artifacts

The collection of antiquities extends back in time for thousands of years (Trigger 1989:27–72). Today, however, the acquisition of antiquities, often by illegal or unethical means, is occurring at unprecedented rates to satisfy the growing interest of collectors and museums in historic or prehistoric items that are prized for their age, rarity, exoticness, or "Aboriginalness." Sometimes Indigenous peoples themselves contribute to the appropriation and commodification of artifacts; the often impoverished Indigenous Central and South Americans known as *huaqueros* loot tombs and sell the artifacts to support their families: "Many of Latin America's indigenous peoples see themselves as the legitimate heirs to both seeds and artifacts, which are conceived of as ancestor's gifts, given to humanity by real or mythological patrons to be harvested, or excavated, as it were, by later generations" (Matsuda 1998:88). "Subsistence digging" also occurs in North America (Hollowell 2003, Staley 1993), and its profits may provide the means of acquiring the knowledge or skills that allow Aboriginal people to improve their circumstances. Zimmer (2003:306–7), for example, reports: "Once a young [Native] woman brought a newly-found artifact to show me, an ivory animal worth many thousands of dollars on the market. 'I know I shouldn't sell this, Julie,' she said, 'but it will help pay for my college education.' " Subsistence digging is not limited to Aboriginal peoples, as is evidenced by the *tombaroli* of Italy and pothunters in the United States, and in some cases Indigenous subsistence diggers do not consider the archaeological remains part of their culture.

The appropriation and commodification of artifacts may also take less obvious forms. For example, reproductions of artifacts in various media and the public dissemination of information, objects, and images derived from the archaeological record are often found among the technologically assisted and mass-produced products introduced into modern society. These include images of artifacts and sites, sometimes including those cherished by or sacred to past or present Indigenous peoples, that appear on postcards, T-shirts, and billboards and in magazine advertisements, books, and films. For example,

Sherwin-Williams uses images of the Upper Paleolithic Lascaux Cave paintings to sell house paint, and AT&T digitally inserts its logo into Egyptian tomb carvings. Through these advertisements, the past is appropriated and commodified in the sense that it is marketed in ways parallel to other, original or more contemporary ideas and resources.

Appropriation and commodification are accompanied by the objectification of the past—a focus on artifacts rather than on the people behind them. In a book on the pictographs of British Columbia, Corner (1968:1) states that "the freedom to wander unrestricted through the rugged and beautiful Kootenay country made me appreciate the feelings of the Indians, and created an intense interest in their life and culture." He goes on to report that "a diligent search of the recorded data on pictographs in North America failed to reveal a simple key that would unlock the mystery of what these fascinating paintings really mean,"[20] overlooking the possibility that contemporary Aboriginal peoples could have assisted him in this effort.

Although anthropologists and archaeologists ought to be more sensitive than others to issues of cultural appropriation and commodification, they, too, sometimes assume that ancient objects become divorced from contemporary cultural impacts when they enter the public domain. When a seated-figurine bowl was illustrated on the program cover of the 1992 Northwest Anthropology Conference, several First Nations individuals in attendance considered this use inappropriate because such bowls still have spiritual value. A similar bowl was illustrated by Winter and Henry (1997) but only with the permission of the Saanich Native Heritage Society. Perhaps the most common example of such appropriation is the use of artifacts and rock art imagery as part of the cover designs of books and journals.[21] If permission to reproduce such artifacts is sought, it is generally from the museum that today curates or owns them.

In marketing the past, the accomplishments of earlier societies are not only removed from their original physical and cultural context but sometimes otherwise altered. The transformation of the unique into the commonplace radically changes the value of things. For centuries, the great Renaissance frescoes of Europe could be viewed only from inside the buildings in which they were painted. Addressing this point, John Berger (1977: 19) writes: "Originally paintings were an integral part of the building for which they were designed.... The uniqueness of every painting was once part of the uniqueness of the place where it resided.... When the camera reproduces a painting, it destroys the uniqueness of its image. Or, more exactly, its meaning multiplies and fragments into many meanings." Berger is writing here of Western art, but his comments pertain also to Indigenous representations, both historic and prehistoric. The same is true of the Upper Paleolithic cave paintings of Lascaux and of Native American rock art, all of which were previously part of fixed landscapes.

Regardless of the original intention of their creators, the appreciation of these representations is very different when they are widely disseminated— and perhaps even altered—through a variety of media. The following anecdote (from Nicholas) illustrates how easy it is to alter an idea expressed in tangible form, how little control we have over dissemination of the original idea, and how difficult it is to make proprietorial claims of an intellectual nature in various hightech media:

About ten years ago I was preparing a lecture on hunter-gatherer economy. I was thinking about "access to the means of production" and other ideas influenced by the work of Karl Marx while making overhead transparencies of !Kung hunters. The next thing I knew, the old boy's head had been pasted onto a hunter's body and then onto an Upper Paleolithic "Venus" figurine. Soon after, I sent copies of this inspired artwork to several colleagues, including Martin Wobst of the University of Massachusetts–Amherst, where I had completed my Ph.D. Last year I learned from Wobst that my Venus/Marx figure had appeared on a T-shirt prepared for the 25th anniversary of the department.

I was amused and honored that this late-night whimsy had its 15 minutes of fame. However, in thinking about IPR issues, I began to wonder where the design on this shirt might ultimately end up. Perhaps an enterprising entrepreneur, seeing someone wearing it, will decide to create a series of T-shirts featuring famous people on Venus-figurine bodies.

The unauthorized appropriation of Aboriginally produced images, whether ancient or modern, has been a topic of discussion in Australia for some time (see Johnson 1996). Much attention has been given to the theft of Aboriginal designs, particularly those created by contemporary Aboriginal artists. Still another dimension of this relates to the theft of intellectual property through the appropriation of Aboriginal art. Brown (1998:219) notes that in a recent legal case in Darwin the plaintiffs were "asking the federal court to recognize the clan's economic and moral rights in the artist's graphic designs, rights tied to the clan's territory and ritual knowledge." At least some pictographs and petroglyphs in North America represent graphic designs tied to traditional territories and the ritual knowledge of past people whose descendants may still occupy that territory. These designs may subsequently appear in books and other media,[22] seldom with attribution to the traditional peoples concerned.

Even when there is approval by Aboriginal persons for the publication of such images or interpretations thereof, is the approval at the level of family, community, tribe, or nation? In some cases it may be Aboriginal peoples themselves that commodify the past. For example, the native people of St. Lawrence Island, Alaska, have been digging and selling artifacts from their ancestral sites for many years (see Hollowell 2003, Hollowell-Zimmer 2001, Staley 1993, Zimmer 2003). However, as Zimmer (2003:307) notes, "Perhaps a Euro-American notion in which objects of material culture are venerated as 'heritage' is somewhat foreign to a people whose heritage is performed and experienced in daily practices like speaking their own language, whaling, eating Native foods, and drum-dancing *sans* tourists."

Appropriation of the North American archaeological record has been facilitated by Indigenous and non-Indigenous parties alike. One example involves the Zia Pueblo sun symbol. Zia Pueblo has demanded $73 million from the state of New Mexico for the use of its *zia* sun symbol on the state flag. The symbol, adopted by the state in 1925, had been developed by Harry Mera, a physician and anthropologist at the Santa Fe Museum of Anthropology, on the basis of a pot on display in the museum that had been made by an anonymous Zia potter in the late 1800s (Healy 2003). (The symbol had likely appeared much earlier.) Another example concerns the cancellation of a mural of images from Pottery Mound ruin commissioned for the new archaeology building at the University of New Mexico in deference to objections raised by Acoma Pueblo. Pottery Mound is an 800-year-old site near Albuquerque that was excavated in the 1950s and 1960s. The Acoma admit that their ancestors had nothing to do with the artwork at the site. A statement by the muralist, Tom Baker, raises an important point beyond the issue of political correctness: "Public Mound images were excavated by a taxpayer-supported institution on public land, and thus are public property" (Duin 2003).

Information

What has occurred with material property is also occurring with the know how of Indigenous peoples. Knowledge that was once restricted to specific cultural systems has now been made widely available, seldom because of decisions of the communities themselves. Immense public interest in things Aboriginal has for centuries prompted collection, study, and even imitation of Native curios and lifeways. This interest is increasingly specialized through fields like anthropology, which aims to understand the totality of humankind through detailed studies of selected societies, often in collaboration with representatives of those societies. In some cases information recorded by anthropologists has been of immense value to community members decades later; that collected and published by Franz Boas (1897, 1969 [1930]) has aided the Kwakiutl of British Columbia in restoring aspects of their ceremonies that had been outlawed in 1885 (Holm 1990). Until the Indian Act was revised in 1951, it was illegal to hold certain ceremonies; individuals or communities who persisted were often jailed and their masks, regalia, and other items confiscated.[23] For the almost 70 years in which they were banned, potlatches and Winter Dances continued secretly, but many of their components were changed or lost in the process. The detailed information collected by Boas and his assistant George Hunt has thus become a vital source for those interested in restoring the ceremonies to their original form. Intellectual aspects of cultural property and cultural identity have been appropriated and sometimes commodified in various ways, including traditional use studies, use of human remains, cultural reconstructions of life (i.e., cultural tourism/living museums), and applications of archaeological research results to modern problems.

Traditional use studies. In British Columbia between 1995 and 2000, provincially funded "traditional use studies" provided Aboriginal communities with the "opportunity" to identify and map the cultural resources in their territories systematically.[24] Through these studies, site-specific biological and cultural information on traditional activities was compiled by the participating community and/or hired consultants. As part of the associated "sharing agreement," the resulting data were submitted to the Provincial Heritage Registered Database for use in the government's natural-resource management decisions. Information-sharing agreements were established through a memorandum of understanding between the province and the Aboriginal community as part of the final phase of the study (i.e., *after* the data had been compiled), but an interim sharing agreement (signed by all parties *prior* to the initial phase of the project) was required for final project funding. Sharing agreements addressed the storage and distribution of inventory data, confidentiality and security, and continued reporting and management of information (Aboriginal Affairs Branch, Ministry of Forests, TUS Program 1996, cited in Markey 2001:71). Issues of data ownership and intellectual property rights were not specifically addressed—a serious omission that was recognized by many First Nations and made them unwilling to participate because of uncertainty about the future use of the data. In her critical analysis of the traditional use study as a model for data gathering and interpretation of traditional ecological knowledge in British Columbia, Markey (2001:14) concludes that such studies "continue to produce inventory-based data, reflecting minimal concern for Aboriginal perspectives and knowledge by taking cultural information out of context."

Appropriation of human remains. The Kennewick Man controversy (Chatters 2000, Preston 1997) has become a landmark case on the disposition of prehistoric human remains. Aboriginal groups in the Northwest have argued in the courts since 1996 that the remains of this 9,000-year-old individual should be repatriated and reburied under the provisions of the NAGPRA, which states that Aboriginal human remains must be turned over to the representative Aboriginal group where affinity can be determined. A group of archaeologists has countered that because of their great age these remains cannot be related to the Aboriginal groups laying claim to them and has sued the U.S. government for the right to study them (*Bonnichsen v United States*, 969 F Supp 628 [1997])[25]—essentially asserting themselves as the rightful owners or stewards of the information contained in the skeletal remains. In September 2000 a federal judge ruled that the remains were to be turned over to the tribal claimants. The case was subsequently appealed. In August 2002 U.S. Magistrate John Jelderks ruled that the skeletal remains could be studied by the archaeologists. The ultimate fate of the remains and the information they embody is uncertain; an appeal of the decision is planned by the tribal claimants.[26] This case has obvious implications for the appropriation of material property and, pending the results of legal decisions on ancestry and custodianship, may raise issues of intellectual property in relation to the appropriation of Indigenous worldview.

Reconstruction of Indigenous lifeways. Cultural tourism has become a significant industry worldwide, and living museums and theme parks are widespread. Many of these include reenactments of life in the past utilizing speech and people in period clothing to represent both the colonizers and the colonized. The "best" of these include or are led by bearers of the culture involved,[27] but some of them blatantly exploit and stereotype Indigenous peoples. Living museums allow visitors to take home the experience of an "authentic" (and safe) encounter with the Other. There is also today a proliferation of Aboriginal heritage parks, tours, workshops, and "experiences" that are Aboriginally conceived, developed, and run.[28] The way in which Aboriginal communities choose to present themselves is critical to whether the experience is appreciated by visitors as one of cultural education and sharing or criticized as cultural "prostitution."

Other examples are worth noting. The German Indian clubs (Calloway, Gmunden, and Zantop 2002, Robbins and Becher 1997–98) consist of individuals who "play Indian" at several removes from the Native Americans they emulate (fig. 3). Going a step farther, the Smokis of the American Southwest have actually appropriated and violated Hopi ceremonies. Founded in 1921 by white businessmen, the Smokis put on public performances that are essentially parodies of the Hopi Snake Dance (Whitely 1997:178). Added to threats to the sanctity of, loss of access to, or destruction of sacred places (e.g., Mt. Graham, Arizona) and the commodification of religious objects, symbolism, and artifacts (Whiteley 1997; Pearlstone 2000, 2001), these activities leave little of the cultural knowledge and property of Southwestern Indigenous peoples unscathed.

Applications of archaeological research. Two types of archaeologically derived information have

FIGURE 3: Campfire, from the series Karl May Festival, by Andrea Robbins and Max Becher 1997–98 (reproduced by permission of the photographers and courtesy of Sonnabend Gallery, New York).

particular relevance in the modern world.[29] The first is information derived from studies of long-term shifts in subsistence practices or settlement patterns, which can be used to evaluate the potential impact of climate change on modern populations. The second is information on prehistoric technology. Both types may be appropriated and commodified.

One example of the development of new ideas through archaeologically obtained knowledge of prehistoric technology is the use of obsidian blades as surgical scalpels. Obsidian was widely utilized for stone blade production in many parts of the world. Aware that such blades had an edge up to 1,000 times sharper than surgical steel, Payson Sheets (1989) developed obsidian scalpels for use in eye surgery, where the shaper edge promotes faster healing and reduces scarring. Even though stone blade production was practiced by virtually all past human societies, this technology was potentially patentable because it represented a new use.[30] Other modern flint-knappers had observed how quickly obsidian cuts healed, but Sheets was the first to capitalize on it. Another example is the reintroduction of raised-field farming techniques by Clark Erickson and his colleagues as a means of assisting native communities to improve their agricultural yields. There is extensive archaeological evidence of raised fields throughout Central and South America (Parsons and Denevan 1967), but this technology appears to have fallen out of use until it was promoted by Erickson and his colleagues (Erickson 1998). This is not the case with the chinampas, a type of raised-field farming constructed in swamps (Coe 1964), that were the economic basis of the Aztec economy in Mexico and of other societies in Central and South America and have continued to be used to the present and introduced into new areas. Does the reintroduction of forgotten raised-field farming represent intellectual property? If so, for whom—the archaeologists or the descendants of the people who developed the technology in the first place? Erickson's (2000) more recent work on precontact artificial fisheries in the Bolivian Amazon suggests yet another area of potentially commercially valuable Indigenous knowledge.

So far we have explored the notion that some products of archaeological research represent cultural and intellectual property according to Janke's (1998) definition and outlined some of the ways in which archaeologically derived knowledge has been appropriated or commodified. We next focus on the means by which Indigenous peoples are seeking (or may seek in future) to regain control over this knowledge through existing legal rights, including intellectual property ownership mechanisms.

Who Owns the Future?

"Everyone now speaks of their culture," says Sahlins (1999:x), "precisely in the context of national or international threats to its existence. This does not mean a simple and nostalgic desire for teepees and tomahawks or some such fetishized repositories of a pristine identity. A 'naïve attempt to hold peoples hostage to their own histories,' such a supposition, Terence Turner remarks, would thereby deprive them of history. What the selfconsciousness of 'culture' does signify is the demand of the peoples for their own space within the world cultural order." A strong association between cultural knowledge and cultural identity is reflected not only in a society's material culture (e.g., the pit house in Interior British Columbia) but in the intellectual aspects of cultural traditions. Language, for example, is a very important contributor to Indigenous cultural identity (see Maffi 2000). Given the strength of this association, it is clear why control of knowledge is at the heart of the issue—not simply for economic reasons but because control is integral to the defini-

tion or restoration of cultural identity for present and future Indigenous societies.

It can be argued that whoever owns (or controls records of) the past also owns or otherwise shapes the future of that past. Archaeologists have, to date, controlled the dissemination of information derived from the archaeological record through publication practices, restriction of access to site locations, and other means. While this management of knowledge has done much to help preserve archaeological resources, it has had several drawbacks. For one, much information has been kept from Indigenous communities, often inadvertently. Since archaeologists are in the position to choose what they will or will not publish, information potentially useful to Indigenous peoples may simply not be available because it fell outside of the interests of the investigator and was not pursued. Access to knowledge is obviously the first of several key steps in establishing control of it. Yet publication itself is a double-edged sword in terms of sharing research findings versus protecting knowledge from third-party exploitation (see Bannister 2000, Bannister and Barrett 2001, n.d., Laird et al. 2002). Beyond simply relying on heritage protection legislation, is it possible to increase Indigenous control of cultural knowledge and property through existing intellectual property laws and complementary nonlegal tools? If so, what are the implications for future archaeological research? In this final section, we explore several current examples that may begin to elucidate answers to these complex questions.

Control through Contracts and Local Protocols for Research

Examples of Indigenous groups' seeking to control access to and/or use of their past are definitely on the rise. Brown (1998:194) cites a 1994 letter to several museums from the chair of the Hopi Tribe that "states the tribe's interest in all published or unpublished field data relating to the Hopi, including notes, drawings, and photographs, particularly those dealing with religious matters." He notes also that the Hopi initiative was soon followed by a declaration issued by a consortium of Apache tribes demanding exclusive decision-making power and control over Apache "cultural property," here defined as "all images, text, ceremonies, music, songs, stories, symbols, beliefs, customs, ideas and other physical and spiritual objects and concepts" relating to the Apache, including any representations of Apache culture offered by Apache or non-Apache people (Inter-Apache Summit on Repatriation 1995:3).

An important question to consider is to what degree archaeological research products might be included here.

Local Indigenous protocols are increasingly being used as the basis for research contracts or agreements between the communities and outside researchers. Protocols have been developed by many Aboriginal groups in British Columbia, and some require a permit in lieu of one issued by the B.C. Heritage Branch under the Heritage Conservation Act. The Sto:lo Nation, for example, states: "We hereby declare that all artifacts recovered from our traditional campsites, ceremonial sites, villages, burial grounds and archaeological sites are the rightful property of the Sto:lo people" (quoted in Mohs 1987:169). The protocol of the Cultural Resources Management Department (CRMD) of the Kamloops Band, Secwepemc Nation, contains even more inclusive terms and provisions for an archaeological permitting system, stating that "all data, maps, journals, and photographs, and other material generated through or as a result of the study are the exclusive property of the Band," that "there shall be joint copyright between the Permittee and the Band over any such publications, unless otherwise agreed between the parties," and that "all material found or generated by the proponent as a result of heritage investigations shall be deemed the property of the Kamloops Indian Band." How effective is this agreement, and what rights are ceded upon signing? The provisions of the archaeological permit refer to physical property/

results but do not specifically mention intellectual property ownership aside from "joint copyright." The provisions do, however, specifically include "data," and the fact that the term is not defined enables the Kamloops Band to interpret it broadly, perhaps allowing some forms of intellectual property to be included.

Should such permits explicitly include reference to intellectual property rights? If so, is it possible or likely that at some point a contemporary Aboriginal group will lay claim to a major archaeological site and exercise exclusive control over the site name, images of the artifacts, or related items? What if there are competing interests due to overlapping land claims (e.g., Franklin and Bunte 1994)? These are complex control issues that have yet to arise. It is important to note, however, that regaining control, such as repatriation of human remains, is often just the beginning of a series of related challenges; control of knowledge or resources without the capacity to manage them can have significant consequences. As Winter and Henry (1997:222) note,

An associated issue is the intrinsic power of excavated materials. While the [Saanich] Society has a responsibility for the preservation of artifacts of cultural, artistic, and historical value to the Saanich people, in some cases it is difficult to accept such objects. Some artifacts carry with them a constellation of responsibilities. To accept care of certain artifacts brings onerous cultural and spiritual obligations. Some need extensive ritual care. Some artifacts may only be returned to individuals who are culturally appropriate by reason of family, lineage, gender, or initiation. Such people may not be available, or may not be willing to personally undertake the effort and personal expense.

Control through Intellectual Property Ownership Mechanisms

Beyond contractual approaches to controlling Indigenous cultural and intellectual property, existing intellectual property ownership tools are beginning to be employed. Academic researchers are increasingly required to negotiate issues related to publication, including standard copyright issues (authorship and moral rights), editorial control (restrictions on publication), and benefit sharing. For example, "joint copyright between the Permittee and the Band" for all resulting publications is required by the heritage investigation permit of the Kamloops Indian Band referred to above. With most archaeological publications, copyright is held by the publishers. With greater collaboration between archaeologists and Aboriginal communities, publishers will need to accommodate the need for more flexible copyright arrangements. This is already under way with some ethnobotany publications (e.g., Turner 1997, 1998). Furthermore, some archaeologists have turned over copyright to the Indigenous peoples with whom they work (e.g., Roberts 2002). Sharing or transferring copyright may require (and benefit from) review by the community collaborator(s) prior to publication—an extension of existing concepts of peer review to include community experts. Such collaborative approaches to publication, however, often require additional time. Another issue is copyright ownership and access to photographs of Aboriginal designs, which raises the question which of these is the true creation or artistic work, the design or the photograph. Here one could suggest a parallel with the patenting of isolated and purified plant chemicals by drug companies that use cultural knowledge as a guide; which creativity is most deserving of protection, the laboratory manipulation or the original knowledge?

Trademark is also gaining recognition as a potentially useful legal tool for protecting Indigenous images and designs. For example, several members of Pauktuutit, a Canadian Inuit women's organization, are currently examining how a variation on trademark that they term a "cultural property mark" might be employed to protect the *amauti*, an innovative traditional form of clothing with both practical and holistic attributes. The concept of a cultural property mark is similar to a trademark but would apply to the collective knowledge of Indigenous peoples rather than the knowledge of individuals or corporations (Blackduck 2001a, b). Aboriginal groups in British Columbia such as the Cowichan Band Council have registered certain words as "certification marks" (another form of trademark) for commercial use. For example, "Cowichan," "Genuine Cowichan," and "Genuine Cowichan Approved" are registered for use in the marketing of handmade clothing created by Coast Salish knitters using traditional materials, methods, and patterns.[31] These marks have potential application in the protection or promotion of other aspects of cultural heritage. While trademark use typically involves protection of exclusive rights to an image intended for commercial purposes, defensive uses of trademark law have been documented. In February 2000 the Snuneymuxw Nation successfully registered some ancient petroglyphs in their traditional territory as "official marks" to prevent their being copied and reproduced by anyone for any purpose, arguing that they are sacred and copying them for any reason would be sacrilegious (Associated Press 2000, Tanner 2000). The Comox Indian Band has protected the placename of a sacred site, Queneesh,[32] as an official mark.

Patents may seem unrelated to archaeological research. At the molecular level, however, archaeological research may involve the recovery of ancient DNA, a potentially patentable material.[33] DNA has, for example, been extracted from 8,000-year-old brain tissue (Doran et al. 1986). Access to and study of DNA from contemporary populations is a very contentious issue, in part because it brings up serious issues of privacy and prior informed consent but also because the genetic information derived through analysis may be seen as a valuable commodity. Given that human genetic material is patentable in Canada, the United States, and many European countries, one can speculate that if, for example, ancient DNA from prehistoric human remains were to play a critical role in informing future medical treatments for contemporary diseases there might be important issues to be resolved regarding both cultural heritage and intellectual property rights. At best, intellectual property and other laws offer a piecemeal approach to protecting certain aspects of cultural heritage. This contrasts with the blanket approach that Brown (2003:209) calls "total heritage protection" and describes as "a benign form of quarantine that safeguards all elements of cultural life. Entire cultures would thus be defined as off-limits to scrutiny and exploitation. Within this sheltering umbrella, communities would remain free to devise appropriate ways to defend their philosophical or scientific or artistic achievements." He points out the contradictions inherent in this approach (pp. 217–18):

> To defend indigenous peoples, it promotes official boundaries that separate one kind of native person from another, and native persons from non-native ones, thereby threatening the fluidity of ethnic and family identities typically found in aboriginal communities. In the name of defending indigenous traditions, it forces the elusive qualities of entire civilizations—everything from attitudes and bodily postures to agricultural techniques—into ready-made legal categories, among which "heritage" and "culture" are only the most far-reaching. In the interest of promoting diversity, Total Heritage Protection imposes procedural norms that have the paradoxical effect of flattening cultural difference.

While much of the recent intellectual property rights discussion has centered on the use or expansion of existing legal mechanisms, Brown (1998:199) contends that this strategy serves primarily to "convert information into property" but that "property discourse *replaces* [emphasis ours] what should be extensive discussion on the moral implications of exposing Native people to unwanted scrutiny, on the one hand, and sequestering public-domain information, on the other." We strongly support Brown's call (p. 202) for "public discussion about mutual respect and the fragility of native cultures

in mass societies." Given that the establishment of an adequate process for such a dialogue has been slow, however, we suggest that the existing legal and nonlegal protection mechanisms discussed herein merit consideration.

Cultural Prospecting? Lessons from Other Disciplines

Non-Indigenous archaeologists have long held a monopoly on the recovery of prehistoric materials and scientific knowledge of past peoples. In general, they have also profited the most from archaeological research in the sense of creating personal careers and building their professional field. Indeed, archaeological exploration of the past could be viewed as cultural prospecting, parallel to biodiversity prospecting. This being the case, are there lessons to be gleaned from the current intellectual property rights debate in ethnobotany? Archaeology is based on physical evidence that is often seen as lacking in contemporary value. In contrast, the intellectual contributions (e.g., language, traditional plant knowledge) of living Indigenous societies are integral to ethonobotany and are in many cases highly regarded in contemporary human and environmental health applications. Some archaeological research products are protected by federal, state, or provincial laws. While such legislation appears to be inadequate to protect cultural and intellectual property, it is often supplemented by well-developed local protocols, contracts, and/or permit systems. By comparison, no provincial or federal policy in Canada specifically limits access to or use of ethnobotanical knowledge or plant biodiversity on public lands. The ethnobotanical research policies and guidelines that have been developed are mainly institutionally derived (i.e., university, industry, professional society). Relevant international statements and declarations are emerging (e.g., *Kari-Oca Declaration* 1992, *Mataatua Declaration* 1993), but protocols developed by Indigenous groups themselves are largely recent developments.[34]

Through publication of their data, archaeologists increase access to the historical record, as archaeological information is often not readily available to communities. Not surprisingly, copyright relating to the publication of results has been largely perceived as the main intellectual property issue, although there is the potential for patent issues and trademark applications are emerging. Indeed, if marketers can seek and often gain legal protection of "proprietary" phrases, symbols, names, and even odors (see Brown 2003:76), then the notion of Indigenous peoples' seeking protection for medicine wheels, rock art, or other aspects of their cultural heritage cannot be viewed as outlandish or unprecedented. In ethnobotany, by comparison, publication raises important issues (see Bannister and Barrett n.d., 2001, Laird et al. 2002), but copyright is viewed as inadequate protection in that it serves only to limit the *physical reproduction* of published works rather than protecting their intellectual components. Copyright is also very difficult to monitor or enforce. Patents are the mechanisms of choice for researchers interested in protecting intellectual property rights to "inventions" with commercial potential based on traditional plant knowledge. Ethnobotanists are increasingly having to consider patent issues and trade secrecy (fiduciary duty) in connection with traditional medicines or foods.

Significant differences between archaeology and ethnobotany are obvious in the types of information sought and the ways in which that information is utilized. Archaeology and ethnobotany approach intellectual property issues from opposite ends of the spectrum—archaeology from the *material* record of *past* culture with supposed *limited* present use and ethnobotany from the *intellectual* aspects (and related biological resources) of *living* (or recently living) peoples with perceived *high* contemporary value. Perhaps the two disciplines can inform one another. Archaeologists have the potential to become leaders in dealing with issues of intellectual property rights in their own field by becoming aware of debates in related disciplines and considering their implications.

Costewardship of the Future

Unless archaeologists consider the implications of existing intellectual property laws and the subject matter that might lead to intellectual property disputes (e.g., publication of academic research, fiduciary duties with regard to secret knowledge, reproduction of images of cultural artifacts or symbols, use of traditional knowledge derived from archaeological digs) they may be caught unawares by restrictions on data access or use imposed on them by tribes that have gained legal rights or developed the capacity to conduct research on their own. The situation is analogous in some respects to the events leading up to drafting of the NAGPRA. For decades professional archaeologists and their antiquarian predecessors were complacent about the recovery and treatment of human skeletal remains, assuming that they had the unlimited right to claim these precontact materials for their own use and that Native Americans had little or no interest in those materials (see Thomas 2000 for overview). Those who held this view were "shocked and outraged" by the ease of passage of this powerful piece of legislation (e.g., Meighan 1992).

We advocate a more active role for archaeologists working with Indigenous peoples (or on Indigenous territories) in considering the implications of their research. We believe that solutions to disputes between archaeologists (or archaeology) and tribes will be found in the recognition of what archaeological knowledge means and what *control* of that knowledge means beyond simply economics or professional rewards and advancement. There must be recognition of ethical obligations at both the individual and the collective level. Adopting participatory research approaches, supporting meaningful collaboration with Indigenous colleagues, sharing decision-making responsibilities and benefits in research processes and outcomes, and working cooperatively with all those who have an interest in Indigenous cultural heritage will be key to identifying, understanding, and addressing the conflicts that may arise in claiming ownership of the past.

Notes

1 This paper has benefited from discussions with many individuals, particularly Michael Brown, Julie Hollowell, Jock Langford, Nola Markey, Claire Smith, and Alison Wylie. We are indebted to Larry Zimmerman, Peter Whiteley, and five anonymous reviewers for their useful comments on a previous version. We also extend our appreciation to the numerous Aboriginal groups and individuals with whom we have worked and discussed many of these issues. This work was supported by the Social Sciences and Humanities Research Council of Canada through a postdoctoral fellowship to K.P. Bannister, British Columbia. Her publications include "Indigenous Knowledge and Traditional Plant Resources of the Secwepemc First Nation," in *Indigenous Intellectual Property Rights: Legal Obstacles and Innovative Solutions*, edited by M. Riley (Walnut Creek: AltaMira Press, in press) and (with K. Barrett), "Weighing the Proverbial 'Ounce of Prevention' versus the 'Pound of Cure' in a Biocultural Context: A Role for the Precautionary Principle in Ethnobiological Research," in *Ethnobotany and Conservation of Biocultural Diversity*, edited by T.J. Carlson and L. Maffi (Advances in Economic Botany 15, in press).

2 We use "Aboriginal," "Indigenous," and "Native" interchangeably. "Aboriginal" tends to be used more commonly in Canada and Australia. In Canada it includes First Nations, Métis, and Inuit.

3 See, for example, *Harvard College v Canada* (Commissioner of Patents) 2002 SCC 76. File No. 28155 December 5 (http://www.texum.umontreal.ca/csc-scc/en/pub/2002/vol4/html/2002scr4_0046.html) and the reexamination of U.S. Plant Patent No. 5,751, the "Da Vine Patent" on the Amazonian rainforest plant *Banisteriopsis caapi*, issued June 17, 1986, to Loren S. Miller and rejected by the U.S. Patent and Trademark Office on November 3, 1999 (CIEL 1999).

4 Bell and Patterson (1999:206) define "Aboriginal cultural property" as "movable objects that have sacred, ceremonial, historical, traditional, or other purposes integral to the culture of a First Nations community and may be viewed as collective property of an Aboriginal people" and continue: "Aboriginal perspectives on identification of cultural property and persons with authority to alienate or convey such property may vary in accordance with the laws, traditions and property systems of the claimant group."

5 This theme is expanded upon in Brown's book *Who Owns Native Culture?* (2003), which is highly recommended as a comprehensive review and discussion of many key issues.

6 Copyright Act. R.S., c. C-30,s. 1, Canada (http://laws.justice.gc.ca/en/C-42/37844.html).

7 A patent is the right to exclude others for a defined period of time (e.g., 20 years in Canada) from making, using, or selling an invention that involves a new process, structure, or function. A trademark is a word, symbol, picture, or group of these used to distinguish the products or services of one individual, organization, or company from those of another. An industrial design protects the shape, pattern, or ornamentation of an industrially produced object. A trade secret is practical knowledge that has commercial value, provides a competitive advantage, and is not widely known (Industry Canada 1995, Posey and Dutfield 1996, Stephenson 1999).

8 However limited the term is, we use "Western" here in its usual colonial/post-colonial sense, as in the distinction between "the West and the Rest" (Sahlins 1976).

9 Asch (1997) has examined the issue of ownership of cultural property in an archaeological context but not that of intellectual property rights per se.

10 We are very much aware that archaeology has frequently been conducted in the context of an unequal power relationship in which descendant communities have had little participation or say. This has been true for Native Americans (e.g., Jemison 1997, Watkins 2000) and African-Americans (e.g., McDavid 2002, Singleton 1995). The situation has changed notably in recent years (see e.g., the Code of Ethics of the World Archaeological Congress).

11 For example, the long-term study and excavation of landfills in the United States by William Rathje has demonstrated their ineffectiveness and contributed to their redesign (Rathje 1991, Rathje and Murphy 1992). Carlson's (1995) study of fish remains from archaeological sites in northeastern North America correlates the substantial—and anomalous—historic salmon population with the Little Ice Age cooling, thereby explaining why many expensive salmon restoration projects may be unlikely to reach projected goals.

12 "Cultural patrimony" is "an object having ongoing historical, traditional, or cultural importance central to the Native American group or culture" (NAGPRA 1990:sec. 2).

13 Export of artifacts out of the province is prohibited by the British Columbia Heritage Conservation Act, while the

export of many materials out of Canada is regulated or prohibited by the Cultural Property Export and Import Act.

[14] We must be careful about making assumptions as to who the descendants of a particular population are. In the Kennewick Man case, there is little scientific evidence that the 9,000-year-old skeletal remains can be directly related to modern Umatilla and other claimants. In the case of the Navajo claim to association with Anasazi sites, archaeological data indicate that it is the Pueblo tribes that are strongly linked to those sites, the Navajo having moved into the Southwest only relatively recently.

[15] The "Mona Lisa," however, is owned by the Louvre and may not be entirely in the public domain in a copyright sense. The museum controls access to it and access to quality reproductions. Petroglyphs have been trademarked (as official marks) in British Columbia and therefore are not necessarily part of our common human heritage.

[16] Morris (1984:11), for example, notes that "ancient peoples believed that time was cyclic in character," ignoring the fact that many contemporary Aboriginal peoples also believe this.

[17] Concerns faced by Indigenous researchers would presumably include some elements from both of these points of view and be further influenced by whether they were members of the communities in which they were working. Such individuals may also expose themselves to criticism for having "sold out."

[18] This is likely the case with the Nlaka'pamux elder Annie York's interpretation of pictographs in her band territory in the Interior Plateau of British Columbia (York, Daly, and Arnett 1993). The degree to which her interpretations of imagery match those of its creators hundreds or thousands of years ago is debatable (Nicholas 2001).

[19] This is but one facet of a larger and more difficult question: If a group "owns" or controls its cultural heritage, should it not have the freedom to do what it wishes with it? Many who agree in principle with this reasoning are dismayed when it is put into practice (for example, when repatriated human remains are reburied).

[20] While many Aboriginal people had commented on the appropriateness of Corner's book, the recent publication of another book on British Columbia rock art (Nankivell and Wyse 2003), this one including GPS locations, has raised the ire of some First Nations.

[21] Including American Antiquity, Australian Archaeology, the Canadian Journal of Archaeology, Latin American Antiquity, the Mid-Continental Journal of Archaeology, and Northeast Anthropology.

[22] The cover of Australian Archaeology shows two stylized human figures that are based on but not direct copies of rock art images. Amy Roberts (personal communication, 2001) notes that Aboriginal people have complained but thinks that this "has to do with the figures' being naked." In 2000, the Australian Archaeological Association membership voted to keep the design.

[23] Many of these materials became part of the collections of the National Museum of Man and the Royal Ontario Museum, among others (Lohnse and Sundt 1990:92).

[24] These land-use and occupancy studies (cancelled in 2002) were a product of British Columbia government policy responses to legal obligations in land-use management as defined by the Court of Appeal in Delgamuukw v The Queen (1993) (Culhane 1998). The goal of the program was "to inventory TUS data to provide the province and industry with the tools to facilitate meaningful consultation with participating First Nations in land use planning" as well as to "[assist] First Nations participating in the treaty process, [and develop] cultural education and capacity" (http://www.for.gov. bc.ca/aab/int_msrs/pim_tus.htm).

[25] D. Ore (1997), cited in the final court brief (http://www. kennwick-man.com/documents/doi.html).

[26] Non-Aboriginal organizations have also made claims, including the Asatru Folk Assembly, which insists that the remains are those of an ancient European: "the Asatru Folk Assembly ... practices an ancient religion known as Asatru, with roots in northern Europe ... Asatru emphasizes the spiritual importance of ancestral bonds. Since Kennewick Man may well be related to modern-day people of European descent, the AFA filed suit in 1996 in federal court to prevent the U.S. government from giving the skeleton to local Indian tribes, and to ensure the remains were studied and results released to the public" (http://www.runestone.org/kmfact.html).

[27] For example, those of African-American slaves at Colonial Williamsburg (Virginia) offered through an interpretive program called "The Other Half Tour."

[28] For example, Xà:ytem (Hatzic Rock) and Tla-o-qui-aht cultural tours by Tla-ook Adventures in British Columbia and the coman-aged Kakadu National Park in Australia.

[29] Archaeological information is also relevant to other realms, such as education.

[30] On the basis of a search of the U.S. Patent Office database (http: //www.uspto.gov/patft/) and personal communication with a representative of Fine Science Tools Inc., a Vancouver-based company that currently sells "Stone Age scalpels" made from obsidian (http: //finescience.com/fst/ScalpelsKnives/10110-01.html), we conclude that obsidian scalpels were not patented.

[31] Canadian Intellectual Property Office website (http://strategis.ic.gc.ca/SSG/0792/trdp079217400e.html).

[32] Canadian Intellectual Property Office website (http://strategis.ic.gc.ca/SSG/0908/trdp090857300e.html).

[33] For example, deCODE Genetics of Delaware has been creating databases of Icelanders' genes and their medical and

genealogical records. The company cross-references these data and markets them and other bioinformatics software products to drug developers (Industry Standard website <http://www.thestandard.com/companies/dossier/0,1922,276205,00.html>). DeCODE "will license the genes that it discovers (all of which it intends to patent) to drug-makers only if they agree to provide medicines developed as a result to all Icelanders without charge" (Gibbs 1998). The Mannverd Association for Ethics in Science and Medicine in Iceland is opposing the databases through a lawsuit on the grounds that they violate human rights (http://mannvernd.is).

34 Examples of protocols or guidelines developed by indigenous groups include *Guidelines for Respecting Cultural Knowledge (Alaska Native Knowledge Network)* (http://www.ankn.uaf.edu/standards/knowledge.html), *Mi'kmaq Research Principles and Protocols* (http://mrc.uccb.ns.ca/mci/default.htm), *Code of Ethics for Researchers Conducting Research Concerning the Ktunaxa Nation* (http://www.law.ualberta.ca/research/aboriginalculturalheritage/casestudies.htm), and *'Namgis First Nation Guidelines for Visiting Researchers/Access to Information* (http://www.law.ualberta.ca/research/aboriginalculturalheritage/casestudies.htm).

References

Andrews, T.D., and J.B. Zoe. 1997. "The *Idaà* Trail: Archaeology and the Dogrib Cultural Landscape, Northwest Territories, Canada," in *At a Crossroads: Archaeologists and First Peoples in Canada*. Edited by G.P. Nicholas and T.D. Andrews, pp. 160–77. Burnaby, BC: Archaeology Press.

Asch, M. 1997. "Cultural Property and the Question of Underlying Title," in *At a Crossroads: Archaeologists and First Peoples in Canada*. Edited by G.P. Nicholas and T.D. Andrews, pp. 266–71. Burnaby, BC: Archaeology Press.

Associated Press. 2000. Indian Band Applies for Trademark on Ancient Petroglyphs. February 16.

Balter, M. 2000. Archaeologists and Rabbis Clash over Human Remains. *Science* 287:34–35.

Bannister, K. 2000. Chemistry rooted in cultural knowledge: Unearthing the links between antimicrobial properties and traditional knowledge in food and medicinal plant resources of the Secwepemc (Shuswap) Aboriginal Nation. Ph.D. diss., University of British Columbia, Vancouver, BC, Canada.

———. 2003. Use of traditional knowledge of Aboriginal peoples for university research: An analysis of academic ethics and research policies in British Columbia, Canada. Commissioned report prepared for the Biodiversity Convention Office for submission to the Convention on Biological Diversity Article 8j. Hull. Quebec.

Bannister, K., and K. Barrett. 2001. Challenging the status quo in ethnobotany: A new paradigm for publication may protect cultural knowledge and traditional resources. *Cultural Survival Quarterly* 24(4):10–13.

———. n.d. "Weighing the proverbial 'ounce of prevention' versus the 'pound of cure' in a biocultural context: A role for the precautionary principle in ethnobiological research," in *Ethnobotany and conservation of biocultural diversity*. Edited by T.J. Carlson and L. Maffi. Advances in Economic Botany 15.

Battiste, M., and J.(S.)Y. henderson. 2000. *Protecting indigenous knowledge and heritage: A global challenge*. Saskatoon: Purich Publishing.

Bell, C.E., and R.K. Patterson. 1999. Aboriginal rights to cultural property. *International Journal of Cultural Property* 8:167–211.

Berger, J. 1977. *Ways of seeing*. New York: Viking Penguin.

Berkes, F. 1993. "Traditional ecological knowledge in perspective," in *Traditional ecological knowledge: Concepts and cases*. Edited by J.T. Inglis, pp. 1–10. Ottawa: Canadian Museum of Nature.

Blackduck, A. 2001a. Protecting Inuit clothing designs: Pauktuutit looks to Panama for legal model. *Nunatsiaq News* [Iqaluit], May 25, Iqaluit. http://www.nunatsiaq.com/nunavut/ nvt10525_091.

———. 2001*b*. Pauktuutit to continue work on Amauti protection: Rankin workshop impresses federal officials. *Nunatsiaq News* [Iqaluit], June 1.

Boas, F. 1897. The social organization and the secret societies of the Kwakiutl Indians. *Report of the U.S. National Museum for 1895*, pp. 311–738. Washington, D.C.

———. 1969 (1930). *The religion of the Kwakiutl Indians.* New York: AMS Press.

Bray, T.L. Editor. 2001. *The future of the past: Archaeologists, Native Americans, and repatriation.* New York: Garland.

Brown, K.S. 1994. Seeing stars: Character and identity in the landscapes of modern Macedonia. *Antiquity* 68:784–96.[yh]

Brown, M.F. 1998. Can culture be copyrighted? Current Anthropology 39:193–222.

———. 2003. *Who owns native culture?* Cambridge: Harvard University Press.

Brush, S., and D. Strabinsky. 1996. *Valuing local knowledge: Indigenous people and intellectual property rights.* Washington, DC: Island Press.

Calloway, C.G., G. Gmunden, and S. Zantop. 2002. *Germans and Indians: Fantasies, encounters, projections.* Lincoln: University of Nebraska Press.

Carlson, C.C. 1995. "The (in)significance of Atlantic salmon in New England," in *New England's creatures: 1400–1900*. Edited by P. Benes, pp. 1–10. Cambridge: Boston University Press.

Carmichael, D.L., J. Hubert, B. Reeves, and A. Schanche. Editors. 1994. *Sacred sites, sacred places.* New York: Routledge.

Cassidy, M., and J. Langford. 1999. *Intellectual property and Aboriginal people: A working paper.* Ottawa: Indian and Northern Affairs Canada.

CBAC (Canadian Biotechnology Advisory Committee). 2001. Biotechnological intellectual property and the patenting of higher life forms. Consultation Document, Ottawa. http://www.cbac-cccb.ca/ IPConsult_eng.htm.

———. 2003. Higher life forms and the Patent Act. Advisory Memorandum, February 24. http://cbac-cccb.ca/epic/internet/ incbac-cccb.nsf/vwGeneratedInterE/ah00217e.html.

Chaloupka, G. 1986. *Burrunguy, Nourlangie Rock.* Darwin: Northart.

Chase, A.K. 1989. "Perceptions of the past among North Queensland Aboriginal people: The intrusion of Europeans and consequent social change," in *Who needs the past? Indigenous values and archaeology.* Edited by R. Layton, pp. 169–79. London: Unwin Hyman.

Chatters, J.C. 2000. The recovery and first analysis of an Early Holocene human skeleton from Kennewick, Washington. *American Antiquity* 65:291–316.

Chatwin, B. 1987. *The songlines.* New York: Penguin Books.

Chippindale, C. 2003. "The ethics of research knowledge," in *Ethical issues in archaeology.* Edited by L.J. Zimmerman, K.D. Vitelli, and J. Hollowell-Zimmer, pp. 239–49. Walnut Creek: AltaMira Press.

Ciel (Centre for International Environmental Law). 1999. US Patent Office admits error, rejects patent claim on sacred "ayahuasca" plant. Centre for International Environmental Law press release, November 4. http:// www.ciel.org/Biodiversity/AyahuascaRejectionPR.html.

Clifford, James. 2004. Looking several ways: Anthropology and Native heritage in Alaska. Current Anthropology 45: 5–30.

Coe, M. 1964. The chinampas of Mexico. *Scientific American* 211(1):90–98.

Corner, J. 1968. *Pictographs (Indian rock paintings) in the interior of British Columbia.* Vernon, BC: Wayside Press.

Culhane, D. 1998. *The pleasure of the crown: Anthropology, law, and First Nations.* Burnaby, BC: Talon.

Davidson, I., C. Lovell-Jones, and R. Bancroft. Editors. 1995. *Archaeologists and aborigines working together.* Armidale: University of New England Press.

Denhez, M. 2000. *Unearthing the law: Archaeological legislation on lands in Canada.* Ottawa: Archaeological Services Branch, Parks Canada.

Doran, G.H., D.N. Dickel, W.E. Ballinger Jr., O.F. Agee, P.J. Laipis, and W.W. Hauswirth. 1986. Anatomical, cellular, and molecular analysis of 8,000-yr-old human brain tissue from the Windover archaeological site. *Nature* 323:803–6.

Dratler, J. 1994. *Licensing of intellectual property.* New York: Law Journal Seminars-Press.

Duin, J. 2003. Tribes veto Southwest mural. *Washington Times*, February 18. http://www.thomasbakerpaintings.com/Washington%20Times%20article.

Erickson, C.L. 1998. "Applied archaeology and rural development: Archaeology's potential contribution to the future," in *Crossing currents: Continuity and change in Latin America.* Edited by M. Whiteford and S. Whiteford, pp. 34–45. Upper Saddle River, NJ: Prentice-Hall.

———. 2000. An artificial landscape-scale fishery in the Bolivian Amazon. *Nature* 408:190–93.

Fagan, B.M. 1997. 9th edition. *In the beginning: An introduction to archaeology.* New York: Longman.

Ferguson, T.J. 1996. Native Americans and the practice of archaeology. *Annual Reviews in Anthropology* 25:63–79.

Finn, Christine. 1997. "Leaving more than footprints": Modern votive offerings at Chaco Canyon prehistoric site. *Antiquity* 71(271):177–78.[so]

Franklin, R., and P. Bunte. 1994. "When sacred land is sacred to three Tribes: San Juan Paiute sacred sites and the Hopi-Navajo-Paiute suit to partition the Arizona Navajo reservation," in *Sacred sites, sacred places.* Edited by D.L. Carmichael, J. Hubert, B. Reeves, and F. Schanche, pp. 245–58. London: Routledge.

Gibbs, W.W. 1998. Natural born guinea pigs: A startup discovers genes for tremor and psoriasis in the DNA of inbred Icelanders. *Scientific American* (online). http://www.sciam.com/1998/0298issue/0298techbus3.html.

Golding, F.N. 1989. "Stonehenge—past and future," in *Archaeological heritage management in the modern world.* Edited by H.F. Cleere, pp. 256–64. London: Unwin Hyman.

Gould, S.J. 1987. *Time's arrow, time's cycle: Myth and metaphor in the discovery of geological time.* Cambridge: Harvard University Press.

Greaves, T. 1994. *Intellectual property rights for indigenous peoples: A sourcebook.* Oklahoma City: Society for Applied Anthropology.

Greer, S. 1997. "Traditional knowledge in site recognition," in *At a crossroads: Archaeologists and First Peoples in Canada.* Edited by G.P. Nicholas and T.D. Andrews, pp. 145–59. Burnaby, BC: Archaeology Press/Simon Fraser University Press.

Hamann, B. 2002. The social life of pre-sunrise things: Indigenous Mesoamerican archaeology. *Current Anthropology* 43: 351–82.

Hamilakis, Y. 1999. *La trahison des archéologues?* Archaeological practice as intellectual activity in post-modernity. *Journal of Mediterranean Archaeology* 12(1):60–79.[yh]

———. 2003. Iraq, stewardship, and the "record": An ethical crisis for archaeology. *Public Archaeology* 3(2):104–11.[yh, so]

Hamilakis, Y., and E. Yalouri. 1996. Archaeology as symbolic capital in modern Greek society. *Antiquity* 70: 117–29.[yh]

Hampton, E., and S. Henderson. 2000. "Discussion paper on indigenous knowledge and intellectual property: Scoping the definitions and issues (executive summary)," in *Protecting knowledge: Traditional resource rights in the new millennium*, pp. i–vi. Vancouver, B.C., Canada.

Healy, D. 2003. The flag of Zia Pueblo. http://users.aol.com/Donh523/navapage/zia.htm.

Helmreich, Stephan. 2003. "Life @sea: Networking marine biodiversity into biotech futures," in *Remaking life and death: Towards an anthropology of the biosciences*. Edited by Sarah Franklin and Margaret Lock, pp. 227–59. Santa Fe: School of American Research. [so]

Hollowell, J.J. 2003. Digging for "old things": Perspectives on a legal market for archaeological materials from Alaska's Bering Strait. Ph.D. diss., Indiana University, Bloomington, Ind.

Hollowell-Zimmer, J.J. 2001. Intellectual property protection for Alaska native arts. *Cultural Survival Quarterly* 24(4).

Holm, B. 1990. "Kwakiutl: Winter ceremonies," in *Handbook of North American Indians*, vol. 7, *Northwest Coast*. Edited by W. Suttles, pp. 378–86. Washington, DC: Smithsonian Institution Press.

Hurst-Thomas, Favid. 2000. *Skull wars: Kennewick Man, archeology, and the battle for Native American identity*. New York: Basic Books. [so]

Industry Canada. 1995. *Canadian patent law*. Canadian Intellectual Property Office, Hull, QC, Canada.

Inter-Apache Summit on Repatriation. 1995. Inter-Apache policy on repatriation and the protection of Apache culture. MS.

Janke, T. 1998. *Our culture. Our future. Report on Australian indigenous cultural and intellectual property rights*. Surrey Hills, N.S.W.: Australian Institute of Aboriginal and Torres Strait Islander Commission/Michael Frankel.

Jemison, G.P. 1997. "Who owns the past?" in *Native Americans and archaeologists: Stepping stones to common ground*. Edited by N. Swidler, K.E. Dongoske, R. Anyon, and A.S. Downer, pp. 57–63. Walnut Creek: AltaMira Press.

Johnson, V. 1996. *Copyrites: Aboriginal art in the age of reproductive technologies (Touring exhibition* 1996 *catalogue)*. Sydney: National Indigenous Arts Advocacy Association and Macquarie University Press.

Jones, S. 1997. The archaeology of ethnicity: Constructing identities in the past and present. New York: Routledge.

Kari-Oca Declaration and Indigenous Peoples Earth Charter. 1992. Kari-Oca: World Conference of Indigenous Peoples on Territory, Environment, Development.

Kritsch, I.D., and A.M. Andre. 1997. "Gwich'in traditional knowledge and heritage studies in the Gwich'in settlement area," in *At a crossroads: Archaeologists and first peoples in Canada*. Edited by G.P. Nicholas and T.D. Andrews, pp. 125–44. Burnaby, BC: Archaeology Press/Simon Fraser University Press.

Laird, S.A., M.N. Alexiades, K.P. Bannister, and D.A. Posey. 2002. "Publication of biodiversity research results and the flow of knowledge," in *Biodiversity and traditional knowledge: Equitable partnerships in practice*. Edited by S.A. Laird, pp. 77–101. London: Earthscan.

Logan, M. 2003. Global systems selling out Indigenous knowledge. Inter Press Service News Agency. http://ipsnews.net/interna.asp?idnewsp21517.

Lohnse, E.S., and F. Sundt. 1990. "History of research: Museum collection," in *Handbook of North American Indians*, vol. 7, *Northwest Coast*. Edited by W. Suttles, pp. 88–97. Washington, D.C.: Smithsonian Institution Press.

Loring, Stephen. 2001. "Repatriation and community anthropology: The Smithsonian Institution's Arctic Studies Center," in *The future of the past: Archaeologists, Native Americans, and repatriation*. Edited by Tamara L. Bray, pp. 185–200. New York: Garland. [mfb]

McDavid, C. 2002. Archaeologies that hurt, descendants that matter: A pragmatic approach to collaboration in the public interpretation of African-American archaeology. *World Archaeology* 34:303–13.

Maffi, L. 2000. Language preservation vs. language maintenance and revitalization: Assessing concepts, approaches, and implications for the language sciences. *International Journal of the Sociology of Language* 142:175–90.

Mann, H. 1997. Intellectual property rights, biodiversity, and indigenous knowledge: A critical analysis in the Canadian context. Report submitted to the Canadian Working Group on Article 8(j) of the Convention on Biological Diversity.

Markey, N. 2001. Data "gathering dust": An analysis of traditional use studies conducted within Aboriginal communities in British Columbia. M.A. thesis, Department of Sociology and Anthropology, Simon Fraser University, Burnaby, BC, Canada.

Mataatua Declaration on Cultural and Intellectual Property Rights of Indigenous Peoples. 1993. Whakatane: Aotearoa/New Zealand. http://users.ox.ac.uk/wgtrr/mataatua.htm.

Matsuda, D. 1998. The ethics of archaeology, subsistence digging, and artifact looting in Latin America: Point, muted counterpoint. *International Journal of Cultural Property* 7:89–97.

Meighan, C.W. 1992. Some scholars' views on reburial. *American Antiquity* 57:704–10.

Merrill, W.L., E.J. Ladd, and T.J. Ferguson. 1992. The return of the *ahayu:da*: Lessons for repatriation from Zuni Pueblo and the Smithsonian Institution. Current Anthropology 34:523–67.

Mihesuah, D.A. 2000. *Repatriation reader: Who owns American Indian remains?* Lincoln: University of Nebraska Press.

Mohs, G. 1987. Spiritual sites, ethnic significance, and native spirituality: The heritage and heritage sites of the Sto:lo Indians of British Columbia. M.A. thesis, Department of Archaeology, Simon Fraser University, Burnaby, BC, Canada.

Morris, R. 1984. *Time's arrows.* New York: Simon and Schuster.

Myers, F.R. 1986. *Pintupi country, Pintupi self: Sentiment, place, and politics among Western Desert Aborigines.* Washington, DC: Smithsonian Institution Press.

NAGPRA (*Native American Graves Protection and Repatriation Act*). 1990. http://www.usbr.gov/nagpra/naglaw.htm.

Nankivell, S., and D. Wyse. 2003. *Exploring B.C.'s pictographs: A guide to native rock art in the British Columbia interior.* Burnaby, BC: Mussio Ventures.

Nicholas, G.P. 2001. The past and future of Indigenous archaeology: Global challenges, North American perspectives, Australian prospects. *Australian Archaeology* 52:29–40.

———. 2003. "Understanding the present, honoring the past," in *Indigenous peoples and archaeology*. Edited by T. Peck, E. Siegfried, and G. Oetelaar. Calgary: University of Calgary Archaeological Association.

———. 2004. "The persistence of memory, the politics of desire: Archaeological impacts on Aboriginal Peoples and their response," in *Indigenous archaeologies: Decolonizing theory and practice*. Edited by C. Smith and H.M. Wobst. London: Routledge. In press.

Nicholas, G.P., and T.D. Andrews. 1997. "On the Edge," in *At a crossroads: Archaeology and First Peoples in Canada*. Edited by G.P. Nicholas and T.D. Andrews, pp. 276–79. Burnaby, B.C.: Archaeology Press/Simon Fraser University.

O'Neill, G. 1994. Cemetery reveals complex aboriginal society. *Science* 264:1403.

Ouzman, Dven. Is audit our object? Archaeology, conservation, sovereignty. *Antiquity* 77(297). http://antiquity.ac.uk/wac5/ouzman.html. [so]

Parsons, J., and W. Denevan. 1967. Pre-Columbian ridged fields. *Scientific American* 217(1):92–101.

Patterson, T.C. 1999. *A social history of anthropology in the United States*. New York: Berg.

Peacock, S. 1998. Putting down roots: The emergence of wild food production on the Canadian Plateau. Ph.D. diss., University of Victoria, Victoria, B.C., Canada.

Pearlstone, Z. 2000. Mail-order "katsinam" and the issue of authenticity. *Journal of the Southwest* 42:801–32.

———. 2001. *Katsina: Commodified and appropriated images of Hopi supernaturals*. Los Angeles: UCLA Fowler Museum of Cultural History.

Pinsky, V., and A. Wylie. 1995. *Critical traditions in contemporary archaeology: Essays in the philosophy, history, and socio-politics of archaeology*. Albuquerque: University of New Mexico Press.

Posey, D.A., and G. Dutfield. 1996. *Beyond intellectual property rights: Toward traditional resource rights*. Ottawa: IDRC.

Preston, D. 1997. The lost man. *New Yorker*, June 16, pp. 70–81.

Ranger, Terence. 1993. "The invention of tradition revisited: The case of colonial Africa," in *Legitimacy and the state in twentieth-century Africa*. Edited by Terence Ranger and Olufemi Vaughan, pp. 62–111. London: Macmillan. [so]

Rathje, W.L. 1991. Once and future landfills. *National Geographic*, May, pp. 116–34.

Rathje, W.L., and C. Murphy. 1992. *Rubbish! The archaeology of garbage*. New York: HarperCollins.

Ritchie, D. 1994. "Principles and practice of site protection laws in Australia," in *Sacred sites, sacred places*. Edited by D.L. Carmichael, J. Hubert, B. Reeves, and A. Schanche, pp. 227–44. London: Routledge.

Robbins, A., and M. Becher. 1997–98. "Karl May Festival," in *German Indians*. Photographic display at Leslie Tonkonw Artworks and Projects, New York. http://robbecher.www4.50megs.com/TonkanowGIimagesframe.html.

Roberts, A. 2002. *Indigenous South Australian perspectives of archaeology project report*. Adelaide: Department of Archaeology, Flinders University.

———. 2003. Knowledge, power, and voice: An investigation of indigenous South Australian perspectives of archaeology. Ph.D. diss., Flinders University, Adelaide, Australia.

Rose, J.C., T.J. Green, and V.D. Green. 1996. NAGPRA is forever: Osteology and the repatriation of skeletons. *Annual Review of Anthropology* 25:81–103.

Sahlins, M. 1976. *Culture and practical reason*. Chicago: University of Chicago Press.

———. 1999. What is anthropological enlightenment? Some lessons of the twentieth century. *Annual Reviews in Anthropology* 29:i–xxiii.

Sheets, P.D. 1989. "Dawn of a new Stone Age in eye surgery," in *Applying anthropology: An introductory reader*. Edited by A. Poloefsky and P.J. Brown, pp. 113–15. Mountain View, CA: Mayfield.

Shennan, S. Editor. 1989. *Archaeological approaches to cultural identity*. London: Unwin Hyman.

Simpson, L.R. 1999. The construction of traditional ecological knowledge: Issues, implications, and insights. Ph.D. diss., University of Manitoba, Winnipeg, Manitoba, Canada.

Singleton, T.A. 1995. The archaeology of slavery in North America. *Annual Review of Anthropology* 24:119–40.

Smith, Benjamin W., J. David Lewis-Williams, Geoffrey Blundell, and Christopher Chippindale. 2000. Archaeology and symbolism in the new South African coat of arms. *Antiquity* 74(284):467–68.[so]

Smith, C.E. 1994. Situating style: An ethnoarchaeological study of social and material context in an Australian Aboriginal artistic system. Ph.D. diss., University of New England, Armidale, Australia.

Staley, D.P. 1993. St. Lawrence Island's subsistence diggers: A new perspective on human effects on archaeological sites. *Journal of Field Archaeology* 20:347–55.

Stanner, W.H.H. 1998. "The dreaming," in *Traditional Aboriginal society*, 2d edition. Edited by W.H. Edwards, pp. 227–38. South Yarra: Macmillan Australia.

Stephenson, D.J., Jr. 1999. "A practical primer on intellectual property rights in a contemporary ethnoecological context," in *Ethnoecology: Situated knowledge/located lives*. Edited by V. Nazarea, pp. 230–48. Tucson: University of Arizona Press.

Strathern, M. 1998. Comment on: Can culture be copyrighted? by Michael Brown. Current Anthropology 39: 216–17.[yh]

———. Editor. 2000. *Audit cultures: Anthropological studies in accountability, ethics, and the academy*. London: Routledge. [so]

Tanner, A. 2000. Image problem. *The Province* [Gabriola Island, BC], February 13.

Thomas, D.H. 1998. 3d edition. *Archaeology*. Fort Worth: Harcourt Brace.

———. 2000. *Skull wars: Kennewick man, archaeology, and the battle for Native American identity*. New York: Basic Books.

Tindale, N.B. 1974. *Aboriginal tribes of Australia: Their terrain, environmental controls, distribution, limits, and proper names*. Canberra: Australian National University Press.

Trigger, B.G. 1989. *A history of archaeological thought*. New York: Cambridge University Press.

Turner, N.J. 1997 (1978). Revised edition. *Food plants of interior First Peoples*. Vancouver: University of British Columbia Press/Victoria: Royal British Columbia Museum.

———. 1998 (1979). Revised edition. *Plant technology of British Columbia first peoples*. Vancouver: University of British Columbia Press/Victoria: Royal British Columbia Museum.

Watkins, J. 2000. *Indigenous archaeology: American Indian values and scientific practice*. Walnut Creek: AltaMira Press.

Wax, M.L. 1991. The ethics of research in American Indian communities. *American Indian Quarterly* 15:431–56.

Whiteley, P. 1997. "The end of anthropology (at Hopi)?" in *Indians and anthropologists: Vine Deloria Jr. and the critique of anthropology*. Edited by T. Biolsi and L.J. Zimmerman, pp. 177–208. Tucson: University of Arizona Press.

Williams, N.M., and D. Mununggurr. 1989. "Understanding Yolngu signs of the past," in *Who needs the past? Indigenous values and archaeology*. Edited by R. Layton, pp. 70–83. London: Unwin Hyman.

Winter, B., and D. Henry. 1997. "The *Sddlnewhala* bowl: Cooperation or compromise?" in *At a crossroads: Archaeology and First Peoples in Canada*. Edited by G.P. Nicholas and T.D. Andrews, pp. 214–23. Burnaby, BC: Archaeology Press/Simon Fraser University Press.

Wood, J.J., and S. Powell. 1993. An ethos for archaeological practice. *Human Organization* 52:405–13.

Wylie, Alison. 2000. Rethinking unity as a working hypothesis for philosophy of science: How archaeologists exploit the disunity of science. *Perspectives on Science* 7:293–317.[so]

———. 2002. "Ethical dilemmas in archaeological practice: The (trans)formation of disciplinary identity," in *Thinking from things: Essays in the philosophy of archaeology*. Compiled by A. Wylie, pp. 229–46. Berkeley: University of California Press.

———. 2004. "The promise and perils of an ethic of stewardship," in *Beyond ethics: Anthropological moralities on the boundaries of the public and the professional*. Edited by Lynn Meskell and Peter Pells. St. Louis: Berg Press. In press.

York, A., R. Daly, and C. Arnett. 1993. *They write their dreams on the rock forever: Rock writings in the Stein River valley of British Columbia.* Vancouver: Talonbooks.

Zimmer, J. J. 2003. "When archaeological artifacts are commodities: Dilemmas faced by native villages of Alaska's Bering Strait," in *Indigenous peoples and archaeology: Proceedings of the 32nd Chacmool conference.* Edited by T. Peck, E. Siegfried, and G. Oetelaar, pp. 298–312. Calgary: Archaeological Association of the University of Calgary.

Zimmerman, L. 1987. The impact of concepts of time and past on the concept of archaeology: Some lessons from the reburial issue. *Archaeological Review of Cambridge* 6(1):42–50.

———. 1997. "Remythologizing the relationship between Indians and archaeologists," in *Native Americans and archaeologists: Stepping stones to common ground.* Edited by N. Swidler, K. Dongoske, R. Anyon, and A. Dower, pp. 44–56. Walnut Creek: AltaMira Press.

Zimmerman, L.J., K.D. Vitelli, and J. Hollowell-Zimmer. Editors. 2003. *Ethical issues in archaeology.* Walnut Creek: AltaMira Press.

PART 3

Working in the Field
and Laboratory

Introduction

The selections in this part of the book were chosen primarily to provide a flavor of field and laboratory work. The first four selections, those by Kelly Dixon, Ronald Lippi, and Cornelius Holtorf, provide views of fieldwork from personal or social perspectives: What is it like to be involved in an archaeological field project? What kinds of things and decisions, both academic and practical, must a fieldworker deal with?

Lithics (stone) and pottery are two of the most frequently encountered categories of material remains from archaeological sites, and the last two selections—a piece about microwear analysis on stone and an overview of pottery studies—were included to provide some insight into the kinds of analyses that can be done with these remains.

"Historical Archaeology Methods: Much More Than Digging with Small Tools"

Kelly J. Dixon

This selection, targeted to a general audience, provides a good overview and case study of the nature of archaeological field and laboratory work. It was originally published as the Introduction to Kelly J. Dixon's *Boomtown Saloons: Archaeology and* *History in Virginia City*, published in 2005, which is based on her Ph.D. dissertation research. Dixon is currently a professor in the department of anthropology at the University of Montana.

•••

Questions to Guide Reading

What skills should a good fieldworker have?
What was the context of the Boston Saloon Project? Why was the site excavated? Who were the excavators? How was the public involved? What were the values being emphasized?
What was covered in the research design?
How were non-archaeologists involved in the project?
What kinds of resources are particularly useful for historical archaeology research projects?
What were the benefits of digging a test pit?
How was the main excavation area chosen?
What do "stratigraphic units" and "pedestaling artifacts" mean?
What is the "Harris Matrix system"?
How was the layer of ash from 1875 important?

•••

The very notion of archaeology evokes images of a field excavation, with people in brimmed hats bent over a gulf of contiguous pits. On hands and knees those dusty individuals delicately wield tools that are ridiculously out of proportion to the amounts of earth they excavate. Their mission: to discover long-lost and unexpected antiquities. For many, these scenes are fascinating to watch—either in person or on any number of entertainingly educational television programs.

In the face of such allure it is common to hear statements like, "I don't know if I could have the patience to sit in a hole all day and do that." For a unique handful of people, being part of such sincere, meticulous explorations is spellbinding. Much to the astonishment of friends and family, those few decide to make a life of archaeology. To do so, they need to learn a comprehensive range of archaeological methods and be aware of the theory lurking in the background.

Ironically, despite the most careful artifact removal and meticulous excavation, the very act of extracting historic or prehistoric objects from buried (or surface) contexts destroys the essence of an archaeological site.[1] Consequently, people working on archaeological projects have a responsibility to ensure that the nonrenewable settings that contained the remains they unearth are recorded in as thorough a manner as possible.

Archaeologists around the world deal with the frustrating reality that their science is inherently destructive. The trade-offs are nevertheless worth it and culminate in the discovery of long-lost and astonishing details about the human time line.[2] Given this rewarding undertaking, archaeologists continue to seek knowledge about the past and keep checks on the destructive nature of their science. Fieldwork is much, much more than digging. As a matter of fact, the most important qualification that one can bring to an excavation is good recording skills. Photographs, maps, detailed notes, and records chronicling the proveniences of a site's artifacts and features are essential for ethical archaeological fieldwork. The ability to keep impeccable records is a cornerstone of field methods and is an important part of the skills commonly taught to university-level students in archaeological field schools.

Public Archaeology

The concept of public archaeology was initially associated with projects undertaken as part of government-mandated salvage operations. Since the 1980s, members of the general public, through the mission of "public archaeology" and related volunteer programs, have also had the opportunity to learn archaeological field methods. The term came to refer to research that engages the public through volunteer programs, site tours, and cooperative work with descendant communities. Such activities were first developed at historic site museums, such as colonial Williamsburg, Monticello, and Mount Vernon, spearheading the new version of public archaeological research projects.[3] In 1993 public archaeology officially appeared in Virginia City, Nevada.

Since Virginia City and colonial sites date from the historic period, the type of archaeology to which many members of the public have been introduced is one that recovers recognizable objects, such as tobacco pipes. The thrill of being able to identify (and identify with) such artifacts is often juxtaposed against the surprise among the public that people carry out archaeological excavations from our relatively recent past. Archaeology has long been associated with far-off places and with sites of longer antiquity than the historic period in North America.[4] Nevertheless, many of the archaeological methods used at various sites and shared with the public can be applied to a range of ruins, be they ancient and exotic or recent and familiar. Archaeology in Virginia City yielded materials that helped to change the familiar and stereotypical conceptions of the "Wild West."[5]

One of the most striking places in the world, Virginia City, Nevada, is both a National Historic Landmark and a place where people live. Consequently, it has many layers. For example, its exterior cover has the enchanting appearance of a nineteenth-century western boomtown laden with saloons, boardwalks, miner-cowboy look-alikes, and a donkey. The place also has an inner layer of being "home" for many people, and it was home to many of their families before them.

Virginia City therefore became an exceptional place to carry out a public archaeology project that involved thousands of passerby tourists, neighboring residences and businesses, and a local community-based volunteer archaeology fieldwork program. Between 1993 and 1995 archaeologist Don Hardesty teamed up with historian and Nevada State Historic Preservation officer Ron James to develop a public archaeology program in the Virginia City National Historic Landmark. The fact that they initiated this project in the middle of the tourist season—and that the program also served as a training ground for archaeology students—was groundbreaking and created a standard for carrying out archaeological research in that community.

I was fortunate enough to begin research there after this paradigm for public archaeology became established. Two saloons were among the sites excavated by Don Hardesty's crews, and I had the opportunity to excavate two other saloons. Because the previous archaeological research had already blazed a path, I came upon a setting with a precedent for public historical archaeology in the mining West, and it had an existing database of saloon artifacts. This book is merely a part of ongoing archaeological research that is being synthesized with western history, and that subsequently contributes to a revisionist western history.[6] And since this book is about archaeology, it only makes sense to rewind to the part of this story that begins with the quintessential picture of archaeology: the fieldwork.

A series of existing documents, including excavation reports and a doctoral dissertation, already provides descriptions of the fieldwork for each saloon project.[7] Rather than repeat and describe the field methods for each saloon excavation here, which could become tedious, I focus in this section on the methods used at the Boston Saloon, which involved a significant public archaeology charter and represents the most recent of the saloon archaeological projects in Virginia City.

Public Archaeology and Field Methods at the Boston Saloon

The Boston Saloon project was the first excavation of an African American saloon in the mining West. In part, it served as a field school for university-level students, working under the instruction of Don Hardesty, to gain hands-on experience with excavation methods.[8] Additionally, the project emphasized the value of archaeological methods for African American history and for western history. It did not limit this approach to field school students, however,

but developed a multifaceted public archaeology program, with more than sixty-five volunteers participating in the fieldwork during the project's five-week period. More than three hundred children came up for brief but helpful visits throughout the summer as well.[9] To efficiently balance this massive public interest, the project's archaeologist and education director had to carefully schedule the visits of groups and volunteers for the summer field season before excavation. This strategy ensured that there were not too many people in too small a dig area.

Another facet of the Boston Saloon public outreach mission focused on the fact that archaeology gives many people—not just those directly involved with a dig—access to tangible remains of the past. The Boston Saloon student and volunteer crew routinely showed and described their findings to thousands of visitors who passed their excavation areas during the course of the five-week excavation. To cater to the people who were curious but who did not approach the excavations too closely, a large sign explaining the project stood at the edge of the site, with brochures about the Boston Saloon project and the role of African Americans in Virginia City attached to it.[10]

Before discussing the public's involvement during fieldwork, it is necessary to back up to the project's planning phase and discuss the public archaeology component at that point. First it was necessary to obtain permission from the owners of private property to conduct a public archaeology project on their land. The McBride family of Virginia City owns the Bucket of Blood Saloon, the property that contained the ruins of the Boston Saloon beneath its asphalt parking lot, and they kindly agreed to let their property be transformed from a parking lot to an archaeological dig during the busy summer tourist season. They agreed—with one major and quite fair condition: that somebody take responsibility for backfilling and repaving their parking lot at the end of the excavation.

After securing permission and appropriate permits, archaeologists do not just go out and randomly plunk holes into the ground in the areas where they believe sites are buried. Rather, they go into the field with a carefully written plan, a "research design." The research design for the Boston Saloon described what was known about that establishment by the spring of 2000, using information that had been gathered primarily from historical records. The design posed a series of questions that could potentially be answered by historical archaeology and then described how the archaeology would be carried out—and by whom—over a certain time line. A public archaeology mission was outlined in the research design, involving an outreach program that would invite African Americans from the area surrounding Virginia City (e.g., Reno, Sparks, and Carson City) to participate in the recovery of their heritage in the mining West, specifically in northern Nevada. The Reno-Sparks chapter of the NAACP aided this effort by distributing flyers about the project at local schools and churches, and the Northern Nevada Black Cultural Awareness Society (NNBCAS) received information packets about the project for their planning and informational purposes. Finally, Ceola Davis, the editor of the monthly newsletter *En Soul*, ran an article about the project in her publication, and this became another crucial level of outreach for the Boston Saloon story.

Continuing the project's charter of public involvement, a number of people from various public and professional backgrounds, including African Americans specializing in history and archaeology,[11] were asked to review and comment on the research design. The intent of this inquiry was to integrate non-Eurocentric ideas into the design, as well as to ensure the project's relevance for the region's African Americans.

After reading a draft of the research design, these individuals made recommendations for how research should be conducted, and their ideas were incorporated into the final plan for the Boston Saloon project.

For example, one of the committee members recommended that security measures be implemented to protect the site before and during fieldwork. Because of a long history of looting in Virginia City, including an incident that took place only a short while before the Boston Saloon was excavated, we were justifiably concerned about uncovering a site that had been capped and therefore well protected from looting by an asphalt parking lot *and* that represented the first of its kind to be examined archaeologically. Thus we explored several options for ensuring the site's protection once the asphalt was removed.

While committee members understood the grave potential for looters to damage freshly uncovered archaeological deposits, one individual expressed an additional concern, explaining that such security measures were essential to protect a heritage that others might seek to damage or erase in the name of racism. She was aware that the project would help to create a new memory in the region that was, in most mainstream circles, not part of the typical western story. This memory of a shared and diverse past in the West was, in the eyes of certain people, better left buried. Perhaps Eurocentrically, I had not even anticipated the possibility of such bigoted, negative reactions to the Boston Saloon project.

Security measures, although costly, therefore became an essential component of the project's public archaeology field methods. The same day that the backhoe lifted the asphalt layer from the Bucket of Blood Saloon's back parking lot, a security fence arrived. The fence surrounded the perimeter of the parking lot until the end of the excavation. The Bucket of Blood Saloon also agreed to have a temporary surveillance camera installed outside one of its upper-story windows. The camera provided twenty-four-hour coverage that, along with the fence, was intended to deter potential looters or vandals. Of course the camera also provided a means of recording and therefore aiding the prosecution of any actual looters and/or vandals.

Historical Research Methods for the Boston Saloon

While the research design outlined the planning process for the Boston Saloon project before anyone put a digging tool into the ground, it would have been impossible to find the right spot to begin excavation without the aid of historical research. Archaeologists researching the historic period would be lost without original records. Although it is necessary to be savvy about the inherent biases of the people who created those accounts, the fact remains that contemporary newspaper articles, maps, photographs, diaries, business directories, tax and property records, and census records are among the major sources that guide archaeological research of historic-period sites.

Such records are the domain of historians, which means archaeologists should consult with those specialists when considering fieldwork on historic sites.[12] Some historians are also aware of how the artifact record can enhance interpretations of the past. For example, soon after the 1997 founding of the Comstock Archaeology Center, Ron James, a historian and a cofounder of that organization, asked for a list of possible historical research topics that would benefit from archaeological research. An investigation of African Americans in the mining West was one of the suggested topics. The scarcity of archaeological investigations of African Americans in that region influenced the decision to prioritize that topic in Virginia City.[13] The initial research goals included a general focus on locating places where African Americans had worked and lived on the Comstock Mining District during the nineteenth century; at this point the research potential of the Boston Saloon was not fully realized.

Many of the kinds of historical records noted above, such as census manuscripts, nineteenth-century business directories, and county records, helped guide the research to find out how many people of African descent had lived in the district during the mining boom and to determine where they lived. We soon learned that African Americans in Virginia

City did not settle in a distinct or designated community as did people of Asian ancestry; the latter, most of whom came from mainland China, resided in the neighborhood known as Chinatown. While single African Americans were primarily dispersed along Virginia City's commercial corridor at that time, families lived in scattered locations downhill from that corridor, in areas with low real estate values on the edge of Chinatown and the mine dumps of the Consolidated Virginia Mine, but integrated within Virginia City's diverse community (Map 0.1). For example, they shared boardinghouses and neighborhoods with European immigrants and European Americans. Although it is inappropriate to overemphasize the degree of integration, especially given the complexity of ethnic relations that likely existed in Virginia City, it is still noteworthy that former slaves rented rooms from and lived next door to Europeans and European Americans.[14]

While the revelation of integration illustrates at least some sophistication on behalf of Comstock society during the Civil War and the Reconstruction era, the potential for mixed deposits deflated hope for archaeological remains that could accurately be linked with African Americans.[15] Furthermore, the many black-owned business enterprises left few traces of their presence from an archaeological point of view because they frequently changed locations. Therefore, the historical records initially suggested that it would be a difficult task to identify African Americans in Virginia City's archaeological record.

After correlating several historical references, Ron James homed in on the site of the Boston Saloon. Multiple lines of evidence, including newspaper articles from the *Territorial Enterprise*, the *Virginia and Truckee Railroad Directory* of 1873–1874, Nevada State Census records from 1875, and Sanborn-Perris Fire Insurance maps all pointed to the location of a saloon that served as the "popular resort for many of the colored population" and that was owned by African American William A.G. Brown.[16]

Oral histories are another valuable historical resource that can provide a layer of meaningful

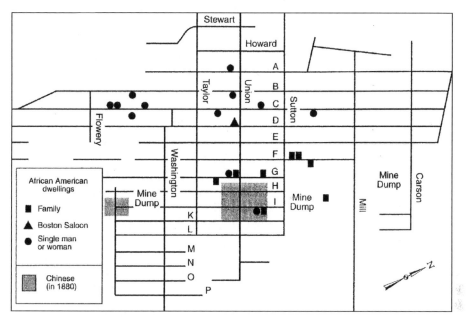

MAP 0.1: Map compiled by Ronald M. James using information from directories, census records, and fire insurance maps to show the various and integrated locations of African American households in Virginia City during 1873–1874. Modified from Ronald M. James, *The Roar and the Silence* (Reno and Las Vegas: University of Nevada Press, 1998), 99; courtesy of the University of Nevada Press.

depth for archaeological excavations. Although such material could potentially have given voice to African Americans in northern Nevada's late-nineteenth- or early-twentieth-century mining communities, the records were lacking.[17]

After the initial research had exhausted the possibility for oral histories and a nationwide press release requesting information about African Americans in Virginia City, Nevada, had been issued, it was clear that only a few lines of historical evidence were available to guide archaeologists in their interpretations of an African American saloon. These records indicated that the Boston Saloon operated at Number 4 South D Street, the southwest corner of D and Union Streets in Virginia City. The long-lived Boston Saloon stayed at that single location throughout most of its existence. This stability made it an anomaly among small businesses in a mining boomtown and—more important for

archaeologists—created a site with sufficient longevity to warrant archaeological investigation.

The current location of Number 4 South D Street is the asphalt parking lot, spanning 18.5 meters by 15.5 meters (61 feet by 51 feet), that sits on the east side of the Bucket of Blood Saloon. In addition to the Boston Saloon, the parking lot covered at least four other structures that were situated on the southwestern corner of D and Union Streets during the period between the 1860s and the 1870s. The site was a garden during the 1930s, a dirt parking lot from the 1950s to the late 1970s, and an asphalt parking lot since about 1980.[18]

Field Methods at the Boston Saloon

Asphalt lots present pretty significant barriers for people who usually dig with trowels. Even so, this difficulty was a minor obstacle compared with the profound potential of recovering the tangible heritage of a group of people who had been excluded—for the most part—from the archaeological stories of the Wild West. We had only to figure out how to remove and replace the parking lot in the name of archaeology. The solution to the problem required some relatively unconventional archaeological techniques, such as using heavy equipment.

Before storming the site with heavy equipment, archaeologists needed to dig a test pit. This crucial prelude to a major excavation helps to determine the nature of buried deposits and provides a preview of the stratigraphic, or layered, appearance of a site.[19] Fortunately, a small patch of ground in the parking lot had not been paved over, so this area was selected as the site for a test pit in 1998, two years before the official parking lot removal and excavation.[20] The test pit revealed a colorful contrast of layers in the earth beneath the parking lot, including a band of gray ash. Beneath that lay a distinct blackened layer, full of charred wood fragments and burned, disfigured splinters from broken glass objects. Just beneath the burn layer, a tiny fragment from the pedestal of a crystal goblet emerged. When combined with Virginia City history, these layers revealed a story that was about to make the pending excavation of the Boston Saloon even more thrilling. The burn layer was a blatant reminder of Virginia City's terrifying and massive Great Fire of 1875.

In the case of the Boston Saloon, that grayish-black temporal marker took on deeper meaning because the establishment's proprietor, William A. G. Brown, had closed his saloon in 1875, just months before the Great Fire, and the fire layer literally capped the remains of the Boston Saloon. Because Brown's establishment had operated for nine years at that single location, material traces of the saloon, such as the pedestal from a crystal wineglass, were lost, thrown out, and subsequently built up in tiny layers until they were covered by the charred wood and ash of the 1875 fire. Realizing this, archaeologists knew that the remains of the saloon were protected

and likely in pristine condition beneath the parking lot. The results of the test excavation deemed it worthwhile and quite essential to undertake a major excavation, starting with the removal of the entire parking lot.[21]

The first step in the excavation of the Boston Saloon, then, was to use a backhoe to remove the parking lot. The backhoe carefully peeled back the asphalt without disturbing any of the earth beneath it. Artifacts immediately became visible, and so the archaeology crew took a conservative position and did not use the backhoe to dig any deeper.

After the removal of the asphalt, the crew established a 1 x 1 meter grid for an open-area excavation, set up a screening area, and erected a tent for the field laboratory. The one-meter squares helped to maintain strict control within the open-area excavation. The grid spanned a 6 x 12 meter area on the ground beneath the parking lot that coincided with the site of the Boston Saloon.

The crew did not excavate several portions of the site, leaving a 1 x 6 meter baulk[22] intact in the center of the excavation grid and a larger, 2 x 6 and 3 x 6 meter baulk along the east-central edge of the grid as a means of preserving portions of the Boston Saloon site for future studies. They also avoided the westernmost portion of the site in the name of additional site preservation and to prevent undermining the Bucket of Blood structure; the field lab was subsequently set up in this area. The crew also avoided the southeastern portion of the parking lot because of time constraints and because the area lay outside the Boston Saloon site. Another unexcavated area was a narrow strip outside the saloon's northern border. The crew avoided this area because of time constraints, because it was not thought to be part of the Boston Saloon site, and because the area was used for screening stations.

As the crew members commenced hand excavation, they realized that the artifacts immediately beneath the asphalt represented displaced deposits in a fill layer. The fill was not part of the site's historic deposits and had obviously been brought in to construct the asphalt parking lot. Once the crew realized how deep the fill layer was, they used a "Bobcat" to peel away the fill material in order to expedite excavation.[23] Once the fill was removed, the crew continued with careful hand excavation in the historic deposits.

The crew dug in stratigraphic units and pedestaled artifacts in situ within each distinct stratigraphic deposit or surface as a means of assuring that the field school students developed careful excavation techniques. *Pedestaling* refers to leaving artifacts where they were uncovered, atop tiny pedestals of earth. Crew members then mapped and photographed each stratigraphic unit and its respective artifact deposits before moving on to underlying contexts. That way, even though the crew removed major portions of the saloon's nineteenth-century deposits, it would be feasible to reconstruct the site by fitting together all of the crew's notes, maps, and photos. While digital photography was available at the time of the Boston Saloon excavation during the summer of 2000, the crew decided to fall back on the more conservative and traditional use of manual cameras with color slides and black-and-white print film.[24]

Even though the excavation crews carefully mapped and photographed hundreds of artifacts as they found them, small items, such as thin glass shards and tiny beads, were often caught by trowel cuts and scooped up in dustpans with ash and clay. These tiny objects were found when the crew carefully screened small fractions of material from their excavation units through one-eighth-inch mesh. The project tracked all excavated artifacts, whether found in situ or in screens, by recording artifact specimen bag and associated provenience information on a master artifact bag sheet.

In addition to keeping strict records regarding the provenience of recovered artifacts, the Boston Saloon excavation employed the Harris Matrix system to document the site's stratigraphic context.[25] The Harris Matrix provides a system for recording the various layers of an archaeological site. Ideally, a site should be excavated by paying attention to the vertical nature of a particular layer and by following the horizontal extent of that layer. That way, an entire stratigraphic context can be excavated as one episode that has a three-dimensional character, and, all artifacts from that episode will be collected as part of a clearly defined deposit.

This method is a challenging undertaking in the learning environment of a field school, though, so the archaeologists laid out a 1 x 1 meter grid to provide student excavators with at least some horizontal area control by assigning everyone respective "squares" in which to excavate. Then they excavated by following the change(s) from one stratigraphic layer, or context, to another. Because of the nature of the open-area excavation, the horizontal contexts were still visible across various contiguous excavation units. For example, the thin 1875 fire layer clearly appeared as a horizontal context; as the crew dug beneath that context, they exposed its vertical context, or depth.

The Harris Matrix system uses the term *context* as a generic term to describe the various types of stratigraphic units that excavators encounter. For example, a context may represent a *deposit* (e.g., ash or clay) or it may represent something like a surface (e.g., floor or ditch within a building foundation). *Context* also refers to an interface, which is the dividing line between deposits; these dividing lines are sometimes described as the surfaces of each subsequent deposit.[26] This means that a *surface* is often referred to as an *interface* when describing the point of contact between deposits. The methods employed for recording the stratigraphic units of the Boston Saloon site represented an attempt to designate a separate context number for each layer and each surface/interface between each layer to provide a separate record for each discrete unit of stratification.[27]

The site's stratigraphic makeup started with a line of fill immediately beneath the asphalt. The fill blanketed the topmost part of the site and was between 25 and 30 centimeters, or roughly one foot, thick. Artifacts contained within this fill included nineteenth-century objects and modern materials such as candy wrappers and plastic drinking cups. While the fill represents a modern occurrence that was necessary for paving the parking lot, the presence of historic artifacts is a clue that the fill itself likely came from somewhere in or around Virginia City.

Beneath the fill, the site's layers revealed two general activity areas. One is the westernmost portion of the excavation grid, where there was a dump and an alley behind the saloon structure. In general, artifacts dating from the 1890s and early 1900s appeared in the shallower portion of the dump, giving way to items from the 1860s and 1870s below. The deepest materials in the dump rested on bedrock, which was 60 centimeters below the surface, demarcating the end of historic cultural deposits in that area. On the basis of the artifact density and dates of the materials, it could be concluded that people threw trash in this dump from the early days of Virginia City's development up to the early twentieth century when the McBride family transformed the area into an orchard. Ash deposits appeared in association with the upper and lower dump deposits and likely represent activities such as burning garbage in the alley. Structure fire probably helped create these two burn deposits, including the well-documented Great Fire of 1875.

A distinct ash deposit appeared in the eastern portion of the site as well. This second portion of the site held the saloon structure, with charred but intact floorboards portraying the most visible remains of that structure. The ash layer and floorboards were 40 centimeters below the surface, beneath a 10-to-15-centimeter-thick deposit of building materials and late-nineteenth-century artifacts. The latter likely represent materials associated with post-1875 occupation of the site, because the ash layer and charred floorboards denote building debris from the 1875 fire.

Because the Boston Saloon closed its doors shortly before that fire, the ashy matrix, as suggested by the pre-excavation test pit, provided a noticeable temporal marker for distinguishing the Boston Saloon from other activities that took place at the corner of D and Union Streets. This is significant because of the complex nature of archaeological deposits in urban settings; businesses move in and out of buildings, and new buildings are constructed atop previous structures in such settings. Indeed, this was the case in Virginia City, which means many activities took place at the corner of D and Union Streets. It was important for the excavation to determine which stratigraphic deposit could be associated with the Boston Saloon's lengthy nine-year tenure at the street corner.

Artifacts from the layer immediately beneath the 1875 fire layer could confidently be associated with the pre-1875 operation of the Boston Saloon at that street corner. Artifact dates correlated with the latter half of the nineteenth century, with a paucity of modern intrusions, providing a confident date range for the stratigraphic layers that held the ruins of the saloon. The fact that the bulk of those artifacts included liquor bottles, glassware, and a handful of food serving vessels provided another type of data, since such items imply saloon activities during the latter portion of the nineteenth century. This evidence, in turn, instilled confidence that the material recovered and analyzed did indeed represent one of the several activities at a bustling Virginia City street corner; and thanks to historical records, it could be verified that the Boston Saloon was one of the operations in that location.

Laboratory Methods and Publication

Contrary to the popular image of archaeologists bent over in dusty pits, most modern-day archaeologists spend more time conducting laboratory analyses, writing reports, and publishing data than they spend in the field. The general rule with archaeological lab methods is that at least three days are needed in the lab for every one day spent in the field. The Boston Saloon project proved that this rule could be extended, for it took students and laboratory employees three years to see the project to completion after returning from the five-week field session.

During this time, the laboratory crew sorted artifacts by material of manufacture and initially classified each object or set of objects according to that material (e.g., glass, ceramic, metal, bone). However, classification systems that account only for materials hinder analyses and are problematic when applied to comparative studies.[28] Because of this, the Boston Saloon's artifact classification system, that is, its catalog of artifacts, was designed to identify the traditional functions of the historic artifacts (e.g., nails and window glass have more explanatory power about a site's makeup when they are categorized in a functional "architectural" category instead of according to the sterile but necessary material functions of metal and glass).[29]

The Boston Saloon's artifact catalog was therefore designed to accommodate such details about the tens of thousands of artifacts recovered from that site. This was the approach taken at the beginning of lab work and continued simultaneously with that work. It meant that at the lab in the University of Nevada's Department of Anthropology a massive artifact catalog and database were created. Lab activities included sorting, cleaning, mending, labeling, and analyzing artifacts, and employing forensic testing and faunal analyses. Finally, the cataloged and cleaned artifacts were prepared for storage and exhibits, with storage box numbers built into the artifact database to allow easy access to each item.

Report preparation and publication is considered the final stage of archaeological research, for this is the medium through which archaeologists compile and interpret their discoveries, or more technically, their data. Don Hardesty, with the assistance of others, prepared a report of his saloon investigations at the Hibernia Brewery and O'Brien and Costello's Saloon and Shooting Gallery.[30] Similarly, I prepared a report that detailed the methods and discoveries at Piper's Old Corner Bar.[31] The data compilation and interpretation of the Boston Saloon site became my doctoral dissertation.[32] In addition to creating reports, archaeologists described research from all of the above investigations at professional conferences and are beginning to publish that research in peer-reviewed journals.[33] This book, along with a proposed exhibit, "Havens in a Heartless World," represents other aspects of the final phase of research, with the goal of making the general results of all four saloon studies accessible to a wide audience.

Even after the preparation of a book like this, archaeological methods are really not exhausted. This publication is merely one person's attempt to make sense of a bulk of archaeological materials with the hope of ever so slightly revising western history. The artifacts are still available for exhibits, for further analysis, for different interpretations, and for other stories about the West. If the archaeologist's methods have been truly successful, artifacts and excavation records will provide material for analysis and comparison for decades or even centuries to come.

Notes

[1] The term *site* is a generic term for a grouping of artifacts or material remains and features that, collectively, demonstrate a concentrated area of human activity in the past. For the most part, it is common archaeological jargon and needs little more definition or discussion. However, some archaeologists argue that the notion of "site" should be discarded altogether in favor of smaller units of analysis: artifacts and the continuous distribution of those artifacts on and near the surface of the earth; for a discussion of this view, see

Robert Dunnell, "The Notion Site," in *Space, Time, and Archaeological Landscapes*, edited by Jacqueline Rossignol and LuAnn Wandsnider, 21–41 (New York: Plenum, 1992); see also James Ebert, *Distributional Archaeology* (Albuquerque: University of New Mexico Press, 1992).

[2] Special thanks to Giles C. Thelen for reminding me of the positive effects of archaeological excavation.

[3] Larry McKee, "Public Archaeology," in *Encyclopedia of Historical Archaeology*, edited by Charles Orser, Jr., 456–458 (London and New York: Routledge, 2002).

4 James Deetz, Foreword to *A Chesapeake Family and Their Slaves: A Study in Historical Archaeology*, by Anne Elizabeth Yentsch, xviii–xx (Cambridge: Cambridge University Press, 1994).

5 Even with the basic methods, each archaeological project tends to treat its resources on a case-by-case basis, slightly modifying standard techniques to work with the nuances of the infinite number of site types.

6 For example, Patricia Nelson Limerick, *The Legacy of Conquest: The Unbroken Past of the American West* (New York: Norton, 1987); Elliott West, *The Way to the West: Essays on the Central Plains* (Albuquerque: University of New Mexico Press, 1995); Mary Martin Murphy, *Mining Cultures: Men, Women, and Leisure in Butte, 1914–1941* (Urbana: University of Illinois Press, 1997); Ronald M. James, *The Roar and the Silence* (Reno and Las Vegas: University of Nevada Press, 1998); Ronald M. James and C. Elizabeth Raymond, eds., *Comstock Women: The Making of a Mining Community* (Reno and Las Vegas: University of Nevada Press, 1998).

7 Donald L. Hardesty et al., *Public Archaeology on the Comstock*, University of Nevada, Reno report prepared for the Nevada State Historic Preservation Office (Carson City: Nevada State Historic Preservation Office, 1996); Kelly J. Dixon et al., "The Archaeology of Piper's Old Corner Bar Virginia City, Nevada," Comstock Archaeology Center Preliminary Report of Investigations (Carson City: Nevada State Historic Preservation Office, 1999); and Kelly J. Dixon, "A Place of Recreation of Our Own." *The Archaeology of the Boston Saloon: Diversity and Leisure in an African American–Owned Saloon, Virginia City, Nevada* (Ann Arbor, MI: University Microfilms International, 2002).

8 In addition to fieldwork, field school students spent time in the University of Nevada's Getchell Library and Special Collections, the Nevada State library and Archives, and the Nevada Historical Society to experience historical research in relation to the site upon which they worked. They prepared notes of their historical research, many of which included maps denoting a reconstruction of businesses and other activities around the Boston Saloon site, to accompany their field notes. Finally, each student turned in a formal paper that addressed an aspect of archaeological fieldwork. Visiting scholars also gave Virginia City field school students, volunteers, and public visitors the opportunity to learn about the different ways in which various archaeologists approach field methods. For example, Adrian and Mary Praetzellis of Sonoma State University provided insights on the methods of conducting urban archaeology and interpreting the complex stratigraphic contexts of an urban site. During his visit, Paul Mullins of Purdue University gave a slide presentation detailing his work with African American archaeology in Annapolis;

this gave students working on the Boston Saloon site an understanding of how their project fit in the bigger picture of African American archaeology.

9 The Boston Saloon Project's education director, Dan Kastens, orchestrated the visits of such large numbers of children, going to many of their schools before the field trips to the site to provide young students with brief overviews of the project and excavation methods.

10 The media were also a consistent presence during the five-week period of excavation. Media coverage of the Boston Saloon project spanned local print and television news, as well as a nationwide range of media outlets such as the *San Francisco Chronicle*, September 19, 2000; the *Boston Globe*, September 12, 2000; *Archaeology*, November/December 2000; and *American Archaeology*, Winter 2000–2001.

11 The committee included Michael S. Coray, special assistant to the president for diversity at the University of Nevada, Reno; Lucy Bouldin, director of the Storey County Library, Virginia City; Ken Dalton of the Reno-Sparks NAACP; Elmer Rusco, professor of political science, University of Nevada, Reno; and Theresa Singleton, Syracuse University, Syracuse, New York; finally Lonnie Feemster, then president of the Reno-Sparks NAACP, received a copy of the research design. In addition, the Comstock Archaeology Center Technical Advisory Board (Ken Fliess, Don Hardesty, Gene Hattori, Ron James, David Landon, Pat Martin, Susan Martin, and Ron Reno) received copies of the research design for review before the fieldwork commenced.

12 Ron James carried out the initial historical investigations that were specifically focused on the Boston Saloon. These are summarized in "African Americans on the Comstock: A New Look," a paper presented at the Conference on Nevada History, in Reno, Nevada, May 1997. In "*Good Times Coming?*" Elmer Rusco provides a history of African Americans in Nevada during the nineteenth century and presents a starting point for understanding African Americans on the Comstock; "*Good Times Coming?*" *Black Nevadans in the Nineteenth Century* (Westport, CT: Greenwood, 1975).

13 The "West" here is defined as the area west of the 100th meridian, and the "mining West" is treated as the extant and ruined remnants of mine operations and boomtowns throughout that region. The literature on African American archaeology reveals many works on African American history in the West; for many African Americans living in the nineteenth century, the West was seen as a place of "economic opportunity and refuge from racial restrictions," yet African American writers' accounts of prejudice reflect the disillusionment that many African Americans experienced after confronting racist restrictions and attitudes. The first quote is taken from Quintard Taylor, *In Search of the Racial*

Frontier: African Americans in the American West, 1528–1990 (New York: Norton, 1998), 81, and the accounts of prejudice came from African American writers, such as Thomas Detter, and were published in the *Pacific Appeal*, February 22, 1868, 2, and October 8, 1870, 1. The *Pacific Appeal* was an African American-edited newspaper that operated out of San Francisco between 1863 and 1883. Its circulation reached various communities throughout northern California and extended to other areas, including Idaho, Nevada, Oregon, Washington, Victoria Island, and Panama. This resource contains an array of primary sources written by people of African ancestry, offering alternative perceptions of life in the West, rather than the more prevalent Eurocentric observations about that region. Despite these and other writings about African Americans from the standpoint of western history, there were only a few archaeological investigations of free black populations in that region: Todd Guenther, "At Home on the Range: Black Settlement in Rural Wyoming, 1850–1950" (master's thesis, University of Wyoming, 1988); Adrian Praetzellis and Mary Praetzellis, "We Were There, Too": Archaeology of an African-American Family in Sacramento, California, Cultural Resources Facility, Anthropological Studies Center (Rohnert Park, CA: Sonoma State University, 1992); Margaret C. Wood, Richard F. Carrillo, Terri McBride, Donna L. Bryant, and William J. Convery III, *Historical Archaeological Testing and Data Recovery for the Broadway Viaduct Replacement Project, Downtown Denver, Colorado: Mitigation of Site 5DV5997*, Archaeological Report No. 99–308 (Westminster, Colorado: SWCA, Inc., Environmental Consultants, 1999); Adrian Praetzellis and Mary Praetzellis, "Mangling Symbols of Gentility in the Wild West," *American Anthropologist* 103 (2001) 3: 645–654. Thus, the archaeological record of African Americans was scant west of the 100th meridian and absolutely lacking in the context of the mining West.

[14] James, *The Roar and the Silence*, 152.

[15] Despite such implied sophistication, people of African descent who lived on and visited the Comstock during the latter part of the nineteenth century found themselves in a complex political climate that overtly and subtly pervaded many aspects of their lives. For example, in *The Roar and the Silence* (7, 152–153), Ron James tells the story of this group on the Comstock to demonstrate an intriguing pattern of integration, marginal survival, and success. On the one hand, they appeared to have more freedom and opportunity on the Comstock than in many other parts of the country in terms of economic successes and overall integrated living, yet their lives were still not as simple or easy as those of their white neighbors before and after 1881. Racist undertones and overtly restrictive attitudes and laws affected the black population there, and their lives featured a complex juxtaposition of integration and prejudice, neighborly acceptance and ill treatment. Such variation in treatment of African Americans in the West was common, experienced by residents of Virginia City, Nevada, and by African American soldiers stationed throughout the West; see Frank N. Schubert, "Black Soldiers on the White Frontier: Some Factors Influencing Race Relations," *Phylon* 32 (Winter 1971): 411.

[16] *Territorial Enterprise*, August 7, 1866.

[17] There are no oral histories on record that represent African Americans living in northern Nevada during the recent past; Thomas King, personal communication, 2002.

[18] Don McBride, personal communication, 2000.

[19] *Stratigraphy* is the description, correlation, and classification of distinct layers of the earth, with each stratum being a homogenous layer that is visually separated from the other layers; see George "Rip" Rapp Jr. and Christopher L. Hill, eds., *Geoarchaeology: The Earth-Science Approach to Archaeological Interpretation* (New Haven, CT: Yale University Press, 1998).

[20] Special thanks to Ron James, Tim McCarthy, and Cal Dillon for their assistance with this testing.

[21] This was made possible after two years of fundraising resulting in grants from the Nevada State Historic Preservation Office, the National Endowment for the Humanities, and private donors.

[22] Also spelled "balk," this term refers to an unexcavated block of earth that archaeologists leave in place between their excavation units. When placed at various intervals throughout an excavation, baulks provide archaeologists with a constant visual reference to the layers they previously exposed.

[23] Special thanks to Ahern Rentals of Gardnerville, Nevada, for donating the use of the Bobcat to assist with this next stage of excavation; also thanks to field school student and project member Diane Willis for contacting Ahern Rentals on behalf of the Boston Saloon project. Gratitude to Larry Buhr for being on hand to operate this machinery.

[24] In retrospect and now well after many archaeologists have made the technological transition to digital photos, high-quality digital photos should have made up another component of the site's photodocumentation. Because they can be viewed instantly, digital photos allow archaeologists to see if their photos turned out "on the spot." When relying on the more traditional, manual camera photography, unless they had the means to develop negatives in the field, archaeologists could not know whether their field photos would turn out. Since they needed to accurately photograph excavated layers before removing them and excavating further, problems like poor photos or overexposed film could ruin the core record-keeping charter of archaeology for the project in question. The instant

feedback available with digital photos allows archaeologists to verify that they have captured the details of the site so that they can move on and excavate the next layer with confidence.

25 Edward Harris, *Principles of Archaeological Stratigraphy*, 2d ed. (London: Academic Press, 1989).

26 Ibid. xiv.

27 The assumption behind this splitting rather than lumping methodology was that it was better to split each stratigraphic context first and then seek similarities among the nature and cultural deposits of each context. Some could then be "lumped" together later; however, if they were lumped together first in the field, potential details of unique context could become lost because of someone's attempt to figure out which general context should be associated with which newly exposed layer; see also Dixon, *"A Place of Recreation of Our Own,"* appendix A, "Stratigraphic Description of the Boston Saloon Site."

28 Roderick Sprague, "A Functional Classification for Artifacts from Nineteenth- and Twentieth-Century Sites," *North American Archaeologist* 2, no. 3 (1980): 251.

29 Ibid., 259.

30 Donald L. Hardesty et al., *Public Archaeology on the Comstock*, University of Nevada, Reno report prepared for the Nevada State Historic Preservation Office (Carson City: Nevada State Historic Preservation Office, 1996).

31 Dixon et al., "The Archaeology of Piper's Old Corner Bar, Virginia City, Nevada."

32 Dixon, *"A Place of Recreation of Our Own."*

33 Donald L. Hardesty and Ronald M. James, "'Can I Buy You a Drink?': The Archaeology of the Saloon on the Comstock's Big Bonanza" (paper presented at the Mining History Association Conference, Nevada City, California, June 1995); Kelly J. Dixon, "The Archaeology of an Upscale Saloon: Purchasing Champagne, Cigars, and Status at Piper's Old Corner Bar" (paper presented at the Society for Historical Archaeology, Atlanta, 1998); Kelly J. Dixon, "Archaeology of the Boston Saloon: An African American Business in a Western Mining Boomtown" (paper presented at the Society for Historical Archaeology, Long Beach, CA, 2001); Kelly J. Dixon, "The Urban Landscape and Sensory Perception of D Street, Virginia City, Nevada" (paper presented at the 35th annual meeting of the Society for Historical Archaeology, Mobile, AL, 2002); Kelly J. Dixon, "Diversity in the Mining West: DNA and Archaeology at the Boston Saloon" (paper presented at Society for Historical Archaeology, Providence, RI, 2003); Kelly J. Dixon, "From Babylonian Taverns to Western Saloons: Establishing a Temporal Context for Social Drinking" (paper presented at Society for Historical Archaeology, St. Louis, MO, 2004); Kelly J. Dixon, "Survival of Biological Evidence on Artifacts: Applying Forensic Techniques at the Boston Saloon," *Historical Archaeology* 39, no. 1 (forthcoming).

"Looking for Sites in All the Right Places"

Ronald D. Lippi

Although excavation is the popular image of archaeological fieldwork, far more of it involves looking for sites. This selection comes from the book *Tropical Forest Archaeology in Western Pichincha, Ecuador* by Ronald Lippi, published in 2004. Lippi is a professor at the University of Wisconsin, Marathon County. The book was published as a case study in archaeology, designed for introductory and intermediate level students.

Questions to Guide Reading

What is the rationale for undertaking a regional survey?
What were the problems associated with the survey?
How was global positioning system technology incorporated into the project?
What were the three broad objectives of the survey?
What does "stratified random quadrat sampling" mean?
What is meant by "opportunistic survey"?
What specific methods were used to look for sites?
Why was the concept of "site" complicated for the project?
What kinds of information were collected when sites were initially discovered?
What were the two main purposes of undertaking subsurface testing at some sites?

The Rationale for a Regional Survey

An archaeological survey is the systematic search for sites. Recent and newly emerging technology—including detailed photography from earth orbit, thermal infrared imagery, ground-penetrating radar, and other remote-sensing devices—has already begun to revolutionize how surveying is done. Nonetheless, these methods are often not available or affordable, nor are they always appropriate. When all is said and done, the classic method of pedestrian surveying—systematically walking over the territory looking for artifacts and features on the surface—remains the most common method of finding sites and was utilized to the extent possible in Western Pichincha.

Prior to the 1960s, surveying was frequently little more than a prelude to excavation. Since that time, surveying, especially of large regions, has emerged as an extremely valuable strategy by itself. Regional surveys provide important data about various kinds of sites in differing habitats throughout a territory, whereas excavations provide detailed data on a single site within a single niche. Moreover, excavating is extremely painstaking, slow, labor-intensive, and costly compared to pedestrian surveying. While excavations certainly provide very useful kinds of information, so do surveys. Among the goals of regional surveys one can list studies of settlement patterns, area population, economic adaptations to natural environments, ethnic boundaries, and human migration patterns, among other important facts.

There are also conservation considerations: sooner or later archaeology students learn the maxim "To excavate a site is to destroy it." Whereas excavation of even a small portion of a site results in the destruction of context and association in the site, surveying and the collection only of surface artifacts are much less destructive of the archaeological record. Modern archaeology has turned more and more from the excavation of sites to their preservation. As the human population continues to grow rapidly and as development threatens an ever-increasing number of sites throughout the world, surveying presents itself as an effective strategy by which to salvage a significant portion of the vanishing archaeological record.

In Ecuador prior to the Western Pichincha Project, surveying had been done only on a much smaller scale, usually within a locality of several square kilometers, but not across an entire region of the country. Choosing to do a regional survey across a territory that was unexplored archaeologically yet was bounded both to the east and the west by known archaeological complexes seemed a reasonable strategy to pursue. Not only could such a project open up a new region to study, but it could also make connections between disparate cultures and begin to form a broader, more complete picture of prehistory in that part of the continent.

Western Pichincha—A Surveyor's Hell?

Accessibility was the first formidable problem encountered as the project got underway. The landscape, particularly of the cloud forest, is extremely rugged; the forest cover throughout many sectors of the region is very dense; and roads are few and far between. Getting into the region and then moving around freely within it were difficult undertakings. During the course of the project, the road problem improved due to the construction of a major highway through the region and the gradual opening up of various secondary roads. This improved access considerably. For example, whereas it used to take four hours to travel by a very bad road from Quito to Mindo, where we spent several months excavating a site, after the new paved highway was constructed, Mindo could be reached comfortably in less than two hours. Nonetheless, during the early years of the project, travel into and through the research region was mostly very slow and restricted.

Having a four-wheel-drive vehicle in decent condition was another prerequisite for travel in the area that turned out to be quite a challenge. For the first two years of the project, I had to use my own vehicle, an old Nissan Patrol (an early, rustic prototype of today's SUVs). The Patrol was in poor condition but was our only means of travel within the region. The vehicle was constantly breaking down on us, and we lost a lot of field time because of it. I tallied more than thirty flat tires before losing count, and on eight occasions the rear axle springs broke and had to be replaced, which should give the reader some indication of the roughness of the roads. We had many other breakdowns, including a gasoline tank that leaked like a sieve and brakes that failed on a hairpin mountain curve, much to our dismay. In subsequent field seasons, we tried to rent a reliable vehicle, but that was always very costly and something of a crapshoot.

While driving around Western Pichincha, we had to negotiate countless "bridges" (and I use the term loosely). Although the bridges on the few main roads were well-built concrete bridges, once we got off the main roads, we encountered bridges that were improvised by the local inhabitants, most of whom did not have motor vehicles and built bridges primarily for pedestrians and horses. The simplest bridges comprised three or four large trees that were felled and positioned to straddle a stream. Sometimes a few wooden planks were laid over the tree trunks, and other times we simply had to steer the vehicle carefully to stay on the trunks. At the opposite extreme were fairly elaborate suspension bridges. These swayed noticeably under the weight of our vehicle and sagged in a very disconcerting manner. One large suspension bridge had originally been built with six huge steel cables, three on each side, from which the bridge was suspended. When a gravel quarry was opened in the area, large dump trucks began using the bridge and strained it so much that only two of the six cables remained.

Perhaps the most interesting bridge was a very nice concrete bridge built in a village that was in a contested part of Western Pichincha; the territory was claimed by both Pichincha and Esmeraldas provinces. Each provincial government in turn tried to lure the villagers to identify with their province through building projects. One province built a one-room school, and the other built a bridge. What was odd about this bridge was that there was no vehicle road into the village, only a narrow horse trail that led directly to this wide, two-lane concrete bridge.

The actual archaeological surveying was done on foot. Often it was pleasant to leave the rattletrap vehicle and bumpy roads and to take off walking along jungle paths. On only one occasion did we borrow a couple of horses to take us into a particularly remote region of forest. Despite the countless footpaths that crisscrossed different sectors of Western Pichincha, the overwhelming majority of the research region, in terms of surface area, could not be directly accessed for pedestrian survey. Following roads and trails necessarily limited the survey to very restricted linear transects, as will be discussed more in the text that follows.

Visibility of the ground surface was the second major difficulty in the pedestrian survey, which relies on visual inspection of the ground for surface artifacts or structures. The dense vegetation severely limited artifact or structure visibility. The ground cover over much of the region is rainforest of one type or another, with dense undergrowth. In areas where the forest has been cleared, one most commonly finds pastureland with high, dense, tropical grasses. Even in the agricultural areas, such as in sugarcane fields and banana or African palm plantations, the soil around the plants and trees is not cultivated, and there is dense weed growth. Large structures, such as tolas, are visible in pastures or other cleared areas, but small structures and surface artifacts are hidden. Only during the very short time that deforestation is in process and before herding or agriculture has gained a foothold—that is, while the terrain is recently cleared—is it feasible to survey the land away from roads and trails. The discovery of such clearings at the right time was due to a combination of perseverance and luck. Even a lost city would be difficult to find under such conditions.

The Ecuadorian Air Force has an inventory of aerial photographs of virtually all of Western Pichincha, and I was able to study those at the Military Geographic Institute in Quito. Although I have some training in inspecting aerial photographs with a stereoscope (an optical device similar to a child's ViewMaster™ that creates the illusion of three-dimensional viewing), the photographs were not useful because of the dense vegetation.

Even when plant cover was sparse or absent, surface artifacts were not always visible because of volcanic activity in the area. The occasional eruption of a few nearby Andean volcanoes over the millennia has buried much of the surface under tephra (volcanic ash, sand, and pumice stone). When it comes to excavations, this stratigraphy of volcanic sediments is actually advantageous, since the ash layers serve as dividing layers of known age. However, the most recent major ashfall (not including two minor ash-falls in 1999) took place in 1660, when Pichincha volcano immediately west of Quito erupted and covered much of Western Pichincha with several centimeters of ash. That means that even the latest pre-Hispanic (pre-1532) occupations in the region, unless the sediments have been eroded or otherwise disturbed, are covered over. This series of ashfalls over time also means that early pre-Hispanic sites are often very deeply buried. For example, a series of ashfalls in the first millennium A.D. deposited as much as 2 m (6 ½ ft.) of ash in some areas of Western Pichincha, so any sites prior to that are very difficult to find.

The third and final major impediment to the surveying of Western Pichincha was the deficiency of maps of the region, which in turn made it difficult to determine the precise location of many sites that were discovered. Although the Military Geographic Institute has worked for decades to produce detailed topographic maps of all of Ecuador, such maps for the eastern half of Western Pichincha were out of date with regard to villages and roads and occasionally slightly unreliable; no topographic maps even existed for the western half of the region. For the western half, topographic maps eventually became available during the later seasons of fieldwork, but all the early work was done without the benefit of such maps. Instead, we relied upon planimetric maps, which lack the topographic (relief) information and were often erroneous, since they were only preliminary maps. The topographic and planimetric maps were mostly at a scale of 1:50,000, although a few topographic maps were available at 1:25,000. The government census bureau also produces maps at a scale of 1:50,000 for use by census workers in rural areas. Although these maps were updated every few years with regard to trails and villages, they were often deficient when it came to natural features of the landscape.

Even when we had reliable topographic maps for a particular sector in which we were looking for archaeological sites, there was typically some imprecision in determining the exact location of those sites

on the maps. That is because most sites were discovered as we walked on foot over roads and trails that may or may not have been shown accurately on the maps. When we discovered a site on or near a road or trail, we still had to determine where we were, and this usually involved triangulation using a compass. I would stand at what appeared to be the middle of the site and take compass readings to two or more landmarks, which usually were mountain peaks but also might be a distant church steeple or some other human-made structure. In some cases, there was no visible landmark, either natural or artificial, because we were too far from such things or because of low clouds or tall trees. In those instances, we had to estimate how far we had walked. In other situations, if a site was discovered relatively near a road, we used the vehicle odometer to give us the distance (to within tenths of kilometers) from a landmark along the road, such as a bridge or kilometer marker. Even this technique failed us when the odometer on the vehicle stopped working for a few weeks.

All in all, we did the best we could in describing how to reach the site and where it was located to make it feasible for us or other researchers to revisit the same site in the future. There can be no guarantee, however, that all the site coordinates are exact.

By the short 1996 season, we were able to take advantage of the relatively new GPS (global positioning system) technology to determine the site coordinates with greater accuracy. The GPS system, developed and maintained by the U.S. Department of Defense, uses a handheld device that receives signals from satellites in earth orbit. The signal from each satellite allows the GPS receiver to calculate the coordinates and elevation of the site. Prior to the year 2000, the U.S. Defense Department, in order to maintain a military advantage, intentionally reduced the accuracy of the system for civilian use so that a site location could usually be determined only to within about 100 meters. As of 2000, that built-in inaccuracy for civilian receivers was removed, so site coordinates in the future should be accurate to within a few meters or less. Because this new technology was not available during most of the survey project and because there has not yet been time to revisit all of the approximately 300 sites, many of the site locations are still only approximations. Also, GPS does not work in canyons, some valleys, or areas of dense forest where the receiver is unable to obtain clear satellite signals. Nonetheless, in 1996 we found that for previously recorded sites where we used GPS to check the coordinates, our earlier estimates were usually very close to the ones obtained through GPS.

The Survey Strategy

The strategy guiding any research project has to be predicated on the goals of the research. Given that nearly all of Western Pichincha was unexplored archaeologically prior to this project, the goals were quite general and broad:

- Salvage part of the North Andean archaeological record by investigating a region of rapid development and concomitant site destruction
- Perform a regional survey in the northern Andes of South America in order to focus on broad cultural development over time and space
- Survey the western flank of the Andes from the summit of the Andes to the Pacific coastal plain to study cultural and developmental similarities and differences with the coast and sierra

Under these broad objectives, more specific goals were laid out prior to the start of the project:

- Determine the antiquity of human occupation of the region
- Identify early agricultural/pottery-making complexes (Formative cultures) that connect the northern sierra Cotocollao culture with well-known Formative coastal cultures, including Valdivia, Machalilla, and Chorrera (all of which were the focus of my previous research)
- Determine the nature of early human adaptation to the different types of rainforest in the region

- Define the various pottery complexes of the region and establish a tentative ceramic chronology for dating sites
- Define distinct prehistoric cultures of the region and determine their spheres of influence
- Catalog extant pre-Columbian structures, including tolas (artificial earthen mounds), house foundations, and forts
- Trace the evolution of trade within the region and with the coast and highlands, and search for trade routes
- Determine the degree of Inca incursion and supremacy in the region

Given these multifarious objectives, the enormous size of the research region, a very limited budget, and the special challenges of accessibility, visibility, and cartography, a regional survey at first glance appears impractical. The standard survey techniques of systematic field walking and shovel testing to locate sites and collect artifacts were unquestionably not feasible. In fact, I spent the first two months of fieldwork in 1984 traveling around Western Pichincha, becoming more familiar with the region and desperately trying to think of new ways to approach a survey in an area where the classic methods were inoperable. By the end of two months, I had a fair idea of specific techniques to use, although our survey methods continued to evolve during the first couple of years.

To give the reader who is unfamiliar with classic archaeological surveying a sense of what should have been done but could not be done, I present Figure 4.1. This map shows the entire research region covered by a grid. Within each major ecological zone, a percentage, say 10%, of randomly selected grid units is marked for systematic surveying. Within each selected grid, the survey team is expected to perform a complete pedestrian survey, visually inspecting the entire surface area and marking and retrieving surface artifacts. In areas with vegetative cover, small test holes dug with

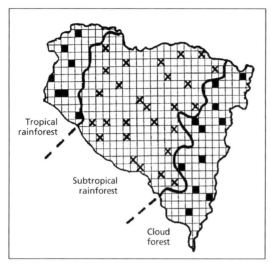

FIGURE 4.1: The Western Pichincha research region with superimposed grid showing areas that might have been surveyed intensively given a systematic stratified quadrat strategy

Tropical rainforest

Subtropical rainforest

Cloud forest

and techniques that provide for surface inspection of any sectors that have been opened up through natural or human disturbance. Whereas a systematic sample is performed so as to provide optimal representative coverage of a region, an opportunistic sample is performed to provide whatever coverage is possible.

The specific methods used in combination that resulted in the opportunistic sample of Figure 4.2 are presented in the following text.

Inspection of Roads

Pedestrian surveys along roads turned out to be the most utilized method of the project. Bulldozers move a considerable amount of soil in creating roads, and often expose archaeological sites in the process. Road building is also accompanied by removal of vegetation within the right-of-way, which facilitates surveying. Artifacts may be visible in road cuts (where the machinery has cut through a hill) as well as in the roadbed. Some roads

a shovel at regular intervals (the shovel-testing method) provide a sampling of what lies near the surface. This strategy is known as a stratified random quadrat sample and is considered one of several desirable strategies that will provide data susceptible to statistical manipulation to represent the entire research region. It is called "stratified" because each environmental zone is sampled independently, "random" because each surveyed grid within each environmental zone is selected using a table of random numbers rather than intuitively, and "quadrat" since the basic survey unit is a quadrat or square. None of this could actually be done for the reasons already noted.

Figure 4.2, on the other hand, is a map of the region showing the land area that was actually surveyed during the various field seasons from 1984 to 1997. Obviously, the survey performed bears no resemblance to the ideal survey. What was actually done I have chosen to refer to as an *opportunistic survey* rather than a systematic one. An opportunistic survey includes those improvised methods

Survey transects

Tulipe area surveyed by Isaacson

FIGURE 4.2: The Western Pichincha research region showing transects actually surveyed on foot using an opportunistic strategy

were covered with gravel or crushed stone brought in from quarries, and those roadbeds were not surveyed due to the possibility of "contamination" (finding artifacts trucked in from a distance). Needless to say, any artifacts found in the dirt roadbeds were generally very fractured due to foot, horse, or vehicular traffic. It is also safe to assume that they were in a secondary context, presumably near to but not in exactly the same position in which they were originally discarded.

Inspection of Footpaths

Various kinds of trails for horses and pedestrians are much more common than vehicular roads, but they are less likely to reveal archaeological sites because they are so narrow and usually do not erode significantly into the surface. Nonetheless, because trails were so common and provided access to many sectors not having roads, this method was frequently used. As will be discussed in Chapter 7, some trails that were quite deeply eroded turned out to be ancient paths.

Inspection of Sites Identified by Local Inhabitants

Whenever residents of the region informed us of possible archaeological sites based on their observations over the years, we made every effort to visit those sites and to authenticate the purported remains. More often than not, these well-intentioned reports turned out to be bogus; as is true in many parts of the world, even well-educated persons with no archaeological experience often mistakenly identify natural objects as artifacts or natural hills as artificial mounds. Reports of mounds almost always turned out to be spurious, in part because many rural Ecuadorians understand the word *tola* slightly differently from the way archaeologists use it, and in part because mounds are often difficult to distinguish from natural features. Even archaeologists working in Ecuador sometimes confuse hills and artificial mounds through only casual observation. Trying to authenticate such information usually led us on a wildgoose chase, but occasionally these reported sites turned out to be valid and worth our trouble.

Using Place Names to Locate Sites

Certain local place names appearing on maps often indicated the presence of a site. For example, Inca forts were typically built on hilltops and consisted of stone walls arranged in concentric ovals. To a casual observer, these ruins may appear from above like a spiral, and they are often called *churos* (snails) on maps because of their shape. The word *tola* frequently occurs on maps; sometimes the name actually marks the location of mounds and sometimes not, perhaps because the mounds have disappeared over time or because someone once mistook a natural elevation for a mound. We were also interested in locating an ancient salt mine or salt spring reported by the Spanish, so we were always suspicious of the Quichua word *cachi* (salt) or *cachiyacu* (salt water) on maps. Even the words *Yumbo* and *Inga* (Inca) appeared in a few places throughout Western Pichincha, leading us to those locations to look for ruins or other evidence of Yumbo or Inca presence.

Systematic Surveying of Cleared Fields

Fields recently cleared of vegetation either for construction or for planting were few, small, and far between, but we always took advantage of such fields when we came across them. Whenever they were encountered, we would systematically walk the clearing and collect artifacts from the exposed surface. It is significant that practically any time we found such a clearing, there was an archaeological site there, suggesting that the prehistoric occupation of Western Pichincha was very widespread. Unfortunately (from an archaeological perspective), such clearings were all too rare.

Searches Based on Ethnohistoric Records

The Spanish colonial record summarized briefly in the previous chapter also provided a basis for surveying. In particular, Yumbo or Nigua villages, even though they are nonexistent today, are referred to, and enough geographic information is included in archival data to suggest their approximate locations. Concerted efforts were made to survey these localities in order to identify the "lost towns." This method was sometimes successful, sometimes not. It was complicated by the aforementioned fact that Indian "towns" in the region were dispersed rather than nucleated; they were not really villages so much as loose clusters of scattered houses.

These various methods used in combination resulted in the survey pattern illustrated in Figure 4.2. While the survey was not systematic in the usual sense of the word, every effort was made to do opportunistic surveys throughout the region, leaving no major sectors completely unexplored. In that sense, the survey was successful. As will be seen in Chapters 7–8, the amount of information obtained from this haphazard survey was very substantial.

Getting Permission

Although an agency of the Ecuadorian government gave us permission to conduct archaeological research in the region, we were responsible, as is usually the case, for getting permission from individual landowners to enter their property. In most cases, however, we crossed private property without being able to detect property lines (fences are not widely used except where cattle have been introduced) and carried out our daily surveys without encountering any owners or caretakers of whom we might ask permission. After all, we were surveying in many areas that are considered wilderness, even though some lands within those areas have been legally purchased or homesteaded or have been claimed by squatters' rights. When we did encounter local inhabitants, we usually took a few

minutes to engage them in conversation, explain our work, ask for permission to walk over their property, and inquire about any sites they might know. During the many seasons of fieldwork, we found the people (whether homesteaders, poor squatters, or wealthy absentee landowners), almost without exception, to be very friendly and cooperative. Rarely were we turned away, and then it was usually by a family that was employed as caretakers for a wealthy landowner who lived in a distant city rather than on his or her land; in these cases, the caretakers usually instructed us to contact the landowner in Quito or elsewhere to get permission.

Cataloging Sites

One of the most fundamental concepts in archaeology is that of the *site*, which is defined as a cluster of artifacts, features, and/or ecofacts[1] that indicate human presence in antiquity. While the concept may seem simple, in the field it can become complicated even during a systematic survey, and downright tricky in a survey such as the one we were performing. Archaeologists do not agree on the minimum density of artifacts for defining a site. The simplest conceivable site might be a single small stone flake in isolation, while the most complex is an ancient city. Finding just one flake in isolation does not tell the archaeologist very much and really reduces the concept of site down to something that may not be at all useful in understanding the past.

The techniques used for finding sites in this densely forested region often revealed only a very small part of what may have been a large site. Perhaps the trail cut through only a corner of a site, thereby explaining why there were so few artifacts. On the other hand, a very small site may have been used by only a few people for a few hours, and the little material found on the surface might be representative of what lies below. In some instances, we followed a road or path for a kilometer or more and found a very low density of artifacts distributed nearly continuously along the trail. Does that distribution signal a very large town, a series of somewhat dispersed farmsteads, or several very small and separate sites that were occupied at different times but which now seem to overlap?

These and similar complexities continually plagued us as we proceeded with the survey. As our procedure evolved over the course of the project, we did not always define sites by the same criteria. Nonetheless, since our objective was not simply to find out how many different sites there were in the region but rather to see how humans utilized space over time, what was most important was simply recording artifacts and features where they were found and then going back and trying to make sense of the distribution.

The only artifacts ever found during the many field seasons were potsherds, and occasionally other ceramic pieces, small stone tools or unused flakes, and ground stone tools. If only one or a few tiny artifacts were found over an area, we began to treat that as an isolated find (as opposed to a "site"), but we cataloged the finds just as we would have cataloged a larger number of artifacts or features such as mounds or stone walls. The only difference is that we expected to learn something useful about the indigenous peoples from sites, whereas isolated finds held little promise. Altogether, we cataloged nearly 300 sites and a couple dozen isolated finds. This does not mean that we discovered some 300 discrete occupations or locales for human activities; what it means is that we identified approximately 300 locations where humans were present in antiquity and left some evidence that we could find on the modern surface.

Upon discovering a site or isolated find, we had to take adequate notes so that detailed site registry forms could be filled out back in Quito. Enough time was spent at each site to describe as precisely as possible the location of the site and directions on how to arrive at it, as well as the apparent size and density of the site (if this could be determined with any confidence). We also described the natural environment, including relief, vegetation, nearby water sources, soil conditions, and the current condition of the site (e.g., banana plantation, disturbed by road cut, severely eroded, disturbed by looters, etc.). Artifacts visible on the surface of the site were collected and labeled for laboratory analysis. If there were few artifacts, as was often the case, we collected whatever we could find. At sites with a dense accumulation of artifacts visible on the ground surface, we began by collecting everything in small areas of the site and then continued by collecting only those artifacts, especially diagnostic potsherds and stone tools, that would be most useful in determining the age and cultural affiliation of the site. If there were any visible structures at the site, such as mounds or walls, they were sketched and photographed. In fact, photographs were taken of nearly every site to augment the written notes. The Archaeology Museum of the Central Bank, for whom we worked during the early years of the project, had its own forms for recording site data, and we used those forms for cataloging all new discoveries.

The National Institute of Cultural Heritage (INPC in Spanish) is the Ecuadorian government agency that oversees archaeological research and grants permits for work such as ours. That agency also maintains a registry of all known archaeological sites in the country. Upon filling out the site forms, we made copies and submitted them to the INPC for filing and reference by other archaeologists.

Sites were coded in three different ways, according to common practice and the requirements of the INPC. Ecuador uses the same system found in most countries of the Americas, in which sites are identified according to local political units. In the United States, this means sites are identified by state, then county, then by a number indicating their order of discovery. For example, the prehistoric city of Cahokia near Collinsville, Illinois, has a site code of 11-Ms-2, where "11" stands for Illinois, "Ms" for Madison County, and "2" for the second archaeological site cataloged in that county. In Ecuador, this system has been adapted to designate the province, the canton, the parish, and the order of discovery. Accordingly, the site P-LB-Mi-7 is the Nambillo site (discussed in Chapters 5–6), which was the seventh site registered in Mindo parish (Mi) of Los Bancos canton (LB) of Pichincha province (P). For the sake of simplicity, I will identify sites in this book at times simply by their parish and number (e.g., Mi-7) instead of writing out the entire designation. Because the central government occasionally creates or realigns cantons and parishes, some sites had to be recodified to reflect changing political boundaries.

The INPC also requires that sites be identified by coordinates, and there are two widely used global coordinate systems. The first is the familiar latitude and longitude system that measures degrees, minutes, and seconds north or south of the equator and east or west of the prime meridian. Because this system uses base 60 and is not readily convertible into common English or metric units, we also use another coordinate system known as UTM (Universal Transverse of Mercator). This numerical system is metric, so the coordinates are directly convertible into meters or kilometers on maps that have a printed kilometer grid on them.

In order to protect unguarded archaeological sites from depredation by looters or tourists, the catalog information, including coordinates, is available only to professional archaeologists.

The Subsurface Testing of the Nambillo Site

Although an enormous amount of information can be obtained through regional surveys, we projected from the beginning of the project the need to do some subsurface testing at one or a few sites fairly early in the project in order to provide supplemental data. The two most important reasons for augmenting the survey data with excavation data are the following. First, the survey stage of the project was expected to lead eventually to an excavation stage,

and it was uncertain how feasible it would be to excavate and find substantial physical remains in this tropical rainforest habitat. The dense vegetation, logistical challenges, acidic soil, and very high humidity all conspire to make excavations difficult and to degrade the physical remains. Doing a test excavation fairly early would help to determine whether an excavation stage of the project would likely be worth the trouble. Our work at the Nambillo site showed us that excavation projects in the region were indeed feasible, that the site was in reasonably good condition despite millennia of volcanic activity and forest growth, and that subsistence data (especially animal bones and charred seeds) were going to be hard to come by in that environment.

Secondly, a significant drawback to survey data based on the collection and study of surface artifacts is that stratigraphic information is excluded. Even though it is possible to establish a chronological sequence for artifacts based on changing styles in surface collections (a method known as "seriation"), it is exceedingly difficult to do unless pottery is abundant and fairly elaborately decorated, which was clearly not going to be the case for most of Western Pichincha. Even when a seriation can be performed, distinguishing between the start and the finish is still dependent on the kind of external data most likely to come from stratigraphic excavations. Only by observing the sequence of pottery styles (or whatever other category of artifacts is being used) in the ground from bottom to top can one be certain that the ordering of artifacts is reliable. By performing limited test excavations at one or a few sites early on, we would then have a sort of anchor upon which to build and refine our ceramic chronology. As it turned out, the excavations at Nambillo provided sufficient pottery in a clear stratigraphic sequence to create a timeline that can be used, at least tentatively, for much of Western Pichincha and that can be related to pottery sequences in neighboring areas.

Note

1. Ecofacts are a category of archaeological data consisting of unmodified materials that were taken to the site by its former occupants or that occur there naturally and help specialists in reconstructing the ancient environment or human activity. Examples are animal bones, fish scales, fossil pollen, and charred plant remains.

"Studying Archaeological Fieldwork in the Field: Views from Monte Polizzo"

Cornelius Holtorf

The study of archaeologists engaged in fieldwork, an area of recent interest, is known as the ethnography of archaeology. This selection by Cornelius Holtorf, a professor at the University of Lund in Sweden, appeared in the edited volume *Ethnographies* *of Archaeological Practice: Cultural Encounters, Material Transformations*, published in 2006. The book was based on presentations on the same topic at the World Archaeology Congress in 2003.

• •

Questions to Guide Reading

What are Holtorf's research methods?
Why is fieldwork considered to be an initiation rite for archaeologists?
What are some elements of the professional culture of field archaeologists?
What kinds of tensions among people were observed?
How does the heavy metal rock group Iron Maiden figure in the article?

• •

Ethnography of archaeology is a new but fast-growing field of interest and approach, investigating the practice and materiality of professional archaeology. Often the focus is on archaeological fieldwork, as the present volume illustrates. My own contribution addresses the question of what kind of experience project members have on an archaeological excavation project. Besides the way a project can be described in academic terms, for example in field reports, I will be asking precisely what it means to participate in an archaeological project from the participants' point of view and what it is they are actually learning during an excavation. This matters particularly when excavations are designed as student training excavations, making it pertinent to study the learning experiences and outcomes.

My case study consists of the ongoing excavations at Monte Polizzo in western Sicily (Morris et al. 2001; Prescott and Mühlenbock 2003; Mühlenbock and Prescott 2004). This large international coproject involving partners in Italy, Norway, Sweden, and the United States is committed to a joint research strategy including common ways of digital recording, scientific sampling, and finds administering. My research extends and complements a number of other studies that have focused on the character of archaeological fieldwork at Monte Polizzo (Avikunthak 2001; Pearson and Shanks 2001, 28–32; Shanks 2001–2003; Holtorf 2002; Shanks 2004, 497–99).

During the summers of 1999 and 2000 I took part in the Monte Polizzo project for four and three weeks respectively. My methodology consisted mostly of participant observation, aided by my camera and a journal. In addition, near the end of both my stays I distributed two-page questionnaires (in English and Italian) to as many project participants as possible. In 1999, I received forty completed questionnaires, in 2000 only eighteen. The questions were a mix of queries about possible improvements for future seasons and questions specifically designed to explore the experience of participating in the project. All my own research was conducted openly and I answered many questions about it. I believe that it was widely understood that everybody could speak to me openly without their interests or reputations being harmed as a consequence, which is why I have anonymized most references to specific people in this paper.

At the time of my research, the community of archaeologists at Monte Polizzo consisted of about fifty-five (in 1999) and over eighty (in 2000) project participants from many countries. About three-quarters were students or recent graduates. Although it was not a homogenous group, but one that differed vastly in academic experience, ranging from undergraduates in other disciplines to various research students in archaeology, anthropology, or classics, all will be called "students" in this chapter. The group of students was the largest and also the one easiest to observe by freely mingling among them, so that it became the main focus of my research. Another reason for not taking into account to the same extent the experiences of the project leaders and various independent experts was that I had no access to their meetings and discussions and a lot of the time I was guessing—with the students—about their true agendas and the precise character of the evidently existing disagreements between them. Since I began my research in 1999, two senior members have resigned from the project.

Overall, my experience in this project was very positive. I met many interesting people from diverse backgrounds, worked at some great locations, was surrounded by much challenging and exciting archaeology, undertook some fantastic excursions to various sites in the area, and benefited a great deal from the good organization of the project. The overall evaluation of the project by other participants was similarly positive. Nevertheless, for heuristic reasons only, I will be saying unproportionally more about those tensions and frictions that arose.

On Archaeological Cultures

Fieldwork has always been considered a crucial part of archaeology's identity, both inside and outside the discipline (Welinder 2000, chapter 4). Among archaeologists, those who do not do fieldwork are often mocked as armchair archaeologists. It is therefore not surprising that practical fieldwork is widely considered of central importance for the training of students. In the field, students become "real" archaeologists by learning the practical skills and methods of academic archaeology. The various universities cooperating at Monte Polizzo made this aspect of fieldwork the key content of their project descriptions. The 1999 field prospectus for Monte Polizzo by Stanford University is an ambitious document, making much of the academic potential of both the site and the project, and again emphasizing field methodology. Likewise, The Sicilian Archaeological Field School run by Michael Kolb of the Northern Illinois University (NIU) invites students to "Learn how to excavate, survey and conduct lab analysis," gaining them six hours of anthropology credits.

When in international coprojects teams from various countries—with their own disciplinary traditions—apply different research methodologies to their own trenches, all sorts of faultlines can emerge that run right across the entire project, creating tensions and animosities on all levels (see, e.g., Hamilton 2000). At Monte Polizzo, as elsewhere, students learned very different kinds of archaeological practice depending on which team they happened to be working with. I remember the disbelief with which a senior team leader looked down on the methodology applied in one particular working area by another team (Pearson and Shanks 2001, 29). I also remember the dismay that was caused when it emerged that the recording of the entire site, managed fully electronically by one team, was duplicated by another team that apparently thought that only their own, traditional recording system could be relied upon. Moreover, there was one area of excavation that some observers considered to be conducted with a very poor excavation methodology indeed.

Going into the field can be considered the principal initiation rite for an apprentice archaeologist, where the professional culture of the discipline is transmitted from one generation to the next (Moser forthcoming; Welinder 2000, 54–60; Carman 2004; see also chapters by Bateman, Carman, Van Reybrouck and Jacobs, and Wilmore in this book). There students learn the unspoken rules, attitudes, and lore of their discipline and they, too, can differ strongly between different archaeological traditions. Stories about the hardship of archaeological fieldwork and anecdotes about students or colleagues that derive from a shared experience of being in the field are popular subjects of conversations among archaeologists of all ages. Personal friendships (and animosities) with future colleagues are established in the field too. The professional culture of archaeology also encompasses such elements as

- ritual feasts;
- digging songs (see also Eibner et al. 1996);
- site-specific vocabulary referring to food (combat bread, cf. Avikunthak 2001), people (Don Kolbo, Pop Karin, Lolita), places (the Swedish hill), things (Banks mobil), or larger issues (the Kristianisation of western Sicily);
- oral traditions, for example, about how the professor bought large numbers of Kinder chocolate eggs in order to get to the toys inside, or how X and Y were secretly interested in each other;
- and behavioral norms including eating manners and dress codes, for various occasions.

Learning such rules of the game, or tacit knowledge, can be of crucial significance in determining whether or not students relish becoming archaeologists and succeed in their subject or not. For "competence in the cultural life of the discipline ... functions as an informal sorting device, often without the sorters and the sorted being aware of the fact" (Gerholm 1985, 2; see also Becher 1989). It is mainly this dimension that makes archaeological fieldwork so significant in educational terms: you learn how to "do" excavation (Carman 2004, 49).

At Monte Polizzo (in 2000), different archaeological cultures could be studied by focusing on distinct working areas on the site (Figure 7.1). The American NIU team engaged in survey work and small excavations at some distance around the main site, so that its members were not normally in sight of the others during working hours. On Monte Polizzo itself, a Scandinavian team of Norwegians from Oslo and Swedes from Göteborg excavated at House 1 and in some trenches nearby. A local Italian team from Palermo dug at Portela St. Anna. A small group of other Sicilians investigated the Necropolis. Finally, another American team, from Stanford University, occupied the Acropolis area and ran the finds lab in the excavation base back in the town of Salemi. Since the various teams did not generally share all their tools and equipment, they might even be kept apart on the basis of their material culture alone and thus be identifiable as archaeological cultures in the conventional sense. The same cultural differences were also manifested in language boundaries that effectively ran both across the mountain and, back in our base in Salemi, across the long table where we ate our main meals together.

In 1999 students were encouraged (and in 2000 allowed) to move between the various working areas of the different teams, in order to be confronted with the variety of traditions and learn about different methodologies, but many never made use of this opportunity. Even those students who did rotate were never left uncertain about which archaeological culture they belonged to themselves. In their questionnaire answers, many mentioned that the student rotation scheme was

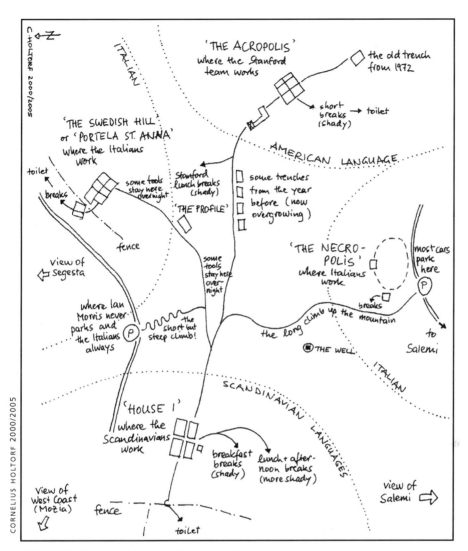

FIGURE 7.1: A sketch map of Monte Polizzo

not working as it should and wished that it be better coordinated by the senior team leaders. My own cultural affiliation was not simple. In 1999, I lived in Göteborg and felt close to the Swedish participants but was officially part of the Stanford team. In 2000, I came from England but was officially part of the Norwegian team.

Fieldwork as a Social Experiment

In the evenings and on weekends, the existing cultural distinctions were played out socially. Sometimes, what members in one team found appropriate was considered offensive, bizarre, or downright embarrassing by others. Toward the end of the 2000 season, for example, the Stanford students publicly awarded various fun awards to members of their team—what others felt would have been appropriate on a scout camp but hardly on a professional excavation project. On another occasion, they commemorated the US Independence Day (July 4) by singing loudly the American national anthem on top of the Italian mountain (see also Holtorf 2002, 68)—to the complete astonishment and disbelief of various onlookers. Some Scandinavians and NIU students, in turn, were considered unwelcoming and cold, even aggressive, because they did not project sufficient friendliness and seemingly lacked requisite small-talk abilities ("Can she actually smile at all?" somebody wondered about a Swede). In another significant episode, one person decided to set fire to the maypole that the Swedes had erected for their midsummer celebrations, even though this was not the Swedish custom and explicitly resented by some of them.

As a result of such experiences, social mixing between members of the various teams only went so far. Sometimes even at the beach they were sitting in separate groups. The reasons for the existing social divisions among the various groups of students were manifold and partly also linked to

- varying durations of participation in the project (in 1999, many Stanford students stayed a considerably shorter time than most others);
- age differences (Scandinavian students were older on average than American students);
- varying personal motivations (for most Stanford students, the project was a holiday experience and a chance to visit Europe—whereas the Scandinavians and NIU students participated in order to advance their archaeological careers);
- the variation in students' social backgrounds and in status of their universities (especially ordinary NIU versus Ivy League-caliber Stanford);
- associations with different Western regions and cultures, and the prejudices associated with them (directed mostly against the Californians);

- varying linguistic abilities and ambitions (whereas some Italians struggled with English as the project's lingua franca, few others were trying to pick up conversational Italian, and the Scandinavians occasionally fell back on their own languages); and
- quite simply the specific mix of characters and personalities involved in each year.

The emerging social tensions were neither unusual nor unexpected. Indeed, one educational rationale for such international cooperation is the desire to confront students with complex social situations, since arguably the experiences gained will help them in their future lives and professional careers. I have no reason to challenge this assumption. But I am not sure if these are merely side issues—however desirable—of international coprojects in archaeology, the main task of which is to understand the past, or if they in fact become the main concern for the project members, against which the daily digging and surveying might seem fairly inconsequential and insignificant. In 1999, every other American who completed my questionnaire described the multinationality of the project in negative terms, and more than half of my sample had reservations about the overall atmosphere within the project.

Tensions can be particularly strong when it comes to perceived or real hierarchies of privileges. By that I do not mean that somebody who returned to the site in the following year could gain status from inside knowledge about the project and life in Salemi, and might thus be able to occupy a particularly prestigious seat at the dinner table (cf. Yarrow, chapter 2), or the supposedly best spot in the house to spend the hot Sicilian summer nights. Problematic, rather, was the fact that the students attended the project under very different financial conditions depending on where they came from. In the Scandinavian tradition, education is provided free of charge and in addition students are eligible for favorable loans to meet their living costs. Most of them participated on the basis that their costs were paid (for instance, by research grants from their university), but a few had paid their own costs in order to participate. Stanford students had everything paid for and additional resources to spend as they needed them, but they of course also paid tuition fees of close to thirty thousand dollars per academic year. NIU's Sicilian Archaeological Field School charged each student several thousand dollars (in 2003, $3,200 plus transatlantic flights) for four weeks of work within the same project. Members of this field school also tended to have less time off than the others, although under the circumstances this was appreciated as "more value for money." Nobody blamed anybody personally for these inequalities—as it was not anybody's personal fault or gain, and more to do with different traditions of educational and research funding—but it nevertheless contributed to erecting boundaries of sheer incomprehension on the one side and maybe some envy on the other. There were other inequalities too.

All students lived together under one roof (with the exception of some of the Italians who commuted from home), but they were often not able to spend their evenings, and especially weekends, together. The key scarce resource was the number of available seats in the cars that were used to shuttle students to the beaches or to undertake excursions to other destinations. Stanford students could draw on seemingly unlimited funds and even hire additional cars when needed, and NIU too was able to supply its paying students with sufficient space in vehicles, which they needed anyway to shuttle people during survey work. The Italians often spent their free time away from the project, but the Scandinavians had only limited funds for transport and that meant that far too often, some of their students had no access to the beach on weekday evenings or were left behind in the excavation house even during weekends. Short-term car hire in Salemi was not available, although students were even willing to pay with their own money. Everybody was aware of this problem and did their best to be as fair as possible, with elaborate booking systems and planning going on all week. The disadvantaged were often those with slightly lower status, who were a little less popular, more shy, or more tired than the others. This issue was the single biggest reason for frustration and friction among students, affecting the entire project. All these sentiments and experiences reflect what Michael Shanks (2004, 498) has called the "political economy" of a project—the existing social order that makes it work.

Effectively, the Monte Polizzo project became a social experiment, with important lessons (hopefully) to be learned and treasured by each participant. Arguably, these social experiences and specific lessons to be learned should be given far more attention by those running such projects. Rather than using cheap (or even lucrative) student labor for opening yet another trench or registering yet another bag of potsherds, the students' field experience might have been vastly improved by devoting as much attention to the time off work as to the time at work. This does not mean that every minute during a project's duration needs to be planned in advance or that there should not be room for spontaneity. But, to me, the Monte Polizzo experience illustrated that training excavations especially are not only about acquiring professional skills and experience but also about learning a professional culture (see also Moser forthcoming; Carman, chapter 8). What this culture will look like in the future depends a lot on how it is transmitted to new recruits. That transmission occurs on excursions and beach visits as much as during working hours.

Training Students During Fieldwork

But how successful was the Monte Polizzo project at teaching students valuable archaeological field skills to which everybody was committed? Despite all the best intentions of the project chiefs, most participants remained largely ignorant not only about the complex historical contexts of the site and the specific academic issues at stake but also about many of the specific methodologies employed to make new contributions to academic knowledge. When asked about the aims of the Monte Polizzo project, the respondents to my questionnaires tended to write in very general terms about learning about the ancient city of Monte Polizzo, about the ancient Elymians (who might once have occupied the site), and about the Iron Age and Bronze Age of Sicily. The senior project leaders did a lot to address this problem—we had weekly or twice-weekly seminars and regular academic lectures. But the problem could not be remedied during any single field season. Specific preparatory courses about the Sicilian past and the methods and techniques used in the project, as they took place in Göteborg in 1999 and as they (Ian Morris tells me) have now been introduced for all participating Stanford students too, are helping to empower all participants as full project members. There were also individual students in various teams who made their field research at Monte Polizzo the subject of their own research, in particular at the master's degree level. But these projects were relatively few and had the value of an added bonus rather than the educational core of the project.

At Monte Polizzo, as so often in archaeology, the site directors and their assistants (effectively the trainee or apprentice site directors) alone carried the burden of writing the all-decisive field reports (see, e.g., Morris et al. 2001; Prescott and Mühlenbock 2003). As principal investigators, they are responsible for the excavation and postexcavation work and can benefit from expert reports that come in long after the fieldwork itself—and therefore the involvement of most of the students—has ended. They carry forward the project from one season to the next and need to justify the progress made in each year to the institutions funding them, to the authorities providing permission, to the academy at large, and to themselves and their own academic careers. It is thus not surprising that, in 2000, one team director and his trusted apprentice regularly went back up the mountain while their students were resting or administering their finds during the hot afternoons. They used this undisturbed time to do much of the

drawing and recording for the planned interim report and presumably subsequent publications. As student error and input concerning the emerging bigger picture are minimized, education is reduced to a favorable mix of labor camp and package holiday, with the accommodation and the served food belonging to one or the other, depending on whom you asked and when. The best students (best in what?) will later become chiefs themselves and perpetuate the system.

In this scheme of things, the large majority of students provide labor, which is largely used to generate primary data, and are given as pleasant an experience as is possible in return, while at the same time being initiated in the professional culture of archaeology, as discussed above. Although student satisfaction with both their own work and the project overall was high, a large majority of my 1999 sample would have appreciated additional teaching, both formal and hands on, about the various methodologies and approaches applied within the project. The extent to which inexperienced students can contribute to archaeological research might be limited, but that is not to say that the professional training outcome could not be improved. In 1999 and 2000, what the archaeological fieldwork at Monte Polizzo actually revealed about the past and the contribution it will make to academic scholarship was almost coincidental to how the project was experienced by many of those participating in it.

Archaeology as an Adventure?

Archaeological fieldwork has traditionally had strong gendered associations and is often perceived as a masculine practice, affecting even recruitment and professional specialization (Woodall and Perricone 1981). Even now, women might occasionally feel pressure to act in more masculine ways on excavations, whereas feminine characteristics in men can be frowned upon (Moser forthcoming). The popular stereotype of the archaeologist is a male hero and adventurer wearing a khaki safari suit and a pith helmet, and carrying a gun. I remember the astonishment in the face of at least one male student who, early during the 2000 season, appeared on Monte Polizzo wearing various practical garments, some in khaki, when it turned out that his project director preferred clothes that had more in common with beachwear than with "suitable" expedition clothing.

I did not particularly focus on gender issues while working on Monte Polizzo but they can be inescapable (see also Avikunthak 2001). Some Italians found it incompatible with their own understanding of gender roles that women in the project were happily doing hard physical work such as deturfing with heavy tools. On the other hand, a few female students occasionally wore skimpy clothes that dazzled some men. Off work there was concern in 1999 about the behavior of young Sicilian men, including local police officers, toward some of our women when the women were walking alone in town. It was thus decreed that among the project participants every woman could request any man to be her escort.

The archaeological romance of eerie adventures in exotic locations, involving treasure hunting and fighting for a good cause, has become a widely applied stereotype of archaeology (Holtorf 2005, chapter 3). In the field, archaeology must be tough and include hardship and sacrifice, for archaeologists prefer to lead lives of exhaustion and earned rewards (see also Larsen et al. n.d.; Welinder 2000, 57–58). In its 2003 online poster, The Sicilian Archaeological Field School emphasized the word "discover," spelled in large letters. Students were then invited to "work and live in a small, medieval village near the Mediterranean" and to "explore ancient temples, ruins and monuments." This is archaeological romance writ large, and not even entirely fictitious. Our daily work involved exhausting physical labor on a mountaintop and a lot of sweating in the merciless midday summer sun of the southern Mediterranean. To compensate (and reward) ourselves we were drinking all sorts of tasty alcoholic drinks such as Zambouka and Limonello during the long and warm Sicilian summer evenings.

Romance and discovery referred mostly to the ongoing search for the best local ice-cream parlor, the coolest pubs (Extra-Bar or Pacha-Bar?), the most beautiful beach, and the most exciting sights in the region. We discovered the Carthaginian town on the small island of Mozia (once crossing over in hired kayaks) and went to explore the caves on the Isle of Lévanzo. We climbed up to the scenic temple of Segesta and walked through the impressively transformed ruins of Gibellina Vecchia. We enjoyed the atmosphere in the little Mediterranean tourist village of Marinella near the beach closest to Salemi and in the medieval town of Erice with the most amazing view over all of western Sicily. Having returned home, former participants often cultivate such memories from the field and revel in the possibility of returning during the following summer.

Some of the most fascinating and memorable discoveries and explorations of the fieldwork season took place both in the local town of Salemi and in the basement of the dig house itself. On the evening of July 9, 1999, for example, a large group of us walked to the ruined castle of Salemi, which we had always wanted to explore. The gate was closed, but adventurous as we were, being the archaeologists in town, we decided to have a look anyway. It was not difficult to climb over the fence and get a look at the entire site. On the way out, there were four people missing. We learned that the local police had detained them for trespassing. They were later released after answering some questions and stating their personal details. As archaeologists, it was said, they should have known that ruined castles can be dangerous to visit and respected that the site was closed. In retrospect, maybe we should not have gone. Our action was certainly never explicitly condoned by any project chief, and Ian Morris tells me now that "everyone currently involved in the project thinks that this was disgraceful behavior, and we deplore it." The episode affected the project's local status and proved embarrassing especially to another senior team member who had been caught in the act with the others. Apparently, even in 2002 when the castle reopened, the event was still remembered. It was an archaeological adventure that none of the involved parties will easily forget.

We also enjoyed exploring the deserted bottom floor of the building in the first and second floors of which we were accommodated. This large space was once used as a clinic and it had obviously not been cleaned up since its closure—only blocked off with bricks in a rudimentary fashion but insufficiently closed to stop us entering through the back door. Like contemporary urban explorers who explore the uncharted areas of our cities (e.g., infiltration.org), we could not resist finding out what lay underneath the floors we called home. We found a mess. One room was full of medical apparatus and papers spread out on the floor. In the center was what looked like a defunct X-ray machine, elsewhere a bone saw. In another room we found an old Italian flag and nearby a plow that was possibly still in occasional use, with access through a locked garage gate. There was much broken glass and other rubbish spread out all around; one room was full of sewage smelling appallingly—we wondered whether this came from our very own toilets. As one participant later remembered, we were living on top of "a classical horror film scenario." Unsurprisingly, one or two students subsequently experienced nightly spooks.

So, What Have We Learned?

Enduring various psychological, physical, social, and cultural ordeals of fieldwork and the rewards one enjoys in compensation are crucial in the participants' experience of it. Within the Monte Polizzo project, there was a certain tension between the explicit archaeological aims of the project, including student training, and what the participants mainly learned and experienced. In effect, students were initiated or further promoted within their own professional culture, gaining social and cultural competency in how to act as an archaeologist and what to treasure in their collective memories. Certain norms, values, customs, and traditions were successfully transmitted to the novices. Exciting adventures were experienced, hardship endured, and pleasures enjoyed so that everybody felt they had proved themselves and been rewarded. All in all, no bad result. Arguably, it is results of precisely that kind that ultimately contribute more to the socialization of archaeologists than any mastered skills or available expertise regarding particular facts or objects found in the ground (Holtorf 2002; Moser forthcoming; cf. Van Reybrouck and Jacobs, chapter 3).

I have argued that emerging academic insights about the past are almost coincidental to what an excavation project is actually about (see also Avikunthak 2001; Shanks 2004; Larsen et al. n.d.). The really significant advances in knowledge are usually established and formulated by the project leaders long after the fieldwork has ended. Only one historic fact was learned by everybody during the excavations in 2000. It impressed some tremendously that Ian Morris, a professor at Stanford University, had in 1979 auditioned for the heavy-metal rock group Iron Maiden (unsuccessfully).

Archaeological fieldwork is not only the sum of applied methods and techniques but also an experience that is significant in many ways other than what it purports to be. I wish that this experience were much more strongly reflected not only in general assessments of what fieldwork is meant to achieve for archaeology but also in the design and evaluation of specific projects.

References

Avikunthak, A. 2001. Rummaging for pasts: Excavating Sicily, digging Bombay. Video film. *Stanford Journal of Archaeology*, archaeology.stanford.edu/journal/newdraft/ashish/index.html (accessed July 17, 2005).

Becher, T. 1989. *Academic tribes and territories: Intellectual enquiry and the cultures of disciplines*. Milton Keynes: Open University Press.

Carman, J. 2004. Excavating excavation: A contribution to the social archaeology of archaeology. In *Digging in the dirt*, ed. G. Carver. BAR S1256. Oxford: Archaeopress.

Eibner, C., H. Fehr, and M. Nadler. 1996. *Baktrer Schnaps und Mammutschinken. Lieder von Archäologen für Archäologen*. Büchenbach, Germany: Dr. Faustus.

Gerholm, T. 1985. On tacit knowledge in academia. In *On communication 3*, ed. L. Gustavsson, 1–15. Selected papers from a seminar arranged by the Department of Communication Studies, May 1984. University of Linköping.

Hamilton, C. 2000. Faultlines: The construction of archaeological knowledge at Çatalhöyük. In *Towards reflexive method in archaeology: The example at Çatalhöyük*, ed. I. Hodder, 119–27. Cambridge, UK: McDonald Institute Monographs.

Holtorf, C. 2002. Notes on the life history of a pot sherd. *Journal of Material Culture* 7:49–71.

———. 2005. *From Stonehenge to Las Vegas: Archaeology as popular culture*. Walnut Creek, Calif.: Altamira Press.

Larsen, J., B. Olsen, A. Hesjedal, and I. Storli. n.d. *Camera archaeologica: Rapport fra et feltarbeid*. Tromsø museums skrifter 23.

Morris, I., T. Jackman, and E. Blake. 2001. Stanford University excavations on the acropolis of Monte Polizzo, Sicily, I: Preliminary report on the 2000 season. *Memoirs of the American Academy in Rome* 46:253–71.

Moser, S. Forthcoming. Gendered dimensions of archaeological practice: The stereotyping of archaeology as fieldwork. In *Practicing archaeology as a feminist*, ed. A. Wylie and M. Conkey. Santa Fe, N.Mex.: School of American Research.

Mühlenbock, C., and C. Prescott, eds. 2004. *The Scandinavian Sicilian Archaeological Project. Archaeological excavations at Monte Polizzo, Sicily. Reports 1998–2001*. Göteborg, Sweden: University of Göteborg, Department of Archaeology.

Pearson, M., and M. Shanks. 2001. *Theatre/Archaeology*. London: Routledge.

Prescott, C., and C. Mühlenbock. 2003. Mt. Polizzo, Sicily: Preliminary views on Elymians and ethnicity, landscape and identity. In *Scandinavian archaeological practice—in theory. Proceedings from the 6th Nordic TAG, Oslo 2001*, ed. J. Bergstøl, 26–37. Olso, Norway: University of Oslo, Department of Archaeology, Art History and Conservation.

Shanks, M. 2001–2003. Sicily—archaeological moments, metamedia.stanford.edu/traumwerk/index.php/Sicily—archaeological moments (accessed July 17, 2005).

———. 2004. Archaeology and Politics. In *A Companion to Archaeology*, ed. J. Bintliff, 490–508. Malden, Mass.: Blackwell.

Welinder, S. 2000. *Arkeologisk yrkesidentitet*. Tromsø, Norway: University of Tromsø, Institute of Archaeology.

Woodall, N., and P. Perricone. 1981. The archeologist as cowboy: The consequence of professional stereotype. *Journal of Field Archaeology* 8:506–9.

"Notes on the Life History of a Pot Sherd"

CORNELIUS HOLTORF

Millions, perhaps billions, of artifacts are dis-covered during archaeological excavations each year. What happens to these artifacts? Cornelius Holtorf, a professor at the University of Lund in Sweden, takes us through the post-discovery life of one such artifact in this innovative account. The article was originally published in a 2002 issue of the interdisciplinary and scholarly *Journal of Material Culture*.

• •

Questions to Guide Reading

What is meant by the "short life history approach" in archaeology, as exemplified by Michael Schiffer?

What is meant by the "long life history approach" in archaeology, as exemplified by Holtorf's study of megalithic monuments?

How does Holtorf's ethnographic approach to studying the potsherd differ from the short and long life history approaches?

What are some of the issues to consider when deciding whether to call something an artifact?

What criteria were used in deciding the potsherd was an artifact, in the field and in the lab?

What happened to the potsherd once it was classified as an artifact?

• •

Introduction

This article is about a fairly ordinary pot sherd found by Erica Grijalva on 4 July 2000. Erica found the sherd while digging in a trench on top of Monte Polizzo—a large hilltop settlement in western Sicily. Most of the occupation deposits on the mountain date to the 6th and 5th centuries BC. That settle-ment was possibly associated with a people known to the Greeks as Elymians who lived in an inland area that was disputed between the Elymians, the Greeks and the Carthaginians. Among the partici-pants of the large international excavation project that now occupies Monte Polizzo every summer, its highest part is known as 'The Acropolis'. This is where, during the summer of 2000, a team led by Ian Morris of Stanford University began their exca-vations. He and his team revealed a semi-circular stone structure on the very top of the mountain, as well as the remains of a rectangular building nearby (Morris et al., forthcoming). In 2001, this building turned out to be one of a complex of at least three

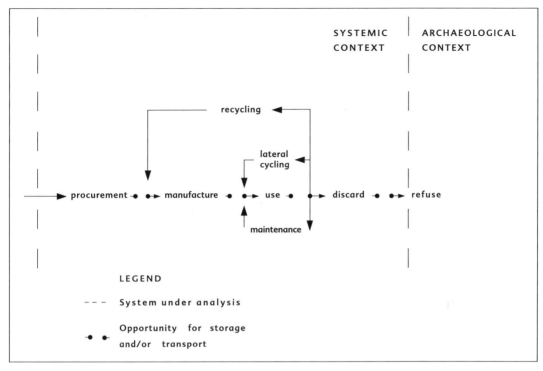

SYSTEMIC CONTEXT | ARCHAEOLOGICAL CONTEXT

recycling

lateral cycling

procurement → manufacture → use → discard → refuse

maintenance

LEGEND

--- System under analysis

Opportunity for storage and/or transport

FIGURE 1: Michael Schiffer's flow model illustrating his 'short' life-history approach to 'durable elements' such as artefacts (1972: Fig. 1). A slightly revised version can be found in LaMotta and Schiffer (2001: Fig. 2.2)

rectilinear rooms with a courtyard and multiple terrace walls (Ian Morris, pers. comm.).

The sherd under scrutiny was found in Layer 8 of Trench 17651 (now known as N106), north of what is probably the outer wall of the rectangular building B 1. Trench supervisor Trinity Jackman said about this layer that 'it consists of pretty fine, sandy material but is initially quite compact. It seems like a fill layer—there is a pit directly to the north east. We are trying to figure out what happened here. It is quite an important area actually.'

I will return to the significance of this sherd later. But first I need to discuss my decision to adopt a particular kind of 'life history' approach. Over the past decade or so, life histories (or biographies) of ancient

sites and artefacts have attracted considerable interest among both archaeologists and anthropologists. Archaeologists infected by this particular intellectual virus range from Michael Schiffer to Michael Shanks, and from Richard Bradley to Julian Thomas and Christopher Tilley. Recently, an entire issue of the journal *World Archaeology*, was dedicated to 'The Cultural Biography of Objects' (Chris Gosden and Yvonne Marshall, eds., 1999). Arguably, the observed popularity of 'life histories' and 'biographies' of things is partly due to some difference in opinion as to what specifically this approach actually stands for. In particular, there are 'short' and 'long' life history approaches.

Short and Long Life Histories of Things

As Michael Schiffer stated recently, it is commonplace in archaeology to make assumptions about the life history of, say, a house or a ceramic jar. Schiffer went on to explain what he meant by that:

> Artifact life histories are usually divided into sets of closely linked activities called processes; in the case of a ceramic jar, processes include the collection of clay and other raw materials, clay preparation, forming the clay into a vessel, smoothing and painting its surface, drying and firing, transport, exchange, use, storage, maintenance, reuse, and discard. (Schiffer with Miller, 1999: 22)

This can be illustrated with a simple flow model (Figure 1). Schiffer considers the 'life history concept' to lie 'at the core' of a behavioral methodology in archaeology, since 'an artifact's life history is the sequence of behaviors (i.e., interactions and activities) that lead from the procurement of raw materials ... to the eventual discard or abandonment of the object in the archaeological record' (LaMotta and Schiffer, 2001: 21). His general idea is to use the life history approach to help account for observable patterns of finds and features on archaeological sites; or—to use his own language—to develop credible, predictive laws about the cultural components of the formation processes of the archaeological record by studying its material elements in their systemic context (Schiffer, 1972; LaMotta and Schiffer, 2001: 21–22). Once the 'durable elements' had left their 'systemic context' and entered the 'archaeological context', they were subject to various natural formation processes which, to Schiffer, represent phases of decay rather than additional episodes of life. It is to Schiffer's credit that he has long been aware that divergences from the standard sequence of processes such as various kinds of discard practices and reuses that might occur (see e.g., Thompson, 1979), quickly add a considerable degree of complexity to the model.[1]

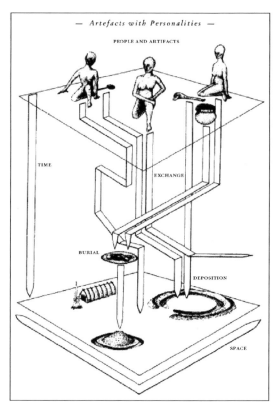

FIGURE 2: Julian Thomas' illustration of the interaction of artefacts, people and places in later Neolithic Britain: a different kind of a 'short' life-history approach. (From Thomas, 1996: Fig. 6.10)

More recently, other archaeologists have looked again at life histories of things, drawing on recent work both in anthropology and in science and technology studies, by scholars such as Igor Kopytoff (1986), Marilyn Strathern (1988) and Bruno Latour (1987). They were hoping to achieve something rather different, namely a better understanding of the various interconnections between the lives of things and the lives of people (Thomas, 1996; Tilley, 1996; Shanks, 1998). As Michael Shanks argued (1998), this required a radical rethinking of the old-established opposition of people and things, and gave new currency to the old post-processual battle cry that material culture is active and meaningfully constituted.

Birth, Childhood	c. 4000–2700	TRB culture, Globular Amphora culture	megaliths built and used as burial sites
Youth	c. 2800–1600	Single Grave culture, early Bronze Age	reused as burial sites *closing of megaliths*
Earlier Adult Life	1200–600 600–1 cal. BC AD 1–600 600–1200	late Bronze Age pre-Roman Iron Age Roman Iron Age (and Migration period) Slavic Period	throughout: secondary burials, finds in and near megaliths, tradition of enclosed burial mounds, imitation of mounds *'paganization' of megaliths?*
Later Adult Life	1200–1400 1400–1750	early German Period later Medieval and early Modern Period	finds in and near megaliths, stones reused *'historizaton' of megaliths*
Old Age	1750–1830 1830–1990 present	Romantic Period Modernity Post-Modernity	appreciated by poets, painters, travellers work by antiquarians and archaeologists, protection *preservation, presentation*

FIGURE 3: My own attempt (Holtorf, 1998: Table 1) at an overview of the 'long' life histories of megalithic monuments in Mecklenburg-Vorpommern (Germany)

Detailed case studies were prepared by Christopher Tilley (1996: chapter 6) and Julian Thomas (1996: chapter 6; see Figure 2). They demonstrated, using the example of Neolithic artefacts, how things in circulation helped to define and redefine relationships between people; how persons can form parts of things, and things form parts of persons: 'I touch an object with my hand and am simultaneously touched by it' (Tilley, 1999: 324).

In contrast to Schiffer's attempt to *infer from* the life histories of things the various contexts of their subsequent deposition, Tilley and Thomas wanted to *learn about* the meanings and social roles of things from their various depositional contexts (Thomas, 1996: 162; Tilley, 1996: 273).[2]

Interestingly, the life history studies I have referred

to so far share the assumption that the life of a thing started at the time of its manufacture and ended at the time of its deposition in the ground. Discarded things are of course subjected to all sorts of natural processes, but their lives are over: they become rubbish, ruins, mummies. However, in an alternative perspective, the life histories of things do not end with deposition but continue until the present-day: activities such as discovery, recovery, analysis, interpretation, archiving and exhibiting are taken to be processes in the lives of things too. Although some examples of such 'long' life histories relate to prehistoric monuments—I think of the work of Richard Bradley (e.g. 1993: chapter 6)—and even to entire landscapes, others followed the changing fortunes of various kinds of artefacts.[3] In my own work on the life histories of megaliths (Holtorf, 1998, 2000–1) I came to the conclusion that whatever we do *with*, and *to*, these monuments today is simply our own contribution to their lives (Figure 3). Like others before us, we 'happen' to ancient monuments or indeed other things, making sense of them and reinterpreting them as we like (see also Shanks, 1998: 25).

The problem with this position is that it was perhaps not radical enough. Although there was some acknowledgement that the past is constructed rather than discovered, the material essence of the thing itself remained unchallenged. We may be able to interpret and 'construct' the meaning of a thing in any way we like, but we are seemingly unable to construct the thing 'itself.' The possibility that the material properties, or identity, of a thing are being renegotiated in different social circumstances has not normally been allowed (but see Shanks, 1998). This was mainly due to the life history metaphor itself. Like human bodies, things that had once been 'born' appeared to have to live as what they happened to be until they died. They may have been seen in different ways along the way, but their material identity was deemed to remain unchangeable and continuous all along: a pot was a pot was a pot. This is particularly problematic for 'long' life histories that explicitly incorporate the present, but the 'short' varieties are faced with the same difficulty, since it is usually assumed that the things being studied today share their very materiality with the things that were once embedded in complex networks of people and things and other meanings. From that viewpoint, it is a realistic task for the relevant specialists to study the material properties of a thing in order to find out *what it is*, for example pot sherd. And then others can go further and think about *what it meant* in a given historical context.

This article takes a different perspective, for I argue that the material identities of things are much more contingent. Consider the following anomalies:

1   Material identities of things can change quickly and without warning, right in front of our eyes—

think of a magician's show: how can we be fooled so easily? But also: how can we be so certain that what we are watching are indeed mere tricks?

2   Widely known material identities of things can begin or end by a few people saying and arguing so and (virtually) all others at some point deciding to agree with them—think of the demise of the four humours of the human body during the 19th century and the emergence and establishment of electrons and black holes in the 20th century. A good archaeological example is the fairly sudden transformation of thunderbolts into stone axes during the late 17th century (Jensen, 2000).

3   Two or more very different material identities may inhabit the same thing—think of fakes and replicas that can have very different effects in different circumstances and for different people (Holtorf and Schadla-Hall, 1999).

A study of the life history of things must therefore not assume anything about *what they are*, but try to understand *how they come to be* ancient artefacts or whatever else. I am arguing for an investigation of the life histories of things as they unfold in the present and extend both into the past and the future. Arguably, this is to study formation processes of the archaeological record in front of our eyes. But it also means to accept that material culture is meaningfully constituted—in the present.

Observing the Lives of Things: An Ethnographic Approach

No life before the moment of discovery can be assumed: any assertions about the origins and, if you will, earlier 'lives' of a thing are the outcome of various processes in its present life. However, I do not mean to imply that the thing did not *exist* previously. The point is rather that this is of no great concern, since *all* the thing's properties and characteristics, including its material identity and age, are ascribed to the thing some time after the moment of its discovery. They are not gradually revealed but slowly assembled (Shanks, 1998). I argue that all ancient sites and artefacts did not have much of a life, as it were, before they were discovered in their present context. All our knowledge, whether certain or speculative, about their past lives are in fact outcomes of their present lives. Of course, things may mean, and be, different things to different people—they can have parallel lives in various present contexts, with varying moments of 'discovery.'

Crucially, this does not imply that a thing's properties and characteristics are completely arbitrary but that they are determined by various factors effective in their present lives. An archaeologist, for example, is constrained in his or her assessment not only by the limits of his own knowledge and experience, but also by available techniques and by the dominant norms and values of academic discourse.

To study such present life stories and associated contexts requires an ethnographic approach, which (a) is much more detailed and therefore smaller in scope than the life history approaches previously mentioned, and (b) employs direct observation and interview as its main methodologies. One of the most important characteristics of the 'ethnographic' method is that the observer maintains an independence from both normative prescriptions of how things ought to function (e.g. Orton et al., 1993) and from the insiders' own perceptions of what they are doing. A similar ethnographic approach relating to the sciences has long been applied by sociologists of science. One of the most influential, so-called 'laboratory studies' is Karin Knorr-Cetina's study of *The Manufacture of Knowledge* (1981, see also 1983). My own approach is something like a laboratory study in the field.

What is to be gained from such research? The greatest benefit is to find out more about what it actually is that archaeologists are doing when they 'study the past.' How do they transform certain things into archaeological evidence? (See also Edgeworth, 1990.) How do they learn what kind of artefacts they are dealing with? And how do they actually get to know their ancientness, i.e., the fact that they are of ancient and not recent age? Contrary to what one might expect, my research results demonstrate that the answer to none of these questions is 'by careful study and analysis'. It will emerge instead that split-second decisions based on established routines and old habits, partly carried out by nonspecialists, account for most of the answers.

I will be focusing on a thing that was quickly to become a 'pot sherd.' It began its life on 4 July 2000, at 11.01 am to be precise. It was 'born' right on top of Monte Polizzo, where Erica Grijalva helped it emerge out of the ground. There were no complications.

What Is an Artefact?

As everybody knows, on an excavation not everything is kept: 'most of what an archaeologist uncovers ends up in fact on the spoil heap' (Johnson, 2001: 76). (One day at Monte Polizzo I kept a bag for things we did not usually keep.) So what made Erica discover and keep this thing?[4]—just for a minute ignoring the fact that I was hovering over Erica and taking pictures of the 'thing' in front of her, then squatting nearby and observing the proceedings. Julian Thomas said (1996: 62) that 'in order to "do archaeology" we have to recognise certain things as representing evidence. Archaeological analysis is consequently a specific form of "clearing" which enables entities to be recognised in a very specific kind of way' (see also Edgeworth, 1990).

In the Monte Polizzo project diggers routinely keep artefacts, bones, and a variety of scientific samples, for example for pollen, charcoal and macrofossil analysis. Such categories are highly contingent. They are adopted by projects because of particular research interests, old habits, established conventions or historical accidents, not because they are necessarily the best possible way to categorize things archaeologists come across (Conolly, 2000; Lucas, 2001: chapter 3). The categories used are subject to change at any time, and they could be very different. Ian Hodder figured (1997: 695) that 'If the object categories on which archaeological research is founded can be seen to be the product of the conventional lenses used in analysis, the door is opened for constructing "new" objects of study which partition the object-world in different and multiscalar ways. "Objects" such as "burning," or "decoration," or "rubbish" cut across the lower-level domains based on conventional artefact categories.' The project Erica was working for did not have any such far-reaching ambitions, although it did (and does) introduce a range of innovative methodologies to Sicilian archaeology.

At the moment the thing was found, Erica had to make the crucial decision as to whether or not that thing was valuable evidence, i.e., an artefact, a bone, a useful sample, or something else worth keeping. This is a routine decision which diggers like Erica make hundreds of times every day. But what is worth keeping anyway? In 1958, Lewis Binford provoked James Griffin when he decided to keep and catalogue large amounts of fire-cracked rock as well as coke bottle tops and nails (Binford, 1972: 128). But value is not only linked to classification. Very small things are often not deemed worth classifying and worth keeping in the same way that others are—which is why on many excavations not all earth is routinely being sieved and why size does matter (Hodder, 1999: 15–17; Orton et al., 1993: 47).

Based on a superficial resemblance to other 'pot sherds', Erica recognized the thing as a pot sherd and deemed it worth keeping. Erica then carefully cleaned away the dirt around it and gradually revealed more and more of what she still believed was a sherd. My watch showed 11.25 am. Often, the initial identification will be revised when more of the object is revealed, or when it is first touched, or when it snaps, or when it is carefully cleaned between the fingers, or when the trench supervisor is consulted. In the space of a split-second, a 'sherd' may thus become 'dirt', or a 'stone' a 'bone', or a 'root' a 'single find'. Clearly this, if anything, is interpretation at the trowel's edge (Figure 4; Hodder, 1997, 1999: chapter 5). Later, people

CH

FIGURE 4: Erica Grijalva is cleaning around the sherd, 4 July 2000, 11.09

may change their minds. Some classifications can later be undone, for example when a sherd is recovered from among the bones, but others are irreversible, for example when a 'sherd' is later discovered on the dirt heap (with the original location unknown).

At 11.43 Erica placed the sherd into the pottery bowl on the side of the trench she was working in. It carried a label stating:

MP 2000
Acropolis
July 4, 2000
Trench 1765
1East Bulk

Later the content of the bowl was transferred into a plastic bag, which was labelled and then carried down the mountain to the car parking place, from where it got a ride directly to the dig house in the nearby town of Salemi. At 15.43 on that same afternoon, Erica began washing 'her' sherds. This gave her a chance to review whether all items in the pottery bag were indeed pot sherds. Any things that she no longer felt were appropriately classified would now have been removed from the bag. A 'bone' would have been removed and put into the bones bag, while a 'pebble' in the bag would in practice probably have been thrown into the bushes behind the table where much of the washing took place. Again, people may later change their views or admit mistakes or others may disagree with their classifications, but probably more often than we would like, facts are created that cannot be undone.

Moreover, there are types of pottery that dissolve in water, and there are types of decoration that suffer from scrubbing, and there are countless little bits and pieces that break off and are thrown out with the water, while other pieces are mixed up during the subsequent drying process in the sun. I remember from my very first excavation in 1986 how a tiny strange thing which my trench supervisor had just identified as the fragment of a bronze fibula a short time later simply disappeared out of my hand, and was never found again. What this means is that a pot is a bone is a piece of dirt is nothing left. At the end of the process of cleaning, inspecting and drying the sherd under investigation was still in the bag, which was good news for my project.

What I have established so far is that the thing, which Erica discovered in the morning on Monte Polizzo, had by the same evening become a clean and dry sherd of pottery in a plastic bag which also contained a number of other sherds found on the same day in the same context. All this was mostly due to Erica Grijalva, an undergraduate student in Mechanical Engineering from Stanford University, California.

Knowing something as a pot sherd is to know a lot already:

> This is a material which is familiar to us, and from the moment when it is turned up by the trowel the way in which we understand it is already constrained by a range of prejudices and understandings. We know certain things about how pottery is made, what it can be used for, and the conditions under which people

can routinely make use of pots. Before we begin, these will inevitably colour the way in which we will interpret the artefact. When the artefact is recovered, it is already a part of a world. (Thomas, 1996: 63)

But the really crucial moment in the life of the sherd lay still ahead.

How Does an Artefact Become Ancient?

Artefacts found on an excavation can be of very different ages—from a few months (or even contemporaneous with the archaeologists) to many millennia. Diggers are usually encouraged to keep and record all artefacts, although most of them would in practice not look twice at rusty nails or beer bottles that are 'obviously' of no great antiquity and therefore not 'worth' keeping (but remember Binford!).[5] Things that derive from the archaeological excavation itself, such as bent nails, small ends of string, or food remains are quickly discarded, too. All such things are often not considered to be finds but 'rubbish.' As a result, the most recent phases of occupation of archaeological sites tend to be systematically undervalued. This raises the question on what grounds diggers are able to identify relatively quickly that one artefact is 'ancient' (which I take to mean from before a possible local person's own memory, i.e., older than 50–80 years), and another one is mere recent rubbish. This is not a trivial question, considering that the digger is not able to apply any kind of sophisticated dating method on site. Instead he or she will glance at the object, maybe remove some dirt that is stuck to it, look again, and usually make a decision after these few moments.

Based on my observations at various excavations I have taken part in (and not applying specifically to Monte Polizzo), diggers come to their decisions about the age of an artefact in a negative way: if it isn't clearly recent, it must be old. Recent artefacts are identified and subsequently discarded if they

1. are positively identified by the digger as belonging to the project (from personal memory),
2. resemble artefacts known to be recent AND come from layers that are likely to be recent (e.g., surface, infills from top layers and so on),
3. are considered as recent by consulted authorities on site (e.g., trench supervisor).

In case of doubt, the object is likely to be kept and treated 'as if ancient,' until it can be reevaluated after washing, possibly consulting further authorities.

The point of this brief discussion is not to complain about any possible misidentifications. It is more interesting to note that by the time a find reaches the finds laboratory and its team, the antiquity of that find has not yet been positively established. The same was true for the 'sherd' I was following (and which by now had become known as 'Cornelius' sherd').[6] Erica of course had never had any doubts about the fact that this was an 'ancient sherd'—just like all the others that she and the other diggers had been recovering for the past few weeks. My own decision to follow this particular thing also relied on my judgment that it was an ancient artefact that would go through the normal process of finds analysis, or I would not have selected it. We could of course both have been proven wrong. For example by a thermoluminescence date for the sherd. But in practice such direct dating methods are not often employed in archaeological projects, and usually restricted to a few carefully selected individual pieces. Instead, finds from Monte Polizzo were usually dated by Emma Blake and her team in the project's finds laboratory. How did they do it?

The Moment of Truth

The moment of truth came one day after the discovery of the sherd, on 5 July 2000 at 13.43, to be precise. The plastic bag with 'my' sherd in it had at that point been opened by Emma Blake, and the contents spread out on a table (Figure 5). With a small team of helpers, one of her main tasks was to

go through all the bags of pottery and enter the information they contained into the project's database. This database would become the primary and most important source of information for later post-excavation analysis. Whatever Emma listed here, would to a large extent determine the information that the project could ever get out of that thing. To paraphrase Douglas Adams, it would be the answer to the question of the meaning of the thing in the universe. Emma came to the conclusion that the answer was 'F 24'—confirming a hunch she had had at 10.55 when she first saw the sherd while putting all the dry sherds in the cassette into the plastic bag (see below). When I asked her, Emma defined F 24 to me as a 'generic, coarse ware, pithos/storage-vessel, grey-red-brown-orange colours, grey core, handmade, undecorated, grog as primary inclusion, a couple of centimetres thick.'

This identification was made in the space of about one second after picking up the sherd and

FIGURE 5: The pot sherd in the finds laboratory, 5 July 2000

looking at it. Emma clearly had a lot of experience, and a lot of intuition. My sherd was neither the first nor the only fabric F 24 she had come across; this was one of the most common fabrics on site and not usually one that was difficult to identify. Hence Emma did not consider it a potentially controversial decision. She did not see a need to consult others in the room for their opinion, but I really do not think that her classification as F 24 could seriously be questioned by anyone. Having said that, it is well known among pottery specialists that the association of pot sherds with a particular fabric type depends partly on the psychology of the person who is associating (Orton et al., 1993: 73).

To complete the process of analysis, the F 24 sherds were weighed, returned to their bag, and the bag was marked 'undiagnostic'. Undiagnostic sherds are those sherds that are effectively not deemed worth being looked at again in any detail (cf. note 6!). By now it was 13.58 and after quarter of an hour of fame the sherd was basically over and done with. What followed was entry of the data on the recording sheet into the computer, and then the bag being stored in a cassette and moved around … and moved around again … for over a week (see below) … until it was moved again, then being transported on 13 July, at 9.58 to be precise, to the local museum where it was carried through the gate at 10.15, and up the stairs, and finally found its final resting place in a large store room—where it is probably still today at the time of writing, almost a year later (Figure 6).

All this may sound pretty mundane and unsurprising. But what had effectively happened is that a thing found in the ground on 4 July 2000 had been authenticated, identified and dated by an archaeological project. When it entered the museum's store room, at 10.16 on 13 July 2000, the thing had become a fragment of a large storage vessel of the Iron Age settlement on top of Monte Polizzo. This transformation was due to specific archaeological formation processes, featuring Erica Grijalva who placed the thing into the right bowls and bags so that it became established as a pot sherd, and Emma Blake who saw

FIGURE 6: The sherd in a labelled plastic bag in a labelled cassette in a store room of the *Museo Civico* in Salemi, 13 July 2000, 10.16

quickly that this sherd was of the fabric F 24. Also important was, of course, that the sherd was meaningfully constituted inasmuch as Erica was working in a particular excavation trench on a particular site, that Emma knew about the origin of the sherd when she made her judgment, and that the cassettes in the museum were clearly labelled as coming from the Monte Polizzo archaeological project.

The Bottom Line

The bottom line of this article is that the lives of artefacts in the present are not half as exciting as those they had in the past. And yet, those past lives are the direct outcome of their present lives. Only with a secure identity as an artefact and its ancientness being established can archaeologists ever hope to involve a thing in any kind of plausible relationships with people of a past period.

As I hope I have shown, these crucial properties of things are not in every case verified through detailed analysis and careful evaluation of the results by an expert in the field who is able to recognize things for *what they are* and therefore *what they were*. Instead, most decisions appear to be made in an ad hoc kind of way and important evaluations emerge as the by-product of unquestioned routine processes. Remember that when Emma was determining the fabric of the sherd, she effectively also verified its ancientness. Such classifications and verifications are contextually specific constructions which bear the mark of the situational contingency by which they are generated.

It was the aim of scientific laboratory studies to study these processes in action (Knorr-Cetina, 1981: 5). 'The result, to summarize it in one sentence, was that nothing extraordinary and nothing "scientific" was happening inside the sacred walls of these temples' (Latour, 1983: 141). This is no less valid in the case of an archaeological excavation. Hopefully this article has demonstrated that an ethnographic life history approach to things can yield interesting insights about the profane practices at work in an excavation project.

The results, I suggest, have more general implications for our understanding of the way we classify and interpret material culture, because scientific practice is not categorically different from anything that is engaged in other (nonscientific) practices (Thomas, 1996: 63). They illustrate in some detail how 'momentary, fluid and flexible' our classifications and interpretations often are (Hodder, 1997). The material identities ascribed to things are not their essential properties but the result of relationships of people and things: their very materiality is potentially multiple and has a history (Thomas, 1996: 70–82; Shanks, 1998).

I do not think that this insight has any grand consequences for the way we should or should not do archaeology in the future. It is more the other way around: the way we will do archaeology in the future may have consequences for our insights about the characteristics of material culture and the practices surrounding its interpretation.

Notes

[1] Other works influenced by Schiffer's life history approach include Lillios (1999) and Walker and Lucero (2000), while Zedeño (1997) has transferred the same general ideas to landscape history which she studied in terms of 'territory formation'. A broadly similar approach on the European continent falls within the realm of archaeological 'source criticism' and is exemplified in Mildenberger's study of the lives of prehistoric stone axes and other artefacts (1969).

[2] A broadly similar approach was adopted by Bradley (1990), Langdon (2001), Jones (2002: chapters 5–7), Strassburg (1998), and Tilley (1999).

[3] Further 'long' life histories relating to monuments were published by Chippindale (1994), Gillings and Pollard (1999), and Karlsson (2001). Nico Roymans studied the life of an entire landscape (1995), while John Edwards applied a similar approach to the city of Córdoba (2001).

For examples relating to artefacts see Rawson (1993) and Burström (1996).

[4] For further discussion of the question how a digger like Erica recognized this thing as a thing and not nothing see Heidegger (1962), Edgeworth (1990), and Thomas (1996: 64–70).

[5] Ian Morris states that at Monte Polizzo 'we have a large and steadily growing collection of beer bottle fragments, barbed wire, shotgun cartridges, and coins dating from the 1970s and 1980s from building A1. The only modern artefact we threw away was a late 1990s pornographic magazine in a very unpleasant state of preservation' (pers. comm).

[6] The Stanford students later awarded me *The Sherd Appreciation Award* for 'seeing beauty in something so dirty, so broken, so common, so ugly and so coarse!'

References

Binford, Lewis (1972) *An Archaeological Perspective*. New York and London: Seminar Press.

Bradley, Richard (1990) *The Passage of Arms. An Archaeological Analysis of Prehistoric Hoards and Votive Deposits.* Cambridge: Cambridge University Press.

Bradley, Richard (1993) *Altering the Earth. The Origins of Monuments in Britain and Continental Europe.* Edinburgh: Society of Antiquaries of Scotland.

Burström, Mats (1996) 'Other Generations' Interpretation and Use of the Past: the Case of the Picture Stones on Gotland', *Current Swedish Archaeology* 4: 21–40.

Chippindale, Christopher (1994) *Stonehenge Complete*. Revised edition. London: Thames and Hudson.

Conolly, James (2000) 'Çatalhöyük and the Archaeological "Object"', in Ian Hodder (ed.) *Towards Reflexive Method in Archaeology: the Example of Çatalhöyük*, pp. 51–56. Cambridge: McDonald Institute of Archaeological Research.

Edgeworth, Matthew (1990) 'Analogy as Practical Reason: the Perception of Objects in Excavation Practice', *Archaeological Review from Cambridge* 9(2): 243–52.

Edwards, John (2001) 'The Changing Use of Worship in Roman and Medieval Córdoba', in Robert Layton, Peter Stone and Julian Thomas (eds) *Destruction and Conservation of Cultural Property*, pp. 221–35. London and New York: Routledge.

Gillings, Mark and Pollard, Joshua (1999) 'Non-portable Stone Artefacts and Context of Meaning: the Tale of Grey Wether (www.museums.ncl.ac.uk/Avebury/stone4.html)', *World Archaeology* 31: 179–93.

Gosden, Chris and Marshall, Yvonne, eds (1999) 'The Cultural Biography of Objects', *World Archaeology* 31(2).

Heidegger, Martin (1962) *Die Frage nach dem Ding*. Tübingen: Niemeyer.

Hodder, Ian (1997) '"Always Momentary, Fluid and Flexible": Towards a Reflexive Excavation Methodology', *Antiquity* 71: 691–700.

Hodder, Ian (1999) *The Archaeological Process. An Introduction*. Oxford: Blackwell.

Holtorf, Cornelius (1998) 'The life history of Megaliths in Mecklenburg-Vorpommern (Germany)', *World Archaeology* 30: 23–38.

Holtorf, Cornelius (2000–1) *Monumental Past: The life history of Megalithic Monuments in Mecklenburg-Vorpommern (Germany)*. Electronic monograph. University of Toronto: Centre for Instructional Technology Development. http://citdpress.utsc.utoronto.ca/holtorf.

Holtorf, Cornelius and Schadla-Hall, Tim (1999) 'Age as Artefact. On Archaeological Authenticity', *European Journal of Archaeology* 2(2): 229–47.

Jensen, Ola (2000) 'The Many Faces of Stone Artefacts: A Case Study of the Shift in the Perception of Thunderbolts in the Late 17th and Early 18th Century', in Ola Jensen and Håkan Karlsson (eds) *Archaeological Conditions. Examples of Epistemology and Ontology*, pp. 129–43. University of Göteborg, Institute of Archaeology.

Johnson, Mark (2001) 'Renovating Hue (Vietnam): Authenticating Destruction, Reconstructing Authenticity', in Robert Layton, Peter Stone and Julian Thomas (eds) *Destruction and Conservation of Cultural Property*, pp. 75–92. London and New York: Routledge.

Jones, Andrew (2002) *Archaeological Theory and Scientific Practice*. Cambridge: Cambridge University Press.

Karlsson, Håkan (2001) 'The Dwarf and the Wine-Cooler: A Biography of a Swedish Megalith and its "Effect-in-history"', in Ola Jensen and Håkan Karlsson (eds) *Archaeological Conditions. Examples of Epistemology and Ontology*, pp. 25–40. University of Göteborg, Institute of Archaeology.

Knorr-Cetina, Karin (1981) *The Manufacture of Knowledge*. Oxford: Pergamon Press.

Knorr-Cetina, Karin (1983) 'The Ethnographic Study of Scientific Work: Towards a Constructivist Interpretation of Science', in Karin Knorr-Cetina and Michael Mulkay (eds) *Science Observed*, pp. 115–40. London: Sage.

Kopytoff, Igor (1986) 'The Cultural Biography of Things: Commoditization as Process', in Arjun Appadurai (ed.) *The Social Life of Things. Commodities in Cultural Perspective*, pp. 64–91. Cambridge: Cambridge University Press.

LaMotta, Vincent and Schiffer, Michael (2001) 'Behavioral Archaeology. Toward a New Synthesis', in Ian Hodder (ed.) *Archaeological Theory Today*, pp. 14–64. Cambridge: Polity.

Langdon, Susan (2001) 'Beyond the Grave: Biographies from Early Greece', *American Journal of Archaeology* 105, 579–606.

Latour, Bruno (1983) 'Give Me a Laboratory and I Will Raise the World', in Karin Knorr-Cetina and Michael Mulkay (eds) *Science Observed*, pp. 141–70. London: Sage.

Latour, Bruno (1987) *Science in Action. How to Follow Scientists and Engineers Through Society*. Milton Keynes: Open University Press.

Lillios, Katina (1999) 'Objects of Memory: The Ethnography and Archaeology of Heirlooms', *Journal of Archaeological Method and Theory* 6, 235–62.

Lucas, Gavin (2001) *Critical Approaches to Fieldwork. Contemporary and Historical Archaeological Practice*. London and New York: Routledge.

Mildenberger, Gerhard (1969) 'Verschleppte Bodenfunde. Ein Beitrag zur Fundkritik', *Bonner Jahrbücher* 169: 1–28.

Morris, Ian, Jackman, Trinity and Blake, Emma (forthcoming) 'Stanford University Excavations on the Acropolis of Monte Polizzo, Sicily: I, Preliminary Report on the 2000 Season', Memoirs of the American Academy in Rome 46.

Orton, Clive, Tyers, Paul and Vince, Alan (1993) *Pottery in Archaeology*. Cambridge: Cambridge University Press.

Pearson, Mike and Michael Shanks (2001) *Theatre/Archaeology*. London: Routledge.

Rawson, Jessica (1993) 'The Ancestry of Chinese Bronze Vessels', in Steven Lubar and David Kingery (eds) *History from Things. Essays on Material Culture*, pp. 51–73. Washington and London: Smithsonian Institution Press.

Roymans, Nico (1995) 'The Cultural Biography of Urnfields and the Long-term History of a Mythical Landscape', *Archaeological Dialogues* 2: 2–38.

Schiffer, Michael (1972) 'Archaeological Context and Systemic Context', *American Antiquity* 37: 156–65.

Schiffer, Michael with Miller, Andrea (1999) *The Material Life of Human Beings. Artifacts, Behavior, and Communication*. London and New York: Routledge.

Shanks, Michael (1998) 'The Life of an Artefact in an Interpretive Archaeology', *Fennoscandia Archaeologica* 15: 15–42.

Strassburg, Jimmy (1998) 'Let the "Axe" Go! Mapping the Meaningful Spectrum of the "Thin-Butted Flint Axe"', in Anna-Carin Andersson, Åsa Gillberg, Ola Jensen, Håkan Karlsson, Magnus Rolöf (eds) *The Kaleidoscopic Past. Proceedings of the 5th Nordic TAG Conference Göteborg, 2–5 April 1997*, pp. 156–69. Göteborg: University of Göteborg, Institute of Archaeology.

Strathern, Marilyn (1988) *The Gender of the Gift*. Berkeley: University of California Press.

Thomas, Julian (1996) *Time, Culture and Identity. An Interpretive Archaeology*. London and New York: Routledge.

Thompson, Michael (1979) *Rubbish Theory. The Creation and Destruction of Value*. Oxford: Oxford University Press.

Tilley, Christopher (1996) *An Ethnography of the Neolithic. Early Prehistoric Societies in Southern Scandinavia*. Cambridge: Cambridge University Press.

Tilley, Christopher (1999) 'Why Things Matter: Some Theses on Material Forms, Mind and Body', in Anders Gustafsson and Håkan Karlsson (eds) *Glyfer och arkeologiska rum—en vänbok till Jarl Nordbladh*, pp. 315–39. Göteborg: University of Göteborg, Institute of Archaeology.

Walker, William and Lucero, Lisa (2000) 'The Depositional History of Ritual and Power', in Marcia-Anne Dobres and John Robb (eds) *Agency in Archaeology*, pp. 130–47. London and New York: Routledge.

Zedeño, María N. (1997) 'Landscapes, Land Use, and the History of Territory Formation: An Example from the Puebloan Southwest', *Journal of Archaeological Method and Theory* 4, 67–103.

"Microwear Polishes on Early Stone Tools from Koobi Fora, Kenya"

Lawrence H. Keeley and Nicholas Toth

Advances in laboratory methods and experimental archaeology in the late twentieth century led to new kinds of analyses, including fresh ways of interpreting the function of tools. Two of the leading researchers in this area were Lawrence Keeley, a professor at the University of Illinois, and Nicholas Toth, now a professor at the University of Indiana. This article on the interpretation of microwear on stone tools originally appeared in a 1981 issue of *Nature*, one of the most prestigious interdisciplinary scientific journals. Not only does the article illustrate one kind of stone tool analysis, it is historically important and it provides a good example of a short scientific report (that is, it clearly identifies the methods, results, and implications of the research).

- -

Questions to Guide Reading

What methods of research were used?
What were the results?
What are the implications of those results?

- -

The functions of the stone artefacts made and used by early hominids has been a matter for speculation. However, recent experimental work has demonstrated that microscopically distinct wear-polishes form on tools of cryptocrystalline silica when used on different materials, and that these microwear polishes survive on ancient implements.[1-3] We have now examined 54 artefacts from five early Pleistocene archaeological sites, dated to 1.5 Myr ago, in the Koobi Fora region of Kenya for microwear polishes and other traces of use. Wear traces were found on nine artefacts, variously resembling traces induced experimentally by cutting soft animal tissue and soft plant material and by scraping and sawing wood. These results greatly extend the time range for which microwear polish analysis is applicable and increase the evidence of early hominid adaptation.

Four of the sites sampled were stratified in fine-grained floodplain deposits adjacent to ancient stream courses (FxJj 18IH, 20M, 20E and 50) and one (FxJj 18GS) was found in river gravels.[4] At sites 20 and especially 50, artefacts have been fitted together to reconstruct total and partial knapping episodes,[5] demonstrating that they were little disturbed by natural forces during or after burial. This conclusion is supported by all other pertinent archaeological and geological evidence. Site 18GS is an exception and, while most artefacts from this location were naturally abraded, one unabraded chert artefact (discussed below) was anomalously fresh.

The assemblages from all these sites are attributed to the Karari Industry,[6] which is regarded as a regional variant of the Olduwan Industrial Complex.[7] K–Ar radioisotope analysis of volcanic marker tuffs, stratified above and below these sites, date them to ~1.5 Myr ago.[8-10]

More than 90% of the artefacts at each site were made of basalt. The surfaces of the basalt pieces had undergone a light chemical dissolution ('weathering'), making them very unsuitable for microwear analysis. A few more resistant materials, including cryptocrystalline silicas and ignimbrites, are found at these and most Koobi Fora sites. Fifty-four non-basalt artefacts, each with one dimension larger than 2 cm and at least one non-cortical edge, were selected (by N.T.) from the five Karari assemblages for microscopic study. Except for one minimally flaked pebble core, all were flakes and flake fragments. A few were retouched.

When examined microscopically, none showed any traces of natural abrasion by wind or water and only five bore evidence of slight chemical weathering (none of these is discussed below). The ridges and edges of all but the latter were microscopically sharp and, at x400 magnification, were indistinguishable from the edges and ridges of freshly struck modern flakes of similar materials. This finding implies that the original surfaces of these artefacts and any wear traces they might bear are likely to have survived intact.

As previous microwear analysis has involved tools of European flint used on materials from a temperate environment 1–3, we 're-calibrated' our inferential base by using experimental tools of Koobi Fora and European cryptocrystalline rocks on plant and animal materials (including the carcass of a circus elephant) from the tropical savanna. (The experiments were conducted by N.T., except for the elephant butchery, at Koobi Fora on local materials.) Wear traces found on the Koobi Fora

experimental tools were identical to those seen on European implements used in analogous ways with two exceptions: (1) the flake surfaces of some of the Koobi Fora chert tools (both experimental and archaeological) show a natural 'greasy' lustre resembling the microwear polish created by low-intensity meat-cutting, effectively raising the threshold of detection for the latter, and (2) the modern grasses cut at Koobi Fora induced the formation of a 'soft-plant' polish much faster than temperate grasses (10 mm of use at Koobi Fora being the equivalent of >1 h of use in Europe).

Both experimental and archaeological specimens were cleaned with ammonia-based detergent, H_2O_2 and dilute Hcl. They were examined with an incident-light microscope at magnifications of x50–x400 before, during and after cleaning. Functional interpretations were based on the reflectivity and texture of the microwear polish, the size and direction of micro-scratches ('striae'), the size and character of the edge damage, and the distribution of all these traces along an edge.[1,2] Nine implements in the sample showed clear microwear traces.

Four implements, three from site 50, showed a rough-textured, 'greasy' microwear polish along one of their edges similar to that induced experimentally by cutting meat and other soft animal tissues. Striae running parallel to the edge and a symmetrical distribution of polish on both edge aspects indicate that all were used with a slicing motion. Coincident with the areas of polish, all the edges bore microscopic damage scars that are typical features of edges used for cutting soft material. Three of the tools have cortical surfaces opposite the used edge that may have served as handles during use. After interpreting the site 50 tools as meat-cutting knives, it was found that two of them were recovered within 1 m of a large bovid humerus showing narrow cutmarks, presumably from a stone knife (ref. 5 and E. Kroll, personal communication).

Two implements had, along portions of their edges, a highly reflective, smooth-textured microwear polish of the type produced by use on soft plant material containing substantial amounts of plant silica. The intensity of the polishes, in contrast to the minimal edge-damage indicating brief usages, suggest that these implements were used to cut the highly siliceous stems of grasses or reeds. Examination of the polish surfaces at higher magnifications with a scanning electron microscope, following the method of Anderson,[11] may reveal undissolved, identifiable phytoliths that could narrow the possibilities. Both pieces bear evidence of use with a slicing motion—striae parallel to their edges and wear traces symmetrically distributed on both edge aspects. The used edges also show the minute damage scars typically resulting from the cutting of soft material. These two tools provide the first direct evidence that early hominids used stone tools to gather or process plant material.

Three pieces show wear polishes of the type produced experimentally by working wood, which resemble those found on implements used for working soft plant material but are less reflective and less developed. Two of these tools were used as scrapers, as they have polish rounding the edge from the ventral aspect, striae at high angles to the edge and 'stepped' damage scars on the dorsal edge aspect. The other implement shows symmetrical wear traces, parallel striae and a few crescent-shaped damage scars, indicating its use as a saw. Except for 'hammerstones' (naturally shaped pebbles used to strike off flakes), these three implements may represent the earliest identified 'tools to make tools.'

Although preliminary, our results are pertinent to the controversy concerning the diet of early hominids and the role of stone tools in their adaption. The detection of wear traces indistinguishable from experimental meat-cutting polishes is strong evidence that early hominids ate meat. Our use-wear data independently corroborate the evidence of the cut-marks found on bones from several early sites, including some of those we sampled. Our evidence documents the use, by early hominids, of stone tools to cut soft plant material, but does not indicate the purpose of this activity. Our identification of a few woodworking tools indicates that by 1.5 Myr ago, some stone tools were probably being used to create wooden implements. If further studies show that such tools are common at early hominid sites, then the manufacture of implements such as digging sticks and spears may eventually be inferred as part of early adaptive patterns.

The discovery that interpretable patterns of microscopic wear can be preserved on cryptocrystalline silica implements even from sites 1.5 Myr old implies that microwear analysis can be profitably applied to suitable stone artefacts of all ages. We should, therefore, be able to document the successive appearance of activities, such as animal butchery, wood working, hide preparation, bone- and antler-working, throughout the entire Palaeolithic. Such investigations will enable archaeologists to discuss with greater certainty crucial aspects of the behavioural repertoire of early hominids.

We thank John W.K. Harris and Richard Leakey for aid and encouragement, Judith Ogden for drawing the illustrations, and especially Glynn Isaac and Tim White for many helpful suggestions. The Koobi Fora Archaeological Project, a joint effort of the National Museums of Kenya and the University of California, Berkeley, is funded by the NSF. Funds for some of the equipment used in this study were provided by the L.S.B. Leakey Foundation.

Notes

[1] Keeley, L.H. *Experimental Determination of Stone Tool Uses: a Microwear Analysis* (University of Chicago Press. 1980).

[2] Keeley, L. H. & Newcomer, M.H. *J. archaeol. Sci.* 4, 29–62 (1977).

[3] Cahen, D., Keeley, L.H. & Van Noten, F.L. *Curr. Anthrop.* 20, 661–683 (1979).

[4] Isaac, G.L. & Harris, J.W.K. in *Koobi Fora Research Project* Vol. 1 (eds Leakey, R.E.F. & Leakey, M.) 64–85 (Clarendon. Oxford. 1978).

5   Bunn, H. *et al. World Archaeol.* 12, 119–136 (1980).

6   Harris, J.W.K. & Isaac, G.L. *Nature* 262, 102–197 (1975).

7   Harris, J.W.K. thesis. Univ. California, Berkeley (1978).

8   Drake, R.E., Curtis, G.H., Cerling, T.E., Cerling, B.W. & Hampel, J. *Nature* 283, 368–372 (1980).

9   Gleadow, A.J.W. *Nature* 284, 225–230 (1980).

10 McDougall, I., Maier, R., Sutherland-Hawkes, P. & Gleadow, A.J.W. *Nature* 284, 230–234 (1980).

11 Anderson, P. *World Archaeol.* 12, 181–194 (1980).

"Pottery and Its History"

PRUDENCE M. RICE

Pottery is one of the most frequently encountered categories of material remains from archaeological sites dating to within the past several thousand years. This selection, which provides a good overview of pottery studies in archaeology, was originally published as the first chapter in the comprehensive *Pottery Analysis: A Sourcebook* by Prudence Rice, a professor at Southern Illinois University, Carbondale. In the Preface, Rice states that the book is directed primarily to archaeologists and other social scientists and is intended as a relatively broad reference work. With its extensive list of references, this selection also introduces readers to the archaeological literature on pottery studies. Although the book was first published in 1987, it has remained one of the standard works on pottery studies in archaeology in the early twenty-first century.

Questions to Guide Reading

What do the words *ceramics, pottery, terra-cotta, earthenware, stoneware, china,* and *porcelain* mean?
What are the approximate dates of the first known ceramics and pottery?
How are the origins and early uses of pottery sometimes explained?
What three main approaches do archaeologists use in the study of pottery?

Pottery was the first synthetic material humans created—artificial stone—and it combines the four basic elements identified by the Greeks: earth, water, fire, and air. As one of many materials within the large sphere of technology known as ceramics, pottery has transformed a broad range of human endeavors, from prehistoric cuisine to the twentieth-century aerospace industry.

Besides prehistoric vessels and fragments, common ceramics include terra-cottas, earthenwares, and stonewares such as craft items and flowerpots, and also china and porcelain tableware. Less obviously, perhaps, ceramics also encompass bricks, roof and floor tiles, sewer pipe, glass, and vitreous plumbing fixtures, as well as cements and plasters, abrasives, refractories, enameled metals, electrical insulation and conduction parts, space-shuttle tiles, spark plugs, and dentures (see Norton 1970, 408–74), and recently ceramic materials have been invented that can bond to living human tissue, opening up new medical applications (Hench and Etheridge 1982, 126–48). The connection between ancient pottery fragments, outer space, and modern medicine may seem tenuous, but it is present in the realm of ceramics.

1.1 Pottery and Ceramics: Definitions and Products

The term "ceramic" derives from the Greek *keramos*, variously translated as "burned stuff" or "earthenware"; it describes a fired product rather than a clay raw material (Oldfather 1920; see also Washburn, Ries, and Day 1920). Although in popular usage ceramics denotes materials made of clay, modern science applies the term far more broadly to chemical compounds combining metallic elements (which give up electrons) with nonmetallic elements (which add or share electrons). Thus one definition calls ceramics "the art and science of making and using solid articles which have as their essential component, and are composed in large part of, inorganic nonmetallic materials" (Kingery, Bowen, and Uhlmann 1976, 3). Although some ceramics are compositionally complex, they may also exist as simple oxides of aluminum (Al_2O_3), magnesium (MgO), or barium ($BaTiO_3$).

The word ceramics has two sets of overlapping meanings, one set common to materials science and another employed in art and archaeology, which complicates its precise definition and usage. In materials science ceramics is a broad generic term, referring either to the entire range of compounds of metals and nonmetals or, sometimes slightly more restrictively, to materials manufactured from silicates (usually clays) and hardened by applying heat. The term also encompasses the research and applied fields developed around these products, that is, ceramic science, ceramic engineering, and ceramic industries. Pottery is one of several specific industries within the overall ceramic field (table 1.1) and includes low- and high-fired tableware, utensils, and tiles; the other ceramic industries manufacture structural, electrical, refractory, or glass products (Grimshaw 1971, 35).

In art and archaeology the term ceramics usually excludes construction or industrial products (cements, bricks, abrasives, etc.) and conforms more closely to dictionary definitions, which emphasize the plastic arts and clay working. Within these fields, ceramics refers to cooking and serving utensils and objets d'art manufactured of clay. Even here the term is sometimes employed more specifically to distinguish ceramics—high-fired, usually glazed, and vitrified—from pottery, which consists of low-fired, unvitrified objects and/or cooking and storage vessels. In Oriental studies an even finer distinction may be made, whereby ceramics denotes glazed and vitrified material intermediate technologically between low-fired pottery and high-fired translucent porcelain.

In terms of these several criteria of function, firing, and composition, prehistoric archaeologists and anthropologists investigating traditional crafts commonly treat only a subset of the diverse field of ceramics, that is, low-fired, unglazed, relatively coarse pottery vessels or art objects. (It is clear, however, that in the historical period as well as in much of Asia, high-fired glazed and vitrified ceramics provide a major component of the data base.) The fine distinction between ceramics and pottery is difficult to uphold in many situations, for example, in time periods or regions where domestic vessels were of vitrified clay. Nevertheless, given both the extremely broad technical meaning and the narrow art-historical meaning of the term ceramics, the bulk of low-fired, unvitrified material treated by anthropologists and prehistoric archaeologists is more properly referred to as pottery.

Prehistoric, historical, and modern pottery and ceramics are grouped into a number of categories called wares or bodies (table 1.2) on the basis of their composition, firing, and surface treatment (see Norton 1970, 1–7). The broadest division is into unvitrified versus vitrified wares, a distinction based on whether the composition and firing are such that the clay melts and fuses into a glassy (i.e., vitreous or vitrified) substance. Low-fired, porous, unvitrified

TABLE 1.1 PRINCIPAL CERAMIC INDUSTRIES

Industry	Product
Structural ceramics	Bricks, tiles, drainpipes, concrete, flowerpots
Pottery	Artware, tableware Terra-cotta Earthenware, glazed and unglazed Stoneware China Porcelain
Refractories	Fireclay bricks, crucibles, insulation
Electrical	Spark plugs
Abrasives	Abrasives
Glass	Glasses, glaze

Source: After Grimshaw 1971, 35.

pottery includes terra-cottas and earthenwares, while high-fired, vitrified ceramics include stonewares and porcelains.

Terra-cottas are relatively coarse, porous wares fired at low temperatures, usually 900°C or less. The earliest fired pottery in all areas of the world falls into this category. Terra-cotta vessels, sculptures, and tiles are generally not covered with a glaze, but they may exhibit several surface treatments that enhance their function. Roughening surfaces by beating with a carved or a cord- or fabric-wrapped paddle can increase the ability of vessels to absorb heat and prevent them from slipping out of the hands when wet. Alternatively, surfaces may be covered with slip or engobe, a liquid solution of fine clays and water that, in addition to cosmetic effects of coloring and smoothing, lowers the vessel's porosity and retards seepage of liquid contents. Terra-cottas are often subsumed within the broader category of earthenwares.

Earthenwares also include porous, unvitrified clay bodies, but they are fired at a wide range of temperatures from 800/900°C or so up to 1100/1200°C. In the lower part of the range they are roughly equivalent to terra-cottas. Earthenwares may be glazed or unglazed; although the body itself is not vitrified, the firing temperature may be high enough to allow a glaze to form properly. These wares

TABLE 1.2 CERAMIC BODIES AND THEIR CHARACTERISTICS

Body Type	Porosity	Firing Range	Typical Applications	Comment
Terra-cotta	High: 30% or more	Well below 1000°C	Flowerpots, roof tiles, bricks, artware; most prehistoric pottery	Unglazed, coarse, and porous; often red-firing
Earthenware	Usually 10%–25%	Wide: 900–1200°C	Coarse: drainpipes, filters, tiles, bricks Fine: wall and floor tiles, majolicas	Glazed or unglazed; body nonvitrified
Stoneware	0.5%–2.0%	Ca. 1200–1350°C	Glazed drainpipes, roof tiles, tableware, artware	Glazed or unglazed; vitrified body
China	Low: usually less than 1%	1100–1200°C	Tableware	White, vitrified
Porcelain	Less than 1%; often nearly 0%	1300–1450°C	Fine tableware; artware; dental, electrical, and chemical equipment	Hard body; fine, white, translucent; "rings" when tapped

are made from "earthenware clays," usually relatively coarse, plastic red-firing primary clays. This category of ceramic material includes a wide range of products, ranging from coarse earthenwares (sometimes called "heavy clay products") such as bricks and tiles to fine earthenwares such as tin-enameled majolicas, made with more refined white-burning clay bodies. Earthenwares have served an enormous variety of household and construction purposes throughout the world for many millennia.

Stonewares are fired at temperatures of roughly 1200 to 1350°C, high enough to achieve at least partial fusion or vitrification of the clay body, depending on its composition. The body is medium coarse and opaque rather than translucent and often is gray or light brown. It is usually composed of "stoneware clays," which are typically sedimentary deposits such as ball clays (see Rhodes 1973, 22), highly plastic and low in iron. Stonewares may be unglazed or may have a lead glaze or, more frequently in modern times, a salt glaze. A distinctive fine, hard, porcelain-like European stoneware is Wedgwood jasper ware, containing high quantities of barium sulfate, which began to be made in England in the mid-eighteenth century.

The pinnacle of the potter's art, at least in terms of technical accomplishments; was reached with the Chinese production of porcelain, a thin, white, translucent vitrified ceramic that is customarily fired at temperatures of 1280–1400°C or higher. Porcelains are made of a white-firing, highly refractory kaolin clay (sometimes called "china clay"), relatively free of impurities, mixed with quartz and with ground, partially decomposed feldspathic rock that acts as a flux. When fired to high temperatures the feldspar melts, giving the product its characteristic translucency, hardness, and melodious ring when tapped. High-fired (but nontranslucent) porcelains in China are well known from the T'ang dynasty in the ninth and tenth centuries A.D. (Hobson 1976, 148), although "protoporcelains" or "porcellanous" stonewares are sometimes claimed to have been manufactured a millennium earlier in the Han dynasty (Laufer 1917; Li Jiazhi 1985, 159).

When Chinese porcelains of the Song, Ming, and later dynasties reached Europe, potters there tried a variety of experiments to achieve the same hardness and translucency, including adding ground glass to the clay, but they met with little success. The translucency of porcelain could be achieved but not the hardness, and the European product up through the eighteenth century was a "soft porcelain" or *pâte tendre* (Kingery and Smith 1985). Porcelains today are composed of 40% to 50% kaolin (sometimes with the addition of a more plastic ball clay), 25% to 30% feldspar, and 20% to 25% quartz or flint (Norton 1970, 336; Rhodes 1973, 53–54). "Bone china" is a late eighteenth-century English innovation in which calcined ox bones provide the desired translucency. Bone china, consisting of 40% to 50% bone ash, today is made almost exclusively in England (Norton 1970, 346–60).

1.2 History of Pottery and Ceramics

It is impossible to trace precisely the beginnings of human exploitation of the world's resources of earthy and clay substances. Although early stone tools from Africa are more than a million years old, the oldest objects of clay that archaeologists have found date only in the tens of thousands of years. Humans may have experimented with soft, plastic earthy materials considerably before this, perhaps hundreds of thousands of years ago, in uses as ephemeral as painting their bodies with colored clays. But the essential features in the history of use of this resource is the application of heat to transform the soft clay into something hard and durable. A relatively recent achievement by the yardstick of prehistory, it is this transformation that allowed broken bits of pottery to survive millennia and come into archaeologists' hands for study.

Any discussion of the history of pottery and ceramics must begin with the recognition of clay itself as a useful raw material (see table 1.3). Clay is certainly one of the most abundant, cheap, and adaptable resources available for human exploitation. Earliest archaeological evidence for its use ties it to the diverse artistic expressions of the Upper Paleolithic period of central and western Europe. Many Paleolithic caves have designs traced into wet clay on walls and floors, in addition to the more familiar animal paintings. At the Tuc d'Audoubert cave in France two modeled bison were found, formed of unfired clay. Among the famous "Venuses"—female figurines with exaggerated sexual characteristics—are specimens formed of fired and unfired clay from Dolní Veˇstonice in Czechoslovakia; dating to about 30,000 B.C. (Zimmerman and Huxtable 1971), some of the figurines were made of clay mixed with crushed mammoth bone.

These examples suggest that by the late Paleolithic period three significant principles of clay use were already known. One is that moist clay is plastic: it can be shaped and formed and will retain that form when dried. Another principle is that fire hardens clay. A third is that adding various substances to clay can improve its properties and usefulness.

The use of clay to make pottery containers does not seem to have originated in any single time and place in human history; rather, the idea seems to have been independently invented in an unknown number of centers. Several scenarios have been proposed to explain the origins of pottery; all are intuitively appealing and may have some basis in fact. Unfortunately, though, simple answers to "Why?" questions in archaeology are not easy to come by, and the whys and hows of pottery origins are no exception. Multiple causes are more probable explanations for almost all prehistoric cultural developments; thus the beginnings of pottery may be a consequence of numerous lines of experimentation and accumulation of practical experience.

One unusual suggestion is that pottery vessels may have developed out of "soil crusts," the surfaces of fine clay deposits that, during sun drying, shrank and warped into shallow bowllike forms (Goffer 1980, 108).

A more typical reconstruction of pottery origins calls attention to the fact that in many parts of the world the earliest pottery known archaeologically occurs in forms or with decorations that resemble earlier containers made of other materials. These pottery skeuomorphs often mimic containers of birchbark (Speck 1931), metal (Trachsler 1965), gourds (Joesink-Mandeville 1973), wood (Mellaart 1965, 220), or soapstone (Griffin 1965, 105–6), or leather bags or baskets. The similarities have led to suggestions that pottery utensils may have developed out of the use of clay to line, mend, or reinforce containers such as baskets (see, e.g., Wormington and Neal 1951, 9). This was once a popular explanation for the origins of Southwestern United States pottery, but the theory was based on the basketlike "corrugated" ceramic wares from this area, which actually occur relatively late in the technological sequence rather than early (Morris 1917; Gifford and Smith 1978).

Alternatively, clay could have been used alone, perhaps to form containers that were only dried and hardened in the sun; these would have served well for holding dry goods such as grains, seeds, nuts, or herbs. In prepottery Neolithic settlements at both Jarmo and Jericho in the Near East, clay-lined storage pits, "baked in place" basins set into house floors, fire pits, and ovens have been found (see Amiran 1965, 242). It is not difficult to imagine that once people recognized the durability and impermeability of the hardened clay that lined these pits they would have experimented with firing clay to create portable containers.

For archaeologists, the problem in all these reconstructions is that unfired clay objects are ephemeral and leave only rare traces in the archaeological record. They are easily broken, crushed, or dissolved by liquid and quickly return to their original state. Thus the early use of clay for making or modifying containers is still poorly documented.

The use of unfired clay for artistic or utilitarian objects is not restricted to the earliest stages of cultural development, however. Unfired clay vessels were

TABLE 1.3 CHRONOLOGICAL SEQUENCE OF DEVELOPMENTS IN POTTERY AND CERAMIC TECHNOLOGY

Development	Europe	Near East	Far East	Western Hemisphere
Fired clay figurines	Dolní Věstonice, Czechoslovakia, 30,000 B.C.			
Pottery		Anatolia, 8500–8000 B.C.	Japan, 10,000 B.C.	Various, 3000–500 B.C.
Kiln	[England, late 1st millennium B.C.]	Iran, 7th millennium B.C.	China, 4800–4200 B.C.	Mexico, A.D. 500
Wheel		3500 B.C.	China, 2600–1700 B.C.	[16th century A.D.]
Brick—adobe		Zagros, 7500–6300 B.C.		Coastal Peru, 900 B.C.; Mexico, 900–800 B.C.
Brick—fired		Sumer, 1500 B.C.		Mexico, A.D. 600–900
Stoneware	Germany, 14th century		China, 1400–1200 B.C.	
Glazes				
Hard		16th century B.C.	China, 1028–927 B.C.	
Lead		100 B.C.	China, 206 B.C.–A.D. 221	
Celadon			China, 4th century	
Fritted			China, 8th century	
Tin	Southern Italy, 13th century England, 17th century	Assyria, 900 B.C.		
Salt	Germany, 16th century			
Porcelain	Germany 1709 France 1768		China, 9–10th century Japan, 1616	
Bone china	England, late 8th century			
Gypsum plaster mold	Italy, 1500			
Jiggering	1700			
Slip casting	1740			
Pyrometric cones	1886			

found in tombs in Nubia from A.D. 300–550 (Williams, Williams, and McMillan 1985, 46); in the Near East unfired clay objects come from excavations into structures dating to the early Sumerian civilization, and a variety of unfired "mud" dishes and other utensils are made by Bedouins in the same area today (Ochsenschlager 1974); and some Eskimo pottery from A.D. 1000 to 1600 was unfired (Stimmell and

Stromberg 1986, 247). Unfired, sun-dried clay objects are made and used today in Papua New Guinea (May and Tuckson 1982, 7). Nonetheless, in most cases it is only when clay items were subjected to fire—intentionally or accidentally, through burning of dried clay parching trays or setting a clay-lined basket too close to the fire—that they survived and allow us to piece together a technological history of pottery.

The appearance of pottery vessels in the archaeological record was at one time interpreted within evolutionary theories as marking the development of human societies out of "Upper Savagery" into "Lower Barbarism" (Morgan 1877), but in more recent thinking pottery is seen as part of the so-called Neolithic technocomplex. This is an assemblage of tools and containers for food preparation and storage, together with the associated technology of their manufacture and use, that correlates in a very general way with worldwide changes in human lifeways at the end of the Paleolithic period or soon thereafter. These changes are dramatic, involving the adoption of food production rather than collecting, and settlement in villages rather than temporary encampments. Although there is no necessary causal relationship between agricultural life and pottery making, it is true that even today pottery is primarily made in sedentary as opposed to nomadic societies (table 1.4). When scrutinized on a smaller scale, however, the Neolithic changes appear as the culmination of a long series of connected adjustments and alterations in social and ecological relationships. The changes took place over several millennia and occurred in different ways at different times in different areas.

Pottery, rather than being a spectacular new achievement at this time, is better considered as a transformed exploitation of an already familiar raw material. The appearance and widespread adoption of fired pottery reflects both continuing and new needs for tools and resources—principally storing and preparing newly important foods such as domesticated grains—and new ways of meeting these needs. In fact one theory of the origins of pottery relates it to the need to detoxify plant foods by heating (Arnold 1985, 129–35). All of this is not to minimize its significance from the viewpoint of the history of technology, however. The technological achievements that underlie pottery making established the foundations for many other ancient and modern technologies such as metallurgy, brick architecture, and engineering.

1.2.1 POTTERY AND CERAMICS IN THE OLD WORLD

1.2.1.1 The Near East

In the Near East, although Paleolithic use of clay has not been documented archaeologically, after about 10,000 B.C. clays were used for a variety of purposes including architecture, pottery, and small modeled clay objects. Their order of appearance varies from region to region within the area.

TABLE 1.4 RELATION BETWEEN POTTERY MAKING AND SEDENTISM AMONG FIFTY-NINE ETHNOGRAPHIC SOCIETIES

	Settlement Type			
	Nonsedentary	Partially Sedentary	Fully Sedentary	Total
Pottery-making societies	2	12	32	46
Non-pottery-making societies	6	4	3	13
Total	8	16	35	59

Source: Arnold 1985, table 5.3. From the Human Relations Area Files Probability Sample Files.

Architectural use of clay is widespread very early (by 7500 B.C.) in all areas of the Near East and calls attention to the integration of clay exploitation with sedentary agricultural settlements. Clay was used by itself or mixed with chaff or straw from the fields as poured or "puddled" adobe for constructing walls of permanent houses, as plaster or mortar over rock or pole walls, and for floors and roofs. Indeed, wheat and barley kernels are often found embedded in the clay of these buildings (Amiran 1965, fig. 1). Adobe bricks began to be used as early as 7500–6300 B.C. in the Zagros area (Schmandt-Besserat 1974). Planoconvex bricks, formed in a mold and dried in the sun, continued to serve in the construction of residences, temples, and burial chambers for millennia; fired bricks were probably regularly in use by 1500 B.C.

Pottery containers appear perhaps as early as 8500–8000 B.C. at Beldibi (Bostanci 1959, 146–47, cited in Schmandt-Besserat 1977a, 133) and Çatal Hüyük (Mellaart 1964, 1965) in southern Turkey, whereas in Syria pottery did not occur until about 6000–5500 B.C. (Schmandt-Besserat 1977b, 40). In the Zagros area, figurines and geometric cones, spheres, and disks were made of clay as early as 8500–7500 B.C., and in the succeeding millennium pottery containers—which may or may not have been fired—began to be made (Schmandt-Besserat 1974). The earliest vessels in the Near East were hand built by coiled or segmental building (Mellaart 1965, 220) and then scraped, paddled, or rubbed to produce an even finish; they were fired without kilns in open bonfires, using wood or dung cakes for fuel. These and later vessels come in a range of shapes, including bowls, cups, and trays, and later are decorated with paint and incised lines. Their decoration depicts a variety of plant and animal forms, human activities, and costuming; and the context of recovery—burials, household activity areas, refuse deposits—provides many clues to their diverse functions.

Despite the common use of fired clay, objects formed of unfired clay continued to be important.

At Çayönü, in Anatolia, in the period about 6500 to 6000 B.C., before the manufacture and use of fired pottery, various unfired clay objects have been found, including models of houses, a bowl formed by lining a basket with clay, animal and human figurines, and a clay-lined bin (Redman 1978, 160).

At a number of sites in the Near East, unfired or low-fired clay tokens, inscribed with various notations, may constitute early records of economic transactions that can be linked to the later development of writing (Schmandt-Besserat 1978; cf. Lieberman 1980). The variety of sizes and shapes of the objects (cones, disks, etc.) may correspond to kinds and quantities of goods. These shapes are echoed in the earliest examples of writing, which appear in cuneiform on clay tablets by the late fourth millennium. When fired, as at Ebla (Tell Mardikh), whether intentionally or accidentally, these clay tablets formed a permanent "library" of knowledge and activities of the time (Matthiae 1977).

Female figurines, "mother goddesses," were widely produced in early agricultural towns and villages in the Near East and may have connections with fertility or household religious practices. Numerous other items of clay were also manufactured, including toys, models of houses, and tools. Among the tools are "administrative artifacts" such as stamp and cylinder seals used for recording and identification in economic transactions, loom weights and spindle whorls used in weaving and spinning, and clay sickles, with inset stone blades, for harvesting grain.

By 1500 B.C. three major characteristics of ceramic manufacture—ancient and modern, craft and industrial—had developed in the Near East. These include the use of kilns (open topped) for firing, the potter's wheel, and glazes. These developments had far-reaching significance in pyrotechnology and in the organization of craft production beyond simply providing household cooking pots and drinking cups.

Kilns, or firing chambers, are significant innovations because the enclosed space concentrates available heat, permitting higher temperatures, better control of the firing process, and more efficient use of fuel. The earliest kilns were probably open topped—either pit kilns or built aboveground—and fulfilled these functions only minimally. Later changes in kiln design, involving enclosed chambers to provide maximum firing control, permitted successful manufacture of high-fired vitrified ceramics. Such high-temperature firing control also contributed to the beginnings of bronze metallurgy (smelting of metal ores) and glassmaking. Several kilns are known from the fifth millennium B.C. in the Near East, and one near Susa in Iran is dated to the seventh millennium B.C. (Majidzadeh 1975–77, 217).

The potter's wheel allowed rapid mass production of standardized forms and development of a ceramic industry serving a large market. The true potter's wheel, on which vessels are "thrown," combines the principle of the pivot, also used in wheeled vehicles, with the principles of rotary and centrifugal motion. It was probably preceded by a "slow wheel," "hand wheel," or tournette on which vessels could be turned during shaping but where the actual rotary force was not a fundamental part of vessel forming as it is in the true wheel. One line of evidence—not entirely reliable—for the use of potter's wheels is the characteristic "rilling" or spiraling ridges on vessel surfaces formed by pressure of the potter's hands during throwing. Archaeological discovery of actual potter's wheels is of course the best evidence of this technique, but those made of wood may not have survived. Wheels or pairs of socketed hand wheels of stone or clay seem to have been common in the Near East after about 3500 B.C. (Amiran and Shenhav 1984; Lobert 1984).

Glazes are vitreous (glassy) coatings melted on the surfaces of vessels to make them watertight. Their manufacture is dependent both on knowledge of how to prepare a substance that will melt to form a glass and on the ability to sustain a high enough temperature in firing so this melting can take place. Glazed faience beads were made in Egypt during the Predynastic period, about 4000–3100 B.C. (see Vandiver 1982), and there is some evidence that alkaline glazed pottery manufacture may have begun about the sixteenth century B.C. in the Near East (Hedges and Moorey 1975).

One of the major kinds of glazes on earthenwares, ancient and modern, is the lead glaze. Lead acts as a flux in glaze composition; that is, it lowers the melting or fusion point of the glaze mixture, allowing it to form a glass at lower temperatures. Lead glazes are generally clear and often green though yellows and reds are also common; copper was a typical colorant. They apparently developed in China during the Han dynasty, 206 B.C. to A.D. 200 (Shangraw 1978, 44), and in the Near East about 100 B.C.

A second kind of earthenware glaze is the tin glaze, a thick white coating made opaque by adding stannic (tin) oxide to a lead glaze. These opaque glazes mask defects in finish or color of the vessel body and provide a clean background for painted decoration, often executed in blue or in polychrome colors. Tin glazes (or enamels) were first used in decorating brick panels by the Assyrians after 900 B.C., then the knowledge of their manufacture was lost until it was rediscovered by Islamic potters in the ninth century A.D. Never popular in China, tin-glazed pottery and tiles were produced in the Islamic Near East and North Africa; knowledge of their manufacture traveled with the Moors to Spain and Italy and later to the New World in the sixteenth century.

1.2.1.2 The Far East

It is in the Far East—primarily China, Korea, and Japan—that the earliest innovations in virtually all stages of the potter's art can be found. Because of these outstanding technical and aesthetic advancements throughout the history of the craft, little attention has been paid to the earliest "primitive" stages, and as a result many questions remain concerning the beginnings of clay use in this area.

The oldest pottery known in Japan is a very well made type called Jo—mon, or "cord pattern," because of its distinctive cord-marked or string-impressed decoration. The dates of Jo—mon pottery are highly controversial, because radiocarbon measurements suggest some pieces may be over twelve thousand years old (Ikawa-Smith 1980, 138). A thermoluminescent dating program on some Jo—mon material, while not yielding evidence of such antiquity, generally supported the radiocarbon ages of the various periods and gave mid-sixth millennium B.C. dates for the earliest Jo—mon period pottery (Ichikawa, Nagatomo, and Hagahara 1978). Jo—mon pottery is hand built and consists primarily of beakers or deep jars with small bases, which often seem unstable and poorly suited for practical use. Although the entire range of early through late Jo—mon pottery is characterized by impressed and modeled (rather than painted) decoration, the most elaborate of these products were produced in the Middle Jo—mon period (second millennium B.C.), with heavy appliquéd fillets and buttons, castellated rims, and deeply incised grooves (see Kidder 1968; Rathbun 1979).

In China little is known of the very earliest stages of the potter's art, though the late prehistoric and historical periods are very well studied. The earliest pottery in the area comes from coastal southeast China

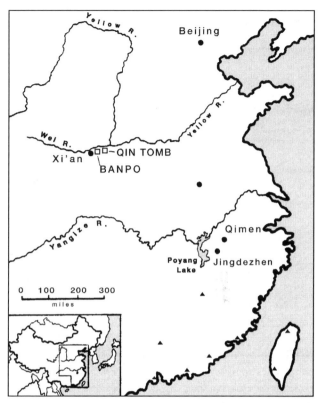

FIGURE 1.1: Map of east-central China, showing locations of interest in ceramic history. Small triangles show locations of sites with early cord-marked pottery.

and adjacent regions and consists of a variety of cord- and shell-marked and incised types (Chang 1977, 85–90). Dating is somewhat uncertain; although dates in the fifth millennium range seem most acceptable, a new radiocarbon determination from the interior of Jiangxi Province gives a date of 6875 ±240 B.C. (Chang 1977, 511). Nine thermoluminescence dates on pottery from Zenpiyan, in Guangxi Province, range from 6990 to 10,340 B.P. (Wang and Zhou 1983, tables 1 and 3).

The best-known early Chinese pottery (see Shangraw 1978) comes from the Yangshao culture in the Yellow River valley (fig. 1.1), between 4800 and 4200 B.C. Potters at Banpo and other Yangshao villages produced beautiful hand-formed jars and

dishes painted with red-and-black geometric decoration, so skillfully made that they could not represent the beginnings of the craft. Furthermore, these wares were fired in small, subterranean horizontal and vertical updraft kilns (fig. 1.2) on the outskirts of the villages (Shangraw 1977); these Neolithic kilns could achieve firing temperatures of 950°C (Li Jiazhi 1985, 143). The date of production of these wares is comparable to the fifth-millennium dates of the early kilns in the Near East. Incised marks on some of the Banpo vessels have been interpreted as maker's marks associated with particular family lines (Chang 1983, 84–86) and may show some relation to later characters, particularly numerals, in Chinese writing (Cheung 1983).

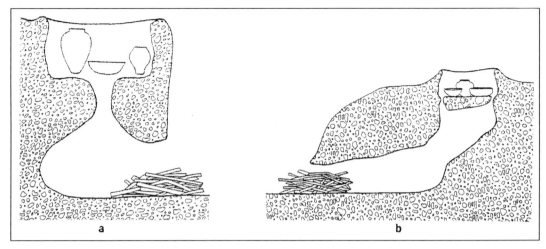

FIGURE 1.2: Reconstruction of early bank kilns found at Banpo, China: *a*, vertical kiln; *b*, horizontal kiln. After Shangraw 1977, 389.

There is little evidence for the beginning of use of the potter's wheel in China. It has recently been suggested that a low, thick-walled dishlike vessel commonly found at Yangshao sites between 4800 and 3600 B.C. may actually have been used as a slow or low-speed wheel (Zhou Zhen-xi 1985). The fast or true wheel was apparently used during the Zhou (Chou) period, roughly the first millennium B.C. (Hobson 1976, 2).

One of the most spectacular finds of archaeological pottery is the army of 7,500 life-size soldiers and horses found in 1974 near Xian, China. Guarding the tomb of Emperor Qin Shi Huang, the first unifier of China in 221 B.C., the terra-cotta army was formed in separate pieces but without molds. Solid or hollow legs support hollow torsos made of coils of clay; heads, arms, and legs were shaped separately, then attached to the bodies with strips of clay; individualized facial features and costume details were sculpted or appliquéd to finish the pieces before firing, then after firing the pieces were painted with red, green, black, and other colors (Hearn 1979, 46–48; Museum of Qin Shi Huang 1981, 11–14).

Chinese ceramic history is marked by numerous technical achievements of lasting impact, particularly in the field of high-fired bodies and in glazes (Li Jiazhi 1985; Zhang Fukang 1985). By the Middle Shang period, between the fifteenth and thirteenth centuries B.C., stonewares were being produced in kilns capable of reaching 1200°C (Li Jiazhi 1985, 144). At about the same time, glazes were produced using a combination of CaO (lime) and wood ash as fluxes (Zhang Fukang 1985, 164, 170), so vessels may have been given a "natural kiln glost" from wood ash during the firing. True hard (feldspathic) glazes began to be used a few centuries later in the Early Western Zhou period (Shangraw 1977, 383; 1978, 43–46).

One of the most beautiful of Chinese wares is celadon, identified by its distinctive sea green, apple green, or olive green glaze. The delicate color, described as "the blue-green color of distant hills," is so similar to jade that the ware was sometimes called "false jade." The origin of the term celadon is uncertain: one theory is that it was named after Saladin, a twelfth-century Islamic potentate, while another calls up the gray-green costume of Celadon, the shepherd hero in a seventeenth-century French pastoral comedy (Wykes-Joyce 1958, 54). Although celadon glaze manufacture has been dated as early as the fourth century A.D. (Mikami 1979, 12), the most famous of the celadons were those produced in the Longquan (Lung Ch'uan) District of the Southern Song dynasty (A.D. 1127–79) and later (Hobson 1976, 16; Li Hu Hou 1985; Vandiver and Kingery 1984). Celadons were widely popular throughout Asia, which can be attributed not only to their beauty but also to their supposed magical or curative powers. It was believed in India and Persia, for example, that a celadon bowl would crack or change color if its contents were poisoned, and a famous Song celadon censer, shaped like a bird, was said to make birds burst into song and to cry out to its owner if danger was near (Spinks 1965, 98–99). Medications were also thought to be more powerful if prepared in a celadon vessel or if such a vessel or its glaze was ground and mixed into the potion (Spinks 1965, 99–100).

The most enduring legacy of Chinese potters is porcelain, originally called *porcellana* (shell) by Marco Polo because of its delicate translucency. The origins of porcelain are uncertain. Historical texts are not conclusive: there is no single Chinese word for porcelain as distinct from other kinds of pottery, although the beginning of a new written character, *tz'u* (or *ts'e*) during the Han dynasty (206 B.C. to A.D. 220) has sometimes been interpreted as signaling the creation of a distinctive new ceramic product (see Hobson 1976, 140–42). Compositionally, some of the hard-fired stoneware ceramics manufactured in this period or earlier (Shang-Zhou) have been called "porcellanous" stoneware (Laufer 1917) or proto-porcelain (Li Jiazhi 1985, 135), but they lack the characteristic white color and translucency of true porcelain. Excavations of tombs in the region of Anyang and Xian in northern China yielded white porcelains, revealing that its manufacture dates as early as the Northern and Sui dynasties (late sixth century A.D.), though no kiln sites of this early date have been found (Li Guozhen and Zhang Xiqiu 1986,

217). Until recently, it was the recovery of Chinese porcelains from outside China that provided the basis for inferring a somewhat later date of production, that of the T'ang dynasty, A.D. 618–906 (Hobson 1976, 148). A set of thirty polychrome porcelain headrests was excavated at an ancient Nara period (A.D. 649–794) temple in Japan (Mikami 1979, 110), and porcelains were also found in the ninth-century Moslem center of Samarra, on the Euphrates River in modern Iraq, which flourished from A.D. 836 to 883 (Wykes-Joyce 1958, 51). White, hard, translucent, and resonant, porcelain reached its finest development in the Song dynasty (A.D. 960–1279) and thereafter and was compared by lyrical Chinese poets to jade, snow, and lotus leaves.

Chinese porcelains are most closely identified with the "imperial kilns" at Jingdezhen (formerly Ching-tê-chên, or Ch'ang-nan). This city (see Tichane 1983) rose from humble origins as an old market town (*chên*) on the east bank of the Chang River in northern Jiangxi (Kiangsi) Province, to become "the metropolis of the ceramic world, whose venerable and glorious traditions outshine Meissen and Sèvres and all the little lights of Europe, and leave them eclipsed and obscure" (Hobson 1976, 152). Although skilled potters were to be found in the area centuries earlier, the meteoric rise of Jingdezhen as one of the world's great potting centers began when Emperor Ching Te (A.D. 1004–7) of the Song dynasty decreed that its kilns should produce wares for the imperial capital (Hobson 1976, 45, 156). Most of the later Chinese export porcelains (see Gordon 1977; Weiss 1971, 44–46) were manufactured at Jingdezhen for shipment to Europe and the New World.

Chinese pottery and porcelains exerted incalculable influence on the ceramic industries of other nations for more than a millennium. The earliest evidence for long-distance export of Chinese products is in the time of the T'ang dynasty, when porcelains came to be popular among the Asian aristocracy (Mikami 1979, 35). Celadons reached Korea by the eleventh century (Mikami 1979, 13), and porcelains arrived there in the fourteenth century. The arrival of Korean potters in Japan, allegedly by force during the "Ceramic Wars" (1592–98) involving trade with Europeans, led to the beginnings of porcelain manufacture there, and the discovery of kaolin clay stimulated the founding of the famous kilns at Arita in 1616 (see Weiss 1971, 48–49). Archaeomagnetic dating has been used to confirm some of the legends surrounding the beginning of porcelain at the time (Fleming 1976, 173).

Contacts with the Near East flourished especially during and after the Mongol Yuan dynasty (A.D. 1280–1367), when there was considerable interchange between the Chinese and Islamic ceramic arts. One significant import from the Near East during this period was pure cobalt pigment—called "Mohammedan blue" or "sacrificial blue" (Zhang Fukang 1985, 173)—for underglaze decoration; the local cobalt in China was contaminated with small amounts of manganese and did not fire well (Wykes-Joyce 1958, 57). The result of this trade was the foundation of the Chinese blue-on-white decorative tradition that has continued to the present (see Weiss 1971, 26–29).

1.2.1.3 Europe and the Mediterranean

Europe was not an independent center of pottery development; the appearance and development of the craft were tied to the broader range of technology associated with agriculture and sedentary life pioneered in the Near East.

Two kinds of pottery in Europe and the classical world, Greek figured pottery and Roman Arretine ware, represent outstanding technical achievements. Both these wares, judged by their firing and other characteristics, probably should be classed as high-fired terra-cottas or low-fired earthenwares. Neither is glazed, though their fine glossy slips have sometimes been erroneously referred to as glazes.

Greek black- and red-figure pottery (Noble 1966; Richter 1976) was manufactured during the sixth through fourth centuries B.C. in Athens. The distinctive painted decoration was applied by potters or by a separate group of vase painters who sometimes signed their work, and the painted scenes depict a variety of activities of Greek life, both ceremonial and prosaic (Beazley 1945; Thompson 1984; Von Bothmer 1985). The occurrence together of

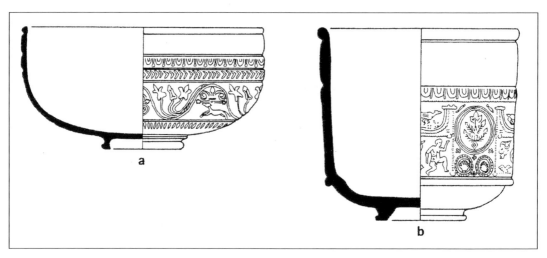

FIGURE 1.3: Gaulish Samian-ware bowls, moldmade with raised decoration and covered with a red slip: a, hemispherical bowl (known as form Drag 37), used in the third century B.C.; b, slightly less common deep bowl (Drag 30) made in the first and second centuries B.C. After Anderson 1984, fig. 27.

both red and black iron paints and slips on these vessels entranced and perplexed scholars for generations, but experiments to reproduce them did not succeed until the early twentieth century (Schumann 1942; Stross and Asaro 1984, 181–83). It was found that the colors and gloss of the paint derived from a particular clay mineral (illite) and from careful control of kiln atmosphere in firing.

Roman Arretine ware dates from the first century B.C. to the fourth century A.D.; the name comes from ancient Arretium (modern Arezzo), a center of production in northern Italy. These beautiful lustrous red bowls and jars were copied at multiple centers of manufacture (Johns 1977a; Peacock 1982, 114–28) and were widely traded throughout Roman Europe. Wares made in what is now France and Germany, for example, are referred to as samian or Gaulish Samian (from Samos) ware (fig. 1.3) or as *terra sigillata* (meaning "clay impressed with designs"). Like the Greek gloss paints, the distinctive red slips of Arretine and Samian wares are fine illite clays fired in a carefully controlled atmosphere at temperatures between 980 and 1260°C (Lawrence and West 1982, 212; Bimson 1956; Tite, Bimson, and Freestone 1982). Vessels were formed in wheel-thrown molds and often feature the name or mark of either the vessel maker or the mold maker on their surface (see Hoffman 1983).

During the Renaissance, the technique of tin glazing moved from the Mahgreb (North Africa) to southern Italy by the fourteenth century (Whitehouse 1980) and then to Spain, France, Germany, and the Netherlands, finally reaching England in the seventeenth century. The type of pottery on which this glaze appears is a fine earthenware known variously as majolica or maiolica, faience, or delft after the hypothesized (and often confused) locations of manufacture or distribution throughout Europe (Wykes-Joyce 1958, 74). Maiorca (or Majorca) is an island from which tin-glazed wares were shipped to Italy, so Italians named the pottery after the island, maiolica; Faenza is a city in Italy from which Italian tin-glazed wares were exported to France, so the French called the pottery faience (not to be confused with a much earlier Egyptian silica-rich glazed material also called faience). Delft wares (Fourest 1980) are later products from the town of Delft in the Netherlands, made in imitation of Chinese blue-and-white porcelains.

European potters continued making tin-glazed earthenwares, and by the fourteenth century Germany had taken the lead in producing a well-developed stoneware. Potters also experimented with reproducing the highly desirable "hard" Oriental porcelains (Weiss 1971, 60–83), but they were hindered in that endeavor by a lack of suitably plastic and white-firing kaolins. Although an experimental porcelain had been made by Grand Duke Francesco Maria de' Medici in Italy in the late sixteenth century (Wykes-Joyce 1958, 78–79; Weiss 1971, 69; Kingery and Smith 1985), it was not until the early eighteenth century that a viable product was achieved. Two Germans, "alchemist" Böttger and physicist von Tschirnhausen, found a local source of kaolin clay that permitted them success in creating a hard, white, translucent porcelain body—a success achieved, according to Böttger's notes, at 5:00 P.M. on January [AU: Date missing] 1708, after a twelve-hour firing (Weiss 1971, 60). With that discovery in 1710 a royal porcelain factory was later established at Meissen, near Dresden (Wykes-Joyce 1958, 136–39). The French continued to produce soft porcelains at Vincennes (d'Albis 1985) and Sèvres until kaolin was discovered at Limoges in 1768, at which point true hard porcelain soon began to be manufactured in that country. In the late 1700s in England, Josiah Spode added calcined ox bones to a porcelainlike fine stoneware body formula, producing "bone china," which is white, translucent, and very hard.

1.2.2 POTTERY IN THE NEW WORLD

In the Western Hemisphere the development of pottery proceeded independent of that in the Old World, and from several apparently unrelated areas of origin. As in the Old World, its beginnings in the New World archaeological record are broadly correlated with the transition to horticulture and sedentary settlement in several regions after the end of the Pleistocene. But because these developments themselves varied considerably in time and mode of occurrence, the association of pottery with them is general, not specific.

Two facts are striking about the development of pottery in the New World as compared with the Old. One is that its earliest appearance is considerably later in the New World, by five thousand years or so. Second, two of the hallmarks of Old World ceramic production, glazes and the potter's wheel, never appeared in the pre-Columbian New World, nor were kilns ever widely used.

Surfaces of aboriginal vessels were covered by clay-rich slips rather than glazes, although vitreous glaze paints were manufactured and used in the Southwestern United States after A.D. 1000 (Shepard 1942a, 1965; DeAtley 1986). A shiny, lead-colored surface appeared on a widespread trade pottery called "Plumbate" in Mesoamerica about A.D. 1000 and is sometimes mistakenly referred to by archaeologists as a glaze. The coating was actually a clay-rich slip, however, its distinctive color and shine resulting from peculiarities in composition and firing (Shepard 1948a), and although it is vitrified in places it is not a true high-fired vitreous glaze. Similarly, potter's wheels were unknown in the New World. Although several devices (e.g., the *kabal* in Yucatán [Thompson 1958] and the *molde* in Oaxaca [Foster 1959] were used by potters to help turn the vessel during forming, the continuous, high-speed rotation of the true wheel was not attained.

Probable pottery kilns have been identified in highland Mexico (Abascal 1975; Payne 1982) as well as a few other areas, and these were primarily used after A.D. 500. In general, however, most New World pottery was fired in open bonfires rather than enclosed chambers. Firing temperatures were most commonly in the range of 700 to 900°C (see Shepard 1976, 84, 87). Stonewares and porcelains were never manufactured in the New World because in the general absence of kilns the consistently high temperatures necessary for vitrification could not be attained, and thus all New World aboriginal pottery falls into the category of terra-cottas or earthenwares. Glazes, wheels, and kilns were introduced to the Americas in the sixteenth century by European explorers and settlers.

Identification of the earliest pottery in the New World is a matter of some disagreement. A very early complex of vessel forms and decorative styles from Valdivia, on the coast of Ecuador, dates to approximately 2500 B.C. (Meggers and Evans 1966). The pottery is similar in some general characteristics (chiefly decoration) to Jo—mon pottery from Japan. This has prompted some speculation that a group of Japanese fishermen blown off course and shipwrecked in this area may have managed to persuade or coerce local inhabitants to make what was to be the first New World pottery. But subsequent excavations at the site revealed an earlier pottery style stratigraphically below the Jo—mon-like material (Bischoff and Viteri-Gamboa 1972), so the Japanese-origins hypothesis is at present given little credence.

The early development of pottery in other areas of the New World at approximately the same time, 2500 to 2000 B.C. or earlier, also supports hypotheses of indigenous development rather than diffusion. These areas of early pottery assemblages include the coast of Colombia (Reichel-Dolmatoff 1961), Pacific coastal Mexico (Brush 1965), and the southeastern United States (Sears and Griffin 1950). Relatively simple forms, often echoing the shapes of gourds or stone bowls, were hand modeled and decorated with incising or, in Mexico, with a red wash or slip. Both the Colombian and the southeastern United States examples were made of clay mixed with plant fibers, stimulating hypotheses that they may represent interrelated technologies resulting from population movements through the Caribbean islands (Bullen and Stoltman 1972).

From these beginnings, the next four thousand years of New World pottery development reveal great elaboration of forms and decoration, particularly in polychrome painting. Architectural uses of clay varied from area to area. Adobe bricks were commonly used in ceremonial buildings on the Peruvian coast, beginning by the Initial Period (1900–1800 B.C.) at the northern site of Las Haldas, whereas in the Andes highlands stone was more typically used. In Mesoamerica stone was employed far more often than adobe; adobe bricks were used in Late Formative period (ca. 900–800 B.C.) ceremonial architecture at Oaxaca (Flannery 1976, 24), and fired bricks are rare, being particularly associated with a Late Classic (ca. A.D. 600–900) lowland site of Comalcalco, in Tabasco, Mexico.

Lacking the wheel and kiln, New World potters were rarely able to attain the same levels of technical achievement and standardized production as did their stoneware- and porcelain-producing Old World contemporaries. In consequence, the artistic and utilitarian excellence of their products, while entirely the equal of Greek figured or Arretine pottery, is often denigrated as "primitive" or simply ignored by Old World scholars. Yet outstanding examples of the potter's craft are to be found all over the ancient New World.

In South America, from 200 B.C. to A.D. 700, Nazca (Proulx 1968) and Moche (Donnan 1965) potters on the coast of Peru produced stirrup-spouted vessels decorated with modeled and painted houses, animals, plants, and human faces so individualized as to suggest actual portraits. These polychrome designs included red, black, brown, yellow, blue, green, pink, and white colors. Other elaborate polychrome vessels, decorated with geometric and stylized natural motifs, were made throughout the Andes up to the coming of the Spaniards.

In Guatemala and Mexico, Maya potters of the Late Classic period civilization, A.D. 600 to 900, produced a variety of bowls and vases with modeled and painted decoration of exceptional technical skill (see Rice 1985). Cylindrical vessels and plates portrayed human and animal figures in a graceful natural style, featuring mythical and ritual scenes such as dances, processions, or royal audiences and often had brief glyphic texts that apparently identified the persons, locations, or events represented

(Coe 1973, 1978; Robicsek and Hales 1981; Quirarte 1979). They were painted with subtly toned pigments, often resist applied and underlying a sheer, glossy pale orange slip. After about A.D. 1000, much of the pottery decoration from Mexico through northern South America changed from multicolored designs to combinations of red, black, and white painting. The Aztecs in central Mexico made and used an orange-paste pottery with painted decoration of fine black lines.

Pueblo pottery in the Southwestern United States from A.D. 700 to 1300 (Dittert and Plog 1980) featured geometric and stylized life-form representations, with polychrome or black-and-white painted decoration. At the same time, in the southeastern and south-central United States, sophisticated plastic decorative techniques, especially incising and modeling, rather than painting were the outstanding modes of embellishment. Modeled heads of dogs or birds were often added to rims of simple globular vessels, or the vessels themselves might be in human or animal form, the features accented by paint or incising (Rice and Cordell 1986).

The prehistoric pottery vessels made in the New World included the standard repertoire of cooking, serving, and storage vessels—plates, bowls, jars, vases, cups—with local variations on shape and elaboration. In addition, braziers, griddles for toasting tortillas or manioc cakes, and "chile grinders" (bowls with incised interiors for grinding chile peppers) were common. Among the more distinctive of the manufactures are pottery incense burners from Mesoamerica, plain vases or bowls with elaborate modeled, ornamented faces and figures of humans and gods (Caso and Bernal 1952). Often two feet or more in height, these censers were painted in bright colors, and openings were placed so that the smoke from the incense would emerge from the figure's nose and mouth. Huge urns were made in South America and used for burials, the deceased being placed inside in a flexed or "fetal" position; elsewhere, smaller vessels were often used to hold cremated remains. Modeled and moldmade figurines of humans and animals and elaborately formed and painted model houses, villages, groups of dancers, and so forth were often found in burials in western Mexico. More utilitarian ceramic manufactures included spindle whorls for spinning cotton fibers, net and line sinkers used in fishing, pipes for smoking, and musical instruments such as whistles, drums, and flutes.

In the early years of the sixteenth century, Europeans arrived in the New World and began exploring and colonizing the land and trading with its native peoples. Their presence is marked by the distribution of European ceramics such as olive jars (Goggin 1970), majolicas (Lister and Lister 1982), stonewares, and porcelains as well as many nonceramic artifacts at missions, forts, trading posts, and settlement locations throughout the Americas. The centuries of European conquest of the native states and chiefdoms had variable effects on the craft of pottery making. Despite the drastic social, demographic, and economic events associated with the conquest—famines, disease, settlement relocation, and depopulation—utilitarian pottery making among the Incas, Mayas, and Aztecs continued virtually unchanged from its pre-European pattern in terms of resources used, form, and decoration. Gradually, however, by introducing the wheel, kilns, and glazes and by stimulating the local manufacture of glazed pottery and tiles for construction and trade, the Spaniards and English transformed and Europeanized the organization and products of the native ceramic craft in the Western Hemisphere.

1.3 Overview of Pottery Studies

Pottery has had a long and varied history of manufacture and use. This range of ceramic products traditionally has been studied from a wide variety of points of view, including artistic, aesthetic, archaeological, historical, classificatory, mechanical, mineralogical, and chemical. Appreciation of the aesthetic qualities of early Chinese porcelains stimu-lated Islamic potters to try to reproduce them in the ninth century. The antiquarianism of the Renaissance and post-Renaissance centuries fostered interest in collecting Greek and Roman wares and an awareness of early civilizations and their achievements. Finally, mineralogical and chemical experiments by western European potters and scientists trying to imitate Far Eastern porcelains led to improvements in their own manufactures, such as bone china.

Modern archaeological studies have generally devoted a great deal of attention—in fact, disproportionate attention—to pottery in their reports, and this is true for myriad reasons. First, pottery has a long history and is found in virtually all parts of the world; its presence is rarely controlled by a particular geological or environmental situation or conditions of preservation. Second, as a function of its physical properties, pottery is essentially nonperishable: although a pot may break, the fragments (called sherds) are virtually indestructible. Third, unlike stone projectile points, which are attractive to collectors and easily gathered for display in decorative "point board" arrangements, sherds are not particularly appealing to pothunters (though unfortunately the same cannot be said of intact vessels). Hence the potsherds are less likely to be selectively removed from sites.

Fourth, in general pottery is not an exotic or highly valued good, like gold or jade, restricted to the residences and tombs of the upper stratum of society. Although certain kinds of pottery may be confined to elite, ceremonial, or mortuary usage—porcelain headrests, figurines, tea jars, life-size statues—pottery as a general artifact class is not so restricted. Pottery served very ordinary, day-to-day functions in cooking, storage, and hygiene for all members of society. Thus archaeologists and anthropologists have encountered a variety of goods made of fired clay, everything from ordinary bowls and jars to baby bottles in Greece (Noble 1972), footscrapers in Pakistan (Rye and Evans 1976, plate 49b–3), and *tangas* or female pubic coverings in Brazil (Palmatary 1950, 327–328).

A final and perhaps most significant reason pottery has been useful to archaeologists is its manufacturing method. Pottery is formed and *in*formed: pottery making is an additive process in which the successive steps are recorded in the final product. The shape, decoration, composition, and manufacturing methods of pottery thus reveal insights—lowly and lofty, sacred and profane—into human behavior and the history of civilizations. Potters' choices of raw materials, shapes to be constructed, kinds of decoration, and location of ornamentation all stand revealed, as do cooking methods, refuse disposal patterns, and occasional evidence of clumsiness and errors in judgment. The sensitivity, spatial as well as temporal, of pottery to changes in such culturally conditioned decisions has fed archaeologists' traditional dependency on this material for defining prehistoric cultures and their interrelations.

Most modern archaeological studies of pottery are based on three approaches: classification, decorative analyses, and compositional studies. Classificatory studies of pottery form and compare groupings of vessels or sherds representative of a particular culture at a particular time. These groupings are the basis for archaeological dating and go back to the late nineteenth-century work of Sir Flinders Petrie in Egypt. Study of the decorative motifs and styles of pottery, whether expressed in painting or in plastic decoration (incising, molding, appliqué), has always yielded insights into the lifeways of a people as well as their aesthetic perceptions and ideological systems. The third and growing focus of pottery study is technological analysis, which focuses on the paste or composition of a ceramic rather than on the way it is decorated or shaped and on the properties conferred by that composition.

Archaeologists' and anthropologists' attention has increasingly turned to pottery manufacture and use among Third and Fourth World groups being rapidly acculturated during the twentieth century. In both hemispheres the traditional craft of the potter, often a household livelihood passed down from generation to generation within a family, is suffering at the hands of modernization. Plastic and metal utensils are relentlessly usurping the utilitarian functions of jars and bowls formerly made of clay, because these new materials permit cheaper, more durable products. Although traditional people everywhere are likely to believe that water is more refreshing when cooled in a porous terra-cotta jar or beans are more flavorful when cooked in an earthenware pot, indulging these preferences is more and more difficult as potters abandon their craft to "progress."

Modern ceramic industries, sensitive to the needs of a technologically oriented society, now produce ovenware, flameware, and freezer-to-stovetop cooking utensils, plumbing fixtures, refractory brick for steel furnaces, dentures, and containers for radioactive waste. Meanwhile, the dwindling numbers of traditional potters turn to producing flowerpots, ashtrays, and figurines for a tourist market that too often has little appreciation for the dignity and history of their craft. Fortunately, the value of studying contemporary potters and their products has not gone unrecognized, both as an aid to archaeological interpretation of the distant past and also in helping many peoples recover part of their heritage before it is irretrievably lost.

References

Abascal, R. 1975. Los hornos prehispanicos en la region de Tlaxcala. *Mesa Redonda* 13: 189-98.

Amiran, R. 1965. The beginnings of pottery-making in the Near East. In *Ceramics and man*, ed. F.R. Matson, 240-47. Chicago: Aldine.

Amiran, R. and D. Shenhav. 1984. Experiments with an ancient potter's wheel. In *Pots and potters: Current approaches in ceramic archaeology*, ed. P.M. Rice, 107-12. UCLA Institute of Archaeology Monograph 24. Los Angeles: University of California.

Anderson, A. 1984. *Interpreting Pottery*. New York: Pica Press.

Arnold, D.E. 1985. *Ceramic theory and cultural process*. Cambridge: Cambridge University Press.

Beazley, J.D. 1945. *Potter and painter in ancient Athens*. Oxford: Oxford University Press.

Bimson, M. 1956. The technique of Greek black and terra sigillata red. *Antiquaries Journal* 36: 200.

Bischoff, H. and J. Viteri-Gamboa. 1972. Pre-Valdivia occupations on the southwest coast of Ecuador. *American Antiquity* 37 (4): 548-51.

Blandino, B. 1984. *Coiled pottery, traditional and contemporary ways*. Radnor, Pa: Chilton.

Bostanci, E.Y. 1959. Researches on the Mediterranean coast of Anatolia: A new Paleolithic site at Beldibi near Antalya. *Anatolia* 4: 129-77.

Brush, C.F. 1965. Pox pottery: Earliest identified Mexican ceramic. *Science* 149: 194-95.

Bullen, R.P. and J.B. Stoltman, eds. 1972. Fiber-tempered pottery in southeastern United States and northern Colombia: Its origins, context, and significance. *Florida Anthropologist* 25 (2), part 2.

Caso, A. and I. Bernal. 1952. *Urnas de Oaxaca*. Memorias 2. Mexico City: Instituto Nacional de Antropologia e Historia.

Chang, K.C. 1977. *The archaeology of ancient China*, 3rd ed. Rev. New Haven: Yale University Press.

———. 1983. *Art, myth, and ritual: The path to political authority in ancient China*. Cambridge: Harvard University Press.

Cheung, K.Y. 1983. Recent archaeological evidence relating to the origin of Chinese characters. In *The origins of Chinese civilization*, ed. K.N. Keightley, 323-91. Berkeley: University of California Press.

Coe, M. 1973. *The Maya scribe and his world*. New York: Grolier Club.

———. 1978. *The lords of the underworld*. Princeton: Princeton University Press.

d'Albis, A. 1985. Steps in the manufacture of the soft-paste porcelain of Vincennes, according to the books of Hellot. In *Ancient technology to modern science*, ed. W.D. Kingery, 257-71. Ceramics and Civilization, vol. 1. Columbus, Ohio: American Ceramics Society.

DeAtley, S.P. 1986. Mix and match: Traditions of glaze paint preparation at Four Mile Ruin, Arizona. In *Technology and style*, ed. W.D. Kingery, 297-329. Ceramics and Civilization, vol. 2. Columbus, Ohio: American Ceramics Society.

Dittert, A.E. and F. Plog. 1980. *Generations in clay: Pueblo pottery of the American Southwest*. Flagstaff, Ariz.: Northland Press.

Donnan, C.B. 1965. Moche ceramic technology. *Nawwpa Pacha* 3: 115–38.

Flannery, K.V., ed. 1976. *The early Mesoamerican village*. New York: Academic Press.

Fleming, S.J. 1976. *Dating in archaeology*. New York: St. Martin's.

Foster, G.M. 1959. The Coyotepec molde and some associated problems of the potter's wheel. *Southwest Journal of Anthropology* 15: 63.

Fourest, H.P. 1980. *Delftware: Faience production at Delft*. New York: Rizzoli Books.

Gifford, C. and W. Smith. 1978. *Gray corrugated pottery from Awatovi and other Jeddito sites in north-eastern Arizona*. Papers of the Peabody Musuem, vol. 69. Cambridge, Mass.: Peabody Museum.

Goffer, Z. 1980. *Archaeological chemistry: A sourcebook on the applications of chemistry to archaeology*. New York: John Wiley.

Goggin, J.M. 1970. The Spanish olive jar, an introductory study. In *Papers in Caribbean anthropology*. Publications in Anthropology no. 62. New Haven: Yale University Press.

Gordon, E. 1977. *Collecting Chinese export porcelain*. New York: Universe Books.

Griffin, J.B. 1965. Ceramic complexity and cultural development: The eastern United States as a case study. In *Ceramics and man*, ed. F.R. Matson, 104-13. Chicago: Aldine.

Grimshaw, R.W. 1971. *The chemistry and physics of clays and other ceramic materials*. 4th ed. New York: John Wiley.

Hammond, N. 1982. *Ancient Maya civilization*. New Brunswick, N.J.: Rutgers University Press.

Hearn, M.K. 1979. An ancient Chinese army rises from underground sentinel duty. *Smithsonian* 10 (8): 39-51.

Hedges, R.E.M. and P.R.S. Moorey. 1975. Pre-Islamic ceramic glazes at Kish and Ninevah in Iraq. *Archaeometry* 17 (1): 25-43.

Hench, L.L. and E.C. Etheridge. 1982. *Biomaterials: An interfacial approach*. Biophysics and Bioengineering Series, vol. 4. New York: Academic Press.

Hobson, R.L. 1976. *Chinese pottery and porcelain: An account of the potter's art in China from primitive times to the present day*. New York: Dover.

Hoffman, B. 1983. Die Rolle handwerklicher Verfahren bei der Formgebung in Serien hergestellter reliefverzierter Terra Sigillata. Ph.D. diss. Ludwig-Maximilian University, Munich.

Ichikawa, Y., T. Nagatomo, and N. Hagahara. 1978. Thermoluminescent dating of Jomon pattern pottery from Taishaka valley. *Archaeometry* 20 (2): 171-76.

Ikawa-Smith, F. 1980. Current issues in Japanese archaeology. *American Scientist* 68 (2): 134-45.

Joesink-Mandeville, L. 1973. The importance of gourd prototypes in the analysis of Mesoamerican ceramics. *Katunob* 8 (3): 47-53.

Johns, C. 1977a. *Arretine and Samian pottery*. London: British Museum.

Kidder, J.E. 1968. *Prehistoric Japanese arts: Jomon pottery*. Tokyo: Kodansha International.

Kingery, W.D., H.K. Bowen, and D.R. Uhlmann. 1976. *Introduction to ceramics*. 2nd ed. New York: John Wiley.

Kingery, W.D. and D. Smith. 1985. The development of European soft-paste (frit) porcelain. In *Ancient technology to modern science*. ed. W.D. Kingery, 273-92. Ceramics and Civilization, vol I. Columbus, Ohio: American Ceramic Society.

Laufer, B. 1917. The beginnings of porcelain in China. Field Museum of Natural History Publication 192. *Anthropological Series* 15 (2): 75-179.

Lawrence, W.G. and R.R. West. 1982. *Ceramic science for the potter*. 2nd ed. Radnor, Pa: Chilton.

Li Guozhen and Zhang Xiqiu. 1986. The development of Chinese white porcelain. In *Technology and style*. ed. W.D. Kingery, 217-36. Ceramics and Civilization, vol. 2. Columbus, Ohio: American Ceramic Society.

Li Hu Hou. 1985. Characteristic elements of Longquan greenware. *Archaeometry* 27 (1): 53-60.

Li Jiazhi. 1985. The evolution of Chinese pottery and porcelain technology. In *Ancient technology to modern science*, ed. W.D. Kingery, 135-62. Ceramics and Civilization, vol. 1. Columbus, Ohio: American Ceramic Society.

Lieberman, S.J. 1980. Of clay pebbles, hollow clay balls, and writing: A Sumerian view. *American Journal of Archaeology* 84 (3): 339-58.

Lister, F.C. and R.H. Lister. 1982. *Sixteenth century Maiolica pottery in the Valley of Mexico*. Anthropological Papers no. 39. Tucson: University of Arizona.

Lobert, H.W. 1984. Types of potter's wheels and the spread of the spindle-wheel in Germany. In *The many dimensions of pottery: Ceramics in archaeology and anthropology*, ed. S.E. van der Leeuw and A.C. Pritchard, 203-30. CINGULA 7. Amsterdam: Institute for Pre- and Proto-history, University of Amsterdam.

Majidzadeh, Y. 1975-77. The development of the pottery kiln in Iran from prehistoric to historical periods. *Paleorient* 3: 207-19.

Matthiae, P. 1977. Tell Mardikh: The archives and palace. *Archaeology* 30 (4): 244-53.

May, P. and M. Tuckson. 1982. *The traditional pottery of Papua New Guinea*. Sydney: Bay Books.

Meggers, B.J. and C. Evans. 1966. A transpacific contact in 3000 B.C. *Scientific American* 214 (1): 28-35.

Mellaart, J. 1964. A Neolithic city in Turkey. *Scientific American* 210 (4): 94-104.

———. 1965. Anatolian pottery as a basis for cultural synthesis. In *Ceramics and man*, ed. F.R. Matson, 218-239. Chicago: Aldine.

Mikami, T. 1979. *The art of Japanese ceramics*. New York: Weatherhill.

Morgan, L.H. 1877. *Ancient Society*. New York: World.

Morris, E.H. 1917. The place of coiled ware in Southwestern pottery. *American Anthropologist* 19(1): 24–29.

Museum of Qin Shi Huang. 1981. *Qin Shi Huang pottery figures of warriors and horses*. Corpus of Data no. 1. Shaanxi, China: Museum of Qin Shi Huang

Noble, J.V. 1966. *The techniques of painted Attic pottery*. New York: Watson-Guptill.

———. 1972. An unusual Attic baby feeder. *American Journal of Archaeology* 76 (4): 437-38.

Norton, F.H. 1970. *Fine Ceramics, technology and applications*. New York: McGraw-Hill.

Ochsenschlager, E. 1974. Mud objects from al-Hiba. *Archaeology* 27 (3): 162-74.

Oldfather, W.A. 1920. A note on the etymology of the word "ceramic." *Journal of the American Ceramic Society* 3: 357-42.

Palmatary, H.C. 1950. *The Pottery of Marajo Island, Brazil*. Transactions of the American Philosophical Society, n.s., vol. 39, part 3. Philadelphia: American Philosophical Society.

Payne, W.O. 1982. Kilns and ceramic technology of ancient Mesoamerica. In *Archaeological ceramics*, ed. J.S. Olin and A.D. Franklin, 189-92. Washington, D.C.: Smithsonian Institution.

Peacock, D.P.S. 1982. *Pottery in the Roman world: an ethnoarchaeological approach*. London: Longmans.

Proulx, D.A. 1968. *Local differences and time differences in Nasca pottery*. Publications in anthropology, vol. 5. Berkeley and Los Angeles: University of California Press.

Quirarte, J. 1979. The representation of underworld processions in Maya vase painting: An iconographic study. In *Maya archaeology and ethnohistory*, ed. N. Hammond and G.R. Willey, 116-48. Austin: University of Texas Press.

Rathbun, W.J. 1979. Impressed and incised decoration on early Japanese pottery. In *Decorative techniques and styles in Asian ceramics*, ed. M. Medley, 34-46. Colloquies on Art and Archaeology in Asia no. 8. London: University of London.

Redman, C.L. 1978. *The rise of civilization*. San Francisco: W.H. Freeman.

Reichel-Dolmatoff, G. 1961. Puerto Hormiga: Un complejo prehistorico marginal de Colombia. *Revista Columbiana de Antropolgia* 10: 347-54.

Rhodes, D. 1973. *Clay and glazes for the potter*, 2nd ed. Philadelphia: Chilton Books.

Rice, P.M. 1985. Maya pottery techniques and technology. In *Ancient technology to modern science*, ed. W.E. Kingery, 113-32. Ceramics and Civilization, vol. 1. Columbus, Ohio: American Ceramic Society.

Rice, P.M. and A.S. Cordell. 1986. Weeden Island pottery: Style, technology, and production. In *Technology and style*, ed. W.D. Kingery, 273-95. Ceramics and Civilization, vol. 2. Columbus, Ohio: American Ceramic Society.

Richter, G. 1976. *Attic red-figure vases*. New Haven: Yale University Press.

Robicsek, F. and D.M. Hales. 1981. *The Maya Book of the Dead: The ceramic codex*. Charlotteseville: University of Virginia Art Museum.

Rye, O.S. and C. Evans. 1976. *Traditional pottery techniques of Pakistan: Field and laboratory studies*. Smithsonian Contributions to Anthropology no. 21. Washington, D.C.: Smithsonian Institution.

Schmandt-Besserat, D. 1974. The use of clay before pottery in the Zagros. *Expedition* 16 (2): 11-17.

———. 1977a. The beginnings of the use of clay in Turkey. *Anatolian Studies* 27: 133-50.

———. 1977b. The earliest use of clay in Syria. *Expedition* 19 (3): 28-42.

————. 1978. The earliest precursor of writing. *Scientific American* 238 (6): 50-59.

Schumann, T. 1942. Oberflachenverzierung in der antiken Topferkust, Terra Sigillata and Griechische Schwartzrotmaleri. *Berichte de Deutsche Keramischen Gesellschaft* 23: 408-26.

Sears, W.H. and J.B. Griffin. 1950. Fiber-tempered pottery of the Southeast. In *Prehistoric pottery of the eastern United States*, ed. J.B. Griffin. Ann Arbor: University of Michigan Press.

Shangraw, C.F. 1977. Early Chinese ceramics and kilns. *Archaeology* 30 (6): 382-93.

————. 1978. *Origins of Chinese ceramics*. New York: China Institute in America.

Shepard, A.O. 1942. *Rio Grande glaze paint ware: A study illustrating the place of ceramic technological analysis in archaeological research*. Publication 526, Contributions to Anthropology 39. Washington, DC: Carnegie Institution of Washington.

————. 1948. *Plumbate: A Mesoamerican trade ware.* Publication 573. Washington, DC: Carnegie Institution of Washington.

————. 1965. Rio Grande glaze-paint pottery: A test of petrographic analysis. In *Ceramics and man*, ed. F.R. Matson, 62-87. Chicago: Aldine.

————. 1976. *Ceramics for the archaeologist*. Washington, D.C.: Carnegie Institution of Washington.

Speck, F.G. 1931. Birch-bark in the ancestry of pottery forms. *Anthropos* 26: 407-11.

Spinks, C.N. 1965. *The ceramic wares of Siam*. Bangkok: Siam Society.

Stimmell, C. and R.L. Stromberg. 1986. A reassessment of Thule Eskimo ceramic technology. In *Technology and style*, ed. R.M. Fulrath and J.A. Pask, 379-405. New York: John Wiley.

Stross, F. and F. Asaro. 1984. Time's wheel runs back or stops: Pottery and clay endure. In *Pots and potters: Current approaches in ceramic archaeology,* ed. P.M. Rice, 179-86. UCLA Institute of Archaeology Monograph 24. Los Angeles: University of California Press.

Thompson, H.A. 1984. The Athenian vase-painters and their neighbors. In *Pots and potters: Current approaches in ceramic archaeology*, ed. P.M. Rice, 7-19. UCLA Institute of Archaeology Monograph 24. Los Angeles: University of California Press.

Thompson, R.H. 1958. Modern Yucatecan Maya pottery making. Memoirs of the SAA, no. 15. *American Antiquity* 23, no. 4, part 2.

Tichane, R. 1983. *Ching-te-chen: View of a porcelain city*. Painted Post: New York State Institute for Glaze Research.

Tite, M.S., M. Bimson, and I.C. Freestone. 1982. An examination of the high gloss surface finishes on Greek Attic and Roman Samian wares. *Archaeometry*: 24 (2): 117-26.

Trachsler, W. 1965. The influence of metalworking on prehistoric pottery: Some observations on Iron Age pottery of the Alpine region. In *Ceramics and man*, ed. F.R. Matson, 140-51. Chicago: Aldine.

Vandiver, P.B. 1982. Technological change in Egyptian faience. In *Archaeological ceramics*, ed. J.S. Olin and A.D. Franklin, 167-79. Washington, D.C.: Smithsonian Institution.

Vandiver, P.B. and W.D. Kingery. 1984. Composition and structure of Chinese Song Dynasty celadon glazes from Longquan. *Ceramic Bulletin* 63 (4): 612-16.

Von Bothmer, D. 1985. *The Amasis painter and his world: Vase painting in the sixth century B.C. Athens*. New York: Thames and Hudson.

Wang, W. and Z. Zhou. 1983. Thermoluminescence dating of Chinese pottery. *Archaeometry* 25 (2): 99-106.

Washburn, E.W., H. Ries, and A.L. Day. 1920. Reports of the committee on definitions of the term "ceramics." *Journal of the American Ceramic Society* 3: 526-36.

Weiss, G. 1971. *The book of porcelain*. Trans. J. Seligman. New York: Praeger.

Whitehouse, D. 1980. Protomajolica. *Faenza* 66: 77-83.

Willey, G.R. 1966. *An introduction to American archaeology*, Vol. 1. *North and Middle America*. Englewood Cliffs, NJ: Prentice-Hall.

Williams, B., W. Williams, and J. McMillan. 1985. Notes on some clays used for pottery in ancient Nubia. In *Ancient technology to modern science*, ed. W.D. Kingery, 43-50. Ceramics and Civilization, vol. 1. Columbus, Ohio: American Ceramic Society.

Wormington, H.M. and A. Neal. 1951. *The story of Pueblo pottery.* Museum Pictorial no. 2. Denver: Museum of Natural History.

Wykes-Joyce, M. 1958. *Seven thousand years of pottery and porcelain.* New York: Philosophical Library.

Zhang Fukang. 1985. The origin and development of traditional Chinese glazes and decorative ceramic colors. In *Ancient technology to modern science*, ed. W.D. Kingery, 163-80. Ceramics and civilization, vol. 1. Columbus, Ohio: American Ceramic Society.

Zhou Zhen-xi. 1985. The origin and early use of throwing wheel in manufacturing of pottery in ancient China. Paper presented at the second international conference on ancient Chinese pottery and porcelain, Beijing.

Zimmerman, D.W. and J. Huxtable. 1971. Thermoluminescence authenticity measurements on core material from the bronze horse of the New York Metropolitan Museum of Art. *Archaeometry* 16 (1).

PART 4

Reconstructing Culture History and Past Lifeways

Introduction

Reconstructing culture history has been a mainstay of archaeological research since the 1800s, and reconstructing past lifeways since the mid-1900s. The selections in this part of the reader have been chosen to reflect the nature of that research. The first selection, by J.A.J. Gowlett, provides an overview of culture history. The second selection, by M.J. Morwood et al., is an example of original, scholarly reporting of a discovery with significant implications for culture history. The remaining selections were chosen from both the scholarly and semi-scholarly literature to give a sampling of how archaeologists reconstruct the social and ideological aspects of past cultures.

"Chronology and the Human Narrative"

J.A.J. GOWLETT

This selection provides an overview of life on Earth for the few million years of human existence. Readers are cautioned that the terminology used for the genera and species of early humans and how to distinguish between them is open to debate. Also, there is little consensus about the dates for many of the events mentioned in the piece. Nevertheless, the basic pattern of development outlined here is generally accepted. The selection was authored by J.A.J. Gowlett, a professor at the University of Liverpool, and was originally published in 2004 in the edited book *A Companion to Archaeology*.

Some key terms that readers may not be familiar with include *Hominids*, a word commonly used to identify the biological family *Hominidae*, to which all members of the genus *Homo*, past and present, belong. *Oldowan, Acheulian,* and *Levallois* are names given to describe different ways of making stone tools and are sometimes referred to as tool traditions, industries, or complexes.

Questions to Guide Reading

What are the names of the hominid genera that predate *Homo*?

From which regions of Africa have most early hominids (predating one million years) been discovered?

What are the approximate dates for the origins of the Oldowan, Acheulian, and Levallois traditions?

What are some of the problems early humans would have had to deal with as they spread around the world?

What dating techniques are mentioned in the article, and when is each most applicable?

In what order and at what approximate date were each of the major continents first occupied by members of the genus *Homo*?

What are the problems associated with determining when and where anatomically modern humans first emerged?

When do modern humans (*Homo sapiens*) first appear in Europe, Africa, the Middle East, Asia, Australia, and the Americas?

What is meant by "Upper Palaeolithic"?

At approximately what date did domestication emerge?

What are the "problems of domestication" for archaeologists?

Hominid Origins

When did the first hominid ancestors diverge from an ape stem? When did the first members of our own genus *Homo* appear? These are fundamental and intriguing questions which can be answered only in general terms, and through the interplay of several techniques. Broadly, we are talking about the period 12–6 million years ago, the later part of the Miocene period and the Pliocene, and there is no great problem in dating the periods as such (papers in Vrba et al. 1996 give a recent view). Through this time, there are sediments on land, and ocean cores. Accurate dating of volcanic events is offered by potassium-argon both in Europe and Africa, and deep sea cores provide a vital additional record that can be cross-linked through palaeomagnetism (Shackleton and Opdyke 1973, 1977; Shackleton 1996). The record of past changes in the earth's magnetism also aids cross-linking or correlation between regions, between sea and land. The ocean cores preserve a palaeotemperature record, and information about wind intensities on land (deMenocal and Bloemendahl 1996). In Africa and Eurasia, the evolution of faunas can be traced, for example the first arrival of the three-toed Hipparion horses in Africa, and then of true horses within the last 10 million years (Bernor and Lipscomb 1996; Hill 1996; Opdyke 1996); or the evolution of primates, which can be seen on and off through the last 40 million years (Simons 1995; Delson 1994).

In this frame, the earliest hominids were long represented just by a gap. The picture has been transformed by the spectacular finds of *Orrorin tugenensis* in Kenya (Senut et al. 2001) and *Sahelanthropus tchadensis* in Chad (Brunet et al. 2002), which at a stroke drive the record back to 7 million years. Otherwise, they are largely absent—as are fossil apes within the last 8 million years, although earlier apes are much more visible. This is partly chance, partly a result of biases in the record, caused by the favored preservation of some habitats over others, and of rocks from some periods rather than others. In general the great Rift Valley system of eastern Africa gives exceptional preservation of sediments through the last 20 million years, but some periods such as 5–10 million years ago are preserved in limited areas (Opdyke 1996; Hill 1996; Hill and Ward 1988).

The new fossil finds can be compared with results of a "molecular clock." Comparisons of DNA and proteins of living species allow good estimates to be made of their relative divergence dates, provided that one or two divergence dates are well established in the fossil record. The divergence date of apes and monkeys at least 30 million years ago allowed calculation of the divergence of apes and hominids, in the range 5–8 million years ago (Sarich and Wilson 1968; Goodman et al. 1989; Jeffreys 1989) (more recent calibrations have not refined these estimates).

The new fossil evidence supports dates at the older end of this range. At present, other well-documented hominid fossils go back to around 4.2–4.6 million years. These are the finds of *Ardipithecus ramidus* from the Awash valley in northern Ethiopia, and of *Australopithecus anamensis* from the south end of Lake Turkana in Kenya (White et al. 1994, 1996; Leakey et al. 1995). Fragmentary remains of a hominid jaw from Lothagam in Kenya (Patterson et al. 1967) suggested the possibility of somewhat earlier hominids, as indicated by the newest finds.

Most early hominids have been found in the Rift Valley of East Africa, but the discovery of finds in Chad confirms that this could be an effect of sampling. With the previous isolated find of *Australopithecus afarensis* from Lake Chad, more than 1,000 kilometers from the Rift, this suggests that the actual hominid distribution may have been much broader, and that sampling factors limit their visibility (Brunet et al. 1995). Even so, the Rift Valley is unparalleled both for preservation and the application of dating methods. The extent of rain forest (the ideal ape habitat) and of savanna and denser bush all varied immensely in the past, so that modern biotopes provide little reliable information about past distributions.

From about 3.5 million years, hominids are well represented down the length of Africa from Ethiopia to South Africa, but there are still intriguing gaps and variations in the quality of dating. There is a lacuna from 2.5–2 million years, with very few fossil finds of any substance. In South Africa the cave sites are very hard to date, although ESR (electron spin resonance) and palaeomagnetism are beginning to help: recent finds of early *Australopithecus* from Sterkfontein have been dated from 2–3.5 million years (Schwarcz et al. 1994; Partridge et al. 1999).

Within the radiation of Australopithecine species, the origin of *Homo*—our own genus—should be a matter of special interest. But this is perhaps as much a problem of classification as of chronology. It may be that scholarship tends to focus on the origins of *Homo* and then of *sapiens* as a direct result of the Linnaean system of classification. This is owed to the eighteenth-century scholar Linnaeus, used universally, and emphasizes the levels of genus and species. Yet palaeontologists are always looking for distinctive features which will help them in arriving at a classification. In this way classification tends to fit itself to the major evolutionary events that are recognizable.

Until recently there were thought to be three species of early *Homo*, present in East Africa at around 1.9 million years ago. These were *Homo habilis*, *Homo rudolfensis*, and *Homo ergaster* (or *erectus*) (Wood 1991, 1992; Rightmire 1990). The implication of such diversity is that a considerable span of time would be needed if these species were to be traced back to some ancestral form of *Homo*, perhaps at 2.5 Ma (millions of years ago) or earlier.

Recent reclassifications—in some ways a return to older views—suggest that the three early species of "*Homo*" are not linked by characters attesting a common origin within *Homo* (Wood and Collard 1999). This implies that two of them should be regarded as varieties of *Australopithecus*, and that *Homo* does not "need" such long chronological roots. On the basis of the evidence now available, it seems that true *Homo* first appears at about 1.9 Ma, around East Turkana in northern Kenya.

In this area the dating of such finds was formerly controversial in itself. Dates for the crucial volcanic ash at East Turkana ranged from 1.8–2.6 million years (Fitch and Miller 1970; Fitch et al. 1976). By 1980 the position was resolved, and a date of around 1.88 million years was established both by potassium-argon and fission track dating (Drake et al. 1980; McDougall et al. 1980; Gleadow 1980). Now the use of the laser-fusion argon technique, the production of large numbers of dates, and chemical "fingerprinting" of volcanic ashes have combined to make the chronologies of East Africa among the most solid. Indeed, the volcanic ashes can also be traced in Arabian Sea cores, providing additional dating evidence and a measure of climatic change. Thus Frank Brown (1996) was able to chart out 25,000 years of deposition with an accuracy and precision which is rarely available except in the last few thousand years.

For most purposes, this record of millennia is more resolution than can be used. There are relatively few early archaeological sites, and we do not understand the variations in their technology. At first, scholars were inclined to suggest that earlier sites would be simpler than later ones. Research in Ethiopia and western Kenya in the 1990s, however, has shown that the early Oldowan tradition has a duration from as much as 2.7 million years down to 1.7 million, and that within this span the very earliest industries show all the skills that were present through almost the next million years (Semaw et al. 1997; Plummer et al. 1999; Harris 1983).

Advances in technological design come only later, with a Developed Oldowan that is dated to ca. 1.6 million years, and the beginnings of the Acheulian hand-axe tradition soon afterwards (Asfaw et al. 1992; Isaac and Curtis 1974; Leakey 1971). These developments are reasonably well dated along the Rift Valley, although the greatest site sequences—at Olduvai Gorge and East Turkana—have a discontinuous record of the events. Olduvai Gorge remains in general the best yardstick for early archaeology (Leakey 1971; Leakey and Roe 1995; Walter et al. 1991), but many other sites have to be linked in to provide a fuller picture.

For the next million years, the main problem for chronology is one of dating sites and distributions rather than "new" phenomena of culture—of these there are very few.

The Spread Around the World

The next great problem is "when did humans spread around the world?" In reality this is a thousand problems (and more). The most accepted outline is that humans originated in Africa, that within the last 2 million years they appear in many parts of the globe, and that in the present day they have a broader distribution than any other mammal (Bar-Yosef 1996a; Clark 1992; Gamble 1993).

Our world has a peculiar geography, which dictates that Africa can be left only through a fairly narrow corridor, unless water transport is used. This position has held for about 5 million years, since the straits opened at the south end of the Red Sea. In glacial phases, however, sea level drops, so that the corridor "out of Africa" would be wider than its present 70 kilometers. Once beyond Africa, there are various routes to the east and north—and ultimately to Europe in the west. Landbridges may have given occasional access to Europe across the Mediterranean, but there is little solid evidence of these. Hominids moving to the north would be pushing into the temperate regions, needing new adaptations to cope with autumn and winter. At times of climatic deterioration, pushing up against glaciers and fearsomely low temperatures, they would certainly be forced south again. The east would seemingly offer easier adaptations—climate, flora, and fauna have more in common with Africa (Cox and Moore 1993). Even so, there is a huge ecological variety to cope with (Clark 1992). As modern hunter-gatherers are supremely well adapted to their environments, it is hard to see how earlier hominids, with far lower cultural capabilities, could have flitted easily from environment to environment. They would need time—but how much time? Here theory is not enough to provide the answers,

and a dated archaeological record is the only thing that can do so.

To weigh up the problem, the main dating tools are palaeomagnetism and K/Ar (Potassium Argon), as for earlier periods. Unfortunately, this limits most dating to areas of Pleistocene volcanic activity. Fortunately, surprisingly many of the areas in question do have some vulcanism, though this is rare in China. Here, however, great sequences of loess sediment are available, which can be dated with high resolution by palaeomagnetism—specifically, magnetostratigraphy (Sun Donghuai et al. 1998). Loess, a fine-grained sediment made up of wind-blown materials transported from the front of ice sheets, can accumulate in thicknesses of thousands of meters, and preserves many archaeological sites (e.g., in Tadzikistan: Schäfer et al. 1996). The main evidence from this period is of stone artefact sites, with very occasional hominid remains.

Assuming that they went first into Asia, when did hominids spread into the Middle East? This question highlights the sampling problem. In the Levant, there are possible stone tools in the Yiron gravels of northwest Israel, dated to about 2.4 million years (Ronen 1991). Thereafter, only the sites of 'Ubeidiya in Israel and Latamne in Syria may break the barrier of 1 million years (Bar-Yosef and Goren-Inbar 1992; Bar-Yosef 1996a). Neither of them is pinned closely by absolute dates, but further north another remarkable site has emerged: Dmanisi in Georgia (Gabunia et al. 2000). Here remains of early *Homo*, early Pleistocene fauna, artefacts and argon-argon dates of 1.8 Ma combine to force a reassessment.

Further afield, however, there are apparently older dates, in an arc, spreading from Spain, across to the Caucasus, China, and through to Java (Swisher et al. 1994). They are spread very wide but very thin, and none is beyond doubt. On the other hand, we can state with some confidence that dates of 1 million years or more are reliable across this huge area. One fairly firm baseline is the Brunhes/Matuyama palaeomagnetic boundary, at 780,000 years (Cande and

Kent 1995). There is a far denser pattern of dates which extend again from Spain to China. Here we have no need to doubt Atapuerca in the west, 'Ubeidiya in the center, or Lantien in the east (Bermudez de Castro et al. 1997; Bar-Yosef and Goren-Inbar 1992; An and Ho 1989; Shaw et al. 1991).

Thus a sort of foundation is emerging: that dates of a million years (or so) can be accepted across a huge zone of the Old World. Considering that the occupation probably did not happen overnight, does this license us to accept any of the older dates? One complication is that occupations may have come and gone with climate change. Truly, resolution of every kind is limited, but here is a tentative evaluation.

First, our global model (level 5) has very few constraints. There are no known archaeological sites older than 2.5 Ma in Africa, but whether or not these exist, there is nothing to rule out equally early sites in parts of Asia and Europe. An implicit model emerged that because the earliest hominids arose in Africa, so should the earliest stone technology—but this is untested assumption.

Then, regional patterns (level 4) in several areas point to dates of greater than 1 million years. Those furthest from Africa—Western Europe and Java—surely increase the likelihood that yet earlier dates should be found in the regions closer to Africa—Dmanisi seems to add support to this idea.

Much more is to appear, but in terms of ideas, it is good to stand back and see what has happened. In the 1950s, people thought that early technology everywhere belonged in the last half-million years. Then compelling scientific dating evidence from Olduvai pushed the African record back to 2 million years—so that the rest of the world had to be occupied later. Now its dates may be catching up (or perhaps we should say "catching back").

Yet these changes of date do not necessarily provide us with a record of progress, such as seen in later periods. Between about 1.5 million and 250,000 years ago, there are very few "new" events to be recorded. Mostly life seems to go on in such a repetitious fashion that—dare we say it—dating is hardly needed.

Variations in preservation account for some of the differences which we do see. The "first" wooden artefacts are clearly not the oldest ever made (400,000 year-old spears are reported by Thieme 1996 from Schöningen in Germany). It is not certain whether humans were building huts, but structures were exceedingly rare until about 400,000 years ago (Nadel and Werker 1999).

Fire offers another controversy: but although the chronology of fire is of great interest, the limits are provided by sampling, and even more by the difficulties of distinguishing between wild fire and domestic fire (Bellomo 1993). There are clusters of sites with fire traces around 1.5–1.0 million years ago in Africa, and at around 0.5 million within Europe and Asia, but between them there is a great gap in the evidence. Nor is there any real prospect, for now, of dating the origins of language, since there is little agreement about what evidence to look for. Anatomists see evidence for and against language in the early Pleistocene, and so have archaeologists (Davidson 1991; Davidson and Noble 1993; Deacon 1997; Dunbar 1996; Graves 1994; Tobias 1991).

Origins of Modern Humans

At some time within the last 200,000 years human beings have emerged who are like us—anatomically modern *Homo sapiens sapiens*. The origins of modern humans present one of the greatest problems of chronology, also introducing new factors of evolutionary process. Broadly speaking, we can state with certainty that the humans of 200,000 years ago around the world were not fully modern; by 100,000 years ago some populations were modern in most details (AMHs=anatomically modern humans), while others, such as the Neanderthals, were considerably more "archaic" looking, and perhaps on their own evolutionary trajectory; and by 30,000 years ago, modern humans prevailed almost everywhere (Mellars and Stringer 1989; papers in Aitken et al. 1993; D'Errico et al. 1998).

The main factors are much as before: sampling

problems, and those of obtaining accurate and precise dating. There is, however, a new component: in the case of a process such as colonization, the task is primarily one of finding the events and dating them. Here we have something more—an evolutionary change, that has to be characterized and assessed both during and through the dating process. To add spice to the problem, there is also the presence of genetic studies—of mitochondrial and nuclear DNA (Richards et al. 1993; Krings et al. 1997). These give information about present-day and some past population relationships, but cannot quite be treated as an additional dating method. Linked directly with dated evidence—especially fossil hominids—they become a far more powerful tool.

Add to this a window of difficulty in applying techniques and the dating picture becomes complex. Potassium-argon is applicable in only a few areas, and there are no major palaeomagnetic boundaries in this period. The main techniques which can be used are those related to uranium-decay: thermoluminescence (TL), ESR, and U-series itself (Aitken 1990; Grün 1989; Grün and Stringer 1991; Schwarcz 1993).

In temperate regions it is also possible to recognize on land the cold and warm stages which appear very clearly in deep sea cores. These oxygen isotope stages are numbered in series backwards from the present interglacial (the Holocene, stage 1), so that warm stages have odd numbers and cold stages even ones. Thus sediments from a warm period can be ascribed first to one of a series of interglacials (say Isotope Stage 9, 11, or 13), and then other dating factors can be brought into play to help decide which stage is involved in particular cases (cf. Shackleton 1996).

From all this a summary of "facts" can be made. Humans of 250,000–200,000 years ago are clearly not modern, anywhere. They have the large brow ridges, flattened cranial vaults, and massive limbs of Middle Pleistocene hominids. By 100,000 years ago, some humans are roughly modern-looking: a little robust in places, but evidently "like us." They

are found scattered across Africa, and in the Middle East, but both sampling and dating is poor elsewhere (Rightmire 1996). In Europe it is good enough to show the continued presence of Neanderthals (Stringer and Gamble 1993; Stringer 1995).

Over the same period, archaeology reveals the adoption of the sophisticated Levallois technique for making stone tools, and the beginnings of regional diversification in tool traditions (Wendorf and Schild 1974; Tuffreau 1992). By 100,000 some stone points look like projectile tips. Burials also appear (Harrold 1980; Bar-Yosef et al. 1992). There is not much else that clearly changes during this period. Thus, both crucial sets of evidence that we are trying to date *change*—perhaps with waves of humans moving around the world—without our being able to characterize very clearly what we are dating (and without having very precise techniques for doing the dating). It is easy to fall back to modern genetic distributions and to use them as a sort of blueprint, adding authority to statements about the past. Thus we have to ask what is the key evidence that certainly belongs in the past, rather than to build a pleasing and plausible story by combining all kinds of evidence at will.

By region the basic evidence can be summarized as follows.

EUROPE

Neanderthals are widespread and well dated, starting with ancestral forms 300,000 years ago, and continuing as the only hominids until about 40,000 years ago. Modern humans then begin to appear. In our finds there is virtually no overlap between the two populations. There is a possible hybrid find from Portugal, where Neanderthals may have hung on until about 25,000 BP (before present) (Duarte et al. 1999).

AFRICA

Scattered finds are reasonably well dated on some sites. Finds around 200,000, such as Kabwe or

Ndutu, are of *Homo sapiens*, but still robust; those around 100,000 such as Omo, Ngaloba, or Jebel Irhoud are more modern-looking but not entirely so (Hublin 1993).

MIDDLE EAST

Finds are almost absent until the period about 100,000 years ago, when a tight group of finds occurs in the caves of Israel, all representing early modern humans (*Homo sapiens sapiens*). The only two finds which could give a picture of a trajectory through time—Tabun and Zuttiyeh—are fragmentary or poorly stratified. At about 60,000 Neanderthals appear in the Middle East; soon afterwards, they appear to be replaced by early modern humans (Vermeersch et al. 1998; Marks 1990; Jelinek 1990).

ASIA

There are remarkably few fossil finds except in Java, China, and then (later) in the region of Australia. In Java, the Solo or Ngandong finds may represent a late *Homo erectus*, but others would see them as an early *sapiens*. In China, early *sapiens* finds date back to 300,000 (Chen and Zhang 1991; Chen et al. 1994), and there is a case for seeing an *in situ* modernization (Stringer 1993). The Australian finds are all of moderns, of varying degrees of robustness, but almost all fall within the last 30,000 years, with the probable exception of one burial from Lake Mungo (Thorne et al. 1999; Stringer 1999).

Two views dominate discussions: (1) that there was a diaspora starting from Africa, the so-called "Out of Africa 2" (or Garden of Eden theory), in which modern humans spread out and replaced all more archaic populations; (2) of multiregionalism, in which the populations of all areas "modernize" in parallel, with a certain amount of gene flow occurring between areas.

It is not plain now that the majority of specialists hold to such simply expressed views. The main planks of replacement are as follows:

1   That genetics points this way: there is less diversity in modern populations than might be expected, but more in Africa than in other regions, suggesting that Africa has the longest history of modern population.
2   African specimens became modern early on, and can be dated reasonably well.
3   Middle Eastern specimens appear modern at an early date (around 100,000).
4   There was replacement in Europe: almost indisputably, Neanderthals in Europe are followed by modern humans at a late date—after 40,000 years ago.

The central difficulty for the replacement scenario is one of chronology: it has had to happen around the whole Old World—and all diversification of modern populations has had to happen since. Australia, for example, has had an occupation by modern humans for at least 40,000 years, perhaps much longer; and yet early modern humans apparently came out of Africa only within the last 100,000 years, and are not clearly seen in the Middle East between 90,000 and 50,000. This pattern creates many global constraints at level 5, some of them glossed over in the replacement debate: was there really enough time for replacement to happen, given the huge distances, and the variety of adaptations that would be needed in the face of varied climates and resources? On the other hand, multiregionalism does not work in Europe—it has a time problem, and now also a genetic problem. First, Neanderthals cannot evolve into modern humans in Europe 40,000 years ago, because modern humans had already evolved somewhere else (Africa or the Middle East): it is exceedingly unlikely that the same species should evolve twice, from different ancestors. The idea of a real and substantial difference between the human varieties is now given extra force by the genetic evidence of mitochondrial DNA. At the very least this shows clearly that the mtDNA of one Neanderthal (the specimen from Neanderthal itself) does not resemble that of modern humans (Krings et al. 1997). Some gene flow between populations of course remains a possibility, but the sudden late appearance of a hybrid population would not affect the basic argument that modern humans appeared first outside Europe (cf. Tattersall and Schwartz 1999).

Would the dates allow alternative interpretations to the most favored scenarios? It is difficult to free ourselves of preconceptions, but there is no doubt that everything hangs not just on a framework of ideas, but also on the dates themselves which have shaped the ideas. Hardly anywhere are Neanderthals and moderns stratified in single sequences, so our trust in the reliability of the dates is crucial. They are amply good enough to make some points about *rates of change*. We can be sure that in Europe Neanderthals evolved gradually over a long period, but that (relatively) the change from Neanderthal to modern came quite fast.

Everything would look simpler if there were a straightforward seriation, especially in the Middle East. In fact we pass from "no evidence" before 200,000; to "equivocal evidence" around 150,000 (Tabun and Zuttiyeh); to early moderns at 100,000; to Neanderthals at 60,000; then apparently around 50,000 to moderns who, apart from their archaeology, are almost invisible for the first few thousand years. This is a great challenge, and a warning not to expect simple solutions elsewhere in the world. In the Middle East, early moderns occur earlier than most if not all Neanderthals—all current explanation has to work around this. They are also older than many European Neanderthals. The Skhul hominids of Israel had been dead for 50,000 years when the Neanderthals of La Ferrassie in France were alive.

African modernization may occur earlier than that of the Middle East. Fragmentary hominid remains are well dated at Klasies River Mouth in South Africa, but few of the other African sites with human remains are very well dated (Smith 1993). What Africa offers is the appearance of continuity, through most of the last half-million years, culminating in modern humans—a gradient that is dated

overall, although its detail lacks precision. The greatest difficulty lies in interpreting events in Asia and beyond—in having time for the diaspora which most scholars now accept. First, there is an almost complete lack of dated hominid finds from the Middle East to China. Then there is the puzzle of the late Neanderthals in the Middle East, around 60,000 years ago. It is almost inconceivable that the eastwards spread of moderns could have come later than this. The alternative is to invoke an earlier spread (or even multiregional origin) of modern humans across Asia, one that is almost invisible in the record, and therefore difficult to date.

The Upper Palaeolithic

Dating of the Upper Palaeolithic can be seen as a sub-problem in the dating of modern humans. Modern humans spread across the world, but the Upper Palaeolithic is a regional phenomenon of Eurasia. It also brings us into the realm of radiocarbon—the chief dating technique of the last 40,000 years—and brings into focus this key question of rates of change. In earlier periods cultural change was so fundamentally slow that a lack of dating precision hardly matters, but as events speed up the need for higher resolution becomes more and more pressing.

The Upper Palaeolithic is a technical and perhaps social phenomenon of a particular part of the world. Historically, it has attracted great attention because it is found in Europe and because of its rich material culture, which embraces symbolism in the record of art. With a lack of knowledge and of chronologies in other parts of the world, the Upper Palaeolithic long stood proxy for the arrival of modern humans in the world. It was the front door to modernity. This picture is now circumscribed and eroded—by newer finds, but just as much so by new dates.

To date it, we must first determine what the Upper Palaeolithic is. In practice archaeologists have tended to treat it as a package of characteristics which occur in the record more or less together. Just as the Neolithic became a package of agriculture and elements of material culture such as pottery, so have ideas of the Upper Palaeolithic moved beyond blade technology. In Europe there are several features in this classic package, including blade industries, prismatic cores, elaborate bone and antler work, arts, and evidence of personal decoration. In contrast, in the Middle East, the chief evidence is of blade industries, with less bonework and art, but again with evidence for social complexity.

It is hard to be utterly consistent in dealing with such a package—even the blade component itself is not always major. But if the term is to be used—and dated—the stone industries have to be taken as having primacy, because they survive the most, and on the most sites. Unfortunately, the beginnings are just too old to be covered reliably by radiocarbon. The oldest known sites are in the Levant, and the likelihood is that they reach back to 50,000 years. This can be said on the basis of radiocarbon dates older than 45,000 from a few sites, and from rare comparisons with uranium-series dates, as at Nahal Zin in Israel (Schwarcz et al. 1979; Schwarcz 1993). Although the number of sites is very small, and there are difficulties in relating the techniques, there is little doubt that the actual technical change from Levallois point to blade industries began at around 50,000 years ago. Once established, the Upper Palaeolithic seems to have spread north and west into Europe, and to have provided the cultural matrix for the introduction of modern humans (Kozlowski 1992, 1999; Rigaud 1989; Mellars 1992).

What chronological problems does all this pose? From the 1980s there came a new demand to think of modern human origins and the origins of the Upper Palaeolithic as separate events. Especially important were dates which broke established patterns, such as those of about 90,000 BP for early bone harpoons at Katanda in the western Rift Valley of Africa (Brooks et al. 1995; Yellen et al. 1995). The implication is that not only were modern humans here, but also with them the technical advances which add up to "modern behaviour"—in this case signaled by the advanced bone toolkit. If this is cor-

rect, we have a set of site evidence (level 3) changing the global view (level 5), but not unassisted by other finds. The early presence of art and bone tools elsewhere suggests that these may have earlier dates than expected, and that in fact they are nothing to do with the "Upper Palaeolithic package," as was always assumed.

There is of course a resistance to reinterpretation. Most prehistorians recognize the need to see the problems of "modern humans" and "Upper Palaeolithic" separately, but the issues tend to recombine. If the central idea is that modern humans emerge from Africa, then it leads to a pressure either to (a) ignore the question of dated archaeological evidence as a tiresome thorn in the side; or (b) find changes of culture which can be linked with the supposed population movement.

Thus, one might link the 90,000-year-old harpoons with 50,000-year-old stone toolkits in the Levant, as the pathway of new "modern" behaviour. But there is virtually no material justification for this, given that the African stone toolkits are so different and no harpoons have been found in the Middle East. Much of the problem is a preoccupation with "modern behaviour." As it cannot be defined, it cannot be dated. It seems much better to concentrate on evidence trait by trait, and to wait for patterns to emerge (Reynolds 1990, 1991; Rigaud 1989). Thus the development in stone tools that leads to blade industries can be documented and dated where it happens and need not be confused with the origins of bone tools, art, or even of modern humans, all of which may have distinct origins, perhaps in different places.

Even accepting this, the dating of the Upper Palaeolithic presents many puzzles. There is a strong tendency, conscious or unconscious, to accept "wave propagation" models when looking at Europe. These are emphasized by the triad of first colonization of the continent (~1 million years?), the appearance of the Upper Palaeolithic and modern humans (~40,000 years), and then of farming (~10,000 years). Europe's shape as a peninsula begs this interpretation, as does the fact that all these phenomena start outside Europe at earlier dates.

Perhaps, of course, the Upper Palaeolithic had a broad origin outside Europe, but dates across Asia are not good enough to pin this down. What we see (or imagine we see) is the thrust across Europe. But here there is another double puzzle. First, the initial Upper Palaeolithic is localized and varied (Kozlowski 1992, 1999). Then there appear to be dates that buck the general trend. If we take one view, dates appear around 45,000 in the southeast, and Spain is not reached until 25,000 years ago. So this Upper Palaeolithic movement takes nearly half of the last 50,000 years. The other view is that hardly a date over 40,000 is firmly established—but that dates of this age appear as early in the extreme west, in northern Spain, as in southeast Europe. This picture is of an Upper Palaeolithic which appears explosively fast across Europe, but then leaves local areas of delayed occupation to be explained (as in the Dordogne in France, or parts of the Peloponnese in Greece).

These differences are huge and have profound implications, not least concerning the demise of the Neanderthals. The difficulties, however, could largely be an artefact of limitations in our dating techniques. Archaeologists need resolution of about 1,000 years, and radiocarbon superficially provides this. Yet the technique is close to its limits. Roughly speaking, these are the activity levels of samples through this period:

32,000: 2 percent modern
37,000: 1 percent modern
42,000: 0.5 percent modern

This means that to achieve accurate measures, laboratories have to reduce contamination levels well below these figures (Olsson 1991; Olsson and Possnert 1992). Although the best laboratories can do this most of the time, it is plain from many dated sequences both that (a) there is variation in dates at a single level, and (b) dates stop getting plainly older towards the bottom of a sequence. The Abri Pataud in southwest France exemplifies both points (Movius 1975; Mellars et al. 1987), which are prima facie evidence that contamination is present.

On this basis one can suggest a model that the Upper Palaeolithic occupation of Europe began by 45,000, and was largely complete by 40,000; in the far reaches of the continent it may have come later, but most variation departing from these figures is probably produced by unduly late dates.

Into New Worlds

As the Upper Palaeolithic was unfolding in Europe, similarly momentous events were taking shape in other corners of the globe—modern humans were making their way far and wide. That these events were contemporaneous is known to us mainly through radiocarbon, but as in Europe, this technique cannot reach back quite far enough to solve some of the major questions.

AUSTRALIA

Recent studies show that *Homo erectus* had reached far out onto the island chains of Indonesia (Morwood et al. 1999), but it was left to *sapiens* to cover the last 100 kilometers of open water to Australia—or rather the landmass of Sahul (Australia and New Guinea combined).

Australia gives us pure prehistory, undisturbed until 1788. The prehistory of Australia again illustrates the problems of sampling resolution. Here the handicap is provided by the scarcity of alternatives to radiocarbon, which clearly does not reach back far enough to chart the earliest occupation. The first archaeological investigators thought that humans had reached Australia within the last few thousand years. Then in the 1960s deep excavations began to show occupations of 20–30,000 years ago (Mulvaney 1969). Eventually, archaeology began to push beyond this framework, but as only radiocarbon was available for dating, there was no means of extending the timescale.

Thus, archaeologists were able to develop a regional chronology (level 4), extending to about 30,000 years. The global constraint at level 5 was that modern humans had been "available" for only 30–40,000 years. In the 1980s this constraint was lifted by earlier dates for modern humans (see above). Older dates in Australia then became a reasonable hypothesis. (Alongside this is the marginal possibility that some premodern population might be found in Australia. Possible hints of this have come through the robust nature of some hominid finds not only in Indonesia but also in Australia itself, but no convincing pattern of evidence has emerged.)

Although deeper roots to the human occupation of Australia have seemed likely, the opportunities for use of appropriate dating techniques are quite restricted. Circumstances allowing the use of K/Ar and palaeomagnetism are minimal. U-series is possible in coastal contexts, but most attempts have been made with thermoluminescence (TL). Unfortunately, this cannot be regarded as a routine dating technique when based on sediments. Fierce arguments have resulted from attempts to date sites such as Jinmium rockshelter in the north (Fullagar et al. 1996; Spooner 1998). The dates in dispute have ranged from 140,000 to 40,000 years. The early occupation of Australia has become as controversial as that of the Americas.

Assessment is not easy at present because the framework is not very tight. Is there reason for doubting that the oldest radiocarbon dates give a true picture? It seems unlikely that they should do so, given that very old dates on the limits of the technique occur on opposite sides of the landmass—from Upper Swann close to Perth, from Ngarrabullgan cave on the Cape York peninsula, and from the Huon peninsula in New Guinea, none of them likely to be first ports of call for early colonists (Pearce and Barbetti 1981; David et al. 1997; Groube et al. 1986).

This is not to say that far older dates are correct. The best chances of occupation of Australia are likely to have come in a cool (glacial) period when sea levels were depressed. The oceans were high, overall, from about 130,000 through to 80,000 years ago. Therefore the period 80–40,000 appears to give the best window of opportunity. Neither the regional pattern of dates, nor the global constraints, argues strongly for an earlier date. This puts the onus on excavators and dating scientists to come up with dated site evidence. At the moment this seems to extend up to 50–60 ka (thousands of years ago). Malakunanja rockshelter in the north has dates in this range (Roberts et al. 1990). These are now supported by dates of approximately 60,000 obtained by a combination of techniques for a human skeleton at Lake Mungo, much further south (Thorne et al. 1999; Stringer 1999). Techniques such as ESR, luminescence, and U-series rarely offer high security when used singly, but in combination they are gradually changing perceptions of the regional model; it seems likely that modern humans were present in Australia long before they reached Europe.

The long aboriginal occupation of Australia provides other challenges to interpretation (Lourandos 1997). What actually happened in this vast field of prehistory? Study requires painstaking application of many hundreds of radiocarbon dates over the whole continent. There are few highlights, but certain important ones in establishing a worldwide picture. These include the dating of rock art (Chippindale et al. 2000; Hedges et al. 1998; Rosenfeld and Smith 1997); also, the extinction of megafauna, which appears in some of the early art. The replacement of technologies can sometimes be charted, but among the myriad cultural events there appear to have been only few that led to distinctive changes in the archaeological record (see below).

THE AMERICAS

The chronology of the first settlement of the Americas has long appeared particularly controversial. Many scholars have believed that the occupation goes back only some 12,000 years, whereas others have argued for a far earlier date (see Bonnichsen and Steele 1994; Bonnichsen 1999). The 12,000 BP benchmark was defined by the dates of ice barriers in the north, the lack of early occupations in the plains of North America, and the "cranky" nature of some claims for earlier sites. For long, the problem of late versus old has appeared to be one for American archaeology specifically, or even for American archaeologists. Now however, it must be admitted that the margins of doubt for the early occupation of Europe, or for the first colonization of Australia, have become at least as great in percentage terms. The unusual feature in the Americas is the "fork" of choice set out by atrocious conditions of the last glacial maximum from about 20,000–15,000 BP. The Bering landbridge was exposed at this time, but initial colonization would be extremely unlikely during the most extreme climate, so perforce it should come earlier or later. Later colonization is problematic, given the huge diversity of subsequent cultures across the Americas, and the short timescale available for achieving it. Earlier colonization also remains problematic, although some sites such as Pedra Furada in Brazil would probably be accepted without question if they were found elsewhere in the world (Guidon and Arnaud 1991). There is one major difference from the Australian controversy. There the early site evidence has been characterized to general satisfaction, but the dates are in dispute. In the Americas, the dates are often acceptable, as at Pedra Furada, but the evidence for human occupation is disputed. Normally, stone age "traditions" can be characterized satisfactorily once a few sites have been found, but it must be admitted that no such recognizable persona has emerged for early American sites. This comes only with the distinctive stone points of the Clovis tradition, beginning about 11–12,000 years ago in the Great Plains, or for material of similar age in South America (Lynch 1980). Human remains are usually recognizable beyond controversy, but in the Americas they have provided little help. Initial amino acid dates proved misleading (Bada and Helfman 1975). None of the radiocarbon dates made possible by accelerator mass spectrometry is so far older than 11,000 BP (Bada et al. 1984; Taylor et al. 1985), although Stafford (1994) has pointed out that poorly preserved older samples would not necessarily yield valid old radiocarbon dates. Perhaps the strongest pointers towards an early occupation via a coastal route (Gruhn 1994) are dates in the south of <10,000 years, which presuppose an earlier entry (e.g., Athens and Ward 1999; Roosevelt et al. 1996). Older dates in North America such as for Tlapacoya or Meadowcroft rockshelter provide further but controversial support for this interpretation (Mirambell 1978; Carlisle and Adovasio 1982).

Again, the global perspective (level 5) can no longer be held as a reason for denying the possibility of early occupation: modern humans were "available" at least 30,000 years ago. As with Australia, the debate is significant partly because of later developments. The Americas—the New World—make up almost 25 percent of total global land area. Although the great majority of recognizable archaeological events fall in the Holocene, the last 10,000 years, the depth of the roots is a critical matter, considering that this region of the world saw its own sequence of megafaunal extinctions, domestication of plants and animals, and the rise of civilizations. Recent years have seen a strengthening of the case for early occupation: perhaps the time has come to accept it as a working hypothesis which still presents curious puzzles.

Problems of Domestication

Amid a host of events that become ever more complex, archaeologists, geologists, and botanists like to have some timelines that are utterly reliable, and that set a frame for further inquiry. The change from Pleistocene to Holocene about 11,000 years ago has long provided one such event on a worldwide scale. The world warmed up, sea levels rose, vegetation changed, and—as it were—humans began to get ready to change everything. Domestication and the origins of agriculture are a large part of this, and have transformed human existence. This makes the chronology of their development an important issue: it reflects other problems. There is space here only for some very general points, the aim being to stand back and consider the frame, rather than looking at the detail. Until the 1950s the view did not depend on radiocarbon—lake varves and pollen plotted out the Holocene. Radiocarbon then showed the Holocene to be about 10,000 years long, and calibration of radiocarbon dates through dendrochronology has added precision to the figures—about 11,600 years BP, "real time" (see Kromer and Spurk 1998; Kromer et al. 1998). The need for such radiocarbon calibration has now been appreciated for thirty years. The basic equations of the technique employ the assumption that past levels of radiocarbon production in the upper atmosphere were equivalent to those of recent times. Dating of tree rings of known age showed that this was not quite the case, and chronologies based on the annual rings of European oaks or American bristlecone pines now allow corrections to be made right through the Holocene. Approximate calibrations of earlier periods can be made from comparisons of U-series dates on coral and radiocarbon dates of the same specimens.

The domesticated plants and animals can be studied in the present in all their diversity, which can now be mapped genetically. To an extent this allows reading of the past, as with human genetics, but crucial archaeological evidence is surprisingly scarce or poorly sampled, or hard to date (Hillman et al. 1993; papers in Gowlett and Hedges 1986). Most plant and animal remains do not survive, and in some of the most critical instances, interpretations may depend upon just one or two charred grains or a few scraps of bone. Direct dating of these by AMS (accelerator) radiocarbon has improved reliability and precision. Wet sieving has also transformed the rates of recovery of plant remains and bone fragments in more recent excavations, such as that at Abu Hureyra in Syria, so that the potential for accurate dating and interpretation has been much improved.

A further problem is that morphological change in early domesticates may be extremely rapid—after many generations, perhaps, of selection and genetic change there may come a virtually instantaneous change in the phenotype, or external appearance (see Hillman 1996). Early maize seems to belie this, as growth in the size of the cobs can be traced through a long period (Beadle 1978), but locally the introduction of maize could be very rapid. Fortunately, it can be pinpointed through studies of stable isotopes of carbon in the bones of people or animals from the relevant sites (Van der Merwe and Vogel 1978; Blake et al. 1992).

Around the world, domestication and agriculture appeared during the early Holocene, so it seemed natural to see this great readjustment as an adaptation to the change: stimulus and response. The near-synchronization of events in the Old and New Worlds appeared to need no more explanation, because this was the start of a new era.

This no longer seems the appropriate frame. A picture is beginning to emerge of continuous developments in the Middle East since the glacial maximum of 20,000 years ago (Harris 1996; Hillman 1996; Sherratt 1997). Radiocarbon dating shows the sophistication of early sites, such as Ohalo II in Israel, dated to 19,000 BP (Nadel and Werker 1999), and Wadi Kubbaniya in Egypt of similar age (Wendorf et al. 1988). At Ohalo there can be seen a range of crafts and signs of intensive food collection, especially of seeds. The following Natufian phase in Israel is also now well dated to the period before the beginning of the Holocene. The question arises: if the Holocene itself was not the trigger of all these developments, why the synchronism at all? Why do comparable developments towards agriculture happen around the world in so many areas, with such synchronism? After precursor phases from about 20,000 to 12,000, all this occurs, broadly, between 12,000 and 8,000 years ago (e.g., Harris 1996). Why not at 30,000, when modern humans were already widely distributed and sophisticated in behavior? These are questions of chronology which go beyond chronology, but their resolution must depend upon high-resolution dating.

There is a growing appreciation that the glacial maximum itself may have been the principal trigger for change. Worldwide, the downturn into atrocious conditions 20,000 years ago, the lowering of sea levels, and then their rapid rise as climate ameliorated, perhaps forced a roughly synchronous set of changes. It may have come naturally to modern humans to react similarly, though independently, in parallel. This may be speculation, but dating evidence—especially unexpectedly early dating evidence for precocious developments, as with yam horticulture in New Guinea—plays a key part in forcing reassessments.

The Home Straight

The last 5,000 years are in many ways the most crucial period of all for chronological study, since they embrace the great bulk of archaeological effort, as well as of developed economies and literate civilization. Clearly, these times need resolved, precise dating, but equally it is a fact that much of the world was in prehistory until the last thousand years, and even within civilizations some circumstances are far fuller with chronological sensitivity than others. A Roman military structure will relate to particular campaigns, and the finds of coins may precisely reflect their span. In contrast, a contemporary native farmstead in the fort's hinterland may remain effectively in Iron Age prehistory, and preserve no equivalent evidence. Glimpses of clarity may be surrounded by utter ignorance. Q. Laberius Durus, a young officer, was killed in a skirmish during Caesar's second expedition to Britain in 54 BC, the first named casualty of any event in Britain, the known rather than the unknown soldier, among all those who must have fallen in this campaign (Caesar, *Gallic Wars* V, 16).

How does archaeology proceed? First, we must understand that approximately three quarters of the world lie outside the historical chronologies; but on the other hand, the period is close enough that (as an ideal) we can look for real calendrical precision (tree rings and ice cores date the entire period at ~1 year precision). Thus, in general:

1 Historical chronologies of ancient civilizations must provide a backbone.
2 Wherever possible, precise natural science chronologies must be brought into play, such as those provided by dendrochronology or volcanic eruptions.
3 In most other circumstances radiocarbon will provide the mainstay of absolute dating, with reasonable precision (usually 100–300 years).
4 There should be numerous opportunities to cross-link dating methods, although on particular sites or in particular areas these may be hard to apply.

The examples given below attempt to follow these points across selected areas of the globe. The chronologies of early civilizations can provide a backbone for the dating of adjacent cultural provinces, but the Egyptologist Ken Kitchen also notes the difficulties (Kitchen 1989, 1991). For the earliest Egyptian dynasties, the errors are potentially of the order of ~300 years—a similar range to that of an average radiocarbon date (+/– 80 years gives a 95 percent confidence range of about 300 years). Thus, if a group of radiocarbon determinations could be associated well enough, the set of dates could give at least equal precision to that of earliest "history."

Cursory study shows that the ancient chronologies are not built up merely from juggling the surviving lists of kings. There is an interplay with archaeological evidence, which can assist in various forms. Some of the best documentary evidence can come when archaeological finds are made in sealed contexts, perhaps related to other datable material. Apart from the manuscripts of the classical world, which have survived in libraries, most other archives have actually been found by archaeological work. This may provide a feedback loop, in which the interpretation of discovered documents allows further fruitful excavation.

Kitchen (1991) stresses the value of synchronisms, or timelines. Those of correspondence, or artefacts, can provide information as effectively as a layer of volcanic ash. Diplomatic exchanges between two monarchs can prove their contemporaneity, even if neither is precisely dated. Similarly, Bronze Age wrecks in the Mediterranean, such as that at Uluburun off Turkey, have provided trade goods from several sources, linked in "systemic context" (cf. Schiffer 1976 for the idea of systemic contexts).

Astronomers were active in early civilizations through the last four to five thousand years, but their observations are not always accurate enough, or precisely described, to allow correlations with known events. Some are easy to pin down, such as the eclipses of the sun, but so many of these happened that confusion can arise. Further back, there are disputes—perhaps this report is a supernova, that one an unknown comet. To summarize, at 2000 BC in Egypt and the Near East, historical chronology is constrained to around ten years. A figure such as King Shamsi-Adad (ca. 1813–1781 BC) can be traced through cuneiform letters found in archaeological excavations, and there is even documentation for his interactions with the kingdom of Dilmun further south in the Gulf (the modern Bahrein), which has not itself yielded documents from this period (Eidem and Hojlund 1993).

If we turn west in the Mediterranean, the record is less precise, notwithstanding the presence of early civilizations such as Mycenae. The resolution is just good enough that Sherratt and Sherratt (1993) can treat the period from 2000 BC onwards roughly by century, the dating based on a mixture of radiocarbon and transferred historical evidence (dated artefacts, including metalwork and pottery, etc.).

European chronologies are stiffened further by dendrochronology, based after all chiefly on the European oak sequences (Baillie 1995). For 2000 BC this could give great precision to the dating of, say, wooden finds preserved in the Swiss lakes. It has the broader importance of providing a precise framework which extends beyond individual finds: dendrochronology is exact. To an extent this record can be cross-linked with the record from Arctic ice cores. Both can give an indication of major volcanic

eruptions. Acidity or tephra are recorded in the ice, while the growth of trees is impaired by reduced sunlight and harsh frosts. Mike Baillie has isolated a series of timelines which seem to point to events of climatic catastrophe. One such, at around 1640 BC, may coincide with, or represent, the eruption of Thera (Santorini), although this is generally no longer considered to have been "catastrophic" for the contemporary Minoan civilization of which Thera was an outpost (see Baillie and Munro 1988; Baillie 1998). Yet such coincidences of events can be deceptive, and disasters can be multiple—Pompeii was rocked by a great earthquake less than twenty years before the eruption of Vesuvius (Potter 1987; Laurence 1994; Fulford and Wallace-Hadrill 1998). Thera erupted in the second millennium BC, but so also did the volcanoes of Iceland, which might be even more likely to affect the Arctic ice cores (see Zielinski and Germani 1998; Buckland et al. 1997). Ultimate precision may be lacking here, but the general picture can be striking in its impact. Lead aerosol records from the ice cores provide a quite remarkable impression of the rises and falls of smelting through the last five thousand years (Figure 12.1).

Such a record treats prehistory and history alike. Elsewhere, there is only prehistory to grapple with. Of hundreds of parts of the globe, we can take for comparison central Africa, and parts of Sahul—the landmass which separated into Australia and New Guinea as seas rose during the early Holocene.

Domesticated plants and animals crept down Africa from about 9,000 years ago, as well evidenced by dated sites from the Sahara down to southern Africa (Robertshaw 1992). At some time came the great expansion that has led to the many Bantu languages of today. Archaeology cannot relate the two. It can aim to date material evidence, such as the earliest pottery in an area, or first traces of domestic animals (Robertshaw 1992). In northern Congo, brave efforts along the tributaries of the Congo River have located "Iron Age" sites, and given a series of dates on pottery, ranging from about 4,000 to 2,000 BP (Eggert 1992). These are probably evidence of an agricultural economy, but they do not date particular peoples. They do not tell us, for example, about the origins of the pygmies. Direct evidence of the latter is provided only by Egyptian tomb paintings—another example of a link between early history and prehistory (Clark 1971).

In Australia and New Guinea the circumstances are somewhat similar but there can be even less "handle" in terms of material culture, except where rock art is abundant, or where environmental evidence provides a framework. Even within the region, there can be great differences between records. On the north coast of New Guinea, the rising Holocene sea flooded a gulf at the mouths of the Sepik and Ramu rivers, producing a shoreline of 6,000 BP which is now some 125 km inland (Swadling 1997). Gradually the shallow embayment silted up, creating a geomorphological history which includes a record of human activity. Midden sites near the shoreline date from 5800 BP onwards. They preserve fish and plant remains in some variety. Pottery, too, is known, from the Lapita tradition, and perhaps an earlier tradition (Swadling 1997; Gosden 1992). A distinctive kind of pottery

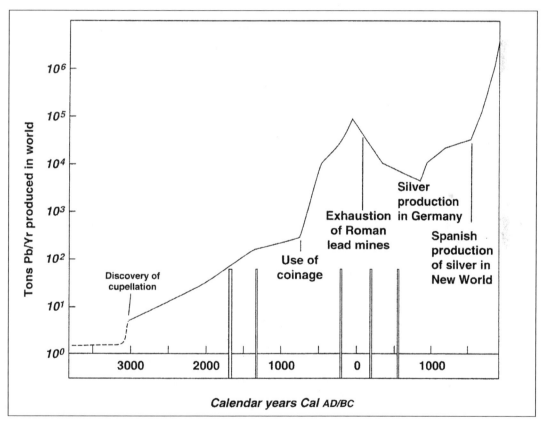

FIGURE 12.1: The lead aerosol record of Arctic ice cores gives a dated index to production of lead and silver through the last 5,000 years (after Settle and Patterson 1980). Marker dates noted by Baillie can be studied against this record. It seems that the effects of volcanic eruptions and dust veils were too localized and short term to have a measurable impact on industrial production (cf. Baillie 1995; Baillie and Munro 1988).

such as Lapita serves to generate its own controversies of origin and dating, much as have the Beakers of Europe (Ambrose 1997; Sand 1997).

This picture, rich in detail, contrasts with southern Australia, where stone tools are virtually the entire record, and do not exhibit much obvious sequential development. There is a dichotomy between early large stone and later small stone or microlithic tool traditions, the latter found in the last three or four thousand years (Bird and Frankel 1991). This means that patterns have to be evaluated without "events." In some areas of Australia traditions of rock art help to furnish such events (Chippindale et al. 2000); although their radiocarbon dating has proved difficult (Hedges et al. 1998; Gillespie 1997). Again, the relationship between humans and environmental change can sometimes help to shape a picture. Dortch (1997a) has studied the distribution of stone fish weirs in the southwest. These would be hard to date by radiocarbon, as they were probably rebuilt many times, but generally they would be set in tidal embayments. Multiple radiocarbon dates show that Lake Clifton, for example, was tidal up to about 4000 BP, when it became a lagoon, thus providing by indirect means a probable minimum age for the weirs. At much the same time in Western Australia, the rising waters of Lake Jasper covered other sites, probably the result of higher water tables as postglacial sea levels rose (Dortch 1997b).

In each area prehistorians have the duty of building up a local record. This brief sampling of examples shows that although their basic task is similar worldwide, the nature of the record varies enormously, even, or perhaps especially, in the last five thousand years—in cultural repertoire, rates of change, in resolution of the events that can be dated, as well as in the means of dating them.

References

Aitken, M.J. 1990. *Science-based Dating in Archaeology*. London: Longman.

Aitken, M.J., C.B. Stringer, and P.A. Mellars (eds.) 1993. *The Origin of Modern Humans and the Impact of Chronometric Dating*. Princeton, NJ: Princeton University Press.

Ambrose, W.R. 1997. "Contradictions in Lapita pottery, a composite clone." *Antiquity*, 71: 525–38.

An Zhizheng and Ho Chuan Kun 1989. "New magnetostratigraphic dates of Lantian Homo erectus." *Quaternary Research*, 32: 213–21.

Andel, T.H. van 1990. "Living in the last high glacial—an interdisciplinary challenge." In O. Soffer and C. Gamble (eds.), *The World at 18000 BP, Vol. 1: High Latitudes*, pp. 24–38. London: Unwin Hyman.

Andel, T.H. van 1998. "Middle and Upper Palaeolithic environments and the calibration of 14C dates beyond 10,000 BP." *Antiquity*, 72: 26–33.

Andrews, P. and P. Banham (eds.) 1999. *Late Cenozoic Environments and Hominid Evolution: A Tribute to Bill Bishop*. London: Geological Society.

Asfaw, B., Y. Beyene, G. Suwa, et al. 1992. "The earliest Acheulean at Konso-Gardula." *Nature*, 360: 732–33.

Asfaw B., T.D. White, C.O. Lovejoy, et al. 1999. "*Australopithecus garhi*: a new species of early hominid from Ethiopia." *Science*, 284: 629–35.

Athens, J.S. and J.V. Ward 1999. "The Late Quaternary of the Western Amazon: climate, vegetation and humans." *Antiquity*, 73: 287–302.

Bada, J.L. and P.M. Helfman 1975. "Amino acid racemization dating of fossil bones." *World Archaeology*, 7: 160–83.

Bada, J.L., R. Gillespie, J.A.J. Gowlett, and R.E.M. Hedges 1984. "Accelerator mass spectrometry radiocarbon ages of amino acid extracts from Californian Palaeoindian skeletons." *Nature*, 312: 442–44.

Bailey, G. (ed.) 1997. *Klithi: Palaeolithic Settlement and Quaternary Landscapes in Northwest Greece. Vol. 1: Excavation and Intra-site Analysis at Klithi.* Cambridge: McDonald Institute for Archaeological Research.

Baillie, M.G.L. 1995. *A Slice Through Time.* London: Routledge.

Baillie, M.G.L. 1998. "Bronze Age myths expose archaeological shortcomings? A reply to Buckland et al. 1997." *Antiquity,* 72: 425–27.

Baillie, M.G.L. and M.A.R. Munro 1988. "Irish tree rings, Santorini and volcanic dust veils." *Nature,* 332: 344–46.

Bard, E., M. Arnold, R.G. Fairbanks, and B. Hamelin 1993. "230th–234U and 14C ages obtained by mass spectrometry on corals." *Radiocarbon,* 35: 191–99.

Barton, C.M., G.A. Clark, and A.E. Cohen 1994. "Art as information: explaining Upper Palaeolithic art in Western Europe." *World Archaeology,* 26 (2): 185–207.

Bar-Yosef, O. 1992. "The role of western Asia in modern human origins." In M.J. Aitken, C.B. Stringer, and P.A. Mellars (eds.), *The Origin of Modern Humans and the Impact of Chronometric Dating,* pp. 132–47. Princeton, NJ: Princeton University Press.

Bar-Yosef, O. 1996a. "The role of climate in the interpretation of human movements and cultural transformations in Western Asia." In E.S. Vrba, G.H. Denton, T.C. Partridge, and L.H. Burckle (eds.), *Palaeoclimate and Evolution, With Emphasis on Human Origins,* pp. 507–23. New Haven, CT: Yale University Press.

Bar-Yosef, O. 1996b. "The impact of Late Pleistocene–Early Holocene climatic changes on humans in Southwest Asia." In L.G. Straus, B.V. Eriksen, J.M. Erlandson, and D.R. Yesner (eds.), *Humans at the End of the Ice Age: The Archaeology of the Pleistocene–Holocene Transition,* pp. 61–78. New York: Plenum Press.

Bar-Yosef, O. and N. Goren-Inbar 1992. *The Lithic Assemblages of the Site of Ubeidiya, Jordan Valley.* Jerusalem: Qedem 34.

Bar-Yosef, O., B. Vandermeersch, B. Arensburg, et al. 1992. "The excavations in Kebara Cave, Mt Carmel." *Current Anthropology,* 33 (5): 497–550.

Beadle, G.W. 1978. "The origin of Zea mays." In D.L. Browman (ed.), *Cultural Continuity in Mesoamerica,* pp. 24–42. The Hague: Mouton.

Belfer-Cohen, A. and O. Bar-Yosef 1999. "The Levantine Aurignacian: 60 years of research." In W. Davies and R. Charles (eds.), *Dorothy Garrod and the Progress of the Palaeolithic,* pp. 118–34. Oxford: Oxbow Books.

Bellomo, R.V. 1993. "A methodological approach for identifying archaeological evidence of fire resulting from human activities." *Journal of Archaeological Science,* 20, 525–55.

Bermudez de Castro, J.M., J. Arsuaga, E. Carbonell, et al. (1997). "A hominid from the lower Pleistocene of Atapuerca, Spain: possible ancestor to Neandertals and modern humans." *Science,* 276: 1392–95.

Bernor, R.L. and D. Lipscomb 1996. "A consideration of Old World hipparionine horse phylogeny and global abiotic processes." In E.S. Vrba, G.H. Denton, T.C. Partridge, and L.H. Burckle (eds.), *Palaeoclimate and Evolution, With Emphasis on Human Origins,* pp. 164–77. New Haven, CT: Yale University Press.

Bird, C.F.M. and D. Frankel 1991. "Problems in constructing a regional sequence: Holocene southeast Australia." *World Archaeology,* 23 (2): 179–92.

Bischoff, J.L., J.F. Garcia, and L.G. Straus 1992. "Uranium-series isochron dating at El Castillo cave (Cantabria, Spain): the 'Acheulean'/'Mousterian' question." *Journal of Archaeological Science,* 19: 49–62.

Bischoff, J.L., R. Merriam, W.M. Childers, and R. Protsch 1976. "Antiquity of man in America indicated by radiometric dates on the Yuha burial site." *Nature,* 261: 128–29.

Bischoff, J.L. and R.J. Rosenbauer 1981. "Uranium series dating of human skeletal remains from the Del Mar and Sunnyvale sites, California." *Science,* 213: 1003–05.

Bishop, W.W. and J.D. Clark (eds.) 1967. *Background to Evolution in Africa.* Chicago: University of Chicago Press.

Blake, B., B.S. Chisholm, J.E. Clark, B. Voorhies, and M.W. Love 1992. "Prehistoric subsistence in the Soconusco region." *Current Anthropology,* 33: 83–94.

Blockley, S.P.E., R.E. Donahue, and A.M. Pollard 2000. "Radiocarbon, calibration and Late Glacial occupation in northwest Europe." *Antiquity*, 74: 112–19.

Bonnichsen, R. (ed.) 1999. *Who Were the First Americans?* Peopling of the Americas Publications. Corvallis: Oregon State University.

Bonnichsen, R. and D.G. Steele (eds.) 1994. *Method and Theory for Investigating the Peopling of the Americas.* Peopling of the Americas Publications. Corvallis: Oregon State University.

Brooks, A.S., D.M. Helgren, J.S. Cramer, et al. 1995. "Dating and context of three Middle Stone Age sites with bone points in the Upper Semliki Valley, Zaire." *Science*, 268: 548–53.

Brown, F.H. 1996. "The potential of the Turkana basin for palaeoclimatic reconstruction in East Africa." In E.S. Vrba, G.H. Denton, T.C. Partridge, and L.H. Burckle (eds.), *Palaeoclimate and Evolution, With Emphasis on Human Origins*, pp. 319–30. New Haven, CT: Yale University Press.

Brown, T.A., R.G. Allaby, K.A. Brown, and M.K. Jones 1993. "Biomolecular archaeology of wheat: past, present and future." *World Archaeology*, 25 (1): 64–73.

Brunet, M., A. Beauvilain, Y. Coppens, et al. 1995. "The first australopithecine 2,500 kilometres west of the rift valley (Chad)." *Nature*, 378: 273–75.

Brunet, M., F. Guy, D. Pilbeam, et al. 2002. "A new hominid from the upper Miocene of Chad, central Africa." *Nature*, 418: 145–51.

Buckland, P.C., A.J. Dugmore, and K.J. Edwards 1997. "Bronze Age myths? Volcanic activity and human response in the Mediterranean and North Atlantic regions." *Antiquity*, 71: 581–93.

Cande, S.C. and D.V. Kent 1995. "Revised calibration of the geomagnetic polarity timescale for the late Cretaceous and Cenozoic." *Journal of Geophysical Research*, 100: 6093–95.

Carlisle, R.C. and J.M. Adovasio 1982. *Collected Papers on the Archaeology of Meadowcroft Rockshelter and the Cross Creek Drainage*, 7th Annual Meeting of the Society for American Archaeology, Minneapolis.

Chen Tiemei, Y. Quan, and W. En 1994. "Antiquity of *Homo sapiens* in China." *Nature*, 368: 55–56.

Chen Tiemei and Zhang Yinyun 1991. "Palaeolithic chronology and the possible coexistence of *Homo erectus* and *Homo sapiens* in China." *World Archaeology*, 23 (2): 147–54.

Chippindale, C., J. de Jongh, J. Flood, and S. Rufolo 2000. "Stratigraphy, Harris matrices and relative dating of Australian rock-art." *Antiquity*, 74: 285–86.

Clark, J.D. 1969. *Kalambo Falls Prehistoric Site, Vol. 1: The Geology, Palaeoecology and Detailed Stratigraphy of the Excavations.* Cambridge: Cambridge University Press.

Clark, J.D. 1971. "A re-examination of the evidence for agricultural origins in the Nile valley." *Proceedings of the Prehistoric Society*, 37 (Part 2): 34–79.

Clark, J.D. 1992. "African and Asian perspectives on the origins of modern humans." In M.J. Aitken, C.B. Stringer, and P.A. Mellars (eds.), *The Origin of Modern Humans and the Impact of Chronometric Dating*, pp. 148–78. Princeton, NJ: Princeton University Press.

Clarke, D.L. 1968. *Analytical Archaeology.* London: Methuen.

Clarke R.J. and P.V. Tobias 1995. "Sterkfontein member 2 foot bones of the oldest South African hominid." *Science*, 269: 521–24.

Cox, C.B. and P.D. Moore 1993. *Biogeography: An Ecological and Evolutionary Approach*, 5th edn. Oxford: Blackwell.

Crawford, G.W. and C. Shen 1998. "The origins of rice agriculture: recent progress in East Asia." *Antiquity*, 72: 858–66.

Dark, P. 2000. "Revised 'absolute' dating of the early Mesolithic site of Star Carr, North Yorkshire, in the light of changes in the early Holocene tree-ring chronology." *Antiquity*, 74: 304–07.

David, B., R. Roberts, C. Tuniz, R. Jones, and J. Head 1997. "New optical and radiocarbon dates from Ngarrabullgan Cave, a Pleistocene archaeological site in Australia: implications for the comparability of time clocks and for the human colonization of Australia." *Antiquity*, 71: 183–88.

Davidson, I. 1991. "The archaeology of language origins: a review." *Antiquity*, 65: 39–48.

Davidson, I. and W. Noble 1993. "Tools and language in human evolution." In K.R. Gibson and T. Ingold (eds.), *Tools, Language and Cognition in Human Evolution*, pp. 363–88. Cambridge: Cambridge University Press.

Deacon, T. 1997. *The Symbolic Species: The Co-Evolution of Language and the Human Brain*. London: Allen Lane.

Delson, E. 1994. "Evolutionary history of the colobine monkeys in palaeoenvironmental perspective." In A.G. Davies and J.F. Oates (eds.), *Colobine Monkeys: Their Ecology, Behaviour and Evolution*, pp. 11–43. Cambridge: Cambridge University Press.

deMenocal, P.B. and J. Bloemendahl 1996. "Plio-Pleistocene climatic variability in subtropical Africa and the paleoenvironment of hominid evolution: a combined data-model approach." In E.S. Vrba, G.H. Denton, T.C. Partridge, and L.H. Burckle (eds.), *Palaeoclimate and Evolution, With Emphasis on Human Origins*, pp. 262–88. New Haven, CT: Yale University Press.

D'Errico, F., J. Zilhao, M. Julien, D. Bafier, and J. Pelegrin 1998. "Neanderthal acculturation in Western Europe? A critical review of the evidence and its interpretation." *Current Anthropology*, 39: 1–44.

Dortch, C.E. 1997a. "New perceptions of the chronology and development of Aboriginal fishing in south-western Australia." *World Archaeology*, 29 (1): 15–35.

Dortch, C.E. 1997b. "Prehistory down under: investigations of submerged Aboriginal sites at Lake Jasper, Western Australia." *Antiquity*, 71: 116–23.

Drake, R.E., G.H. Curtis, T. Cerling, B.W. Cerling, and J. Hampel 1980. "KBS tuff dating and geochronology of tuffaceous sediments in the Koobi Fora and Shungura formations, East Africa." *Nature*, 283: 368–72.

Duarte C., J. Mauricio, P.B. Pettitt et al. 1999. "The early upper Paleolithic human skeleton from the Abrigo do Lagar Velho (Portugal) and modern human emergence in Iberia." *Proceedings of the National Academy of Sciences USA*, 96: 7604–09.

Dunbar, R. 1996. *Grooming, Gossip and the Evolution of Language*. London: Faber and Faber.

Edwards, R.L., J.W. Beck, G.S. Burr et al. 1993. "A large drop in atmospheric 14C/12C and reduced melting in the Younger Dryas, documented with 230th ages of corals." *Science*, 260: 962–67.

Eggert, M.K.H. 1992. "The Central African rain forest: historical speculation and archaeological facts." *World Archaeology*, 24 (1): 1–24.

Eidem, J. and F. Hojlund 1993. "Trade or diplomacy? Assyria and Dilmun in the eighteenth century BC." *World Archaeology*, 24 (3): 441–48.

El Mansouri, M., El Fouikar, A., and B. Saint-Martin 1996. "Correlation between 14C ages and aspartic acid racemization at the Upper Palaeolithic site of the Abri Pataud (Dordogne, France)." *Journal of Archaeological Science*, 23: 803–09.

Ericson, J.E., L. Pandolfi, and C. Patterson 1982. "Pyrotechnology of copper extraction: methods of detection and implications." In T.A. Wertime and S.F. Wertime (eds.), *Early Pyrotechnology: The Evolution of the First Fire-Using Industries*, pp. 193–203. Washington, DC: Smithsonian Institution Press.

Fitch, F.J., P.J. Hooker, and J.A. Miller 1976. "Argon-40/Argon-39 dating of KBS Tuff in Koobi for a formation, East Rudolf, Kenya." *Nature*, 263: 740–44.

Fitch, F.J. and J.A. Miller 1970. "Radioisotopic age determinations of Lake Rudolf artefact site." *Nature*, 226: 226–28.

Fulford, M. and A. Wallace-Hadrill 1998. "Unpeeling Pompeii." *Antiquity*, 72: 128–45.

Fullagar, R.L.K., D.M. Price, and L.M. Head 1996. "Early human occupation of northern Australia: archaeology and thermoluminescence dating of Jinmium rock-shelter, Northern Territory." *Antiquity*, 70: 751–73.

Gabunia, L., A. Vekua, D. Lordkipanidze, et al. 2000. "Earliest Pleistocene hominid cranial remains from Dmanisi, Republic of Georgia: taxonomy, geological setting, and age." *Science*, 288: 1019–25.

Gamble, C. 1993. *Timewalkers*. London: Alan Sutton.

Geel, B. van, J. van der Plicht, M.R. Kilian, et al. 1998. "The sharp rise of Δ14C ca. 800 cal BC: possible causes, related climatic teleconnections and the impact on human environments." *Radiocarbon*, 40 (1): 535–50.

Geyh, M.A. and C. Schlüchter 1998. "Calibration of the 14C time scale beyond 22,000 BP." *Radiocarbon*, 40 (1): 475–82.

Gibert, J., L. Gibert, A. Iglesias, and E. Maestro 1998. "Two 'Oldowan' assemblages in the Plio-Pleistocene deposits of the Orce region, southeast Spain." *Antiquity*, 72: 17–25.

Gillespie, R. 1997. "On human blood, rock art and calcium oxalate: further studies on organic carbon content and radiocarbon, age of materials relating to Australian rock art." *Antiquity*, 71: 430–37.

Gleadow, A.J.W. 1980. "Fission track age of the KBS Tuff and associated hominid remains in northern Kenya." *Nature*, 284: 225–30.

Goodman, M., B.F. Koop, J. Czelusniak, et al. 1989. "Molecular phylogeny of the family of apes and humans." *Genome*, 31: 316–35.

Görsdorf, J., G. Dreyer, and U. Hartung 1998. "New 14C dating of the archaic royal necropolis Umm el-Qaab at Abydos (Egypt)." *Radiocarbon*, 40 (1): 641.

Gosden, C. 1992. "Production systems and the colonization of the western Pacific." *World Archaeology*, 24 (1): 55–69.

Gowlett, J.A.J., J.W.K. Harris, D. Walton, and B.A. Wood 1981. "Early archaeological sites, hominid remains and traces of fire from Chesowanja, Kenya." *Nature*, 294: 125–29.

Gowlett, J.A.J. and R.E.M. Hedges (eds.) 1986. *Archaeological Results from Accelerator Dating*. Oxford: Oxford University Committee for Archaeology Monograph Series, No. 11.

Gowlett, J.A.J., R.E.M. Hedges, and R.A. Housley 1997. "Klithi: the AMS radiocarbon dating programme for the site and its environs." In G. Bailey (ed.), *Klithi: Palaeolithic Settlement and Quaternary Landscapes in Northwest Greece, Vol. 1: Excavation and Intra-site Analysis at Klithi*, pp. 27–39. Cambridge: McDonald Institute for Archaeological Research.

Graves, P. 1994. "Flakes and ladders: what the archaeological record cannot tell us about the origins of language." *World Archaeology*, 26 (2): 158–71.

Groube, L., J. Chappell, J. Muke, and D. Price 1986. "40,000-year-old human occupation site at Huon Peninsula, Papua New Guinea." *Nature*, 324: 453–55.

Gruhn, R. 1994. "The Pacific coast route of initial entry: an overview." In R. Bonnichsen and D.G. Steele (eds.), *Method and Theory for Investigating the Peopling of the Americas*, pp. 249–56. Peopling of the Americas Publications. Corvallis: Oregon State University.

Grün, R. 1989. "Present status of ESR-dating." *Applied Radiation and Isotopes*, 10–12, 1045–55.

Grün, R. and C.B. Stringer 1991. "Electron spin resonance dating and the origin of modern humans." *Archaeometry*, 33: 153–99.

Guidon, N. and B. Arnaud 1991. "The chronology of the New World: two faces of one reality." *World Archaeology*, 23 (2): 167–78.

Harris, D.R. (ed.) 1996. *The Origins and Spread of Agriculture and Pastoralism in Eurasia*. London: University College London Press.

Harris, J.W.K. 1983. "Cultural beginnings: Plio-Pleistocene archaeological occurrences from the Afar, Ethiopia." *African Archaeological Review*, 1: 3–31.

Harrold, F.B. 1980. "A comparative analysis of Eurasian Palaeolithic burials." *World Archaeology*, 12 (2): 195–211.

Hay, R.L. 1976. *Geology of the Olduvai Gorge*. Berkeley: University of California Press.

Hedges, R.E.M., C. Bronk Ramsey, G.J. van Klinken, et al. 1998. "Methodological issues in the 14C dating of rock painting." *Radiocarbon*, 40 (1): 35–44.

Hedges, R.E.M. and J.A.J. Gowlett 1986. "Radiocarbon dating by accelerator mass spectrometry." *Scientific American*, 254: 100–07.

Hedges, R.E.M., M.J. Humm, J. Foreman, G.J. van Klinken, and C.R. Bronk 1992. "Developments in sample combustion to carbon dioxide, and in the Oxford AMS carbon dioxide ion source system." *Radiocarbon*, 34 (3): 306–11.

Hedges, R.E.M. and G.J. van Klinken 1992. "A review of current approaches in the pretreatment of bone for radiocarbon dating by AMS." *Radiocarbon*, 34 (3): 279–91.

Heinzelin, J. de, J.D. Clark, T. White, et al. 1999. "Environment and behavior of 2.5 million-year-old Bouri hominids." *Science*, 284: 625–29.

Hill, A. 1996. "Faunal and environmental change in the Neogene of East Africa: evidence from the Tugen Hills sequence, Baringo District, Kenya." In E.S. Vrba, G.H. Denton, T.C. Partridge, and L.H. Burckle (eds.), *Palaeoclimate and Evolution, With Emphasis on Human Origins*, pp. 178–93. New Haven, CT: Yale University Press.

Hill, A. and S. Ward 1988. "Origin of the Hominidae: the record of African large hominoid evolution between 14My and 4My." *Yearbook of Physical Anthropology*, 31: 49–83.

Hillman, G. 1996. "Late Pleistocene changes in wild plant-foods available to hunter-gatherers of the northern Fertile Crescent: possible preludes to cereal cultivation." In D.R. Harris (ed.), *The Origins and Spread of Agriculture and Pastoralism in Eurasia*, pp. 159–203. London: University College London Press.

Hillman, G., S. Wales, F. McLaren, J. Evans, and A. Butler 1993. "Identifying problematic remains of ancient plant foods: a comparison of the role of chemical, histological and morphological criteria." *World Archaeology*, 25 (1): 94–121.

Housley, R.A., C.S. Gamble, and P. Pettitt 2000. "Reply to Blockley, Donahue and Pollard." *Antiquity*, 74: 119–21.

Housley, R.A., C.S. Gamble, M. Street, and P. Pettitt 1997. "Radiocarbon evidence for the late glacial human recolonization of northern Europe." *Proceedings of the Prehistoric Society*, 63: 25–54.

Huang, W., R. Ciochon, Y. Gu, R. Larick, Q. Fang, H.P. Schwarcz, et al. 1995. "Early *Homo* and associated artefacts from Asia." *Nature*, 378: 275–40.

Hublin, J.J. 1993. "Recent human evolution in northwestern Africa." In M.J. Aitken, C.B. Stringer, and P.A. Mellars (eds.), *The Origin of Modern Humans and the Impact of Chronometric Dating*, pp. 118–31. Princeton, NJ: Princeton University Press.

Hublin, J., F. Spoor, M. Braun, F. Zonneveld, and S. Condemi 1996. "A late Neanderthal associated with Upper Palaeolithic artefacts." *Nature*, 381: 224–26.

Huxtable, J. and R.M. Jacobi 1982. "Thermoluminescence dating of burned flints from a British Mesolithic site: Longmoor Inclosure, East Hampshire." *Archaeometry*, 24 (2): 164–69.

Isaac, G.L. and G.H. Curtis 1974. "Age of Early Acheulian industries from the Peninj Group, Tanzania." *Nature*, 249: 624–27.

Jeffreys, A.J. 1989. "Molecular biology and human evolution." In J.R. Durant (ed.), *Human Origins*, pp. 217–52. Oxford: Clarendon Press.

Jelinek, A.J. 1990. "The Amudian in the context of the Mugharan tradition at the Tabun Cave (Mount Carmel), Israel." In P.A. Mellars (ed.), *The Emergence of Modern Humans*, pp. 81–90. Edinburgh: Edinburgh University Press.

Johanson, D.C., E.T. Masao, G.G. Eck, et al. 1987. "New partial skeleton of *Homo habilis* from Olduvai gorge, Tanzania." *Nature*, 327: 205–09.

Khan, F. and J.A.J. Gowlett 1997. "Age-depth relationships in the radiocarbon dates from Sanghao Cave, Pakistan." *Archaeological Science, Conference Proceedings, Liverpool 1995*: 182–87.

Kimbel, W.H., D.C. Johanson, and Y. Rak 1994. "The first skull and other new discoveries of *Australopithecus afarensis* at Hadar, Ethiopia." *Nature*, 368: 449–51.

Kimbel, W.H., R.C. Walter, D.C. Johanson, et al. 1996. "Late Pliocene *Homo* and Oldowan tools from the Hadar formation (kada hadar member), Ethiopia." *Journal of Human Evolution*, 31: 549–61.

Kitagawa, H. and J. van der Plicht 1998. "Extension of the 14C calibration curve to ca. 40,000 cal BC by a 40,000-year varve chronology from Lake Suigetsu, Japan." *Radiocarbon*, 40 (1): 505–15.

Kitchen, K.A. 1989. "The basics of Egyptian chronology in relation to the Bronze Age." In P. Aström (ed.), *High, Middle or Low? Acts of an International Colloquium on Absolute Chronology held at the University of Gothenburg, 1987*, pp. 37–55. Gottenburg: Paul Aströms Förlag.

Kitchen, K.A. 1991. "The chronology of ancient Egypt." *World Archaeology*, 23 (2): 201–08.

Kozlowski, J.K. 1992. "The Balkans in the Middle and Upper Palaeolithic: the gate to Europe or a cul-de-sac?" *Proceedings of the Prehistoric Society*, 38: 1–20.

Kozlowski, J.K. 1999. "The evolution of the Balkan Aurignacian." In W. Davies and R. Charles (eds.), *Dorothy Garrod and the Progress of the Palaeolithic*, pp. 97–117. Oxford: Oxbow Books.

Krings, M., A. Stone, R.W. Schmitz, et al. 1997. "Neandertal DNA sequences and the origin of modern humans." *Cell*, 90: 19–30.

Kromer, B. and M. Spurk 1998. "Revision and tentative extension of the tree-ring based 14C calibration, 9200–11955 Cal. BP." *Radiocarbon*, 40: 1117–25.

Kromer, B., M. Spurk, S. Remmele, M. Barbetti, and V. Toniello 1998. "Segments of atmospheric 14C change as derived from Late Glacial and Early Holocene floating tree-ring series." *Radiocarbon*, 40 (1): 351–58.

Kuhn, S.L., M.C. Stiner, and E. Güleç 1999. "Initial Upper Palaeolithic in south-central Turkey and its regional context: a preliminary report." *Antiquity*, 73: 505–17.

Kuzmin, Y.V. and L.A. Orlova 2000. "The Neolithization of Siberia and the Russian Far East." *Antiquity*, 74: 356–64.

Lange, M. 1998. "Wadi Shaw 82/52: 14C dates from a predynastic site in northwest Sudan, supporting the Egyptian historical chronology." *Radiocarbon*, 40 (1): 687.

Laurence, R. 1994. *Roman Pompeii: Space and Society*. London: Routledge.

Leakey, M.D. 1971. *Olduvai Gorge, Vol. 3: Excavations in Beds I and II, 1960–1963*. Cambridge: Cambridge University Press.

Leakey, M.D. and D.A. Roe 1995. *Olduvai Gorge, Vol. 5*. Cambridge: Cambridge University Press.

Leakey, M.G., C.S. Feibel, I. McDougall, and A.C. Walker 1995. "New four-million-year-old hominid species from Kanapoi and Allia bay, Kenya." *Nature*, 376: 565–71.

Lourandos, H. 1997. *Continent of Hunter-Gatherers*. Cambridge: Cambridge University Press.

Lynch, T.F. (ed.) 1980. *Guitarrero Cave: Early Man in the Andes*. New York: Academic Press.

McBurney, C.B.M. 1967. *The Haua Fteah*. Cambridge: Cambridge University Press.

McDougall, I., R. Maier, P. Sutherland-Hawkes, and A.J.W. Gleadow 1980. "K-Ar age estimate for the KBS Tuff, East Turkana, Kenya." *Nature*, 284: 230–34.

McHenry, H.M. and L.R. Berger 1998. "Body proportions in *Australopithecus afarensis* and *A. africanus* and the origin of the genus *Homo*." *Journal of Human Evolution*, 35: 1–22.

Malone, C. (ed.) 1998. "Rice domestication: special section." *Antiquity*, 72: 857–907.

Manning, S.W. and B. Weninger 1992. "A light in the dark: archaeological wiggle matching and the absolute chronology of the close of the Aegean Late Bronze Age." *Antiquity*, 66: 636–63.

Marks, A.E. 1990. "The Middle and Upper Palaeolithic of the Near East and the Nile Valley: the problem of cultural transformation." In P.A. Mellars (ed.), *The Emergence of Modern Humans*, pp. 56–80. Edinburgh: Edinburgh University Press.

Mellars, P.A. 1992. "Archaeology and the population dispersal hypothesis of modern human origins in Europe." In M.J. Aitken, C.B. Stringer, and P.A. Mellars (eds.), *The Origin of Modern Humans and the Impact of Chronometric Dating*, pp. 196–216. Princeton, NJ: Princeton University Press.

Mellars, P.A. 1996. *The Neanderthal Legacy*. Princeton, NJ: Princeton University Press.

Mellars, P.A., H.M. Bricker, J.A.J. Gowlett, and R.E.M. Hedges 1987. "Radiocarbon accelerator dating of French Upper Palaeolithic sites." *Current Anthropology*, 29 (1): 128–32.

Mellars, P. and C. Stringer (eds.) 1989. *The Human Revolution: Behavioral and Biological Perspectives on the Origins of Modern Humans.* Edinburgh: Edinburgh University Press.

Mercier, N., H. Valladas, G. Valladas, et al. 1995. "TL dates of burnt flints from Jelinek's excavations at Tabun and their implications." *Journal of Archaeological Science*, 22: 495–509.

Mirambell, L. 1978. "Tlapacoya: A late Pleistocene site in central Mexico." In A.L. Bryan (ed.), *Early Man in America from a Circum-Pacific Perspective*, pp. 221–30. Occasional Papers No. 1, Department of Anthropology, University of Alberta, Edmonton.

Morwood, M.J., F. Aziz, F. Nasruddin, et al. 1999. "Archaeological and palaeontological research in central Flores, east Indonesia: results of fieldwork 1997–98." *Antiquity*, 73: 273–86.

Movius, H. 1949. "The Lower Palaeolithic cultures of southern and eastern Asia." *Transactions of the American Philosophical Society*, n.s. 38 (4): 329–420.

Movius, H.L., Jr. 1975. "A summary of the stratigraphic sequence." In H.L. Movius, Jr. (ed.), *Excavation of the Abri Pataud, Les Eyzies (Dordogne)*. American School of Prehistoric Research, Bulletin No. 30: 7–18.

Mulvaney, J. 1969. *The Prehistory of Australia*, 1st edn. London: Thames and Hudson.

Nadel, D. and E. Werker 1999. "The oldest ever brush hut plant remains from Ohalo II, Jordan Valley, Israel (19,000 BP)." *Antiquity*, 73: 755–64.

Neftel, A., H. Oeschger, J. Scwander, B. Stauffer, and R. Zumbrunn 1982. "Ice core sample measurements give atmospheric CO_2 content during the past 40,000 yr." *Nature*, 295: 220–23.

O'Connor, T.P. 1997. "Working at relationships: another look at animal domestication." *Antiquity*, 71: 149–56.

Olsson, I.U. 1991. "On the calculation of old ages and the reliability of given ages." In B.G. Andersen, and L.-K. Königsson (eds.), *Late Quaternary Stratigraphy in the Nordic Countries 150,000–15,000 BP. Striae* (Uppsala) 34: 53–58.

Olsson, I.U. and G. Possnert 1992. "The interpretation of 14C measurements on pre-Holocene samples." *Sveriges Geologiska Undersökning*, Ser. Ca. 81: 201–08.

Opdyke, N. 1996. "Mammalian migration and climate over the last seven million years." In E.S. Vrba, G.H. Denton, T.C. Partridge, and L.H. Burckle (eds.), *Palaeoclimate and Evolution, With Emphasis on Human Origins*, pp. 109–14. New Haven, CT: Yale University Press.

Palmqvist, P. 1997. "A critical re-evaluation of the evidence for the presence of hominids in lower Pleistocene times at Venta Micena, southern Spain." *Journal of Human Evolution*, 33: 83–89.

Partridge, T.C., J. Shaw, D. Heslop, and R.J. Clarke 1999. "The new hominid skeleton from Sterkfontein, South Africa: age and preliminary assessment." *Journal of Quaternary Science*, 14: 293–98.

Patterson, B., A.K. Behrensmeyer, and W.D. Sill 1970. "Geology and fauna of a new Pliocene locality in north-western Kenya." *Nature*, 226: 918–21.

Patterson, B. and W.W. Howells 1967. "Hominid humeral fragment from early Pleistocene of northwestern Kenya." *Science*, 156: 64–66.

Pearce, R.H. and M. Barbetti 1981. "A 38,000-year-old archaeological site at Upper Swan, Western Australia." *Archaeology in Oceania*, 14, 18–24.

Pearson, G.W., J.R. Pilcher, and M.G.L. Baillie 1983. "High precision 14C measurement of Irish oaks to show the natural 14C variations from 200 BC to 4000 BC." *Radiocarbon*, 25: 179–86.

Pettitt, P.R. 1997. "High resolution Neanderthals? Interpreting Middle Palaeolithic intrasite spatial data." *World Archaeology*, 29 (2): 208–24.

Plicht, J. van der 1999. "Radiocarbon calibration for the Middle/Upper Palaeolithic: a comment." *Antiquity*, 73: 119–23.

Plummer, T., L.C. Bishop, P. Ditchfield, and J. Hicks 1999. "Research on Late Pliocene Oldowan sites at Kanjera South, Kenya." *Journal of Human Evolution*, 36: 151–70.

Potter, T.W. 1987. *Roman Italy*. London: British Museum Publications.

Raynal, J.-P., L. Magoga, F.-Z. Sbihi-Alaoui, and D. Geraads 1995. "The earliest occupation of Atlantic Morocco: the Casablanca evidence." In W. Roebroeks and T. van Kolfschoten (eds.), *The Earliest Occupation of Europe: Proceedings of the European Science, Foundation Workshop at Tautavel (France), 1993. Analecta Praehistorica Leidensia*, 27: 255–62. Leiden: University of Leiden.

Renfrew, A.C. 1968. "Wessex without Mycenae." *Annual of the British School at Athens*, 63: 277–85.

Reynolds, T. 1990. "The Middle-Upper Palaeolithic transition in southwestern France: interpreting the lithic evidence." In P.A. Mellars (ed.), *The Emergence of Modern Humans*, pp. 262–75. Edinburgh: Edinburgh University Press.

Reynolds, T.E.G. 1991. "Revolution or resolution? The archaeology of modern human origins." *World Archaeology*, 23 (2): 155–66.

Richards, M., K. Smalley, B. Sykes, and R. Hedges 1993. "Archaeology and genetics: analysing DNA from skeletal remains." *World Archaeology*, 25 (1): 18–28.

Rigaud, J.-P. 1989. "From the Middle to the Upper Palaeolithic: transition or convergence?" In E. Trinkaus (ed.), *The Emergence of Modern Humans*, pp. 142–53. Cambridge: Cambridge University Press.

Rightmire, G.P. 1990. *The Evolution of Homo Erectus*. Cambridge: Cambridge University Press.

Rightmire, G.P. 1996. "The human cranium from Bodo, Ethiopia: evidence for speciation in the Middle Pleistocene?" *Journal of Human Evolution*, 31: 21–39.

Roberts, R.G., R. Jones, and M. Smith 1990. "Thermoluminescence dating of a 50,000-year-old human occupation site in northern Australia." *Nature*, 345: 153–56.

Robertshaw, P. 1992. "Radiocarbon dating and the prehistory of sub-saharan Africa." In R.E. Taylor, A. Long, and R.S. Kra (eds.), *Radiocarbon, After Four Decades: An Interdisciplinary Perspective*, pp. 335–51. New York: Springer-Verlag.

Roebroeks, W. 1996. "The English Palaeolithic record: absence of evidence, evidence of absence and the first occupation of Europe." In C.S. Gamble and A.J. Lawson (eds.), *The English Palaeolithic Reviewed*, pp. 57–62. Salisbury: Wessex Archaeology.

Roebroeks, W., N.J. Conard, and T. van Kolfschoten 1992. "Dense forests, cold steppes, and the Palaeolithic settlement of northern Europe." *Current Anthropology*, 33: 551–86.

Roebroeks, W. and T. van Kolfschoten (eds.) 1995. *The Earliest Occupation of Europe: Proceedings of the European Science Foundation Workshop at Tautavel (France), 1993. Analecta Praehistorica Leidensia*, 27. Leiden: University of Leiden.

Ronen, A. 1991. "The Yiron-Gravel lithic assemblage: artifacts older than 2.4 My in Israel." *Archäologisches Korrespondenzblatt*, 21: 159–64.

Roosevelt, A.C., M. Lima da Costa, C.L. Machado, et al. 1996. "Paleoindian cave dwellers in the Amazon: the peopling of the Americas." *Science*, 272: 373–84.

Rosenfeld, A. and C. Smith 1997. "Recent developments in radiocarbon and stylistic methods of dating rockart." *Antiquity*, 71: 405–11.

Sand, C. 1997. "The chronology of Lapita ware in New Caledonia." *Antiquity*, 71: 539–47.

Sarich, V.M. and A.C. Wilson 1968. "Immunological time scale for hominid evolution." *Science*, 158: 1200–02.

Schäfer, J., P.M. Sosin, and V.A. Ranov 1996. "Neue Untersuchungen zum Lösspaläolithikum am Obi-Mazar, Tadzikistan." *Archäologisches Korrespondenzblatt*, 26: 97–109.

Schick, K. and D. Zhuan 1993. "Early Paleolithic of China and eastern Asia." In J.D. Fleagle (ed.), *Evolutionary Anthropology*, 2 (1): 22–35. New York: Wiley-Liss.

Schiffer, M.B. 1976. *Behavioral Archaeology*. New York: Academic Press.

Schild, R., E. Wendorf, and A. Close 1992. "Northern and eastern Africa climate changes between 140,000 and 12,000 years ago." In F. Klees and R. Kuper (eds.), *New Light on the Northeast African Past*, pp. 81–96. Köln: Heinrich-Barth-Institut.

Schwarcz, H.P. 1993. "Uranium-series dating and the origin of modern man." In M.J. Aitken, C.B. Stringer, and P.A. Mellars (eds.), *The Origin of Modern Humans and the Impact of Chronometric Dating*, pp. 12–26. Princeton, NJ: Princeton University Press.

Schwarcz, H.P., B. Blackwell, P. Goldberg, and A.E. Marks 1979. "Uranium series dating of travertine from archaeological sites, Nahal Zin, Israel." *Nature*, 277: 558–60.

Schwarcz, H.P., R. Grün, and P.V. Tobias 1994. "ESR dating studies of the australopithecine site of Sterkfontein, South Africa." *Journal of Human Evolution*, 26: 175–81.

Sealy, J.C. and N.J. van der Merwe 1985. "Isotope assessment of Holocene human diets in the southwestern Cape, South Africa." *Nature*, 315: 138–40.

Semaw, S., P.R. Renne, J.W.K. Harris, et al. 1997. "2.5 million-year-old stone tools from Gona, Ethiopia." *Nature*, 385: 333–36.

Senut, B., M. Pickford, D. Gommery, et al. 2001. "First hominid from the Miocene (Lukeino Formation, Kenya)." *Comptes rendus des séances de l'académie des sciences*, 332: 137–44.

Settle, D.M. and C.C. Patterson 1980. "Lead in Albacore: guide to lead pollution in Americans." *Science*, 207: 1171.

Shackleton, N.J. 1996. "New data on the evolution of Pliocene climatic variability." In E.S. Vrba, G.H. Denton, T.C. Partridge, and L.H. Burckle (eds.), *Palaeoclimate and Evolution, With Emphasis on Human Origins*, pp. 242–48. New Haven, CT: Yale University Press.

Shackleton, N.J. and N.D. Opdyke 1973. "Oxygen isotope and palaeomagnetic stratigraphy of Equatorial Pacific core V28–238." *Quaternary Research*, 3: 39–55.

Shackleton, N.J. and N.D. Opdyke 1977. "Oxygen isotope and palaeomagnetic evidence for early Northern Hemisphere glaciation." *Nature*, 270: 216–19.

Shaw, J., Z. Hongbo, and A. Zisheng 1991. "Magnetic dating of early man in China." *Archaeometry*, 90: 589–95.

Sherratt, A. 1997. "Climatic cycles and behavioral revolutions: the emergence of modern humans and the beginning of farming." *Antiquity*, 71: 271–87.

Sherratt, S. and A. Sherratt 1993. "The growth of the Mediterranean economy in the early first millennium BC." *World Archaeology*, 24 (3): 361–78.

Simons, E. 1995. "Egyptian Oligocene primates: a review." *Yearbook of Physical Anthropology*, 38: 199–238.

Smith, F.H. 1993. "Models and realities in modern human origins: the African fossil evidence." In M.J. Aitken, C.B. Stringer, and P.A. Mellars (eds.), *The Origin of Modern Humans and the Impact of Chronometric Dating*, pp. 234–48. Princeton, NJ: Princeton University Press.

Soffer, O. and C. Gamble (eds.) 1990. *The World at 18000 BP*, 2 vols. London: Unwin Hyman.

Spooner, N. 1998. "Human occupation at Jinmium, northern Australia: 116,000 years ago or much less?" *Antiquity*, 72: 173–78.

Stafford, T.W. 1994. "Accelerator C-14 dating of human fossil skeletons: assessing accuracy and results on New World specimens." In R. Bonnichsen and D.G. Steele (eds.), *Method and Theory for Investigating the Peopling of the Americas*, pp. 45–55. Peopling of the Americas Publications. Corvallis: Oregon State University.

Stern, N. 1994. "The implications of time-averaging for reconstructing the land-use patterns of early tool-using hominids." In J.S. Oliver, N.E. Sikes, and K.M. Stewart (eds.), *Early Hominid Behavioral Ecology. Journal of Human Evolution*, 27: 89–105.

Stocker, T.F. and D.G. Wright 1998. "The effect of a succession of ocean ventilation changes on 14C." *Radiocarbon*, 40 (1): 359–66.

Straus, L.G., B.V. Eriksen, J.M. Erlandson, and D.R. Yesner (eds.) 1996. *Humans at the End of the Ice Age: The Archaeology of the Pleistocene-Holocene Transition.* New York: Plenum Press.

Stringer, C.B. 1993. "Reconstructing recent human evolution." In M.J. Aitken, C.B. Stringer, and P.A. Mellars (eds.), *The Origin of Modern Humans and the Impact of Chronometric Dating,* pp. 179–95. Princeton, NJ: Princeton University Press.

Stringer, C.B. 1995. "Replacement, continuity and the origin of *Homo sapiens.*" In G. Bräuer and F.H. Smith (eds.), *Continuity or Replacement,* pp. 9–24. Rotterdam: Balkema.

Stringer, C.B. 1999. "Has Australia backdated the Human Revolution?" *Antiquity,* 73: 876–79.

Stringer, C.B. and C. Gamble 1993. *In Search of the Neanderthals.* London: Thames and Hudson.

Sun Donghuai, A. Zhisheng, J. Shaw, J. Bloemendal, and S. Youbin 1998. "Magnetostratigraphy and palaeoclimatic significance of Late Tertiary aeolian sequences in the Chinese Loess Plateau." *Geophysics Journal International,* 134: 207–12.

Suwa, G., B. Asfaw, Y. Beyene, et al. 1997. "The first skull of Australopithecus boisei." *Nature,* 389: 489–92.

Svoboda, J. 1994. *Paleolit Moravy a Slezska (The Paleolithic of Moravia and Silesia),* vol. 1. Brno: Dolni Vestonice Studies.

Swadling, P. 1997. "Changing shorelines and cultural orientations in the Sepik-Ramu, Papua New Guinea: implications for pacific prehistory." *World Archaeology,* 29 (1): 1–14.

Swisher, G.C., G.H. Curtis, T. Jacob, et al. 1994. "Age of the earliest known hominids in Java, Indonesia." *Science,* 263: 1118–21.

Tattersall, I. and J.H. Schwartz 1999. "Hominids and hybrids: the place of Neanderthals in human evolution." *Proceedings of the National Academy of Sciences,* 96: 7117–19.

Taylor, R.E., L.A. Payen, C.A. Prior, et al. 1985. "Major revisions in the Pleistocene age assignments for North American human skeletons: None older than 11,000 14C years BP." *American Antiquity,* 50 (1): 136–40.

Terrell, J.E. and R.L. Welsch 1997. "Lapita and the temporal geography of prehistory." *Antiquity,* 71: 548–72.

Thieme, H. 1996. "Altpaläolithische Wurfspeere aus Schöningen, Niedersachsen—ein Vorbericht." *Archäologisches Korrespondenzblatt,* 26 (4): 377–93.

Thorne, A., R. Grün, G. Mortimer, et al. 1999. "Australia's oldest human remains: age of the Lake Mungo 3 skeleton." *Journal of Human Evolution,* 36: 591–612.

Tobias, P.V. 1991. "The emergence of spoken language in hominid evolution." In J.D. Clark (ed.), *Approaches to Understanding Early Hominid Life-ways in the African Savanna,* pp. 67–78. Römisch-Germanisches Zentralmuseum Forschungsinstitut für Vor-und Früh-geschichte in Verbindung mit der UISSP, 11 Kongress, Mainz, 31 August—5 September 1987, Monographien Band 19. Bonn: Dr Rudolf Habelt GMBH.

Tuffreau, A. 1992. "L'Acheuléen en Europe occidentale d'après les données du bassin de la Somme." In C. Peretto (ed.), *Il piu antico popolamento della valle Padana nel quadro delle conoscenze Europee: Monte Poggiolo,* pp. 41–45. Milan: Jaca Book.

Tuffreau, A., A. Lamotte, and A.-L. Marcy 1997. "Land-use and site function in Acheulean complexes of the Somme valley." *World Archaeology,* 29 (2): 225–41.

Tushingham, A.M. and W.R. Peltier 1993. "Implications of the radiocarbon timescale for ice-sheet chronology and sea-level change." *Quaternary Research,* 39: 125–29.

Valladas, H. 1981. "Datation par thermoluminescence de grès brûlés de foyers de quatre gisements du Magdalénien final du Bassin Parisien." *Comptes rendus de l'académie de sciences, Paris,* series 11, 292: 355–58.

Van der Merwe, N.J. and J.C. Vogel 1978. "13C content of human collagen as a measure of prehistoric diet in woodland North America." *Nature,* 276: 813–16.

Vermeersch, P.M., E. Paulissen, S. Stokes, et al. 1998. "A Middle Palaeolithic burial of a modern human at Taramsa Hill, Egypt." *Antiquity,* 72: 475–84.

Voelker, A.H.L., M. Sarnthein, P. M. Grootes, et al. 1998. "Correlation of marine 14C ages from the Nordic Seas with the GISP₂ isotope record: Implications for 14C calibration beyond 25 ka BP." *Radiocarbon*, 40 (1): 517–34.

Vrba, E.S., G.H. Denton, T.C. Partridge, and L.H. Burckle (eds.) 1996. *Palaeoclimate and Evolution, With Emphasis on Human Origins*. New Haven, CT: Yale University Press.

Walter, R.C., P.C. Manega, R.L. Hay, et al. 1991. "Laser-fusion 40Ar/39Ar dating of Bed I, Olduvai Gorge, Tanzania." *Nature*, 354: 145–49.

Wanpo, H., R. Ciochon, G. Yumin, et al. 1995. "Early Homo and associated artefacts from Asia." *Nature*, 378: 275–78.

Wendorf, F. and R. Schild 1974. *A Middle Stone Age Sequence from the Central Rift Valley, Ethiopia*. Warsaw: Institute for History and Material Culture, Polish National Academy.

Wendorf, F., R. Schild, A.E. Close, et al. 1988. "New radiocarbon dates and Late Palaeolithic diet at Wadi Kubbaniya, Egypt." *Antiquity*, 62: 279–83.

White, T.D., B. Asfaw, and G. Suwa 1996. "Ardipithecus ramidus: a root species for Australopithecus." In F. Facchini (ed.), *The First Humans and Their Cultural Manifestations. The Colloquia of the XIII International Congress of Prehistoric and Protohistoric Sciences, Forli, Italy*, pp. 15–23. Forli: ABACO.

White, T.D., G. Suwa, and B. Asfaw 1994. "*Australopithecus ramidus*, a new species of early hominid from Aramis, Ethiopia." *Nature*, 371: 306–12.

Wolde, G., T.D. White, G. Suwa, et al. 1994. "Ecological and temporal context of early Pliocene hominids at Aramis, Ethiopia." *Nature*, 371: 330–33.

Wolpoff, M.H. 1992. "Theories of modern human origins." In G. Bräuer and F.H. Smith (eds.), *Continuity or Replacement: Controversies in Homo Sapiens Evolution*, pp. 25–63. Rotterdam: A.A. Balkema.

Wood, B.A. 1991. *Koobi Fora Research Project, Vol. 4: Hominid Cranial Remains*. Oxford: Clarendon Press.

Wood, B.A. 1992. "Origin and evolution of the genus Homo." *Nature*, 355: 783–90.

Wood, B.A. and M. Collard 1999. "The human genus." *Science*, 284: 65–71.

Yellen, J.E., A.S. Brooks, E. Cornelissen, et al. 1995. "A Middle Stone Age worked bone industry from Katanda, Upper Semliki Valley, Zaire." *Science*, 268: 553–56.

Zaitseva, G.I., S.S. Vasiliev, L.S. Marsadolov, et al. 1998. "A tree-ring and 14C chronology of the key Sayan-Altai monuments." *Radiocarbon*, 40 (1): 571–80.

Zhimin, A. 1991. "Radiocarbon dating and the prehistoric archaeology of China." *World Archaeology*, 23 (2): 193–200.

Zielinski, G.A. and M.S. Germani 1998. "New ice-core evidence challenges the 1620s BC age for the Santorini (Minoan) eruption." *Journal of Archaeological Science*, 25: 279–89.

"Archaeology and Age of a New Hominin from Flores in Eastern Indonesia"

M.J. Morwood, R.P. Soejono, R.G. Roberts, T. Sutikna, C.S.M. Turney, K.E. Westaway, W.J. Rink, J.-x. Zhao, G.D. van den Bergh, Rokus Awe Due, D.R. Hobbs, M.W. Moore, M.I. Bird, and L.K. Fifield

One of the most exciting and potentially significant archaeological events of the early twenty-first century has been the discovery of the skeletal remains and associated tools of what is reported to be a previously unknown species of human called *Homo floresiensis*, who may have lived as recently as 13,000 years ago. This selection, which appeared in a 2004 issue of the scholarly journal *Nature*, was the first to focus on the archaeology of the finds. A separate article on the human skeletal remains was published in the same issue. The authors of the piece reproduced here are an international team associated with universities and research institutes in Australia, Canada, Indonesia, the Netherlands, and the United Kingdom.

Some words that readers may not be familiar with include *Hominin*, a biological classification to which all humans and their closely related ancestors belong, and *faunal*, which means animal.

Readers are cautioned that the assignment of the skeletal remains and associated artifacts to *Homo floresiensis* is highly contentious.

• •

Questions to Guide Reading

What were the research goals of the project?
What dating techniques were used?
Why were some of the faunal remains thought to be associated with human behavior?
What kinds of stone tools were evident?

• •

Excavations at Liang Bua, a large limestone cave on the island of Flores in eastern Indonesia, have yielded evidence for a population of tiny hominins, sufficiently distinct anatomically to be assigned to a new species, *Homo floresiensis*.[1] The finds comprise the cranial and some post-cranial remains of one individual, as well as a premolar from another individual in older deposits. Here we describe their context, implications and the remaining archaeological uncertainties. Dating by radiocarbon (^{14}C),

luminescence, uranium-series and electron spin resonance (ESR) methods indicates that *H. floresiensis* existed from before 38,000 years ago (kyr) until at least 18 kyr. Associated deposits contain stone artefacts and animal remains, including Komodo dragon and an endemic, dwarfed species of *Stegodon*. *H. floresiensis* originated from an early dispersal of *Homo erectus* (including specimens referred to as *Homo ergaster* and *Homo georgicus*)[1] that reached Flores, and then survived on this island refuge until relatively recently. It overlapped significantly in time with *Homo sapiens* in the region,[2,3] but we do not know if or how the two species interacted.

Liang Bua is a cave formed in Miocene limestone on Flores, an island in eastern Indonesia located midway between the Asian and Australian continents (Fig. 1). The cave is situated 14 km north of Ruteng and 25 km from the north coast, overlooking the Wae Racang river valley at an altitude of 500 m above sea level (08° 31' 50.4" S, 120°26' 36.9" E). It is 30 m wide and 25 m high at the entrance, and up to 40 m deep (Fig. 2). Formed as an underground cavern by karst dissolution, the northern end was then exposed by invasion of the Wae Racang. This river now lies 200 m distant from and 30 m below Liang Bua, but five river terraces at different elevations in the valley indicate a complex process of incision over a substantial period.

Our research at Liang Bua aims to recover evidence for the history of hominin evolution, dispersal and cultural and environmental change on Flores—an island with evidence of Early Pleistocene hominin occupation by 840 kyr.[4,5] Work involved removing backfill from four previously excavated Sectors (I, III, IV and VII) and then continuing the excavations. We have reached a maximum depth of 11 m without encountering bedrock.

Thus far, the most significant find at Liang Bua is a hominin skeleton in Sector VII, close to the east wall. Remains include a skull, mandible, pelvis and leg bones, some of which were still articulated when discovered (Fig. 3), with sufficient distinctive features to be designated a new hominin species, *Homo floresiensis*.[1]

Sector VII, 2 m by 2 m in area, was excavated to red clay containing water-rolled boulders at 7.2 m depth (Fig. 4). The skeleton, together with animal remains and stone artefacts, was deposited on a gently sloping surface in dark-brown silty clay at 5.9 m depth, then covered by slope wash sediments. There was no stratigraphic or artefactual evidence for deliberate burial. The overlying layers of clay, silt and rockfall show that this slope was maintained until light-brown and grey ('white') tuffaceous silts settled in the lower, northern part of Sector VII. These tuffaceous silts were derived from volcanic eruptions and occur elsewhere in the cave, providing a useful stratigraphic marker horizon that is bracketed by ages of 13 and 11 calibrated kyr (Supplementary Table 1a) from associated charcoal, using acid-base wet oxidation, stepped-combustion (ABOX-SC) [14]C (refs 6, 7 and Supplementary Information). From 4 m depth to the surface, deposits are horizontally laid and the same stratigraphic sequence extends across the cave floor, indicating a consistent pattern of sediment accumulation.

Radiocarbon and luminescence dating methods were used to infer the age of the hominin remains (Supplementary Table 1a, b), which, given their completeness and degree of articulation, must have been covered by fine sediments soon after death, when still partially fleshed. Three charcoal samples from the lowermost excavated deposits in Sector VII were pretreated and graphitized using the ABOX-SC method, and the ^{14}C content of the most reliable component was measured by accelerator mass spectrometry. The two samples associated with the skeleton (ANUA-27116 and ANUA-27117) yielded statistically indistinguishable calibrated ages centred on 18 kyr (68% confidence intervals: 18.7–17.9 and 18.2–17.4 cal kyr, respectively).

Luminescence dating of sediments was used to confirm the validity of these ^{14}C ages; in particular that 'infinitely old' charcoal had not been contaminated by radiocarbon of Holocene age, resulting in the unexpectedly young ages for a hominin skeleton with so many primitive traits. Optical dating[8,9] of potassium-rich feldspar grains, using the infrared stimulated luminescence (IRSL) emissions, yielded ages of 14 ^2 (LBS7-40a) and 6.8 ^0.8 (LBS7-42a) kyr for samples collected above and alongside the skeleton, respectively. Both samples exhibited significant anomalous fading (see Supplementary Information), which will cause the measured ages to be too young, but we could not reliably extend

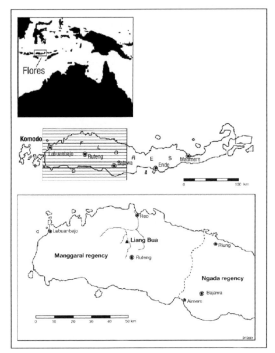

FIGURE 1: General location of Flores in eastern Indonesia, and Liang Bua in western Flores.

the measured fading rates to geological timescales using available fading-correction models.[10] Both IRSL ages, therefore, should be viewed as minimum estimates of the time since the sediments were last exposed to sunlight.

Maximum ages for sediment deposition were obtained using the light-sensitive red thermoluminescence (TL) emissions from grains of quartz.[11,12] The TL signal is less easily bleached than the IRSL signal, but does not suffer from anomalous fading. The TL ages for the two samples—38 ^8 (LBS7-40b) and 35 ^4 (LBS7-42b) kyr— are statistically indistinguishable, supporting our contention that the body was rapidly buried soon after death. The TL and IRSL ages bracket the time of deposition of the hominin-bearing sediments to between 35 ^4 and 14 ^2 kyr, which is consistent with the ^{14}C ages centred on 18 kyr.

Diagnostic evidence for *H. floresiensis* is also found at Liang Bua in deposits of greater age, showing that we are not dealing with an abnormal individual but a long-standing population. At 4.3 m depth in Sector IV, deposits beneath a stratigraphic unconformity yielded a mandibular left premolar with the same distinctive morphology as premolars in the complete hominin mandible from Sector VII. Flowstone stratigraphically overlying the unconformity returned a thermal ionization mass spectrometry (TIMS) uranium-series age of 37.7 ^0.2 kyr

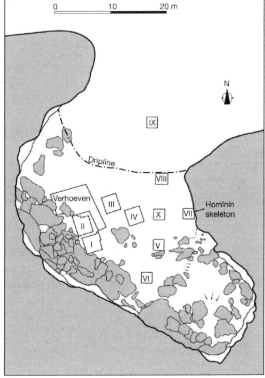

FIGURE 2: Plan of Liang Bua showing the locations of the excavated areas (Sectors) and the hominin skeleton (in Sector VII). Father Theodor Verhoeven carried out the first large-scale work at the site in 1965, and R.P. Soejono excavated ten Sectors between 1978 and 1989. Beginning in 2001, we extended the excavations in Sectors I, III, IV and VII.

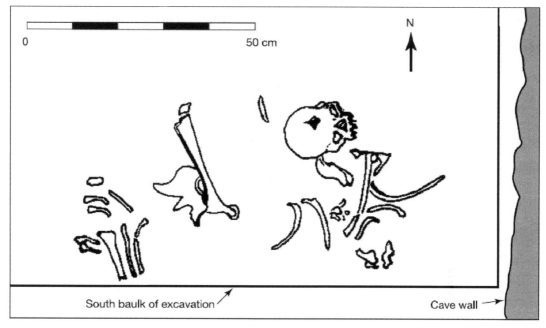

FIGURE 3: Plan of the hominin skeleton as found during excavation at Sector VII at Liang Bua. The relationships between skeletal elements and their proximity to the east and south baulks are shown. The right tibia and fibula were flexed beneath the corresponding femur and patella. Additional skeletal remains, such as the arms, may lie in unexcavated deposits immediately to the south.

(sample LB-JR-6A/13–23, Supplementary Table 1c), which provides a minimum extension of the time range for *H. floresiensis*.

In addition, a juvenile *Stegodon* molar from 4.5 m depth, just below the isolated hominin premolar, yielded a coupled ESR/uranium-series age of 74[thorn]¹⁴ kyr (sample LB-JR-8a, Supplementary Table 1e). Hominin remains excavated from between this dated level and 7.5 m depth, for which a maximum age of 95 ^13kyr for sediment deposition was obtained by TL dating (sample LBS4-32a, Supplementary Table 1b), are not yet species-diagnostic. They include, however, from a depth of 5.8 m, the radius of an adult with an estimated height of about 1 m (ref. 1) that we provisionally assign to *H. floresiensis* because of its size; the holotype lacks arms for direct comparison. If confirmed, this iden-

tification would extend the minimum antiquity of *H. floresiensis* to about 74kyr.

Concerning the behavioural context of *H. floresiensis*, associated small faunal remains include those of fish, frog, snake, tortoise, varanids, birds, rodents and bats. Many are likely to have accumulated through natural processes, but some bones are charred, which is unlikely to have occurred naturally on a bare cave floor.

The only large animals in the Pleistocene deposits are Komodo dragon and another, even larger varanid, as well as an endemic, dwarfed species of *Stegodon*. At least 17 individuals of *Stegodon* are represented in Sector IV, and at least 9 in Sector VII. The extent of dental wear on *Stegodon* molars also indicates that most individuals were juveniles (Age Group 1 of ref. 13), with 30% (five individuals) in

Sector IV being neonates. Adults are only represented by two poorly preserved post-cranial elements and a single molar-ridge fragment. Other large mammals, such as macaque monkey, deer, pig and porcupine, first appear in the overlying Holocene deposits, which lack evidence for *H. floresiensis*. These animals were almost certainly translocated to Flores by *H. sapiens*.

Pleistocene deposits in Sector VII contain relatively few stone artefacts; only 32 were found in the same level as the hominin skeleton. In Sector IV, however, dense concentrations of stone artefacts occur in the same level as *H. floresiensis*—up to 5,500 artefacts per cubic metre. Simple flakes predominate, struck bifacially from small radial cores and mainly on volcanics and chert, but there is also a more formal component found only with evidence of *Stegodon*, including points, perforators, blades and microblades that were probably hafted as barbs (Fig. 5). In all excavated Sectors, this 'big game' stone artefact technology continues from the oldest cultural deposits, dated from about 95 to 74 kyr, until the disappearance of *Stegodon* about 12 kyr, immediately below the 'white' tuffaceous silts derived from volcanic eruptions that coincide with the extinction of this species. The juxtaposition of these distinctive stone tools with *Stegodon* remains suggests that hominins at the site in the Late Pleistocene were selectively hunting juvenile *Stegodon*.

The chronologies for Sectors IV and VII show that *H. floresiensis* was at the site from before 38 kyr until at least 18 kyr—long after the 55 to 35 kyr time of arrival of *H. sapiens* in the region[2,3,7,14–18]. None of the hominin remains found in the Pleistocene deposits, however, could be attributed to *H. sapiens*. In the absence of such evidence, we conclude that *H. floresiensis* made the associated stone artefacts.

Stone artefacts produced by much heavier percussion also occur in older deposits at Liang Bua. At the rear of the cave, for example, river-laid conglomerates contain stone artefacts, including a massive chopper. TIMS uranium-series dating of overlying flowstones indicates that these artefacts are older than 102.4 ^0.6 kyr (sample LB-JR-10B/3–8, Supplementary Table 1c), but we do not know which hominin species manufactured them.

Further afield, the Soa Basin, which lies 50 km to the east of Liang Bua, has sites of Early and Middle Pleistocene age, where the remains of Komodo dragon and *Stegodon* occur in association with simple, flaked stone artifacts.[4,5] It has been assumed that *H. erectus* made these artifacts.[19–21] The morphological traits of *H. floresiensis* at Liang Bua are consistent with *H. erectus* as an ancestral candidate, but the potential time-depth of hominin occupation of Flores means that, at this stage, we can only speculate as to which species made the Soa Basin artefacts.

Liang Bua provides evidence for distinctive hominins descended from an ancestral *H. erectus* population that survived until at least 18 kyr, overlapping significantly in time with *H. sapiens*. We interpret *H. floresiensis* as a relict lineage that reached, and was preserved on, a Wallacean island refuge—in the same way that Flores was a refuge for *Stegodon*, the only other large land mammal on the island during the Pleistocene. In isolation, these populations underwent protracted, endemic change; Flores was home to the smallest known species of the genera *Homo*[1] and *Stegodon*.[13]

On present evidence, the genetic and cultural isolation of Flores was only subsequently breached when *H. sapiens* appeared in eastern Asia with watercraft. How a population of tiny, small-brained hominins then survived for tens of millennia alongside *H. sapiens* remains unclear, as there is currently no evidence for the nature of their interaction; it may have involved little or no direct contact, symbiosis, competition or predation.

The cognitive capabilities of early hominins, however, should not be underestimated, as indicated by the technology of the stone artefacts associated with *H. floresiensis* at Liang Bua. It is also significant that hominins were able to colonize Flores by the Early Pleistocene,[4,5] whereas the required sea crossings were beyond the dispersal

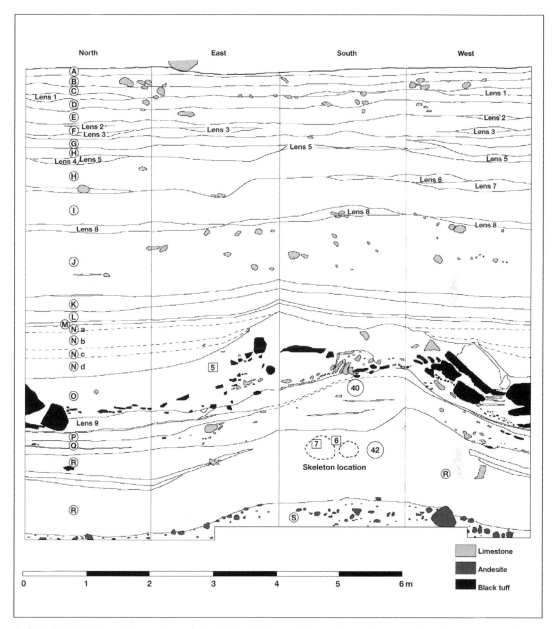

FIGURE 4: Stratigraphic section of the Sector VII excavation at Liang Bua, showing the location of the hominin skeleton. Layer key: A, coarse silt; B, silt; C–K, coarse silts; L, tuffaceous silt; M, clay; N (a–d), 'white' tuffaceous silts; O, clay and rubble; P, clay; Q, silty clay; R, sandy clay; S, clay with water-rolled volcanic boulders. The circles enclosing the numbers 40 and 42 indicate the locations of luminescence samples LBS7-40 and LBS7-42, respectively, and the squares enclosing the numbers 5, 6 and 7 denote the locations of ^{14}C samples ANUA-27115, ANUA-27116 and ANUA-27117, respectively.

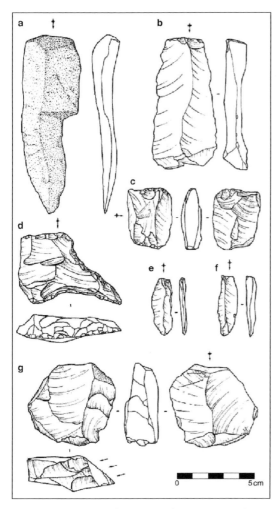

abilities of most other land animals, even during glacial periods of lowered sea level.

Clearly, the history of hominin occupation, evolution and cultural change on Flores, and by implication other Wallacean islands, is of much greater complexity than hitherto believed. For example, Lombok and Sumbawa are obvious stepping-stone islands for the hominin colonization of Flores from continental Asia and Java. If early hominin populations survived long-term on these islands, they would have been subject to the same insular speciation pressures evident in *H. floresiensis*. Size reduction is a predictable evolutionary trend, but other trends will reflect island-specific adaptations, demographic changes and the impacts of catastrophic events, such as volcanic eruptions.

FIGURE 5: Range of stone artefacts associated with remains of *H. floresiensis* and *Stegodon*. a, b, Macroblades. c, Bipolar core. d, Perforator. e, f, Microblades. g, Burin core for producing microblades. Arrows indicate position of striking platforms, where knappers detached the flakes from cores by direct percussion using hammerstones.

Notes

1 Brown, P. et al. A new small-bodied hominin from the Late Pleistocene of Flores, Indonesia. Nature 431, 1055–1061 (2004).

2 Barker, G. et al. The Niah Cave Project: the second (2001) season of fieldwork. SarawakMus.J. 56 (new ser. 77), 37–119 (2001).

3 Bowler, J.M. et al. New ages for human occupation and climatic change at Lake Mungo, Australia. Nature 421, 837–840 (2003).

4 Morwood, M.J., O'Sullivan, P.B., Aziz, F. & Raza, A. Fission-track ages of stone tools and fossils on the east Indonesian island of Flores. Nature 392, 173–176 (1998).

5 Morwood, M.J. et al. Archaeological and palaeontological research in central Flores, east Indonesia: results of fieldwork, 1997–98. Antiquity 73, 273–286 (1999).

6 Bird, M.I. et al. Radiocarbon dating of "old" charcoal using a wet oxidation, stepped-combustion procedure. Radiocarbon 41, 127–140 (1999).

7 Turney, C.S.M. et al. Early human occupation at Devil's Lair, southwestern Australia 50,000 years ago. Quaternary Research 55, 3–13 (2001).

8 Aitken, M.J. An Introduction to Optical Dating (Oxford Univ. Press, Oxford, 1998).

9 Bøtter-Jensen, L., McKeever, S.W.S. & Wintle, A.G. Optically Stimulated Luminescence Dosimetry (Elsevier Science, Amsterdam, 2003).

10 Huntley, D.J. & Lamothe, M. Ubiquity of anomalous fading in K-feldspars and the measurement and correction for it in optical dating. Can. J. Earth Sci. 38, 1093–1106 (2001).

11 Franklin, A.D., Prescott, J.R. & Robertson, G.B. Comparison of blue and red TL from quartz. Radiat. Meas. 32, 633–639 (2000).

12 Stokes, S. & Fattahi, M. Red emission luminescence from quartz and feldspar for dating applications: an overview. Radiat. Meas. 37, 383–395 (2003).

13 van den Bergh, G.D. The Late Neogene elephantoid-bearing faunas of Indonesia and their palaeozoogeographic implications. A study of the terrestrial faunal succession of Sulawesi, Flores and Java, including evidence for early hominid dispersal east of Wallace's Line. Scripta Geologica 117, 1–419 (1999).

14 Roberts, R.G., Jones, R. & Smith, M. A. Thermoluminescence dating of a 50,000 year-old human occupation site in northern Australia. Nature 345, 153–156 (1990).

15 Roberts, R.G. et al. The human colonisation of Australia: optical dates of 53,000 and 60,000 years bracket human arrival at Deaf Adder Gorge, Northern Territory. Quaternary Sci. Rev. 13, 575–583 (1994).

16 Gillespie, R. Dating the first Australians. Radiocarbon 44, 455–472 (2002).

17 O'Connor, S., Spriggs, M. & Veth, P. Excavation at Lene Hara Cave establishes occupation in East Timor at least 30,000–35,000 years ago. Antiquity 76, 45–49 (2002).

18 O'Connell, J.F. & Allen, J. Dating the colonization of Sahul (Pleistocene Australia–New Guinea): a review of recent research. J. Archaeol. Sci. 31, 835–853 (2004).

19 Maringer, J. & Verhoeven, Th. Die steinartefakte aus der Stegodon-fossilschicht von Mengeruda auf Flores, Indonesien. Anthropos 65, 229–247 (1970).

20 Sondaar, P.Y. et al. Middle Pleistocene faunal turnover and colonisation of Flores (Indonesia) by Homo erectus. C.R. Acad. Sci. Paris (Se´rie II) 319, 1255–1262 (1994).

21 O'Sullivan, P.B. et al. Archaeological implications of the geology and chronology of the Soa Basin, Flores, Indonesia. Geology 29, 607–610 (2001).

Acknowledgements

Our work is funded by a Discovery Project grant to M.J.M. from the Australian Research Council (ARC), and by grants from the University of New England (M.J.M.) and the University of Wollongong (R.G.R.). R.G.R. holds an ARC Senior Research Fellowship, and C.S.M.T. and J.-x.Z. hold ARC Queen Elizabeth II Fellowships. C.S.M.T. also acknowledges the support of the Australian Academy of Science (J.G. Russell Award), the Natural Environment Research Council and Queen's University Belfast. The 2003 excavations at Liang Bua were undertaken under Indonesian Centre for Archaeology Permit Number 1178/SB/PUS/BD/24.VI/ 2003. Other participants included Jatmiko, E. Wahyu Saptomo, S. Wasisto, A. Gampar, C. Lentfer, N. Polhaupessy, K. Grant, B. Walker, A. Brumm, Rikus, Deus, Leo, Ansel, Agus, Seus, Camellus, Gaba, Rius, Beni and Piet. H. Yoshida and J. Abrantes assisted with IRSL and TL analyses, J. Olley made the high-resolution gamma spectrometry measurements, D. Huntley and O. Lian provided advice on anomalous fading, and R. Bailey suggested the isothermal measurement of red TL. Wasisto, M. Roach and K. Morwood assisted with the stratigraphic sections, plans and stone artefact drawings, and P. Brown and P. Jordan commented on earlier drafts of this paper.

Author Contributions

M.J.M., R.P.S. and R.G.R. planned and now co-ordinate the research program funded by the ARC Discovery Project grant, which includes the Liang Bua project. T.S. directed aspects of the excavations and analyses. Ages were provided by R.G.R. and K.E.W. (luminescence); C.S.M.T., M.I.B. and L.K.F. (^{14}C); W.J.R. (ESR); and J.-x.Z. (uranium-series). R.A.D. and G.D.v.d.B. analysed the faunal remains, and M.W.M. the stone artefacts. D.R.H. supervised the stratigraphic section drawings and other aspects of the project.

"Gender in Inuit Burial Practices"

Barbara A. Crass

Many archaeologists study human burials for the wealth of information they can provide about the cultures of peoples. The major categories of evidence at burials include human biological remains, grave goods (things buried with the body), and treatment of the body. In this selection, archaeologist Barbara Crass shows how Inuit concepts of gender and religion are reflected in burials.

The article originally appeared in the edited volume *Reading the Body: Representations and Remains in the Archaeological Record*, published in 2000. Some words that readers may not be familiar with include *ethnography*, which is a written description of a culture based on firsthand observation by an anthropologist, and *cairns*, which are accumulations of stones created by humans, often used to cover burials.

Questions to Guide Reading

What are some examples of the lack of strong gender differentiation in Inuit society?
How do the patterns of both cairn and in-ground burials, such as orientation of the body and number and kind of grave goods, make sense in terms of gender differences in Inuit society?
How do the burial patterns make sense in terms of Inuit religious beliefs?

Arctic hunter-gatherer societies such as the Inuit are often described as having a strongly gendered division of labor (Burch 1988; Riches 1982; Watanabe 1968). This economic interdependency is, however, often portrayed in excessively simplistic terms, with men hunting and women staying home to process meat and tend the house and children. The actual relationship between economic organization and gender differentiation, as in any society, is considerably more complex. In Euro-American culture, for example, economic tasks are no longer strictly differentiated by sex, yet our names are quite gender-specific, and many activities are still viewed as "unmanly" or "unladylike." In contrast, in a hunting society such as the Inuit, where we might expect a high degree of differentiation in economic sex roles, there is little if any gender differentiation in personal names.

A simplistic man-the-hunter and woman-the-gatherer model obviously does not necessarily correlate with gender differentiation in other contexts, or, in fact, with actual performance of economic activities. Analysis of burial context and grave goods among Inuit burials shows that this lack of strong differentiation is also manifest in burial treatment. Apparently, in Inuit society, beliefs about the afterlife and about the economic complementarity of men and women are expressed in language and action as well as in the treatment of the dead.

Gender Differentiation in Inuit Society

The lack of strong gender differentiation seen in many aspects of Inuit society may stem in part from Inuit conceptions of the afterlife and the continued role of the dead among the living. In Inuit society, names are seen as holding part of a person's essence, or *inua*, which exists apart from that person's gender identity. When a newborn is given the name of a recently deceased relative or community member, the Inuit believe that the child acquires some of the wisdom, skills, and characteristics of the deceased, regardless of the deceased person's biological sex. In essence, the child becomes a living representative of the dead person (Weyer 1932:293). This practice results in the child assuming multiple roles and relationships with members of the community, regardless of the child's sex or age.

As one example, Stefansson knew an Inuit couple who had a seven-year-old son, "whose father called him stepmother and whose mother called him aunt, for those were their respective relationships to the woman whose soul was the boy's guardian" (1926:401). The use of relationship terms, such as "aunt" instead of "son," indicate that the nature of the relationship is more important than the sex of the individual (Giffen 1930:58). The lack of pronouns for specifying gender in Eskimo[1] languages (Barker 1995; Birket-Smith 1928; Fortescue 1984) is, thus, not surprising since individual people can have multiple gender identities. This idea that a person could have multiple gender identities, with no one of these identities paramount in importance, results in a lack of attention to the gender of English pronouns among bilingual speakers. For example, when speaking English, the Inuit commonly substitute "he" for "she" and vice versa (Barker 1995:90).

This lack of strong gender differentiation in Inuit society, demonstrated in the realm of language and personal names, is also apparent in people's activities. Even economic activities that one might suppose would be more strictly differentiated by sex are not assigned to mutually exclusive gender categories. A careful reading of early ethnographies reveals that activities such as hunting and domestic tasks are not ascribed solely to members of one sex. For example, Diamond Jenness noted that the division of labor in Inuit society was fluid and flexible. Despite a general attribution of domestic tasks as "women's work," he personally knew of a man who lived alone, hunted successfully, and managed to cook and mend his clothes (1957:140). He also met women who performed "men's work": they shot birds, hunted caribou with the men, and even stalked seals on the ice. Perhaps more important, Jenness commented, "The Eskimos seemed to consider this all natural" (1957:177).

Furthermore, activities that were commonly considered to be "men's work" or "women's work" were not ranked in terms of relative worth. For example, Patrick H. Ray, a member of the Point Barrow Expedition in 1885, reported: "The women as a rule seem to have an equal voice in the direction of affairs, when once admitted to the position of wife, and in each village there are a number of old women who are treated with the greatest consideration by all, they being credited with wonderful powers of divination, and are consulted in all important affairs.... The wife is invariably consulted when any trade is to be made, and the husband never thinks of closing a bargain of any importance without her consent" (1988:xcvi–xcvii).

These and other observations suggest that our models of the sexual division of labor among hunter-gatherers need revision. Native and non-native scholars have recently described the traditional roles of men and women in Inuit society not as a sexual division of labor but as two complementary forms of one function. This complementarity is expressed in a Yupik man's statement that "the man's success as a hunter was just as much her [the woman's] responsibility. They made up a team, complemented each other, and were very much equal in standing" (Kawagley 1995:20). Barbara Bodenhorn (1990) further describes the interdependent and complementary roles that an Inuit husband and wife must perform in order to have a successful hunt. According to her informants, the husband goes out and kills the game, but the wife is the one who attracts the game. The animals are pleased by the carefully sewn clothing that she makes for the hunter and are attracted to the woman's generosity and attention to ritual responsibilities. The animal is thus considered to give itself to the wife, even though the husband strikes the fatal blow.

Given the lack of strong gender differentiation in these linguistic, economic, and political realms, it seems likely that Inuit burial assemblages would also lack strong gender differentiation. Inuit burials are generally of two types: underground burials and burials in cairns. Burials are also often found with grave goods. This chapter examines the relationships between burial type and grave goods and the sex of the skeletal remains.

The Archaeological Data

In this study, only sites where the human remains were sexed by a physical anthropologist or other trained individual were selected. Burials for which the sex assignment was likely or possibly based on grave goods were eliminated. These burials date from the first century A.D. to the late nineteenth century, or within the Thule culture phase (Dumond 1987). Burials that date after the introduction of Christianity into this region were not included in this study.

The sites studied here include Ekwen (Arutiunov and Sergeyev 1975) and Uelen (Arutiunov and Sergeyev 1969) cemeteries from Siberia; the Gamble area of St. Lawrence Island, Alaska (Bandi 1984 and Hofmann-Wyss 1987); Igluligardjuk, Inuksivk, Kamarvik, Kulaituijavik, and Silumiut on Chesterfield Inlet, Canada (McCartney 1971 and Merbs 1964, 1967,

1968); Niutang and Tasioya on Baffin Island (Salter 1984) and Southampton Island, Canada (Collins 1955, Collins and Emerson 1954, Emerson 1954). From each of these sites (Fig. 6.1), all of the burials containing sexed human remains were selected. Grave goods and skeletal orientation were analyzed, although the orientation was not known for all the burials.

The sites neatly divide into two ethnic/geographic groups: Siberian Yupik and Canadian Inuit. The Siberian Yupik lived in Siberia and on St. Lawrence Island in Alaska. The people lived in permanent settlements and used in-ground burials. The Inuit in Eastern Canada were seasonally mobile and buried their dead in above-ground stone cairns.

A total of 496 individuals were included in the study: 248 males and 248 females. Of these 496 individual burials, 326 (65.7 percent) had grave goods (164 males and 162 females). Obviously, the decision to bury someone with or without grave goods was not based on the deceased's sex. Approximately 150 different possible artifacts and materials were studied to see if any sexual differentiation existed. The artifacts represented all classes of goods; they included land and sea hunting items, sled and dog tack, lamps and household goods, sewing and skin processing tools, fishing gear, bird-hunting gear, containers, toys, ceremonial items, jewelry, figurines, and carving tools. Other items found as grave goods included worked bone, antler and ivory, ivory tusks, ochre, metal, soapstone, pyrite, graphite, jade, and quartz crystals. The number of males and females who had these grave goods was tested by the chi square test, with significance set at p].025. Here, the total number of each item in any particular burial was not considered; rather, each grave was scored as having or not having an item.

Out of 150 possible burial items, only thirteen items showed any significant association with the sex of the individual: ten items were consistently associated with males and three items with females (Table 6.1). Although hunting items were all associated with males, not all male burials had hunting items, and only one hunting tool, a seal scratcher,

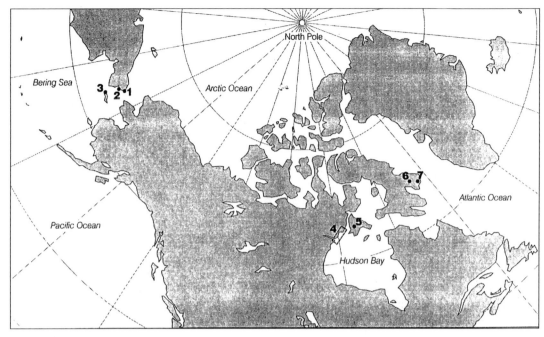

FIGURE 6.1: Site locations in the Arctic used in this study: (1) Ekwen, Siberia; (2) Uelen, Siberia; (3) the Gamble area of St. Lawrence Island, Alaska; (4) Igluligardjuk, Inuksivk, Kamarvik, Kulaituijavik, and Silumiut on Chesterfield Inlet, Canada; (5) Southampton Island, Canada; (6) Tasioya, Baffin Island, Canada; and (7) Niutang, Baffin Island, Canada (map drawn by the author).

was found exclusively with males (four males, no females). The only other item found exclusively in burials of one sex was a sinew twister (no males, two females). Only these two items were found solely in burials of one sex. All the other items and materials were represented with both males and females.

Although these data show that there were few differences in the types of burial goods included in male and female burials, there were some gender differences in the number of burial goods, particularly among the cairn burials. For burials in cairns, the mean number of grave goods was 2.5 per female cairn and 7.6 per male cairn. Four male cairns were exceptionally rich, however, containing 59, 73, 76, and 96 grave goods, respectively. If these 4 cairns containing 59 or more grave goods are omitted from analysis, the mean number of goods in a male cairn

burial is 3.4 items. It thus appears that only a slightly greater number of grave goods were generally placed in male cairns, although some males were apparently treated differently. A possible explanation for the male cairns with exceptional numbers of grave goods may be that these individuals had a higher status (such as shaman or whaling captain).

In-ground burials yielded greater numbers of items in both male and female graves, but the distribution of these goods by sex was more nearly equal. The mean number of grave goods in in-ground graves was 17.9 per female grave and 24.2 per male grave, a result that suggests that male burials in graves had more items. Again, however, several graves were exceptional: one female grave contained 167 items; two male graves contained 61 items; the rest contained 71, 78, 90, 92, 94, 101, 113,

TABLE 6.1 SIGNIFICANT ITEMS FOUND WITH MALE AND FEMALE BURIALS

	Male	Female	Chi-square Significance
Harpoon head	60	36	>.01
Arrowheads	28	11	>.01
Drill parts	26	12	>.025
Adze	22	11	>.025
Socket piece	21	9	>.025
Ice probe	21	9	>.025
Shaft	17	6	>.025
Winged object	15	4	>.01
Wound pin	9	2	>.025
Ulu	14	29	>.025
Mattock	12	29	>.01
Needle	11	24	>.025
Antler	38	19	>.01

116, and 136 items. If these exceptional graves are ignored, the mean number of items per burial is nearly identical: 16 items in female graves and 15.3 items in male graves.

In-ground graves, therefore, show slightly less differentiation between males and females both in terms of the numbers of items typically found in graves and in the representation of at least one female among the graves with exceptional numbers of items. It is also interesting that the one exceptional female grave had considerably more items that the richest of the exceptional male graves. The large number of burial items, as well as other unusual features of this grave, suggests that this woman may have had a special role during life, perhaps that of a shaman (Arutiunov and Sergeyev 1975).

The different types of burials (cairn and in-ground) are also associated with differences in the orientation of the body. Skeletal orientation in the cairn burials shows a distinct northeast-southwest orientation for male burials: 35 of the 57 males (61

percent) were oriented with the head positioned from north-northeast to east (p].001). The majority of these burials were adult males. This preferred orientation is not as strongly expressed among the females in cairn burials, but chi square tests show that the orientation of females is nonrandom (p].025). Females thus exhibit greater variety in skeletal orientation. In particular, a small number of female cairn burials were oriented with the skull positioned to the west or south-southwest.

Bodies in in-ground graves do not adhere to such a strong pattern of orientation. In addition, little difference is apparent between the male and female graves. However, for neither sex is the orientation of the body completely random (p].001). Apparently, in-ground graves were constructed with less regard to a preferred orientation of the body, or else there were a number of acceptable alternative body orientations, no one of which was strongly preferred.

Inuit Belief and Mortuary Ritual

Some of this observed patterning in mortuary treatment makes sense in terms of Inuit religious beliefs. Early ethnographic data agree that the Inuit had no concept similar to a Judeo-Christian afterworld such as Heaven or Hell, but did believe in an afterlife (Weyer 1932). The afterlife was in another realm: at worst, filled with fewer hardships than life on earth; at best, filled with abundant game and warm, sunny skies. In general, Inuit groups had two afterlife realms, one in the sky and one under the sea or land. The destination of a soul to any one sphere depended as much on the matter of death as on the person's earthly conduct. Those who died a violent death, such as victims of murder, drowning, and hunting accidents, and women who died in childbirth, would go to the Land of the Day, or east. The Land of the Day is a supercelestial realm ruled by the Moon, which according to Inuit mythology is a male figure (Merkur 1991). The realm is filled with sunlight, mountains, rivers, warmth and herds of caribou. In contrast, those who died a nonviolent death would go to the Land of the Sea, or west (Merkur 1991). The Land of the Sea was envisioned as a dark, gloomy, monotonous realm ruled by the Sea Woman who also controls the sea mammals.

The orientation of the body after death would be important in that it would direct the soul to the proper afterlife realm. One of the early ethnographic reports suggests that orientation of burials adhered to this patterning, although several sources describe a more complex system in which the age of the deceased was also an important factor affecting grave orientation (see Lyon 1825:371). Merbs (1996) has recently argued that archaeological cairn burials near Chesterfield Inlet exhibit a preferred orientation that can be attributed to the violent or nonviolent nature of the individual's death.

The data presented in this study supports this proposed differentiation in skeletal orientation for bodies in the cairn burials. In the cairns, both males and females are most commonly oriented with the skull to the north-northeast to east. The majority of the males in this grouping are adult males, the age group at highest risk for a violent death. The women in this grouping are also primarily adults. While women can die violent deaths from drowning, murder, or hunting accidents, the most likely cause of violent death would be childbirth. An equal-sized cluster of adult women deviates from this pattern, with the skull oriented to the west or south-southwest. This group of women would presumably be those who died a nonviolent death.

Inuit mythology and beliefs about the afterlife can also help explain some of the patterned representation of different kinds of objects in the graves. Antler, for example, was found only in male burials. Other valuable material, such as ivory, was found with both males and females. McGhee (1977) has suggested that these items in particular have gendered significance, with ivory and antler symbolizing female and male respectively. The burials in this study did not exhibit such a simple correlation. I suggest that these two materials represent not just one or another sex or sex role, but rather symbolize the economic and social interdependence between men and women.

This suggestion is based on McGhee's (1977) elegant model of the Inuit worldview, in which the environment is centered around a dichotomy between the land and the sea. Taboos, such as the widespread prohibition against cooking caribou and sea mammal meat together, exist to keep separate land and sea mammals. Another example of such a taboo would be the prohibition against working on sealskin clothing during caribou hunts, and conversely, working on caribou clothing while on the sea ice.

Various myths also support this theory. As mentioned earlier, two afterlife realms are known among the Inuit: one on land, ruled by a male and filled with caribou; the other in the sea, ruled by a woman and filled with sea mammals. The myth of the origin of the walrus and caribou describes how during a famine an old woman (or sometimes the Sea Woman) took two pieces of fat and threw one on the water where it turned into a walrus that swam away. The other piece she threw onto the land, where it turned into a caribou and attacked her. She knocked out the caribou's teeth and has disliked caribou ever since (McGhee 1977:147).

In this model, seemingly dichotomous units are actually interdependent units. Thus, the sea and the land are separate, but together represent the world; in the supernatural world, the Moon Man and Sea Woman combined represent the afterlife realms. This interrelationship among seemingly separate and opposite characteristics is also expressed in everyday life: sea animals and land animals together represent food and other crucial resources. Thus, caribou and walrus, or their respective products, antler and ivory, together make human life possible. Similarly, man and woman together, separate but independent, represent a powerful team that can most effectively utilize these resources.

Conclusion

Hunting societies such as the Inuit are sometimes presented as societies with rigid economic sex roles that sharply distinguish male hunters from females who gather plant foods and process the results of male hunting. The ethnographic data presented here, ranging from ideology to reports of actual activity patterns, demonstrate the pervasive inaccuracies in such a simplistic view of this society. Analysis of burials also shows that there are no strongly significant differences in the treatment of males and females after death, whether they are buried in cairns or in below-ground burials. Some of the observed variation in skeletal orientation seen in male and female cairns can be explained not in terms of sex difference, but in terms of the circumstances of the individual's deaths. The orientation of in-ground graves reveals a more complex and yet unexplained pattern.

Inuit myths present a view of males and females being equally powerful, yet forming an interdependent unit necessary for survival. This worldview seems to have structured actual economic activities, beliefs about male and female economic contributions, and mortuary ritual. Traditional life for Inuit hunter-and-gatherers was filled with uncertainty and risks. A tremendous degree of cooperation was necessary for survival, so sexual differences had to be used advantageously. Unequal treatment in any form would only lessen the odds for survival. This principle seems to contribute to the general lack of distinctive mortuary assemblage for male and female burials in this study.

A comment, made by Bilby in 1923 when discussing female representation in Eskimo folk tales, was more insightful than he had realized: "One of [the tales] might almost point to a feminist movement in the Arctics! [sic]" (Bilby 1923:104). Apparently the Inuit female had more equality with males in her society than did American women of the 1920s.

Note

1 The term *Eskimo* is used to denote the Eskimo language family, which includes Inupiaq dialects (spoken in Northern Alaska, Canada, and Greenland), Central Yupik (spoken in Southwestern Alaska), and Siberian Yupik (spoken in Siberia and St. Lawrence Island, Alaska).

References

Arutiunov, Sergei A. and Dorian A. Sergeyev. 1969. *Drevnie kul'tury Aziatskik Eskimosov* (Uelenski Mogil'nik). (Ancient Cultures of the Asiatic Eskimo). Nauka, Moscow.

———. 1975. *Problemy etnicheskoi istorii Beringo mor'ia. Ekvenskii Mogil'nik.* (Problems of the Ethnic History of the Bering Sea: The Ekven Cemetery). Nauka, Moscow.

Bandi, Hans-Georg. 1984. *St. Lorenz Insel-Studien. Berner Beitrage zur archaologischen und nologischen Erforschung des Beringstrassengebietes. Band I. Allgemeine Einfuhrung und Graberfunde bei Gambell am Nordwestkap der St. Lorenz Insel, Alaska.* Verlag Paul Haupt. Bern and Stuttgart, Germany.

Barker, Robin. 1995. Seeing Wisely, Crying Wolf: A Cautionary Tale on the Euro-Yup'ik Border. In *When Our Words Return: Writing, Hearing, and Remembering Oral Traditions of Alaska and the Yukon*, edited by Phyllis Morrow and William Sneider, pp. 79–98. Utah State University Press, Logan.

Bilby, Julian William. 1923. *Among Unknown Eskimo: An Account of Twelve Years Intimate Relations with the Primitive Eskimo of Ice-Bound Baffin Land, with a Description of Their Ways of Living, Hunting Customs, and Beliefs.* J.B. Lippincott, Philadelphia.

Birket-Smith, Kaj. 1928. *Five Hundred Eskimo Words: A Complete Vocabulary from Greenland and Central Eskimo Dialects*. Gyldendalske Boghandel, Nordisk Forlag, Copenhagen, Denmark.

Bodenhorn, Barbara. 1990. "I'm Not the Great Hunter, My Wife Is": Inupiat and Anthropological Models of Gender. *Inuit Studies* 14 (1-2): 55–74.

Burch, Ernest S., Jr. 1988. *The Eskimos*. University of Oklahoma Press, Norman.

Collins, Henry B., Jr. 1955. *Field Notes, Native Point, Southampton Island, 1954 and 1955*. Manuscript on file (MS no. 1974). Document Collection, Information Management Services, Canadian Museum of Civilization, Quebec, Canada.

Collins, Henry B., Jr. and J.N. Emerson. 1954. *Tunirmiut I Site, Native Point*. Manuscript on file (MS no. 1523, Book 1). Document Collection, Information Management Services, Canadian Museum of Civilization, Quebec, Canada.

Dumond, Don. 1987. *The Eskimos and Aleuts*. Thames and Hudson, London.

Emerson, J.N. 1954. *Field Notes, Tunirmiut (T1) Burial 2, Southampton Island, 1954*. Manuscript on file (MS no. 1973). Document Collection, Information Management Services, Canadian Museum of Civilization, Quebec, Canada.

Fortescue, Michael. 1984. *West Greenlandic*. Croom Helm, London.

Giffen, Naomi M. 1930. *The Roles of Men and Women in Eskimo Culture*. University of Chicago Press, Chicago.

Hofmann-Wyss, Anna Barbara. 1987. *St. Lorenz Insel-Studien. Berner Beitrage zur archaologischen und ethnologischen Erforschung des Bereingstrassengebietes. Band II. Prahistorische Eskimograber an der Dovelavik Bay und bei Kitnepaluk im Westen der St. Lorenz Insel, Alaska*. Verlag Paul Haupt, Bern and Stuttgart, Germany.

Jenness, Diamond. 1957. *Dawn in Arctic Alaska*. University of Chicago Press, Chicago.

Kawagley, A. Oscar. 1995. *A Yupik Worldview: A Pathway to Ecology and Spirit*. Waveland Press, Prospect Heights, Ill.

Lyon, George Frances. 1825. *The Private Journal of Captain G.F. Lyon, of H.M.S. Hecla, During the Recent Voyage of Discovery under Captain Parry*. 2nd ed. J. Murray, London.

McCartney, Allen P. 1971. Thule Eskimo Prehistory Along Northwestern Hudson Bay. Ph.D. dissertation, University of Wisconsin—Madison. University Microfilms, Ann Arbor, Mich.

McGhee, Robert. 1977. Ivory for the Sea Woman: The Symbolic Attributes of a Prehistoric Technology. *Canadian Journal of Archaeology* 1: 141–149.

Merbs, Charles F. 1964. *Summary of Field Work*. Manuscript on file (MS no. 603), Document Collection, Information Management Services, Canadian Museum of Civilization, Quebec, Canada.

——. 1967. *Human Burials of Silumiut, A Thule Culture Site North of Chesterfield Inlet, Northwest Territories, Preliminary Report*. Manuscript on file (MS no. 605), Document Collection, Information Management Services, Canadian Museum of Civilization, Quebec, Canada.

——. 1968. *Eskimo Burial Studies: The Kamarvik and Silumiut Sites, Preliminary Report*. Manuscript on file (MS no. 607), Document Collection, Information Management Services, Canadian Museum of Civilization, Quebec, Canada.

——. 1996. Thule Concepts of Gender and the Souls of the Dead. Paper presented at the Sixty-first Annual Meeting of the Society for American Archaeology, New Orleans.

Merkur, Daniel. 1991. *Powers Which We Do Not Know: The Gods and Spirits of the Inuit*. University of Idaho Press, Moscow.

Ray, Patrick H. 1988. Ethnographic Sketch of the Natives of Point Barrow in Murdoch, John. *Ethnological Results of the Point Barrow Expedition*. Smithsonian Institution Press, Washington, DC.

Riches, David. 1982. *Northern Nomadic Hunter-Gatherers: A Humanistic Approach*. Academic Press, New York.

Salter, Elizabeth Mary. 1984. Skeletal Biology of Cumberland Sound, Baffin Island, NWT. Ph.D. dissertation, Department of Anthropology, University of Toronto, Ontario, Canada.

Stefansson, Vilhjalmur. 1926. *My Life with the Eskimo.* Macmillan, New York.

Watanabe, Hitoshi. 1968. Subsistence and Ecology of Northern Food Gatherers with Special Reference to the Ainu. In *Man the Hunter*, edited by Richard B. Lee and I. Devore, pp. 69–77. Aldine Publishing Company, Chicago.

Weyer, Edward M., Jr. 1932. *The Eskimos: Their Environment and Folkways.* Yale University Press, New Haven.

"Women and Men at Çatalhöyük"

Ian Hodder

Archaeologists use many lines of evidence in reconstructing past lifeways. This selection shows how diet, skeletal remains, burials, allocation of household space, and symbols can be used to determine the relative status of men and women. The article focuses on the site of Çatalhöyük, one of the best known and intensively excavated archaeological sites of the Stone Age. The author, Ian Hodder, is one of the most influential archaeologists of the last few decades, known primarily for his leading role in the rise of post-processual archaeology in the 1980s, which challenged archaeologists to work towards such things as reconstructing gender. Hodder is now a professor at Stanford. The article initially appeared in a 2004 issue of *Scientific American*, a monthly magazine targeted to readers with a general interest in science.

Questions to Guide Reading

What is the location and age of Çatalhöyük?

What were the contributions of James Mellaart and Marija Gimbutas? Are their interpretations supported by more recent work?

How are diet, skeletal remains, burials, the use of household space, and symbols (including art) used to determine the relative status of men and women at Çatalhöyük?

How does agriculture factor into the relative status of men and women at Çatalhöyük?

Nine thousand years ago on the plains of central Turkey, a group of Neolithic people settled at the edge of a river. The town they built there—now known as Çatalhöyük ("chah-tahl-HU-yook")—grew to about 8,000 people and 2,000 houses. Crammed within 26 acres, roughly the size of 24 football fields, the later town contained no streets; people had to move about on the roofs. When they entered the houses down a stairway from the roof, they descended into a domestic space that was full of painting and sculpture—primarily depicting bulls, deer, leopards, vultures and human figures.

These late Stone Age settlers had finely polished stone tools, and they had domesticated cereals and sheep. In addition, they hunted wild cattle, pigs and horses and made use of many wild plants. The site is not the earliest agricultural settlement, but its large size at an early date and its elaborate art mean that it has always played a part in discussions about early farmers and their way of life.

One of the questions in which Çatalhöyük was immediately embroiled was the role of women in early agricultural societies. A long tradition in European thought holds that most of these societies were matriarchies (women were the leaders, descent was through the female line, and inheritance passed from mother to daughters) and that they worshipped a powerful mother goddess. The idea of an agricultural phase in which the goddess was a potent symbol became a central tenet of the New Age goddess movements in the last decades of the 20th century, and many goddess tours have visited Çatalhöyük to pray, to hold circle dances and to feel the sway of the goddess.

Was Çatalhöyük the bastion of female power it has been thought to be? The resumption of excavations at the site in the 1990s, after a gap of a quarter of a century, has turned up fresh evidence of the relative power of the sexes at this place in central Turkey 9,000 years ago, and we can begin to answer this question—and to paint a picture of what it was like to be a woman or a man at Çatalhöyük.

The Mother Goddess

Research on earlier and later agricultural sites provided some context for thinking about this question—and warned against expecting clear-cut answers. Before the 18th century, scholars in Europe had believed, based on Aristotle and interpretations of the Bible, that the political development of society began with patriarchy. During the 18th century,

CLAY STATUETTE of a voluptuous female figure supported by leopards was found in a grain bin, where it may have been placed to promote the fertility of the crops by sympathetic magic. The interpretation of the figure when it was discovered during the first excavations in the early 1960s was that it was the mother goddess. Today it is seen more in terms of the symbolic importance of women. At 16.5 centimeters high, it is one of the largest figures found at the site.

however, reports from North America told of societies that traced heritage through the female line, and in the early 19th century a Swiss jurist named Johann Bachofen argued that a phase of women's social power had preceded the patriarchal family. These ideas influenced many scholars in the second

Overview/Life circa 7000 B.C.E.

- A 9,000-year-old site at Çatalhöyük in Turkey reveals a curious town of thousands of houses crammed together with no streets between them.
- Inhabitants climbed down stairways from the roof to enter dwellings filled with wall paintings and sculptures.

- The lives of men and women in the town do not appear to have differed greatly. One or the other sex may have exercised more power in certain spheres—men in hunting, women in growing plants, for example—over various periods in the town's history, but both sexes played key roles in social and religious life.

half of the 19th century and throughout the 20th century, including Sigmund Freud and archaeologists such as V. Gordon Childe and Jacques Cauvin.

The first excavator at Çatalhöyük was James Mellaart of the University of London, who, with his wife, Arlette, worked at the site from 1961 to 1965. He was steeped in the scholarship of the European tradition, so it is not surprising that when he discovered opulent female imagery, such as the figurine on the previous page, he presumed that it represented the mother goddess. The powerful naked woman sitting on a seat of felines (probably leopards), with her hands resting on their heads, seems to conjure up precisely the tamer of nature.

Mellaart's publications about the site, complete with images of potent women, reached a wide audience, but it was another archaeologist who most effectively took up the mother goddess view of Çatalhöyük. Marija Gimbutas of the University of California at Los Angeles in a number of publications, including her 1974 book *Gods and Goddesses of Old Europe,* argued forcefully for an early phase of matriarchal society, evident at Çatalhöyük but also found across Europe with the advance of agriculture. Patriarchal societies came later, she contended, in conjunction with metallurgy, horse riding and warring.

More recently, cultural anthropologists—who compare and analyze societies—have withdrawn from making such sweeping generalizations, because human groups living today or in the recent past offer a diverse picture of the roles of the two sexes. Furthermore, cultural anthropology provides no substantiated claims for true matriarchies. The record does show, however, that in most recent and contemporary societies women have some form of authority or that women at certain stages in their lives, or in certain contexts, have power. Rather than talking simplistically about matriarchies and patriarchies, we should expect, according to the ethnographic evidence, a more complicated picture, which is just what we find at Çatalhöyük.

You Are What You Eat

So far excavations at Çatalhöyük have extended over only 4 percent of the site. We have discovered 18 levels of habitation (each built on top of the previous level), covering a total of about 1,200 years. Most of our understanding comes from the middle and earlier levels, which have been examined most closely.

Some of our strongest scientific evidence about the relative status of men and women in the early and middle levels of Çatalhöyük concerns diet. If women and men lived notably different lives, and if one or the other was dominant, then we might expect to uncover disparities in diet, with the dominant group having more access to certain foods, such as meat or better joints of meat. So we have searched hard for such evidence, but we have not uncovered clear differences.

Two of my colleagues, Michael P. Richards of the University of Bradford in England and Jessica A. Pearson, now at the University of Liverpool, have analyzed the stable isotopes in ancient bones at Çatalhöyük to discover what people ate. The inhabitants of the settlement buried their dead underneath the floors of the houses, and in one building we found 62 bodies. The analysis of these skeletons detected no statistical variation between the isotopes in male and female bones. The same is true of the teeth, which were studied by Basak Boz, a graduate student at Hacettepe University in Ankara, in collaboration with Peter Andrews and Theya Molleson of the Natural History Museum in London. Women tend to have more cavities than men, but in terms of wear on the teeth the researchers found no difference.

By analyzing the patterns of wear and tear on the bones, Molleson has also been able to demonstrate that the people seem to have carried out very similar tasks during their lives [see "The Eloquent Bones of Abu Hureyra," by Theya Molleson; Scientific American, August 1994]. An intriguing piece of evidence supports this finding. Andrews and Molleson had noticed a black deposit often lining the inside of the ribs, which when analyzed proved to include carbon. The inhabitants of Çatalhöyük lived in small houses with little draft and with much smoke from the fire. Indeed, the wall plasters were covered with soot. The same soot got into people's lungs.

The hole in the roof through which inhabitants entered their houses was also where the smoke from the fire came out. Winters in the area are extremely cold, so families may have spent a great deal of time indoors, breathing smoky air. As a result, soot built up in their lungs. After burial and during the decay of the body, the soot was deposited on the inside of the ribs. But—and this is the crucial point for our purposes—both men and women had soot on their ribs. This finding implies that we cannot argue, for example, that men had more of an outdoor and women more of an indoor life. In fact, they appear to have lived quite similar lives in terms of the amount of time spent in the house.

The study of the human remains showed that men were taller than women, but the variation in size was slight. The bones reveal that women were sometimes fatter in relation to their height than men. So perhaps there is some truth to the images of "fat ladies" seen in the figurines discovered by Mellaart. But overall, various lines of evidence suggest similar diets and lifestyles for women and men. We see little indication that the sexes had specialized tasks or that daily life was highly gendered.

This is not to argue that differences based on sex did not exist. An obvious one relates to childbirth. Study of the human bones has shown a high rate of infant and child mortality and several cases of burials of women with babies, perhaps indicating

MAP: ÇATALHÖYÜK originally lay beside a river and was surrounded by marshland. Today the river has dried up, and the area, 3,000 feet above sea level on the Anatolian plateau, is covered by fertile wheat fields.

death during childbirth. But dietary and bone analyses give no clear sign that any divergence in lifestyle between women and men was translated into differences of status or power.

In Life and in Death

We sought more information on status by looking into a custom at Çatalhöyük that seems bizarre from a 21st century perspective. Archaeologists have excavated burials of headless bodies at the site. Most people were buried with their heads intact, and they were left like that. But in some cases, perhaps a year or so after burial, the grave was reopened and the head was cut off with a knife, leaving cut marks on the bones. These heads were then used for ceremonial purposes. They were sometimes later left as part of abandonment rituals in houses. These practices are part of a wider tradition among the early farmers of Turkey and the Near East. At such places as Jericho, the skulls were plastered to re-create human features of the face.

It appears likely that the heads were removed from notable individuals—perhaps literally family or lineage "heads." So it was of great interest to find that skulls of both men and women were circulated and curated, thus suggesting that lineage or family could be traced through both female and male lines.

We reach a similar conclusion when we consider another aspect of burial. The 62 burials in one building that I mentioned earlier largely occurred below platforms and spaces around the edges of the main room. A particular platform would serve for a time for burial and then go out of use. It is possible that the death of a particular person, specifically the last one buried in a spot, influenced when the shift in use took place—and these last-buried individuals are both male and female.

Archaeologists are accustomed to studying the layout of graves and of the artifacts in them to assess social distinctions. We have looked carefully to see whether men are always buried in one part of the room and women in another, whether men are

buried on their left side and women on their right, whether men face one direction and women another, whether certain artifacts are found in the graves of men and others in the graves of women. Naomi Hamilton, while a postgraduate student at the University of Edinburgh, searched for such patterning. Look as she might, she could not tease out any clear distinctions. In one way, this is very frustrating, but in other ways, it is fascinating. It suggests a society in which sex is relatively unimportant in assigning social roles.

The burials imply equality, but what about the use of space within the houses during life? Archaeologists

BODIES of family members, such as this nine-month-old child, were usually laid on one side, often placed in a basket or on a reed mat and then buried under the floors and sleeping platforms of the dwellings. The lime plaster floors above the burials and the smoke from the ovens may have masked the odor of decay.

have often argued, on the basis of much contemporary study of small-scale, non-Western societies, that men would have made the stone tools, whereas women would have made the pots and done much of the cooking. The trouble with such assumptions is that one can always find ethnographic examples in which the roles are reversed. But let us for the moment allow that some sexual division of labor may have existed at Çatalhöyük when it came to activities inside the house. Each domicile contains a hearth or oven.

Around the oven we find large accumulations of ashy rake-out material from the fire as well as the remains of cooking and processing cereals. So, we might conclude, the area around the oven was for food processing, and it was mainly the domain of women. One piece of evidence could be taken to support such a view: neonate burials frequently occur near the ovens.

But the ashy rake-outs also contain high densities of obsidian that had been flaked and knapped to make stone tools. The obsidian was traded from Cappadocia in central Turkey and then placed beneath the floor near the oven until pieces were taken out and made into tools. Such trading and tool production are often the province of men. If this was so at Çatalhöyük, then forming the obsidian into tools does not seem to have taken place in an area separate from that linked to domestic activity. Whether men or women made the stone tools, we find no indication of a clear separation of roles and tasks in any of the levels that have been excavated to date.

Life is Short, Art is Long

The picture looks quite coherent thus far. When we examine how people lived their daily lives—what they ate, what they did, where they were buried, who was paramount in terms of lineage and family—we see little in the way of radical division between men and women, no evidence for either patriarchy or matriarchy.

But in the world of symbolic representation and art, we see something quite different. Here the realms of influence seem distinct. Consider first the males of the community. The abundant paintings appear to concentrate on men. By and large, the paintings do not portray women, whereas they include many figures of men, often clad in leopard skins, hunting or teasing wild animals. In some panels, these images are unmistakably men because they are bearded.

Indeed, much of the art is very masculine, and much is concerned with wild animals, a number of them male—bulls and stags with erect penises, for example. The numerous animal heads fixed to walls of the houses are mostly those of wild bulls and rams. This male focus of the art has a long tradition in Anatolia. Excavations at the earlier site of Göbekli in southeastern Turkey have found fantastic images of wild animals, often with erect penises, as well as stone phalluses around the site.

Nerissa Russell of Cornell University and Louise Martin of University College London have identified concentrations of the bones of large wild animals— mainly bulls—at Çatalhöyük. These deposits, which contain higher proportions of bull bones than do those from daily meals, seem to be the residues from special feasts. The many paintings depicting groups of men and bulls could well commemorate such feasts or other rituals, as could the heads of bulls and other wild animals that were installed in the houses and plastered and painted.

As we have seen, however, the isotopic analysis of the human remains indicates no differences in the diets of the sexes, leading us to conclude that women as well as men participated in eating at these events. Only in the art connected with hunting and feasting do we see a distinction.

And what of the powerful female figure on the seat of leopards? Surely that indicates a strong image of women. Moreover, a recent find at Çatalhöyük reinforces this presumption: we discovered an intriguing female figurine that has a wild seed lodged in its back [see illustration below]. This connection between women and plants is also evident in the place that the famous "goddess" with leopards was found: a grain bin. And the few paintings that unmistakably depict women appear to show them gathering plants.

But aside from these few examples, the art and symbolism on the whole downplay or even deny the significance of agriculture. The houses are filled with symbolic representation: in many dwellings, one seems hardly able to move without facing some bull's head or painting. Yet in all this, the grain stores are never elaborated with any form of symbolism. The domestic pots are not painted or decorated; neither are the baskets used to store grains. The entire area of plants and agriculture is marginal in the art and symbolism. The artistic evidence, then, points to a divided world, one dominated by males

RECENT FINDING of a female figurine, only 2.8 centimeters high, with a seed embedded in her back suggests the important role women played in the nascent domestication of plants at Çatalhöyük.

and their activities involving hunting and wild animals and the other, less frequently portrayed world involving women and plants.

The situation is of course more complicated than this simple division implies. We must consider, too, the evolution of this society as it is revealed in the various levels of occupation. The figurines of fat ladies, and especially the woman on leopards found in a grain bin, as well as the woman with a grain lodged in her back, come from the upper levels of the site—specifically, the most recent three or four in the total of 18. Although agriculture and domesticated plants had existed for centuries, key aspects of social life, as revealed in the art and in the remains of feasts, continued to focus on wild animals. In the upper levels of Çatalhöyük, however, we may be observing agricultural products becoming more central to the life of the community, with rituals taking place that involved farming. We also see in the art, particularly in the figurines, women linked to the growing of plants.

This prominence of agriculture and the role women play in it is part of a wider set of changes that occur in the upper levels of the site. In particular, we find large-scale ovens outside the houses, in courtyards, which may indicate some specialization in food production. Certainly the specialization in the manufacture of stone tools and pottery increases in these upper levels. And stamp seals appear, suggesting a greater sense of ownership. It is in this overall context that we see gender divisions becoming more marked and a specific female domain—growing plants for food—becoming more manifest.

So the picture of women and men at Çatalhöyük is complex—in a way that echoes some of the conclusions I mentioned earlier that anthropologists have reached about the allocation of power between the sexes. We are not witnessing a patriarchy or a matriarchy. What we are seeing is perhaps more interesting—a society in which, in many areas, the question of whether you were a man or a woman did not determine the life you could lead.

Both men and women could carry out a series of roles and enjoy a range of positions, from making tools to grinding grain and baking to heading a household. The depictions of feasting rituals imply that men dominated in this realm. But we can discern no sign that they had an overarching influence on other areas of life. And in any case, such male dominance came to be contested when, several millennia after the domestication of cereals, plant agriculture began to play a fuller part in the life of the community.

At this point, women and plants are linked in the art, but even here, whether the dominance of women in agriculture had much effect on other aspects of life must await further scientific study. In particular, we have much less information from the upper levels, where we found the fat ladies and the large-scale ovens, than we do from the earlier levels, where we have analyzed bones and teeth. Only when excavation of the upper levels is renewed over the next five years will we be able to see how this story of the emergence of images of powerful women unfolds.

PAINTING of an enormous red bull (the now extinct aurochs, *Bos primigenius*) occupied the wall of one house. The bull itself is more than six feet long, and the disproportionately small size of the male figures that surround it suggests the awe that the creature inspired. The painting may commemorate a feast or other ritual.

At Home in the Stone Age

In 1958 archaeologists discovered a late stone age settlement on a mound rising out of the plain in central Turkey. To their surprise, the site, which dated back to 7000 B.C.E., turned out to be far more than a village; it could rightfully be called a town. Çatalhöyük ("forked mound") had been a community of several thousand inhabitants who had an impressive social organization, a rich religious life, a high level of technology (weaving, pottery, obsidian tools), and a genius for painting and sculpture.

Researchers eventually identified 18 superimposed building levels on the 26-acre site. The habit of building one structure on top of another, using the old walls as foundations, led to a certain uniformity of plan. But by subdividing rooms or joining others together and by creating an open space in place of one or more rooms, the builders managed to vary the plans of individual levels considerably, and pleasant irregularities break the monotony of row after row of dwellings.

Nevertheless, orderliness and planning prevail: in the standard layout of houses, in the size of bricks, in the heights of panels, doorways, hearths and ovens, even in the size of rooms. The houses themselves range in size from about 11 to 48 square meters, but they are invariably rectangular. Constructed of timber frames, sun-dried mud bricks, reeds and plaster, all the buildings appear to have been only one story high. Bundles of reeds formed the flat roofs, with a thick mud cover on top and a mat below to prevent bits of reeds from falling on the inhabitants.

Entry through the roof is one of the most characteristic features of the buildings; other access was rare. Each house had a wooden stairway made of squared timber, one side of which rested along the south wall, where it has left an easily recognizable diagonal mark in the plaster. The stairs descended from a hole in the roof, and through this same opening the smoke from the hearth, oven and lamps escaped. Movable ladders provided access to the roofs from outside the town. The interiors were rich in sculptures and wall paintings—the first paintings ever found on constructed walls. The main room served as the area for cooking, eating, sleeping and many other activities. The kitchen was always along the south side, to allow smoke to escape through the entrance hole in the roof. Secondary rooms, used for storage, were entered from the main room through low doorways; one could move through them only by squatting or crawling.

Along the walls of the main room were built-in, raised platforms for sitting, working and sleeping. These were as carefully plastered as the rest of the dwelling, and they were often covered with reed or rush matting as a base for cushions, textiles and bedding. No single building provided sleeping space for more than eight people, and in most cases the family was probably smaller. Below these platforms the dead lay buried. The bodies were tightly wrapped in a crouched position and often placed in baskets.

So far no wells have been discovered. But some buildings had toilet areas; the material was taken out and put in disposal heaps used for both sanitation and rubbish. The thick ash deposits in these heaps made efficient sterilizers. Houses were kept scrupulously clean; remains of meals such as broken bones are a rarity in any building.

Nothing suggests that defense was the reason for the peculiar way in which the people of Çatalhöyük constructed dwellings with sole entry through the roof. Nor is there evidence of any sack or massacre during the 1,200 years of the town's existence so far explored. At present, the most likely explanation for the close huddling of houses is that people wanted to be buried on or near their ancestors. As nearby spaces for building new dwellings disappeared, the cramming in of houses meant that the only access possible was from the roof. What caused the final abandonment of the settlement is still far from clear.

ARCHAEOLOGISTS working at Çatalhöyük have reconstructed a typical house. They plastered the internal walls and the built-in furniture and then smoothed them with rubbing stones. Then they experimented with pigment mixes to replicate wall paintings. Using both dung and various kinds of wood, the researchers lit the oven and analyzed the residue to see how it compared with the archaeological remains of burned fuel. The house has provided insight into the use and feel of the interior space and raised many questions about light sources and problems of air circulation when the ovens were in use.

"African American Ethnicity"

Timothy Baumann

Archaeologists often attempt to reconstruct many kinds of identity in the archaeological record, including descent groups, gender, and ethnic groups. This selection focuses on identifying African American ethnicity. It was first published in a 2004 issue of *The SAA Archaeological Record*, a publication of the Society for American Archaeology, and is a good example of semi-scholarly archaeological literature. Timothy Baumann is a professor at the University of Missouri, St Louis.

• •

Questions to Guide Reading

What is meant by "African American ethnicity" and "African American archaeology"?
What three forms of ethnic markers are used in reconstructing African American ethnicity?
What is the "acculturation model," and what is the "creolization model"? How have these models been used in the archaeology of African Americans?
What is the "dominance and resistance model"?

• •

How did African American ethnicity develop in the New World? How has archaeology contributed to our understanding of this cultural process? In this article, a summary is provided of archaeological approaches to identify and explain African American ethnicity.

The Genesis of African American Ethnicity

The history of African American cultural origins and identity has been a much-debated topic over the last century. According to Sidney Mintz and Richard Price (1976), the origins of African American culture began in West Africa and quickly developed in the New World. As Africans were forced into slavery, they were separated from their family, friends, and their *ethnos*. Thus, in order to survive, they had to quickly adapt by bonding with strangers in the slave dungeons of Africa or on slave ships. Many of these slaves spoke different languages, followed different religious practices, and were mortal enemies. Despite these differences, they forged bonds through pidgin languages and common cultural practices. After arriving in the New World, these enslaved Africans continued to rapidly develop into a new cultural community. The speed of this cultural transformation from African to African American ethnicity was much quicker than that of European colonists, who were not enslaved and who settled the New World with those of the same cultural background. European colonists were very homogeneous in their cultural traditions, while Africans were much more diverse in their cultural origins (Mintz and Price 1976:3).

African American Archaeology

African American archaeology has been defined by Theresa Singleton and Mark Bograd (1995:1) as "the study of material culture to describe and interpret the diverse experiences of African Americans and the social processes that affected their lives." The development of African American archaeology as a serious subfield of historical archaeology only occurred in the last 40 years. The first African American archaeological research began with plantation and slavery studies in the Deep South and the Caribbean. Current African American research has expanded across the US and beyond the "big house" to include urban slavery, post-emancipation settlements, western frontier experiences, industrial sites, and turn-of-the-century tenant farmers.

Archaeological strategies for studying African Americans have developed along two lines of inquiry: (1) the study of everyday life, and (2) social stratification studies. The study of everyday life has included questions of subsistence (Rietz et al. 1985), housing (Otto 1984), material possessions (Kelso 1986), and health (Gibbs et al. 1980; Rathbun 1987). Social stratification studies have addressed issues of class (Otto 1984), creolization/acculturation (Ferguson 1992; Otto 1984; Wheaton and Garrow 1985), gender (Galle and Young 2004), power and resistance (Orser 1988, 1991), race and racism (Babson 1990; Mullins 1999), and ethnicity. The latter has been the primary focus of social stratification studies in African American archaeology.

"Ethnic Markers"

Ethnic studies in African American archaeology have focused more often on defining "ethnic markers,"

or objects that can be linked to Africa or African American culture, and less time on understanding the underlying processes that formed these patterns. Archaeologists looking for ethnic markers have been defined as *separatists*, who "interpret the African American experience as a separate national experience" from Euro-Americans (Singleton 1998:172). In contrast, when "ethnic markers" are not visible in the archaeological record, archaeologists have often taken an *integrationist* perspective, "viewing cultural contact between Africans and Europeans within an assimilation model where Africans are absorbed into the dominant European culture" (Singleton 1998:172).

African American ethnic markers have been defined archaeologically in three forms. First, ethnicity has been linked to objects made in or indigenous to Africa but that are found in the New World. For example, Jerome Handler and Frederick Lange (1978) uncovered an African clay pipe from Ghana in a Barbados slave cemetery. Second, African American ethnicity can be expressed through objects made in the New World that exhibit African styles, forms, or influence. An example is provided by Matthew Emerson (1999), who recorded seventeenth-century clay pipes in the Chesapeake Bay Region made in European forms but exhibiting West African-styled decorative motifs. African American ethnicity has also been associated with non-African materials that were used in distinctive African ways. This third form of ethnicity is the most difficult to see archaeologically. However, it is likely the most prevalent type of ethnicity that was expressed materially by frequency ratios or spatial contexts. For example, the research of John Otto (1984) at Cannon's Point plantation compared the material remains of the planter, overseer, and slave households and suggested that African foodway traditions of gumbos and stews were recognizable in the higher ratio of European-made bowls to plates found in the slave quarters.

The main critique of African American "ethnic marker" studies in archaeology has been that they are too shallow or over-simplified (Babson 1990;

Singleton 1995; Singleton and Bograd 1995). Little effort has been made to explain the underlying cultural process that causes some cultural patterns to be retained while others are forgotten or transformed.

Cultural Process of Ethnicity

In African American archaeology, there are three explanatory paradigms that address the underlying processes of African American ethnicity: (1) acculturation, (2) creolization, and (3) dominance and resistance (Singleton 1998).

ACCULTURATION

Acculturation was originally defined by Redfield et al. (1936:149) as "those phenomena, which result when groups of individuals having different cultures come into continuous first-hand contact, with subsequent changes in the original cultural patterns of either or both groups." Today, the term "acculturation" has been linked to ethnocentric viewpoints of culture contact in which a dominant culture assimilates a minority group, erasing the differences between these groups. In archaeology, the acculturation model can be seen in the archaeology of the Yaughan and Curriboo plantations in South Carolina (Wheaton and Garrow 1985). Excavations at these plantations recorded the acculturation of enslaved Africans through the transition from African-style houses made of wattle and daub to European architectural forms, and from colonoware ceramics, a low-fired earthenware based on African traditions, to European-made ceramics, which were mass-produced.

Acculturation is viewed as a unidirectional model with objects, technology, and ideology only coming from the top down. "The problem inherent in applying acculturation models in this context is that such models fail to examine the agency or human action of the colonized, enslaved, or missionized. *Acculturation* assumes that the simple replacement of African-influenced items with European items

FIGURE 1: African American family in Arrow Rock, Missouri (circa 1916).

was an indication of cultural change and a loss of cultural identity" (Singleton 1998:176). In reaction to this critique, more recent studies have attempted to recognize that enslaved Africans did not relinquish their cultural identity but instead applied new cultural meanings to non-African objects (Brown and Cooper 1990; Ferguson 1992).

CREOLIZATION

A Creolization model recognizes that cultural interaction is not a one-way street, as seen in acculturation, but is a two-way relationship with objects, technology, and ideas exchanged between two or more individuals or groups (Ferguson 1992). This interaction model is not normally an equal exchange, but it does recognize human agency as well as the transformation of a cultural identity to include borrowed ideas and objects. To date, the creolization model is the best approach to understanding the interaction of enslaved Africans and other cultural groups in the New World.

There are three basic forms of creolization: (1) linguistics, (2) studies of self-identified creole peoples, and (3) racial terminology (Dawdy 2000). Linguistically, creolization is a "recombination of new elements within a conservative cultural grammar" (Dawdy 2000:1). This is often associated with creole or pidgin languages that combine elements of two or more languages, such as the Gullah language on St. Helena Island of South Carolina, which is a combination of African languages and English. The second form is "synonymous with the adaptation and development of a distinct colonial culture that does not necessarily result from ethnic and racial mixing" (Dawdy 2000:1). The final form of creolization suggests "hybridity and syncretism" combining genetic and cultural traits. Most studies combine all three of these definitions.

The linguistic model of creolization has been applied most often in historical archaeology, where

FIGURE 2: Crystals and beads, like these from a Postbellum community in Arrow Rock, Missouri, have been linked to African American ethnic traditions.

artifacts replace language and these objects formulate a cultural grammar (Deagan 1983). Leland Ferguson (1992) has been the leading proponent of creolization and its application to African American archaeology. In his analysis of the transformation from African to African American ethnic identity, Ferguson (1992:150) suggested that creolization recognizes the "free-will, imagination, and creativity of non-Europeans" in cultural contact and exchange and the development of "new cultures from diverse elements." He analyzed colonoware pottery of enslaved Africans in South Carolina, Georgia, and the Chesapeake Bay area. The colonoware was created in the New World through an African pottery tradition and ideology, but it is often found creolized with European forms (e.g., teapot). Despite the transition to more Euramerican material culture, enslaved Africans did not use or view these structures in the same way as Euramericans. Enslaved Africans filtered their environment through their own identity and worldview. In this sense, objects can have multiple uses or meanings (Gundaker 2000).

Singleton (1995:133) has been critical of Ferguson's creolization explanation because "it gives primacy to evidence supporting the continuity of an African heritage rather than its discontinuity and reconfiguration" and "evidence of both should enter into the analysis of creolization." Thus, Singleton argues that the study of ethnicity should examine and explain both the cultural traditions that persist and the ones that are forgotten or transformed. Following the same line of reasoning, Singleton (1998:178) argues that in African American archaeology, creolization has focused on how enslaved Africans creolized European traditions but very little work has been done to document European creolization of African traditions. Ferguson (1992) and Anne Yentsch (1994) have begun this discussion in the area of foodways, but more work is still needed. The research of Sian Jones (1997) also provides a solution to Singleton's critique. Jones argues that the use of practice theory and its concept of the *habitus* can be used to view the development, reproduction, and transformation of identity through a sociohistorical or diachronic approach addressing the long-term change among ethnic groups.

DOMINANCE AND RESISTANCE

The social interaction between Africans and Europeans in the New World was primarily a power relationship of dominance (master) and resistance (enslaved). Paynter and McGuire (1991) state that domination is the exercise of power through the control of resources including class, race, and gender relationships. Resistance can be viewed in two extremes: (1) open defiance or (2) overt resistance. Open defiance is a conscious and sometimes violent decision to rebel against the dominant culture or class. Overt resistance can be either conscious or subconscious reactions to the dominant, including slowed work production, deliberate breaking of equipment, faked sickness, and even the retention of cultural traditions. It is in this interplay that material culture is manipulated and new identities are formed and transformed.

Within this hegemonic approach, archaeologists have attempted to view "how dominant groups exert their power and how subordinate groups resist such power" (Singleton 1998:179). Examples in African American archaeological research have included housing (McKee 1992), landscape studies (Epperson 1990; Orser 1988), and foodways (McKee 1999). Within the latter, the formation of "soul food" may provide the best example of African American identity (Franklin 2001). The term "soul food" was coined in the 1960s as an outgrowth of ethnic pride and revitalization of African American identity, but its origins go back to slavery: in reaction to enslavement and racism, African American cooks created new recipes. This food tradition provided nutritional needs of the body as well as sociocultural and psychological needs of the soul by forming personal and community identity in the face of oppression.

Conclusion

Despite having nothing more than the clothes on their backs, enslaved Africans retained their cultural identity through their memories, and once transported to the New World, their cultural self was used to adapt to a new environment and transform them into a new ethnic group. The major critique of African American ethnic studies has been that it is often oversimplified, focusing on the identification of "ethnic markers," and it does not address a historical perspective on the transformation of ethnic communities. Archaeological attempts to understand the underlying processes of ethnicity have led to cultural contact studies focusing on acculturation, creolization, and dominance/resistance models. In the end, the search for material correlates of African American ethnicity may be a futile effort, as it is only one level of social stratification or inequality (Berreman 1981). Other social factors can equally and simultaneously affect the material record, including age, consumer choice, kinship, socioeconomic status, gender, race, and occupation. Future research needs to not only understand the formation processes of ethnicity but also the interwovenness of ethnicity with other forms of social stratification, which together generate cultural identity.

References

Babson, David
1990 The Archaeology of Racism and Ethnicity on Southern Plantations. *Historical Archaeology* 24(4):20–28.

Berreman, Gerald D.
1981 Social Inequality: Across-Cultural Approach. In *Social Inequality: Comparative and Developmental Approaches*, edited by G. Berreman, pp. 3–40. Academic Press, New York.

Brown, Kenneth L., and Doreen C. Cooper
1990 Structural Continuity in an African American Slave and Tenant Community. *Historical Archaeology* 24(4):7–19.

Dawdy, Shannon Lee
2000 Preface. *Historical Archaeology* 34(3):1–4.

Deagan, Kathleen
1983 *Spanish St. Augustine: The Archaeology of a Colonial Creole Community*. Academic Press, New York.

Emerson, Matthew
1999 African Inspirations in New World Art and Artifact: Decorated Pipes from the Chesapeake. In "*I, Too, Am American": Archaeological Studies of African American Life*, edited by T. Singleton, pp. 47–82. University Press of Virginia, Charlottesville.

Epperson, Terrence W.
1990 Race and the Disciplines of the Plantation. *Historical Archaeology* 24(4):29–36.

Ferguson, Leland
1992 *Uncommon Ground: Archaeology and Early African America, 1650–1800*. Smithsonian Institution Press, Washington, DC.

Franklin, Maria
2001 The Archaeological Dimensions of Soul Food: Interpreting Race, Culture, and Afro-Virginian Identity. In *Race and the Archaeology of Identity*, edited by C.E. Orser Jr., pp. 88–107. The University of Utah Press, Salt Lake City.

Galle, Jillian E., and Amy L. Young
2004 *Engendering African American Archaeology: A Southern Perspective*. The University of Tennessee Press, Knoxville.

Gibbs, Tyson, Kathleen Cargill, Leslie Sue Lieberman, and Elizabeth Rietz
1980 Nutrition in a Slave Population: An Anthropological Examination. *Medical Anthropology* 4(2):175–262.

Gundaker, Grey
2000 Discussion: Creolization, Complexity, and Time. *Historical Archaeology* 34(3):124–133.

Handler, Jerome S., and Frederick W. Lange
1978 *Plantation Slavery in Barbados: An Archaeological and Historical Investigation*. Harvard University Press, Cambridge, Massachusetts.

Jones, Sian
1997 *The Archaeology of Ethnicity: Constructing Identities in the Past and Present*. Routledge Press, London and New York.

Kelso, William M.
1986 Mullberry Row: Slave Life at Thomas Jefferson's Monticello. *Archaeology* 39(5):28–35.

McKee, Larry
1992 The Ideals and Realities behind the Design and Use of 19th-Century Virginia Slave Cabins. In *The Art and Mystery of Historical Archaeology: Essays in Honor of Jim Deetz*, edited by A. Yentsch and M.C. Beaudry, pp. 195–213. CRC Press, Boca Raton, Florida.

1999 Food Supply and Plantation Social Order: An Archaeological Perspective. In "*I, Too, Am America": Archaeological Studies of African American Life*, edited by T. Singleton, pp. 218–239. University Press of Virginia, Charlottesville.

Mintz, Sidney W., and Richard Price
1976 *The Birth of African American Culture: An Anthropological Perspective*. Beacon Press, Boston, Massachusetts.

Mullins, Paul
1999 *Race and Affluence: An Archaeology of African America and Consumer Culture*. Kluwer Academic/Plenum Publishers, New York.

Orser, Charles
1988 Toward a Theory of Power for Historical Archaeology: Plantations and Space. In *Recovery of Meaning: Historical Archaeology in the Eastern United States*, edited by M.P. Leone and P.B. Potter, Jr., pp. 314–343. Smithsonian Institution Press, Washington, DC.

1991 The Continued Pattern of Dominance: Landlord and Tenant on the Postbellum Cotton Plantation. In *The Archaeology of Inequality*, edited by R.H. McGuire and R. Paynter, pp. 40–54. Basil Blackwell, New York.

Otto, John S.
1984 *Cannon's Point Plantation, 1794–1860: Living Conditions and Status Patterns in the Old South*. Studies in Historical Archaeology Series. Academic Press, Orlando, Florida.

Paynter, Robert, and Randall McGuire
1991 The Archaeology of Inequality: Material Culture, Domination, and Resistance. In *The Archaeology of Inequality*, edited by R. McGuire and R. Paynter, pp. 1–27. Blackwell, Oxford and Cambridge.

Rathbun, Ted A.
1987 Health and Disease in a South Carolina Plantation: 1840–1870. *American Journal of Physical Anthropology* 74:239–253.

Redfield, Robert, Ralph Linton, and Melville Herskovits
1936 Memorandum for the Study of Acculturation. *American Anthropologist* 38:149–152.

Rietz, Elizabeth J., Tyson Gibbs, and Ted A. Rathbun
1985 Archaeological Evidence for Subsistence on Coastal Plantations. In *The Archaeology of Slavery and Plantation Life*, edited by T.A. Singleton, pp. 163–191. Academic Press, Orlando, Florida.

Singleton, Theresa
1995 The Archaeology of Slavery in North America. *Annual Review of Anthropology* 24:119–140.

1998 Cultural Interaction and African American Identity in Plantation Archaeology. In *Studies in Culture Contact: Interaction, Culture Change, and Archaeology*. Occasional Paper No. 25, edited by J. Cusick, pp. 172–188. Center for Archaeological Investigations, Southern Illinois University, Carbondale.

Singleton, Theresa, and Mark D. Bograd
1995 *The Archaeology of the African Diaspora in the Americas*. Guides to the Archaeological Literature of the Immigrant Experience in America No. 2. The Society for Historical Archaeology.

Wheaton, Thomas R., and Patrick H. Garrow
1985 Acculturation and the Archaeological Record in the Carolina Lowcountry. In *The Archaeology of Slavery and Plantation Life*, edited by T. Singleton, pp. 239–260. Academic Press, Orlando, Florida.

Yentsch, Anne
1994 *A Chesapeake Family and Their Slaves: A Study in Historical Archaeology*. Cambridge University Press, New York.

"Pirate Imagery"

Lawrence E. Babits, Joshua B. Howard, and Matthew Brenckle

The study of pirates has enormous popular appeal, but until recently, very few scholarly treatments of pirates could be found in the archaeological literature. This selection comes from the first edited volume devoted exclusively to the archaeology of piracy, *X Marks the Spot: The Archaeology of Piracy*, published in 2006. Although it focuses on pirates, the selection illustrates well the problems associated with identifying subgroups within societies; that is, subgroups are often very, very difficult to recognize archaeologically.

Questions to Guide Reading

Why is it difficult to identify pirates in the archaeological record?

What is the problem with using the following items to identify pirates: clothing, the inventory of goods on a ship, physical characteristics of the ship, and weaponry?

As pirate shipwrecks continue to be sought, found, and investigated, a close look at what might constitute a distinctive pirate assemblage is necessary. The act of piracy, a legal construction, rather than any concrete artifact distinguished pirates from everyday sailors. Three lines of nondocumentary evidence exist: the personnel, the ship itself, and the artifacts. While sailors were distinguished from landsmen by their clothing and tools, there is little artifactual evidence to distinguish sailors from pirates. What survives in a shipwreck is not likely to demonstrate conclusively that the wreck was manned by pirates.

The Beaufort Inlet wreck site publicly identified as Blackbeard's *Queen Anne's Revenge* by the governor of North Carolina has the same problem. While Governor Hunt had obvious reasons for claiming

that *Queen Anne's Revenge* had been found, he was responding to an older popular imagery that we are all familiar with, even if the objects did not survive nearly 300 years under water. A similar observation can be made for the *Whydah*, a known pirate vessel identified by its bell and its public imagery, including one book about its discovery, *The Pirate Prince* (Clifford 1993).

Today's children know what a pirate looks like long before they learn any names or details about piracy. In part, this is attributable to James Barrie's *Peter Pan* (1987; originally published in 1904) and Robert Louis Stevenson's *Treasure Island* (1965; originally published in 1883). Captain Hook is relevant here because he was Blackbeard's bo'sun (Barrie 1987:44). Aside from an "iron claw" replacing his right hand, Hook's distinguishing attribute was that "he somewhat aped the attire associated with the name of Charles II" (Barrie 1987:52), a flamboyant, late seventeenth-century style that included much lace. Hook's pirates were a "villainous-looking lot," one in particular with "great arms bare, pieces of eight in his ears ... [a] gigantic man" (Barrie 1987:50–51).

As they get older, children graduate to Robert Louis Stevenson's *Treasure Island* and Long John Silver. Captain Silver's distinguishing attributes (depending on the written version rather than films) produce a standardized pirate figure, but with one leg and a Devonshire accent, drawing out the *r*s until they are almost words in themselves. It is not simply Silver's appearance that is striking. The book begins with nautical references and Captain Billy Bones, "a tall strong, heavy, nut-brown man, his tarry pigtail falling over the shoulders of his soiled blue coat, his hands ragged and scarred, with black, broken nails, and the sabre cut across one cheek" (Stevenson 1965:11). The description continues: "[H]is great sinewy arm ... was tattooed in several places. 'Here's luck,' 'A fair wind,' and 'Billy Bones his fancy,' were very neatly and clearly executed on the forearm; and up near the shoulder there was a sketch of a gallows and a man hanging from it" (Stevenson 1965:22).

Bones was being stalked by his former crew mates, led by Long John Silver, "the ship's cook, Barbecue, as the men called him" (Stevenson 1965:66). "His left leg was cut off close by the hip, and under the left shoulder he carried a crutch ... He was very tall and strong" (Stevenson 1965:54). "Aboard ship he carried his crutch by a lanyard round his neck, to have both hands as free as possible" (Stevenson 1965:66). "He was tricked out in his best; an immense blue coat, thick with brass buttons, hung as long as to his knees, and a fine laced hat was set on the back of his head" (Stevenson 1965:122). The long coat fits within late seventeenth- and early eighteenth-century styles, and the wooden leg is typical of ships' cooks retained after injury in the Royal Navy. Silver owned a parrot named Captain Flint that squawked "Pieces of eight! Pieces

of eight" (Stevenson 1965:67). Silver, Captain Hook, and Blackbeard are linked via Israel Hands, a known Blackbeard crewman. In *Peter Pan*, Captain Hook was said to have been Blackbeard's bo'sun and "the only man of whom Barbecue [Silver] was afraid" (Barrie 1987:44, 51).

Stevenson's pirates included Black Dog, "a pale, tallowy creature, wanting two fingers of the left hand, and though he wore a cutlass, he did not look much like a fighter. I had always my eye open for seafaring men, with one leg or two, and I remember this one puzzled me. He was not sailorly, and yet he had a smack of the sea about him too" (Stevenson 1965:18). Blind Pew lost his eyesight in the same broadside that took away Long John Silver's leg. "He was hunched, as if with age or weakness, and wore a huge old tattered seacloak with a hood that made him appear positively deformed" (Stevenson 1965:27). Others are described as "mahogany faced," muscular and tattooed; but if they were not identified as pirates, the descriptions would fit law-abiding sailors.

The television film *Goonies* includes many pirate caricatures, including One Eyed Willie, clothed in Jacobean finery, sitting at a jewel-laden table on board his vessel. Popular imagery is fairly consistent in showing a pirate leader as a flawed gentleman and his crew as tarred, sunbronzed, tattooed, hook-armed, wooden-legged, eyepatch-wearing seadogs. This image translated to a terrestrial funeral in *Cold Mountain*, when a dead preacher has two pennies placed on his eyes when one eye started to open, because "to have covered the opening eye would have looked strange and piratical" (Frazier 1997:30).

Walking the plank is one part of the popular image of piracy. Although this action has been discounted as myth, at least one example from a later period involving mutinous privateers does exist:

... two Days ago Capt. Davise in the employ of Mr. Stanly arrived from the french West Indies—he brings an acct of a matter similar to this exactly—a vessel of the United States put into St. Thomas's the Capt. went ashore & the majority of the seamen being English they mutinied lashed a plank on the Bows and told the mate to take his choice either to walk over Board or navigate that vessel into Tarbola, the latter alternative of course was embraced ... the young Gent son of our printer and of exceeding good character offers to make oath to and I believe has or is to do. (Nash 1777:719–20)

While twentieth-century images are well known, they follow the tradition of earlier pirate imagery. Charles Johnson's 1724 book *A General History of the Pyrates* (1972; Charles Johnson is assumed to be a pseudonym for Daniel Defoe) went through many editions; as styles changed, so did the book's illustrations. Johnson's illustrations showed popular sailor images and identified them as pirates. Without this identification, they would just be sailors.

A pirate's clothing and accoutrements were no different from those of law-abiding sailors on a merchantman or man-of-war. The sailor's short clothes distinguished him from the landsman, with his long clothes (Lavery 1989:204; Rodger 1986:64). As sailor styles changed, similar clothing was worn by pirates, who, after all, were sailors. In fact, pirates are often shown dressed in later clothing more typical of a book's publication date than of their own time.

Images of Blackbeard are a case in point. The 1724 image shows him wearing a thrumm, the seventeenth-century sailor's hat (Johnson 1972:72). In 1740 he is wearing a low cocked hat (Botting et al. 1978:136); but by the 1780s he has a full cocked hat (Cordingly 1995). His coat length also varies according to current styles.

While sea officers' clothing tended to change more rapidly, in keeping with current styles, sailors were notoriously conservative in terms of their functional clothing, although they often wore garish items when going ashore. Traditional clothing elements like loose trousers, short jackets, and monmouth caps or thrumms readily identified sailors. A fan (ca. 1740) in the collections of Colonial Williamsburg shows both sailors and soldiers in typical attire. The sailors had short jackets, caps, and loose breeches or very short trousers, while the soldiers wore longer coats

and tight-fitting breeches (Baumgarten 1986:45, 66). The weaponry is too vague to identify precisely, other than as flintlocks.

Pirates thus are impossible to tell from common sailors by their dress. At Ocracoke Inlet, where Blackbeard was killed, one of Lieutenant Maynard's crew was shot by a fellow Royal Navy sailor, who took "him by mistake for one of the pirates" (Lee 1997:122). Sailor's clothing alone (buttons, hooks, eyes, buckles, and so forth) therefore cannot be linked with piracy either. A pirate's personal weaponry reflects that available to any sailor.

The generalized imagery is all well and good for the public but insufficient for scientific archaeological reporting. For an archaeologist, faced with differential preservation, the popular image is of little help. Cloth rarely survives in the archaeological record, wood floats away, and iron decays. That takes care of the flag, eye patch, wooden leg, and hook. Unless a fortuitous site formation process occurred, as in the sinking of the English collier *General Carleton of Whitby* in 1785 (Babits and Ossowski 1999), little identifiable clothing will survive.

When the *General Carleton* sank on September 1785 in the Baltic Sea, a barrel of birch tar spilled over several clothing items, including hats, gloves, jackets, vests, breeches, stockings, shoes, and at least one shirt. As part of the wrecking process, the tar mixed with sand and metallic artifacts, resulting in a concretion from which the clothing was later extracted. Wool and leather clothing survived, along with a silk ribbon; cotton, hemp, and linen material did not survive, leaving some items disassembled because the thread was linen (Babits and Ossowski 1999). These clothing items exhibit damage, repair, or adjustment, indicating that they were being used by sailors rather than stowed for later issue or sale. As a collection of clothing items in everyday use, the *General Carleton* assemblage is as remarkable for the eighteenth century as the *Mary Rose* (McKee 1972; Rule 1982) and *San Juan* (Davis 1997) are for the sixteenth century, the *Vasa* (Franzen 1966; Kaijser et al. 1982; Skenback 1983) and *Kronan* (Einarsson 1997) for the seventeenth, and the *Bertrand* (Petsche 1974) for the nineteenth.

Piracy is robbery at sea without a letter of marque and reprisal or commission. As a physical activity, piracy does not survive in the archaeological record. So how does one tell a pirate from a sailor in terms of a wreck's artifacts? More importantly, how does one tell if a wreck is a former pirate ship? An examination of what survives, has been documented, and has been found on "pirate sites," such as Beaufort Inlet and the *Whydah*, might prove instructive.

Any vessel used by pirates may or may not have been modified. Modifications included cutting down the forecastle or the stern castle, adding gun and sweep ports, and shifting masts (Botting et al. 1978:133; Johnson 1972:64). Although many archaeologists will not admit it, most nautical archaeology has very little to do with a vessel above the bilge, except in those unusual instances where a vessel was quickly buried or lay in very cold water. Human activity was concentrated and distinctive embellishment was placed well above the waterline in most vessels. When ships burned, wrecked, or rotted away, only the lowest portions survived in the mud or sand. If a wreck was accessible, it was repeatedly scavenged for usable material.

With the exception of a ship that came to rest on its side or was rapidly buried, virtually the only evidence of typical pirate modifications would be mast steps, timbers attached to the keel or keelson (the spine of a vessel) to support the mast. Masts were also inserted into a mortise on the keel or keelson. How does one tell if mast steps were added or put out of use, much less that they were a modification to convert a merchant vessel to a pirate ship? An armed merchantman, especially a slaver or a privateer, has many similar attributes (speed, large human spaces, heavy armament), for precisely the same reasons.

Artifacts may provide clues. If a vessel's history is known, any recovered artifacts should reflect that history. For the *Queen Anne's Revenge* and the *Whydah*, artifacts should reflect a ship outfitted in Europe for the slave trade that made voyages to the Caribbean via West Africa and returned (Clifford 1993; Lee 1997:14; Mettas 1978:16, 37, 56; Moore 1989). Most basic ship accoutrements should be English or French. Other artifacts should relate to the slave trade. The *Henrietta Marie* might well serve as a starting point for comparative purposes, because it contained numerous items used in the slave trade (Moore 1989). The *Whydah*, a slaver before being converted into a pirate vessel, contains artifacts linking slavery with piracy (Clifford 1993). Again, the question can be raised, what if the captured slaver *La Concorde* was swapped out for another vessel, which then sailed north as the *Queen Anne's Revenge* to terrorize Charleston? There ought to be items taken from European and American vessels after a slaver turned pirate. A listing of captured vessels should reflect these origins.

The Beaufort Inlet Wreck and *Whydah* sites yielded ceramics, including salt-glazed stoneware and redware. These are typical ceramics from Western Europe for the early eighteenth century and appear on terrestrial sites from Rhode Island to Brazil. There were also pewter objects and lead sounding weights. The barrel hoops and anchors are not distinctive, at least as far as they have been examined. The artifacts represent a generic nautical assemblage, except for the bell and the pewter plates.

Weaponry may provide clues because it is large, resistant to decay, and diagnostic for time and place. Pirate weaponry might include weapons of several nationalities and sizes. In contrast, an armed merchantman, privateer, or man-of-war would have adequate shot for a set of standardized guns. Pirates might be presumed to have a variety of weapons, captured as they upgraded their vessel and personal weapons. They may have shifted weaponry from one vessel to another to create a more powerful armament. A mix of older pieces as well as up-to-date cannon might be found. This interpretation is partially based on a 1718 pirate vessel inventory (Pennsylvania 1718) and an Alabama pirate inventory (Sands 1818) (tables 13.1 and 13.2).

The Pennsylvania inventory shows ten cannon,

two swivels, and three patereros. The patereros were obsolete by 1718, but they had particular value as rapid firing, lightly charged, antipersonnel breech loaders. The Pennsylvania inventory also suggests that the pirates planned on fighting on only one side of their ship because there were only four sponges and five pass boxes. The Pennsylvania inventory also shows thirty muskets, five blunderbusses, five pistols, and seven cutlasses, plus fifty-three hand grenades (Pennsylvania 1718). A hundred years later, an Alabama pirate vessel had a similar diverse weapons assemblage, described as "11 old guns, 10 pistols, 2 Sords [sic]" (Sands 1818).

A number of weaponry-related artifacts have been recovered from both the Beaufort Inlet wreck and *Whydah* sites. For Beaufort Inlet, these include seven cannon, touch-hole covers, smaller shot, and cannonballs ranging in size from two to twenty-four pounds. The touch-hole aprons on both sites are virtually identical (Hamilton et al. 1992:66–71), and their curvature fits recovered cannon vents. Two recovered *QAR* cannon are six-pounders. Preliminary measurements on the cannon, including at least seventeen still on site, suggest that, while there are several lengths, the bores all seem to be about four inches or two inches. These are consistent with six-pounder to nine-pounder cannon and lighter swivel guns. The range of cannon seems fairly uniform and may reflect the original armament that might have been carried aboard the slaver *La Concorde*. For Beaufort Inlet, upgraded weaponry might be questioned, because the *La Concorde* was well armed, and any newer, larger guns may have been saved prior to abandoning the *Queen Anne's Revenge*. But what if the *La Concorde* was exchanged for a better, cleaner vessel, uncontaminated with the human waste left on a slaver, before Blackbeard ran his flagship aground off Beaufort?

Cannonballs certainly reflect the diversity expected aboard a large vessel with upgraded armament, but this is misleading. The 24-pound shot on the Beaufort Inlet wreck may be intrusive, since nearby Fort Macon had eighteen 24-pounders. In 1862 Union forces attacked Beaufort Inlet and exchanged artillery fire

TABLE 13.1. PENNSYLVANIA PIRATE INVENTORY, 1718

10 Great Guns & Carriages	4 Sponges
2 Swivel Guns	2 Crows
3 Pateraroes	0 Organ Barrels
4 Chambers	7 Cutlasses
30 Muskets	5 Great Gun Cartridge Boxes
5 Blunderbusses	8 Cartridge Boxes for small arms
5 Pistols	
53 hand Granadoes	4 Old Chambers
2 Barrl. Powder	20 Guns Tackles
4 Caggs of Catridge	10 Breechins
2 Powder Horns	2 Guns, Worm & Ladle
Acct. of Sails, Rigging & Stores	
1 Main Sail	2 Runners & Tackles
1 ffore sail	a Small Quantity of Tallow
1 Jib	& Tobacco
2 fflying Jibbs	3 Compasses
1 Top Sail	1 Doctor's Chest
1 Sprit Sail	1 Black fflagg
1 Square Sail	1 Red fflagg
1 boat Main Sail & ffore Sail	2 Ensignes
22 Spare Blocks	2 Pendants
1 Topmast Stay	8 Stoppers
1 ffore halliards	1 fflying Jibb halliards
1 Topping Lift	1 main Halliards
2 Grinding Stones	1 main Down Hall
24 Water Casks	1 Jib Sheet, the other for
1 barl. of Tar & a peice [sic]	Bow fast
30 barl. of Powder	1 Flying Tack
7 Dead Eyes	1 Fish Hook & Pendant
1 Kittle	2 Pump Spears
2 iron potts	1 Broad Ax
3 Anchors	1 Wood Ax
1 Cables [sic]	1 hand saw
1 old piece of junk	1 pair of Canhooks
13 planks	1 hammer
2 Top Sail Sheets	1 Auger
1 Boom Tackle	1 plain
13 bbr. of Beef & pork	Some Iron work & Lumber

Source: Pennsylvania 1718.

TABLE 13.2. ALABAMA PIRATE INVENTORY, 1818

4 Mosquito Bar	2 pr Pantaloons
1 Piece Gingaws	2 Vest & one Coat
1 Bed Sack	9 Bags
11 Old Guns	10 Pistols
1 Spade and Hatech [sic]	2 Sords [sic]
1 Quadrant	2 Compasses
2 Charts	8 Kegs
1 Sail Bag	1 Boat with 3 sails & 9 oars
2 Hatchets	1 Hammer
1 Hand Lead	1 Small box containing Sundry Articles

Source: Sands 1818.

with Fort Macon for almost two days. During the bombardment, Fort Macon's gunners fired 24-pound shot at the Union fleet standing 1.25 miles offshore, the location of the Beaufort Inlet site. Unless a 24-pounder cannon is found on site, it is more likely that this cannonball is an 1862 Confederate projectile.

The 6-pound balls match some recovered cannon. The smaller shot could have been grape shot or have been used in the lighter swivel guns common to eighteenth-century vessels. Two possible *QAR* hand grenades might be misinterpretations. They were not solid balls; cloth impressions were on both clusters' outer matrix; and X-rays showed a variety of shot present. The *Whydah* did have hand grenades, hollow iron balls with wooden fuse plugs. Pirates also used bags of shot more than men-of-war did because they were made up easily. They wanted to capture vessels, not sink them; a premium was thus placed on disabled rigging or maimed crewmen. Bag shot was certainly used on the 1718 *Whydah*, a vessel positively identified as a pirate. Bag shot was used on privateers as late as 1814, however: "a twenty-four pounder ... was loaded with an immense quantity of grape and buck shot, balls and bullets of every description" (Savannah 1814:3).

Further examination of lead shot in concreted clusters shows several size groups, including swan

shot, buck shot, and two larger ball types in the .54–.60 and the .69–.88 caliber ranges. The shot diameters provide keys about other weaponry on board, including shoulder arms. Gun experts can identify at least three musket sizes and two pistol sizes in these ranges. Far more interesting is that all the shot above a half-inch diameter is very poorly mold cast, often misshapen, and many still have sprues. These shot were probably wasters; but instead of being recast, they were bagged for antipersonnel use.

The only *QAR* firearm recovered is a blunderbuss that could take many different shot sizes, including all those found. Other small arms have been identified by parts found in concretions, including at least one musket. Statements about the identity of Beaufort Inlet site are confirmed by examining the *Whydah*, where guns, pistols, weapons parts, a cartridge box, and shot were found.

Knives and cutlasses should be found as well, but it is hardly valid to suggest that these were present only on pirate ships. An unknown 1779 North Carolina armed merchantman that ran aground yielded a pair of swivels, several small arms, pistols, blunderbusses, and cutlasses (Virginia Gazette 1779). This salvaged goods list reads much like a pirate inventory, confirming the similarity between the two groups of seafarers:

> Sundry dry goods, consisting of a variety of articles, a parcel of nails, several small arms, pistols, blunderbusses, cutlasses, and a quantity of powder, and many other articles saved from the brigantine Dispatch, William Sarjeant master, lately chased on shore, and stranded on the coast of North Carolina. And on Thursday the 14th of October, will also be sold at the South Quay, a quantity of rum, molasses, nails, canvas, osnabrugs, etc. also the rigging and sails, part of which are quite new, with a ten inch cable also new, an anchor of 800 wt. and a pair of swivels, also saved from the said brigantine. It is hoped that the skippers on the said vessels will be so obliging as to attend at Petersburg on the above day that some measures may be adopted for adjusting their respective proportions

in the value of goods saved. (Virginia Gazette, 2 October 1779)

Information recovered to date is insufficient to support any specific identification of pirates from an artifact assemblage. Thus far, the mix of artifacts on the Beaufort Inlet site is not diagnostic for Blackbeard, except for the date. On the *Whydah*, the ship's bell was recovered, thus identifying the wreck as a ship used by pirates. Although the Beaufort Inlet artifacts may have been used by pirates, so far nothing has been identified that is specifically diagnostic for pirates as opposed to seamen in general.

Any suggested pirate ship or pirate artifact model includes precisely those items that an armed merchantman would have: a mix of cannon of different sizes, often from different nations, loaded with shot designed to damage a vessel's rigging and personnel. Personal weaponry such as pistols, cutlasses, and knives would be found on any vessel. Sailors' clothing is different from landsmen's but is neither uniform nor identifiable specifically as a pirate's. Without supporting documentation and artifacts clearly linked to a specific vessel identified as a pirate vessel, attributing any artifacts to a pirate crew is very subjective.

To return to the public imagery of pirates, what we need to find is subject to differential preservation—but it could be found. We might find a purser's cabin preserved because a barrel of tar soaked its contents. Here we might find arm hooks, wooden legs, and eye patches. If so, we might also expect the skeleton of a wooden-legged seafarer draped over the wheel, with a parrot skeleton on his shoulder. In many ways, the imagery is summarized by Clive Cussler in *Trojan Odyssey*:

She was a square-rigged barque with three masts and a shallow draft, a favorite vessel of pirates before the seventeen hundreds. The foresails and topsails were billowing in a nonexistent breeze. She mounted ten guns, five run out on the main deck on both sides. Men with bandannas around their head were standing on the quarterdeck, waving swords. High on her mainmast, a huge black flag with a fiendishly grinning skull dripping blood stood straight out as if the ship was sailing against a headwind ... "Look at the man in the scarlet suit and tell me what you see" ... "A man with a feathered hat" ... "He has a peg leg and a hook on his right hand." "Don't forget the eye patch" ... "all that's missing is a parrot on one shoulder" ... "A bit stereotyped, don't you think?" ... captain with his Treasure Island Long John Silver peg leg, Peter Pan hook and Horatio Nelson eye patch. And then there was the flag. (Cussler 2003:210–12)

Digression into fiction is not flippant. Pirate imagery was largely generated by fictional and semifictional accounts. Pirates were sailors first, and their vessels were in contemporary use. Even if it is not a pirate ship, the Beaufort Inlet site is important because it is the oldest wreck yet found in North Carolina. Pirates are just extra titillation to generate public interest and funding. Only after asking very specific questions about just what specifically distinguishes a pirate's belongings from a legal sailor's material culture will we know what is diagnostic for pirate vessels.

References

Babits, Lawrence E. and Waldemar Ossowski. 1999. 1785 Common Sailor's Clothing and a Ship's Camboose from the *General Carleton of Whitby*. In *Underwater Archaeology Proceedings from the Society for Historical Archaeology Conference, Richmond, Virginia*, edited by Adrian Askins Neidinger and Matthew A. Russell, pp. 115–22. Society for Historical Archaeology.

Barrie, James Matthew. 1987. *Peter Pan*. Mahwah, NJ: Watermill Press.

Baumgarten, Linda. 1986. *Eighteeenth-Century Clothing at Williamsburg.* Williamsburg, VA: Colonial Williamsburg.

Botting, Douglas, and the editors of Time-Life Books. 1978. *The Pirates.* The Seafarers Series. Alexandria, VA: Time-Life Books.

Clifford, Barry. 1993. *The Pirate Prince: Discovering the Priceless Treasures of the Sunken Ship Whydah.* New York: Simon and Schuster.

Cordingly, David. 1995. *Under the Black Flag: The Romance and the Reality of Life among the Pirates.* New York: Harcourt Brace.

Cussler, Clive. 2003. *Trojan Odyssey.* New York: G.P. Putnam's Sons.

Davis, Stephen. 1997. Piecing Together the Past: Footwear and Other Artefacts from the Wreck of a 16th Century Spanish Basque Galleon. In *Artefacts from Wrecks*, edited by Mark Redknap, pp 110–20. Oxbow Monograph 84. Oxford: Short Run Press.

Einarsson, Lars. 1997. Artefacts from the *Kronan* (1676): Categories, Preservation and Social Structure. In *Artefacts from Wrecks*, edited by Mark Redknap, pp 209–18. Oxbow Monograph 84. Oxford: Short Run Press.

Franzen, Anders. 1966. *The Warship Vasa: Deep Diving and Marine Archaeology in Stockholm.* Stockholm: Nordstedts Bonniers, P.A. Nordstedts and Soners Forlag.

Frazier, Charles. 1997. *Cold Mountain.* New York: Atlantic Monthly Press.

Hamilton, Christopher E., Regina Binder, and Garreth McNair-Lewis. 1992. *Final Report of Archaeological Data Recovery: Catalog/Inventory, The Whydah Shipwreck Site WLF-HA-1.* Report Submitted to US Army Corps of Engineers, Waltham, Mass., and South Chatham, Mass.: Maritime Underwater Surveys, Inc.

Johnson, Charles (Daniel Defoe). 1972. *A General History of Pyrates.* Edited by Manuel Schonhorn. Columbia: University of South Carolina Press.

Kaijser, Ingrid, Ernst Nathort-Boos, and Inga-Lill Persson. 1982. *Ur Sjomannens Kista och Tunna.* Wasastudier 10. Stockholm: Statens Sjohistoriska Museum.

Lavery, Brian. 1989. *Nelson's Navy.* Anapolis, MD: Naval Institute Press.

Lee, Robert E. 1997. *Blackbeard the Pirate: A Reappraisal of His Life and Time.* Winston-Salem, NC: John F. Blair.

McKee, Alexander. 1972. *King Henry VIII's Mary Rose.* London: Souvenir Press.

Mettas, Jean de. 1978. *Répertoire des expéditions négrières françaises au XVIIIe siècle.* Nantes, France: Société Française d'Histoire d'Outre-Mer.

Moore, David. 1989. Anatomy of a 17th Century Slave Ship: Historical and Archaeological Investigations of the *Henrietta Marie.* M.A. thesis, Department of History, East Carolina University, Greenville, NC.

Nash, Abner. 1777. Letter from Abner Nash to ?, dated 19 April 1777. *State Records of North Carolina* 11: 719–20.

Pennsylvania, 1718. Pirate Vessel Inventory. *Minutes of the Provincial Council of Pennsylvania*, vol. 3, p. 53. Philadelphia, 1852. Reprint, New York: AMS Press, 1968.

Petsche, Jerome. 1974. *The Steamboat Bertrand.* Washington, DC: Government Printing Office.

Rodger, N.A.M. 1986. *The Wooden World.* Glasgow, Scotland: Fontana Press, William Collins Sons and Company.

Rule, Margaret. 1982. *The Mary Rose: The Excavation and Raising of Henry VIII's Flagship.* Annapolis, MD: Naval Institute Press.

Sands, A.L. 1818. Inventory of Pirate's Property. A.L. Sands Papers, Yale University, New Haven, CT.

Savannah. 1814. *Republican Savannah (Georgia) and Evening Ledger,* August 20.

Skenback, Urban. 1983. *Sjofolk ock Knektar pa Wasa.* Wasastudier 11. Stockholm: Statens Sjohistoriska Museum.

Stevenson, Robert Louis. 1965. *Treasure Island.* New York: Signet, New American Library.

Virginia Gazette. 1779. *Virginia Gazette* (Williamsburg), October 2.

"The Archaeology of Religion"

Colin Renfrew

The reconstruction of ideology, including religious beliefs and practices (sometimes known as cognitive archaeology), became a major theme of research in the late twentieth century. This selection outlines some of the issues archaeologists consider and some of the practical aspects of archaeological investigations of religion. The author, Colin Renfrew, is one of the most prominent archaeologists of the past several decades. Renfrew retired from the University of Cambridge in 2004. The selection first appeared in the volume *The Ancient Mind: Elements of Cognitive Archaeology*, published in 1994.

Questions to Guide Reading

According to Renfrew, what are the key components of religion?
What are the archaeological indicators of ritual?
Why does Renfrew think burials should be considered under the rubric of religion?

Any attempt to encompass the archaeology of mind must inevitably consider the archaeological approach towards religion. For if the archaeology of mind, as envisaged in chapter 1, may be considered in terms of a series of functions of the symbol, of various ways in which symbols may operate, the role of symbols in coping with the unknown and with the supernatural is surely one of the more significant (see Renfrew and Bahn 1991: 358–63). But there is the danger here that we may carry to the inquiry our own culturally-encapsulated, and therefore perhaps stereotyped, view of what religion is. Through our acquaintance, in the first instance, with the great religions of the Book (Judaism, Christianity, Islam), all of which proclaim a unitary deity, we undoubtedly begin from a very special viewpoint. Even some acquaintance with other great, contemporary faiths such as the Buddhist, Hindu, Jam and Zoroastrian, serves in some ways to reinforce the impression of coherently codified (and thus literate), authoritative systems of belief, operating often in an urban context. A preliminary knowledge of the religious systems and the pantheons of Ancient Egypt, Greece and Rome might, at first, reinforce this view of text-based, well-delineated and formalized structures of belief. Clearly, however, the studies of cultural anthropologists have much to tell us about the religious systems of non-urban societies and of social groups operating on a basis of band or tribal organisation, so that some of these preconceptions can be counteracted and the effects of literacy discounted.

A more serious difficulty perhaps accompanies our very conceptualization of 'religion' itself, as a distinguishable, and in some senses separable, field of human activity. For we shall soon note that, from the standpoint of the archaeologist, religious activities are potentially open to observation only when they might be identifiable as religions by an observer at the time in question. Places set aside for religious observances and objects used specifically for cult purposes may, in favourable circumstances, be recognized as such. Such identification is much less easy when the locus of religious activity has a whole range of other functions, or when the artefacts used there also have other, secular uses. The problem of the 'embeddedness' of cult activity within the other activities of daily life is thus a very real one. And just as economic anthropologists warn us that the economy in simpler, non-state economies is often inextricably embedded within the matrix of the social organization, so might we anticipate that the same could apply to cult observance. The very term 'religion', conceived as a separate dimension or sub-system of the society, could thus prove to be something of a misconception, even among those communities where the supernatural plays a significant role in shaping the thoughts and actions of its individuals.

These, however, are inescapable constraints: at least we can try to be aware of them. We should therefore concede that in many societies the religious life is more varied and more widespread than we might realize, especially if it has this quality of embeddedness.

In all attempts to investigate the early past there is the risk that we first conceptualize, setting up a whole series of categories of our own construction, and then order our data (our observations bearing upon the past) in terms of such categories. The past is then presented in these terms, and it is easy to assume that our description is telling us about the way the past was and the way it was ordered. In some cases, however, all that we are seeing is a reflection and an exemplification of our own a priori categories. Such criticisms have, for instance, been made of the term 'chiefdom,' much used for a while among evolutionary anthropologists, and still useful among archaeologists. But it has been pointed out, with some justice, that it can be a cumbersome exercise to set up elaborate criteria by which a chiefdom may be recognized, and then to spend much time and effort arguing whether this culture or that society is to be regarded as a chiefdom against the standard of those criteria. The ultimate moral must be that such classifications are not useful in themselves. Classifications are of value only if they are put to some use once they are established. These cautionary thoughts are perhaps easier to formulate than they are to apply in practice, but right at the outset of our consideration of the archaeology of religion, it should be acknowledged that the very use of the category 'religion' inevitably influences some aspects of the discussion.

Aspects of Religion

Religion is not an easy term to define. But it clearly implies some framework of beliefs. These cannot, however, be restricted to general philosophic beliefs about the world or about the way it works. They must relate to forces which are not merely those of the everyday material world, but which go beyond it and transcend it.

The Shorter Oxford Dictionary offers one convenient definition (Onions 1973: 1978) for religion: 'Action or conduct indicating a belief in, or reverence for, and desire to please, a divine ruling power ... Recognition on the part of man of some higher unseen power as having control of his destiny and as being entitled to obedience, reverence and worship.' This convenient definition has many merits, but not all its components may be of universal validity. For instance, there are some oriental belief systems (such as that following Confucius) which are generally recognized as religious but which avoid specific divinities and where such powers as are postulated are immanent, not readily to be separated from other aspects of the world with which they are to be associated.

To speak of the 'supernatural' in such a case might be misleading if it were taken to imply a belief in spirits or other separable entities. But the Shorter Oxford Dictionary definition for 'supernatural' is perhaps a broadly acceptable one (Onions 1973: 2193): 'That is above nature; transcending the power of the ordinary course of nature.' Transcendence does not necessarily imply separation.

These are important and basic points. Durkheim, for instance (1965: 47) was able to define religion without reference to the supernatural (although he could not avoid the term 'sacred'). Geertz (1966: 4) offers a definition which indeed avoids the supernatural and the sacred, but which is so lacking in focus that it could apply to secular ritual or even to the system of values which is used to uphold a monetary economy. Such a definition lacks any sense of what must surely be a component of any religion: the individual religious experience.

RELIGIOUS EXPERIENCE

Central to the notion of religion is that of a personal experience for the individual which seems to him or her not only important, but of a larger significance. This is a feature carefully discussed by Rudolf Otto (1917) in a work which still makes valid points, where he laid emphasis on the sense of the numinous which he viewed as central to religious experience. It cannot be escaped that when we allow ourselves to speak of the religions of early societies we are making something of a cross-cultural assumption, namely that there was indeed some variety of numinous experience enjoyed by the members of those societies, some sense of mystery and of external, non-human power. We do not need to assert that such a power has any real existence—that is a matter for the individual's religious beliefs today. But to talk of the archaeology of religion presupposes that religious experience was available then as now. This is a point which it would be very difficult to demonstrate, although such an experience is certainly perfectly plausible as a motivating

force for some of the symbolic monuments which we may observe from the past. But the existence of such an experience in the past seems to be an assumption which the student of early religion has to make: there is a uniformitarian assumption there which needs to be recognized.

This is a question which I believe was largely avoided by Durkheim, and then less subtly (and less successfully) by Geertz, in the discussions cited above. Both avoided placing such religious experience as a central feature of their definition of religion, preferring instead to see religion rather as a social phenomenon. But it seems to me that when we are speaking of the belief systems of other people, while we do not need, ourselves, to share or even to understand those beliefs very well, we can scarcely avoid the view that they, the participants in the culture, did indeed themselves believe them. While other aspects of the diagram offered by Rappaport (1971a, 1971b) may be open to discussion, the place within it of religious experience seems appropriate.

MYSTERY AND PURPOSE IN THE HUMAN CONDITION

Every religion, by definition, involves a system of beliefs which offers answers to profound existential questions. Indeed most religions provide, at the individual and at the collective level, answers to those basic existential questions posed so effectively by Paul Gauguin in the title to one of his canvasses: 'Where do we come from? Where are we? Where are we going?' Most religious systems offer a coherent view of the nature of the present world, of the origins of the world and of future human destiny. At a personal level also the mysteries of birth, death and of what happens after death, are resolved.

It should be noted here that the answers supplied by religious belief systems to these questions, and in particular those of origin, are often provided in mythological form. The 'answer' takes the form of a history, a kind of historical narrative. But the personages are not simply historical people. They have a greater significance, indeed for the community or culture in question a universal significance. The answers to general questions are not general propositions, as they have become for us in the aftermath of the scientific revolution, following Descartes and Newton. They are specific, narrative propositions, as Frankfort *et al.* (1949) have so clearly shown. But they do serve to answer the questions.

Most religions indicate also how we can take steps to harmonize with the world, and often, through this process how we, through our actions (or our prayers) can influence the world in a manner favourable to our own aspirations. Such concerns lead naturally to ethical concerns, towards beliefs about how our actions

should be governed. And consequent upon a view of how we should regulate our own actions comes the notion of social sanctions to ensure that they do indeed conform with such precepts and, in some cases, the notion of divine sanctions towards the same end.

Archaeological recovery of these belief systems may, in most cases, be exceedingly difficult. But it is a principal purpose of the present discussion to identify various aspects inherent within most or all religions, which we can expect to accompany those other aspects which may be more readily identifiable in the archaeological record.

As we shall see below, iconographic representation is one of the most promising routes towards

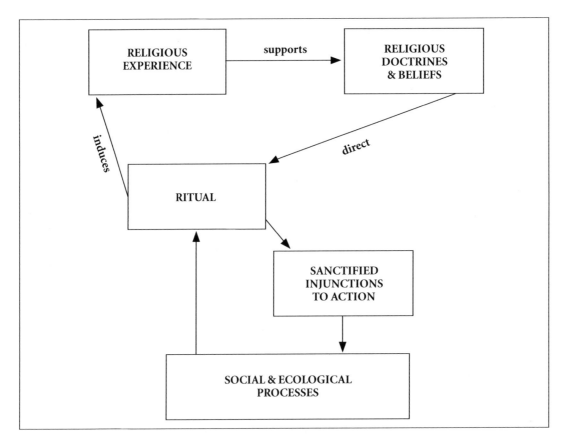

FIGURE 6.1: Religion as interpreted by Rappaport: beliefs direct ritual which induces religious experience. (After Renfrew and Bahn 1991: 358.)

the detail of some belief systems. Interpretations may often be difficult but, in some cases, we may be able to detect reference to what may be recurrent (although not, of course, universal) themes across cultures. One such theme, the passage of the 'soul' or 'spirit' after corporeal death, is familiar in Christian iconography through depictions of the judgement day, of which the celebrated 'Last Judgement' by Michelangelo is one of the more recent. Analogous concepts may be found in Mesoamerican depictions, and they are, of course, a recurrent preoccupation in the mural decoration of Egyptian tombs and sarcophagi, as well as in papyrus texts of the Book of the Dead.

THE SOCIAL ASPECT

Central to the notion of religion, although not well brought out in the definition by Onions cited earlier, is the circumstance that it is a *shared* belief system. Religion in this sense implies a community of believers: Durkheim (1965) speaks of 'beliefs and practices which unite into one single moral community called a Church, all those who adhere to them'.

This view of religion as a social and cultural phenomenon is naturally one which preoccupies the cultural anthropologist. It is, of course, important to the archaeologist who, as noted earlier, hopes to define actions, ritual actions, which were carried out at specific places in special ways. The setting apart of the place, and the special distinctive manner of the actions, will always be important for the detection process, the recognition process undertaken by the archaeologist. Of course Durkheim intended the term 'church' purely in the social sense, to indicate a community of persons. But the term 'church' in our language, as in several others, implies also a special place dedicated by those persons for special activities, rituals, undertaken in relationship to the beliefs shared by that community. These activities are, in most religions, formalized. They are carefully prescribed and accompanied also by proscriptions (things which must not be done, forbidden words, taboos). As

noted, they often take place in special places, in the manner established by tradition and by doctrine. They are also coherently time-structured: they take place at special times of day, on special days of the week and at special occasions in the year.

These generalizations are of crucial importance to the archaeologist, although there has been very little broad, theoretical discussion of them. For it is usually through the investment of effort into the construction of special places (whose remains may be preserved), through the use of special equipment in rituals at those places (which may also be preserved), in the development of iconic representations for use in such places, and in some cases through the depiction of such rituals, that we have our principal insights into past religions. These matters are further discussed in the next section.

Another important and very interesting social aspect of most religions is that the belief system, as it relates to the supernatural, is inevitably related in some ways to the social reality of the culture. Karl Marx, one of the first thinkers to deal seriously with the sociology of thought (Marx and Engels 1977) saw the religious beliefs of a society as part of the ideological superstructure which he viewed as arising from the relations of production within a given social formation. One does not need to follow all his assumptions to see that there is much in this idea. Whether man is made in the image of God or vice versa, it is certainly the case that the deities of many human societies have been conceived of as anthropomorphic, although animal gods (theriomorphic) are at least as common. The notion of a hierarchy of divinities is one which comes more easily to a society which is itself hierarchically structured, for instance to a state society. It is difficult to imagine such a feature in an egalitarian society organized at band level.

THE FUNCTIONS AND CONSEQUENCES OF RELIGION

Various thinkers have considered religious systems not from the standpoint of the content of their belief structures nor of their communal behaviour, but in terms of their consequences for society as a whole. Within the Marxist view, for instance, with its emphasis upon class antagonisms, religion is viewed as a means, developed by the elite, for the manipulation of the masses. Within most state societies it is indeed the case that the ruler (the 'king') has a special place in relation to the leading religious specialist (the 'chief priest') and in many state societies the two offices converge (the 'priest-king'), sometimes with the deity ruling through this head of state (a theocracy), or at least inspiring and sanctioning his actions (the 'divine right' of kings). Marxist archaeologists have also applied such ideas to societies generally regarded as essentially egalitarian, where, for instance, the elders are seen as using religious beliefs to ensure their own favoured and privileged position in relation to younger members of society (Tilley 1984). A very different view of religion is taken by anthropologists working broadly in the 'functionalist' tradition of Malinowski, for whom religious beliefs and rituals are useful in governing and regulating various aspects of the social system (e.g., Rappaport 1971a). The earlier 'functionalist' view saw religion as useful in ensuring the smooth functioning of society by ensuring some considerable degree of community of belief, some acceptance of the social system and hence some general social solidarity among members of the community. More recent work, notably by Rappaport, would accord religious beliefs a further, more active role, in bringing into play mechanisms of a broadly homeostatic nature whose timing is governed by ritual.

A further, broadly evolutionary, perspective has been proposed by Lachmann (1983) who contrasts the variability in all human behaviour with that among species where quite complicated social behaviour is genetically determined, for instance among bees. In his perspective there are enormous advantages in cultural evolution, precisely in the special human ability to learn, and thus to change the whole behaviour of society in the space of just a couple of generations. But there are penalties too, in terms of lack of stability of behaviour and in the risk that valuable information, no longer stored in the genome, may become lost between generations. It is here that the devices used by religion for the very long-term storage of information may be particularly useful. For, as Lachmann stresses, it is through religion that 'ancient wisdom' is most effectively stored and transmitted. Much of the repetition associated with religious ritual may be regarded as 'redundant' in the information theory sense, and secure transmission is thereby more adequately assured. It is the case that the oral transmission of religious knowledge has been shown to be enormously effective. The Hymns of the Rigveda, recorded in archaic Vedic Sanskrit, were preserved orally for many centuries before being set down in writing about the fifth century BC at a time when classical Sanskrit was already in use. Much of their vocabulary was by that time not well understood, but later scholarly study has shown the accuracy of transmission to be remarkably high. This gives support to Lachmann's view that a coherent religious system, with its high survival value, confers a selective advantage upon the society which possesses it.

In general, the wider effects of religious beliefs have been little considered by archaeologists. Yet clearly frameworks of religious belief provided strong motivational contexts for many aspects of the behaviour of ancient societies. This has been well documented, for instance, for the case of the ancient Maya (Schele and Miller 1986) and the role of sacred concepts, both in the development of urbanism and in its specific forms, has been emphasized by a number of authors, including Wheatley (1971). For the traditional Marxist historian these may be mere epiphenomena, where the superstructure follows the economic infrastructure, but neo-Marxist thinkers are inclined to give greater causal weight to ideational factors. For the functionalist there is a similar inclination to see symbolic factors as contributing to greater efficiency in the culture system and thus having an adaptive value, but perhaps not much more than this. Such a view seems related to the Binfordian notion that ideational and religious aspects are akin to 'palaeopsychology' (see chapter 1), and that more basic causal factors reside in the ecological relationship between humans and their environment.

Today, however, within the framework of cognitive-processual archaeology, such assessments seem deficient. It is no longer sufficient to see the ideational component of early societies (including their religions) as simply some superstructural reflection of the more substantial infrastructure, albeit one that is readily subverted by the dominant elite in their ceaseless application of the class war. Nor can religion be seen as purely and simply a device for promoting efficiency, or even for lengthening the memory span of society within an evolutionary context. The causes of religious change are not well understood and, indeed, have scarcely been addressed in any coherent way. Even the notion of the evolution (in the sense of gradual, endogenously-produced change) of religious beliefs and practices has scarcely been developed. It is often, in practice, widely assumed that any new religious form has an outside origin; the local factors favouring or resisting change have not yet been analysed in detail. But the religious system of an early society can no longer be considered a secondary factor in the explanation of culture change.

Recognizing Religion

Some of the foregoing discussion may seem a shade premature, when it is quite evident that the identification and elucidation of early cult practices from the archaeological record is a challenging task, and the analysis of the belief systems which sustain them an even more difficult problem. The appropriate methodology for these tasks is only now being developed, and the focus of attention has so far been upon the recognition of cult (Renfrew 1985: chapter 1; Renfrew and Bahn 1991) rather than upon any attempted inference towards the belief system underlying it. So far, as we shall see in the next section, this has been examined largely in the context of the analysis of the iconography of depictions in which aspects of the world are figuratively represented.

Constraints of space preclude the detailed analysis here of the problems which face the archaeologist seeking to identify sanctuaries or other places devoted primarily to cult practice and to recognize the equipment of cult. The nub of the matter was touched on above, in the discussion of the social aspect of religion. As noted, it is, in general, only where religious practices involve either the use of special artefacts or special places, or both, that we can hope to discern them archaeologically. The logic of the inquiry must, I believe, start from the general properties of religious belief and of cult practice as discussed in the earlier section. This is not to assert that all the belief systems involved are similar or even comparable, but it does imply that the term 'religion' carries with it certain correlates which are certainly general if not necessarily universal and by which the investigation can be advanced. I have argued (Renfrew 1985) that cult observances employ a range of attention focusing devices. When sacred ritual takes place, it is situated at the boundary between this world and the other, supernatural world: the very act of religious observance ensures that the celebrant is situated within this liminal zone or boundary area which itself possesses certain characteristic features. And the purpose of much religious ritual is to secure the attention (if one may put it that way) of the deity or of the transcendental forces which are invoked. This, in general, requires the active participation of the celebrants in speech acts (or song acts) and in a range of ritually determined actions, which may also involve the making of offerings, whether of food or drink, or of material goods. Such considerations as these can allow the formulation of a series of indicators, which can reasonably suggest to the archaeologist that religious ritual has taken place. It is not intended that these should be used as a mechanical check list, nor is any particular 'score' to be regarded as conclusive. But any archaeological recognition of ritual and hence of religion, is likely to be based upon such indications, as well as upon information from representational schemes of painting or other depictions, and on information from such texts as may survive.

Archaeological indicators of ritual (from Renfrew and Bahn 1991: 359–60)

Focusing of attention

(1) Ritual may take place in a spot with special, natural associations (e.g., a cave, a grove of trees, a spring or a mountain-top).
(2) Alternatively, ritual may take place in a special building set apart for sacred functions (e.g., a temple or church).
(3) The structure and equipment used for the ritual may employ attention-focusing devices, reflected in the architecture, special fixtures (e.g., altars, benches, hearths) and in movable equipment (e.g., lamps, gongs and bells, ritual vessels, censers, altar cloths, and all the paraphernalia of ritual).
(4) The sacred zone is likely to be rich in repeated symbols (i.e., 'redundancy').

Boundary zone between this world and the next

(5) Ritual may involve both conspicuous public display (and expenditure) and hidden exclusive mysteries, whose practice will be reflected in the architecture.
(6) Concepts of cleanliness and pollution may be reflected in the facilities (e.g., pools or basins of water) and maintenance of the sacred area.

Presence of the deity

(7) The association with a deity or deities may be reflected in the use of a cult image or a representation of the deity in abstract form (e.g., the Christian Chi-Rho symbol).
(8) The ritualistic symbols will often relate iconographically to the deities worshipped and to their associated myth. Animal symbolism (of real or mythical animal) may often be used,

with particular animals relating to specific deities or powers.

(9) The ritualistic symbols may relate to those seen also in funerary ritual and in other rites of passage.

Participation and offering

(10) Worship will involve prayer and special movements—gestures of adoration—and these may be reflected in the art or iconography or decorations or images.
(11) The ritual may employ various devices for inducting religious experience (e.g., dance, music, drugs and the infliction of pain).
(12) The sacrifice of animals or humans may be practised.
(13) Food and drink may be brought and possibly consumed as offerings or burned/poured away.
(14) Other material objects may be brought and offered (votives). The act of offering may entail breaking and hiding or discard.
(15) Great investment of wealth may be reflected both in the equipment used and in the offerings made.
(16) Great investment of wealth and resources may be reflected in the structure itself and its facilities.

These then are some of the categories of information which may be useful to the archaeologist. It is not, however, the presence or absence of specific diagnostic criteria of this kind which are significant, but rather the documentation of repeated actions of a symbolic nature which are directed, it may be inferred, towards non-terrestrial and therefore transcendent forces.

The negative form employed in the term 'non-terrestrial' has a wider implication. For if a given practice, which might otherwise be taken to have a religious function, can be explained in other, 'functional' terms, such an explanation is likely to be the preferred one. I am not confident of the logical strength of that assertion, but it certainly reflects the prevailing process of archaeological inference whereby, if a feature cannot plausibly be explained in rational, 'functional' terms, then it may be ascribed a 'ritual' function. The archaeological category 'ritual' thus often becomes an essentially residual one, defined principally by the absence of something else, namely a good alternative explanation. The purpose of the foregoing list of indications is to counter, in part, this prevailing attitude. But at the last analysis, is that attitude altogether misguided?

The question is complicated further by the important and difficult question of play. For it is the very nature of actions undertaken in play that they are in some sense symbolic. In many cases they mimic other actions, and in that sense represent and thus symbolize them. In other cases the play is undertaken following well-defined rules. These are rules which generate repetitions (redundancies) of action and often give rise to special modes of behaviour including gestures which may be analogous to those of ritual. Play will certainly use attention-focusing devices and often involves the participation of most of those present. Special equipment is used, very much as for religious rituals, and play often takes place in a special location which, while not precisely a 'liminal zone' in the sense used earlier, may nonetheless partake of some of its qualities. When, for instance, the play is conducted between potentially hostile teams, it may have to take place on neutral ground which is, indeed, in a boundary area of some kind. For all these reasons, the distinction between play and religious ritual is, in practice, a difficult one archaeologically, just as is the distinction between toys and cult images (although the two categories need not be entirely exclusive anyway). At a last analysis it may well be found that in several ways play and religious (and other) ritual are indeed homomorphic: that is to say they share the same forms. Both are symbolic, metaphorical. Perhaps therefore they are not always exclusive. Certainly religious rituals may often have as participants individuals who do not subscribe

fully to the belief systems which those rituals are supposed to proclaim. Is such participation so different from play? And while a high seriousness of purpose, and dedication towards a transcendental entity, may well be the key discriminating factor between them play too can be a serious business. In Mexico as in Turkey, lives have been lost in recent years in disputes between supporters of rival football teams.

A further area of human activity also deserves to be brought into the discussion at this point: burial. The disposal of the dead is generally considered, by archaeologists, under a different rubric from that of religion. This may be the case because burials, like death, are of frequent occurrence. But that is hardly a persuasive reason. Nearly every burial, however, constitutes a highly symbolic act. That is to say it has a purpose not simply to get rid of a lifeless and possibly noisome corpse (which can be done in a number of effective and inexpensive ways). Many burials involve a considerable investment of effort and the use of well-defined symbolism. Of course the investment, as has been well argued, may have the twin objectives of enhancing the status of the person undertaking it (the person doing the burying, rather than the one who gets buried) and of securing rights to the property of the deceased. Neither of these need involve religious concepts. But at the same time, where there is a belief in an afterlife, it is likely to have an influence upon the details of the practice of burial. Other aspects of the burial may also be symbolic of the world-view of the community since burial is the last of all rites of passage and the most permanent.

So far most of the discussion by archaeologists seeking a theoretical context within which to consider burial has centred upon the social questions touched upon above: questions of prestige, of social persona and of property (Binford 1971; Saxe 1970; Chapman, Kinnes and Randsborg 1981). The emphasis has been very much upon 'tombs for the living' to use Fleming's telling phrase (Fleming 1973). But it is easily forgotten, amongst all this Binfordian talk, that tombs may indeed also be for the dead. Their construction and the other circumstances of burial may reflect (and have a role in developing) a belief system relating as much to eternal values as to the present secular world. Moreover, it may not be unduly naive to bypass the cynicism of Marx and to suggest that many members of society actually did hold the purported beliefs in question—persons of high rank as well as low. The celebrated paper by Ucko on this topic (Ucko 1969), in its presentation of many different circumstances and of varied responses to circumstances, served to give the impression that the relationship between form of burial, form of religious belief and form of society was in general not a coherently patterned one. But while the relationships may certainly differ, that need not imply that patterning is lacking. There is much to learn, I believe, about ancient belief systems, including systems of religious belief, by drawing on the detailed study of ancient burial practices. The relationships remain to be investigated in a systematic way.

The Iconography of Religion

The most coherent insights into the belief systems of the past must come, if we exclude from the discussion the information available from written texts, from the analysis of symbolic systems. In such systems a coherent, non-verbal language is employed in such a way that someone familiar with the conventions can understand the significance of the symbols (i.e., what they signify). In many cases the propositions which are asserted are not novel: the principle of redundancy in religious ritual extends to representation, and the divine sentences may be repeated just as often and as authoritatively as the calligraphic inscriptions in an Islamic holy place.

Nor need it follow that the symbols which we seek to understand are directly representational in the figurative sense. It is not necessary that we recognize human beings, or deities, or forms which depict entities already known to us from the world of nature. Recently I spent a very interesting afternoon with George Eogan examining the incised schemata visible on the kerbstones which surround the great passage grave of Knowth in the Boyne Valley in Ireland (Eogan 1986). Although the precise significance of these designs is not yet clear—that is to say what, as signs, they signify—there is the strong intuition, not yet made formally explicit, that there is in operation here some coherent system, consistently used.

Much the same can be said for the cup-and-ring markings of the British Bronze Age which have recently been subjected to study by Richard Bradley (this volume). The close study of the contexts of occurrence may, in favourable cases, reveal correlations which give indications of the way these symbols were used. As noted in chapter 1, to seek to attain their meaning in any complete sense (as it would have been understood by their makers) is hardly a feasible undertaking.

More complex figurative systems, although rarer, may offer commensurately greater rewards (in the sense of more complex analyses of 'meaning', when that term is understood in the more restricted sense of limited but coherent interpretation, rather than comprehensive insight). Constraints of space prevent a fuller discussion here of these problems, for which a coherent methodology has not in any case yet been established.

It is already clear, however, that the interpretation of complicated figurative schemes depends crucially upon the successful identification of the successive representations of repeatedly occurring individuals, whether these are humans, deities or mythological persons. In favourable circumstances a clue may be given by specific attributes, such as those which accompany individual saints in Christian iconography (often the instruments of martyrdom, as for St Catherine of Alexandria and her wheel). In the Maya case, the juxtaposition of specific glyphs along with royal representations has now allowed the elucidation of what are, in effect, narrative cycles for the reigns of individual kings (Schele and Miller 1986). The great fresco cycles in Byzantine churches can certainly be read in this way, although it must be admitted that in such cases it certainly helps the viewer to know the basic story first. Indeed, in many cases where depictions are used in a religious context, their role is to reinforce what is already known and perhaps to act as a mnemonic. Partly for this reason they may not always supply sufficient information to make reasonable inferences possible for the uninitiated.

For the archaeologist, for whom such symbolic material is rarely abundant, one crucial question is the extent to which evidence from different sites may justifiably be brought together under simultaneous consideration, to provide a corpus of material sufficient to allow for systematic analysis. The analogy may perhaps be drawn with a number of small archives, each consisting of just a few tablets found at various different sites, and all in what is thought to be a single script. To what extent can this body of material be amalgamated? In the case of written records the answer can be provided internally, as it were, by close study of the script employed on the tablets from the various locations whose unity or diversity can thus be evaluated. In the case of iconic representations, however, the answer is not always so clear. This question is equivalent to asking whether the same system of beliefs, and the same symbolic system for linking the signifier and the thing signified, are in operation at the various sites. A categorical answer is not always possible, but where a considerable range of specific symbols is found in each location, with a good degree of overlap between them, it may be reasonable to infer, in some instances, that a single coherent system is in operation.

These are crucial questions for the archaeological interpretation of data bearing upon early religions. They, and others like them, have not, in general, yet been very clearly addressed. As noted in chapter 1, the methodology of cognitive-processual archaeology is still underdeveloped. But already it is clear that in many cases there is patterning there among the data. This is an inviting field of study.

References

Binford, L.R. 1971. Mortuary practices: their study and potential. In *Approaches to the social dimensions of mortuary practices*, ed. J.A. Brown, pp. 6–29 (Memoirs of the Society for American Archaeology 25).

Chapman, R., I. Kinnes and K. Randsborg (eds.) 1981. *The archaeology of death*. Cambridge, Cambridge University Press.

Durkheim, E. 1965. *The elementary forms of religious life* (translated by J.W. Swain). New York, Free Press [first published 1912].

Eogan, G. 1986. *Knowth and the passage-tombs of Ireland*. London, Thames and Hudson.

Fleming, A. 1973. Tombs for the living. *Man* 8: 177–93.

Frankfort, H., H.A. Frankfort, J.A. Wilson and T. Jacobsen 1949. *Before philosophy*. Harmondsworth, Penguin [first published in 1946 as *The intellectual adventure of ancient man*, Chicago, University of Chicago Press].

Geertz, C. 1966. Religion as a cultural system. In *Anthropological approaches to the study of religion* (ASA Monographs 3), ed. M. Banton, pp. 1–46. London, Tavistock.

Lachmann, P.J. 1983. Why religions? An evolutionary view of the behaviour of bees and men. *Cambridge Review*, 28 January 1983: 22–6.

Marx, K. and F. Engels 1977. *The German ideology* (edited by C.J. Arthur). London, Lawrence and Wishart.

Onions, C.T. (ed.) 1973. *The shorter Oxford dictionary*. Oxford, Clarendon Press.

Otto, R. 1959. *The idea of the holy*. Harmondsworth, Penguin (1st edn, 1917).

Rappaport, R.A. 1971a. Ritual, sanctity and cybernetics. *American Anthropologist* 73: 59–76.

———. 1971b. The sacred in human evolution. *Annual Review of Ecology and Systematics* 2: 23–44.

Renfrew, C. 1985. *The archaeology of cult*. London, Thames and Hudson.

Renfrew, C. and P. Bahn 1991. *Archaeology, theories, methods and practice*. London, Thames and Hudson.

Saxe, A.A. 1970. Social dimensions of mortuary practices. Ph.D. dissertation, University of Michigan.

Schele, L. and M.E. Miller 1986. *The blood of kings, dynasty and ritual in Maya art*. New York, Brazilier.

Tilley, C. 1984. Ideology and the legitimation of power in the Middle Neolithic of Sweden. In *Ideology, power and prehistory*, ed. D. Miller and C. Tilley, pp. 111–46. Cambridge, Cambridge University Press.

Ucko, P. 1969. Ethnography and archaeological interpretation of funerary remains. *World Archaeology* 1: 262–80.

Wheatley, P. 1971. *The pivot of the four quarters*. Edinburgh, Edinburgh University Press.

PART 5

Explaining Things of Archaeological Interest

Introduction

Why do some cultural patterns such as warfare, the origins of agriculture, and the collapse of civilizations occur in some circumstances but not in others? As all students of archaeology will inevitably realize, consensus rarely exists about the answers to these questions. Facts never speak for themselves, and numerous things may influence archaeologists' interpretations, including the framework they use to research a topic, the kinds of evidence they search for, and their and assumptions and biases.

In this final part of the reader, the selections by Peter Kosso and Richard Wilk were chosen to provide some basic understanding about the nature of archaeological explanations. The selections by Stephen Lekson, Brian Hayden, and Jared Diamond provide some examples of those explanations.

"The Epistemology of Archaeology"

Peter Kosso

This selection gives some insight into scholarly archaeological reasoning. It was written by Peter Kosso, a professor in the department of philosophy at Northern Arizona University, and originally appeared in the edited volume *Archaeological Fantasies: How Pseudoarchaeology Misrepresents the Past and Misleads the Public*, published in 2006.

....

Questions to Guide Reading

What is Kosso's stated purpose in writing the selection?
What are the inherent difficulties in knowing what happened, when it happened, and why?
How can these difficulties be overcome using material evidence?
What is meant by the phrase "the epistemology of archaeology"?
What makes one belief more justifiable than another in archaeology?
When considering the pyramids at Giza, why is the standard model considered the best?
What are some of the problems with the standard model for explaining the pyramids?
What are the problems with the alternative model proposed by Graham Hancock and
   Robert Bauval?

....

Knowledge welcomes challenges. If we claim to know something, rather than simply believe it or think it or wish it, we must be willing to confront potentially challenging evidence and alternative ideas. This is not merely a politeness but a prerequisite to the distinction between knowledge and opinion, and it is true for new, hypothetical ideas as well as for well-established, widely believed ideas.

The responsibility for accepting a challenge comes with the right to claim knowledge. But this does not mean that theorizing in science, archaeology, or history is a free-for-all of skepticism where nothing can be known because everything can be challenged. There are definite standards of appropriate challenge and standards for evaluating how well a challenge has been met. We can tell what counts as good evidence and how evidence supports or undermines a theory. And we can assess the relevance between different ideas to see if they are compatible or contradictory, supportive or refuting. In other words, we can tell and we can agree to what extent the appropriate challenges to a theory have been met and hence to what extent we are justified in believing the theory.

The purpose of this introductory chapter is to demonstrate that these standards of justification exist and to clarify what they are. With a focus on archaeology and the use of material evidence to know what happened in the human past, we will see that there are ways to distinguish plausible from implausible theories. Some descriptions of the human past are more likely than others to be accurate. Assessing the likelihood of accuracy is the topic of this chapter.

There are two parts to the chapter. The first is a general account of the epistemology of the human past, that is, an outline of how archaeological knowledge is possible and how it works. This starts with a description of the inherent difficulties in knowing what happened, when, and why. And it continues with a look at how those difficulties can be overcome using material and in some cases textual evidence. The key is an understanding of the criteria of credible, meaningful evidence and of the procedures and standards of acceptability of a theory about the past. The second part of the chapter is a brief application of the epistemology to the specific case of the pyramids at Giza. Who built the pyramids, when, how, and for what purpose? It is not so much the answers to these questions that are the concern here as it is the reasons for believing the answers. Why is one account of the ancient Egyptian pyramids more justified, more likely to be accurate, than the others? This is the question we will answer.

The Epistemology of Archaeology

Epistemology is the systematic study of knowledge. The key concern is to distinguish knowledge, on the one hand, from mere belief, opinion, dogma, and wishful thinking, on the other. This distinction is described under the concept of justification, the good reason for believing something to be true. Justification of a belief, the modern rendition of Plato's epistemic requirement of a *logos*, is about meeting the standards of evidence and reason that indicate likelihood of accuracy (Plato *Theaetetus* 201d). Meeting the standards of justification never guarantees the truth, the accuracy of a belief. Humans are not that good at knowing. Justification is not foolproof, and it comes in degrees. Beliefs, descriptive claims about aspects of the world, can be more or less justified. I know, for example, that the table before me has four legs. This is a highly justified claim. I also know that this same table is made of atoms and they in turn are made of quarks and electrons. This claim has some justification (it is not pure guesswork) but less justification than the claim about the number of legs.

The business of epistemology is to show that there is a correlation between being more justified and being more likely to be true. Justification is therefore most useful as a comparative rather than absolute tool. When given a choice between conflicting descriptions of the same thing, the reasonable thing to do is to endorse the more justified.

Justification comes in degrees, but truth does not. A proposition, a descriptive claim about some aspect of the world, is either true or false. This table either has four legs, or it does not. But justification for the claim comes in degrees. In fact, I have more justification for the truth of this claim than you do, since I can see the four legs directly, while you are relying on the good faith of my testimony. Maybe one of the legs broke off years ago, and I have propped that corner up on a stack of books. The amount of justification for a claim will depend on the amount and quality of evidence, and on the compatibility of the claim with other things in one's network of understanding (for example, your general understanding of the concept of a table, the tendency of people like me to salvage broken furniture, and so on).

More justification is better, since it raises the likelihood of accuracy. But it is certainly possible for a well-justified belief to be false. Based on the evidence of dark clouds, the sound of thunder, and the fact of a thunder shower every afternoon for the past week, I am very justified in believing that it is about to rain on me. The belief is justified but false if the storm happens to miss me this time. It is the task of the systematic disciplines, the natural sciences, studies of the past such as history and archaeology, and the like, to refine carefully the content of justification, the evidence and the network of theoretical beliefs, to bring justification into ever closer correlation with truth.

There is no certainty in science, in archaeology, or in life. Any claim that transcends immediate experience or basic logic is at risk of being wrong. You anticipate that first sip of orange juice in the morning, knowing that it will be both tasty and healthy. But even this is to some small degree uncertain, since all your evidence is of previous encounters with orange juice, not this one. It is conceivable, though very unlikely, that something has changed, in orange juice or in your own body, that will affect how your body interacts with the drink. We live with this degree of uncertainty in our daily lives, and we still claim to know that orange juice is safe and good to drink.

The point about uncertainty and knowledge and orange juice is to preempt a common fallacy, which is a fallacy to argue (or assume) that since there is no certainty, there is no reason to believe anything. The most common form of this fallacy is the argument (or assumption) that since no descriptive claim about the world is justified with certainty, then all descriptive claims are alike in the sense that any one is as justified as any other. This often then cascades into an opportunity to endorse one's own wishful thinking or to indulge in imagination or even political expediency. If all ideas are equal, then why not believe mine? But not all ideas are equal. There is more reason to believe some than others, even if none is perfectly justified to the point of certainty. I suppose, for example, that the idea of bacteria causing disease is somewhat uncertain. Few people actually see these things in action destroying cells. But I will have my surgery in sterile conditions rather than in the garage. The degrees of justification are important.

Knowing that we must attend to the degrees of justification of beliefs, we now need to understand what makes a belief more justified, particularly in the case of archaeology.

THE CHALLENGES TO KNOWLEDGE

Consider the challenges to justifying the everyday knowledge of our present surroundings, for that will put the challenge of archaeology into helpful perspective. What we see, the evidence of the world around us, is a series of episodic images of the surfaces of things, images that change as we move around and change our own perspective. But what we claim to know is a world of enduring, three-dimensional objects that exist independent of us and our way of looking at them. There is an informational gap between the appearance of things and the reality we know, and somehow we manage to cross the gap by using the evidence (the appearances) and our ability to reason.

The situation is similar, although perhaps more challenging, in science. Here the knowledge claims are more ambitious in that they stray further from what is immediately observed. Things like black holes, curved space-time, and the long process of biological evolution are not only unobserved, they are largely unobservable (although evolutionary microbial adaptation is observable). The theoretical descriptions are based on observations and evidence, or it would not be science. But it is important to note that the observations themselves are influenced by theory. Scientific evidence, after all, is neither haphazard nor uninterpreted, and some prior conceptual understanding of nature will inform decisions about what to observe, which observations are credible, what the observation means, and how what is observed is causally (and hence informationally) linked to what is not observed. Theory is necessary to turn mindless sensations into meaningful evidence. This is a warning against a pure or naive empiricism as a model of scientific method. Observations are not foundational in the sense of being of indubitable epistemic authority. Justification does not flow just one way, from evidence to theory. The epistemic relation is reciprocal in that (revisable) theoretical information is used to make the most of observation, which is in turn used to suggest and test theories.

The predicament is the same for knowledge of the human past, where the people and events of interest are unobservable. What we do observe is evidence in textual and physical remains. Each of these forms of evidence has its strengths and its weaknesses. Textual evidence, the currency of history, ranges from something as candid and mundane as a shopping list to more self-conscious and remarkable records such as treaties and historical narratives. It has the potential to be explicit and precise, telling us just what people were doing and what was on their minds. But historical evidence is intentional in a way that archaeological evidence is not. Writers in the past could choose what they wanted to disclose and how it should sound. This makes the written record vulnerable to a subjectivity under the influence of the people in the past, people with ideas and values that we might not understand. Material evidence, the stuff of archaeology, is less at risk of this complication, since it is largely unintended. Archaeology often amounts to digging through rubbish and wreckage, what remains of daily life, not because it was chosen for posterity but because certain conditions have left it intact. Thus archaeology can offer a more candid image of the past, but it is generally less clear and less explicit than the textual record. Material evidence requires more interpretation. It usually takes an expert, that is, someone with sufficient background knowledge to call on, to tell us what a particular object is, how old it is, how it was used, and so on. Archaeological finds give up information about the past only if we have some contextual information to add into the interpretative process.

Interpretation of evidence is key in both history and archaeology. What we find, that is, what can be observed, must be described in terms intelligible to us. We have to describe the past in our own terms, with our own conceptual categories, so we risk importing some of our own values. This means that we risk imposing ourselves on the past, seeing and describing it as our own world in different circumstances. It presents a challenge to distinguish between discovery and invention, between finding out what really happened and making things up in a way that accommodates our own sensibilities.

The subjective component of using our own concepts and background knowledge to interpret the past is unavoidable. But the goal is to understand the past on its own terms, to get information from the past itself. This is an aspect of what Thomas Kuhn called the "essential tension," the need to impose some old information on evidence in order to get new information out (Kuhn 1977). It is an essential part of the challenge to discovering things about nature or the human past.

It is important to be realistic about the challenges to knowledge in archaeology. We should neither underestimate nor exaggerate them. Evaluating archaeological claims is not as easy as a directive to get some evidence, and if there is none then your claim is false or if there is any at all then your claim is true. It is more challenging, and more complicated, than this. Evidence comes in degrees of indirectness, and hence degrees of authority. Evidence must be interpreted. And we need to understand how evidence meets theory, that is, what it is to confirm or falsify a theory.

But it is not impossible to meet the challenges, to deal with the essential tension, and to use evidence to distinguish the more from the less justified archaeological claims. There are many cases where we can clearly tell that the requirements of justification are being met. The claim that there was a Nazi Holocaust is clearly justified. The claim that there were New World civilizations before the arrival of Europeans is clearly justified. And so on. But then there are cases where we still struggle for justification, for example in determining how long human beings have been in the Americas. A good strategy for epistemology is to examine the successful cases to distill the methods and standards of appraisal at work there, and then apply those to the troublesome cases.

All of this talk about justification as an indication of a match between what we say happened and the facts of what really happened presumes that there are definitive facts. We do not create facts about the past by virtue of producing descriptions, any more than we create events in the present simply by describing them. There are facts about much of what happens in the present, and we have thoughts, motives, and values regarding what happens. To suppose less of people in the past would be a kind of arrogance.

The facts of the past are independent of us. The goal is to create descriptions that match, and to be able to tell when we have got one that matches. Different situations differ in degree of difficulty, from the account of basic physical events to the understanding of motives and values. The degree of difficulty changes from case to case, but the basic method of justification remains the same. It is that basic method, the way that archaeology can assess the credibility of claims about the past, that we turn to next.

MEETING THE CHALLENGES

Evidence is the key. Evidence is what separates fiction from non-fiction, make-believe from theory. But the relation between evidence and theory is rich and complex, and to understand method in archaeology we need to know about both the nature of evidence and its use.

Archaeological evidence is not foundational in the sense of being self-sufficient in information or credibility. Evidence itself must be justified and interpreted. Consider the most basic kinds of observations in archaeology, things like potsherds, worked stone, and wall foundations. Even these descriptions, using these terms, rely on the expertise of archaeologists, and this imports their background knowledge into the interpretative process.

An expert sees a sherd rather than a lump of ceramic, or sees the stone as worked rather than naturally broken. To see these objects as evidence of activities in the past requires a context, including claims about activities in the past. And these contextual claims, the background knowledge, must be supported by evidence, which must be interpreted and justified with the help of some background knowledge. There is no end to it, no foundation. The relation between evidence and theory is incorrigibly one of reciprocity, and the structure of justification is one of coherence.

Even information as basic as dating an artefact involves this coherence structure. In some cases, such as radiometric dating and dendrochronology, the background knowledge is supplied by the physical sciences. These highlight the epistemic value in having an independent source of support for the evidence. In cases of historical archaeology, dating of the physical remains can sometimes be helped by association with textual evidence. And in still other archaeological cases, dating of the evidence is by comparison with other objects, comparanda, that have been otherwise dated. Meaningful comparisons depend on classifications of types of artefact into identifiable categories, and this is done using terms and concepts based on current theories. In all these ways, dating archaeological evidence is done under the influence of some theoretical background that is itself continually reassessed as new evidence is found in new contexts.

Describing the evidence for what it is is similarly influenced. Labeling something as an amphora fragment, for example, rather than a lump of hard, powdery red stuff, requires some background knowledge, some expertise. This particular amphora fragment might be used as evidence for a theory about trade or about agriculture, but first we need to know the basics of what an amphora looks like and even something about the deposition and preservation of this one. This supporting information, which links the fragment in hand to the object of interest, is what Lewis Binford calls the "middle-range theory" (Binford 1977: 7). It is the information that traces the causal chain from, in this case, the amphora and its use in the past to the sherd and its recovery in the present.

Here is an example of this important part of archaeological method, this middle-range theory. Survey archaeologists in Greece interpret a concentration of potsherds as evidence of a site of human activity, but what can be said of a tenuous but fairly uniform scatter of sherds found in areas between these sites? With the middle-range understanding that ancient Greeks often mixed broken pottery in with the manure from domestic animals and then spread the manure as fertilizer on cultivated land, the off-site sherds become evidence of cultivation. And knowing how much land was under cultivation then functions as evidence for claims about the socio-economic situation of ancient Greece. None of this is certain, and the middle-range analysis is much more complex than simply sherds mean cultivation. But it is a good case of using theory to enrich the informational content of data, and this is characteristic of the empirical base of archaeology.

An important constraint on middle-range theories is independence. They should be justified on independent grounds, by appeal to evidence other than the evidence to which they give meaning and credibility. The former evidence will rely on other middle-range theories, indicating that the essence of justification is broad coherence between ideas, including theoretical descriptions of aspects of the past and more immediate descriptions of objects found in the present. Justification is not an isolated relation between a theory and its evidence. Nor is it unidirectional, from evidence to theory. Justification goes both ways; a theory gains justification from evidence and, typically, will also be used to help to justify some other evidence. And this usefulness, success as a middle-range theory, contributes to the justification of a theory, since it enhances the overall coherence of our network of beliefs about the past. Justification is a holistic phenomenon.

All of this is also true in the physical sciences. Observation is not evidence without some theoretical support. In physics, for example, the sketchy tracks through a particle detector are not evidence for or against any theory unless they can be identified as tracks of this or that particular particle, and this requires a theoretical understanding of how the detector works and how the tracks are formed. And those theories, drawn from chemistry and electrodynamics, are supported by their own independent evidence. And that evidence is influenced by theoretical background knowledge, and so on. This networking is the basic structure of scientific method, and it is coherence in the network that is its justification.

The important point about archaeology is this: descriptive claims about the past must be supported by evidence, but the evidence is always indirect to some extent. It is both physically and informationally removed from the activities of interest. So what we do observe, the immediate data, serve as evidence only with some theoretical support to make the link to the past.

To say that a theory is supported by some particular evidence is to say that the theory explains or predicts the evidence. The evidence is what one would expect to find if what the theory says happened actually happened. Successfully explaining or predicting some evidence is by no means certain proof that the theory is true, since there are always alternative explanations for what is observed and always alternative theories that make the same predictions. A false theory can make true predictions. After all, the tooth-fairy theory fully explains the appearance of the nickel the last time you lost a tooth and will successfully predict the next nickel with the next tooth. Furthermore, predicting some evidence that does not appear is not certain disproof of a theory. A true theory can make a false prediction. This is largely because of the complexity in interpreting the evidence and the potential ambiguity in determining what any particular observation means. The middle-range theories involved could be wrong. If evidence conflicts with theory, perhaps the theory is true but the evidence is misunderstood.

Evidence, either for or against a theory, is never decisive. Even outright lack of evidence is not in itself a conclusive reason to reject a theory when there is good reason for the expected evidence to be missing. In archaeology, evidence can be lost to looting, natural degradation or displacement, or other confounding factors. Evidence is still necessary, and a theory with a record of failed predictions and unexplained missing evidence is a failure. But a single anomaly, in the sense of missing or contrary evidence, is usually not in itself reason to reject a theory. The exception to this is where there is no plausible explanation for why the evidence is missing. A theory describing a huge ancient city of stone buildings predicts literally tons of sturdy and stationary debris. If they are not to be found, the theory is not to be believed. A civilization that lasts for thousands of years with the technological wherewithal to construct huge monuments of stone will not simply disappear without a trace. Such a theory, as we will encounter in an alternative to the accepted account of the pyramids at Giza, lacks justification entirely.

Again, the situation is similar to the one in the physical sciences. Evidence, taken one at a time, neither confirms nor disconfirms a theory. Here is a quick example. The spectrum of electromagnetic radiation emitted by the Sun is good evidence for the theory that the source of the Sun's energy is nuclear fusion taking place at its core. The fusion would explain the details of the spectrum. But this evidence is not decisive, and it is important to know that for a long time there was some important missing evidence as well. The theory predicts the production of particles called neutrinos and their detection here on Earth, but these neutrinos were not detected, despite decades of careful attempts (Bahcall 1990). This missing evidence, even though its absence was not explained, did not force the abandonment of the fusion theory. Nor should it

have, since contrary or missing evidence is ambiguous as to which of the many theories involved is inaccurate. Revised middle-range theories and new techniques of detection have finally revealed the predicted neutrinos (Schwarzschild 2002).

The point about the role of evidence in archaeology is this: it would be too simplistic to evaluate a description of the past by saying that if there is evidence on the theory's behalf then it is justified and if there is no evidence then it is not justified and should be rejected. This is the naive empiricism I warned against earlier. It is too simplistic for two kinds of reason. First, evidence comes in degrees of directness and credibility, so different evidence will have different degrees of authority over theory. The degrees are based on the links between the evidence and other ideas in our web of understanding. Second, testing a theory can never be left to a single piece of evidence. Justification comes from links to a large variety of evidence, each in turn linked to independent theories, and so on. Justification is a spread-out property of the web.

Historian E.H. Carr (1961: 37) described this situation as an essential reciprocity between theory and evidence. It may seem like a circular relation of theory justifying evidence and evidence justifying theory, but it is a harmless circle. It is unavoidable and even necessary, as we use what we already know to enhance the meaning and assess the reliability of the new things we discover.

The circularity is a form of what is elsewhere called the hermeneutic circle, and hermeneutics is a helpful model for the structure of justification in archaeology. Hermeneutics is about code breaking as a way of translating an unfamiliar language. Individual symbols on the page must be understood as a means to knowing the larger meaning of the text. We have to know the letters and words individually in order to find the plot and the message. And we first get an idea of the meaning of individual symbols by seeing how they are situated in the larger text. Syntactic patterns are noted, and hypothesized meanings must function together to generate a text that makes sense. In other words, our preliminary understanding of the large-scale meanings influences the interpretation of the small-scale symbols. And the understanding of the large-scale is built up from meaningful individual symbols. In this way, there is a reciprocity between the global, abstract interpretation of the content of the text and the more localized and specific assignments of meanings to the marks on the page.

This is hermeneutics, and it works. It works because of two important constraints. First, any assignment of meaning, either to individual symbols or to the larger ideas of the text, is revisable. And, second, the developing translation of the text must be coherent. It must make sense. It must be generally free of contradictions, and there must be connections between one part of the text and others. What it says here ought to explain or at least be related to what it says there. If the text is not making sense, then revision is called for, although it is usually unclear exactly what aspect of the translation needs to be revised. And even if things are making sense and the picture is coherent, we must keep reading. This is the hermeneutic version of always being open to new challenges. The best way to justify the accuracy of a hypothesized translation is to apply it to new examples of the language to see if those make sense. And the hermeneutic justification is at its best when the coherence is far and wide. That is, the understanding of the big picture is supported by many different parts of the text and not just a single passage. This is the independence in the justification process that was required of middle-range theory.

These same conditions apply to the hermeneutic model of archaeological method. All claims about the past and even about the evidence are, to varying degrees, revisable. This is knowledge welcoming challenge. But the willingness to revise is not wishy-washy, because there are constraining data, observations of the material remains. These are analogous to the individual marks on a page to be translated by hermeneutic methods. Descriptions of the

past, our theories of what happened, are analogous to the larger message of the text. The hermeneutic reciprocity between individual symbol and global meaning shows up in archaeology as reciprocity between evidence and theory. The goal, and the criterion of justification, is far-reaching coherence. The evidence and theories must make sense in terms of fitting into an extensive network of evidential and theoretical claims.

There are different kinds of links in the network, different components of coherence. A theory could explain or predict specific evidence. This is what we mean in saying that a theory is tested and (to some extent) confirmed by evidence. A theory could be used to give meaning and credibility to specific evidence. This is using a theory as a middle-range theory. Or a theory could relate more directly to another theory, as different parts of a translated text should be relevant to one another. All of these links contribute to justification in the form of far-reaching coherence.

There is also the requirement to continue to confront new evidence, to keep reading. By exposing ideas on what happened in the past to unforeseen challenges in the present, theories are less likely to harbor inaccuracies. It is not a stagnant or complacent coherence that indicates accuracy; it is a dynamic coherence, coherence maintained through ongoing empirical challenges, that is the hallmark of justification.

When a theory makes a prediction that contrasts with what is actually observed, or when the description of one aspect of the past contradicts the description of another, the coherence of the network is reduced and something must be revised. But what? Which part of the description is more likely to be inaccurate? Is it the theory or the observation that needs to be questioned and revised? These kinds of questions are answered by noting that in any network of ideas, some ideas are more deeply entrenched and hence less vulnerable than others to rejection or revision. No claim in the system is foundational in the sense of being immune from doubt, rejection, or revision. But some carry more weight than others. They have more epistemic authority by virtue of having more links into the network. To change or discard a well-connected idea would have far-reaching impact, since many of those ideas connected to it would have to be revised as well. Tampering with the well entrenched tends to decrease rather than increase overall coherence, hence defeating the purpose of the revision.

The relative weight of a claim is not based on a sociological entrenchment. It is not about how many people endorse the claim, or how long the claim has been believed. Rather, it is an epistemic entrenchment. It is about how many other ideas and observations in our network are linked to this one. How many things does this theory explain? How many things contribute to explaining this theory? And so on. Theories used as middle-range theories tend to have a lot of this kind of weight, since they have two kinds of links in the network. They are tested by evidence, and they are used to give meaning to other evidence.

A quick example will illustrate the usefulness of this idea of epistemic weight. There is a great deal of evidence and theory put together over decades of research about the rise of agriculture in Eurasia and the Americas. These fit coherently with ideas about continent-specific cultural innovations, including the development of writing. All of this is broadly coherent and hence well justified. The suggestion that a lost continent of Atlantis is the source of all civilization renders it all incoherent. The resulting system of beliefs is a significant loss of coherence, since it leaves unanswered, that is, unconnected, the central question of the ultimate source of Atlantis' civilization.

The variable weighting of ideas within the coherent network is also helpful in dealing with anomalies, that is, failed explanations or the absence of evidence where it was expected. If the theory is otherwise well connected, well entrenched, it is reasonable to retain it despite the anomaly. Only if more anomalies accumulate for the same theory

will they collectively come up with the epistemic authority to force a revision or rejection of the theory. But if the theory itself is peripheral in the web, if it is only sparsely connected to other ideas, then a single anomaly is important. In this case, the evidence must be taken seriously, and rejection of the theory may well be warranted.

Again, we are warned against naive or isolated empiricism or falsificationism as a model of method in archaeology. Justification comes in degrees, measured by embeddedness in our existing web of understanding. Having evidence for a theory comes in degrees, not just in the amount of evidence but in the directness and embeddedness of its interpretation. Evidence can be found to support almost any claim; what counts is how much strain the interpretation of that evidence puts on the coherence of the rest of our network of beliefs. Furthermore, almost any credible theory has some confounding or missing evidence, and it would be misleading and unreasonable to cite a single anomaly as cause to abandon an otherwise well-supported idea. In archaeology as in the physical sciences, justification cannot be isolated to single cases of evidence.

In sum, the epistemology of archaeology, the model of how archaeological claims about the past are justified, works like this. Theory, description of the past, requires evidence, both as motivation and subsequent testing. And evidence requires theory to make it meaningful and credible. This is the essential reciprocity. It is necessary bootstrapping, but it is not defeatingly circular as long as we insist on independence between the theory supporting a bit of evidence and the theory it is evidence for. The standard of acceptance of ideas, the measure of justification, is participation in a broadly coherent network of theories and evidential claims, a coherence that persists even as more observations are added. This is the dynamic nature of coherence. When there is a conflict between a theory and some evidence, sometimes it is the theory that must be revised, and sometimes it is the evidence that must be reinterpreted or rejected outright. The ruling is influenced by the epistemic weight of the competing claims, since that is a reflection of the overall coherence in the larger network.

It is important to acknowledge the complication and potential ambiguity in justifying archaeological knowledge. Denying or ignoring the difficulties risks defending our own claims too simply, or, perhaps worse, rejecting what we do not agree with too casually.

An Example:
The Pyramids at Giza

The preceding model of justification in archaeology has been very general and abstract, and its clarity and plausibility may have suffered for it. So let us apply it to a real example, the pyramids at Giza in Egypt. Answers to the most basic questions are not without some controversy. Who built the pyramids, when, how, and why? Recall that our interest here is not in the content of the conclusions but in how they are reached.

The pyramids offer a good case to demonstrate the important epistemological aspects of archaeology. One reason is that there is significant uncertainty about them. Some of the most basic and important questions are without good answers. It is not that there are no hypotheses, for example as to how the pyramids were built. But of several hypotheses, none stands out as being significantly more justified, that is, better linked into a coherent system of beliefs, than the others. We will want to resist filling this void with our own favorite fantasy.

Even for the descriptive claims that are justified, and are clearly more justified than their alternatives, there is no certainty. None of the answers to the important questions is beyond all doubt whatsoever. Nothing interesting ever is. And again, we should resist exploiting the uncertainty in what is said about the pyramids to make room for our own wishful thinking.

We will see in the case of the pyramids that the only way to understand and to justify the claims made about the past is in the larger context. They must be regarded and evaluated as a big group rather than individually or in isolated pairs of one idea and one bit of evidence. It would be misleading, for example, to try to understand and justify claims about just one of the pyramids, or even about just the three large pyramids at Giza. The necessary context is much broader. Each pyramid is situated in a surrounding complex of burials, buildings, and sometimes boats, and interpreting one of the pyramids alone would be like translating a single line of text without putting it into its larger literary context. There are other Egyptian pyramids, and what we say about the three at Giza must make sense, must be coherent, with what we say about the others. And there is the general social and cultural context of Egypt at the time of the pyramids. Claims about the nature of Egyptian society, technology, government, religion, and so on are all relevant to understanding the pyramids. What is theorized about the pyramids must be coherent with the way in which other aspects of Egyptian civilization are described.

No theory or evidence is justified in isolation, but this does not imply that justification demands the consideration of all possible data. Some details are irrelevant, and it can be a difficult and potentially question-begging decision whether or not to take a particular aspect of the situation seriously. For example, all three of the pyramids at Giza have been measured with great precision. We know their dimensions, their orientations, their slopes, and so on. Several theories have been proposed that explain the design principles of the pyramids, why they were built, based on impressive numerical correlations in the dimensions. Roger Herz-Fischler surveys several such theories specific to the largest of the pyramids at Giza. These include the Pi-theory, which purports to show that the pyramid builders must have known the value of π, since "the circumference of a circle with radius equal to the height is [very nearly] equal to the perimeter of the base of the pyramid" (Herz-Fischler 2000: 67). Herz-Fischler describes fifteen such proposals for the design plan of the Great Pyramid, all of which highlight correlations in dimensional details that Egyptologists regard as unimportant. This shows an important aspect of archaeology and science, that the selection of data is influenced by the theories that one already believes. And sometimes this can degrade the objectivity of the process, if selecting evidence is self-serving. But in this case, Herz-Fischler uses an independent means of evaluating the relevance of these data. He provides a statistical analysis of the proposed correlations and shows that none of the fifteen stands out as being more significant than any of the others (Ibid.: 29).

Again, the moral of this story is that justification of a theory is not to be found in an isolated, narrow look at a single aspect of a single pyramid. It must be based on extensive coherence in a broad context. We will see that the generally accepted account of the building of the pyramids is well justified in this holistic way. With conscious reference to modern physics, I will call this account the standard model.

The standard model of the three main pyramids at Giza describes them as being three tombs. The largest, the Great Pyramid, was built to be a tomb for the pharaoh Khufu. The slightly smaller pyramid that is associated with the sphinx was built as a tomb for the pharaoh Khafre, one of Khufu's sons. And the smallest of the three pyramids is the tomb of Menkaure. Each pyramid was built during the reign of the pharaoh, although there is no way to tell if they were done exactly on time. The standard model puts the dates of the three pharaohs at roughly 2550–2528 BC, 2520–2494 BC, and 2490–2472 BC, respectively. This precision is probably unwarranted, and the exact dates are still a topic of discussion and revision, but it is clear that the pyramids were built roughly 4,500 years ago and each took roughly a generation to construct.

This answers the question of when the pyramids were built. To describe them as tombs answers why, although more details on the motives are elusive. Why did they choose the particular pyramid shape in which to entomb the pharaoh? What does the pyramid mean to the Egyptians? These remain important outstanding questions and are the subject of ongoing debate.

Who built the pyramids? According to the standard model, they were built by mortal Egyptians, the minions of the pharaohs. How did they do it? What sort of social organization, technology, and labor schedule did they use to accomplish this enormous task? The Great Pyramid of Khufu is usually estimated to be made of 2.3 million blocks of limestone and granite (this total has recently been revised upward to nearly four million; see Sakovich 2002), weighing up to 80 tons apiece. These had to be quarried, delivered, shaped, lifted (eventually up to the peak at 146 meters), and carefully placed. All this was done without the use of iron tools or wheeled carts, and done in a period of about twenty years. How was it done? The candid answer is that we do not really know. The details of construction are not clearly or securely understood. This is not to say that there are no good ideas on the methods of construction or no tested hypotheses. There are. A huge nearby quarry has been found, and there is reason to believe that ramps were used to haul wooden sledges on rollers to raise the blocks into position. But the description of how the pyramids were built is still a work in progress within the standard model.

Most important for understanding the epistemology of archaeology is understanding the reasons for believing that the standard model is accurate. Given the imprecision of the dates and the incompleteness in describing the methods, what justification is there for endorsing the model at all?

There are many pieces of evidence in support of the standard model. None is singularly sufficient for justifying the account of the pyramids, and none stands on its own in the sense of being free of some theoretical interpretation. That is the way it is with evidence. It is only by considering the whole, coherent, far-reaching network of claims into which the model fits that we appreciate its justification.

Each of the three pyramids has an interior chamber that contained a sarcophagus. This would seem to be decisive for the ascription as tombs, except that none of the sarcophagi contained bones when it was discovered. (Well, bones of a bull were found in the sarcophagus of the Khafre pyramid, and human bones dating to the Christian era in that of Menkaure.) So there is work to be done to show that each of the stone boxes is in fact a sarcophagus, placed in the pyramid at the time it was built rather than added later. How, in other words, are these data, these stone boxes, evidence of the pyramids being built for the purpose of being tombs for the pharaohs?

The boxes are identified as sarcophagi because they resemble boxes from elsewhere in Egypt found in clear contexts as burials. Some of these held bodies of Egyptians; some were in other Egyptian pyramids; and some were in situations with textual references to death and burial. In other words, there are similar objects in Egypt, some found in pyramids, that are independently interpreted to be sarcophagi. This use of comparanda, comparable objects with independent middle-range theories to give them meaning, is a standard of archaeological method. It is not that the standard model identifies the pyramids as tombs, uses this as the reason to call the boxes sarcophagi, and then cites the sarcophagi as the proof that the pyramids are tombs. This circularity is prevented by insisting that the interpretations, of pyramids and sarcophagi, fit into a much broader picture that includes other pyramids, other contexts, and, importantly, other kinds of data.

Another noteworthy detail is that the sarcophagus in the interior chamber of the Great Pyramid is too big to fit through the passageway leading to the outside. The sarcophagus had to have been put in place during construction of the pyramid, indicating that the pyramid was not only *used* as a tomb, but was indeed *built* as a tomb.

Now consider the evidence of the Giza pyramids in the larger context of other Egyptian pyramids. Although the Giza pyramids are the largest and most famous, there is a line of development starting with *mastabas* and developing into step pyramids. Some

of these other pyramids were discovered with entombed bodies in the interior chambers. Some were inscribed with so-called Pyramid Texts. These texts are on interior walls of pyramids, and although they are difficult to interpret, they are generally about "the ruler and his life in the beyond" (Verner 1997: 41). Furthermore, the texts are written to be read in a direction starting at the interior of the pyramid and moving to the outside, as if to guide the entombed king in his passage to the next world.

A few individual pyramids have distinctive features that support the general interpretation of pyramids as tombs and even suggest clues about the methods of construction. Papyri have been found near the pyramid of Neferirkare, for example, describing activities associated with the pyramid. These temple archives list religious duties and festivals, equipment of worship, and even some architectural details of the temple. The point is that the textual evidence associated with this one pyramid, together with the similarity between this pyramid and others, helps us to understand and justify statements about Egyptian pyramids generally.

There are similar clues about construction techniques. The use of ramps, for example, is described in the Anastasi papyrus. It even includes specific dimensions of ramps. And there are physical remains of ramps still in place on the Red Pyramid. Since it is likely that different pyramids, with different sizes and shapes, required somewhat different building methods, generalization might be unwarranted. But the textual reference to ramps and the few remains make the theory of ramps at the Giza pyramids at least worth pursuing.

Each of the pyramids at Giza fits into its own broad context of smaller satellite pyramids and surrounding buildings. It is important to consider the evidence of the pyramid complex and not just the pyramid itself. Each of the pyramids at Giza is within a necropolis. They are surrounded by lesser pyramids, tombs, and *mastabas* that function as burials of the king's family and associates. Some of these sites are inscribed, and in some cases with reference to the king for whom the large pyramid is a tomb. A good example of this is in the Queen's pyramids around the Great Pyramid of Khufu, in particular in the chamber of Hetepheres.

Recent excavations at Giza have revealed settlements of the many workers who built the pyramids. There are houses for the work crews, as well as bakeries and cemeteries with inscribed titles such as "overseer of the side of the pyramid," "overseer of masonry," and "director for the king's work" (Hawass 1997: 41). The numbers of workers estimated to have lived in the settlements is commensurate with estimates of the number of people at work on the pyramid at any time. This is a good example of testing a hypothesis by what philosophers of science call the hypothetico-deductive method. A prediction is rendered, namely that if there were so many men at work on the pyramids then there would have to be material remains of their housing and life support, and then one looks to see if the prediction is true. In this case it is. This does not mean that the hypothesis is surely true, but it is some addition to the justification, some part of the reason to believe it to be true.

One last piece of evidence in favor of the standard model is worth mentioning. Some Egyptologists claim it to be decisive proof that the Great Pyramid was built to be a tomb for the pharaoh Khufu. This is the graffiti in a relieving chamber above the king's burial chamber, which gives names of some work crews and names Khufu himself. The key is that the relieving chamber has no entrance. It is a space above the burial chamber that deflects the enormous weight away from the ceiling, an artefact of engineering never meant to be entered. It was originally accessible only during the construction of the pyramid. And here is a series of so-called builders' marks and the cartouche of Khufu. According to Mark Lehner, the graffiti and the fact that no one had been in the chamber between the time the pyramid was built and 1837, when an explorer blasted his way in, "clinches the ascription of this pyramid to the 4th-dynasty Pharaoh, Khufu" (Lehner 1997: 53). Indeed, some quarry marks are even found on the sides of blocks; they could not have

been put there after the pyramid was built. It is tempting to regard the graffiti as singularly decisive for the standard model, but a more realistic evaluation is that it is neither decisive nor singular. The standard model does not depend on this single piece of evidence, convincing as it is. These graffiti do not have to bear the full burden of proof, since they fit wonderfully with both the standard model and with other pieces of evidence. There are workers' graffiti on some of the other pyramids, for example, thus enhancing the credibility of them all.

Like any scientific description of events that cannot be observed, the standard model of the pyramids at Giza has some anomalies, some recalcitrant evidence and even parts of the theory that do not quite fit. Radiometric dating of mortar in the Great Pyramid is one example. The dates are roughly 400 years earlier than the reign of Khufu. This is an important problem, and it cannot be ignored or minimized. It does not force the rejection of the standard model, but some part of the theoretical network must be revised. It is unlikely, and unreasonable, to revise the account of radioactive decay and techniques of radiometric dating, since these ideas are so extensively and coherently connected in theoretical systems of both physics and archaeology. Perhaps, instead, the evidence suggests a recalibration of the dates of the pharaohs. Or perhaps, much more profound changes to the standard model are in order, to the extent that the pyramids were not built during the lifetime of the pharaoh and hence were not built as his tomb. A third possibility for fitting the radiometric dates coherently into the model is to reassess the middle-range theory describing the making and use of mortar. If the mortar incorporates older organic material, the mortar itself could be much newer than the radiometric dates indicate. The important point here is that the evidence is both important and at odds with the standard model. It is also ambiguous, in that the evidence alone does not tell us what part of the model, or what other participating theories, need to be rejected or revised.

Another anomaly for the standard model of the pyramids at Giza is that none of the three sarcophagi were discovered to have bones of a pharaoh, and none of the three pyramids held a statue of a pharaoh. However, this missing evidence is plausibly explained by looting. The pyramids are highly visible and irresistible targets for treasure hunters, and, over 4,000 years, anything of value or interest that is movable has been removed. All that remains are the multi-ton stones, although even some of those have been taken for use elsewhere. This is typical in archaeology. Much of the most informative evidence is in the mundane, the objects of no value to robbers and collectors. The workers' settlements associated with the pyramids, for example, are of lower profile and lesser value to looters, but they will probably be high-yielding and very interesting sources of archaeological evidence.

And, finally, there is an important drawback to the standard model in that it cannot yet describe how the pyramids were constructed. There are convincing and clear answers to the questions of who, why, and when (roughly), but not how. Were ramps used on the huge pyramids at Giza? If so, the ramps themselves would have to have been enormous and so long as to extend beyond the quarry. There should be tons of debris from the mud-brick ramps. The debris is not there, and its absence cannot be blamed on looting. Perhaps the ramps wrapped around the pyramid in a way that required less material. Perhaps, but this is largely speculative and without evidential support. In its current state, the standard model is without a clear mechanism for building the pyramids.

This gap in the description of the pyramids is one reason I like to call it the standard model, to make an explicit analogy with physics. Physicists refer to the current description of elementary particles and processes as the standard model. It talks about forces, fields, particles, masses, charges, and so on (see Weinberg 1992). Many aspects of the standard model in physics are well justified in the sense of theoretical and evidential coherence. But some

important details are still unclear. For example, there is no detailed evidence for a fundamental process called symmetry breaking, which is theorized as the source of mass. Mass is not an unimportant detail in understanding matter and interactions, yet this unfinished business in the standard model is not reason to scrap the whole thing. Like the standard model of the pyramids, there is a large network of interrelated, coherent ideas and claims, both theoretical and observational. That is what gives the model its justification. No single anomaly or uncertainty should force its undoing.

Justification is most useful as a comparative tool, so it is appropriate to ask how the justification of the standard model of the pyramids compares with alternatives. Consider the theory proposed and defended by Graham Hancock and Robert Bauval in *The Message of the Sphinx* (Hancock and Bauval 1997). This is a good comparison, since it is the confluence of two streams of "alternative" ideas that are well publicized and highly detailed.

The alternative model is this. The entire pyramid complex at Giza is an "astronomical theme park" (Ibid.: 78), begun around 10,500 BC. The pyramids were not built as tombs but as models of stars, in particular, the stars in Orion's belt (for details of this so-called Orion correlation theory, see Chapter 10). The pyramids begun in 10,500 BC but were finished only in 2,500 BC. They were then used as tombs. The pyramid complex is a message from a lost civilization, with the pattern of stars as its telltale date, since only in 10,500 BC would the stars in the sky match the pattern on the ground.

Two main lines of evidence are cited in support of this proposition, the astronomical alignment and the technological impossibility for Egyptian civilization, as we know it to have been in 2,500 BC, to have built the pyramids. Both of these are given as reasons to push the starting date of the pyramids back by 8,000 years to an otherwise hidden civilization, although neither gives any reason for adding the extra interpretative step that the monuments are a message to the future.

Consider the evidence on its merits. There are narrow shafts in the Great Pyramid that angle up from the King's Chamber and the Queen's Chamber on the north and south sides. These point to important stars, or to where the stars were located in the sky in 2,500 BC. This indicates a stellar orientation of the pyramid. Furthermore, the three pyramids are said to be an exact reproduction of the stars in the belt of Orion, an important constellation to the Egyptians. The position of Orion was most appropriate for this match in 10,500 BC, thus allegedly dating the layout of the pyramid complex. There is a problem though. Orion's belt shows two big stars and a little one, with a subtle bend to the north. The line linking the two bigger pyramids, Khufu and Khafre, to the smaller one, Menkaure, has a bend to the south. The pyramids are not an image of Orion's belt; they are backwards (Krupp 2003). Justification in archaeology depends on coherence of theory and evidence in a broad network of ideas, and the most basic component of coherence is logical consistency. But here is a case of evidence that is outright inconsistent. The diagonal shafts in the pyramids orient the monuments north on the ground to north in the sky, but the alleged match to Orion's belt requires that we flip things over to align north to south.

Then there is the argument that construction projects so enormous and so precise as the pyramids could not have been designed and completed by Egyptians in 2,500 BC, and certainly not in the twenty or thirty years described by the standard model. Here is a clear case of exploiting some uncertainty to make room for a radical alternative theory. Radiocarbon dating of the mortar in the Great Pyramid may challenge traditional dating by a few hundred years, but it is no reason at all to move the date back by *eight thousand years*. And questions about the building techniques may force some revisions in the web of understanding of ancient Egypt and the standard model, but they do not warrant positing an entire new civilization. This would require far-reaching and profound revisions in the web, unwarranted by any anomalies we see today.

The most glaring deficiency in the justification of the Hancock–Bauval model is basic: there is no evidence for the hypothesized civilization other than the pyramid complex itself. There is no reason at all why evidence of 8,000 years of "continuous transmission of advanced scientific and engineering knowledge ... and thus the continuous presence in Egypt" (Hancock and Bauval 1997: 248) should be completely absent. The evidence at Giza is all we have to motivate the theory of the astronomical message from a lost civilization. The theory is used to interpret this evidence, which is in turn the main evidence cited in support of the theory. This is circularity of reasoning at its most insular and self-serving. It lacks the most important ingredients of justification, extensive links to other ideas and independent evidence. It is isolated in its own small web of ideas. It is at odds with the wider understanding of the history of Egypt, including the pyramids at places other than Giza and the archaeological and textual evidence of Egyptian culture. The result is intractable dissonance rather than coherence in the larger web of understanding.

Given the evidence available and the standards of comparing justification, the standard model is the responsible choice. In this case, it is simply a matter of following the advice of the eighteenth-century Scottish philosopher David Hume: "A wise man, therefore, proportions his belief to the evidence" (Hume 1993 [1777]: 73).

The case of the pyramids at Giza, together with the analogy with the standard model of particle physics, displays the important aspects of epistemology of archaeology and science. No single piece of evidence confirms the model or any other description of the past. No single piece of evidence (or missing evidence) falsifies it either. No part of the model is above questioning, revision, or rejection. But some aspects are more secure than others, and this is measured by the security of connection with a coherent network of beliefs. When in doubt, suspect the loosely connected and peripheral ideas. Justification is rooted in the overall coherence between beliefs.

References

Bahcall, J. (1990) "The solar-neutrino problem." *Scientific American,* May: 54–61.

Binford, L. (1977) "General introduction." in L. Binford (ed.), *For Theory Building in Archaeology.* New York: Academic Press.

Carr, E.H. (1961) *What Is History?* New York: Vintage Books.

Hancock, G. and Bauval, R. (1997) *The Message of the Sphinx: A Quest for the Hidden Legacy of Mankind.* New York: Crown; published in the UK as *Keeper of Genesis: A Quest for the Hidden Legacy of Mankind.* London: Heinemann.

Hawass, Z. (1997) "Tombs of the pyramid builders." *Archaeology* 50 (1): 31–8.

Herz-Fischler, R. (2000) *The Shape of the Great Pyramid.* Waterloo: Wilfrid Laurier University Press.

Hume, D. (1993) *An Enquiry Concerning Human Understanding.* Indianapolis: Hackett.

Krupp, E. (2003) "Astronomical integrity at Giza." Available at <http://www.antiquityofman.com/Krupp_refutes_Bauval_and_Roy.html>.

Kuhn, T. (1977) *The Essential Tension.* Chicago: University of Chicago Press.

Lehner, M. (1997) *The Complete Pyramids.* London: Thames and Hudson.

Plato (1992) *Theaetus,* translated by B. Williams. Indianapolis: Hackett.

Sakovich, A. (2002) "Counting the stones: how many blocks comprise Khufu's pyramid?" *KMT* 13.3: 53–7.

Schwarzschild, B. (2002) "Direct measurement of the sun's total neutrino output confirms flavor metamorphosis." *Physics Today* (July): 13–15.

Verner, M. (1997) *The Pyramids,* translated by S. Rendall. New York: Grove Press.

Weinberg, S. (1992) *Dreams of a Final Theory.* New York: Pantheon.

"The Ancient Maya and the Political Present"

RICHARD R. WILK

Archaeological explanations are filled with bias, not always explicit. Major kinds of bias include the inherent bias of the archaeological record (e.g., stone preserves better than bone), the bias of the theoretical frameworks used, and biases of age, gender, ethnicity, training, and education on the part of the researcher. Yet another kind of bias is that of time and place, meaning that where and when an archaeologist is situated is likely to influence the kinds of explanations he or she develops or follows. This bias is illustrated in this selection, using explanations for the collapse of the Maya civilizations as an example.

Richard Wilk is a professor of anthropology at Indiana University, and this article originally appeared in a 1985 issue of the scholarly *Journal of Anthropological Research*. Many pieces have been written about potential bias in archaeological interpretation since, but they lack the clarity of this article.

Questions to Guide Reading

What is meant by the statement that archaeology is essentially a "reflexive science"?
What was Wilk's method of research?
How are archaeological explanations for the Maya collapse correlated with recent history in the United States?

Can archaeologists depict the past with any accuracy, and is that their goal? Where do archaeologists' ideas come from in the first place? This paper suggests that archaeological discourse has a dual nature: at the same time that it pursues objective, verifiable knowledge about the past, it also conducts an informal and often hidden political and philosophical debate about the major issues of contemporary life. This paper investigates this second, hidden dialogue within a single subfield of archaeology, Maya prehistory. What gives power to the past, and to archaeology, is the way it is used to political and philosophical ends. The task is to recognize the nature of the dialogue and to take responsibility for it.

Professional archaeologists are accustomed to changing explanations and theories; they interpret such change as a sign of progress in the discipline. Consciously or unconsciously, archaeologists tend to see the constant proposal, evaluation, and rejection of new ideas and theories as a part of the scientific method, one which leads us gradually closer to objective truth.[1] Yet to many laymen, amateurs, and students, the frequent change of explanations and reconstructions of the past (excluding of course those based on "new discoveries") is somewhat bewildering. The perception that the latest theory is likely to be short lived and that all aspects of the past are subject to interpretation does not instill in nonarchaeologists a fascination with archaeological methodology or epistemology. Rather it leads to cynicism—to the perception that views of the past are determined by fashion, by competition for status within the profession (between individuals and/or groups and schools), by borrowing from other disciplines, or by a reluctant accommodation to new discoveries. The credibility of archaeology suffers when serious scholarship is perceived to be some sort of arcane game.[2]

Defensiveness in the face of such criticism leads many archaeologists to emphasize the part of their work which is rigorous and scientific. Frequent assertions by professionals that archaeological hypotheses are formulated and evaluated in an objective and scientific manner are a direct bolster to the "progressivist" view that archaeology is gradually homing in on explanations that are right and true. This is an implicit, and sometimes explicit, denial of the substance of the lay critiques—that archaeologists are just making up stories about the past.

In this paper I suggest that neither the critique or the defense do justice to the true complexity (or beauty) of archaeologists' relationships to the past. The process of explaining the past is not a frivolous game, but neither is it a simple scientific quest for objective truth. There are elements of truth in lay perceptions of the profession: hypotheses about and explanations for the past are not generated in an abstract, objective way, and the acceptance and/or rejection of these hypotheses is not necessarily based on rigorous scientific testing. But to accept this as fact does not require that we adopt the cynical pose that all prehistory is just academic gamesmanship lacking in any scientific credibility.

Archaeology has a dual nature; it simultaneously engages in a fairly rigorous pursuit of objective facts about the past and an informal and sometimes hidden dialogue on contemporary politics, philosophy, religion, and other important subjects. It is this second dialogue, based on archaeologists' perceptions of the present and their experience of the world (including their experience of fieldwork), which brings motivation, passion, interest, and relevance to the whole enterprise. This is what makes archaeology an essentially "reflexive" science, one which reflects back on the present as much light as it sheds on the past.

I have no intention of taking an extreme position like that of some anthropologists (e.g., Sahlins 1976:220), who feel that the past is nothing but a cultural construct, lacking any objective reality. This would be as fallacious as insisting that the past is like an object which the archaeologist merely uncovers and puts together like a broken pot. The true situation is much more complex and messy. Objective knowledge of the past is interwoven and intertwined with reflexive commentary, and for usual intents and purposes it should probably remain so.

In this paper, however, I will try to disentangle, isolate, and dissect the reflexive component of a particular corpus of archaeological explanation of the past. My intent is not to single out one group of archaeologists and point an accusing finger or hold anyone up for ridicule. Certainly any other group of archaeologists would serve just as well. I have chosen Mayan prehistory only because I know this literature best.

The point is to untie the reflexive element of archaeology from its status as a naive lay criticism, to show that it really (even "objectively") exists. Once the topic can be discussed freely, we may reach the conclusion that there is nothing shameful about a certain lack of objectivity in our choice of explanations and hypotheses concerning the past. Rather than being considered a pollution of science, the reflexivity of archaeology should be viewed, I believe, as the very element which makes it interesting and relevant. The ultimate point is not that we have to do something about the situation, but instead that we may be able to draw upon it and convert it into a strength.

Conventional Wisdom on the Sources of Theory

Considering how much introspection has gone into recent archaeological writing, the endless discussions of epistemology and the place of archaeology in the philosophy of science, it is strange to find so little has been written on the ultimate origins and sources of explanation and theory. We have heard a great deal about what to do with an explanation, a hypothesis, or a model once it has been found or formulated. But where do they come from in the first place?[3]

One of the major elements of the self-conscious scientism of the "New Archaeology" was a critique of inductive reasoning, then seen to be a characteristic of the old cultural-historical approach (see, for example, Watson, LeBlanc, and Redman 1971:28; Fritz and Plog 1970:411–12). Binford (1968) and others thought that the idea of archaeological explanations emerging from data through empirical analysis was bogus; when "old archaeologists" said their theory emerged from the data they were really using a whole series of unspoken, implicit assumptions, which could never be tested because they remained concealed.

So the "New Archaeology" was involved in a critique of the origins of explanation and theory from the start. What alternative was offered to "unscientific" inductive generalizations based on shaky assumptions? There were two. One was to be explicit about assumptions, to differentiate between what was a hypothesis to be tested and what was data, and to be conscious of the process by which hypotheses are constructed and used (best exemplified by the arguments in Watson, LeBlanc, and Redman 1971). The other was a bit more contentious and considerably more muddled—a call for a "deductive nomothetic" methodology by which specific hypotheses about prehistory would be derived from "established social-science laws"

(Trigger 1973:107). Rather than generate their own hypotheses from observations of the past, archaeologists were to derive explanations from elsewhere and then explicitly test them; following Hempel, a past phenomenon would be explained when it was subsumed under such general laws.

But where *were* the general laws of society? The very existence of such laws had been a subject of heated debate since the Enlightenment. Sociocultural anthropology only offered some cross-cultural statistical regularities which were not particularly useful (e.g., Murdock 1949 and the Human Relations Area Files research). For a while there appeared lists of where the laws were going to come from: cultural evolutionism, general systems theory, locational analysis, demography, and population theory (see Trigger 1973:101–4; Leone 1972:25; Redman 1973:11–20; Watson, LeBlanc, and Redman 1971). But it became clear that these bodies of knowledge had only general, and often untested, assumptions to offer rather than hard "laws," and they were often contradictory. Furthermore, there was some dissatisfaction with the idea that archaeologists could only test the laws produced by others—they should be able to be law producers as well as law consumers (Reid, Rathje, and Schiffer 1974).

Finally, a common position on the sources of theory and law was borrowed from the philosophers of science: that it *did not matter* where hypotheses came from, whether from general laws, from observation, or from imagination. Scientists should only be concerned with how hypotheses were tested (Hempel 1966:15, 16; Binford 1977:2) not where they came from. Using this logic, Watson, LeBlanc, and Redman (1971:33, 7–8) condemned "old archaeologists" for unscientific derivation of explanations and hypotheses *and* followed Hempel in stating that the sources or derivations of hypotheses are unimportant. So the critique that the "old archaeologists'" hypotheses were derived incorrectly was negated almost as soon as it was raised.

The acceptance of Hempel's assertion that the origin of theory and explanation is irrelevant to science masks the importance of the issue of where archaeologists' ideas come from. Binford still takes archaeologists to task for being empiricists and thinking that theory emerges from observations and generalizations. He recently has restated his belief that "theory represents *inventions* of the human mind.... We invent, rather than discover, theories or parts of theories" (Binford 1985:583). Binford is remarkably consistent in his critique, but like most other archaeological theorists he leaves unexamined here the issue of *how* those theories are invented. Do they appear in the brain by divine inspiration, by dint of training in a good graduate school, or by some more complex mechanism that does not invite close examination?

Conventional histories of archaeology, like histories of anthropology in general, take what could be called a "normal science" view of the origin of hypotheses (see, for example, Willey and Sabloff 1973; Bernal 1980). Scientists work within a scientific milieu, deriving and testing hypotheses within the traditions of their own field or subfield. They get their ideas from each other, directly or indirectly, and the coherence of this transmission allows the identification of "schools" and lines of descent from one group of scholars to another. Through a series of "begots" the historian traces ideas back to influential scholars through their students, keeping things well within the bounds of the discipline (Willey and Sabloff 1973:187). Of course at times there is cross-fertilization between disciplines, the collision or melding of different research traditions, and even unaccountable wild innovation.[4] These histories depict a discipline somewhat isolated from the world, engaged in dialogue with itself and a few close relatives, with an occasional visitor from far away dropping by for a chat. While contemporary politics and cultural currents could influence archaeological debates and archaeology could be turned to political purposes (as in early disputes over American Indian origins, see Willey and Sabloff 1973), these influences are considered indirect in modern times. And some archaeologists find

even the possibility of such influence to be very threatening to their image of objective science (e.g., Ford 1973).

In the last few years however, archaeology has become more introspective, and alternative histories of the field have appeared. Several recent analyses of "regional traditions of archaeological research" make strong cases for direct influence of political change on archaeology (see Trigger and Glover 1981; Trigger 1981; Chang 1981; Lorenzo 1981a; Bulkin, Klejn, and Lebedev 1982; Bar-Yosef and Mazar 1982). The best cases are made for the Soviet Union and China, though Israel should be a strong runner-up in the race for direct political involvement in the interpretation of prehistory. In a similar vein, Kristiansen (1981) offers a perceptive analysis of the history of Danish archaeology, paying close attention to the class position of the archaeologists and their audience and to the cultural and political content of research and publications.

Contemporary research has also been the target of sociopolitical analysis, in which the social role and status of the profession is shown to have guided the choice of research areas, topics, and methods (see Lorenzo 1981b and papers in Gero, Lacy, and Blakey 1983). But even these finely textured and highly introspective analyses do not go so far as to suggest that the actual *content* of explanation and theory is affected or determined by contemporary events. They suggest that archaeology may be politically motivated or serve political purposes; presumably this occurs because archaeologists are aware of who they are and what the past signifies. But it is another thing to say that the theories, explanations, ideas, and specific reconstructions of past events are unconsciously but directly reflecting current events.

Just such an argument is offered by Trigger (1981), who, for example, links the popularity of catastrophe theory among prehistorians with the increasing perception that Western society is heading towards a (presumably nuclear) catastrophe. Similarly, Leone (1972:24) suggests that interest in general systems theory stems from "the pervasiveness of certain aspects of technology in modern American Culture." And Rathje and Schiffer (1982) link interest in migration in early archaeology to waves of immigrants coming to the United States and interest in diffusion to colonialism. Tenuous and isolated connections such as these may appear to have only a minor influence on the main flow of archaeological discourse. If one believes that social science is generally objective and value free, then a few minor connections between current events and the interpretation of the past can be excused as regrettable, but understandable, deviations.

An alternative view is that archaeology, like other social sciences, *always* draws on current events, and politics as a source of general orientation, as criteria for the choice of research questions, and as sources of specific hypotheses and explanations about prehistory. From this perspective, the depiction of the past is inseparable from the present in which it is presented (Leone 1981). The empirical question then becomes one of just how close the link between present and past really is. I will suggest that the connections are much more common, specific, and direct than most archaeologists accept.

While the thematic connections I draw are more direct, I do not think that they flow from the conscious expression of political philosophy by archaeologists. Rather, I believe that correlations between what happens in the present and what is depicted to have happened in the past flow from unconscious processes. The exact nature of these processes remains obscure, but they clearly involve the application of ideas, conclusions, and questions derived from daily life and thought about current events to the professional work of archaeology.

The Present in the Past: The Maya Case

The analysis that follows is meant to be indicative rather than exhaustive. I have not pried into the private papers or unpublished thoughts of any Mayanists, but have instead depended on the writings which best present current "mainstream" interpretation and explanation to other archaeologists and the public.[5] Mainstream Maya archaeology is best represented in English by a series of influential topical and synthetic volumes, which usually include papers presented at conferences (such as those at Cambridge University or the School of American Research). The participants include a mixture of older established authorities, a highly competitive middle-aged peer group involved in active fieldwork, and a few younger, ambitious researchers who are trying to establish their reputations. Papers in the major journals are also important but tend to be much less adventuresome and more oriented towards the presentation of data. It should be noted that these sources generally do not include the work of French- and Spanish-speaking Mesoamericanists, whose contributions are therefore not included in my analysis.

Maya archaeology is a particularly good field in which to study the influence of the present on the past, because Classic Maya culture is known entirely through archaeological rather than historical evidence. To be sure, ethnographic analogy plays some part, but most prehistorians have assumed a major disjunction to exist between the Maya of history and tradition and those of the Classic period, a barrier which conveniently corresponds with the "collapse" of Classic Maya society just before the earliest reliable ethnohistoric evidence. The reality or solidity of this barrier has always been a matter of some dispute.

In the early years, when little actual excavation had been done, the imagination could run riot, and images of the past tell more about the culture of the prehistorian than about the Maya. For the first half of this century, Maya archaeology was more a means of escaping the present than a reflection of it, and there are few direct parallels between current events and theories of the past. Rather, the past comes across as an antithesis of the present, as a model of how things could or should be in opposition to the way they are. Early views of the "Old Empire" as being ruled by theological lords of the jungle, a unique, peaceful, and artistic group holding sway by dint of their intellectual accomplishments (i.e., the ritual calendar), are clearly projections. They fit well with an early twentieth-century disillusionment with the lack of harmony and spiritual values in the industrial age, attributes which had supposedly been lost in the recent past.

Becker (1979) has published a particularly astute analysis of the Maya archaeology of the "middle period" from 1924 to 1945. He traces clear connections between upper-class anti-urbanism and J. Eric Thompson's highly influential model depicting Maya cities as empty "Ceremonial Centers" where only a religious elite resided (Becker 1979:10–12). Thompson (1927) also popularized the idea that the Classic Maya collapse was the result of class warfare, as the peasants overthrew an oppressive elite. Becker traces this theory to Thompson's class background and early experience on his family's Argentine estate and also to contemporary political events during Thompson's career. "The beginnings of Thompson's popular peasant revolt theory could have been the historical events taking place in modern, not ancient, Mexico" (Becker 1979:13).

When an ethnographer drew on experience with "untouched" Maya in the highlands to support the view that the ancient Maya were an egalitarian, agrarian, and nonurban society, building only religious monuments, the same kinds of projection were operating (see Vogt 1961, 1964). We might ask why this model was so popular and lasted so long (see Sanders and Price 1968; Price 1974), even after its ethnographic basis was cast into doubt (Harris 1964:26–31). I think the answer is that the image of village democracy, of egalitarian, rural people managing their own affairs without the interference of political ideologies, was an important one in the age of the Peace Corps (founded 1961). Here was a model of democracy at the village level, a system which led to the construction of massive monuments and sophisticated art on a voluntary basis, without coercion, bureaucracy, class structure, or powerful leaders. Here, ancient history served as an antithesis to the present, an instructive example of how things could be.

The parallels between historical events and archaeological interpretation become more pronounced and direct during the late sixties, at the very time that "relevance" became an important concern of college students and teachers. Certainly the overriding historical event at this time, from the standpoint of the academic community, was the growing escalation of the war in Vietnam. And indeed, the ancient Maya also went through a period of militarization.

While the Bonampak murals depicting violent Maya conflicts had been known since 1946, they were not interpreted as evidence for widespread Maya warfare. Stelae portraying bound war captives under the feet of spear-wielding rulers were also ignored. Instead it was long believed that "The Maya ... were one of the least warlike nations who ever existed" (Gann and Thompson 1931:63). Suddenly, in the late sixties interpretations began to change, and the militaristic aspects of Maya history assumed a new prominence. Fortifications were discovered at major sites; they had been walked over many times before but were never recognized before (see Puleston and Callender 1967; Webster 1972).

The first use of warfare to explain Maya prehistory in a systematic way was in 1964 in a paper entitled "The End of Classic Maya Culture" by George Cowgill. In the same year, Adams published an interpretation of ceramic evidence that led him to posit a foreign invasion of the Maya Lowlands just before the collapse. Was it a coincidence that this was the year of the Gulf of Tonkin Resolution, when American troop strength in Vietnam surpassed fifty thousand? As the war in Vietnam escalated, so did the number of papers which included warfare as a major element of Classic Maya history. Invasion by a foreign imperialist power from a more developed area was an accepted part of Classic Maya prehistory by 1967 (see Sabloff and Willey 1967), the year when U.S. troop strength in Vietnam reached a peak of half a million.

At first, warfare and invasion were implicated in the *collapse* of Maya civilization (see Thompson

1970; Sabloff and Willey 1967; Adams 1971) and were considered disruptive influences, symptoms of pathology. Shortly, however, conflict was elevated from a symptom of collapse to a general principle of cultural evolution, an essential part of the causal process in the *origin* of the Maya state (see Webster 1972, 1974, 1975, 1977; Adams 1977a). Again, foreign imperialist invaders with economic motives, this time from Teotihuacan, were part of the process. Thus warfare was transformed from an aberration into a functional part of cultural evolution, a development which occurred elsewhere in anthropology as well (see Carneiro 1970; Chagnon 1967).

By the end of the 1960s and during the early 1970s, intellectual Americans became involved in a series of debates which were concerned with national and even global policy. Trigger (1981) links these debates, which he calls "middle class movements," to pessimism about the future and lack of confidence in technological progress. While the precise causes are likely more complex than he suggests, each of these debates was immediately reflected in thought about the Maya past. Opposition to the Vietnam War and a deep concern with the effects of militarization on contemporary society were certainly middle-class movements, and they are reflected in interpretations of prehistory.

While ecological protectionism arose as a national issue in the early sixties, the danger to America's natural environment did not become a pressing national (and political) concern until the late sixties, culminating with the establishment of the Environmental Protection Agency in 1970.[6] The peak of the movement came in the early seventies with the Endangered Species Act of 1973 and the Safe Drinking Water Act of 1974. Environmental issues became blended with those of energy, overpopulation, and resource scarcity after the oil embargo of 1973; no new significant environmental legislation was passed after 1974.[7]

Beginning around 1962 (see Cowgill 1962; Sanders 1962, 1963; Sanders and Price 1968), ecological and environmental causality came to Mesoamerican prehistory. In this early stage, environment was seen mainly as a limitation on cultural growth in a conventional cultural-ecological framework based on the ideas of Meggers (1954).[8] But as the idea of environmental destruction (rather than environmental limitation) became entrenched in the popular mind, the ancient Maya began to have more difficult relations with their rain forest habitat.

Sanders (1972, 1973) restated his earlier work more forcefully, claiming that agricultural overexploitation had led to environmental degradation through grass invasion and erosion. Despite the lack of material evidence, ecological catastrophe continued to be popular as at least a contributing factor in explaining the Maya collapse (e.g., Turner 1974; Harrison 1977; Rice 1978). The logical underpinnings of such arguments are made clear in statements such as this: "Following this [systems] model it is assumed that each sociocultural system seeks equilibrium or harmony with its environment" (Sharer 1977:541). Involved here are important philosophical and political issues of balance and harmony and the dire consequences of disrupting that balance.

Interest in environmental matters was expressed in other ways. Although supported by remarkably little hard evidence, papers on ancient Maya agriculture burgeoned in number, peaking in 1975–76 (perhaps related to the "back to the land" movement?). Others (e.g., Hosler, Sabloff, and Runge 1977) drew elaborate flow charts which showed how everything was related to everything else. The end of the Vietnam War and the rise of the environmental movement were paralleled in Maya archaeology by a shift from "external" to "internal" models of culture change (see Sharer 1977; compare Puleston and Puleston 1971 with Puleston 1979: 70; Adams 1973 with Adams 1981; or Cowgill 1964 with Cowgill 1979).

Closely interwoven with themes of environmental disruption are those of runaway population growth, leading to stress on resources, social decay, and impending crisis. Given intellectual armor by Ehrlich (1968) and works like *The Limits to Growth* (Meadows et al. 1972), population increase became a common explanation for starvation and poverty around the world. At the same time, population growth became a significant explanatory variable in Maya prehistory. Again the emphasis was first on population growth as a danger, contributing to the instability of Maya society and eventually to its downfall (see several papers in Culbert 1973; Culbert 1974; and earlier works by Sanders). But population growth was quickly transformed, admittedly under the influence of Boserup's (1965) work, into the driving force of cultural evolution, responsible for the rise of Maya civilization (see papers in Adams 1977b and in Harrison and Turner 1978). Despite a general lack of data to support these hypotheses (see Cowgill 1975), for a brief period they achieved the status of a universal explanation.

In passing I should mention another human-environmental interaction which achieved prominence during the late 1960s (especially on college campuses): widespread use of hallucinogenic and euphoric drugs. Ancient Mesoamerica quickly produced its own literature on the subject, including discussions of the importance of hallucinogens in the art and iconography of ancient cultures (see Furst 1970, 1972; Dobkin de Rios 1974).

The stirrings of the women's movement also had a brief impact on the ancient Maya, as Molloy and Rathje (1974) proposed that "sexploitation" was a part of the Classic political system. It has not been until much more recently, however, that studies of women in Maya society have become more common (see Pohl and Feldman 1982; Nimis 1982). A real feminist critique of Maya archaeology has yet to be published however.[9]

It is interesting that the late 1970s, an uncertain time in American politics, was also an uncertain time in archaeology. An "empirical revival" of sorts seems to have occurred. While new discoveries were being made, especially in the fields of Maya origins and agricultural production, no clear, new explanatory trends developed. The Hammond and Willey volume of 1979 is remarkably free of the ecological and population pressure models of earlier years. But already in this volume were the seeds of future

developments, in a paper on the Maya collapse by Dennis Puleston (1979). He suggested that religious prophesies forecasting the doom of Maya society actually had a strong influence on pushing the society to its destruction. One can almost visualize the Maya priests scurrying around taking survivalist courses and reading up on how to prosper during the coming Postclassic years.

Puleston's paper was both a sensitive reaction to contemporary changes in the American political and social environment and a harbinger of things to come. With the growing conservatism and the increasing power of fundamentalist religious movements in American society, religion began to figure more prominently in prehistory as well (see, e.g., Marcus 1978; Coe 1981). Freidel (1979, 1981a, 1981b) argued that ideology, particularly the religious ideology of the politically powerful, was far more important in shaping Classic society than was population growth or pressure on resources. Indeed, a spate of anti-ecological models has spread all over Mesoamerica, each stressing the importance of political and religious ideology over economic maximization (see, e.g., Brumfiel 1983; Blanton 1980; Kowalewski 1980; Freidel and Scarborough 1982). The study of elites and elite culture became respectable once again, after years of emphasis on the common folk, and the tracing of kingly lineages became increasingly popular (see, e.g., Haviland 1981; Adams and Smith 1981).

To religious fundamentalism, the "New Right" political agenda of the late 1970s and early 1980s adds an emphasis on the family as a basic building block of society and a belief that "big government" is responsible for America's economic decline. Each of these auxiliary themes is reflected in recent explanations of the Maya past. It is remarkable just how little interest Mayanists have shown in Maya family and household organization through the years, but this has changed recently. I (Wilk and Rathje 1982) am guilty of pushing the household and family as important units in understanding Maya prehistory but had little difficulty finding others to participate in a symposium on "Mesoamerican Houses and

Households" co-organized with Wendy Ashmore at the 1983 meetings of the Society for American Archaeology (soon to be an edited volume).

Furthermore, the current idea that big government and the expense of supporting it are a burden on the populace seems to be reflected in recent work on the origin and demise of the Maya state. Where, previously, political elites were considered functional (contributing to the maintenance of the system), now they appear as pernicious growths, maintaining themselves at the expense of the body politic through force (see Haas 1981). The "peasants-rebelling-against-the-burden-of-elite" argument for the collapse of Maya society has been revived (see Hamblin and Pitcher 1980). Cowgill (1979:62) hypothesizes that the Maya collapse came about when the elite drove the system into the ground in their efforts to expand the size and scope of the state. Hosler, Sabloff, and Runge (1977:560) blame the collapse on "inadequacy of bureaucratic technology." How long will it be before the Maya collapse is interpreted as an attempt to "get government off the backs" of the ancient Maya, perhaps accompanied by a tax rebellion?

Figure 1 summarizes the close correspondence between current events and explanations in Maya archaeology. I have taken seven major edited volumes of papers by prominent Mayanists and have placed them on a time line according to when the papers were presented at symposia or submitted for publication, rather than when they were actually published. The papers in each volume were then placed in categories according to explanatory content. A single paper was allowed to count in several categories if it was judged to deal with each in a substantive way.[10] The volumes are close to a standardized sample, as they tend to draw on the same small community of scholars, and the editors in each case tried to present current views and "hot" topics.

The trends are clear and correspondences are striking. Most important is the sequencing of peaks of interest, first in warfare, then in ecology, and lastly in religion. Also evident by the late 1970s is an unexplained drop in the number of explanatory papers and a return to earlier interests in culture history, architecture, art, and ceramics. Does this mean that the period of correspondence between Maya archaeology and current events is over? Or is there instead a shift to new topics and explanations which are difficult to establish or understand through lack of perspective? It does seem a general rule that it becomes more difficult to pick out trends as we get closer to the present.

Some Tentative Conclusions

I do not intend to prove that *every* explanation offered by Mayanists has its ultimate source on the pages of *Time* magazine; many do arise from elsewhere in the profession, from anthropology, and through genuine original thought. On the other hand, almost every trend of importance in recent United States history finds some reflection, sometimes after a lag of a few years, in learned analyses of the rise and fall of ancient Maya civilization.

But does the existence of this relationship mean that the field is methodologically bankrupt? Is it true that "the past is an empty stage to be filled with actors and actions dictated by our means and desires" (Fritz 1973:76) and that all explanations are therefore open to attack as projections (or at best collective representations)? Certainly, Binford and Sabloff (1982) seem to think that such arguments are attacks on the "rationality" of the field. They respond by emphasizing the importance of regional traditions of anthropology and of the paradigms of culture which guide archaeological research and by arguing for "middle-range" studies as solutions to the limitations of world view.

Several sociological aspects of the archaeological profession promote reflexivity and hinder objectivity. The rewards of the field, prestige and position, go to those who propose new explanations, who have intriguing and relevant hypotheses, and not to those who slowly and ploddingly test those hypotheses (Flannery 1982). As competition for positions and

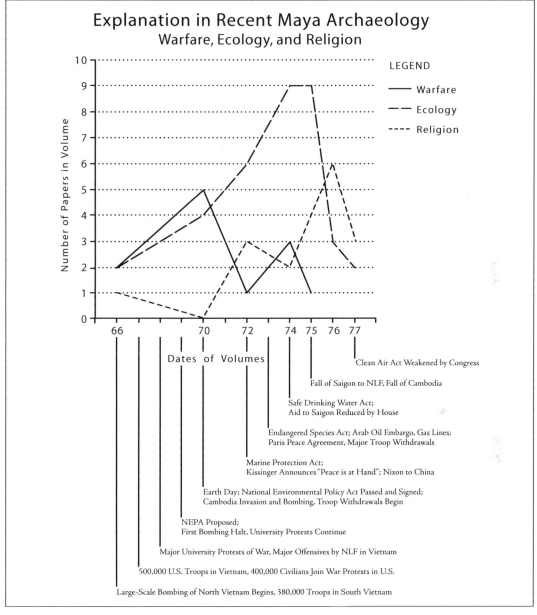

FIGURE 1: Explanation in Recent Maya Archaeology: Warfare, Ecology, and Religion

research funding increases, we can therefore expect more pressure for new explanations; and there are a limited number of sources for these. Scholars can hardly be blamed for looking to modern America (even if unconsciously) for inspiration.

Furthermore, most of the explanations and

hypotheses being proposed are not subject to disproof with present techniques and knowledge, considering the general lack of bridging arguments and middle-range theory (Ascher 1961; Binford and Sabloff 1982). Explanation can therefore accumulate much faster than it can be evaluated; in the absence of disproof we have only disapproval. The stage is ideally set for trendy scenarios of the past, evaluated on the basis of what sounds good; and that is likely to be something which relates directly to the commonsense, everyday experience of the reader. This may be why recent archaeology has depended on quite mundane models of past peoples, forgetting just how exotic and bizarre the ethnographic record can be. Explanations have to appeal to common experience.

That is perhaps the "dark side" of the picture I have painted, one which certainly alarms some of the leaders of our field (Flannery 1982; Binford and Sabloff 1982). As I said in the introduction to this paper, the changeability of the past in the hands of archaeologists can also lead to cynicism and disillusion on the part of lay people and academics in other fields. But there is another side to the matter, for it is the very fact that the past is to a certain extent a reflection of the present that makes the past so fascinating. If the past bore no relation to the present, and it can certainly be argued that the connection between the ancient Maya and modern Americans is tenuous (though Rathje [1982] disagrees), it would be dreadfully boring, even to archaeologists. By their commitment to studying the past as a profession, archaeologists affirm that there *is* a connection between past and present and that it is important and relevant. They tend to believe that the appreciation of the past has a positive social role to play in the present.

Instead of being an escape from the present, the past today serves specific purposes, in a social and political sense. The purposes can be generally lumped into "past as charter" and "past as bad example." In the first, the past, as a reflection of the present, serves to legitimize present courses of action or circumstances, much as the Old Testament is used by the state of Israel. In the second, the past is also a reflection of the present but serves as a source of moral or pragmatic lessons showing why a present policy, action, or trend is wrong or deleterious. In *both* cases, the connection between past and present must be shown before the lesson can be drawn. Is it any wonder that archaeologists participate in the process by drawing their hypotheses and explanations from the present?

There is no reason for archaeologists to be defensive about explicitly or implicitly drawing on their personal, cultural, and political experience in their professional work. Like Hodder (1985), I think we should drop the pretense of absolute objectivity. Further, I suggest that drawing on present experience and interests is hardly "unscientific" and that it strengthens, rather than weakens, our work. The connection between present and past is a source of power, the power to offer legitimacy or attack it. Archaeologists have no monopoly on this power (though they do tend to resent others who intrude on their control of the past), but they do have a strong claim to it. Rather than condemning those who "pervert" the past to their own political purposes (Ford 1973), we should acknowledge that there is *no* neutral, value-free, or nonpolitical past—that if we take the present out of the past we are left with a dry, empty husk. The challenge is to be aware of the weight of the task and to take responsibility for the power inherent in interpreting the past. Let us not forget Orwell's epigram from *Nineteen Eighty-Four*: "Who controls the past, controls the future: who controls the present, controls the past" (Orwell 1949:251).

Notes

1. A version of this paper was presented at the 1983 meetings of the American Anthropological Association in Chicago. Many of the ideas presented here were developed during conversations with Diane Gifford, though they do not necessarily reflect her opinions. I want to thank Hal Wilhite, Orvar Löfgren, Robert Netting, Cheryl Claasen, Warren DeBoer, Anne Pyburn, Matt Cartmill, David Freidel, Bill Rathje, Michael Schiffer, and three anonymous reviewers who read and offered useful comments on various drafts of this paper. I particularly appreciate Freidel's support and interest, though he is far from agreement with the contents of the paper.

2. This perception is not limited entirely to laymen and students. The lead article in archaeology's major journal recently suggested that explanation in Maya archaeology has followed a circular pattern, with old ideas being rejected, allowed to rest, and then recycled, through ignorance and blind reaction against predecessors' theories (Marcus 1983).

3. It is remarkable that Salmon's recent (1982) study of archaeology from the perspective of the philosophy of science is almost devoid of any discussion about the origins of hypotheses. Apparently the issue is philosophically trivial, whatever its historical importance.

4. The lineal transmission of ideas from teacher to student seems to be the prevailing folk model among archaeologists. A rival model sees a source of innovation in the rebellion of students against their teachers (Binford 1972).

5. It would indeed be a fascinating study to look at the papers in Maya studies which have been rejected by the major journals or which were never even submitted by authors. It would also be interesting to contrast the content of the writings of North American Mesoamericanists with Mexican and French work to see if the different cultural backgrounds affect the explanatory content.

6. Rachel Carson's *Silent Spring* was published in 1962.

7. After 1975, in fact, most new legislation weakened existing environmental law. The Clean Air Act amendments of 1977 weakened standards and controls established in 1970.

8. A much earlier period had seen a good deal of descriptive work on the Maya rain forest environment and Maya agriculture (e.g., Lundell 1934, 1937; Roys 1931). This work seems largely devoted to showing that the Maya environment wasn't quite as hostile as it appears and that it was quite capable of supporting a civilization, a position that was later attacked by Meggers. There is no space in this paper to discuss how this whole environmental limitation argument is related to the great highland/lowland division between archaeologists in Mesoamerica.

9. An earlier paper on women in Maya art by Proskouriakoff (1964) merely points out that women did indeed exist in Classic times, a fact that had been mostly overlooked until then.

10. For the purposes of Figure 1, the categories have been condensed. Invasion and warfare are conflated, as are agriculture and population growth in the category of ecology. In each volume the majority of papers were concerned with the "three C's" (ceramics, chronology, culture history), while a minority (not tabulated) dealt with sundry topics like art history and trade. Tabulations for the 1966 papers (Bullard 1970) are somewhat more tentative than for later volumes. Because of the overwhelming culture-historical orientation of that volume, it contained only slight discussion of warfare, ecology, or religion. The dates for environmental events are mainly from Vig and Kraft (1984), while the Vietnam War was covered in Isaacs (1983) and Amter (1984). The volumes' proper references, the number of substantive papers in each (excluding introductions and summary papers), and the date the papers were presented or submitted for publication are as follows: Bullard 1970, 10 papers, submitted 1966; Culbert 1973, 15 papers, conference 1970; Hammond 1974, 14 papers, conference 1972; Adams 1977b, 13 papers, conference 1974; Hammond 1977, 22 papers, submitted 1975; Hammond and Willey 1979, 13 papers, conference 1976; Ashmore 1981, 13 papers, conference 1977.

References

Adams, R.E.W., 1964, The Ceramic Sequence at Altar de Sacrificios and Its Implications. Pp. 371–78 in 35th International Congress of Americanists, vol. 1. Mexico City: Instituto Nacional de Antropología e Historia.

Adams, R.E.W., 1971, The Ceramics of Altar de Sacrificios, Guatemala. Papers of the Peabody Museum 63(1). Harvard University, Cambridge, Mass.

Adams, R.E.W., 1973, Maya Collapse: Transformation and Termination in the Ceramic Sequence at Altar de Sacrificios. Pp. 133–64 in The Classic Maya Collapse (ed. by T.P. Culbert). Albuquerque: University of New Mexico Press.

Adams, R.E.W., 1977a, Rio Bec Archaeology and the Rise of Maya Civilization. Pp. 77–99 in The Origins of Maya Civilization (ed. by R.E.W. Adams). Albuquerque: University of New Mexico Press.

Adams, R.E.W., ed., 1977b, The Origins of Maya Civilization. Albuquerque: University of New Mexico Press.

Adams, R.E.W., 1981, Settlement Patterns of the Central Yucatan and Southern Campeche Regions. Pp. 211–58 in Lowland Maya Settlement Patterns (ed. by W. Ashmore). Albuquerque: University of New Mexico Press.

Adams, R.E.W., and W. Smith, 1981, Feudal Models for Classic Maya Civilization. Pp. 335–50 in Lowland Maya Settlement Patterns (ed. by W. Ashmore). Albuquerque: University of New Mexico Press.

Amter, J.A., 1984, Vietnam Verdict. New York: Continuum.

Ascher, R., 1961, Analogy in Archaeological Interpretation. Southwestern Journal of Anthropology 17(4): 317–24.

Ashmore, W., ed., 1981, Lowland Maya Settlement Patterns. Albuquerque: University of New Mexico Press.

Bar-Yosef, O., and A. Mazar, 1982, Israeli Archaeology. World Archaeology 13(3): 310–26.

Becker, M., 1979, Priests, Peasants, and Ceremonial Centers: The Intellectual History of a Model. Pp. 3–20 in Maya Archaeology and Ethnohistory (ed. by N. Hammond and G. Willey). Austin: University of Texas Press.

Bernal, I., 1980, A History of Mexican Archaeology. London: Thames and Hudson.

Binford, L.R., 1968, Some Comments on Historical Versus Processual Archeology. Southwestern Journal of Anthropology 24: 267–75.

Binford, L.R., 1972, An Archaeological Perspective. New York: Seminar Press.

Binford, L.R., 1977, General Introduction. Pp. 1–10 in For Theory Building in Archaeology (ed. by L.R. Binford). New York: Academic Press.

Binford, L.R., 1985, "Brand X" Versus the Recommended Product. American Antiquity 50(3): 580–90.

Binford, L.R., and J. Sabloff, 1982, Paradigms, Systematics, and Archaeology. Journal of Anthropological Research 38(2): 137–53.

Blanton, R.E., 1980, Cultural Ecology Reconsidered. American Antiquity 45(1): 145–51.

Boserup, E., 1965, The Conditions of Agricultural Growth. Chicago: Aldine.

Brumfiel, E., 1983, Aztec State Making: Ecology, Structure, and the Origin of the State. American Anthropologist 85(2): 261–84.

Bulkin, V.A., L. Klejn, and G. Lebedev, 1982, Attainments and Problems of Soviet Archaeology. World Archaeology 13(3): 272–96.

Bullard, W., ed., 1970, Monographs and Papers in Maya Archaeology. Papers of the Peabody Museum 61. Harvard University, Cambridge, Mass.

Carneiro, R., 1970, A Theory of the Origin of the State. Science 169(3947): 733–38.

Carson, R., 1962, Silent Spring. Boston: Houghton-Mifflin.

Chagnon, N., 1967, Yanomamo Social Organization and Warfare. Natural History 76: 44–48.

Chang, K.C., 1981, Archaeology and Chinese Historiography. World Archaeology 13(2): 156–70.

Coe, M., 1981, Religion and the Rise of Mesoamerican States. Pp. 157–71 in The Transition to Statehood in the New World (ed. by G. Jones and R. Kautz). Cambridge, Eng.: Cambridge University Press.

Cowgill, G.L., 1964, The End of Classic Maya Culture: A Review of Recent Evidence. Southwestern Journal of Anthropology 20(2): 145–59.

Cowgill, G.L., 1975, On Causes and Consequences of Ancient and Modern Population Changes. American Anthropologist 77: 505–25.

Cowgill, G.L., 1979, Teotihuacan, Internal Militaristic Competition, and the Fall of the Classic Maya. Pp. 51–62 in Maya Archaeology and Ethnohistory (ed. by N. Hammond and G. Willey). Austin: University of Texas Press.

Cowgill, U.M., 1962, An Agricultural Study of the Southern Maya Lowlands. American Anthropologist 64: 273–86.

Culbert, T.P., ed., 1973, The Classic Maya Collapse. Albuquerque: University of New Mexico Press.

Culbert, T.P. 1974, The Lost Civilization: The Story of the Classic Maya. New York: Harper and Row.

Dobkin de Rios, M., 1974, The Influence of Psychotropic Flora and Fauna on Maya Religion. Current Anthropology 15(2): 147–64.

Ehrlich, R., 1968, The Population Bomb. New York: Ballantine Books.

Flannery, K., 1982, The Golden Marshalltown: A Parable for the Archaeology of the 1980s. American Anthropologist 84(2): 265–78.

Ford, R., 1973, Archeology Serving Humanity. Pp. 83–94 in Research and Theory in Current Archaeology (ed. by C. Redman). New York: John Wiley and Sons.

Freidel, D.A., 1979, Culture Areas and Interaction Spheres: Contrasting Approaches to Lowland Maya Evolution in Light of the Evidence from Cerros, Northern Belize. American Antiquity 44(1): 36–54.

Freidel, D.A., 1981a, The Political Economics of Residential Dispersion Among the Lowland Maya. Pp. 371–84 in Lowland Maya Settlement Patterns (ed. by W. Ashmore). Albuquerque: University of New Mexico Press.

Freidel, D.A., 1981b, Civilization as a State of Mind: The Cultural Evolution of the Lowland Maya. Pp. 188–227 in The Transition to Statehood in the New World (ed. by G. Jones and R. Kautz). Cambridge, Eng.: Cambridge University Press.

Freidel, D.A., and V. Scarborough, 1982, Subsistence, Trade and Development of the Coastal Maya. Pp. 131–56 in Maya Subsistence (ed. by K. Flannery). New York: Academic Press.

Fritz, J.M., 1973, Relevance, Archaeology and Subsistence Theory. Pp. 59–82 in Research and Theory in Current Archaeology (ed. by C. Redman). New York: John Wiley and Sons.

Fritz, J., and F. Plog, 1970, The Nature of Archaeological Explanation. American Antiquity 35: 405–12.

Furst, P., 1970, The Tsite (Erythrina spp.) of the Popol Vuh and other Psychotropic Plants in Pre-Columbian Art. Paper presented at the Annual Meeting of the Society for American Archaeology, Mexico City.

Furst, P., ed., 1972, Flesh of the Gods. New York: Praeger.

Gann, T., and J.E. Thompson, 1931, The History of the Maya, from the Earliest Time to the Present Day. New York: Scribner's.

Gero, J., D. Lacy, and M. Blakey, eds., 1983, The Socio-Politics of Archaeology. Anthropological Research Report, no. 23. University of Massachusetts, Amherst, Mass.

Haas, J., 1981, Class Conflict and the State in the New World. Pp. 80–104 in The Transition to Statehood in the New World (ed. by G. Jones and R. Kautz). Cambridge, Eng.: Cambridge University Press.

Hamblin, R., and B. Pitcher, 1980, The Classic Maya Collapse: Testing Class Conflict Hypotheses. American Antiquity 45(2): 246–67.

Hammond, N., ed., 1974, Mesoamerican Archaeology: New Approaches. Austin: University of Texas Press.

Hammond, N., ed., 1977, Social Process in Maya Prehistory. London: Academic Press.

Hammond, N., and G.R. Willey, eds., 1979, Maya Archaeology and Ethnohistory. Austin: University of Texas Press.

Harris, M., 1964, Patterns of Race in the Americas. New York: Walker and Company.

Harrison, P., 1977, The Rise of the Bajos and the Fall of the Maya. Pp. 470–509 in Social Process in Maya Prehistory (ed. by N. Hammond). London: Academic Press.

Harrison, P., and B.L. Turner II, eds., 1978, Pre-Hispanic Maya Agriculture. Albuquerque: University of New Mexico Press.

Haviland, W., 1981, Dower Houses and Minor Centers at Tikal, Guatemala: An Investigation into the Identification of Valid Units in Settlement Hierarchies. Pp. 89–120 in Lowland Maya Settlement Patterns (ed. by W. Ashmore). Albuquerque: University of New Mexico Press.

Hempel, C.G., 1966, Philosophy of Natural Science. Englewood Cliffs, N.J.: Prentice-Hall.

Hodder, I., 1985, Postprocessual Archaeology. Pp. 1–26 in Advances in Archaeological Method and Theory, vol. 8 (ed. by M. Schiffer). New York: Academic Press.

Hosler, D., J. Sabloff, and D. Runge, 1977, Situation Model Development: A Case Study of the Classic Maya Collapse. Pp. 553–90 in Social Process in Maya Prehistory (ed. by N. Hammond). London: Academic Press.

Isaacs, A.R., 1983, Without Honor. Baltimore, Md.: Johns Hopkins University Press.

Kowalewski, S., 1980, Population-Resource Balances in Period 1 of Oaxaca, Mexico. American Antiquity 45(1): 151–64.

Kristiansen, K., 1981, A Social History of Danish Archaeology (1805–1975). Pp. 20–44 in Towards a History of Archaeology (ed. by G. Daniel). London: Thames and Hudson.

Leone, M., 1972, Issues in Anthropological Archaeology. Pp. 14–27 in Contemporary Archaeology (ed. by M. Leone). Carbondale, Ill.: Southern Illinois University Press.

Leone, M., 1981, Archaeology's Relationship to the Present and the Past. Pp. 5–14 in Modern Material Culture: The Archaeology of US (ed. by R. Gould and M. Schiffer). New York: Academic Press.

Lorenzo, J., 1981a, Archaeology South of the Rio Grande. World Archaeology 13(2): 190–209.

Lorenzo, J., 1981b, Notes on the History of Ibero-American Archaeology. Pp. 133–45 in Towards a History of Archaeology (ed. by G. Daniel). London: Thames and Hudson.

Lundell, C.L., 1934, The Agriculture of the Maya. Southwest Review 19: 65–77.

Lundell, C.L., 1937, The Vegetation of the Peten. Publication 478. Washington, DC: Carnegie Institution of Washington.

Marcus, J., 1978, Archaeology and Religion: A Comparison of the Zapotec and Maya. World Archaeology 10: 172–91.

Marcus, J., 1983, Lowland Maya Archaeology at the Crossroads. American Antiquity 48(3): 454–88.

Meadows, D.H., D.L. Meadows, J. Randers, and W.W. Behrens III, 1972, The Limits to Growth: A Report for the Club of Rome's Project on the Predicament of Mankind. New York: Universe Books.

Meggers, B., 1954, Environmental Limitation in the Development of Culture. American Anthropologist 56(5): 801–24.

Molloy, J.P., and W.L. Rathje, 1974, Sexploitation Among the Late Classic Maya. Pp. 431–44 in Mesoamerican Archaeology: New Approaches (ed. by N. Hammond). Austin: University of Texas Press.

Murdock, G.P., 1949, Social Structure. New York: Macmillan.

Nimis, M.M., 1982, The Contemporary Role of Women in Lowland Maya Livestock Production. Pp. 313–26 in Maya Subsistence (ed. by K. Flannery). New York: Academic Press.

Orwell, G., 1949, Nineteen Eighty-Four. New York: Harcourt, Brace and World.

Pohl, M., and L. Feldman, 1982, The Traditional Role of Women and Animals in Lowland Maya Economy. Pp. 295–312 in Maya Subsistence (ed. by K. Flannery). New York: Academic Press.

Price, B., 1974, The Burden of the Cargo: Ethnographic Models and Archaeological Inference. Pp. 445–66 in Mesoamerican Archeology: New Approaches (ed. by N. Hammond). Austin: University of Texas Press.

Proskouriakoff, T., 1964, Portraits of Women in Maya Art. Pp. 81–99 in Essays in Pre-Columbian Art and Archaeology (ed. by S.K. Lothrop and others). Cambridge, Mass.: Harvard University Press.

Puleston, D., 1979, An Epistemological Pathology and the Collapse, or Why the Maya Kept the Short Count. Pp. 63–74 in Maya Archaeology and Ethnohistory (ed. by N. Hammond and G. Willey). Austin: University of Texas Press.

Puleston, D., and D.W. Callender, Jr., 1967, Defensive Earthworks at Tikal. Expedition 9: 40–48.

Puleston, O., and D. Puleston, 1971, An Ecological Approach to the Origins of Maya Civilization. Archaeology 24: 330–37.

Rathje, W., 1982, Braniff's Ruin. Early Man (Autumn) 1982: 14–15.

Rathje, W., and M. Schiffer, 1982, Archaeology. New York: Harcourt, Brace, Jovanovich.

Redman, C., 1973, Research and Theory in Current Archaeology: An Introduction. Pp. 5–20 in Research and Theory in Current Archaeology (ed. by C. Redman). New York: Wiley and Sons.

Reid, J.J., W.L. Rathje, and M.B. Schiffer, 1974, Expanding Archaeology. American Antiquity 39: 125–26.

Rice, D.S., 1978, Population Growth and Subsistence Alternatives in a Tropical Lacustrine Environment. Pp. 35–62 in Pre-Hispanic Maya Agriculture (ed. by P. Harrison and B.L. Turner). Albuquerque: University of New Mexico Press.

Roys, R.L., 1931, The Ethno-Botany of the Maya. Middle American Research Series, Publication no. 2. Tulane University, New Orleans, La.

Sabloff, J., and G.R. Willey, 1967, The Collapse of Maya Civilization in the Southern Lowlands: A Consideration of History and Process. Southwestern Journal of Anthropology 23(4): 311–36.

Sahlins, M., 1976, Culture and Practical Reason. Chicago: University of Chicago Press.

Salmon, M., 1982, Philosophy and Archaeology. New York: Academic Press.

Sanders, W.T., 1962, Cultural Ecology of the Maya Lowlands, Part 1. Estudios de Cultura Maya 2: 79–121.

Sanders, W.T., 1963, Cultural Ecology of the Maya Lowlands, Part 2. Estudios de Cultura Maya 3: 203–41.

Sanders, W.T., 1972, Population, Agricultural History, and Societal Evolution in Mesoamerica. Pp. 101–53 in Population Growth: Anthropological Implications (ed. by B. Spooner). Cambridge, Mass.: M.I.T. Press.

Sanders, W.T., 1973, The Cultural Ecology of the Lowland Maya: A Reevaluation. Pp. 325–66 in The Classic Maya Collapse (ed. by T.P. Culbert). Albuquerque: University of New Mexico Press.

Sanders, W.T., and B. Price, 1968, Mesoamerica: The Evolution of a Civilization. New York: Random House.

Sharer, R.J., 1977, The Maya Collapse Revisited: Internal and External Perspectives. Pp. 532–52 in Social Process in Maya Prehistory (ed. by N. Hammond). London: Academic Press.

Thompson, J.E.S., 1927, The Civilization of the Mayas. Anthropology Leaflet 25. Chicago: Field Museum of Natural History.

Thompson, J.E.S., 1970, Maya History and Religion. Norman: University of Oklahoma Press.

Trigger, B., 1973, The Future of Archaeology is the Past. Pp. 95–112 in Research and Theory in Current Archaeology (ed. by C. Redman). New York: Wiley and Sons.

Trigger, B., 1981, Anglo American Archaeology. World Archaeology 13(2): 138–55.

Trigger, B., and I. Glover, 1981, Editorial: Regional Traditions of Archaeological Research. World Archaeology 13(2): 133–37.

Turner, B.L., 1974, Prehistoric Intensive Agriculture in the Maya Lowlands. Science 185: 118–24.

Vig, N., and M. Kraft, 1984, Environmental Policy from the Seventies to the Eighties. Pp. 3–27 in Environmental Policy in the 1980s (ed. by N. Vig and M. Kraft). Washington, DC: CQ Press.

Vogt, E.Z., 1961, Some Aspects of Zinacantan Settlement Patterns and Ceremonial Organization. Estudios de Cultura Maya 1: 131–45.

Vogt, E.Z., 1964, Some Implications of Zinacantan Social Structure for the Study of the Ancient Maya. Pp. 307–19 in 35th International Congress of Americanists, vol. 1. Mexico City: Instituto Nacional de Antropología e Historia.

Watson, P.J., S. LeBlanc, and C. Redman, 1971, Explanation in Archeology: An Explicitly Scientific Approach. New York: Columbia University Press.

Webster, D.L., 1972, The Fortifications of Becan, Campeche, Mexico. Ph.D. diss., University of Minnesota, Minneapolis.

Webster, D.L., 1974, The Fortifications of Becan, Campeche, Mexico. Publication 31, Middle American Research Institute, Tulane University, New Orleans, La.

Webster, D.L., 1975, Warfare and the Origin of the State: A Reconsideration. American Antiquity 40: 464–70.

Webster, D.L., 1977, Warfare and the Evolution of Maya Civilization. Pp. 335–72 in The Origins of Maya Civilization (ed. by R.E.W. Adams). Albuquerque: University of New Mexico Press.

Wilk, R.R., and W. Rathje, 1982, Household Archaeology. American Behavioral Scientist 25(6): 617–40.

Willey, G.R., and J. Sabloff, 1973, A History of American Archaeology. San Francisco: W.H. Freeman.

"War in the Southwest, War in the World"

STEPHEN H. LEKSON

This selection provides some insight into archaeological thinking about warfare, including alternative approaches to understanding its causes. Author Stephen Lekson is a professor and curator of anthropology at the University of Colorado. This piece originally appeared in a 2002 issue of *American Antiquity*, a scholarly journal published by the Society for American Archaeology.

....

Questions to Guide Reading

What were Lekson's research methods?

What is the time range and geographic location of the Pueblo peoples?

What is Lawrence Keeley's view of warfare in prehistory?

What are some examples of "resource unpredictability" and how can it be identified archaeologically?

How can the "socialization for mistrust and fear" be identified archaeologically?

How is cannibalism explained?

....

The study of warfare in the ancient Pueblos of the U.S. Southwest has become politicized and contentious, and southwestern data are only rarely used to address larger anthropological theories of war. A cross-cultural model of violence proposed by Carol and Melvin Ember (1992) suggests that war in pre-state societies is predicted by resource unpredictability and socialization for fear. The Ember and Ember model is evaluated using syntheses of southwestern warfare by Steven LeBlanc (1999), environmental variability by Jeffrey Dean (1988, 1996), and political history by Stephen Lekson (1999). The fit between the southwestern data and the model is close, and supports the Ember and Ember model.

The past decade has seen renewed archaeological interest in warfare in the ancient U.S. Southwest (Haas 1990; Haas and Creamer 1993; LeBlanc 1999; Lipe 1995; Rice and LeBlanc 2001; Schaafsma 2000; Turner and Turner 1999; Wilcox and Haas 1994). A region conventionally considered peaceful is emerging as periodically violent. Southwestern warfare receives media attention, and, in its most sensational presentations (Preston 1998; Turner 1999), accounts of warfare and possible cannibalism polarize archaeology and offend Native Americans. The furor caused by journalistic presentations of these subjects, however, does not diminish their importance. As Haas (1990), Kantner (1999), LeBlanc

(1999) and, earlier, Kroeber and Fontana (1986) have demonstrated, the study of violence in the ancient Southwest can contribute to larger anthropological questions about warfare.

There is, of course, no anthropological unanimity on war's causes (see, for example, Ferguson 1984; Ferrill 1997; Haas 1990; Keeley 1996; Kelly 2000; Otterbein 1973, 1997; Reyna and Downs 1994). If consideration is extended to other disciplines that study warfare (economics, history, military science, political science, philosophy, psychology, sociology, and others), the range of ideas is staggering. Many theories about warfare fall into two major approaches: ideas that favor internal biological or psychological causes, and ideas that favor external institutional or environmental causes. Arguments from either perspective are often presented as exclusive: that is, external or internal factors are presented as paramount. In this paper, I will use southwestern prehistoric data to evaluate one cross-cultural study that links the origins of warfare to *both* external environmental and internal psychological factors, developed by Carol Ember and Melvin Ember (1992).

In the Ember and Ember model, the primary external environmental factor is *resource unpredictability*. Is resource unpredictability correlated with southwestern war? The southwestern data used here to evaluate warfare and resource unpredictability are, principally, Steven LeBlanc's (1999) recent summary of violence in the Southwest and Jeffrey Dean's dendroclimatological reconstructions of ancient southwestern climate (Dean 1988, 1996). A secondary factor in Ember and Ember's study implicates internal psychological conditions with the onset or prevalence of warfare. This factor is *socialization for mistrust or fear*. My reconstruction of the political history of the ancient Southwest (Lekson 1999) will be used to evaluate Ember and Ember's second, internal proposition about the causes of war.

The Ember and Ember study is particularly interesting in that it addresses both external, environmental causes and internal, psychological causes. It is only one alternative in the vast literature on war,

but Ember and Ember's cross-cultural methodology is singularly well-suited to archaeological application and testing (Ember and Ember 1995).

The southwestern studies that form the core of my analysis are subject to various and numerous criticisms, but these works provide remarkably (even uniquely) broad syntheses of key themes useful for the evaluation of the Ember and Ember model. Wide-ranging synthetic studies—such as those of LeBlanc and my own work—are always vulnerable to alternate interpretations of details and particulars; but, as we shall see, the conclusions of the studies I use here are remarkably congruent. The mutual agreement of these independent studies must not be accepted uncritically as representing a true interpretation of the past, but their complementarity is heartening.

This article is not an attempt to develop an encompassing model for violence and warfare in the Southwest. It is only an application of the Ember and Ember model to southwestern data—no more and no less. Nor does it present startling new data; the data considered here come from published, peer-reviewed studies, cited and quoted throughout. The paper begins with a brief review of relevant southwestern prehistory. It then summarizes Ember and Ember's study of warfare in non-state societies, and their conclusions linking (primarily) environmental factors and violence and (secondarily) psychological factors and violence. Dean's dendroclimatology and LeBlanc's study of warfare in the ancient Southwest will then be presented to evaluate the environmental aspects of the Ember and Ember model. My version of Pueblo political history is then integrated with chronologies of violence and warfare to address the psychological conclusions of the Ember and Ember study.

A particular appeal of the Ember and Ember model for southwestern archaeology is this: it works. As we shall see, there is a reasonably good fit between their model and our data. That fit, of course, is no reason to ignore imperfections in either the model or the data, but it happens so seldom that it seems worthy of remark.

The Southwest, In Brief

The archaeology of Pueblo peoples is well summarized by Cordell (1994, 1997), Plog (1997), and Reid and Whittlesey (1997). Here I provide an extremely brief version of later Pueblo history and geography, for readers who may be unfamiliar with the region. This paper does not address the Hohokam (the ancient peoples of southern Arizona), and they are absent from this review. Note that all dates in this paper are A.D.

Southwestern archaeology is doubly fortunate in that it has a great deal of high-quality field research and high-resolution dendrochronology, which provides both precise tree-ring dates and (as discussed below) fine-grained climatic data. The prehistory of the Southwest is also relatively uncomplicated, in contrast to the Basin of Mexico, the Tigris-Euphrates, or many other areas with longer sequences and more complex developments. The Southwest provides a simple and relatively clear archaeological record. This is not to diminish the remarkable achievements of ancient southwestern peoples (or modern archaeologists); indeed, the Southwest's simplicity and the quality and quantity of its archaeological data make the Southwest a useful place for investigating complicated matters, and war is a complicated matter.

Today, Pueblo peoples live in about 30 towns in 19 tribal clusters, along a 500-km-long arc from the Hopi villages of Arizona to Taos Pueblo in New Mexico (Figure 1). The modern Pueblo groups are the cultural heirs of a tradition of small farming villages that reaches back in time at least 1,500 years, and extended in space over the "Four Corners" areas of Utah and Colorado, most of New Mexico and Arizona, and the northern part of Chihuahua. It is useful to divide this vast area into northern and southern parts (Figure 1). The northern half of the Pueblo region corresponds, roughly, to the southern portion of the Colorado Plateau and includes the present Pueblos. The southern half includes the mountainous Mogollon uplands and the upper margins of the Sonoran and Chihuahuan deserts.

Most towns in the southern Pueblo world had been abandoned about 1450, but at the time of Spanish contact, Pueblo peoples were living in the northernmost reaches of the Chihuahuan deserts in south-central New Mexico. Those southern villages did not survive colonization. The entire region is arid. Agriculture in the south was closely linked to rivers and canal irrigation, but "dry farming" (relying primarily on rainfall) was a major element of subsistence in the northern Pueblo world.

Pueblo traditional histories recount high degrees of population movement and migrations by large groups. Many pueblos grew to several thousands of residents by the fifteenth and sixteenth centuries, despite the "abandonment" of the Four Corners area at the end of the fourteenth century, the "abandonment" of the southern Pueblo region in the fifteenth century, and other population disruptions.

Various areas within the Pueblo world were archaeologically prominent at different times. Chaco Canyon was very important in the tenth and eleventh century. For over a century, archaeologists explored and excavated at Chaco (Frazier 1999; Lister and Lister 1981). Judge (1989) provides a particularly useful summary, and I follow his chronology here (see also Crown and Judge 1991; Lekson et al. 1988). Chaco's massive buildings and its remarkable network of "roads"—linear earthen features that extend great distances—and far-flung Chaco-like structures ("outliers") have suggested to many archaeologists that Chaco was the center of a large region.

Chaco's end in the early or mid twelfth century was followed by the rise of remarkable cliff-sheltered villages in southwestern Colorado and across the Four Corners area. The cliff-dwellings date principally to the late twelfth and thirteenth century. The largest villages of this era, however, were huge "open" sites that were up to five times the size of the largest cliff-dwellings. The twelfth and thirteenth centuries saw the emergence (or solidification) of localized traditions—"Kayenta," "Mesa Verde," "Tularosa," and the like—several of which continued down into the historic Pueblos. An excellent

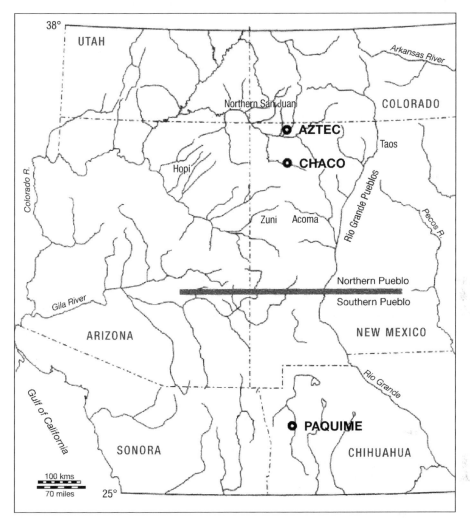

FIGURE 1: Southwest United States and Northwest Mexico, with selected towns, sites, and regions.

summary of the Pueblo world during this period is provided by Adler (1996).

One of the very largest thirteenth-century sites, discussed below, was the misnamed Aztec Ruins complex in northwestern New Mexico. The major excavations at Aztec Ruins were the work of Earl Morris; Morris's work was summarized in Lister and Lister (1987). Recent thinking is summarized by McKenna and Toll (2001). Aztec Ruins, during the

twelfth and thirteenth century, included six-to-eight structures comparable to the massive Chacoan buildings of the preceding century and scores of smaller structures. Building ceased at Aztec Ruins about 1275, a date coinciding with the "Great Drought" of ca. 1275–1300 and the final abandonment of the Four Corners region.

The fourteenth and fifteenth centuries saw the development of Pueblos along the Rio Grande, at

Acoma, Zuni and the Hopi mesas, as well as significant population centers in the southern Pueblo area in the Mogollon uplands and northern Chihuahua. Many of these towns and village clusters emerged from local traditions; others were significantly affected by the late-thirteenth-century population movements out of the Four Corners area and (later, and less certainly) by fifteenth-century movements out of the southern Pueblo region. Sites reached very large sizes: the largest prehistoric Pueblos date to the fourteenth and fifteenth centuries. One of these is a site that is emerging as truly important in southwestern archaeology: Paquimé, near the town of Casas Grandes in Chihuahua, Mexico. Paquimé is only a little more than 100 km south of the international border, but southwestern archaeologists did not begin to understand the site until the late 1960s, when Charles Di Peso of the Amerind Foundation excavated about one-third of the ruin. His monumental report (Di Peso 1974) is the principal account of the site, supplemented by recent research (Schaafsma and Riley 1999; Whalen and Minnis 2001). The city of Paquimé was abandoned about 1450, along with much of the southern Pueblo world. The northern Pueblos continued to grow and flourish until the arrival of the Spanish in the late sixteenth century.

This brief survey, of course, does not attempt to digest the cultural history or the voluminous archaeology of the Pueblo Southwest. It simply outlines the chronology and geography of Pueblo prehistory, and introduces principal sites pertinent to the analysis of violence and warfare in the Southwest, to which we now turn.

Cross-Cultural Studies of Warfare in Non-State Societies

One of the most influential recent syntheses of warfare in non-state societies is Lawrence Keeley's (1996) *War Before Civilization*. Keeley makes a strong case that "archaeologists of the postwar period had artificially 'pacified the past' and shared a pervasive bias against the possibility of prehistoric warfare" (Keeley 1996:vii). In contrast to that received view, he argues that "peaceful prestate societies were very rare; warfare between them was very frequent" (Keeley 1996:174). Keeley's study documents the prevalence of war across a wide range of societies in a broad range of times, as a corrective to the vast literature on war that is based, he argues, on fatally insufficient data. Misunderstandings of the violent nature and high frequency of war in non-state societies have, in Keeley's opinion, undermined classical and contemporary theory on war. (See Otterbein 1997 for a critique of Keeley, and a more moderate reading of war in pre-state societies.)

The Pueblo Indians of the U.S. Southwest are famously peaceful. Pueblos of the late-nineteenth and early twentieth century were offered as models for nonviolent society (Benedict 1989 [1934]). Was this always the case? Steven LeBlanc (1999) argues that Keeley's thesis applies to the U.S. Southwest: LeBlanc concludes that the ancient Southwest was as violent as other agricultural, non-state societies.

For Keeley, the theoretical search for causes of warfare is confounded by the complexity of the phenomenon, pervasive across many varied societies and different environments. The richness and variety of Keeley's data defeat the simple causal arguments of past theories: "the essential focus of almost all of these arguments has been the perennial question: what causes war? ... no complex phenomenon [such as war] can have a single cause" (Keeley 1996:17). Perhaps the Southwest, in its simplicity and archaeological clarity, will prove a useful place to investigate war's causes. I turn now to a study comparable to Keeley's in breadth, which reached tentative conclusions about the causes of war. These conclusions can be evaluated using southwestern data.

Carol Ember and Melvin Ember (1992; see also Ember 1982) conducted a broad cross-cultural study of the predictors of warfare in non-state societies, by evaluating standardized coefficients in a multiple regression analysis of cross-cultural data mostly from the Human Relations Area File Collection of

Ethnography. They concluded, "war may be caused by a fear of nature and a partially resultant fear of others. A history of unpredictable natural disasters strongly predicts more war, as does socialization for mistrust (but less strongly)" (Ember and Ember 1992:242). That is, they concluded that two factors most strongly predicted the presence of war in nonstate societies.

The two strongest predictors of warfare were "resource unpredictability" ($R = 0.631, p$ [0.001) and "socialization for mistrust" ($R = 0.1352, p$ [0.025) (Ember and Ember 1992:Table 1). Resource unpredictability refers to "nonchronic resource problems created by natural disasters" (Ember and Ember 1992:250). Socialization for mistrust is a psychological result of enculturation: "people who grow up to be mistrustful of others, and who therefore fear others, may be more likely to go to war than to negotiate or to seek conciliation" (Ember and Ember 1992:245). They argue from their analysis that socialization for mistrust is "more likely a cause than a consequence of war" (Ember and Ember 1992:254). For reasons that will become clear, I recast "socialization for mistrust" as "socialization for fear."

Each of these factors will be discussed at more length below, but please review the Ember and Ember article for the larger arguments behind these two conclusions, which I accept here as hypotheses. Can we test these hypotheses with the archaeological record of the U.S. Southwest? I will first discuss resource unpredictability, and then turn to socialization for fear.

Resource Unpredictability

Resource unpredictability is a far more familiar theme in archaeology than socialization for fear. Rainfall farming (or "dry farming") was apparently the major agricultural strategy in the northern Pueblo region (Cordell 1997; Plog 1997; Reid and Whittlesey 1997). Absent investment in canal irrigation, rainfall was probably the most important environmental parameter that affected crop pro-

duction through various "dry-farming" strategies. Salinated soils, unseasonable frosts, insect infestations, and other natural disasters undoubtedly impacted crops, but year-to-year, rainfall was probably the principal concern of farmers and their leaders. Today, much Pueblo ceremonialism encourages or insures rainfall.

Because of the very close linkage between precipitation and farming success, resource unpredictability should be reflected in dendroclimatology, the reconstruction of past climate through tree-ring analysis. Dendroclimatology provides annual and even seasonal projections of precipitation, with great precision. The remarkable dendroclimatological record in the Southwest was summarized in a widely cited paper by Jeffrey Dean (1988). Dean defined periods of "high temporal variability" in tree-ring departures (averaged decadally); that is, spans in which year-to-year variation was highly variable. Variation in tree-ring departures reflects comparably high temporal variability in various parameters of annual rainfall that, in the arid Southwest, has a direct relationship to crop production in "dry-farming" societies of the ancient Pueblo region (e.g., Van West 1996). In a later paper, Dean (1996) presents additional data on seasonal variation, that is, patterns of seasonal dominance of precipitation—a key factor in the success of "dry farming." In this section, I will briefly discuss conventional archaeological interpretations of environmental risk, and then use data from Dean's 1988 and 1996 papers to construct a chronology of resource unpredictability.

"High temporal variability," as presented by Dean (1988, 1996) is a composite measure, defined by visual inspection of a number of parallel tree-ring sequences. (Spatial variability is also important, but beyond the goals of my paper.) In periods of "high temporal variability," change from high to low tree-ring indices was rapid, taking place over scales of one to ten years. "High temporal variability" was defined in contrast to "low temporal variability," when change took place over several decades. In short, "high temporal variability" meant rapid, short-term oscillations of precipitation, while "low temporal variability" meant longer term, more stable regimes. Cultural systems could *adapt* to either circumstance—the principal argument of Dean and his colleagues (see chapters in Gumerman 1988).

Viewed from the longer term, southwestern societies did indeed adapt—by creating new storage technologies, intensifying agricultural practices, by migrating to new places, or by dissolving into new social formations. These adaptations, while real, are best perceived from the distance of history: a pattern invisible to people when they lived it, and unknown to us before we detected it (to paraphrase Kubler 1962:13). But from the perspective of the individual farmer, living in the pattern "low temporal variability" must have been perceived as more predictable or more constant than regimes of "high temporal variability." In regimes of "low temporal variability," good times stayed good and bad times stayed bad. Subsistence decisions could be made with a reasonable degree of predictability. In regimes of high temporal variability, the only constant was change. A farmer would never know what the next year might bring, and any decision could easily be wrong. Risk—both real and perceived—was high.

It is possible to adapt to circumstance of high-temporal variability by developing storage, reciprocity, and other adaptationist scenarios (as Dean and others have demonstrated). It is also possible to respond to those circumstances by raiding and warfare, as Billman et al. (2000) and Haas and Creamer (1993) suggest for the Pueblo Southwest, or by developing a degree of political complexity, as Judge (1979) and Lekson (1999) have suggested for Chaco.

Southwestern archaeology has long favored storage, agricultural intensification, and other economic adaptations to environmental risk over political or power responses. A fair gauge of southwestern thinking can be found in the ten papers compiled in *Evolving Complexity and Environmental Risk in the Prehistoric Southwest* (Tainter and Tainter 1996). These studies address "resource uncertainty," "risk," and "subsistence stress" (all of which encompass various forms of resource unpredictability). Political hierarchy and warfare barely break the surface (most notably in Kohler and Van West 1996:183; and in Tainter's introduction to the volume), and are generally ignored as an alternative to adaptationist responses to environmental risk. Linda Cordell, in her concluding remarks to this important volume, notes the relative unimportance of political models:

> Regional social dynamics and hierarchical systems of social control are not considered important to the kinds of strategies implemented in response to stress.... despite more than a decade of discussing the Chaco Phenomenon and the possibility of the existence of regionally based systems in the fourteenth century, most archaeologists are probably not convinced that these had any meaningful impacts on local behaviors [Cordell 1996:254].

In contrast, I will argue that regional political structures were major factors in management of risk and response to resource unpredictability in the ancient Southwest.

Resource unpredictability, as defined by Ember and Ember, includes natural disasters: volcanoes, floods, plagues of locusts, and other epic calamities. Resource unpredictability need not be quite so dramatic, particularly for marginal environments. In deserts, slight variations in rainfall can make the difference between subsistence success and failure. We are accustomed to think of risk in the ancient Southwest in terms of droughts. The Southwest is a desert; that is, drought is a constant. Sustained severe droughts with "low temporal variability"—such as the so-called Great Drought of ca. 1275–1300, could be accommodated by movement or by the development of new technologies, such as irrigation. That is, a series of dry years became *predictable*, and societies and individuals made decisions based on the perceived likelihood of another bad year. (Prolonged periods of higher rainfall were also, presumably, circumstances to which ancient societies could adjust, presumably with more satisfaction.)

But rapid and effectively unpredictable oscillations between "wet" and "dry" years—Dean's periods of "high temporal variability"—would challenge conventional social responses and perhaps exceed existing strategies for subsistence adjustments.

Thus, Dean's periods of "high temporal variability" in tree-ring departures can be taken as proxy measures of resource unpredictability. Periods of "high temporal variability" as defined by Dean (1988:138) fall at approximately 310–380, 750–1000, 1350–1560, and 1730–1825. That periodization will be modified, slightly, here to reflect an additional form of unpredictability: seasonal variability of precipitation. Dean (1996) identified two basic regimes of seasonality. In the north and west Southwest, precipitation was generally "bimodal" (evenly divided between winter and summer), while in the east and south precipitation was "summer dominant" (Dean 1996:Fig. 5). Those patterns held over almost all the dendroclimatological record; that is, they were effectively *predictable* over long periods of time. At ca. 1250, however, those long-standing patterns were disrupted; that is, they became strikingly *unpredictable*. "Between about A.D. 1250 and 1450 ... the long-term pattern [of seasonal precipitation] broke down into chaotic distributions ... that exhibit no local geographic patterning" (Dean 1996:43). From 1250 to 1450, the Pueblo people experienced resource unpredictability of a type unique in later southwestern prehistory: "a 200-year, regional-scale disruption of a climatic pattern that characterized the Southwest for the preceding 550 years [A.D. 700 to 1250] and the following 550 years [A.D. 1450 to present]" (Dean 1996:43; see also Ahlstrom et al. 1995). It should be noted that the analysis of seasonal variability was conducted by a principal component analysis of overlapped centuries, and therefore is potentially less precise than the decadal analysis of rainfall variability, discussed above. The onset date of 1250 is therefore approximate.

"High temporal variability" in tree-ring departures happened at least four times in the dendroclimatological record, as noted above. High seasonal variability, however, was unique, at the regional scale; that is, it happened only once, from 1250 to 1450. Note the slight but significant differences between the period of "high temporal variability" at 1350–1560 and the episode of high seasonal variability at 1250–1450, and particularly the difference between the inceptions of each, at 1350 and at 1250. While "high temporal variability" (i.e., unpredictability) in tree-ring departures began about 1350, significant unpredictability in seasonal precipitation patterns began about 1250. There is, of course, no reason why the two should coincide; the point here is that two different kinds of resource unpredictability are indicated that, in tandem, suggest an inclusive episode of significant resource unpredictability from 1250 to 1575 caused by *both* "high temporal" and chaotic seasonal variability. Thus, in combination, the indicated periods of resource unpredictability from both causes become: 310–380, 750–1000, 1250–1560, and 1730–1825.

Violence and Warfare

Against periods of resource unpredictability, as defined above, we can contrast data from Steven LeBlanc's (1999) survey of *Prehistoric Warfare in the American Southwest*. LeBlanc defined three periods of warfare in the ancient Southwest: Early (0–900), Middle (900–1150), and Late (1250–Spanish contact). The missing "interim" period 1150–1250 was "particularly difficult to characterize in terms of warfare" (LeBlanc 1999:153); I will return to the 1150–1250 period below. LeBlanc characterized these periods by labels: Early, "Endemic warfare"; Middle, "Pax With a Twist"; and Late, "Crisis and Catastrophe" (LeBlanc 1999).

A wide range of behaviors is subsumed by terms such as "warfare" and "violence." LeBlanc refers to violence in both Early and Late periods as warfare. I prefer terms reflecting the very different nature of violence in those two periods (congruent with LeBlanc's presentation): in the Early period, a lower level of *raiding and feuding*, comprising sporadic, situational, tit-for-tat conflicts on a family or small-group scale; and in the Late period, real war, consisting of large, intense, institutionalized combat on village or even multiple-village scales. Yet a third form of violence characterized the Middle period: executions. These executions were the grim "twist" in LeBlanc's "Pax with a twist." All three forms of violence will be discussed at more length, below.

LeBlanc's Early period was marked by intermittent but persistent violence: endemic raiding and feuding. The severity of this violence was not constant through the Early period. LeBlanc notes that, within the long Early period (0–900), there was marked "increase in the level of warfare during the late Pueblo I period—in the late 700s and 800s" (LeBlanc 1999:145). I therefore divide LeBlanc's long Early period into two subperiods, 0 to late 700s and late 700s to 900, with increased evidence for raiding- and feuding-scale violence during the later subperiod. "It is unclear, at this point, why the rate of warfare intensified at that time [late 700s] or why it was so abruptly terminated [about 900]" (LeBlanc 1999:146). Neither of my changes—substituting "feuding and raiding" for LeBlanc's "endemic warfare" and the temporal recognition of intensified violence during the late 700s—alters LeBlanc's general characterizations and conclusions about the Early period.

For his Middle period, LeBlanc amends my old phrase "Pax Chaco" to "Pax with a twist"—and there was indeed a "twist" (executions, discussed at length below). Otherwise, the Middle period from 900 to 1150 was "an era of unprecedented peace" (LeBlanc 1999:196). A wide range of archaeological data, summarized by LeBlanc, strongly suggests an abrupt and dramatic end to Early period raiding. In the Middle period, few homes were burned and violent trauma is rare. Middle period settlement can be fairly characterized as small single-family or extended family homes, scattered around the countryside in non-defensive locales. Often, these were loosely clustered in communities around Chaco "outliers," but this settlement pattern does not suggest concern for war or violence. In summary, LeBlanc's Middle period

was characterized by the absence of warfare and the presence of peace—but *not* the absolute absence of violence (as described below) from 900 to 1150.

Middle period peace probably persisted beyond 1150, through the hazy "interim" period from 1150 to 1250. LeBlanc states, of this interim period, that violence was "present, but barely visible in the archaeological record," compared to spectacularly evident warfare after 1250 (LeBlanc 1999:195). Low visibility, I think, represents low occurrence: the interim was, from the evidence, largely an extension of the Pax Chaco. As I will argue below, political patterns that characterized Chaco from about 900 to 1125 continued at Aztec Ruins from about 1110 to 1275—throughout the interim period. The "Pax Chaco" continued, I think, as a failed "Pax Aztec." Therefore, I will extend the Middle period through the 1150–1250 "interim": for this paper, the Middle period dates from 900 to 1250. I do not think my extension of LeBlanc's Middle period alters his recognition of a remarkable episode in southwestern prehistory. LeBlanc rightly concludes that the Middle period—"ten generations of a virtual absence of war, ... worthy of serious study"—was an exceptional event (LeBlanc 1999:313). Adding several more generations of peace makes the Middle period even more remarkable.

In contrast to this remarkable era of peace, LeBlanc defines a limited but very specific form of violence that characterized the Middle period and accompanied the Pax Chaco. Against the *absence* of warfare in the Middle period, LeBlanc notes the *presence* of a disturbing form of social violence: a series of group executions recognized over much of the northern Pueblo area between the late 900s and 1250 by LeBlanc (1999:162–186), by Turner and Turner (1999), by White (1992), and by Kuckelman et al. (2000). (I am not aware of incidents of this type of violence in the southern Pueblo world in the Middle period.) While a few incidents of this type of violence are known before and after the Middle period, archaeological evidence indicates that these events were sharply concentrated in the Middle period.

This form of violence was limited in scope. Turner and Turner (1999) note only about 75 possible instances, and re-analysis may reduce this number (see Billman et al. 2000). While few in number, the events were spectacularly brutal. In LeBlanc's words: "the bodies of humans were treated the same as carcasses of animals" (LeBlanc 1999: 172). Small groups of people were executed, dismembered, mutilated, and, less certainly, cannibalized. White describes the archaeological remains of these events at a small pueblo in southwestern Colorado, dated to ca. 1100:

> Scattered "bone beds" were found in several locations on the site. There is a clear dichotomy between these remains [of about 30 individuals] and the intentional, primary burials [of two individuals]. Unlike the primary burials, there was no association or articulation of skeletal elements, and multiple individuals were mixed together in the scattered bone beds. It is inferred that the fragmentation of these remains was not the result of sediment pressure because fragments of individual skeletal elements were found widely separated.... Elements in the bone beds manifest burning and trauma. There is no evidence of purposive burial and no evidence of in situ burning [White 1992:52–53].

This pattern has been documented throughout the Northern San Juan region by Kuckelman et al. (2000:159): "these characteristics indicate that much of the violence during this time was intended to do more than simply kill people." Kuckelman and her colleagues refer to these situations as "extreme processing," which they abbreviate as "EP." These events require a label to differentiate them from raiding and warfare, and following their terminology, I will call these executions "EP Events."

While the brutal nature of EP Events is beyond doubt, claims of cannibalism remain controversial. No claims have been made for subsistence cannibalism; almost all authors who positively consider evidence of cannibalism (Billman et al. 2000; Kantner 1999; LeBlanc 1999; Turner and Turner 1999) argue that the violence that culminated in cannibalism was an instrument of political power: a tactic of terror or intimidation. Other archaeologists have suggested that Middle period EP Events might also reflect witchcraft executions, without cannibalism (Bullock 1998; Darling 1999; Dongoske et al. 2000; Walker 1998), a subject to which we will return below. For the purposes of this paper, the reality or nonreality of cannibalism is not important.

LeBlanc's final Late period (1250–Spanish Contact) was marked by large-scale warfare: village against village and even multiple-village alliances against single villages or enemy alliances (see also Upham 1982). The scale and nature of southwestern violence reached levels that can appropriately be called warfare, in contrast to Early period raiding and feuding, and Middle period EP Events. LeBlanc sees large-scale warfare beginning in 1250 and continuing until Spanish Contact (which, hereafter, I date approximately to 1600) and beyond. It is notable that modern Pueblo stories and histories clearly recount warfare on dramatically larger scales during the Late period (Haas and Creamer 1997).

In summary, I recast LeBlanc's chronology (with my minimal revisions) thus:

0–late 700s	early Early period	Low-level raiding and feuding
late 700s–900	late Early period	Escalating raiding and feuding
900–1250	Middle period	Peace with EP Events
1250–1600	Late period	Village or alliance warfare

Resource Unpredictability and Warfare, Compared

With these chronologies in hand, we can evaluate the Ember and Ember model by comparing

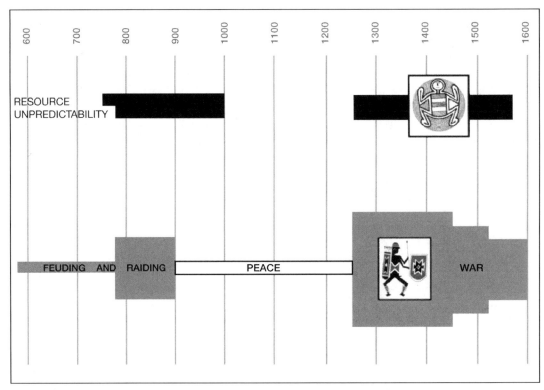

FIGURE 2: Schematic chronologies of resource unpredictability and violence. Periodization of resource unpredictability modified from Dean (1988,1996); of raiding/feuding and warfare modified from LeBlanc (1999). See text for details. Note the approximate coincidence of periods of violence and periods of resource unpredictability and escalation of violence from raiding/feuding (early) to warfare (late).

resource unpredictability with violence and warfare in the Pueblo Southwest (Figure 2). Recall that Dean defined four periods of "high temporal variability," which I have amended to incorporate Dean's (1996) era of high seasonal variability, thus: 310–380, 750–1000, 1250–1560, and 1750–1825. Do these periods of resource unpredictability correspond to periods of warfare and violence? Taken in order,

310–380: Dean's first period of high temporal variability falls in the early part of LeBlanc's Early period (0–late 700s), for which there are few data. It is impossible to evaluate whether Dean's span of 310–380 corresponds to any increase against a background

of what appears to be "endemic" low-level raiding and feuding.

750–1000: Dean's 750–1000 period of high temporal variability corresponds to the second part of LeBlanc's Early period (late 700s to 900), which was marked by a notable increase in the levels of feuding and raiding. There is a disjuncture of about one century between the end of Early period violence (at 900) and the end of high temporal variability (at 1000). We will revisit this disjuncture below.

1000–1250: The period from 1000 to 1250 was *not* marked by high resource unpredictability. It represents a 250-year span between two of Dean's periods of unpredictability. LeBlanc's peaceful Middle period (as extended by me to 900–1250) corresponds closely to this favorable climatic span, with the exception of the disjuncture mentioned above. The Middle period was "an era of unprecedented peace," punctuated by EP Events. Resource predictability and peace, therefore, co-occurred.

1250–1560: Dean's span of "high temporal variability" from 1350 to 1560 (expanded by me to include "high seasonal variability" from 1250 to 1450) corresponds closely to LeBlanc's Late period (1250–1600). The Late period was marked by village-on-village and alliance-on-alliance warfare—"crisis and catastrophe," in LeBlanc's words.

1730–1825: LeBlanc does not extend his analysis beyond Spanish contact, so Dean's final period of "high temporal variability" is not applicable here. A brief survey of colonial history does *not* suggest a close correlation of high temporal variability and violence in the Spanish and Mexican Southwest. The Ember and Ember model, developed from non-state data, should not be expected to apply to the colonized Southwest after 1600, with the possibility of bulk transportation of foodstuffs.

While not precise, the correspondences of LeBlanc's periods of Early period raiding, Middle period peace, and Late period warfare to Dean's periods of resource unpredictability are striking. Imprecision, in this comparison, should be evaluated in view of the nature of the two rather different chronologies: dendroclimatology is far more precise than cultural periodization. Moreover, "lag times" and temporal mismatches between causes and effects must be considered (and should be expected) in any model of past behaviors that are not completely mechanistic—people take time to react, and may react inappropriately or maladaptively to environmental change. I will argue, below, that the disjunctures have important implications for the second, psychological factor in the Ember and Ember model. For the present, however, comparison of LeBlanc's and Dean's analyses strongly support Ember and Ember's conclusion that resource unpredictability is a strong predictor of violence. Violence correlates well with resource unpredictably between 750 and 1600 in the Pueblo Southwest, as do peace and resource predictability.

Socialization for Fear

Resource unpredictability is an external or environmental cause of warfare and violence; many theorists (including Ember and Ember) argue for the importance of internal, psychological causes. The fit between resource unpredictability and violence, while close, is not chronologically precise. I believe that the observed disjunctures in the timing of resource unpredictability and violence have implications for internal predictors or causes.

In the Ember and Ember model, internal causes are psychological: socialization for fear. "Fear appears to be a common thread in the two obtained predictors of war—fear of nature and fear of others" (Ember and Ember 1992:256). Recall that Ember and Ember considered socialization "less strong" than resource unpredictability, but socialization for fear was still a significant predictor of war. Further, Ember and Ember argued that socialization for fear was, statistically and theoretically, a cause rather than a consequence of warfare. They discussed the relationship of resource scarcity and socialization for fear:

> There is some evidence suggesting that fear of others may be at least partially a result of fear of resource scarcity; if people have a history of resource problems, their fear of scarcity may spill over into fear of others. In any case, mistrustful adults may be more likely to respond aggressively to the arousal of any fears, and therefore socialization for mistrust may lead to more war [Ember and Ember 1992:245].

How can we detect socialization for mistrust or fear, archaeologically? Socialization—"the process through which people and especially children are made to take on the ideas and behaviors appropriate to life in a particular society" (Toren 1996:512)—occurs throughout the life cycle in all social settings, but childhood and family contexts are fundamental (e.g., Poole 1994). Family contexts are the domain of household archaeology. While household archaeology may prove useful in addressing this question, I look here for socialization as it might be institutionalized outside (above) the family and particularly in adult social contexts. These contexts could include ritual and ceremonial institutions (known to be important for socialization in modern Pueblos) and political institutions (perhaps more important in ancient Pueblo societies [Lekson 1999]). I focus here on the latter, and specifically on politically driven socialization. Politics is an adult occupation; war is politics by other means.

Recall that the nature of violence differed significantly from period to period. Early period violence was feuding and raiding. The Middle period was peaceful, but punctuated by EP Events. The Late period was characterized by widespread village-on-village or alliance-on-alliance conflict. Early period and Middle period violence might not qualify as "war" under some definitions, but Late period violence was inarguably real warfare. Why did real warfare emerge during the Late period? The much higher escalated scale of Late period warfare may be related to socialization for mistrust or fear, particularly at the political level. To understand how this might have been so, I will digress briefly into a political history of the Pueblo Southwest. The chronology of political socialization for fear will then be compared to the nature of violence.

I have presented elsewhere (Lekson 1999) a political history of the Pueblo Southwest that, like any such broad-scale essay, is susceptible to criticism in detail. Various aspects of my argument may ultimately prove incorrect, but I believe that the larger patterns identified are consistent with the record as we now know it, and may well survive as reasonable readings of the past. I refer the reader to the original monograph (Lekson 1999) for the detailed argument and the data supporting it, which I summarize here.

There were, I argue, three sequential major regional centers or capitals of the Pueblo Southwest:

Chaco (ca. 900–1125), Aztec Ruins (ca. 1110–1275), and Paquimé (ca. 1250 to 1450) (Figure 1). Each center was the clear primate settlement of its place and time; each was the center of large but different regions. Chaco, Aztec, and Paquimé were, in Paul Wheatley's term, "ceremonial cities" (Wheatley 1971), but they were also, to varying degrees, political and economic centers. Through time (that is, from Chaco to Aztec to Paquimé) the basis of power shifted from strongly political to largely commercial. At the same time, the subsistence technologies supporting their near-urban populations (ca. 3,000–5,000 people) shifted from rainfall farming at Chaco, to small-scale irrigation at Aztec Ruins, to large-scale canal irrigation at Paquimé. The centers became increasingly self-reliant for subsistence support. I further argue that these three centers were historically linked, with the leaders of each referring symbolically to the preceding center for legitimation of power. That point, though interesting, is irrelevant to the present argument.

The political history corresponds reasonably well to the chronology of resource unpredictability and warfare, outlined above. Construction at Chaco begins about 900 (or even 850 [Windes and Ford 1996]). At about 900, two centuries of Early period intense raiding ended "abruptly" (LeBlanc's word). With the end of resource unpredictability at 1000, Chaco expands to became a major regional center (ca. 1020; Judge 1989). The coincidence of the end of Early period feuding/raiding, the rise of Chaco, and changes in resource predictability is close, if not precise. The end of Chaco and the beginning of Aztec do not correspond to any major changes in resource unpredictability, and the nature of violence (EP Events in an era of peace) continues unchanged until the final decades of Aztec's span, a subject to which I will return below. The end of Aztec as a regional center and the rise, far to the south, of Paquimé corresponds well to the return of resource unpredictability and the explosion of warfare in the northern Pueblo world.

The nature of Chacoan polity is a matter of much debate. Judge (1989) and others see Chaco as a benign center of ritual and ceremony, but I argue that the evidence points to more formal, hierarchical political structure (Lekson 1999; see also Sebastian 1992). The reality of political power seems evident in Chaco's architecture and high-status burials, and Chacoan roads and outlier Great Houses suggest strong regional control. I suggest that, within the larger context of Pueblo history, Chaco represented a high degree of political centralization. Aztec Ruins, in my reconstruction, attempted to perpetuate Chacoan regional dominance, but with less success. Chaco was a relatively effective central political power; Aztec tried to be, but failed. Patterns of Middle period violence may provide insights on the nature of the Chaco and Aztec polities.

The Middle period peace prevailed from 900 to about 1250, interrupted by several score EP Events of execution and mutilations. While I focus here on adult contexts, it is important to note that children were not immune from this violence: "The common inclusion of women and children that met violent death is an important characteristic of the violence in the Northern San Juan Region" (Kuckelman et al. 2000:153). I suggest that EP Events represent coercive force directed by and perhaps emanating first from Chaco and, later, from Aztec Ruins. Less than an army, but more effective than local villagers, forces from Chaco and (later) Aztec made brutal examples of families and households who, for whatever reasons, were deemed inimical to the Chacoan world order. This reconstruction is tame in comparison to Turner and Turner's (1999:480) "cannibal warrior cult" from Mexico, but consistent with the arguments of LeBlanc (1999) and Kantner (1999). As factors of politically driven socialization, it is reasonable to assume that knowledge of EP Events was widespread within and among communities; that is, everyone knew about the executions, and many—children and adults—may have actually witnessed these brutal events.

This form of social violence might have been framed as witchcraft executions (Bullock 1998; Darling 1999; Dongoske et al. 2000; Walker 1998). If

so, the Middle period witnessed an astonishing explosion of witchcraft. That attribution does negate the political implications of Middle period violence. Political power was almost certainly intertwined with religious and ceremonial systems. Political offenders might well have been condemned and punished as witches, or religious apostates, since an offense against the political power might also be seen as an offense against the ideological and ceremonial system. Parallels between the EP Events seen by LeBlanc and by Turner and Turner and socially sanctioned violence of historic Pueblo against witches might reflect punishments developed first for ancient crimes against the state (or at least against the polity), retained on later, smaller Pueblo village scales. I intend here no disrespect for Pueblo past (and present) with this discussion; I merely wish to communicate the possible comparability of Middle period EP Events and later witchcraft executions.

Middle period violence, I suggest, was institutionalized and controlled by central political authorities at Chaco and Aztec. It was a strong tool for enculturating "ideas and behaviors appropriate to life in a particular society" (that is, socialization) and for maintaining the structure of political power. EP Events occurred mainly (indeed, almost entirely) during the Middle period, and during a time otherwise remarkable for the absence of war and violence. Over the course of many decades, generations matured and reproduced amid general peace and economic prosperity, punctuated by rare but brutal EP Events, in which whole families and residence groups were executed and brutalized. Thus, Middle period violence constituted a dramatic socialization for fear, a topic to which I will return.

A central authority, I argue, was enforcing peace and social order by coercion, and EP Events are the most spectacular archaeological evidence of that coercive control. These were hierarchical political decisions, and therefore perhaps only distantly related to environmental perturbations. Indeed, EP Events were not correlated with or caused by resource unpredictability. I will argue that EP Events were politically driven, and their effects in socialization for fear was an important cause for elevated levels of warfare during the Late period.

Socialization for Fear and Warfare, Compared

Politically driven socialization for fear may be reflected in two intriguing chronological disjunctures, summarized here and discussed at more length below. First, a significant period of resource unpredictability ended about 1000, while Early period violence ended and Chaco began about 900, a century earlier. Second, construction at Aztec Ruins continued until at least 1275 (and perhaps even later), while a period of intense resource unpredictability and coincident Late period warfare began about 1250, decades earlier.

The first disjuncture, between initial construction at Chaco and "Pax Chaco" at 900, and the end of resource unpredictability at 1000, has implications for the noncorrelation of EP Events with resource unpredictability. Most scholars date the beginning of intense EP Events at about 900 (LeBlanc 1999; Kuckelman et al. 2000; Turner and Turner 1999). Large-scale construction also began at Chaco at or shortly before 900. Neither EP Events nor the rise of Chaco appear to be coincident with the end of resource unpredictability, and instead both begin solidly within a period of high unpredictability.

According to an early (and unfairly discarded) model of Chacoan development (Judge 1979; Judge et al. 1981), Chaco arose about 900 as a cultural mechanism specifically to cope with resource unpredictability within the relatively small area of the San Juan Basin. That is, Chaco began as a small-scale political solution to problems of uneven food production within its immediate area (that is, the San Juan Basin). I argue elsewhere that, despite criticisms, this model for the tenth-century origins of Chaco remains valid (Lekson 1999; Malville 2001). That is, Chaco was a response to ongoing resource unpredictability, and it managed that unpre-

dictability successfully for about a century (that is, from 900 to 1000). Chaco rose as a political solution to raiding and feuding caused (at least in part) by resource unpredictability. It appears likely that mechanisms of control included coercive force. Early period raiding and feuding ceased when EP Events of the Middle period began, and I do not believe the timing was coincidental.

Following Judge's (1989) chronology, Chaco expanded beyond the ecological limits of the San Juan Basin only after 1000; that is, after the 750–1000 episode of high temporal variability ended. Chaco's political structure, developed in the tenth century, evolved in remarkable ways after the onset of more favorable climatic conditions about 1000. I believe the political system at Chaco was deliberately perpetuated and expanded beyond its original, environmental contexts. Mechanisms of political control developed to suppress raiding and feuding also continued in the improved environment of the Middle period: incidence of EP Events increased after 1000 (LeBlanc 1999; Kuckelman et al. 2000; Turner and Turner 1999). The shift in power from Chaco to Aztec was a political act (influenced by a short, twelfth-century drought, to be sure [Lekson 1999]), uncorrelated to resource unpredictability.

The onset of Late period village-scale warfare about 1250 correlates well with the reappearance of resource unpredictability, resulting from both chaotic seasonal variability and high temporal variability in rainfall (1250–1560). Large-scale construction, in contrast, continued at Aztec until 1275—the second temporal disjuncture. I argue that Aztec attempted to perpetuate Chaco's central political power and failed (Lekson 1999). The scale and scope of Aztec's political dominance never reached that of Chaco's; however, I believe Aztec's influence extended over most of the northern San Juan region. In the northern San Juan area, the period from 1150 to 1300 "includes fewer cases of extreme perimortem processing, [and relatively more] association of violent death with burned or partly burned structures, antemortem trauma, and at least one village-wide massacre.... This violence could have been the result of escalating violence between sociopolitically equal settlement groups" (Kuckelman et al. 2000:159). At about 1250, rainfall farming became increasingly problematic and intervillage warfare began.

The disjuncture between both the onset of war and resource unpredictability at 1250 contrasted to continued construction at Aztec until 1275 can be understood as evidence of political failure. The end of regional order does not result in the immediate abandonment of the center (consider Rome). Capitals are, by definition, important places and often overlap symbolically and temporally, and even spatially (Rapoport 1993). Old capitals are used in various ways to legitimize new capitals: the "new Rome," the "new Jerusalem," and so forth. There was, indeed, temporal overlap between the sequential centers which I construe to be capitals: the rise of the new center did not preclude continued construction at the prior center. This overlap should not surprise us: important places remain important, even in decline (or ruin). Construction continued at Aztec even after the natural and social environments began to deteriorate at 1250; leaders and decision makers did not have the benefit of our dendroclimatological retrodictions and did not realize that Aztec's run was over.

Political disintegration, environmental deterioration, and rising levels of warfare all surely contributed to the "abandonment" of the Four Corners. The details of that event, or series of events, are beyond the scope of this paper (see Duff and Wilshusen 2000; Lekson and Cameron 1995; Lipe 1995; Lipe and Varien 1999). It is important to note that the remarkable increase in intensity and scale of Late period violence after centuries of Middle period peace surely played a role in the totality and finality of the out-migration from the Four Corners area. At least 20,000 people left the Four Corners and joined existing communities in the areas of the modern Pueblos or created new towns in new places, as far south as modern Safford, Arizona and Magdalena, New Mexico (Wilson 1995; Woodson 1999). The population move-

ments of 1250–1300 may have exacerbated environmental difficulties and escalated war's scale and intensity. In addition, those displacements created circumstances for sociopolitical change. The northern Pueblo area—once almost entirely subsumed in the Chacoan region—was characterized after 1250 by a breakdown of large-scale regional polities, and balkanized into a dozen smaller subregional traditions (Adler 1996; Lekson 1996). Nothing like Chaco or Aztec ever appeared again in the northern Pueblo world, from Hopi to the Rio Grande.

Sometime after 1200, and probably about 1250, a capital and political formation on the scale of Chaco and Aztec reappeared, but much farther south, at Paquimé in Chihuahua, Mexico. Paquimé's span from about 1250 to 1450 was remarkably coincident to the first half of LeBlanc's Late period (1250–1600) of village-on-village and alliance-on-alliance warfare across the northern Southwest. Paquimé probably traded with those northern villages, but I argue that Paquimé stayed out of the northern "troubles" (Lekson 1999). Paquimé was the third and final capital in my reconstruction of southwestern political history (Lekson 1999); but, far to the south, Paquimé's influence on contemporary northern Pueblos was probably far more commercial than political.

The Late period in the northern Pueblo world is accurately described by LeBlanc as a time of "crisis and catastrophe." The span 1250–1600 was marked by warfare on scales unprecedented in southwestern prehistory. Why did violence escalate to real war during the Late period? Why did Late period violence not return to the raiding and feuding that typified the Early period?

There were, of course, several important environmental and historical parameters that differed between the Early and Middle periods. Absolute population levels and regional densities were probably significantly higher in the Late period than in the Early period, although it is difficult to reach archaeological consensus in matters of population size (Adler 1996; Nelson et al. 1994). The nature of resource unpredictability had also changed: in addition to "high annual variability" from 1350 to 1575, from 1250 to 1450 there was also a disruption of long-standing patterns of seasonal variability in precipitation, unique in dendroclimatological record (Dean 1996).

There were more people (probably) and harder times (certainly), but, against this, it appears that Late period Puebloan peoples adopted a wide range of new agricultural technologies and those technologies apparently worked: population is generally assumed to have continued to grow until the late fifteenth century. Whatever the causes of Late period warfare, those causes did not prevent Pueblo populations from increasing and, indeed, thriving. Following the Ember and Ember model, I suggest that there were other, less-material factors influencing the severity of Late period warfare.

Psychological or internal causes may in part explain the intensification of warfare during the Late period: socialization for fear. Recall that Ember and Ember (1992) noted that this factor was "less strong" than resource unpredictability, but socialization for fear was still a highly significant predictor of war. Recall also that Ember and Ember argued that socialization for fear was, statistically and theoretically, a cause rather than a consequence of warfare (Ember and Ember 1992:245).

That conclusion may apply to the Late period, heir to the institutions and legacies of the Middle period. The Middle period was a period of peace, but it was marked by politically motivated socialization for fear: EP Events. I suggested that people knew (and were intended to know) about these events, and I assume that people learned (and were expected to learn) the social rules and contexts that provoked or caused them. EP Events were deliberate acts of socialization. The phrase EP Events is a sanitized term for truly horrible incidents. The killings were terrible: witch or political enemy, the victims were terrorized and brutalized. The events must have been as chilling and awful as political executions of twentieth-century nation-states. EP Events of the Middle period suggest, almost

inescapably, socialization for fear of old and young, adults and children. How could Puebloan people during the otherwise peaceful Middle period not live in fear—in fear of their own society? The causes of Middle period EP Events are of intense interest but, for evaluating the Ember and Ember model, they are to some degree irrelevant. Political "death squads" or witchcraft "inquisitions": the constant threat of socially sanctioned violence—whatever its source—would almost certainly create a climate of mistrust and fear.

Returning to Ember and Ember's model, recall that socialization for fear predicted warfare rather than the reverse. Recall also that the end of the Middle period was also the end of centralized political control in the northern Pueblo world. The strong central role of Chaco was diminished in its successor, Aztec; and by about 1250, Aztec had ceased to be an effective regional center. Socialization for fear, which had effectively controlled raiding and warfare, gave way to large-scale village warfare, far more violent than the endemic raiding and feuding of the Early period (Figure 3). While there were other important factors (e.g., larger population and high seasonal variability, discussed above), it is worth considering socialization for fear as one *cause* of village-on-village warfare in the Late period. Three and one-half centuries of Middle period EP Events must have produced lasting cultural patterns—internal causes—that exacerbated and escalated warfare in the Late period. When Aztec ceased to function as a regional center, the political controls that had enforced peace in the Middle period disappeared and violence erupted on unprecedented levels: real war came to the Southwest.

A frequent criticism of cross-cultural analyses, such as the Ember and Ember study used here, is the general absence of history or sequence, and the consequent confusion of cause and effect. Does war cause fear, or does fear cause war? The chronology of violence and politics in the northern Pueblo world supports, to a degree, Ember and Ember: the increased intensity of warfare in the Late period

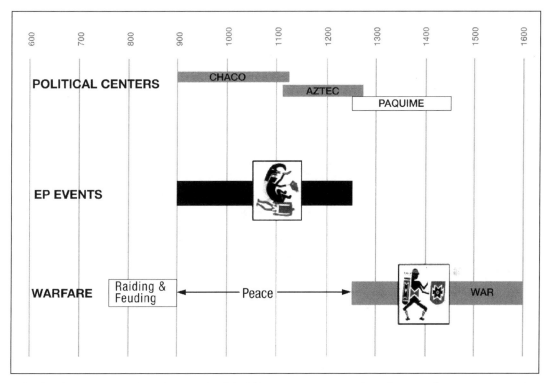

FIGURE 3: Schematic chronologies of political history, EP Events, and warfare. Northern centers are shown in gray, southern center shown in white. EP Events modified from LeBlanc (1999), Turner and Turner (1999), and Kuckelman et al. (2000). See text for details. Note that village-on-village and alliance warfare begins about 1250, approximately coincident with the end of northern centers and "EP Events."

was conditioned by the history, institutions, and psychology of the Middle period—the Pax Chaco with its politically driven use of political force—and the cultural legacy of over three centuries of socialization for fear.

Conclusions

How might the emerging recognition and study of violence in southwestern prehistory contribute to larger anthropological questions of warfare? Alone, lurid and controversial stories of cannibalism add little of value. Set within larger histories of politics, warfare, and ideology, the new southwestern data may, in fact, have something to contribute.

Steven LeBlanc in *Prehistoric Warfare in the American Southwest* differentiates theories about war that are fundamentally "materialist" versus those that are "nonmaterialist" (LeBlanc 1999:308ff.), closely paralleling Ember and Ember's "external" and "internal" categories. Among the former, we would find theories built around resource scarcity or evolutionary fitness; "nonmaterialist" theories, on the other hand, emphasize psychological or ideological factors. Often, these approaches are seen as exclusive and contradictory. The application of the Ember and Ember study to the Southwest suggests the utility of both: resource unpredictability is external and materialist, while socialization for fear is internal and nonmaterialist. Together, these two factors may better explain warfare in the ancient Southwest than models emphasizing only one school of thought. Referring to a slightly different dichotomy, Lawrence Keeley (1996:17) notes "the anthropological debates about the causes of warfare may represent a classic case of unacknowledged complementarity."

References

Adler, M.A. (editor)
  1996 *The Prehistoric Pueblo World A.D. 1150–1350*. University of Arizona Press, Tucson.
Ahlstrom, R.V.N., C.R. Van West, and J.S. Dean
  1995 Environmental and Chronological Factors in the Mesa Verde-Northern Rio Grande Migration. *Journal of Anthropological Archaeology* 14:125–142.
Benedict, R.
  1989 [1934] *Patterns of Culture*. Houghton Mifflin, Boston.
Billman, B.R., P.M. Lambert, and B.L. Leonard
  2000 Cannibalism, Warfare, and Drought in the Mesa Verde Region during the Twelfth Century A.D. *American Antiquity* 65:145–178.
Bullock, P.Y.
  1998 Does the Reality of Anasazi Violence Prove the Myth of Anasazi Cannibalism? In *Deciphering Anasazi Violence*, edited by P.Y. Bullock, pp. 35–51. HRM Books, Santa Fe, New Mexico.
Cordell, L.S.
  1994 *Ancient Pueblo People*. St. Remy Press, Montreal.
  1996 Models and Frameworks for Archaeological Analysis of Resource Stress in the American Southwest. In *Evolving Complexity and Environmental Risk in the Prehistoric Southwest*, edited by J.A. Tainter and B. Bagley Tainter, pp. 251–265. Addison-Wesley, Reading, Massachusetts.
  1997 *Archaeology of the Southwest*. 2nd edition. Academic Press, San Diego.
Crown, P.L., and W.J. Judge (editors)
  1991 *Chaco and Hohokam*. School of American Research Press, Santa Fe, New Mexico.
Darling, J.A.
  1999 Mass Inhumation and the Execution of Witches in the American Southwest. *American Anthropologist* 100:732–752.
Dean, J.S.
  1988 Dendrochronology and Paleoenvironmental Reconstruction on the Colorado Plateau. In *The Anasazi in a Changing Environment*, edited by G.J. Gumerman, pp. 119–167. Cambridge University Press, Cambridge.
  1996 Demography, Environment, and Subsistence Stress. In *Evolving Complexity and Environmental Risk in the Prehistoric Southwest*, edited by J.A. Tainter and B. Bagley Tainter, pp. 25–56. Addison-Wesley, Reading, Massachusetts.
Di Peso, C.C.
  1974 *Casas Grandes*. Amerind Foundation, Dragoon, Arizona.
Dongoske, K.E., D.L. Martin, and T.J. Ferguson
  2000 Critique of the Claim of Cannibalism at Cowboy Wash. *American Antiquity* 65:179–190.
Duff, A.J., and R.H. Wilshusen
  2000 Prehistoric Population Dynamics in the Northern San Juan Region, A.D. 950–1300. *The Kiva* 66:167–190.
Ember, M.
  1982 Statistical Evidence for an Ecological Explanation of Warfare. *American Anthropologist* 84:645–649.
Ember, C.R., and M. Ember
  1992 Resource Unpredictability, Mistrust, and War. *Journal of Conflict Resolution* 36:242–262.

Ember, M., and C.R. Ember

1995 Worldwide Cross-Cultural Studies and Their Relevance for Archaeology. *Journal of Archaeological Research* 3:87–111.

Ferguson, R.B.

1984 Introduction: Studying War. In *Warfare, Culture and Environment*, edited by R.B. Ferguson, pp. 1–81. Academic Press, Orlando.

Ferguson, T.J., and B.R. Hart

1985 *A Zuni Atlas*. University of Oklahoma Press, Norman.

Ferrill, A.

1997 *The Origins of War: From the Stone Age to Alexander the Great*. Westview Press, Boulder, Colorado.

Frazier, K.

1999 *People of Chaco*. 2nd edition. W.W. Norton, New York.

Gumerman, G.J. (editor)

1988 *The Anasazi in a Changing Environment*. Cambridge University Press, Cambridge.

Haas, J. (editor)

1990 *The Anthropology of War*. Cambridge University Press, Cambridge, U.K.

Haas, J., and W. Creamer

1993 *Stress and Warfare Among the Kayenta Anasazi of the Thirteenth Century A.D.* Fieldiana, Anthropology New Series 21. Field Museum of Natural History, Chicago.

1997 Warfare Among the Pueblos. *Ethnohistory* 44:235–261.

Judge, W.J.

1979 The Development of a Complex Cultural Ecosystem in the Chaco Basin, New Mexico. In *Proceedings of the First Conference on Scientific Research in the National Parks*, edited by R.M. Linn, pp. 901–906. National Park Service, Washington, D.C.

1989 Chaco—San Juan Basin. In *Dynamics of Southwest Prehistory*, edited by L.S. Cordell and G.J. Gumerman, pp. 209–261. Smithsonian Institution Press, Washington, D.C.

Judge, W.J., W.B. Gillespie, S.H. Lekson, and H.W. Toll III

1981 Tenth-century Developments in Chaco Canyon. In Collected Papers in Honor of Erik Kellerman Reed, edited by A.H. Schroeder, pp. 65–98. *Papers of the Archaeological Society of New Mexico* 6. Archaeological Society of New Mexico, Albuquerque.

Kantner, J.

1999 Survival Cannibalism or Sociopolitical Intimidation? *Human Nature* 10:1–50.

Keeley, L.H.

1996 *War Before Civilization*. Oxford University Press, New York.

Kelly, R.C.

2000 *Warless Societies and the Origin of War*. University of Michigan Press, Ann Arbor.

Kohler, T.A., and C.R. Van West

1996 The Calculus of Self-Interest in the Development of Cooperation: Sociopolitical Development and Risk Among the Northern Anasazi. In *Evolving Complexity and Environmental Risk in the Prehistoric Southwest*, edited by J.A. Tainter and B. Bagley Tainter, pp. 169–196. Addison-Wesley, Reading, Massachusetts.

Kroeber, C.B., and B.L. Fontana

1986 *Massacre on the Gila: An Account of the Last Major Battle Between American Indians, With Reflections on the Origin of War*. University of Arizona Press, Tucson.

Kubler, G.

1962 *The Shape of Time*. Yale University Press, New Haven.

Kuckelman, K.A., R.R. Lightfoot, and D.L. Martin

2000 Changing Patterns of Violence in the Northern San Juan Region. *The Kiva* 66:147–165.

LeBlanc, S.A.

1999 *Prehistoric Warfare in the American Southwest*. University of Utah Press, Salt Lake City.

Lekson, S.H.

1996 The Pueblo Southwest After A.D. 1150. In *Interpreting Southwestern Diversity*, edited by P.R. Fish and J.J. Reid, pp. 41–44. Anthropological Research Paper 48. Arizona State University, Tempe.

1999 *The Chaco Meridian*. Altamira Press, Walnut Creek, California.

Lekson, S.H., and C.M. Cameron

1995 The Abandonment of Chaco Canyon, the Mesa Verde Migrations, and the Reorganization of the Pueblo World. *Journal of Anthropological Archaeology* 14:184–202.

Lekson, S.H., J.R. Stein, T. Windes, and W. James Judge

1988 The Chaco Canyon Community. *Scientific American* 259:100–109.

Lipe, W.D.

1995 The Depopulation of the Northern San Juan: Conditions in the Turbulent 1200s. *Journal of Anthropological Archaeology* 14:143–169.

Lipe, W.D., and M.D. Varien

1999 Pueblo III (A.D. 1150–1300). In *Colorado Prehistory: A Context for the Southern Colorado River Basin*, edited by W.D. Lipe, M.D. Varien, and R.H. Wilshusen, pp. 290–352. Colorado Council of Professional Archaeologists, Denver.

Lister, R.H., and F.C. Lister

1981 *Chaco Canyon*. University of New Mexico Press, Albuquerque.

1987 *Aztec Ruins on the Animas*. University of New Mexico Press, Albuquerque.

Malville, Nancy J.

2001 Long-Distance Transport of Bulk Goods in the Prehispanic American Southwest. *Journal of Anthropological Archaeology* 20:230–243.

McKenna, P.J., and H.W. Toll III

2001 Regional Patterns of Great House Development Among the Totah Anasazi, New Mexico. In *Anasazi Regional Organization and the Chaco System*, 2nd edition, edited by D.E. Doyel, pp. 133–143. Maxwell Museum of Anthropology Anthropological Papers No. 5. Maxwell Museum of Anthropology, Albuquerque.

Nelson, B.A., T.A. Kohler, and K.W. Kintigh

1994 Demographic Alternatives. In *Understanding Complexity in the Prehistoric Southwest*, edited by G. Gumerman and M. Gell-Mann, pp. 113–146. Addison-Wesley, Reading, Massachusetts.

Otterbein, K.F.

1973 The Anthropology of War. In *Handbook of Social and Cultural Anthropology*, edited by J.J. Honigmann, pp. 923–958. Rand McNally, Chicago.

1997 The Origins of War. *Critical Review* 11: 251–277.

Plog, S.

1997 *Ancient Peoples of the American Southwest*. Thames and Hudson, London.

Poole, F.J.P.

1994 Socialization, Enculturation, and the Development of Personal Identity. In *Companion Encyclopedia of Anthropology*, edited by T. Ingold, pp. 831–860. Routledge, London.

Preston, D.

1998 Cannibals of the Canyon. *New Yorker* 74(37):76–89.

Rapoport, A.

1993 On the Nature of Capital and Their Physical Expression. In *Capital Cities*, edited by J. Taylor, J.G. Lengelle, and C. Andrew, pp. 31–67. Carleton University Press, Ottawa.

Reid, I., and S. Whittlesey

1997 *The Archaeology of Ancient Arizona*. University of Arizona Press, Tucson.

Reyna, S.P., and R.E. Downs (editors)

    1994 *Studying War: Anthropological Perspectives*. Gordon and Breach, Amsterdam.

Rice, G., and S.A. LeBlanc (editors)

    2001 *Deadly Landscapes: Case Studies in Prehistoric Southwestern Warfare*. University of Utah Press, Salt Lake City.

Schaafsma, C.F., and C.L. Riley (editors)

    1999 *The Casas Grandes World*. University of Utah Press, Salt Lake City.

Schaafsma, P.

    2000 *Warrior, Shield, and Star: Imagery and Ideology of Pueblo Warfare*. Western Edge Press, Santa Fe, New Mexico.

Sebastian, L.

    1992 *The Chaco Anasazi: Sociopolitical Evolution in the Prehistoric Southwest*. Cambridge University Press, Cambridge, UK.

Tainter, J.A., and B. Bagley Tainter (editors)

    1996 *Evolving Complexity and Environmental Risk in the Prehistoric Southwest*. Addison-Wesley, Reading, Massachusetts.

Toren, C.

    1996 Socialization. In *Encyclopedia of Social and Cultural Anthropology*, edited by A. Banard and J. Spencer, pp. 512–514. Routledge, London.

Turner, C.G., II

    1999 A Reign of Terror. *Discovering Archaeology* 1:48–51.

Turner, C.G., II, and J.A. Turner

    1999 *Man Corn*. University of Utah Press, Salt Lake City.

Upham, S.

    1982 *Polities and Power*. Academic Press, New York.

Van West, C.R.

    1996 Agricultural Potential and Carrying Capacity in Southwestern Colorado, A.D. 901–1300. In *The Prehistoric Pueblo World A.D. 1150–1350*, edited by M.A. Adler, pp. 214–227. University of Arizona Press, Tucson.

Walker, W.H.

    1998 Where Are the Witches of Prehistory? *Journal of Archaeological Method and Theory* 5:245–308.

Whalen, M.E., and P.E. Minnis

    2001 *Casas Grandes and Its Hinterland: Prehistoric Regional Organization in Northwest New Mexico*. University of Arizona Press, Tucson.

Wheatley, P.

    1971 *The Pivot of the Four Quarters*. Aldine, Chicago.

White, T.D.

    1992 *Prehistoric Cannibalism at Mancos 5MTUMR–2346*. Princeton University Press, Princeton.

Wilcox, D., and J. Haas

    1994 The Scream of the Butterfly: Competition and Conflict in the Prehistoric Southwest. In *Themes in Southwest Prehistory*, edited by G.J. Gumerman, pp. 211–238. School of American Research Press, Santa Fe, New Mexico.

Wilson, J.P.

    1995 Prehistory of the Gallinas Mountains, Socorro County. In *Of Pots and Rocks: Papers in Honor of A. Helene Warren*, edited by Meliha S. Duran and David T. Kirkpatrick, pp. 189–210. Papers of the Archaeological Society of New Mexico 21, Albuquerque.

Windes, T.C., and D. Ford

    1996 The Chaco Wood Project: The Chronometric Reappraisal of Pueblo Bonito. *American Antiquity* 61:295–310.

Woodson, M.K.

    1999 Migrations in Late Anasazi Prehistory: the Evidence from The Goat Hill Site. *The Kiva* 65:63–84.

"Were Luxury Foods the First Domesticates? Ethnoarchaeological Perspectives from Southeast Asia"

Brian Hayden

Explaining the conditions that led to the domestication of plants and animals remains a major topic of theoretical interest in archaeology. While domestication certainly has some benefits, such as the ability to create more food than occurs naturally, it also has negative impacts, such as creating more work and worse health for many. Some archaeological explanations suggest that domestication may have been a by-product of other activities, such as the cultivation of plants for their hallucinogenic or alcoholic properties. Many explanations propose that resource depletion caused by environmental changes or increasing populations was the catalyst. Other explanations, such as the one described here, suggest that the origin of domestication is correlated with feasting.

This selection by Brian Hayden, a professor of archaeology at Simon Fraser University in Canada, originally appeared in a 2003 issue of the scholarly journal *World Archaeology*.

Questions to Guide Reading

What is the thesis of the article?
According to Hayden, what are the three important advantages of raising animals for feasts?
On what basis does Hayden claim that domesticated rice may have originated as a luxury food?
What alternative views or hypotheses of domestication are discussed in the article?
How is Hayden's hypothesis supported ethnographically and archaeologically?

Abstract

There are important reasons for considering the first domesticated plants and animals as luxury foods primarily used in feasting. Using Southeast Asian tribal society as a case study, it is demonstrated that all the domesticated animals and the most important of the domesticated plants constitute forms of wealth that are primarily or exclusively used in feasting contexts. In addition, numerous studies have demonstrated that feasting generates powerful forces that intensify and increase resource production of luxury foods as well as staples. Such forces ultimately can lead to the domestication of wild species and the transformation of luxury foods into staple foods.

Keywords

Domestication; Southeast Asia; feasting; rice; intensification; ethnoarchaeology.

Introduction

One aspect of the model of cultural change that I have espoused is that there is a built-in tendency for luxury items, including foods, to become common fare wherever technological or genetic advances can reduce production costs (Hayden 1998). This is largely due to self-interested aggrandizers attempting to maintain prestigious displays while minimizing costs. Although this strategy is beneficial to aggrandizers in the short run, in the long run it leads to the transformation of many prestigious luxury items, such as metals, glass and textiles, into cheap throwaway items. Foods that begin as luxury items often become banal mundane staples that are taken for granted. Outcomes from this process can be easily chronicled in any major food store today. White bread, which was once reserved only for the elites of Europe, has now become the Wonderbread plague. Chocolate, once reserved for Mesoamerican elites, is now the bane of the overfed multitude. Oversized, out-of-season fruits and vegetables which once only graced the tables of kings and nobles have become everyday fare. Fat-rich meats, which formerly were used only for special occasions or for the highest ranks of society, are now commonplace for all but the poorest and produce coronary and arterial diseases on a wide scale. Wines and spirits that played crucial roles in feasts for elites (Dietler 1990) have now become the profane intoxicants of households throughout the industrial world. In short, our eating habits today largely are the result of, and reflect, the luxury foods of the past.

Thus, it seems that many foods that are taken for granted as everyday fare by today's urbane citizens really originated as costly delicacies in earlier societies. I suggest that early domesticates were developed as luxury foods and that the primary context for their consumption was in feasting. Feasts not only provide the vehicle for the use of luxury foods, but also the very reason for their existence. I shall use a number of examples from the tribal cultures of Southeast Asia to illustrate these propositions. Following the lead of earlier researchers who suggested that initial domestication was linked to feasting or the prestige use of foods (Bender 1978; Lewthwaite 1986; Runnels and Van Andel 1988), I have investigated the dynamics of tribal feasting in this region over the last eight years.

In my ethnoarchaeological approach, I and my students have endeavoured to develop models of community organization that are relevant to understanding prehistoric village life. We selected communities that were among the most traditional in terms of subsistence economy, socio-political structure, customs and ritual life. We undertook many household interviews in order to obtain a solid understanding of the subsistence economy of the communities with special attention paid to variability between households and constraints on the production of specific types of foods. We then tried to understand the basic aspects of the social and political structures of those communities from household and administrative perspectives and how these aspects were tied into subsistence production. We have conducted studies at several levels of socio-political complexity and surplus production, including studies among the transegalitarian Akha hill tribes of north-western Thailand, the (formerly) simple chiefdom-level polities of the Torajan highlands in Sulawesi and the chiefdom-level polities of Futuna in French Polynesia.

Transegalitarian societies (whether hunter/gatherers, horticulturalists or pastoralists) are those that have significant socio-economic inequalities (therefore are not egalitarian), but lack true socio-economic stratification or classes such as occur in chiefdom societies. Transegalitarian societies are characterized by private ownership of resources and produce, prestige objects, unstable socio-economic hierarchies, the production of surpluses, economically based competition and a wide range of feasting behaviour, usually including some ostentatious displays. I suggest that contemporary traditional Southeast Asian transegalitarian communities provide useful models for understanding the nature of prehistoric societies that first domesticated plants and animals and produced the first luxury foods. While improved plant varieties and technology, especially metal tools, have certainly increased the productive potentials of food production since early prehistoric times, many groups have expanded into environments that never could have been productive before the advent of metals. Thus, in contemporary marginal areas, the net productivity of communities is probably not very different from the levels characteristic of the best environments in early food-producing communities. It can be argued that the basic socio-political adaptations of marginal groups today and early groups that first domesticated plants and animals are probably similar, including feasting patterns and the use of luxury foods.

Some of the major conclusions that I and my students have developed are that feasts are critical for the conversion of surplus production into social and political ties through the creation of debt relationships and the display of mutual support (Adams 2001; Clarke 2001; Perodie 2001; Hayden 2001a). Feasting relationships are fundamental to structuring power relationships within communities, and have even been described as an institution comparable to parliamentary democracy (Clarke 2001). Typically, support networks and competition between networks operate primarily at the level of lineages or corporate kindreds (such as the tongkonans in the Torajan area), with only a loose correspondence between individual household production and feasting activity. However, in all situations, it is clear that feasting constitutes the single most important consumption activity of surpluses and that there is significant competition to display wealth at the most important feasts. Feasts can also be used to underwrite major labour-intensive projects such as house building, irrigation works, planting and harvesting (Dietler and Herbich 2001; Dietler 1990).

Because the main goal in most alliance-building feasts is to impress guests favourably with the productive abilities of the hosts and their allies, specialty foods are a central feature of these feasts. Let us examine the luxury foods used in Southeast Asian feasts from this perspective. The major traditional luxury foods include meat from domestic animals, rice alcohol, dried fish, various types of rice, tobacco or opium and various sauces. In this article, I shall concentrate on domesticated animals and rice.

Southeast Asian Luxury Foods

ANIMALS

Although Smith (2001) and Zeder (2001) have recently argued that water buffaloes, cattle, pigs and chickens were not domesticated as feasting foods, but provided protein for everyday nutritional needs, it can be pointed out that meat protein is hardly required for survival. Many societies throughout the world subsist with little or no meat protein in their diets. Even Bushman hunter/gatherers kill surprisingly few animals throughout the year, only 0.6 large animals per man per year (Lee 1979: 243). Hawkes et al. (2001: 685–7) report similar but not quite so extreme success (failure) rates among the Aché and Hadza. Meat, especially meat with a high fat content, is a special food that has always been relished. Because of this special role, it should not be surprising to find that domestic animals throughout tribal Southeast Asia are used primarily or, more commonly, *exclusively* for special occasions, notably feasts. The size of the feasting group and the importance of impressing guests largely determine the size, number and value of the animals to be sacrificed. Tribal members explicitly view the raising of domesticated animals as non-essential for subsistence, and explicitly speak of raising domestic animals as similar to putting money (surpluses) in the bank (Falvey 1977: 22–3, 38, 40, 86; Shubert 1986: 81). They use domestic animals to broker alliances, obtain marriage partners, solicit favours, create debts and impress guests at feasts. In Southeast Asia, Izikowitz (1951: 358) observes, raising water buffalo and growing rice are the major means by which people acquire wealth, and feasts are necessary to raise one's status to that of a rich man, entitling individuals to be judges and use the most desirable swiddens (1951: 116–17, 209).

Thus, domestic animals are killed *only* in the context of feasts and sacrifices. This, in fact, is a behavioural pattern which is so overwhelmingly common in tribal and peasant cultures throughout the world, whether in New Guinea (Blanton and Taylor 1995), Crete (Keswani 1994), rural France (personal observations) or Turkey, that the onus is clearly upon critics like Zeder to explain why the situation should have been different in earlier transegalitarian societies. Her suggestion that domesticated animals would not require much labour to raise does not take into account the need for winter fodder (for which wild animals would traditionally have migrated to other areas), nor does it take into account the very significant risks of owning medium or large-sized domesticated animals—risks involving loss of investment as well as damage to other families' crops (Starr 1987; Hayden 2001b). In fact, it may well be that it was the high risk costs associated with keeping destructive animals such as cattle, pigs, goats and sheep that deterred their domestication in situations where highly productive wild stands of plants were being managed, as suggested by Willcox (1996, 1998: 33, 1999) for the Fertile Crescent during the Epipalaeolithic. If there were cost and risk impediments to raising animals, what benefits could have overcome these disadvantages?

Raising animals for feasts has these important advantages:

1 Animal flesh is inherently desirable in most traditional societies, whether hunter/gatherer or horticultural (Hayden 1981; Speth and Spielmann 1983). The most critical aspect is the fat content, which renders meat protein digestible and delicious. Most importantly, the fat content of domestic animals can be elevated to much higher levels than among animals in the wild.

2 Surplus agricultural production can be invested and stored in domesticated animals, just as money can be put in the bank. Animals can subsequently be consumed to impress guests, given away or used to create debts.

3 Timing and the ability to amass surpluses for use at specified times are critical elements in holding alliance and competitive feasts. Procurement of wild animals is fraught with uncertainties and could rarely be used as a reliable basis for holding feasts. Domesticated animals, on the other hand, can be used whenever necessary.

From an ethnoarchaeological point of view, the case for the domestication of animals as luxury foods seems incontrovertible. The desire to quickly produce more animals suitable for feasting, in fact, appears to be one of the major motivating factors for the intensification of *agricultural* production (to feed animals) in East Africa (Hakansson 1994, 1995) as well as New Guinea (Blanton and Taylor 1995; Modjeska 1982), and also appears to play a key role in the production of maize and rice in Southeast Asia (Falvey 1977).

RICE

While the case for the feasting role of the first domesticated animals may be robust, the case for rice (and other cereals in the world) may appear more equivocal at first glance. Yet, the notion that rice may have originated as a luxury food is worth pursuing in order to see if, in fact, it can profitably be viewed from this perspective.

Rice may be taken for granted today as a basic ubiquitous staple in Asian diets (as argued by Smith 2001: 212); however, there are strong indications that this has not always been the case. The contemporary ubiquity of rice, I would argue, is the product of a long series of intensification events that have transformed rice from a highly valued special context food into one that is commonplace and often devalued, as is also the case with chocolate, bread, meat and beer. Examining the role of rice among Southeast Asian hill tribes should be particularly instructive since one locus of domestication is postulated to have been in the homeland of the hill tribes—the Himalayan foothills stretching from Burma through northern Thailand and into South China (Chang 1989). Alternatively, many hill tribes, such as the Akha, Hmong and Yao, originated from the Yangtzi River basin, which is postulated to be another hearth of rice domestication (Lu 1999: 72–3, 86–99, 115–16, 127). Early traditions of rice production and use may well have persisted among the more marginal groups in this heartland of rice domestication and among their descendants who now occupy the Himalayan foothills. Although many Asian scholars assume that wild wet rice was the first domesticate, in my estimation, it is equally or more reasonable to view wild hill rice as being the first form of domesticated rice.

What are the reasons for thinking that rice was at the outset a highly valued and relatively expensive crop to produce (in terms of time and effort)—a luxury crop that might well have been used primarily in feasting contexts? First of all, it is a cereal grain, and, as with wheat or maize, the inherent balance of lipids to protein and starch seems to exert a natural appeal to people's palates similar in nature to the innate attraction of rich and fast-burning foods. Thus, rice has a natural good taste, especially the less refined varieties such as the hill rices.

Second, people plant as much rice as they can, but they rarely have enough for daily meals throughout the year. They are limited in the amount that they can produce by soil fertility and the amount of manpower that can be assembled at key bottleneck periods (notably planting and harvesting: Falvey 1977: 55; Condominas 1977). The same appears to have been true for early wheat producers in Europe (Gregg 1988: 156, 161).

Third, and perhaps most important, growing rice is not really necessary for survival in the region. The poor, who have little or no rice, survive by harvesting wild forest products or growing other, less labour-intensive crops such as manioc. At times of rice and other crop failures, most people survive by reverting to the collection of wild forest products. Up until recently there were relatively widespread, albeit dispersed, hunter/gatherer groups in the mountains of Southeast Asia, such as the Mlabri, who survived off wild forest produce and perhaps represented marginalized former horticulturalists. Archaeologists should focus on these models of societies when considering early agriculture.

Fourth, rice, like wheat and maize, is widely used for the production of alcohol, which is one of the most important constituents of all feasts in grain-producing regions (e.g., Katz and Voigt 1986; Dietler 1990; Dietler and Herbich 2001). As others have noted (Katz and Voigt 1986; Stevens 1987; Dietler 1990), alcohol production is entirely based on surplus grain and thus is largely restricted to those who are relatively well off and can afford to use up their surpluses in this fashion.

Fifth, like other important grains (wheat and maize), rice holds a special place in the ritual and ideological life of Hill Tribes. There are special planting, maturation and harvesting rituals for rice that do not exist for any other plants. There are special varieties of rice (sticky types) that are sacred and must be used in rituals. Rice is the only plant that has a soul like human beings (Izikowitz 1951: 244). The same also seems to be true of pre-industrial wheat in Europe as well as maize in Mesoamerica where it was given a deity status.

Sixth, my investigations have shown that rice is an absolutely required central element in all feasting rituals among Southeast Asian hill tribes (see also Fox 1992: 77; Gunawan 1998: 18).

Seventh, even today in the hill tribes and related traditional communities, there is a strong emic value put on the consumption of rice. I have seen rice avidly sought after by guests (especially the poor) at feasts as though it was of extreme value. It is also worth noting that the poor frequently do not have rice, or certainly not enough rice to last them throughout the year, and not as much rice as they want. In some areas such as the Torajan Highlands of Sulawesi, I was told that, before modern hybrids were introduced, only the rich had rice in any significant quantities. In the Philippines, too, rice was a high-status food served primarily at feasts (Junker 2001: 289).

Eighth, rice can always be exchanged for other commodities due to its high prestige value, whereas other food crops cannot always be confidently exchanged for commodities. Therefore, areas that could produce surpluses of rice in most years did so, as was the case with the Lamet (Izikowitz 1951). Even in some areas that produce surplus rice, like Sumba, people eat as much maize and root crops as possible for daily meals in order to save rice for feasts or to trade rice for water buffaloes and horses (Gunawan 1998: 23). It seems entirely probable that in former times, before industrially grown rice became available, the exchange rate for rice would have been much higher than its current value, just as the availability of commercial salt has impoverished many traditional communities that had control over lucrative pre-industrial salt sources.

Ninth, and finally, the special role of rice in traditional economies of the area is highlighted by the fact that other crops are more reliable and provide more calories than rice. Manioc is perhaps the most interesting example, since I have been told that hill tribe families can never starve in the region due to the ease and reliability of growing manioc (Maneeprasert, R. pers. com.); and, in fact, starvation seems to be a very rare occurrence, although failures of the rice crops are relatively commonplace.

Thus, while rice is highly desired and prestigious, it also requires a high labour investment compared to other foods like manioc. In addition, as with the raising of cattle, there are many risks involved in growing rice. These include droughts, inadequate temperatures, insect infestations, depredations by rodents, incursions by wild and domestic animals and birds, and diseases. As Bogucki (1999: 197) has argued, domesticates by nature are high-risk, unstable products, and this is especially true of rice. Thus,

one may ask why people cultivated rice to begin with. I suggest that growing rice really only makes sense initially as a prestige crop grown to impress guests at feasts. It may have also been highly valued for its ability to produce alcohol and to increase the growth and reproduction rates of cattle or swine, as is the case among the transegalitarian cattle raisers studied by Hakansson (1994, 1995). In the societies studied by Hakansson, irrigation was developed to increase millet production or acquisition so that cattle production could be increased. In Southeast Asia, feeding pigs maize is similarly critical (Hayden 2001b). These socio-political models of forces driving the intensification of rice production in Asia might well be taken into consideration in future evaluations of rice intensification.

It is clear that the increases in labour costs (represented by the initial cultivation and domestication of rice and its subsequent augmented productivity via irrigation) must have been outweighed by the increases in wealth, power and socio-political fitness that successful growers and users of rice experienced via their deployment of rice in exchanges, feasting and related socio-political struggles.

In sum, I think a good case can be made that rice has traditionally held a highly valued position in Southeast Asia, that it was a relatively costly and high-risk plant to cultivate, and that it was initially used in special contexts such as feasting and drinking. This seems likely for regions of low productivity today such as the mountains, but I think it is also likely to have characterized the initial phases of domestication of rice no matter what the geography. Limited technology (the lack of irrigation or metal tools for clearing forests or spading dense wetland root systems) and the lower yield of the initial varieties of rice must have made early production much more precarious and costly than today, even in favourable environments. By way of comparison, Mexican maize farmers today do not consider it worthwhile to farm land with less than a 200–250 ton yield per hectare. Yet, according to estimates, initial domesticated varieties of maize yielded only about 60–80 tons per hectare (Flannery 1973: 297–8). If early domesticated forms of rice exhibited similar low levels of productivity, they would certainly not have been worth cultivating as staples. Moreover, the widespread similarity in emic importance and rituals surrounding rice and its use in feasting throughout tribal Asia strongly argue for an early role of rice as a prestige feasting food throughout the area. While technological improvements such as irrigation have made it possible to intensify rice production in highly productive areas, the advent of metal tools and cheap iron has only recently made rice cultivation marginally feasible in the areas of lower productivity. It is in these regions that the older patterns of rice cultivation and use may have persisted.

Implications for the Transition from Foraging to Farming

It is worth pausing to determine whether the widespread contemporary view of the common, 'mundane' role of species that were first domesticated is perhaps not overly ethnocentric or obscuring of past realities. On the basis of research in Southeast Asia, it seems likely that many of the domesticated foods that we take for granted today as being staple subsistence items probably originated as luxury foods among transegalitarian hunter/gatherers and horticulturalists. The specific context in which these foods repeatedly appear ethnographically is that of feasts. This phenomenon has long been remarked upon by anthropologists working in Southeast Asia with regard to animal domesticates (e.g., Leach 1954; Izikowitz 1951; Falvey 1977). Equally good arguments can be advanced for a similar luxury food role for rice and alcohol. Although we are still in the exploratory stages of understanding how and why this situation emerged, there is no compelling reason to believe that it was different in prehistory. A number of alternative scenarios within the feasting-and-surplus model for the domestication of luxury (and non-luxury plants) are possible. It is

far too early to tell which of these may best fit the actual archaeological record or to dismiss any of them out of hand. What is required is an ongoing dialogue and openness to theoretical and research exploration. The basic scenario of feasts supported by surpluses and the drive to produce ever more in order to impress potential or actual allies (Hayden 1990, 1995a, 1995b) is very different from the traditional climatic or population pressure stress models of domestication.

In terms of the Eurasian Neolithic, the feasting model implies that all domesticated animals were consumed in feasting contexts; however, archaeologically, faunal remains may be relatively uniform between households due to households taking turns in hosting feasts, gifting of major cuts of meat and scavenging. Nevertheless, household food preparation or serving-vessel sizes should reflect feasting activities and there may be prestige displays of feasting remains such as the bucrania in Çatal Hüyük households. On a larger scale, feasting remains should be relatively apparent at major ceremonial sites such as causewayed enclosures or tomb sites. Special attention should also be paid to the Neolithic role of cereals since these may have been used primarily for making beer or bread for feasts (both labour-intensive preparations). The enduring minor importance of domesticated cereals in the overall subsistence of a number of early Neolithic communities seems to imply such a role, leading some analysts to argue that these were essentially hunting and gathering economies (Thomas 1991: 25; Lidén 1995: 411; Willcox 1999: 494; Hauptmann 1999: 78; Cauvin et al. 1999: 101; Esin and Harmankaya 1999: 115; Özdogan 1999: 234–5; Stafford 1999: 13, 134–5). However, even substantial consumption of cereals at later times may be related to the growing of cereals for brewing since many societies obtain up to 20-30 per cent of their calories in the form of beer at feasts (Dietler 2001: 81–2).

Because domestication is often viewed as one outcome of resource intensification, it is worth emphasizing that ethnographers of transegalitarian societies have repeatedly observed that the primary force behind intensified subsistence production is not food shortage, but the desire to obtain social and political advantages—to obtain the most desirable mates, to create the most advantageous alliances, to wield the most political power. This pattern is documented in Southeast Asia (Izikowitz 1951: 341, 354), New Guinea (Modjeska 1982; Blanton and Taylor 1995), the Philippines (Junker 2001: 295ff.), the Northwest Coast (Perodie 2001), Europe (Jennbert 1984, 1987), East Africa (Hakansson 1994, 1995), Polynesia (Earle 1977), Coastal California (Blackburn 1976: 242) and elsewhere (e.g., Runnels and Van Andel 1988 for Greece). As Hakansson (1994: 264) observes for East Africa, in a vein reminiscent of Izikowitz, labour is the main bottleneck in these transegalitarian societies, and, thus, there is constant pressure for more wives and higher bride prices. There are never enough cattle for brides or other socio-political goals, and people constantly try to obtain more wives via the exchange of surpluses or valuables for cattle or by means of raiding. It is common in these situations for families to go heavily into debt for competitive displays, once again creating powerful pressures to increase production by whatever means possible in order to pay off the debts.

Whether defence, procurement of brides, political advantage or other goals were the major adaptive driving forces, it is clear, as Hakansson (1994: 271) has noted, that these demands pushed the economic systems to their limits in a relentless juggernaut of pressure to intensify production. As he and I have noted, the resulting facts and scenarios do not support population pressure models of intensification at all.

If domestication had occurred but once in human history, the population pressure approach might be credible. However, the fact that domestication occurred multiple times in multiple locations throughout the world in the short span of a few thousand years indicates that very fundamental changes and forces were at work. Many of the first domesticates in most regions of the world are clearly luxury foods or prestige items (e.g., gourds, dogs), while other initial domesticates may have been luxury foods or staples used either directly in feasts or indirectly to underwrite feasts. Both Smith (2001) and Zeder (2001) reject this feasting model of domestication and claim that none of the early domesticates can be viewed as luxury foods. They also argue that early food-producing communities were not socially or economically complex enough to support intensifying feasting systems. From the ethnoarchaeological and archaeological data that I am familiar with, their assessment seems far too premature, perhaps resulting from too narrow a focus on archaeological objects as objects. Surely, we need to concentrate on the human behaviour and culture that those artefacts represent, and ethnoarchaeology provides a valuable key in that undertaking.

Acknowledgements

The Canadian SSHRC provided funding for my research on feasting, and many colleagues in Thailand were instrumental in helping formulate or refine concepts and gather data, especially Ralana Maneeprasert, Lindsey Falvey, Theera Visitpanich, as well as Tran Quoc Vuong in Vietnam and Stanislaus Sandarupa in Sulawesi.

References

Adams, R. 2001. Ethnoarchaeology of Torajan feasts. Unpublished master's thesis. Burnaby, British Columbia: Simon Fraser University.

Bender, B. 1978. Gatherer-hunter to farmer: a social perspective. *World Archaeology*, 10: 204–22.

Blackburn, T. 1976. Ceremonial integration and social interaction in Aboriginal California. In *Native Californians: A Theoretical Retrospective* (eds L. Bean and T. Blackburn). Socorro, N. Mexico: Ballena Press, pp. 225–43.

Blanton, R. and Taylor, J. 1995. Patterns of exchange and the social production of pigs in highland New Guinea: their relevance to questions about the origins and evolution of agriculture. *Journal of Archaeological Research*, 3: 113–45

Bogucki, P. 1999. *The Origins of Human Society*. Malden, MA: Blackwell.

Cauvin, J., Aurenche, O., Cauvin, M-C. and Balkan-Atli, N. 1999. The pre-pottery site of Cafer Höyük. In *Neolithic in Turkey* (eds M. Özdogan and N. Basgelen). Istanbul: Arkeoloji ve Sanat Yayinlari, pp. 87–104.

Chang, T.T. 1989. Domestication and the spread of the cultivated rices. In *Foraging and Farming: The Evolution of Plant Exploitation* (eds D. Harris and G. Hillman). London: Unwin Hyman, pp. 408–17.

Clarke, M. 2001. Akha feasting: an ethnoarchaeological perspective. In *Feasts: Archaeological and Ethnographic Perspectives on Food, Politics, and Power* (eds M. Dietler and B. Hayden). Washington, DC: Smithsonian Institution Press, pp. 144–67.

Condominas, G. 1977. *We Have Eaten the Forest*. New York: Hill & Wang.

Dietler, M. 1990. Driven by drink: the role of drinking in the political economy and the case of early Iron Age France. *Journal of Anthropological Archaeology*, 9: 352–406.

Dietler, M. 2001. Theorizing the feast: rituals of consumption, commensal politics, and power in African contexts. In *Feasts: Archaeological and Ethnographic Perspectives on Food, Politics, and Power* (eds M. Dietler and B. Hayden). Washington, DC: Smithsonian Institution Press, pp. 65–114.

Dietler, M. and Herbich, I. 2001. Feasts and labor mobilization: dissecting a fundamental economic practice. In *Feasts: Archaeological and Ethnographic Perspectives on Food, Politics, and Power* (eds M. Dietler and B. Hayden). Washington, DC: Smithsonian Institution Press, pp. 240–64.

Earle, T. 1977. A reappraisal of redistribution: complex Hawaiian chiefdoms. In *Exchange Systems in Prehistory* (eds T. Earle and J. Ericson). New York: Academic Press, pp. 213–29.

Esin, U. and Harmankaya, S. 1999. Asikli. In *Neolithic in Turkey* (eds M. Özdogan and N. Basgelen). Istanbul: Arkeoloji ve Sanat Yayinlari, pp. 115–32.

Falvey, L. 1977. *Ruminants in the Highlands of Northern Thailand*. Thai-Australian Highland Agronomy Project. Chiang Mai: Tribal Research Institute, Chiang Mai University.

Flannery, K. 1973. The origins of agriculture. *Annual Review of Anthropology*, 2: 271–310.

Fox, J. 1992. The heritage of traditional agriculture in Eastern Indonesia: lexical evidence and the indications of rituals from the outer arc of the lesser Sundas. In *The Heritage of Traditional Agriculture among the Western Austronesians* (ed. J. Fox). Canberra: Australian National University, pp. 67–88.

Gregg, A. 1988. *Foragers and Farmers*. Chicago: University of Chicago Press.

Gunawan, I. 1998. *Hierarchy and Balance: A Study of Wanokoka Social Organization*. Canberra: Australian National University.

Hakansson, N.T. 1994. Grain, cattle, and power: social processes of intensive cultivation and exchange in precolonial western Kenya. *Journal of Anthropological Research*, 50: 249–76.

Hakansson, N.T. 1995. Irrigation, population pressure, and exchange in precolonial Pare, Tanzania. *Research in Economic Anthropology*, 16: 297–323.

Hauptmann, H. 1999. The Urfa region. In *Neolithic in Turkey* (eds M. Özdogan and N. Basgelen). Istanbul: Arkeoloji ve Sanat Yayinlari, pp. 65–86.

Hawkes, K., O'Connell, J. and Blurton Jones, N. 2001. Hunting and nuclear families. *Current Anthropology*, 42: 681–709.

Hayden, B. 1981. Subsistence and ecological adaptations of modern hunter/gatherers. In *Omnivorous Primates* (eds R. Harding and G. Teleki). New York: Columbia University Press, pp. 344–421.

Hayden, B. 1990. Nimrods, piscators, pluckers, and planters: the emergence of food production. *Journal of Anthropological Archaeology*, 9: 31–69.

Hayden, B. 1995a. A new overview of domestication. In *Last Hunters—First Farmers* (eds T. Price and A. Gebauer). Santa Fe, New Mexico: American Research Press, pp. 273–99.

Hayden, B. 1995b. Pathways to power: principles for creating socioeconomic inequalities. In *Foundations of Social Inequality* (eds T. Price and G. Feinman). New York: Plenum Press, pp. 15–86.

Hayden, B. 1998. Practical and prestige technologies: the evolution of material systems. *Journal of Archaeological Method and Theory*, 5: 1–55.

Hayden, B. 2001a. Fabulous feasts: a prolegomenon to the importance of feasting. In *Feasts: Archaeological and Ethnographic Perspectives on Food, Politics, and Power* (eds M. Dietler and B. Hayden). Washington, DC: Smithsonian Institution Press, pp. 23–64.

Hayden, B. 2001b. The dynamics of wealth and poverty in the transegalitarian societies of Southeast Asia. *Antiquity*, 75: 571–81.

Izikowitz, K. 1951. *Lamet: Hill Peasants in French Indonesia*. Uppsala: Goteborg.

Jennbert, K. 1984. *Den Productiva Gavan*. Lund: Acta Arcaeologica Lundensia, No. 16.

Jennbert, K. 1987. Neolithisation processes in the Nordic area. *Uddevalla*, 21–35.

Junker, L. 2001. The evolution of ritual feasting systems in prehispanic Philippine chiefdoms. In *Feasts: Archaeological and Ethnographic Perspectives on Food, Politics, and Power* (eds M. Dietler and B. Hayden). Washington, DC: Smithsonian Institution Press, pp. 267–310.

Katz, S. and Voigt, M. 1986. Bread and beer: the early use of cereals in human diet. *Expedition*, 28(2): 23–34.

Keswani, P. 1994. The social context of animal husbandry in early agricultural societies. *Journal of Anthropological Archaeology*, 13: 255–77.

Leach, E.R. 1954. *Political Systems of Highland Burma*. Boston, MA: Beacon Press.

Lee, R. 1979. *The !Kung San: Men and Women, and Work in a Foraging Society*. Cambridge: Cambridge University Press.

Lewthwaite, J. 1986. The transition to food production: a Mediterranean perspective. In *Hunters in Transition* (ed. M. Zvelebil). Cambridge: University of Cambridge Press, pp. 53–66.

Lidén, K. 1995. Megaliths, agriculture, and social complexity. *Journal of Anthropological Archaeology*, 14: 404–17.

Lu, T. 1999. *The Transition from Foraging to Farming and the Origin of Agriculture in China*. Oxford: British Archaeological Reports, International Series 774.

Modjeska, N. 1982. Production and inequality: perspectives from Central New Guinea. In *Inequality in New Guinea Highlands Societies* (ed. A. Strathern). Cambridge: Cambridge University Press, pp. 50–108.

Özdogan, M. 1999. Concluding remarks. In *Neolithic in Turkey* (eds M. Özdogan and N. Basgelen). Istanbul: Arkeoloji ve Sanat Yayinlari, pp. 225–36.

Perodie, J. 2001. Feasting for prosperity: a study of southern Northwest Coast feasting. In *Feasts: Archaeological and Ethnographic Perspectives on Food, Politics, and Power* (eds M. Dietler and B. Hayden). Washington, DC: Smithsonian Institution Press, pp. 185–214.

Runnels, C. and Andel, T. van. 1988. Trade and the origins of agriculture in the eastern Mediterranean. *Journal of Mediterranean Archaeology*, 1(1): 83–109.

Shubert, B. 1986. *Proposals for Farming Systems-Oriented Crop Research of Wawi Highland Agriculture Research Station in Northern Thailand*. Berlin: Center for Advanced Training in Agricultural Development, Technical University of Berlin.

Smith, B. 2001. The transition to food production. In *Archaeology at the Millennium* (eds G. Feinman and T. Price). New York: Kluwer Academic/Plenum, pp. 199–230.

Speth, J. and Spielmann, K. 1983. Energy source, protein metabolism, and hunter-gatherer subsistence strategies. *Journal of Anthropological Archaeology*, 2: 1–31.

Stafford, M. 1999. *From Forager to Farmer in Flint*. Aarhus: Aarhus University Press.

Starr, M. 1987. Risk, environmental variability and drought-induced impoverishment: the pastoral economy of central Niger. *Africa*, 57(1): 29–50.

Stevens, W. 1987. Does civilization owe a debt to beer? *New York Times* 24 March: 20.

Thomas, J. 1991. *Rethinking the Neolithic*. Cambridge: Cambridge University Press.

Willcox, G. 1996. Evidence for plant exploitation and vegetation history from three Early Neolithic pre-pottery sites on the Euphrates (Syria). *Vegetation History and Archaeobotany*, 5: 143–52.

Willcox, G. 1998. Archaeobotanical evidence for the beginnings of agriculture in Southwest Asia. In *The Origins of Agriculture and Crop Domestication* (eds A. Damania, J. Valkoun, G. Willcox and C. Qualset). London: International Center for Agricultural Research in the Dry Areas, Food and Agriculture Organization of the UN, pp. 25–38.

Willcox, G. 1999. Agrarian change and the beginnings of cultivation in the Near East. In *The Prehistory of Food* (eds C. Gosden and J. Hather). London: Routledge, pp. 478–500.

Zeder, M. 2001. Feast or forage, the transition to agriculture in the Near East. Paper presented at the annual meetings of the Society for American Archaeology, New Orleans.

"The Maya Collapses"

Jared Diamond

Along with the origin of agriculture, the collapse of civilizations is one of the major topics of theoretical interest in archaeology. Archaeologists have proposed many catalysts for collapse, including drought, epidemic diseases to crops, soil nutrient depletion through overuse, overpopulation, collapse of trading networks, internal conflict, warfare, and excessive time devoted to religious activities, but there is no consensus on what caused the collapse of any single civilization or what causes collapse in general.

This selection originally appeared as Chapter 5 in Jared Diamond's popular book *Collapse: How Societies Choose to Fail or Succeed*, published in 2005. In the book's Introduction, Diamond outlines a five-point framework of factors that may contribute to a society's collapse: 1) environmental damage, 2) climate change, 3) hostile neighbors, 4) friendly trade partners, and 5) the society's response to environmental change. Diamond contends that the first four factors may or may not be significant, but the fifth (the society's response) is always significant.

Jared Diamond is currently a professor of geography at the University of California, Los Angeles (UCLA). He was formerly a professor of physiology at the same university and is a widely published author of articles and books on humans in antiquity. Readers are cautioned that while some archaeologists see value in his work, it has also received some severe criticism from within the field.

Questions to Guide Reading

When and in what geographic area did the peoples of the Classic Maya civilization live?

What are some of the major archaeological sites associated with the Maya?

How does Diamond explain the collapse of the Maya?

How does Diamond use material remains to support his views? (i.e., What kinds of physical evidence does he use and how does he use it?)

What does Diamond mean by the "Classic Maya collapse"?

What five reasons does Diamond cite to say that the story of the Maya collapse is complicated?

What does Diamond have to say about the roles of drought and warfare?

What are the "five strands" of Diamond's conclusion about the collapse of the Maya?

On what basis do you think some archaeologists criticize Diamond's explanation?

By now, millions of modern tourists have visited ruins of the ancient Maya civilization that collapsed over a thousand years ago in Mexico's Yucatán Peninsula and adjacent parts of Central America. All of us love a romantic mystery, and the Maya offer us one at our doorstep, almost as close for Americans as the Anasazi ruins. To visit a former Maya city, we need only board a direct flight from the U.S. to the modern Mexican state capital city of Mérida, jump into a rental car or minibus, and drive an hour on a paved highway.

Today, many Maya ruins, with their great temples and monuments, still lie surrounded by jungle, far from current human settlement (Plate 12). Yet they were once the sites of the New World's most advanced Native American civilization before European arrival, and the only one with extensive deciphered written texts. How could ancient peoples have supported urban societies in areas where few farmers eke out a living today? The Maya cities impress us not only with that mystery and with their beauty, but also because they are "pure" archaeological sites. That is, their locations became depopulated, so they were not covered up by later buildings as were so many other ancient cities, like the Aztec capital of Tenochtitlán (now buried under modern Mexico City) and Rome.

Maya cities remained deserted, hidden by trees, and virtually unknown to the outside world until rediscovered in 1839 by a rich American lawyer named John Stephens, together with the English draftsman Frederick Catherwood. Having heard rumors of ruins in the jungle, Stephens got President Martin Van Buren to appoint him ambassador to the Confederation of Central American Republics, an amorphous political entity then extending from modern Guatemala to Nicaragua, as a front for his archaeological explorations. Stephens and Catherwood ended up exploring 44 sites and cities. From the extraordinary quality of the buildings and the art, they realized that these were not the work of savages (in their words) but of a vanished high civilization. They recognized that some of the carvings on the stone monuments constituted writing, and they correctly guessed that it related historical events and the names of people. On his return, Stephens wrote two travel books, illustrated by Catherwood and describing the ruins, that became best sellers.

A few quotes from Stephens's writings will give a sense of the romantic appeal of the Maya: "The city was desolate. No remnant of this race hangs round the ruins, with traditions handed down from father to son and from generation to generation. It lay before us like a shattered bark in the midst of the ocean, her mast gone, her name effaced, her crew perished, and none to tell whence she came, to whom she belonged, how long on her journey, or what caused her destruction.... Architecture, sculpture, and painting, all the arts which embellish life, had flourished in this overgrown forest; orators, warriors, and statesmen, beauty, ambition, and glory had lived and passed away, and none knew that such things had been, or could tell of their past existence.... Here were the remains of a cultivated, polished, and peculiar people, who had passed through all the stages incident to the rise and fall of nations; reached their golden age, and perished.... We went up to their desolate temples and fallen altars; and wherever we moved we saw the evidence of their taste, their skill in arts.... We called back into life the strange people who gazed in sadness from the wall; pictured them, in fanciful costumes and adorned with plumes of feather, ascending the terraces of the palace and the steps leading to the temples.... In the romance of the world's history nothing ever impressed me more forcibly than the spectacle of this once great and lovely city, overturned, desolate, and lost, ... overgrown with trees for miles around, and without even a name to distinguish it." Those sensations are what tourists drawn to Maya ruins still feel today, and why we find the Maya collapse so fascinating.

The Maya story has several advantages for all of us interested in prehistoric collapses. First, the Maya written records that have survived, although frustratingly incomplete, are still useful for reconstructing Maya history in much greater detail than we can reconstruct Easter Island, or even Anasazi history with its tree rings and packrat middens. The great art and architecture of Maya cities have resulted in far more archaeologists studying the Maya than would have been the case if they had just been illiterate hunter-gatherers living in archaeologically invisible hovels. Climatologists and paleoecologists have recently been able to recognize several signals of ancient climate and environmental changes that contributed to the Maya collapse. Finally, today there are still Maya people living in their ancient homeland and speaking Maya languages. Because much ancient Maya culture survived the collapse, early European visitors to the homeland recorded information about contemporary Maya society that played a vital role in our understanding ancient Maya society. The first Maya contact with Europeans came already in 1502, just 10 years after Christopher Columbus's "discovery" of the New World, when Columbus on the last of his four voyages captured a trading canoe that may have been Maya. In 1527 the Spanish began in earnest to conquer the Maya, but it was not until 1697 that they subdued the last principality. Thus, the Spanish had opportunities to observe independent Maya societies for a period of nearly two centuries. Especially important, both for bad and for good, was the bishop Diego de Landa, who resided in the Yucatán Peninsula for most of the years from 1549 to 1578. On the one hand, in one of history's worst acts of cultural vandalism, he burned all Maya manuscripts that he could locate in his effort to eliminate "paganism," so that only four survive today. On the other hand, he wrote a detailed account of Maya society, and he obtained from an informant a garbled explanation of Maya writing that eventually, nearly four centuries later, turned out to offer clues to its decipherment.

A further reason for our devoting a chapter to the Maya is to provide an antidote to our other chapters on past societies, which consist disproportionately of small societies in somewhat fragile and geographically isolated environments, and

behind the cutting edge of contemporary technology and culture. The Maya were none of those things. Instead, they were culturally the most advanced society (or among the most advanced ones) in the pre-Columbian New World, the only one with extensive preserved writing, and located within one of the two heartlands of New World civilization (Mesoamerica). While their environment did present some problems associated with its karst terrain and unpredictably fluctuating rainfall, it does not rank as notably fragile by world standards, and it was certainly less fragile than the environments of ancient Easter Island, the Anasazi area, Greenland, or modern Australia. Lest one be misled into thinking that crashes are a risk only for small peripheral societies in fragile areas, the Maya warn us that crashes can also befall the most advanced and creative societies.

From the perspective of our five-point framework for understanding societal collapses, the Maya illustrate four of our points. They did damage their environment, especially by deforestation and erosion. Climate changes (droughts) did contribute to the Maya collapse, probably repeatedly. Hostilities among the Maya themselves did play a large role. Finally, political/cultural factors, especially the competition among kings and nobles that led to a chronic emphasis on war and erecting monuments rather than on solving underlying problems, also contributed. The remaining item on our five-point list, trade or cessation of trade with external friendly societies, does not appear to have been essential in sustaining the Maya or in causing their downfall. While obsidian (their preferred raw material for making into stone tools), jade, gold, and shells were imported into the Maya area, the latter three items were non-essential luxuries. Obsidian tools remained widely distributed in the Maya area long after the political collapse, so obsidian was evidently never in short supply.

To understand the Maya, let's begin by considering their environment, which we think of as "jungle" or "tropical rainforest." That's not true, and the reason why not proves to be important. Properly speaking, tropical rainforests grow in high-rainfall equatorial areas that remain wet or humid all year round. But the Maya homeland lies more than a thousand miles from the equator, at latitudes 17° to 22° N, in a habitat termed a "seasonal tropical forest." That is, while there does tend to be a rainy season from May to October, there is also a dry season from January through April. If one focuses on the wet months, one calls the Maya homeland a "seasonal tropical forest"; if one focuses on the dry months, one could instead describe it as a "seasonal desert."

From north to south in the Yucatán Peninsula, rainfall increases from 18 to 100 inches per year, and the soils become thicker, so that the southern peninsula was agriculturally more productive and supported denser populations. But rainfall in the Maya homeland is unpredictably variable between years; some recent years have had three or four times more rain than other years. Also, the timing of rainfall within the year is somewhat unpredictable, so it can easily happen that farmers plant their crops in anticipation of rain and then the rains do not come when expected. As a result, modern farmers attempting to grow corn in the ancient Maya homelands have faced frequent crop failures, especially in the north. The ancient Maya were presumably more experienced and did better, but nevertheless they too must have faced risks of crop failures from droughts and hurricanes.

Although southern Maya areas received more rainfall than northern areas, problems of water were paradoxically more severe in the wet south. While that made things hard for ancient Maya living in the south, it has also made things hard for modern archaeologists who have difficulty understanding why ancient droughts would have caused bigger problems in the wet south than in the dry north. The likely explanation is that a lens of freshwater underlies the Yucatán Peninsula, but surface elevation increases from north to south, so that as one moves south the land surface lies increasingly higher above the water table. In the northern peninsula the elevation is sufficiently low that the ancient Maya were able to reach the water table at deep sinkholes called cenotes, or at deep caves; all tourists who have visited the Maya city of Chichén Itzá will remember the great cenotes there. In low-elevation north coastal areas without sinkholes, the Maya may have been able to get down to the water table by digging wells up to 75 feet deep. Water is readily available in many parts of Belize that have rivers, along the Usumacinta River in the west, and around a few lakes in the Petén area of the south. But much of the south lies too high above the water table for cenotes or wells to reach down to it. Making matters worse, most of the Yucatán Peninsula consists of karst, a porous sponge-like limestone terrain where rain runs straight into the ground and where little or no surface water remains available.

How did those dense southern Maya populations deal with their resulting water problem? It initially surprises us that many of their cities were not built next to the few rivers but instead on promontories in rolling uplands. The explanation is that the Maya excavated depressions, modified natural depressions, and then plugged up leaks in the karst by plastering the bottoms of the depressions in order to create cisterns and reservoirs, which collected rain from large plastered catchment basins and stored it for use in the dry season. For example, reservoirs at the Maya city of Tikal held enough water to meet the drinking water needs of about 10,000 people for a period of 18 months. At the city of Coba the Maya built dikes around a lake in order to raise its level and make their water supply more reliable. But the inhabitants of Tikal and other cities dependent on reservoirs for drinking water would still have been in deep trouble if 18 months passed without rain in a prolonged drought. A shorter drought in which they exhausted their stored food supplies might already have gotten them in deep trouble through starvation, because growing crops required rain rather than reservoirs.

Of particular importance for our purposes are the details of Maya agriculture, which was based on crops domesticated in Mexico—especially corn,

—MAYA SITES—

Gulf of Mexico

• Mérida

CHICHÉN ITZÁ ◆

COBA ◆

PUUC
REGION

20°

*Bay of
Campeche*

18°

MEXICO

CALAKMUL ◆

EL MIRADOR ◆

PALENQUE ◆

BELIZE

Usumacinta River

PETÉN
AREA

TIKAL ◆

Lake Petén Itzá

BONAMPAK ◆

CARACOL ◆

16°

QUIRIGUA ◆

GUATEMALA

◆ COPÁN

HONDURAS

Pacific Ocean

14°

UNITED STATES

*Gulf of
Mexico*

Atlantic Ocean

CENTRAL AMERICA

Caribbean Sea

Pacific Ocean

0 Miles   50   100   150

0 Kilometers   150

92°   90°   88°   © 2004 Jeffrey L. Ward

Map of Maya Sites

with beans being second in importance. For the elite as well as commoners, corn constituted at least 70% of the Maya diet, as deduced from isotope analyses of ancient Maya skeletons. Their sole domestic animals were the dog, turkey, Muscovy duck, and a stingless bee yielding honey, while their most important wild meat source was deer that they hunted, plus fish at some sites. However, the few animal bones at Maya archaeological sites suggest that the quantity of meat available to the Maya was low. Venison was mainly a luxury food for the elite.

It was formerly believed that Maya farming was based on slash-and-burn agriculture (so-called swidden agriculture) in which forest is cleared and burned, crops are grown in the resulting field for a year or a few years until the soil is exhausted, and then the field is abandoned for a long fallow period of 15 or 20 years until regrowth of wild vegetation restores fertility to the soil. Because most of the landscape under a swidden agricultural system is fallow at any given time, it can support only modest population densities. Thus, it was a surprise for archaeologists to discover that ancient Maya population densities, estimated from numbers of stone foundations of farmhouses, were often far higher than what swidden agriculture could support. The actual values are the subject of much dispute and evidently varied among areas, but frequently cited estimates reach 250 to 750, possibly even 1,500, people per square mile. (For comparison, even today the two most densely populated countries in Africa, Rwanda and Burundi, have population densities of only about 750 and 540 people per square mile, respectively.) Hence the ancient Maya must have had some means of increasing agricultural production beyond what was possible through swidden alone.

Many Maya areas do show remains of agricultural structures designed to increase production, such as terracing of hill slopes to retain soil and moisture, irrigation systems, and arrays of canals and drained or raised fields. The latter systems, which are well attested elsewhere in the world and which require a lot of labor to construct, but which

reward the labor with increased food production, involve digging canals to drain a waterlogged area, fertilizing and raising the level of the fields between the canals by dumping muck and water hyacinths dredged out of canals onto the fields, and thereby keeping the fields themselves from being inundated. Besides harvesting crops grown over the fields, farmers with raised fields also "grow" wild fish and turtles in the canals (actually, let them grow themselves) as an additional food source. However, other Maya areas, such as the well-studied cities of Copán and Tikal, show little archaeological evidence of terracing, irrigation, or raised- or drained-field systems. Instead, their inhabitants must have used archaeologically invisible means to increase food production, by mulching, floodwater farming, shortening the time that a field is left fallow, and tilling the soil to restore soil fertility, or in the extreme omitting the fallow period entirely and growing crops every year, or in especially moist areas growing two crops per year.

Socially stratified societies, including modern American and European society, consist of farmers who produce food, plus non-farmers such as bureaucrats and soldiers who do not produce food but merely consume the food grown by the farmers and are in effect parasites on farmers. Hence in any stratified society the farmers must grow enough surplus food to meet not only their own needs but also those of the other consumers. The number of non-producing consumers that can be supported depends on the society's agricultural productivity. In the United States today, with its highly efficient agriculture, farmers make up only 2% of our population, and each farmer can feed on the average 125 other people (American non-farmers plus people in export markets overseas). Ancient Egyptian agriculture, although much less efficient than modern mechanized agriculture, was still efficient enough for an Egyptian peasant to produce five times the food required for himself and his family. But a Maya peasant could produce only twice the needs of himself and his family. At least

70% of Maya society consisted of peasants. That's because Maya agriculture suffered from several limitations.

First, it yielded little protein. Corn, by far the dominant crop, has a lower protein content than the Old World staples of wheat and barley. The few edible domestic animals already mentioned included no large ones and yielded much less meat than did Old World cows, sheep, pigs, and goats. The Maya depended on a narrower range of crops than did Andean farmers (who in addition to corn also had potatoes, high-protein quinoa, and many other plants, plus llamas for meat), and much narrower again than the variety of crops in China and in western Eurasia.

Another limitation was that Maya corn agriculture was less intensive and productive than the Aztecs' *chinampas* (a very productive type of raised-field agriculture), the raised fields of the Tiwanaku civilization of the Andes, Moche irrigation on the coast of Peru, or fields tilled by animal-drawn plows over much of Eurasia.

Still a further limitation arose from the humid climate of the Maya area, which made it difficult to store corn beyond a year, whereas the Anasazi living in the dry climate of the U.S. Southwest could store it for three years.

Finally, unlike Andean Indians with their llamas, and unlike Old World peoples with their horses, oxen, donkeys, and camels, the Maya had no animal-powered transport or plows. All overland transport for the Maya went on the backs of human porters. But if you send out a porter carrying a load of corn to accompany an army into the field, some of that load of corn is required to feed the porter himself on the trip out, and some more to feed him on the trip back, leaving only a fraction of the load available to feed the army. The longer the trip, the less of the load is left over from the porter's own requirements. Beyond a march of a few days to a week, it becomes uneconomical to send porters carrying corn to provision armies or markets. Thus, the modest productivity of Maya agriculture, and their

lack of draft animals, severely limited the duration and distance possible for their military campaigns.

We are accustomed to thinking of military success as determined by quality of weaponry, rather than by food supply. But a clear example of how improvements in food supply may decisively increase military success comes from the history of Maori New Zealand. The Maori are the Polynesian people who were the first to settle New Zealand. Traditionally, they fought frequent fierce wars against each other, but only against closely neighboring tribes. Those wars were limited by the modest productivity of their agriculture, whose staple crop was sweet potatoes. It was not possible to grow enough sweet potatoes to feed an army in the field for a long time or on distant marches. When Europeans arrived in New Zealand, they brought potatoes, which beginning around 1815 considerably increased Maori crop yields. Maori could now grow enough food to supply armies in the field for many weeks. The result was a 15-year period in Maori history, from 1818 until 1833, when Maori tribes that had acquired potatoes and guns from the English sent armies out on raids to attack tribes hundreds of miles away that had not yet acquired potatoes and guns. Thus, the potato's productivity relieved previous limitations on Maori warfare, similar to the limitations that low-productivity corn agriculture imposed on Maya warfare.

Those food supply considerations may contribute to explaining why Maya society remained politically divided among small kingdoms that were perpetually at war with each other, and that never became unified into large empires like the Aztec Empire of the Valley of Mexico (fed with the help of their *chinampa* agriculture and other forms of intensification) or the Inca Empire of the Andes (fed by more diverse crops carried by llamas over well-built roads). Maya armies and bureaucracies remained small and unable to mount lengthy campaigns over long distances. (Even much later, in 1848, when the Maya revolted against their Mexican overlords and a Maya army seemed to be on the verge of victory, the army had to break off fighting and go home to harvest another crop of corn.) Many Maya kingdoms held populations of only up to 25,000 to 50,000 people, none over half a million, within a radius of two or three days' walk from the king's palace. (The actual numbers are again highly controversial among archaeologists.) From the tops of the temples of some Maya kingdoms, it was possible to see the temples of the nearest kingdom. Maya cities remained small (mostly less than one square mile in area), without the large populations and big markets of Teotihuacán and Tenochtitlán in the Valley of Mexico, or of Chan-Chan and Cuzco in Peru, and without archaeological evidence of the royally managed food storage and trade that characterized ancient Greece and Mesopotamia.

Now for a quick crash-course in Maya history. The Maya area is part of the larger ancient Native American cultural region known as Mesoamerica, which extended approximately from Central Mexico to Honduras and constituted (along with the Andes of South America) one of the two New World centers of innovation before European arrival. The Maya shared much in common with other Mesoamerican societies not only in what they possessed, but also in what they lacked. For example, surprisingly to modern Westerners with expectations based on Old World civilizations, Mesoamerican societies lacked metal tools, pulleys and other machines, wheels (except locally as toys), boats with sails, and domestic animals large enough to carry loads or pull a plow. All of those great Maya temples were constructed by stone and wooden tools and by human muscle power alone.

Of the ingredients of Maya civilization, many were acquired by the Maya from elsewhere in Mesoamerica. For instance, Mesoamerican agriculture, cities, and writing first arose outside the Maya area itself, in valleys and coastal lowlands to the west and southwest, where corn and beans and squash were domesticated and became important dietary components by 3000 B.C., pottery arose around 2500 B.C., villages by 1500 B.C., cities among

the Olmecs by 1200 B.C., writing appeared among the Zapotecs in Oaxaca around or after 600 B.C., and the first states arose around 300 B.C. Two complementary calendars, a solar calendar of 365 days and a ritual calendar of 260 days, also arose outside the Maya area. Other elements of Maya civilization were either invented, perfected, or modified by the Maya themselves.

Within the Maya area, villages and pottery appeared around or after 1000 B.C., substantial buildings around 500 B.C., and writing around 400 B.C. All preserved ancient Maya writing, constituting a total of about 15,000 inscriptions, is on stone and pottery and deals only with kings, nobles, and their conquests (Plate 13). There is not a single mention of commoners. When Spaniards arrived, the Maya were still using bark paper coated with plaster to write books, of which the sole four that escaped Bishop Landa's fires turned out to be treatises on astronomy and the calendar. The ancient Maya also had had such bark-paper books, often depicted on their pottery, but only decayed remains of them have survived in tombs.

The famous Maya Long Count calendar begins on August 11, 3114 B.C.—just as our own calendar begins on January 1 of the first year of the Christian era. We know the significance to us of that day-zero of our calendar: it's the supposed beginning of the year in which Christ was born. Presumably the Maya also attached some significance to their own day zero, but we don't know what it was. The first preserved Long Count date is only A.D. 197 for a monument in the Maya area and 36 B.C. outside the Maya area, indicating that the Long Count calendar's day-zero was backdated to August 11, 3114 B.C. long after the facts; there was no writing anywhere in the New World then, nor would there be for 2,500 years after that date.

Our calendar is divided into units of days, weeks, months, years, decades, centuries, and millennia: for example, the date of February 19, 2003, on which I wrote the first draft of this paragraph, means the 19th day of the second month in the third year of the first decade of the first century of the third millennium beginning with the birth of Christ. Similarly, the Maya Long Count calendar named dates in units of days (*kin*), 20 days (*uinal*), 360 days (*tun*), 7,200 days or approximately 20 years (*katunn*), and 144,000 days or approximately 400 years (*baktun*). All of Maya history falls into baktuns 8, 9, and 10.

The so-called Classic period of Maya civilization begins in baktun 8, around A.D. 250, when evidence for the first kings and dynasties appears. Among the glyphs (written signs) on Maya monuments, students of Maya writing recognized a few dozen, each of which was concentrated in its own geographic area, and which are now considered to have had the approximate meaning of dynasties or kingdoms. In addition to Maya kings having their own name glyphs and palaces, many nobles also had their own inscriptions and palaces. In Maya society the king also functioned as high priest carrying the responsibility to attend to astronomical and calendrical rituals, and thereby to bring rain and prosperity, which the king claimed to have the supernatural power to deliver because of his asserted family relationship to the gods. That is, there was a tacitly understood quid pro quo: the reason why the peasants supported the luxurious lifestyle of the king and his court, fed him corn and venison, and built his palaces was because he had made implicit big promises to the peasants. As we shall see, kings got into trouble with their peasants if a drought came, because that was tantamount to the breaking of a royal promise.

From A.D. 250 onwards, the Maya population (as judged from the number of archaeologically attested house sites), the number of monuments and buildings, and the number of Long Count dates on monuments and pottery increased almost exponentially, to reach peak numbers in the 8th century A.D. The largest monuments were erected towards the end of that Classic period. Numbers of all three of those indicators of a complex society declined throughout the 9th century, until the last known Long Count date on any monument fell in baktun 10, in the year A.D. 909. That decline of Maya population, architecture, and the Long Count calendar constitutes what is known as the Classic Maya collapse.

As an example of the collapse, let's consider in more detail a small but densely built city whose ruins now lie in western Honduras at a site known as Copán, and described in two recent books by archaeologist David Webster. For agricultural purposes the best land in the Copán area consists of five pockets of flat land with fertile alluvial soil along a river valley, with a tiny total area of only 10 square miles; the largest of those five pockets, known as the Copán pocket, has an area of only 5 square miles. Much of the land around Copán consists of steep hills, and nearly half of the hill area has a slope above 16% (approximately double the slope of the steepest grade that you are likely to encounter on an American highway). Soil in the hills is less fertile, more acidic, and poorer in phosphate than valley soil. Today, corn yields from valley-bottom fields are two or three times those of fields on hill slopes, which suffer rapid erosion and lose three-quarters of their productivity within a decade of farming.

As judged by numbers of house sites, population growth in the Copán Valley rose steeply from the 5th century up to a peak estimated at around 27,000 people at A.D. 750–900. Maya written history at Copán begins in the year with a Long Count date corresponding to A.D. 426, when later monuments record retrospectively that some person related to nobles at Tikal and Teotihuacán arrived. Construction of royal monuments glorifying kings was especially massive between A.D. 650 and 750. After A.D. 700, nobles other than kings also got into the act and began erecting their own palaces, of which there were about twenty by the year A.D. 800, when one of those palaces is known to have consisted of 50 buildings with room for about 250 people. All of those nobles and their courts would have increased the burden that the king and his own court imposed on the peasants. The last big buildings at Copán were put up around A.D. 800, and the last Long Count date on an incomplete altar possibly bearing a king's name has the date of A.D. 822.

Archaeological surveys of different types of habitats in the Copán Valley show that they were occupied in a regular sequence. The first area farmed was the large Copán pocket of valley bottomland, followed by occupation of the other four bottomland pockets. During that time the human population was growing, but there was not yet occupation of the hills. Hence that increased population must have been accommodated by intensifying production in the bottomland pockets by some combination of shorter fallow periods, double-cropping, and possibly some irrigation.

By the year A.D. 650, people started to occupy the hill slopes, but those hill sites were cultivated only for about a century. The percentage of Copán's total population that was in the hills, rather than in the valleys, reached a maximum of 41%, then declined until the population again became concentrated in the valley pockets. What caused that pullback of population from the hills? Excavation of the foundations of buildings in the valley floor showed that they became covered with sediment during the 8th century, meaning that the hill slopes were getting eroded and probably also leached of nutrients. Those acidic infertile hill soils were being carried down into the valley and blanketing the more fertile valley soils, where they would have reduced agricultural yields. This ancient quick abandonment of hillsides coincides with modern Maya experience that fields in the hills have low fertility and that their soils become rapidly exhausted.

The reason for that erosion of the hillsides is clear: the forests that formerly covered them and protected their soils were being cut down. Dated pollen samples show that the pine forests originally covering the upper elevations of the hill slopes were eventually all cleared. Calculation suggests that most of those felled pine trees were being burned for fuel, while the rest were used for construction or for making plaster. At other Maya sites from the pre-Classic era, where the Maya went overboard in lavish use of thick plaster

on buildings, plaster production may have been a major cause of deforestation. Besides causing sediment accumulation in the valleys and depriving valley inhabitants of wood supplies, that deforestation may have begun to cause a "man-made drought" in the valley bottom, because forests play a major role in water cycling, such that massive deforestation tends to result in lowered rainfall.

Hundreds of skeletons recovered from Copán archaeological sites have been studied for signs of disease and malnutrition, such as porous bones and stress lines in the teeth. These skeletal signs show that the health of Copán's inhabitants deteriorated from A.D. 650 to 850, both among the elite and among the commoners, although the health of commoners was worse.

Recall that Copán's population was increasing steeply while the hills were being occupied. The subsequent abandonment of all of those fields in the hills meant that the burden of feeding the extra population formerly dependent on the hills now fell increasingly on the valley floor, and that more and more people were competing for the food grown on those 10 square miles of valley bottomland. That would have led to fighting among the farmers themselves for the best land, or for any land, just as in modern Rwanda (Chapter 10). Because Copán's king was failing to deliver on his promises of rain and prosperity in return for the power and luxuries that he claimed, he would have been the scapegoat for this agricultural failure. That may explain why the last that we hear from any Copán king is A.D. 822 (that last Long Count date at Copán), and why the royal palace was burned around A.D. 850. However, the continued production of some luxury goods suggests that some nobles managed to carry on with their lifestyle after the king's downfall, until around A.D. 975.

To judge from datable pieces of obsidian, Copán's total population decreased more gradually than did its signs of kings and nobles. The estimated population in the year A.D. 950 was still around 15,000, or 54% of the peak population of 27,000. That population continued to dwindle, until there are no more signs of anyone in the Copán Valley by around A.D. 1250. The reappearance of pollen from forest trees thereafter provides independent evidence that the valley became virtually empty of people, and that the forests could at last begin to recover.

The general outline of Maya history that I have just related, and the example of Copán's history in particular, illustrates why we talk about "the Maya collapse." But the story grows more complicated, for at least five reasons.

First, there was not only that enormous Classic collapse, but at least two previous smaller collapses at some sites, one around the year A.D. 150 when El Mirador and some other Maya cities collapsed (the so-called pre-Classic collapse), the other (the so-called Maya hiatus) in the late 6th century and early 7th century, a period when no monuments were erected at the well-studied site of Tikal. There were also some post-Classic collapses in areas whose populations survived the Classic collapse or increased after it—such as the fall of Chichén Itzá around 1250 and of Mayapán around 1450.

Second, the Classic collapse was obviously not complete, because there were hundreds of thousands of Maya who met and fought the Spaniards— far fewer Maya than during the Classic peak, but still far more people than in the other ancient societies discussed in detail in this book. Those survivors were concentrated in areas with stable water supplies, especially in the north with its cenotes, the coastal lowlands with their wells, near a southern lake, and along rivers and lagoons at lower elevations. However, population otherwise disappeared almost completely in what previously had been the Maya heartland in the south.

Third, the collapse of population (as gauged by numbers of house sites and of obsidian tools) was in some cases much slower than the decline in numbers of Long Count dates, as I already mentioned for Copán. What collapsed quickly during the Classic collapse was the institution of kingship and the Long Count calendar.

Fourth, many apparent collapses of cities were really nothing more than "power cycling": i.e., particular cities becoming more powerful, then declining or getting conquered, and then rising again and conquering their neighbors, without changes in the whole population. For example, in the year 562 Tikal was defeated by its rivals Caracol and Calakmul, and its king was captured and killed. However, Tikal then gradually gained strength again and finally conquered its rivals in 695, long before Tikal joined many other Maya cities in the Classic collapse (last dated Tikal monuments A.D. 869). Similarly, Copán grew in power until the year 738, when its king Waxaklahuun Ub'aah K'awil (a name better known to Maya enthusiasts today by its unforgettable translation of "18 Rabbit") was captured and put to death by the rival city of Quirigua, but then Copán thrived during the following half-century under more fortunate kings.

Finally, cities in different parts of the Maya area rose and fell on different trajectories. For example, the Puuc region in the northwest Yucatán Peninsula, after being almost empty of people in the year 700, exploded in population after 750 while the southern cities were collapsing, peaked in population between 900 and 925, and then collapsed in turn between 950 and 1000. El Mirador, a huge site in the center of the Maya area with one of the world's largest pyramids, was settled in 200 B.C. and abandoned around A.D. 150, long before the rise of Copán. Chichén Itzá in the northern peninsula grew after A.D. 850 and was the main northern center around 1000, only to be destroyed in a civil war around 1250.

Some archaeologists focus on these five types of complications and don't want to recognize a Classic Maya collapse at all. But this overlooks the obvious facts that cry out for explanation: the disappearance of between 90 and 99% of the Maya population after A.D. 800, especially in the formerly most densely populated area of the southern lowlands, and the disappearance of kings, Long Count calendars, and other complex political and cultural institutions. That's why we talk about a Classic

Maya collapse, a collapse both of population and of culture that needs explaining.

Two other phenomena that I have mentioned briefly as contributing to Maya collapses require more discussion: the roles of warfare and of drought.

Archaeologists for a long time believed the ancient Maya to be gentle and peaceful people. We now know that Maya warfare was intense, chronic, and unresolvable, because limitations of food supply and transportation made it impossible for any Maya principality to unite the whole region in an empire, in the way that the Aztecs and Incas united Central Mexico and the Andes, respectively. The archaeological record shows that wars became more intense and frequent towards the time of the Classic collapse. That evidence comes from discoveries of several types over the last 55 years: archaeological excavations of massive fortifications surrounding many Maya sites; vivid depictions of warfare and captives on stone monuments, vases (Plate 14), and on the famous painted murals discovered in 1946 at Bonampak; and the decipherment of Maya writing, much of which proved to consist of royal inscriptions boasting of conquests. Maya kings fought to take one another captive, one of the unfortunate losers being Copán's King 18 Rabbit. Captives were tortured in unpleasant ways depicted clearly on the monuments and murals (such as yanking fingers out of sockets, pulling out teeth, cutting off the lower jaw, trimming off the lips and fingertips, pulling out the fingernails, and driving a pin through the lips), culminating (sometimes several years later) in the sacrifice of the captive in other equally unpleasant ways (such as tying the captive up into a ball by binding the arms and legs together, then rolling the balled-up captive down the steep stone staircase of a temple).

Maya warfare involved several well-documented types of violence: wars between separate kingdoms; attempts of cities within a kingdom to secede by revolting against the capital; and civil wars resulting from frequent violent attempts by would-be kings to usurp the throne. All of these types were described or depicted on monuments, because they involved kings and nobles. Not considered worthy of description, but probably even more frequent, were fights between commoners over land, as overpopulation became excessive and as land became scarce.

The other phenomenon important to understanding Maya collapses is the repeated occurrence of droughts, studied especially by Mark Brenner, David Hodell, the late Edward Deevey, and their colleagues at the University of Florida, and discussed in a recent book by Richardson Gill. Cores bored into layers of sediments at the bottoms of Maya lakes yield many measurements that let us infer droughts and environmental changes. For example, gypsum (a.k.a. calcium sulfate) precipitates out of solution in a lake into sediments when lake water becomes concentrated by evaporation during a drought. Water containing the heavy form of oxygen known as the isotope oxygen-18 also becomes concentrated during droughts, while water containing the lighter isotope oxygen-16 evaporates away. Molluscs and crustacea living in the lake take up oxygen to lay down in their shells, which remain preserved in the lake sediments, waiting for climatologists to analyze for those oxygen isotopes long after the little animals have died. Radiocarbon dating of a sediment layer identifies the approximate year when the drought or rainfall conditions inferred from those gypsum and oxygen isotope measurements were prevailing. The same lake sediment cores provide palynologists with information about deforestation (which shows up as a decrease in pollen from forest trees at the expense of an increase in grass pollen), and also soil erosion (which shows up as a thick clay deposit and minerals from the washed-down soil).

Based on these studies of radiocarbon-dated layers from lake sediment cores, climatologists and paleoecologists conclude that the Maya area was relatively wet from about 5500 B.C. until 500 B.C. The following period from 475 to 250 B.C., just before the rise of pre–Classic Maya civilization, was dry. The pre-Classic rise may have been facilitated by the return of wetter conditions after 250 B.C., but then a drought from A.D. 125 until A.D. 250 was associated with the pre-Classic collapse at El Mirador and other sites. That collapse was followed by the resumption of wetter conditions and of the buildup of Classic Maya cities, temporarily interrupted by a drought around A.D. 600 corresponding to a decline at Tikal and some other sites. Finally, around A.D. 760 there began the worst drought in the last 7,000 years, peaking around the year A.D. 800, and suspiciously associated with the Classic collapse.

Careful analysis of the frequency of droughts in the Maya area shows a tendency for them to recur at intervals of about 208 years. Those drought cycles may result from small variations in the sun's radiation, possibly made more severe in the Maya area as a result of the rainfall gradient in the Yucatán (drier in the north, wetter in the south) shifting southwards. One might expect those changes in the sun's radiation to affect not just the Maya region but, to varying degrees, the whole world. In fact, climatologists have noted that some other famous collapses of prehistoric civilizations far from the Maya realm appear to coincide with the peaks of those drought cycles, such as the collapse of the world's first empire (the Akkadian Empire of Mesopotamia) around 2170 B.C., the collapse of Moche IV civilization on the Peruvian coast around A.D. 600, and the collapse of Tiwanaku civilization in the Andes around A.D. 1100.

In the most naïve form of the hypothesis that drought contributed to causing the Classic collapse, one could imagine a single drought around A.D. 800 uniformly affecting the whole realm and triggering the fall of all Maya centers simultaneously. Actually, as we have seen, the Classic collapse hit different centers at slightly different times in the period A.D. 760–910, while sparing other centers. That fact makes many Maya specialists skeptical of a role of drought.

But a properly cautious climatologist would not state the drought hypothesis in that implausibly oversimplified form. Finer-resolution variation in rainfall from one year to the next can be calculated from annually banded sediments that rivers wash into ocean basins near the coast. These yield the conclusion that "The Drought" around A.D. 800 actually had four peaks, the first of them less severe: two dry years around A.D. 760, then an even drier decade around A.D. 810–820, three drier years around A.D. 860, and six drier years around A.D. 910. Interestingly, Richardson Gill concluded, from the latest dates on stone monuments at various large Maya centers, that collapse dates vary among sites and fall into three clusters: around A.D. 810, 860, and 910, in agreement with the dates for the three most severe droughts. It would not be at all surprising if a drought in any given year varied locally in its severity, hence if a series of droughts caused different Maya centers to collapse in different years, while sparing centers with reliable water supplies such as cenotes, wells, and lakes.

The area most affected by the Classic collapse was the southern lowlands, probably for the two reasons already mentioned: it was the area with the densest population, and it may also have had the most severe water problems because it lay too high above the water table for water to be obtained from cenotes or wells when the rains failed. The southern lowlands lost more than 99% of their population in the course of the Classic collapse. For example, the population of the Central Petén at the peak of the Classic Maya period is variously estimated at between 3,000,000 and 14,000,000 people, but there were only about 30,000 people there at the time that the Spanish arrived. When Cortés and his Spanish army passed through the Central Petén in 1524 and 1525, they nearly starved because they encountered so few villages from which to acquire corn. Cortés passed within a few miles of the ruins of the great Classic cities of Tikal and Palenque, but he heard or saw nothing of them because they were covered by jungle and almost nobody was living in the vicinity.

How did such a huge population of millions of people disappear? We asked ourselves that same question about the disappearance of Chaco Canyon's (admittedly smaller) Anasazi population in Chapter 4. By analogy with the cases of the Anasazi and of subsequent Pueblo Indian societies during droughts in the U.S. Southwest, we infer that some people from the southern Maya lowlands survived by fleeing to areas of the northern Yucatán endowed with cenotes or wells, where a rapid population increase took place around the time of the Maya collapse. But there is no sign of all those millions of southern lowland inhabitants surviving to be accommodated as immigrants in the north, just as there is no sign of thousands of Anasazi refugees being received as immigrants into surviving pueblos. As in the U.S. Southwest during droughts, some of that Maya population decrease surely involved people dying of starvation or thirst, or killing each other in struggles over increasingly scarce resources. The other part of the decrease may reflect a slower decrease in the birthrate or child survival rate over the course of many decades. That is, depopulation probably involved both a higher death rate and a lower birth rate.

In the Maya area as elsewhere, the past is a lesson for the present. From the time of Spanish arrival, the Central Petén's population declined further to about 3,000 in A.D. 1714, as a result of deaths from diseases and other causes associated with Spanish occupation. By the 1960s, the Central Petén's population had risen back only to 25,000, still less than 1% of what it had been at the Classic Maya peak. Thereafter, however, immigrants flooded into the Central Petén, building up its population to about 300,000 in the 1980s, and ushering in a new era of deforestation and erosion. Today, half of the Petén is once again deforested and ecologically degraded. One-quarter of all the forests of Honduras were destroyed between 1964 and 1989.

To summarize the Classic Maya collapse, we can tentatively identify five strands. I acknowledge, however, that Maya archaeologists still disagree vigorously among themselves—in part, because the different strands evidently varied in importance among different parts of the Maya realm; because detailed archaeological studies are available for only some Maya sites; and because it remains puzzling why most of the Maya heartland remained nearly empty of population and failed to recover after the collapse and after regrowth of forests.

With those caveats, it appears to me that one strand consisted of population growth outstripping available resources: a dilemma similar to the one foreseen by Thomas Malthus in 1798 and being played out today in Rwanda (Chapter 10), Haiti (Chapter 11), and elsewhere. As the archaeologist David Webster succinctly puts it, "Too many farmers grew too many crops on too much of the landscape." Compounding that mismatch between population and resources was the second strand: the effects of deforestation and hillside erosion, which caused a decrease in the amount of useable farmland at a time when more rather than less farmland was needed, and possibly exacerbated by an anthropogenic drought resulting from deforestation, by soil nutrient depletion and other soil problems, and by the struggle to prevent bracken ferns from overrunning the fields.

The third strand consisted of increased fighting, as more and more people fought over fewer resources. Maya warfare, already endemic, peaked just before the collapse. That is not surprising when one reflects that at least 5,000,000 people, perhaps many more, were crammed into an area smaller than the state of Colorado (104,000 square miles). That warfare would have decreased further the amount of land available for agriculture, by creating no-man's lands between principalities where it was now unsafe to farm. Bringing matters to a head was the strand of climate change. The drought at the time of the Classic collapse was not the first drought that the Maya had lived through, but it was the most severe. At the time of previous droughts, there were still uninhabited parts of the Maya landscape, and people at a site affected by drought could save themselves by moving to another site. However, by the time of the Classic collapse the landscape was now full, there was no useful unoccupied land in the vicinity on which to begin anew, and the whole population could not be accommodated in the few areas that continued to have reliable water supplies.

As our fifth strand, we have to wonder why the kings and nobles failed to recognize and solve these seemingly obvious problems undermining their society. Their attention was evidently focused on their short-term concerns of enriching themselves, waging wars, erecting monuments, competing with each other, and extracting enough food from the peasants to support all those activities. Like most leaders throughout human history, the Maya kings and nobles did not heed long-term problems, insofar as they perceived them. We shall return to this theme in Chapter 14.

Finally, while we still have some other past societies to consider in this book before we switch our attention to the modern world, we must already be struck by some parallels between the Maya and the past societies discussed in Chapters 2–4. As on Easter Island, Mangareva, and among the Anasazi,

Maya environmental and population problems led to increasing warfare and civil strife. As on Easter Island and at Chaco Canyon, Maya peak population numbers were followed swiftly by political and social collapse. Paralleling the eventual extension of agriculture from Easter Island's coastal lowlands to its uplands, and from the Mimbres floodplain to the hills, Copán's inhabitants also expanded from the floodplain to the more fragile hill slopes, leaving them with a larger population to feed when the agricultural boom in the hills went bust. Like Easter Island chiefs erecting ever larger statues, eventually crowned by pukao, and like Anasazi elite treating themselves to necklaces of 2,000 turquoise beads, Maya kings sought to outdo each other with more and more impressive temples, covered with thicker and thicker plaster—reminiscent in turn of the extravagant conspicuous consumption by modern American CEOs. The passivity of Easter chiefs and Maya kings in the face of the real big threats to their societies completes our list of disquieting parallels.